KNOWLEDGE-ORIENTED APPLICATIONS IN DATA MINING

Edited by **Kimito Funatsu**
and **Kiyoshi Hasegawa**

Knowledge-Oriented Applications in Data Mining

Edited by Kimito Funatsu and Kiyoshi Hasegawa

Published by InTech

Janeza Trdine 9, 51000 Rijeka, Croatia

Publishing Process Manager Ana Nikolic

Technical Editor Teodora Smiljanic

Cover Designer InTech Design Team

Additional hard copies can be obtained from orders@intechopen.com

Knowledge-Oriented Applications in Data Mining, Edited by Kimito Funatsu and Kiyoshi Hasegawa
p. cm.
ISBN 978-953-307-154-1

Meet the editors

Prof. Kimito Funatsu was born on December 3, 1955 in Japan. He received his Doctor degree (Dr. Sci.; physical organic chemistry) from Kyushu University which is one of the oldest imperial universities (1983) and joined Prof. Shin-ichi Sasaki's group, Toyohashi University of Technology (1984) as research-associate. During researching in Prof. Sasaki's group he worked on chemoinformatics field, i.e., Structure elucidation system CHEMICS, organic synthesis design system AIPHOS, molecular design. In 1990 he took the post of associate-professor. In 2004 he moved to The University of Tokyo as full Professor to continue the same research work. Recently he is trying material design and soft sensor. He is a chair of division of chemical information and computer sciences, Chemical Society of Japan.

Dr. Kiyoshi Hasegawa was born on August 18, 1963 in Kanazawa, Japan. He received his Ph.D. from Toyohashi University of Technology (1995) and worked at Biostructure group in Chugai Pharmaceutical Company in Japan. While working in Chugai, he spent three months at Swiss Basel Research Center in Roche for developing new de novo design program (2003). He is now principal scientist in his group and is involved in many SBDD projects. He is also the Roche data mining working group member and the secretary general of Japan Chemical Information Science. His interests are de novo design, Chemogenomics, data mining and web application.

Contents

Preface

Data mining, a branch of computer science and artificial intelligence, is the process of extracting patterns from data. Data mining is seen as an increasingly important tool to transform a huge amount of data into a knowledge form giving an informational advantage. Reflecting this conceptualization, people consider data mining to be just one step in a larger process known as knowledge discovery in databases (KDD). Data mining is currently used in a wide range of practices from business to scientific discovery.

The progress of data mining technology and large public popularity establish a need for a comprehensive text on the subject. The series of books entitled by 'Data Mining' address the need by presenting in-depth description of novel mining algorithms and many useful applications.

The first book (New Fundamental Technologies in Data Mining) is organized into two parts. The first part presents database management systems (DBMS). Before data mining algorithms can be used, a target data set must be assembled. As data mining can only uncover patterns already present in the data, the target dataset must be large enough to contain these patterns. For this purpose, some unique DBMS have been developed over past decades. They consist of software that operates databases, providing storage, access, security, backup and other facilities. DBMS can be categorized according to the database model that they support, such as relational or XML, the types of computer they support, such as a server cluster or a mobile phone, the query languages that access the database, such as SQL or XQuery, performance trade-offs, such as maximum scale or maximum speed or others.

The second part is based on explaining new data analysis techniques. Data mining involves the use of sophisticated data analysis techniques to discover relationships in large data sets. In general, they commonly involve four classes of tasks: (1) Clustering is the task of discovering groups and structures in the data that are in some way or another "similar" without using known structures in the data. Data visualization tools are followed after making clustering operations. (2) Classification is the task of generalizing known structure to apply to new data. (3) Regression attempts to find a function which models the data with the least error. (4) Association rule searches for relationships between variables.

The second book (Knowledge-Oriented Applications in Data Mining) is based on introducing several scientific applications using data mining. Data mining is used for a variety of purposes in both private and public sectors. Industries such as banking, insurance, medicine, and retailing use data mining to reduce costs, enhance research, and increase sales. For example, pharmaceutical companies use data mining of chemical compounds and genetic material to help guide research on new treatments for diseases. In the public sector, data mining applications were initially used as a means to detect fraud and waste, but they have grown also to be used for purposes such as measuring and improving program performance. It has been reported that data mining has helped the federal government recover millions of dollars in fraudulent Medicare payments.

In data mining, there are implementation and oversight issues that can influence the success of an application. One issue is data quality, which refers to the accuracy and completeness of the data. The second issue is the interoperability of the data mining techniques and databases being used by different people. The third issue is mission creep, or the use of data for purposes other than for which the data were originally collected. The fourth issue is privacy. Questions that may be considered include the degree to which government agencies should use and mix commercial data with government data, whether data sources are being used for purposes other than those for which they were originally designed.

In addition to understanding each part deeply, the two books present useful hints and strategies to solving problems in the following chapters. The contributing authors have highlighted many future research directions that will foster multi-disciplinary collaborations and hence will lead to significant development in the field of data mining.

January, 2011

Kimito Funatsu
The University of Tokyo, Department of Chemical System Engineering, Japan

Kiyoshi Hasegawa
Chugai Pharmaceutical Company, Kamakura Research Laboratories, Japan

1

Data Mining Classification Techniques for Human Talent Forecasting

Hamidah Jantan[1], Abdul Razak Hamdan[2] and Zulaiha Ali Othman[2]
[1]Faculty of Computer and Mathematical Sciences UiTM, Terengganu, 23000 Dungun, Terengganu,
[2]Faculty of Information Science and Technology UKM, 43600 Bangi, Selangor, Malaysia

1. Introduction

In knowledge management process, data mining technique can be used to extract and discover the valuable and meaningful knowledge from a large amount of data. Nowadays, data mining has given a great deal of concern and attention in the information industry and in society as a whole. This technique is an approach that is currently receiving great attention in data analysis and it has been recognized as a newly emerging analysis tool (Osei-Bryson, 2010; Park, 2001; Sinha, 2008; Tso & Yau, 2007; Wan, 2009; Zanakis, 2005; Zhuang et al., 2009). Additionally, among the major tasks in data mining are classification and prediction; concept description; rule association; cluster analysis; outlier analysis; trend and evaluation analysis; statistical analysis and others. Classification and prediction tasks are among the popular tasks in data mining; and widely used in many areas especially for trend analysis and future planning. In fact, classification technique is supervised learning, which is the class level or prediction target is already known. As a result, the classification model which is represented through rules structures will be constructed in the classification process. In this case, the constructed model will be representing the precious knowledge and it can be used for future planning.

There are many areas which adapted this approach to solve their problems such as in finance, medical, marketing, stock, telecommunication, manufacturing, health care, customer relationship and etc. However, the data mining application has not attracted much attention from people in Human Resource (HR) field (Chien & Chen, 2008; Ranjan, 2008). Besides that, in our previous study, most of the prediction applications are used to predict stock, demand, rate, risk, event and others; but there are quite limited studies on human prediction. In addition prediction applications are mainly developed in business and industrious fields; and quite restricted studies involved human talent in an organization (Jantan et al., 2009). HR data can provide a rich resource for knowledge discovery and for decision support system development.

Recently, an organization has to struggle effectively in term of cost, quality, service or innovation. All these depend on having enough right people with the right skills, employed in the appropriate locations at appropriate point of time. In HR, among the challenges of HR professionals are managing an organization talent known as talent management. Talent management involves a lot of managerial decisions and these types of decisions are very uncertain and difficult. Besides that, these decisions depend on various factors such as human experience, knowledge, preference and judgment. The process to identify the existing talent in an organization is among the top talent management challenges and the important issue (A TP Track Research Report 2005). In addition, talent management is defined as an outcome to ensure the right person is in the right job (Cubbingham, 2007). Talent in an organization is evaluated based on the position that he/she holds, and the position is represented by the talent ability that he/she has. Due to those reasons, this study attempts to use classification techniques in data mining to handle issue on talent forecasting. In this study, academic talent type of data in higher learning institution has been chosen as the datasets to represent human talent. As a result, the purpose of this article is to suggest the potential classification techniques for human talent forecasting through some experiments using selected classification algorithms.

This chapter is organized as follows. The second section describes the related work on classification and prediction in data mining; researches on data mining in HR especially for talent management; and human talent forecasting using data mining technique. The third section discusses on experiment setup in this study. Next, the forth section shows experiment results and discussions. Then, section five suggests some related future works. Finally, the paper ends at Section 6 with the concluding remarks acknowledged.

2. Related work

2.1 Classification and prediction in data mining

Data mining tasks are generally categorized as clustering, association, classification and prediction (Chien & Chen, 2008; Ranjan, 2008). Over the years, data mining has evolved various techniques to perform the tasks that include database oriented techniques, statistic, machine learning, pattern recognition, neural network, rough set and etc. Database or data warehouse are rich with hidden information that can be used to provide intelligent decision making. Intelligent decision refers to the ability to make automated decision that is quite similar to human decision. Classification and prediction in machine learning are among the techniques that can produce intelligent decision. At this time, many classification and prediction techniques have been proposed by researchers in machine learning, pattern recognition and statistics.

Classification and prediction in data mining are two forms of data analysis that can be used to extract models to describe important data classes or to predict future data trends (Han & Kamber, 2006). The classification process has two phases; the first phase is learning process, the training data will be analyzed by the classification algorithm. The learned model or classifier shall be represented in the form of classification rules. Next, the second phase is classification process where the test data are used to estimate the accuracy of the classification model or classifier. If the accuracy is considered acceptable, the rules can be applied to the classification of new data (Fig. 1).

Several techniques that are used for data classification are decision tree, Bayesian methods, Bayesian network, rule-based algorithms, neural network, support vector machine, association rule mining, k-nearest-neighbor, case-based reasoning, genetic algorithms, rough sets, and fuzzy logic. In this study, we attempt to use three main classification techniques i.e. decision tree, neural network and k-nearest-neighbor. However, decision tree and neural network are found useful in developing predictive models in many fields(Tso & Yau, 2007). The advantage of decision tree technique is that it does not require any domain knowledge or parameter setting, and is appropriate for exploratory knowledge discovery. The second technique is neural-network which has high tolerance of noisy data as well as the ability to classify pattern on which they have not been trained. It can be used when we have little knowledge of the relationship between attributes and classes. Next, the K-nearest-neighbor technique is an instance-based learning using distance metric to measure the similarity of instances. All these three classification techniques have their own advantages and disadvantages, for that reasons, this study endeavor to explore these classification techniques for human talent data. Besides that, data mining technique has been applied in many fields, but its application in HR is very rare (Chien & Chen, 2008).

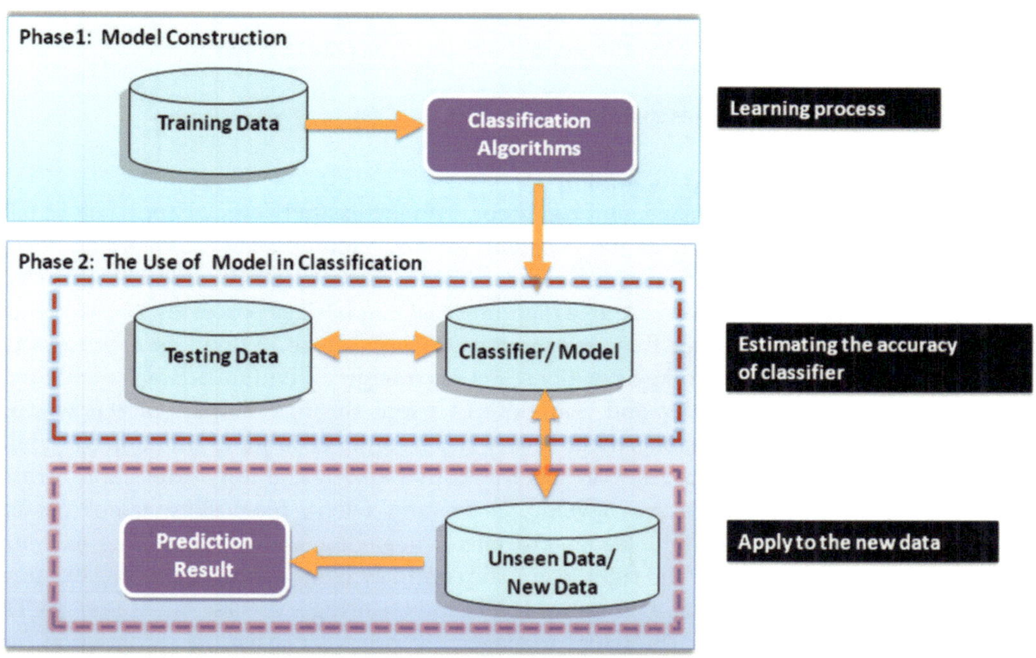

Fig. 1. Classification and Prediction in Data Mining

Recently, there are some researches that show great interest on solving HR problems using data mining approach (Ranjan, 2008). Table 1 lists some of the tasks in human resource that use data mining technique, and it shows there are quite limited studies on data mining in human resource domain. In addition, until now there are quite limited discussions on talent management such as for talent forecasting, career planning and talent recruitment use data mining approach. In HR, data mining technique used focuses on personnel selection especially to choose the right candidates for a job. The classification and prediction in data mining for HR problems are infrequent and there are some examples such as to predict the length of service, sales premium, to persistence indices of insurance agents and analyze miss-operation behaviors of operators (Chien & Chen, 2008). Due to these reasons, this study attempts to use data mining classification techniques to forecast potential employees as substantial of talent management task using the past experience knowledge.

HR Task	Data Mining Technique
Personnel selection	Decision tree (Chien & Chen, 2008), Fuzzy Logic and Data Mining (Tai & Hsu, 2005) Rough Set Theory(Chien & Chen, 2007)
Training	Association rule mining (Chen et al., 2007)
Employee Development	Fuzzy Data Mining and Fuzzy Artificial Neural Network (Huang et al., 2006) Decision Tree (Tung et al., 2005)
Performance Evaluation	Potential to use Decision Tree (Zhao, 2008)

Table 1. Data mining Techniques in HRM.

2.2 Talent management and data mining

In any organization, talent management has become an increasingly crucial approach in HR functions. Talent is considered as the capability of any individual to make a significant difference to the current and future performance of the organization (Lynne, 2005). In fact, managing talent involves human resource planning that emphasizes processes for managing people in organization. Besides that, talent management can be defined as a process to ensure leadership continuity in key positions and encourage individual advancement; and decision to manage supply, demand and flow of talent through human capital engine (Cubbingham, 2007). Talent management is very crucial and needs some attention from HR professionals. TP Track Research Report has found that among the top current and future talent management challenges are developing existing talent; forecasting talent needs; attracting and retaining the right leadership talent; engaging talent; identifying existing talent; attracting and retaining the right leadership and key contributor; deploying existing talent; lack of leadership capability at senior levels and ensuring a diverse talent pool (A TP Track Research Report 2005). The talent management process consists of recognizing the key talent areas in the organization, identifying the people in the organization who constitute key talent, and conducting development activities for the talent pool to retain and engage them and also have them ready to move into more significant roles (Cubbingham, 2007) (Fig. 2). These processes involve HR activities that need to be integrated into an effective system (CHINA UPDATE, 2007) (Fig. 2).

In this study, we focus on one of the talent management challenges i.e. to identify the existing talent regarding the key talent in an organization by predicting their performance using previous employee performance records in databases. In this case, we use the past related employee data regarding on their talent by using classification technique in data mining.

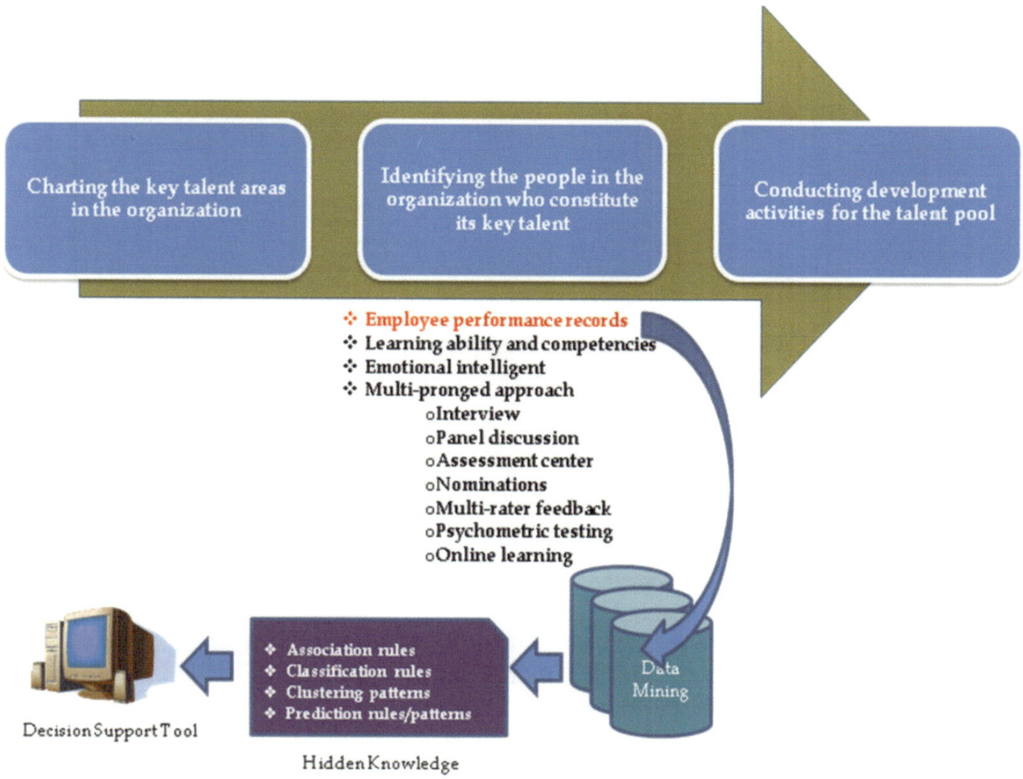

Fig. 2. Data mining and Talent Management

2.3 Human talent forecasting

Recently, with the new demand and increased visibility, HR seeks a more strategic role by turning to data mining methods (Ranjan, 2008). This can be done by discovering generated patterns as useful knowledge from the existing data in HR databases. Thus, this study concentrates on identifying the patterns that relate to the human talent. The patterns can be generated by using some of the major data mining techniques such as clustering to list the employees with similar characteristics, to group the performances and etc. From the association technique, patterns that are discovered can be used to associate the employee's profile for the most appropriate program/job, associated with employee's attitude toperformance and etc. In prediction and classification task, the pattern discovered can be used to predict the percentage accuracy in employee's performance, behavior, and attitudes, predict the performance progress throughout the performance period, and also identify the best profile for different employee and etc. (Fig. 3). The match of data mining problems and talent management needs are very crucial. Therefore, it is very important to determine the suitable data mining techniques for talent management problems.

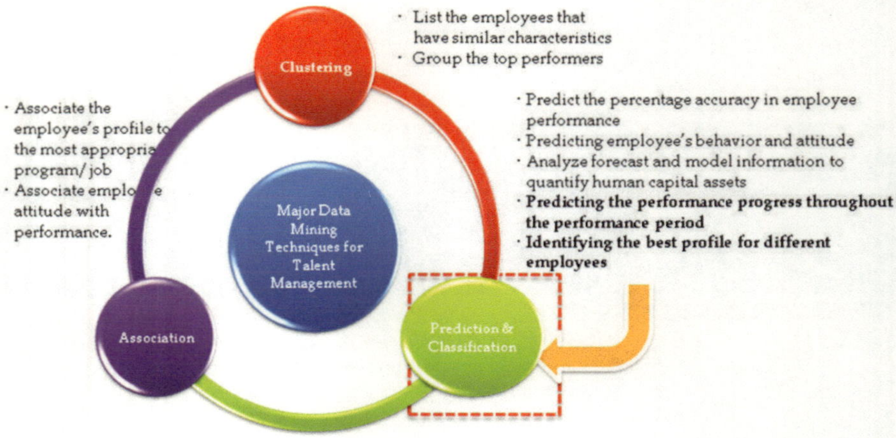

Fig. 3. Data mining Tasks for Talent Management

3. Experiment setup

This experiment attempts to propose the potential data mining classifier for human talent data. The proposed classifier can be used to generate talent performance classification patterns from employee's performance databases. Subsequently, the generated classification patterns can be employed in decision support tool for human talent prediction. The basic process for classification and prediction in data mining has been discussed in the related work (Fig. 1). The experiment setup in this study has several tasks such as simulated data construction, outlier placing, attribute reduction and accuracy of model determination as shown in Fig. 4. However, due to the difficulties to get real data from HR department, because of the confidentiality and security issues, for the exploratory purposes, this study simulates two human talent datasets

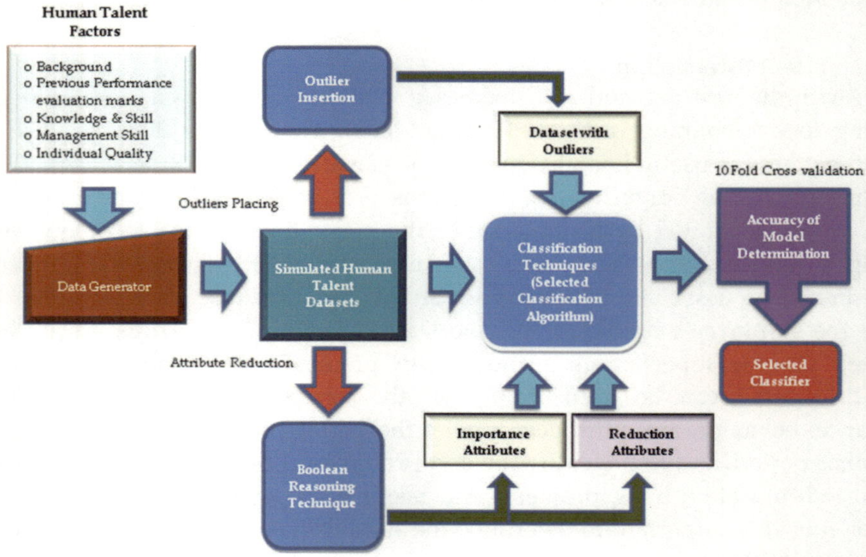

Fig. 4. Experiment Setup

using dataset rule generator shown in Table 2. The first dataset contains one hundred data (*dataset1*) and the second dataset has a thousand performance data (*dataset2*) based on human talent performance factors. In many cases, simulated or syntactic data is an ideal data and can produce a good data mining model. For that reason, in this study uses outlier placing task for *dataset1* to handle that issue and that new dataset known as *dataset3*.

In this experiment, the selected classification techniques used are based on the common techniques used for classification and prediction in data mining. As mentioned earlier in related work, the classification techniques chosen are neural network which is quite popular in data mining community and used as pattern classification technique (Witten & Frank, 2005). The decision tree known as 'divide-and-conquer' approach is from a set of independent instances for classification and the nearest neighbor is for classification that are based on the distance metric. Table 3 summarizes the selected classification techniques in data mining, such as decision tree, neural network and nearest neighbor. In this study, we attempt to use C4.5 and Random Forest for decision tree category; Multilayer Perceptron (MLP) and Radial Basic Function Network (RBFC) for neural network category; and K-Star for the nearest neighbor category.

Factor and Attributes	Rules
Background/ Demographic (D1-D8) (a1-a8) Class level - D4/a4	D1 = RANDBETWEEN (1950-1983), D2 = RANDBETWEEN (1,2,3,4), D3 = RANDBETWEEN (0,1), D4 = RANDBETWEEN ((1-4), D5= RANDBETWEEN (1975-2008) and G2 = IF (D5-D1<25 THEN D1+25 ELSE D5) I2 = G2+RANDBETWEEN(5,10) D6 = IF(I2>2008 THEN 0 ELSE I2) K2= G2+RANDBETWEEN(6,15) D7 = IF(K2>2008THEN 0 ELSE K2) M2= G2+RANDBETWEEN(10,30) D8 = IF(M2>2008 THEN 0 ELSE M2)
Previous performance evaluation (DP1-DP15) (a9-a22)	{DP1,DP15}= RANDBETWEEN (75-100)
Knowledge and skill (PQA-PQH) (a23-a42)	{ PQA,PQC1,PQC2,PQC3,PQD1, PQD2,PQD3,PQE1,PQE2,PQE, PQE4,PQE5,PQF1,PQF2,PQG1, PQG2,PQH1,PQH2,PQH3,PQH4} =RANDBETWEEN (1-10)
Management skill (PQB, AC1-AC5) (a43 -a48)	{PQB }=RANDBETWEEN(1-10) {AC1, AC2,AC3,AC4,AC5}= RANDBETWEEN (0-5)
Individual Quality (T1-T2, SO, AA1-AA2) (a49-a53)	{T1,T2} = RANDBETWEEN (1-10) {SO,AA1,AA2} = RANDBETWEEN (0-5)

Table 2. Rules to Generate Simulated Dataset

Data Mining Techniques	Classification Algorithm
Decision Tree	• *C4.5* (Decision tree induction – the target is nominal and the inputs may be nominal or interval. Sometimes the size of the induced trees is significantly reduced when a different pruning strategy is adopted). • *Random forest* (Choose a test based on a given number of random features at each node, performing no pruning. Random forest constructs random forest by bagging ensembles of random trees).
Neural Network	• *Multi Layer Perceptron* (An accurate predictor for underlying classification problem. Given a fixed network structure, we must determine appropriate weights for the connections in the network). • *Radial Basic Function Network* (Another popular type of feed forward network, which has two layers, not counting the input layer, and differs from a multilayer perceptron in the way that the hidden units perform computations).
Nearest Neighbor	• *K*Star* (An instance-based learning using distance metric to measure the similarity of instances and generalized distance function based on transformation

Table 3. Selected Classification Algorithm

The human talent factor in this case study is for academic talent in higher learning institution. The academic talent factors are extracted from the common practice for evaluation, performance evaluation documents and expertise experiences. Besides the human performance factors, the talent background and management skill are also considered in the process to identify the potential talent. In this experiment, the training dataset contains 53 related attributes from five performance factors demonstrated in Table 4. The target class for the dataset is the academic position (*D4*) which is representing as professor, associate professor, senior lecturer and lecturer. The classification technique used is based on 10 fold cross validation training and test dataset. In this experiment, the data mining tools used are WEKA and ROSETTA toolkit. This experiment has two phases; the first phase is to identify the possible techniques using selected classifier algorithm for full attributes of data. In this case, we use all the attributes which are defined before for the full dataset.

Besides that, this experiment concentrates on the accuracy of selected classifiers in order to identify potential classifier algorithm for the datasets. The accuracy of classifier is based on the percentage of test set samples that are correctly classified. The second phase of experiment is to compare the accuracy of classifier for attribute reduction. In this case, Boolean reasoning technique is used to select the most relevant or important attributes from the dataset. The attribute reduction phase is divided into two stages. The first stage is attribute reduction using the shortest length attribute, which is used by many researches in attribute reduction process. The aim of this process is to determine the important attributes for the data set, which is known as attribute reduction dataset (AR). The second stage is for

Factor and Attributes	Variable Name	Meaning
Background (7)	D1,D2,D3,D5,D6, D7,D8	Age ,Race, Gender, Year of service, Year of Promotion 1, Year of Promotion 2, Year of Promotion 3
Previous performance evaluation (15)	DP1,DP2,DP3, DP4,DP5,DP6, DP7,DP8,PP9, DP10, DP11,DP12, DP13,DP14, DP15	Performance evaluation marks for 15 years
Knowledge and skill (20)	PQA,PQC1,PQC2, PQC3,PQD1, PQD2,PQD3,PQE1, PQE2,PQE, PQE4,PQE5,PQF1, PQF2,PQG1, PQG2,PQH1,PQH2, PQH3,PQH4	Professional qualification (Teaching, supervising, research, publication and conferences)
Management skill (6)	PQB,AC1,AC2,AC3,AC4,AC5	Student obligation and administrative tasks
Individual Quality (5)	T1,T2,SO,AA1,AA2	Training, award and appreciation

Table 4. Factors and Attributes for Academic Talent

the combination of important attribute which is known as importance attributes dataset (IA). In this case, we attempt to study the accuracy of the classifier using all importance attributes. Finally, the experiment results for each phase is evaluated using the statistical significant test in order to determine the most significant classifier for each of datasets and it will be considered as the potential classifier for human talent data.

4. Result and discussion

In this experiment, the accuracy of classification techniques is based on the selected classifier algorithm. In the first phase, the accuracy for each of the classifier algorithm for full attributes for three datasets is shown in Table 5. The results for full attribute present the highest accuracy of model is C4.5 (95.14%, 99.90% and 90.54%) which is the results could be considered as an indicator to the potential classification algorithm for human talent data (Fig. 5.).

Classification Algorithm	Dataset1	Dataset2	Dataset3
C4.5	95.14	99.90	90.54
Random forest	74.91	95.43	71.80
Multi Layer Perceptron (MLP)	87.16	99.84	84.55
Radial Basis Function Network	91.45	99.98	87.09
K-Star	92.06	97.83	87.79

Table 5. Accuracy of Model for Full Attributes

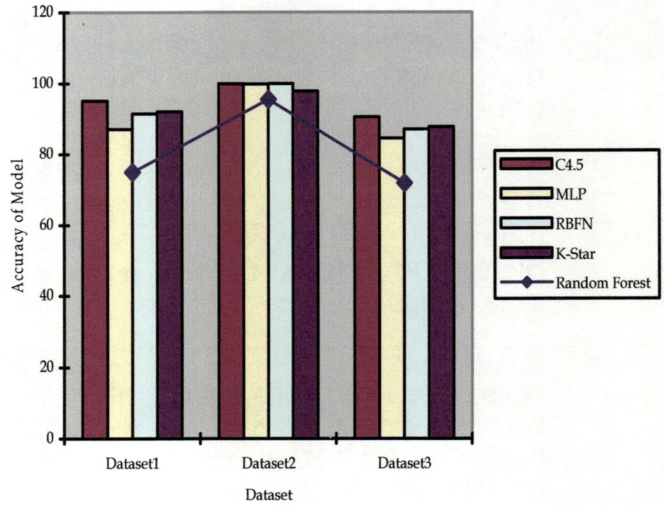

Fig. 5. Accuracy of Model for Full Attributes

The result for full attributes shows us the more data that we used (*dataset2*) in training process the highest accuracy of model can be developed. Besides that, the accuracy for dataset3 which contains outliers is slightly down for all classifiers, this result demonstrates the effect of outliers in dataset for accuracy of the model. The second phase of the experiment is considered as a relevant analysis process in order to determine the accuracy of the selected classification technique using datasets with attribute reduction. In this experiment, we focus on dataset1 and dataset2. The purpose of attribute reduction process is to select the most relevant attribute in the dataset. The reduction process is implemented using Boolean reasoning technique. Through attribute reduction, we can decrease the preprocessing and processing time and space. Table 6. shows the relevant analysis results for attribute reduction, five (5) attributes are selected, all the attributes are from the background factor. By using these attributes reduction variables, the second phase of experiment is implemented. The aim of this experiment is to find out the accuracy of the classification techniques with attribute reduction using the shortest length attributes and combination of the important attributes after reduction process.

Variable Name	Meaning
D1,D5,D6,D7,D8	Age, Year of service, Year of Promotion 1, Year of Promotion 2, Year of Promotion 3

Table 6. Important Attributes from Atribut Reduction

Table 7. shows the accuracy of the classification algorithm with attribute reduction for the shortest length methods (AR dataset). The C4.5 classifier has the highest percentage of accuracy in the first stage of second phase experiment (Table 7.) but the accuracy has declined at this stage.

Classification Algorithm	Dataset1	Dataset2
C4.5	61.06	63.21
Random forest	58.85	62.49
Multi Layer Perceptron (MLP)	55.32	60.16
Radial Basis Function Network(RBFN)	59.52	64.05
K-Star	60.22	63.92

Table 7. Accuracy of Model for Attribute Reduction

In this experiment, the result indicates more attributes used in dataset that will affect the accuracy of the classifier. Consequently, this result illustrates most of the attributes in dataset are important and should be considered. However, with the combination of attributes from reduction process (IA dataset) in the second stage of experiment, the accuracy of classifier is higher compared to the shortest length attributes (AR dataset). Table 8. shows the accuracy of classifier for importance attributes for *dataset1* and *dataset2*. The C4.5 classifier has the highest accuracy for both datasets at this stage of experiment. Fig. 6. shows the accuracy of model for AR datasets and IA datasets in the second phase experiment.

Classification Algorithm	Dataset1	Dataset2
C4.5	95.63	99.89
Random forest	86.50	99.88
Multi Layer Perceptron (MLP)	79.49	99.91
Radial Basis Function Network(RBFN)	84.41	99.96
K-Star	78.40	99.95

Table 8. Accuracy of Model for Importance Attribute

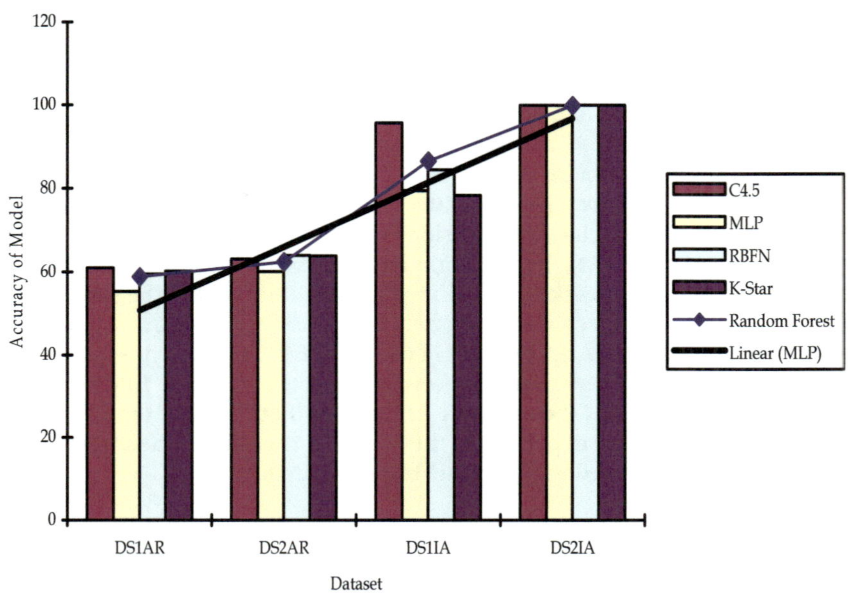

Fig. 6. The Accuracy of Model for Attribute Reduction and Importance Attributes

Consecutively, to propose the potential classifier for human talent data, the statistical significant test is conducted using t-test evaluation. By using the pair t-test as shown in Table 9, a positive mean difference in accuracy shows that the C4.5 has the highest value of positive mean which is significantly better than other classifiers. For the accuracy criterion, C4.5 is significantly better than Random Forest and MLP, with a p-value < 0.05. In addition, decision tree can produce a model which may represent interpretable rules or logic statement and can be performed without complicated computations and the technique can be used for both continuous and categorical variables. This technique is more suitable for predicting categorical outcomes and less appropriate for application to time series data (Tso & Yau, 2007). Besides that, the decision tree classifiers are a quite popular technique because the construction of tree does not require any domain knowledge or parameter setting, and therefore is appropriate for exploratory knowledge discovery.

	Paired Samples	Mean	SD	t	df	p-value
Pair 1	C4.5 – Random Forest	7.93000	8.45564	2.481	6	*0.048
Pair 2	C4.5 - MLP	5.56286	5.56322	2.646	6	*0.038
Pair 3	C4.5 - RBFN	2.70143	4.15154	1.722	6	0.136
Pair 4	C4.5 - KStar	3.60000	6.17387	1.543	6	0.174

SD: Standard Deviation; t: significant ratio; df: degrees of freedom; p: significant 2-tailed value;
* most significant

Table 9. Pair T-Test Result on Accuracy of Model for C4.5

In these experiments, we observe the great potential to use C4.5 classification algorithm in the next stage of data mining process i.e. prediction using the constructed classification model. Besides that, these results also show about the suitability of C4.5 classifier for the human talent datasets.

5. Future works

In this study, due to the difficulties to obtain human talent data, we have to simulate the data for exploratory purposes and setup the classification experiment using the data. In this case, knowledge discovered or constructed classification model by using the proposed classifier for the datasets cannot be used to represent the real problems. In future works, the similar experiment setup can be applied to the real data in order to use classification model constructed by the proposed classifier. Besides that, other Data mining techniques such as Support Vector Machine (SVM), Fuzzy logic and Artificial Immune System (AIS) should also be considered for future work on classification techniques using the same dataset.

In some cases, the attribute relevancy has also become a factor on the accuracy of the classification algorithm. In the next experiment, the attribute reduction process should be applied to other reduction techniques in order to confirm these findings whether the number of attributes will affect the accuracy of the classifier. Besides that, the C4.5 classifier has the highest accuracy in the experiment; the accuracy for other decision tree classifier also needs to be experimented in order to validate these findings.

6. Conclusion

This article has described the significance of the study using data mining for talent management especially for classification and prediction. However, there should be more data mining techniques applied to the different problem domains in HR field of research in order to broaden our horizon of academic and practice work on data mining in HR. In addition, C4.5 classifier algorithm is the potential classifier in this experiment. Thus, this technique can be used for real human talent data in the next prediction phase i.e classification rules construction. These generated classification rules can be used to predict the potential talent for the specific task in an organization. In HRM, there are several tasks that can be solved using this approach, for examples, selecting new employees, matching people to jobs, planning career paths, planning training needs for new and senior employee, predicting employee performance, predicting future employee and etc. In conclusion, the ability to continuously change and obtain new understanding about classification and prediction in HR field has thus, become the major contribution to HR data mining.

7. References

A TP Track Research Report (2005). *Talent Management: A State of the Art*: Tower Perrin HR Services.

Chen, K. K., Chen, M. Y., Wu, H. J., & Lee, Y. L. (2007). *Constructing a Web-based Employee Training Expert System with Data Mining Approach.* Paper presented at the Paper in The 9th IEEE International Conference on E-Commerce Technology and The 4th IEEE International Conference on Enterprise Computing, E-Commerce and E-Services (CEC-EEE 2007).

Chien, C. F., & Chen, L. F. (2007). Using Rough Set Theory to Recruit and Retain High-Potential Talents for Semiconductor Manufacturing. *IEEE Transactions on Semiconductor Manufacturing, 20*(4), 528-541.

Chien, C. F., & Chen, L. F. (2008). Data mining to improve personnel selection and enhance human capital: A case study in high-technology industry. *Expert Systems and Applications, 34*(1), 380-290.

CHINA UPDATE. (2007). HR News for Your Organization : The Tower Perrin Asia Talent Management Study. Retrieved from www.towersperrin.com. 7/1/2008.

Cubbingham, I. (2007). Talent Management : Making it real. *Development and Learning in Organizations, 21*(2), 4-6.

Han, J., & Kamber, M. (2006). *Data Mining: Concepts and Techniques.* San Francisco: Morgan Kaufmann Publisher.

Huang, M. J., Tsou, Y. L., & Lee, S. C. (2006). Integrating fuzzy data mining and fuzzy artificial neural networks for discovering implicit knowledge. *Knowledge-Based Systems, 19*(6), 396-403.

Jantan, H., Hamdan, A. R., & Othman, Z. A. (2008). *Data Mining Techniques for Performance Prediction in Human Resource Application.* Paper presented at the 1st Seminar on Data Mining and Optimization, Selangor.

Jantan, H., Hamdan, A. R., & Othman, Z. A. (2009, 25-27 February 2009). *Knowledge Discovery Techniques for Talent Forecasting in Human Resource Application.* Paper presented at the World Academy of Science, Engineering and Technology, Penang, Malaysia.

Lynne, M. (2005). *Talent Management Value Imperatives : Strategies for Execution*: The Conference Board.

Osei-Bryson, K.-M. (2010). Towards supporting expert evaluation of clustering results using a data mining process model. *Information Sciences, 180*(3), 414-431.

Park, S. C., Piramuthu, S., & Shaw, M.J. (2001). Dynamic rule refinement in knoledge-based data mining systems. *Decision Support System, 31*(2), 205-222.

Ranjan, J. (2008). Data Mining Techniques for better decisions in Human Resource Management Systems. *International Journal of Business Information Systems, 3*(5), 464-481.

Sinha, A. P., & Zhao, H. (2008). Incorporating domain knowledge into data mining classifiers: An application in indirect lending. *Decision Support System, 46*(1), 287-299.

Tai, W. S., & Hsu, C. C. (2005). A Realistic Personnel Selection Tool Based on Fuzzy Data Mining Method. Retrieved from www.atlantis-press.com/php/download_papaer?id=46, 9/1/2008.

Tso, G. K. F., & Yau, K. K. W. (2007). Predicting electricity energy consumption: A comparison of regression analysis, decision tree and neural networks. *Energy, 32*, 1761-1768.

Tung, K. Y., Huang, I. C., Chen, S. L., & Shih, C. T. (2005). Mining the Generation Xer's job attitudes by artificial neural network and decision tree - empirical evidence in Taiwan. *Expert Systems and Applications, 29*(4), 783-794.

Wan, S., & Lei, T.C. (2009). A knowledge-based decision support system to analyze the debris-flow problems at Chen-Yu-Lan River, Taiwan. *Knowledge-Based System, 22*(8), 580-588.

Witten, I. H., & Frank, E. (2005). *Data Mining: Practical Machine Learning Tools and Techniques*. San Francisco: Morgan Kaufmann Publisher.

Zanakis, S. H., Fernandez, I.B. (2005). Competitiveness of nations: A knowledge discovery examination. *European Journal of Operational Research, 166*(1), 185-211.

Zhao, X. (2008). *An Empirical Study of Data Mining in Performance Evaluation of HRM*. Paper presented at the International Symposium on Intelligent Information Technology Application Workshops, Hangzhou, China.

Zhuang, Z. Y., Churilov, L., Burstein, F., & Sikaris, K. (2009). Combining data mining and case-based reasoning for intelligent decision support for pathology ordering by general practitioners. *European Journal of Operational Research, 195*, 662-675.

2

New Implementations of Data Mining in a Plethora of Human Activities

Alberto Ochoa[1,2], Julio Ponce[3,4], Francisco Ornelas[4], Rubén Jaramillo[7], Ramón Zataraín[5], María Barrón[5], Claudia Gómez[6], José Martínez[6] and Arturo Elias[3]

[1]*Juarez City University*
[2]*UNICAMP Instituto de Computacão*
[3]*Aguascalientes University*
[4]*Cuauhtémoc University*
[5]*ITC*
[6]*ITCM*
[7]*CIMAT*
[1,3,4,5,6,7]*México*
[2]*Brazil*

1. Introduction

The fast growth of the societies along with the development and use of the technology, due to this at the moment have much information which can be analyzed in the search of relevant informationto make predictions or decision making. Knowledge Discovery and Data Mining are powerful data analysis tools. The term Data mining is used to describe the non-trivial extraction of implicit, Data Mining is a discovery process in large and complex data set, refers to extracting knowledge from data bases. Data mining is a multidisciplinary field with many techniques. Whit this techniques you can create a mining model that describe the data that you will use (Ponce et al., 2009a).

Typical Data Mining techniques include clustering, association rule mining, classification, and regression.

We show an overview of some algorithms that used the data mining to solve problems that arisen from the human activities like: Electrical Power Design, Trash Collectors Routes, Frauds in Saving Houses, Vehicle Routing Problem.

One of the reasons why the Data Mining techniques are widely used is that there is a need to transform a large amount of data on information and knowledge useful.

Having a large amount of data and not have tools that can process a phenomenon has been described as rich in data but poverty in information (Han & Kamber, 2006). This steady growth of data, which is stored in large databases, has exceeded the ability of human beings to understand. Moreover, various problems they might present a constant stream of data, which may be more difficult to analyze the power of information.

1.1 Tree decisions to improve electrical power design

A decision tree (DT) is a directed acyclic graph, consisting of a node called root, which has no input arcs, and a set of nodes that have an entrance arch. Those nodes with output arcs are called internal nodes or nodes of evidence and those with no output arcs are known as leaf nodes or terminal nodes of decision (Rokach & Maimon, 2005).

The main objectives pursued by creating a DT (Safavian & Landgrebe, 1991) are:

- Correctly classify the largest number of objects in the training set (TS).
- Generalize, during construction of the tree, the TS to ensure that new objects are classified with the highest percentage of correct answers possible.
- If the dataset is dynamic, the structure of DT should be upgraded easily.

An algorithm for decision tree generation consists of two stages: the first is the induction stage of the tree and the second stage of classification. In the first stage is constructed decision tree from training set, commonly each internal node of the tree is composed of an attribute of the portion of the test and training set present in the node is divided according to the values that can take that attribute. The construction of the tree starts generating its root node, choosing a test attribute and partitioning the training set into two or more subsets, for each partition generates a new node and so on. When nodes are more objects of a class generate an internal node, when it contains objects of a class, they form a sheet which is assigned the class label. In the second stage of the algorithm, each new object is classified by the tree constructed, the tree is traversed from the root to a leaf node, from which membership is determined to some kind of object. The way forward in the tree is determined by decisions made at each internal node, according to attribute this to the test.

Pattern Recognition one of the most studied problems is the supervised classification, where it is known that a universe of objects is grouped into a given number of classes which have of each, a sample of known objects belong to it and the problem is given a new order to establish their relationships with each of those classes (Ruiz et al., 1999).

Supervised classification algorithms are designed to determine the membership of an object (described by a set of attributes) to one or more classes, based on the information contained in a previously classified set of objects (training set - TS).

Among the algorithms used for solving supervised classification are decision trees. A decision tree is a structure that consists of nodes (internal and leaves) and arches. Its internal nodes are characterized by one or more attributes of these nodes test and emerge one or more arcs. These arcs have an associated attribute value test and these values determine which path to follow in the path of the tree.

Leaf nodes contain information that determines the object belongs to a class. The main characteristics of a decision tree are: simple construction, no need to predetermine parameters for their construction, can treat multi-class problems the same way he works with two-class problems, ability to be represented by a set of rules and the easy interpretation of its structure.

1.1.1 Classifications of decision trees

There are various classifications of decision trees, for example according to the number of test attributes in their internal nodes there are two types of trees:

- Single-valued: only contain a test attribute on each node. Examples of these algorithms include ID3 (Mitchell, 1997), C4.5 (Quinlan, 1993), CART (Breiman et al., 1984), FACT (Vanichsetakul & Loh, 1988), QUEST (Shis & Loh, 1988), Model Trees (Shou et al., 2005),

CTC (Perez et al., 2007), ID5R (Utgoff, 1989), ITI (Utgoff et al., 1997), UFFT (Gama & Medes, 2005), StreamTree (Jin & Agrawal, 2003), FDT (Janikowo, 1998), G-DT (Pedrycz, 2005) and Spider (Wang, et al., 2007).

- Multivalued: they have to a subset of attributes in each of its nodes. For example, PT2 (Utgoff & Brodley,1990), LMDT (Utgoff & Brodley,1995), GALE (Llora & Wilson, 2004) and C-DT.

According to the type of decision made by the tree, there are two types of trees:

- Fuzzy: give a degree of membership of each class of the data set, for example, C-DT, FDT, G-DT and Spider.
- Drives: assign the object belongs to only one class, so the object is or does not belong to a class, are examples of such algorithms: ID3, C4.5, CART, FACT, QUEST, Model Trees, CTC, LMDT, GALE, ID5R, ITI, UFFT, and StreamTree PT2.

The algorithms for generation of decision trees can be classified according to their ability to process dynamic data sets, i.e. sets in which lets you add new objects.
According to this there are two types of algorithms for generation of decision trees:

- Incremental: can handle dynamic data sets which are getting a partial solution as they are looking at the objects. Examples of such algorithms are: ID5R, ITI, UFFT, and StreamTree PT2.
- No Incremental: can only work on static data sets as needed for the solution to the dataset in its entirety. Examples include: ID3, C4.5, CART, FACT, QUEST, Model Trees, CTC, FDT, G-DT, Spider LMDT, GALE and C-DT.

1.1.2 Decision tree application

To diagnose the electric power apparatus, the decision tree method can be a highly recommended classification tool because it provides the if-then-rule in visible, and thus we may have a possibility to connect the physical phenomena to the observed signals. The most important point in constructing the diagnosing system is to make clear the relations between the faults and the corresponding signals. Such a database system can be built up in the laboratory using a model electric power apparatus, and we have made it. The next important thing is the feature extraction (Llora & Wilson, 2004).

2. Trash collectors routes organized by profiles

Waste. It is something that we produce as part of everyday living, but we do not normally think too much about our waste. Actually many cities generates a waste stream of great complexity, toxicity, and volume (see fig. 1). It includes municipal solid waste, industrial solid waste, hazardous waste, and other specialty wastes, such as medical, nuclear, mining, agricultural waste, construction and demolition (C&D) waste, household waste, etc. (OECD, 2008).
In the management of solid waste have the problem relates to the household waste is the individual decision-making over waste generation and disposal. When the people decide how much to consume and what to consume, they do not take into account how much waste they produce.
Therefore garbage collection is a very complex (even though in most cases do not perceive it) as not only identify routes used by vehicles for this purpose (which by itself is highly complex, to be taken into consideration many factors including the capability of vehicles, the

amount of waste that can each container, the type of waste, which is held in each container, the distance between containers, street address, etc.), but to determine what the best way to make such collection (Marquez, 2009).
Currently a major concern in the world is the way which must be stored, recycled or destroy the waste that we produce (as they have done studies that indicate that the daily waste production per person is about an extra kilogram to the produced in the manufacture of the products we use daily) which starts with the garbage collection process.
There are many algorithms and techniques being used to improve the collection process, creating different routes on the basis of the different profiles from those who generate the garbage and of the type of waste, some of these algorithms and techniques are: Ant Colony Algorithms, Hybrid Genetic Algorithms, Data Mining, among others.

Fig. 1. Example of composition by weight of household garbage

3. Fraud analysis in saving houses

Fraud is an illegal activity, which has many variants and is almost as old as mankind. Fraud tries to take advantage in some way, usually economic, by the fraudster with respect to the shame. Specifically in the case of plastic card fraud there are several variants (Sánchez et al., 2009). The total cost of plastic card fraud is bigger respect to other forms of payment. The first line of defence against fraud is based on preventive measures such as the Chip and PIN cards. Next step is formed by methods employed to identify potential fraud trying to minimize potential losses. These methods are called fraud detection systems (FDS), and a variety of ways are used to detect the most behavior potential fraudulent.

3.1 Techniques for detection of frauds

There are two major frameworks to detect fraud through statistical methods. If fraud is conducted in a known way, the pattern recognition techniques are typically used, especially supervised classification schemes (Whitrow et al., 2009). On the other hand if the way in which fraud is not know, for example, when there are new fraudulent behaviors, outlier analysis methods are recommended (Kou et al., 2004). Previous research has established that the use of outlier analysis is one of the best techniques for the detection of fraud in general. Some studies show simple techniques for anomaly detection analysis to discover plastic card fraud. (Juszczak et al., 2008). However, to establish patterns to identify anomalies, these patterns are learned by the fraudsters and then they change the way to make de fraud. Other problem with this approach is not always abnormal behaviors are fraudulent, so a successful system must locate the true positive events, that is, transactions that are detected as fraud, but they really are fraud and not only appear to be fraudulent. Time is a factor against it, because to reduce losses, fraud detection should be done as quickly as possible. In practical applications it is possible to use supervised and unsupervised methods together.

3.1.1 Clustering

The clustering is primarily a technique of unsupervised approach, even if the semi-supervised clustering has also been studied frequently (Basu et al., 2004). Although often clustering and anomaly detection appear to be fundamentally different from one another, have developed many techniques to detect anomalies based on clustering, which can be grouped into three categories which depend on three different assumptions regarding (Chandola et al., 2009):

a. Normal data instances belong to a pooled data set, while the anomalies do not belong to any group clustered.
b. Normal instances of data are close to the cluster centroids, while anomalies are further away from these centroids.
c. The normal data belongs to large, dense clusters, whereas the anomalies belong to small and sparse clusters.

Each of the above assumptions has their own forms of detect outliers which have advantages and disadvantages between them.

3.1.2 Hybrid systems

However, as in many aspects of artificial intelligence, the hybridization is a very current trend to detect abnormalities. The reason is because many developed algorithms do not follow entirely the concepts of a simple classical metaheuristic (Lozano et al., 2010), to solve this problem is looking for the best from a combination of metaheuristics (and any other kind of optimization methods) that perform together to complement each other and produce a profitable synergy, to which is called hybridization (Raidl, 2006).

Some possible reasons for the hybridization are (Grosan et al., 2007):

1. Improve the performance of evolutionary algorithms.
2. Improve the quality of solutions obtained by evolutionary algorithms.
3. Incorporate evolutionary algorithms as part of a larger system.

In this way, Evolutionary Algorithms (EAs) have been the most frequently technique of hybridization used for clustering. However previous research in this respect has been limited to the single objective case: criteria based on cluster compactness have been the objectives most commonly employed, as the measures provide smooth incremental guidance in all parts of search space.

Since many years ago there has been a growing interest in developing and applying of EAs in multi-objective optimization (Deb, 2001).

The recent studies on evolutionary algorithms have shown that the population-based algorithms are potential candidate to solve multi-objective optimization problems and can be efficiently used to eliminate most of the difficulties of classical single objective methods such as the sensitivity to the shape of the Pareto-optimal front and the necessity of multiple runs to find multiple Pareto-optimal solutions.

In general, the goal of a multi-objective optimization algorithm is not only to guide the search towards the Pareto-optimal front but also to maintain population diversity in the set of the Pareto optimal solutions. In this way the following three main goals need to be achieved:

- Maximize the number of elements of the Pareto optimal set found.
- Minimize the distance of the Pareto front produced by the algorithm with respect to the true (global) Pareto front (assuming we know its location).
- Maximize the spreads of solutions found, so that we can have a distribution of vectors as smooth and uniform as possible (Dehuri et al., 2009).

So it looks like a good proposal to develop a FDS with a foundation of multi-objective clustering, which places the problem of detecting fraud in an appropriate context to reality. In the same way, the system is strengthened through hybridization using PSO for the creation of clusters, and then finds the anomalies using the clustering outlier concept.

The FDS is running on the plastic card issuing institution. When a transaction arrived is sent to the FDS to be verified, the FDS receives the card details and purchase value to verify if the transaction is genuine, by calculating the anomalies, based on the expenditure profile of each cardholder, purchasing and billing locations, time of purchase, etc. When FDS confirms that the transaction is malicious, it activates an alarm and the financial institution decline the transaction. The cardholder concerned is contacted and alerted about the possibility that your card is at risk.

To find information dynamically observation for individual transactions of the cardholder, stored transactions are subject to a clustering algorithm. In general, transactions are stored in a database of the financial institution, which contain too many attributes. Although there are several factors to consider, many proposals working only with the transaction amount, with the idea of reducing the dimensionality of the problem. However, to improve the accuracy of the system is recommended to use other factors such as location and time of the transaction. So, if the purchase amount exceeds a certain value, the time between the uses of the card is low or the locations where different transactions are distant are facts to consider activating the alarm. Therefore, the alarm must be activated with a high level of accuracy.

Overall accuracy is simply the percentage of correct predictions of a classifier on a test set of "ground truth". TP means the rate of predicting "true positives" (the ratio of correctly predicted frauds over all of the true frauds), FP means the rate of predicting "false positives" (the ratio of incorrectly predicted frauds over those test examples that were not frauds, otherwise known as the "false alarm rate") (Stolfo et al., 1997).

Other two types of rates are considered for the results delivered by FDS, FN means the rate of predicting "false negatives" (the ratio of no predicted frauds over all the true frauds) and TN means the rate of predicting "true negatives" (the ratio of normal transactions detected). Table I shows the classification rate of results obtained by the FDS after analyzing a transaction.

Once clusters are established, new transaction is entered and evaluated in the FDS, to see if it belongs to a cluster set or is outside of it, seeing the transaction as an anomaly and becoming a candidate to be fraudulent. All this required the calculation of anomalies through the clustering of transaction information through a multi-objective Pareto front with the support of Particle Swarm Optimization (PSO).

Outcome	Classification
Miss	False Negative (FN)
False Alarm	False Positive (FP)
Hit	True Positive (TP)
Normal	True Negative (TN)

Table 1. Classification rate of results.

The accuracy of the FDS is represented as the fraction of total transactions (both genuine and fraudulent) that are detected as correct, which can be expressed as follows (Stolfo et al., 2000). The equation 1 shows the way to computing the precision.

$$Precision = \frac{\#\ of\ TN + \#\ of\ TP}{Total\ of\ carry\ out\ transaction} \tag{1}$$

Fig. 2 shows the idea of the full flow of the process proposed for the FDS. As shown in the figure, the FDS is divided into two parts, one that involves the creation of clusters and the second in the detection of anomalies.
Transactions outside of clusters are candidates to be considered fraudulent, however as mentioned above the accuracy of the system is a factor to be considered, which is expected to maximize in order to increase the functionality of the FDS.

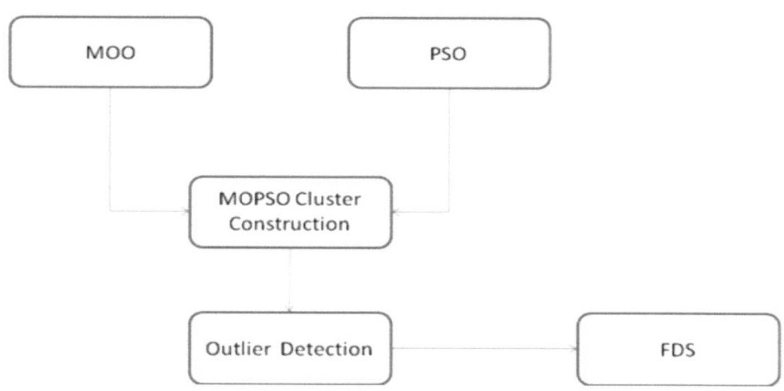

Fig. 2. Research model

4. Data mining in vehicle routing problem

With the rapid development of the World-Wide Web (WWW), the increased popularity and ease of use of its tools, the World-Wide Web is becoming the most important media for collecting, sharing and distributing information. Progress in digital data acquisition and storage technology has resulted in the growth of huge distributed databases. Due that interest has grown in the possibility of tapping these data, of extracting from them information that might be of value to the owner of the database.
The discipline concerned with this task has become known as data mining, is the analysis of observational data sets to find unsuspected relationships and to summarize the data in novel ways that are both understandable and useful to the data owner. The relationships and summaries derived through a data mining exercise are often referred to as models or

patterns. Examples include linear equations, rules, clusters, graphs, tree structures and recurrent patterns in time series.
These patterns provide knowledge on the application domain that is represented by the document collection. Such a pattern can also be seen as a query or implying a query that, when addressed to the collection, retrieves a set of documents. Thus the data mining tools also identify interesting queries which can be used to browse the collection. The system searches for interesting concept sets and relations between concept sets, using explicit bias for capturing interestingness. A set of concepts (terms, phrases or keywords) directly corresponds to a query that can be placed to the document collection for retrieving those documents that contain all the concepts of the set.
In this work, a new ant-colony algorithm, Adaptive Neighboring-Ant Search (AdaNAS), for the semantic query routing problem (SQRP) in a P2P network is presented. The proposed algorithm incorporates an adaptive control parameter tuning technique for runtime estimation of the time-to-live (TTL) of the ants. AdaNAS uses three strategies that take advantage of the local environment: learning, characterization, and exploration. Two classical learning rules are used to gain experience on past performance using three new learning functions based on the distance travelled and the resources found by the ants. These strategies are aimed to produce a greater amount of results in a lesser amount of time. The time-to-live (TTL) parameter is tuned at runtime, though a deterministic rule based on the information acquired by these three local strategies.

4.1 Semantic Query Routing Problem (SQRP)

SQRP is the problem of locating information in a network based on a query formed by keywords. The goal in SQRP is to determine shorter routes from a node that issues a query to those nodes of the network that can appropriately answer the query by providing the requested information. Each query traverses the network, moving from the initiating node to a neighboring node and then to a neighbor of a neighbor and so forth, until it locates the requested resource or gives up in its absence. Due to the complexity of the problem (Amaral, 2004) (Lui et al., 2005) (Tempich et al., 2004), (Wu et al., 2006) solutions proposed to SQRP typically limit to special cases.

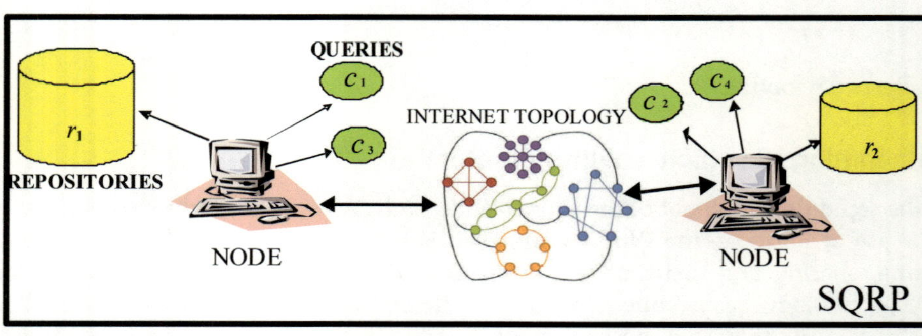

Fig. 3. SQRP Componets

The general strategies of SQRP algorithms are the following. Each node maintains a local database of documents r_i called the repository. The search mechanism is based on nodes sending messages to the neighboring nodes to query the contents of their repositories. The queries q_i are messages that contain keywords that describe for possible matches. If this examination produces results to the query, the node responds by creating another message informing the node that launched the query of the resources available in the responding node. If there are no results or there are too few results, the node that received the query forwards it to one or more of its neighbors. This process is repeated until some predefined stopping criteria is reached. An important observation is that in a P2P network the connection pattern varies among the net (heterogeneous topology), moreover the connections may change in time, and this may alter the routes available for messages to take. As showed in the Figure 1 each node has associated a database of documents ri (repository). Those are available to all nodes connected in the network. A node seeks information at the repository sending messages to its nodes neighbors.

4.2 Neighboring-Ant Search (NAS)

NAS (Cruz et al., 2008) is also an ant-colony system, but incorporates a local structural measure to guide the ants towards nodes that have better connectivity. The algorithm has three main phases: an evaluation phase that examines the local repository and incorporates the classical lookahead technique (Mihail etal., 2004), a transition phase in which the query propagates in the network until its TTL is reached, and a retrieval phase in which the pheromone tables are updated.

Most relevant aspects of former works have been incorporated into the proposed NAS algorithm. The framework of AntNet algorithm is modified to correspond to the problem conditions: in AntNet the final addresses are known, while NAS algorithm does not has a priori knowledge of where the resources are located. On the other hand, differently to AntSearch, the SemAnt algorithm and NAS are focused on the same problem conditions, and both use algorithms based on AntNet algorithm. However, the difference between the SemAnt and NAS is that SemAnt only learns from past experience, whereas NAS takes advantage of the local environment. This means that the search in NAS takes place in terms of the classic local exploration method of Lookahead (Mihail et al., 2004), the local structural metric DDC (Ortega, 2009) its measures the differences between the degree of a node and the degree of its neighbors, and three local functions of the past algorithm performance.

4.3 Adaptative Neighboring-Ant Search (AdaNAS)

AdaNAS is a metaheuristic algorithm, where a set of independent agents called ants cooperate indirectly and sporadically to achieve a common goal.

The algorithm has two objectives: it seeks to maximize the number of resources found by the ants and to minimize the number of steps taken by the ants. AdaNAS guides the queries toward nodes that have better connectivity using the local structural metric degree; in addition, it uses the well known lookahead technique, which, by means of data structures, allows to know the repository of the neighboring nodes of a specific node.

The algorithm performs in parallel all the queries using query ants. Each node has only a query ant, which generates a Forward Ant for attending only one user query, assigning the searched keyword t to the Forward Ant. Moreover the query ants realize periodically the local pheromone evaporation of the node where it is. In the Algorithm is shown the process realized by the Forward Ant. As can be observed all Forward Ants act in parallel. In an initial phase (lines 4-8), the ant checks the local repository, and if it founds matching documents then creates a backward ant. Afterwards, it realizes the search process (lines 9-25) while it has live and has not found R documents. The search process has three sections: Evaluation of results, evaluation and application of the extension of TTL and selection of next node (lines 24-28).

The first section, the evaluation of results (lines 10-15) implements the classical Lookahead technique. That is, the ant x located in a node r, checks the lookahead structure, that indicates how many matching documents are in each neighbor node of r. This function needs three parameters: the current node (r), the keyword (t) and the set of known nodes (known) by the ant. The set known indicates what nodes the lookahead function should ignore, because their matching documents have already taken into account. If some resource is found, the Forward Ant creates a backward ant and updates the quantity of found matching documents.

Algorithm: Forward ant algorithm

```
1  in parallel for each Forward Ant x(r,t,R)
2  initialization: TTL = TTLmax, hops= 0
3  initialization: path=r, Λ=r, known=r
4  Results= get_ local_ documents(r)
5  if results > 0 then
6     create backward ant y(path, results, t)
7     activate y
8  End
9  while TTL < 0 and results < R do
10    La_ results= look ahead(r,t,known)
11    if la results > 0 then
12      create backward ant y(path, la results, t)
13      activate y
14      results   results + la results
15    End
16    if TTL > 0 then
17      TTL= TTL - 1
18    Else
19      if (results < R) and ( ΔTTL(x, results, hops) > 0) then
20        TTL= TTL + ΔTTL(x, results, hops)
21       change parameters: q= 1, Wdeg =0, β2=0
22      End
23     End
24 Hops= hops + 1
25 Known= known∪[ ( r ∪ Γ(r))
25 Λ = Λ ∪ r
27 r = ℓ(x,r,t)
28 add to path(r)
29 End
30 create update ant z(x, path, t)
31 activate z
32 kill x
33 end of in parallel
```

Fig. 4. AdaNAS algorithm

The second section (lines 16-23) is evaluation and application of the extension of TTL. In this section the ant verifies if TTL reaches zero, if it is true, the ant intends to extend its life, if it can do it, it changes the normal transition rule modifying some parameters (line 21) in order to create the modified transition rule. The third section of the search process phase is the selection of the next node. Here, the transition rule (normal or modified) is applied for selecting the next node and some structures are updated. The final phase occurs when the search process finishes; then, the Forward Ant creates an update ant for doing the pheromone update.

Figure 5 shows the results of the different experiments applied to NAS and AdaNAS on thirty runnings for each ninety different instances generated with the characteristics showed in (Cruz et al., 2004). It can been seen from it that on all the instances the AdaNAS algorithm outperforms NAS. On average, AdaNAS had an efficiency 81% better than NAS. The topology and the repositories were created static, whereas the queries were launched randomly during the simulation. Each simulation was run for 15,000 queries during 500 time units, each unit has 100ms. The average performance was studied by computing three performance measures of each 100 queries. Average efficiency, defined as the average of resources found per traversed edge (hits/hops).

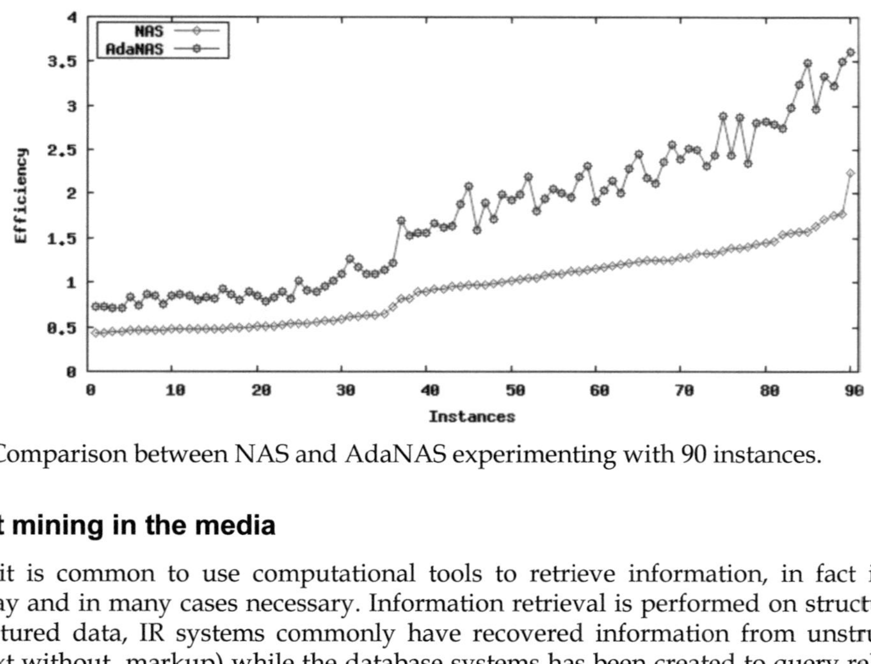

Fig. 5. Comparison between NAS and AdaNAS experimenting with 90 instances.

5. Text mining in the media

Today it is common to use computational tools to retrieve information, in fact it is an everyday and in many cases necessary. Information retrieval is performed on structured or unstructured data, IR systems commonly have recovered information from unstructured text (text without markup) while the database systems has been created to query relational data (sets of records that have values for predefined) , the principal differences between are in terms of retrieval model, data structures and query language. (Christopher et al., 2009).

According to the literature reviewed, nowadays do not exist techniques for Natural Language Processing to achieve 100% accurate results, either with the statistical approach, or the linguistic approach, in such a situation some researchers have blended both techniques (Chaudhuri et al. , 2006) (Gonzalez et al., 2007) (Vallez & Pedraza, 2007). For example, in (Sayyadian, 2004) they propose several methods to exploit structured information in databases and present a query expansion mechanism based on information extraction from structured data. The experimental results obtained show that using more structured information to expand the textual queries to improve performance in the recovery of entities in texts.

It is common that the amount of data with which one interacts is considerably larger and cannot be worked and in some cases it would be very difficult to work with these manually, in addition, these digital resources increase rapidly every day, reason by which the World Wide Web has become so popular, and is notorious as well as increased information systems. Because of this, it is very important to retrieve information efficiently (Hristidis & Papakonstantinou, 2002).

The search motor of Google, is the clearest example of how a computational tool can facilitate a user the information retrieval, unfortunately does not allow elaborate searches successfully, since it is designed mainly to operate with key words on documentary data bases; email servers are other type of tools very useful and popular.

Due to the diversity of existing digital media (heterogeneous data) has been investigated in diverse areas, as much in information retrieval as in natural language processing, whose final objective is to facilitate access to information and improve performance . In (Vallez & Pedraza, 2007) classified research areas as follows:

- The information extraction is the removal of a text or a set of texts entities, events and relationships between existing elements.
- The generation of summaries must like objective condense the most relevant information of a text. The techniques used vary according to compression rate, the purpose of summary, the genre of the text, the language (or languages) of the source texts, among other factors.
- The quest for answers can give a concrete answer to the question raised by the user, is important that the information needs to be well defined: dates, places, people, etc.
- The multilingual information retrieval consists of the possibility of recovering information although the question and/or the documents are in different languages, situation that reigns at the moment in the Web.

Automatic classification techniques Search text automatically assign a set of documents to predefined classification categories, mainly by using statistical techniques, processing and parameterization.

IR systems not only seek to identify only one object in a collection, but several items that can answer the query that satisfy user requirements, objects are usually text documents, but may be of multimedia content such as image, video or audio. For recovery to be efficient, the data are transformed into adequate representation, in addition, to answer satisfactorily the demands made by the user, the system can use various techniques and models, for example, the statistical processing that represents the classical model the information retrieval systems. In (Noy, 2006) use data mining to test their analytical approach, whereas in (Oren, 2002) use the genetic programming paradigm with satisfactory results.

In (Iskandar, 2007) "The retrieval strategy has been evaluated using Wikipedia, a social media collection that is an online encyclopedia. Social media describes the online tools and platforms that people use to share opinions, insights, experiences, and perspectives with each other. Social media can take many different forms, including text, images, audio, and video. Popular social mediums include blogs, message boards, podcasts, wikis, and blogs", see Figure 6.

5.1 Experiments

We simulated by means of the developed tool -WREID- the expectations of successfully in a circuit of Wrestling and interests of obtain popularity based on their performance associated with specific features. One of most interesting characteristics observed in the experimental

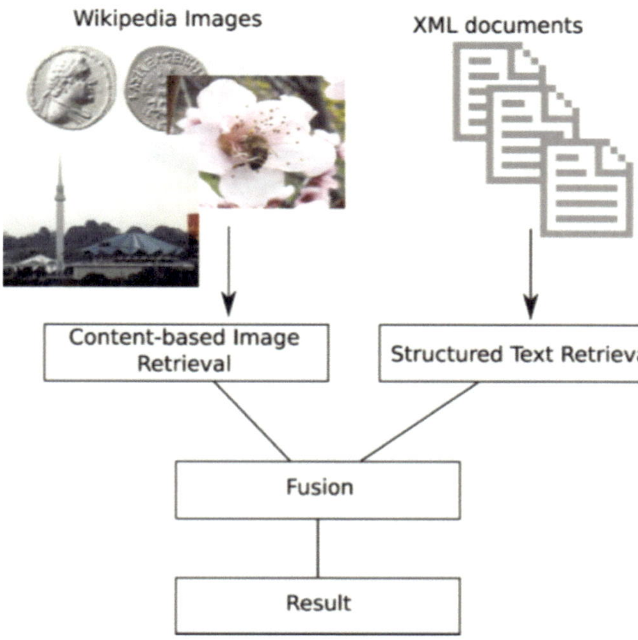

Fig. 6. Social Media Retrieval using image features and structured text

analysis were the diversity of cultural patterns established by each society because the selection of different attributes in a potential best wrestler: Agility, ability to fight, Emotional Control, Force, Stamina, Speed, Intelligence. The structured scenes associated the agents cannot be reproduced in general, so that the time and space belong to a given moment in them. They represent a unique form, needs and innovator of adaptive behavior which solves a followed computational problem of a complex change of relations. Using Social Data Mining implementing with agents was possible simulate the behavior of many followers in the selection of a best wrestler and determinate whom people support this professional career. With respect at Node attributes, we summarize the measures required to describe individual nodes of a graph. They allow identifying elements by their topological properties. The degree -or connectivity- (k_i) of a node v_i is defined as the number of edges of this node. From the adjacency matrix, we easily obtain the degree of a given node as:

$$k_i = \sum_{j=1}^{N} a_{ij} \tag{2}$$

See examples of k values in figure 7. For directed graphs, we distinguish between incoming and outgoing links. Thus, we specify the degree of a node in its *indegree, ini k* , and *outdegree,* k_i^{out} . The *clustering coefficient* C_i is a local measure quantifying the likelihood that neighboring nodes of *vi* are connected with each other. It is calculated by dividing the number of neighbors of *vi* that are actually connected among them, *n*, with all possible combinations excluding autoloops, i.e., *ki(ki-1)*. Formally, we have:

$$C_i = \frac{2n}{k_i(k_i - 1)} \tag{3}$$

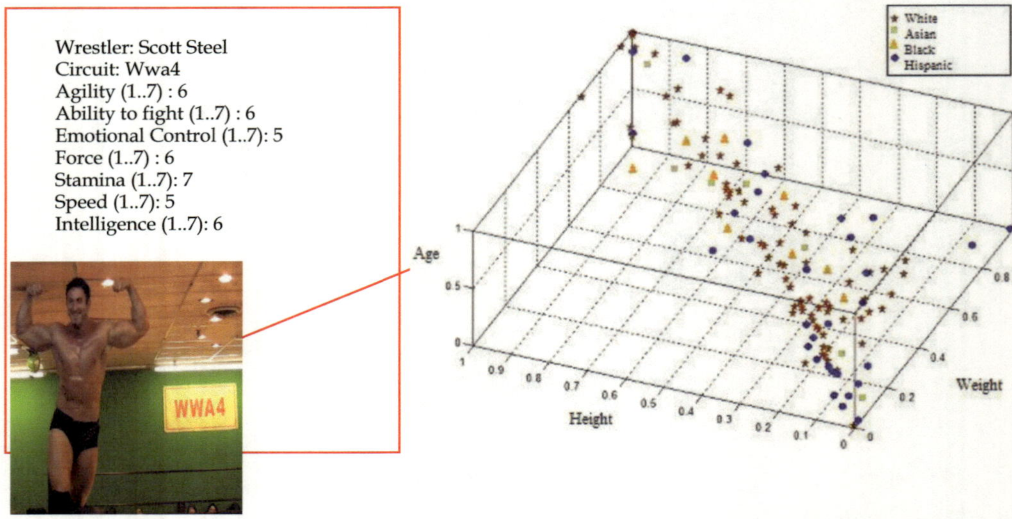

Fig. 7. Individual features of an element and classification of wrestling performance to a sample of 127 Wrestlers.

We first observe that Professional Wrestler Idol (support in features related with age, height and weight are considered) always plays a very significant role, which should of course not be surprising. Hidden patterns observed in the agents are related with size of circuit, match records and cultural distances (ethnicity), and the expectative of selection of a good wrestler whit specific attributes. The nodes with more value in their degree are considered more popular and obtain the best contracts. To get some insight, we run 100 regressions on 100 random samples of half the number of observations, and count the number of times each parameter affect the graph built. A Wrestler with the features similar to Scott Steel was selected as the most popular by the majority of societies because the attributes offered by it are adequate for others. In Figure 7 is shown the results of a sample of American Wrestlers.

6. Data mining with Ant Colony and Genetic Algorithm

6.1 Artificial Ant Colony

This section describes the principles of any Ant System (AS), a meta-heuristic algorithm based in the form in how the natural ants find food sources. The description starts with the ant metaphor, which is a model of this behavior. Then, it follows a discussion of how AS has evolved, and show as the ant algorithms can be applied to the Data Mining process. The Ant System was inspired by collective behavior of certain real ants (forager ants). While they are traveling in search of food, they deposit a chemical substance called pheromone on the traversed path. The communication through the pheromone is an effective way of coordinating the activities of these insects. For this reason, pheromone rapidly influences the behavior of each ant: they will choose the paths where is the biggest pheromone concentration. The behavior of real ants to search food is modeled as a probabilistic process. When there are paths without any amount of pheromone, the ants explores the neighboring area in a totally random way. In presence of an amount of pheromone, the ants follow a path with a probability based in the pheromone concentration. The ants deposit additional pheromone concentrations during his travels. Since the pheromone evaporates, the pheromone concentration in non-used paths tends to disappear slowly. The Ant System (AS) or Ant Colony Optimization (ACO) was introduced by Marco Dorigo (Dorigo, 1991). The Ant System is inspired in the natural optimization process of real ants to create paths. This type of algorithms can be applied to the solution of many combinatorial optimization problems. The artificial ants, repeat the search process to find solutions. Each ant builds a possible solution to the optimization problem. The ants share information through the pheromone, which is a common memory (global information) that can be accessed by all. The Ant System is a multi-agent system, where the ant-agents have simple behavior but the interactions between they have like result a complex behavior of the whole ant colony. They need the collaboration of whole colony to get the final objective. The AS was originally proposed to solve the Traveling Salesman Problem (TSP), and the Quadratic Assignment Problem (QAP). Now exist a lot of applications like scheduling, machine learning, data mining, and others. There are several variants of AS designed to solve specific problems or to extend the characteristics of the basic algorithm (Ochoa et al., 2010). Some of the most important variants of AS in order of appearance are. Ant Colony Optimization (ACO) was introduced initially by Dorigo (Dorigo, 1991), the Ant-Q algorithm designed by Gambardela and Dorigo (Gambardela, 1995), Max-Min Ant System algorithm (MMAS) was developed by Stützle and Hoose (Stützle, 1996), other variant of AS, named ASrank, was developed by Bullnheimer, Hartl and Strauss (Bullnheimer et al., 1997).

Actually exist some AS to solve task of Data Mining, like classified and clustering, some of this algorithms are: ANT-LGP, ANT-BASED Clustering, AntClass, Ant-Miner, others.

The maximum clique problem is a problem classified within the NP-Hard problems; this problem has real applications eg: Codes Theory, Errors Diagnosis, Computer Vision, Clustering Analysis, Information Retrieval, Learning Automatic, Data Mining, among others. Therefore it is important to use new heuristic and/or meta-heuristics techniques to try to solve this problem (Ponce et al., 2009b). The general Ant Colony Algorithm for the maximum clique problem proposed by Fenet and Solnon (Fenet and Solnon, 2003). The proposed algorithm is based on the Ant Algorithm created to solve the clique maximum; the construction process is showed in figure 8.

To initialize the pheromone signs
To place Ants Randomly
Repeat
For k en 1..nb Ants **do**:
Build the clique (Solution) C_k
Update the pheromone signs $\{C_1, \ldots, C_{nbAnts}\}$
If is the first iteration to keep in lists all the solutions without repeating no one
Else only are added to the list the solutions that not exist in the list
Until Reaching the Number of Cycles or Finding the optimum solution

Fig. 8. Pseudo code of Ant Clustering Algorithm.

Construction of cliques: An initial vertex is selected randomly to put an ant, and iteratively it chooses vertices to add to clique of a set of candidates (all the vertices that are connected with all vertices of the partial clique), to see figure 9.

Choose the first vertex randomly $v_f \in V$
$C \leftarrow \{v_f\}$

Candidates ← $\{v_i / (v_f, v_i) \in E\}$
While Candidate $\neq 0$ **do**
Choose a vertex $v_i \in$ Candidates with a probability p(v_i), see Ec. (2)
$C \leftarrow C \cup \{v_i\}$
Candidates ← Candidates $\cap \{v_j / (v_i, v_j) \in E\}$
End While
Return C

Fig. 9. Construction of Clique.

This Ant Colony Algorithm can be using to realize data clustering by the natural form that have a clique.

6.2 Genetic Algorithm with migration operator

Genetic Algorithms are algorithms that group techniques or methods based on natural evolution and genetics, taking as basis the "Theory of Evolution of Species" proposed by Charles Darwin and the discoveries made by Gregor Mendel in the field of genetics. (Holland, 1975) (Goldberg, 1989).

As in nature, the AG's evolving populations of individuals (possible solutions) usually of better quality solutions through operators for evaluation, selection, crossover and mutation. These have proved to be a good tool for solving optimization problems. Unfortunately one of its major limitations is that due to the loss of genetic diversity due to inbreeding between individuals within populations is that they tend to converge to local optima. For this reason we have proposed hybrid genetic algorithms somehow preventing the loss of diversity and achieve more efficient and fast tools.

Of these proposals are currently working largely with AG's side, where it seeks to improve the diversity of populations and their performance, this dividing both the computational load of each of the operators on different nodes for an intensification of themselves or by dividing the initial population in subpopulations that evolve individually until certain criteria laid down in that share some of the best individuals (Whitley et al., 1998) (Lu and Areibi, 2004) (Tzung-Pei et al., 2007).

Also have the AG's with immigration adapters that have a major population and a population parallel evolve independently and each number of generations are immigrants the best individuals of the population parallel to the main population (as shown in Figure 10), allowing the introduction of new genetic material in the major population allowing a greater diversity (Ornelas et al., 2009).

To evolve independently and through the parallel population has no influence from the main population evolves in a totally different which results in a process called speciation that is that genetic material that evolved independently in different conditions generates new species with very different characteristics that depend largely on the adaptive process.

The AG's with adaptive migration have been used to solve optimal route generation, water distribution networks and wastewater, design postcards, in data mining processes, among others.

These algorithms are currently used in data mining to make the process of cauterization and classification of information, and thanks to the way they work can process large volumes of information without extensive searches, which is of great importance because by the volume of information that is currently in the databases is impossible to use this type of research.

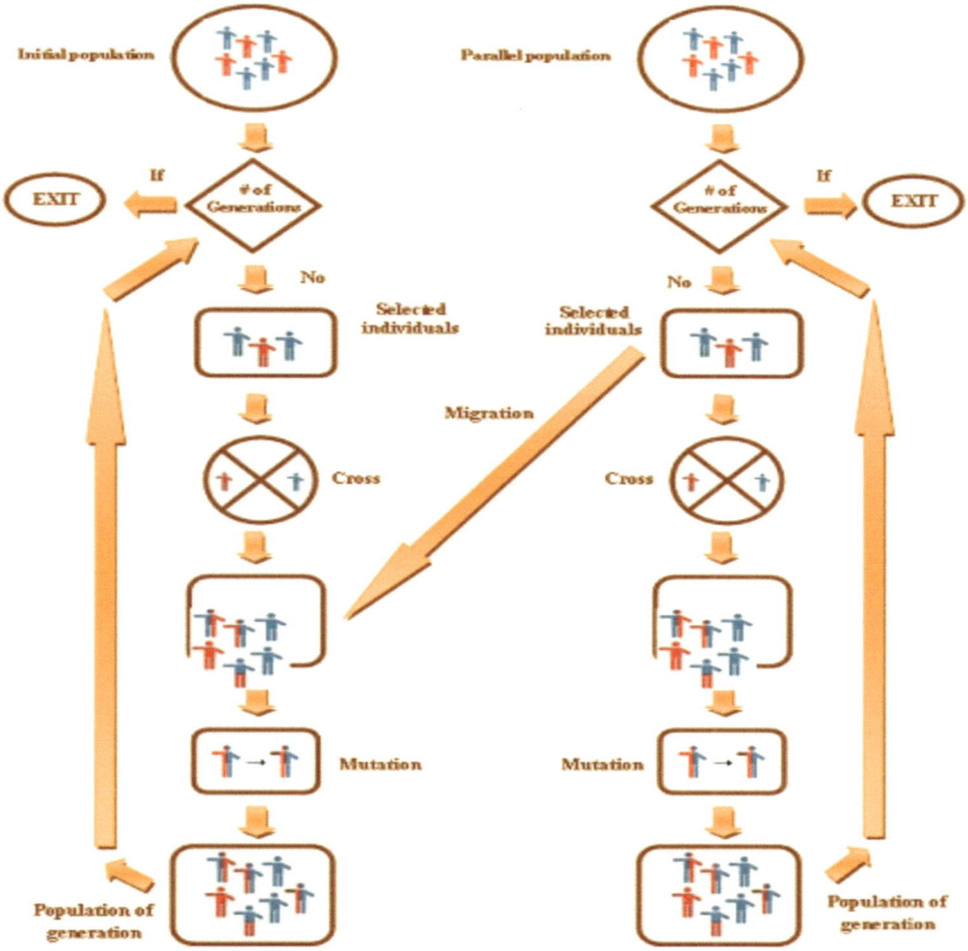

Fig. 10. Diagram of the AG's model with adaptive migration.

7. Intelligent Tutor Systems

Intelligent Tutoring Systems (ITS) are those computer systems that provide students with direct customization instructions or feedback without human intervention. ITSs were conceived around 1970, but not popularized until the 90's. They have four modules: the Interface Module, the Expert Module, the Student Module, and the Tutor Module. The Interface Module controls the communication between the student and the Intelligent Tutor System; the Expert Module contains a domain model that describes the knowledge or behavior that represents a high expert in the domain; the Student Module describes the student knowledge, behavior, etc.; and the Tutor Module is responsible for simulating the task of a teacher.

In this section, we present EDUCA, a Web 2.0 software tool to allow a community of authors and learners to create, share, and view learning materials and web resources for authoring Intelligent Tutoring Systems which combine collaborative, mobile and e-learning methods.

EDUCA applies different artificial intelligence techniques like a neural network and a genetic algorithm for selecting the best learning style or a recommendation-web mining system for adding and searching new learning resources.
Figure 11 illustrates the overall architecture of EDUCA. As we can observe, there are two authors: the main tutor (a teacher or instructor) and the community of learners. The student or learner is an important author of the course and participate actively adding learning resources to the courses. The learner has a user profile with information like the GPA, the particular learning style, or the recommended resources to the course. When the authors add learning material, they first create four different instances corresponding to four different learning styles according to Felder-Silverman Learner Style Model (Felder and Silverman, 1988). When a mobile course is exported to a mobile device, a XML interpreter is added to the course. A SCORM file for the course can also be exported. Once a course is created, a Course Publication Module saves it into a Course Repository. Whenever a learner accesses a course, a recommender system implemented in EDUCA presents links or Web sites with learning material related to the current topic. Such material is stored in a resource repository of EDUCA, which was searched previously by using Web mining techniques implemented also in EDUCA.

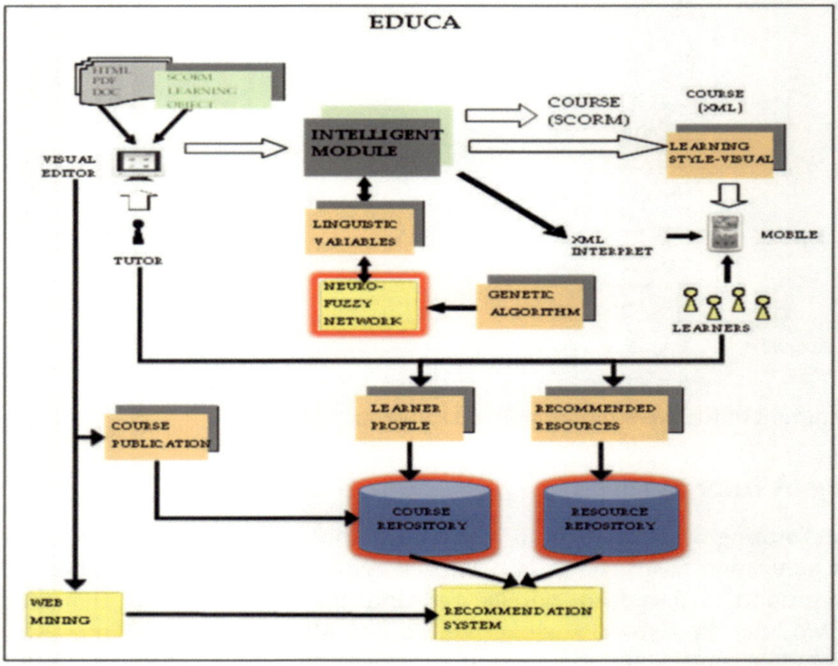

Fig. 11. EDUCA Architecture

We implemented a fuzzy-neural network using the fuzzy input values previously defined. The output of the network is the learning style for each student using a course. We also implemented a genetic algorithm (Bucket Sort) for the optimization of the weights used in the network. The network was trained for 800 generations using a population of 150 chromosomes. In order to train the network, we created three set of courses for high school students. Each course was presented in four different teaching styles according to the

Felder-Silverman model. When a mobile course is exported to a mobile device, a XML interpreter is added to the course. A SCORM file for the course can also be exported. Once a course is created, a Course Publication Module saves it into a Course Repository. Whenever a learner accesses a course, a recommender system implemented in EDUCA presents links or Web sites with learning material related to the current topic. Such material is stored in a resource repository of EDUCA, which was searched previously by using Web mining techniques implemented also in EDUCA.
We tested the tool with 15 professors/teachers and their respective students of different teaching levels. They developed different kinds of courses like a GNU/Linux course, a Basic Math Operation course, and learning material for preparation to the Mexico's Admission-Test for College EXANI-II. The students participated by reading, evaluating and adding material (Web resources) to the courses. Next, we present an example of how an author creates/updates learning material for a Basic Math course (figure 12). We first create the structure of the course (left-top). Then, we add learning material for each learning style (right-top and left-bottom). In this stage, we also assign fuzzy set values to each linguistic variable, and use recommended and actual resources for inclusion in the course. Last, we export and display the course (right-bottom).

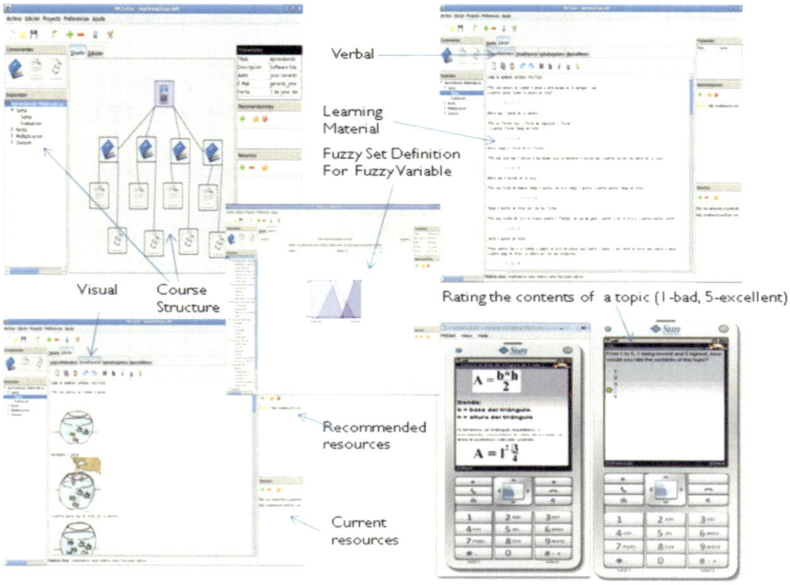

Fig. 12. Authoring Learning Material

8. Conclusion and the future research

Nowadays exist a lot of applications in real life problems, where is possible used data mining to analyse data base to obtain important information in different areas, in this chapter was present some algorithms and applications that us data mining such as like Electrical Power Design, Trash Collectors Routes, Fraud Analysis, Vehicle Routing Problem, Text Mining in the Media, Intelligent Tutor Systems, Ant Colony Optimization, Genetic Algorithms, Particle Swarm Optimization and Web Mining Techniques.

As shown there are multiple areas in which data mining can be used to retrieve information that is not easy to detect with the naked eye using different tools and algorithms.
We describe how decision trees work where structures are used if-then and allow the creation of recommender systems to facilitate decision making, such as diagnostic system for identifying electrical signals the device occurrence, related to physical phenomena and provide a quick and better solution to the problem presented.
For the problem of garbage collection to do a catheterization to determine how best to plan it based on the type of waste, areas collection, type and number of vehicles used for this purpose, among others, using algorithms such as Ant Colony Optimization, Genetic Algorithms and Particle Swarm Optimization.
Once clustered can use these same tools to generate optimal routes that shorten the distance travelled, fuel consumption, deterioration of vehicles, among others.
The methodologies for the detection of fraud have their own strengths and weaknesses characteristics. The overall strength of FDS using anomaly detection is the adaptability to new patterns fraudsters, in the particular case of this study is strengthened with the application of hybridization clustering processes giving a greater dynamism to the system and making it look like a promising component within the fraud detection systems with potential advantages in regard to: upgrade and management of the heterogeneity of customers and their transactions, achieving a better accuracy in the results, and greater dynamism in the system.
Additionally, the multi-objective approach place it in a better position compared to other systems, due to the characteristics of fraud detection problem where there are several factors to consider for best results.
For the solution of SQRP, we proposed a novel algorithm called AdaNAS that is based on existing ant-colony algorithms. This algorithm incorporates parameters adaptive control techniques to estimate a proper TTL value for dynamic text query routing. In addition, it incorporates local ruler that take advantage of the environment on local level, three functions were used to learn from past performance. This combination resulted in a lower hop count and an improved hit count, outperforming the NAS algorithm. Our experiments confirmed that the proposed techniques are more effective at improving search efficiency. Specifically the AdaNAS algorithm in the efficiency showed an improvement of the 81% in the performance efficiency over the NAS algorithm.
Using Social Data Mining in Media Richness we improve the understanding of change for the best paradigm substantially, because we classify the communities of agents appropriately based on their related attributes approach, this allows determine a "American Wrestler Idol" which exists with base on the determination of acceptance function by part of the remaining communities to demonstrate best performance. Each year 7000 new wrestlers arrive to different American Wrestling Circuits. Social Data Mining offers a powerful alternative for optimization problems, for that reason it provides a comprehensible panoramic of the cultural phenomenon (Ochoa et al., 2006). This technique lead us about the possibility of the experimental knowledge generation, created by the community of agents for a given application domain. How much the degree of this knowledge is cognitive for the community of agents is a topic for future work. The answer can be similar to the involved in the hard work of communication between two different societies and their respective perspectives. A new Artificial Intelligence that can be in charge of these systems, continues being distant into the horizon, in the same way that we still lack of methods to understand the original and peculiar things of each society.

As future work is to continue working with various tools and algorithms that allow us to improve data mining and this allowed us to knowledge based on information extracted from databases (information that can not be extracted directly and that features not visible to the naked eye) to improve many existing systems and create developments that take into account factors that so far can not be displayed using other tools.
Applied the models proposed in several areas for example establishing the need for FDS to be increasingly proactive in order to adapt to the greatest extent possible so changing the behaviour presented by fraudsters or in singers of Mexican Society and determine the possible "New Musical Idols or Bands" where only 27% record their second album, this for different genders according theirs profiles, the principal problem is the confidentially of this information and its use for this propose.

9. References

Amaral, L. and Ottino, J. (2004) Complex systems and networks: Challenges and opportunities for chemical and biological engineers. *Chemical Engineering Scientist*, 59:1653–1666.

Basu, S.; Bilenko, M. and Mooney R. (2004). A probabilistic framework for semi-supervised clustering. *Proceedings of the Tenth ACM SIGKDD international Conference on Knowledge Discovery and Data Mining*. Seattle, WA : ACM, press, pp. 59-68.

Breiman, L.; Friedman, J. and Olshen, R. (1984). Classification and Regression Trees, *Wadsworth International Group*. Belmont, CA.

Bullnheimer, B.; Hartl, R. and Strauss C. (1997). A New Rank Based Version of the Ant System: A Computational Study, *Technical report*, Institute of Management Science, University of Vienna, Austria, 1997.

Chandola, V.; Banerjee A. and Kumar, V. (2009). Anomaly detection: A survey. *Journal of Computing Surveys*. ACM. pp. 1-58.

Chaudhuri, S.; Das, G.; Hristidis, V. and Weikum, G. (2006). Probabilistic information retrieval approach for ranking of database query results, *ACM Trans. Database Syst.*, 31(3), pp. 1134-1168

Cruz, L.; Gómez, C.; Aguirre, M.; Schaeffer, S.; Turrubiates, T.; Ortega, R. and Fraire, H.(2008). NAS algorithm for semantic query routing systems in complex networks. *In DCAI*, volume 50 of Advances in Soft Computing, pages 284–292. Springer.

Deb, K. (2001). Multi-objective optimization using evolutionary algorithms, Book Chichester, Uk : John Wiley and Sons.

Dehuri, S. and Cho, S.B. (2009). Multi-criterion Pareto based particle swarm optimized polynomial neural network for classification: A review and state-of-the-art, *Journal of Computer Science Review*. pp. 19-40.

Dorigo, M. (1991). Positive Feedback as a Search Strategy. *Technical Report*. No. 91-016. Politecnico Di Milano, Italy.

Felder, R. and Silverman, L. (1988). Learning and Teaching Styles In Engineering Education, *Journal of Engineering Education*. North Carolina State University and Institute for the Study of Advanced Development.. 78(7), pp. 674_681.

Fenet, S. and Solnon, C. (2003) Searching for Maximum Cliques with Ant Colony Optimization, *EvoWorkshops 2003*, LNCS 2611, 236–245.

Gama, J. and Medes, P. (2005) Learning decision trees from dynamic data streams. *Journal of Universal Computer Science*.

Gambardella, L.M. and Dorigo M.(1995). Ant-Q: A Reinforcement Learning Approach to the Traveling Salesman Problem. *Proceedings of ML-95, Twelfth International Conference on Machine Learning, Tahoe City*, CA, A. Prieditis and S. Russell (Eds.), Morgan Kaufmann, pp. 252-260.

Goldberg, D.(1989). Genetic Algorithms in Search, Optimization, and Machine Learning. *Addison Wesley*. ISBN: 0-201-15767-5..

González, J.J.; Pazos, R.; Gelbukh, A.; Sidorov, G.; Fraire, H. and Cruz, I. (2007). Prepositions and Conjunctions in a Natural Language Interfaces to Databases, *Lecture Notes in Computer Science*, Vol. 4743, pp. 173-182.

Grosan, C. and Abraham, A.(2007) Hybrid evolutionary algorithms: methodologies, architectures, and reviews. Hybrid evolutionary algorithms. Book auth. Grosan C., Abraham A. and Ishibuchi H.. - Berlin : Springer Verlag-Heidelberg.

Han, J. and Kamber, M. (2006). Data Mining, Concepts and Techniques. *Morgan Kaufmann Publishers is an imprint of Elsevie*r. ISBN 13: 978-1-55860-901-3, ISBN 10: 1-55860-901-6.

Holland J. (1975). Adaptation in Natural and Artificial Systems An Introductory Analysis with Applications to Biology, Control, and Artificial Intelligence. *The University of Michigan Press*.

Hristidis, V. and Papakonstantinou, Y. (2002). Discover: Keyword Search in Relational Databases, *VLDB '02: Proc. of the 28th International Conference on Very Large Data Bases*, Hong Kong, China, pp. 670-681.

Iskandar, D.; Pehcevski, J.; Thom, J. and Tahaghoghi, S. (2007). Social Media Retrieval using Image Features and Structured Text, *In N. Fuhr, M. Lalmas, and A. Trotman (eds).*

Janikowo, C. (2008) Fuzzy decision trees: Issues and methods. IEEE Transactions on Systems, Man and Cybernetics - Part B: Cybernetics. 28-1. 1.14.

Juszczak, P.; Adams, N.; Hand, D.; Whitrow, C. and Weston, D. (2008). Off-the-peg and bespoke classifiers for fraud detection. *Computational Statistics & Data Analysi* –Vol. 52. pp. 4521-4532.

Jin, R. and Agrawal, G. (2003) Efficient decision tree construction on streaming data. *In Proceedings of the Ninth ACM SIGKDD International Conference on Knowledge Discovery and Data Mining*. pp. 571 576.

Kou, Y.; Sirwongwattana, C. and Huang, S. (2004). Survey of fraud detection techniques. *IEEE International Conference on Networking, Sensing and Control*. Taipei : IEEE press, pp. 749-754. ISSN: 1810-7869. Print ISBN: 0-7803-8193-9.

Liu, L.; XiaoLong, J. and Kwock, C. (2005). Autonomy oriented computing — from problem solving to complex system modeling. *In Springer Science + Business Media Inc*, pages 27–54.

Llora, X. and Wilson, S. (2004). Mixed Decision Trees: Minimizing Knowledge representation bias in LCS. *Genetic and Evolutionary Computation. GECCO*. Lecture Notes in Computer Science –Vol. 3103/2204. pp. 797 809.

Lozano, M. and García, C. (2010). Hybrid metaheuristics with evolutionary algorithms specializing in intensification and diversification: Overview and progress report. *In Journal of Computers and Operations Research*. pp. 481-497.

Lu, G. and Areibi, S.(2004). An Island-Based GA Implementation for VLSI Standard-Cell Placement. *In GECCO 2004*. K. Deb et al. (Eds.), LNCS 3103, pp. 1138–1150, Springer-Verlag, 2004.

Manning, C.; Raghavan, P. and Schütze, H. (2009). An Introduction to Information Retrieval, *Cambridge University Press*, Cambridge, England, pag.195.

Márquez, M. Y. (2009). Determinación de perfiles de generación de RSD por tipología familiar a través de minería de datos: Estudios de casos en tres comunidades de Mexicali, B. C. *Tesis Doctoral*. UABC.

Michlmayr, E. (2007). Ant Algorithms for Self-Organization in Social Networks. *PhD thesis*, Vienna University of Technology.

Mihail, M.; Saberi, A. and Tetali, P.(2004). Random walks with lookahead in power law random graphs. Internet Mathematics, 3, 2004.

Mitchell, T. (1997). Machine Learning. McGraw Hill.

Noy, A.; Raban, D. and Ravid, G. (2006). Testing Social Theories in CMC through Gaming and Simulation. *Journal of Simulation and Gaming*, 37(2), pp. 174-194.

OECD (2008) Household Behaviour and the Environment.

Ochoa, A.; Hernández, A.; Cruz, L.; Ponce, J.; Montes, F.; Li, L. and Janacek, L. (2010) New Achievements in Evolutionary Computation, *Book edited by: Peter Korosec*, ISBN 978-953-307-053-7, pp. 318, INTECH, Croatia, downloaded from SCIYO.COM

Ochoa, A.; Sehr, M.; Sarchimelia, M.; Meriam, G. et al. (2006). Italianitá: Discovering a Pygmalion effect on Italian Communities Using Data Mining. *In Proceedings of CORE'2006*.

Oren, N. (2002). Improving the effectiveness of Information Retrieval with Genetic Programming, *MSc research report*, University of the Witwatersrand, South Africa.

Ortega, R.(2009) Estudio de las Propiedades Topológicas en Redes Complejas con Diferente Distribución del Grado y su Aplicación en la Búsqueda de Recursos Distribuidos. *PhD thesis*, Instituto Politécnico Nacional, México.

Ornelas, F.; Padilla, A.; Padilla F.; Ponce de León E. and Ochoa, A. (2009) Genetic Algorithm using Migration and Modified GSX as Support. *Artificial Intelliigence & Applications, Book Edited by: A. Gelbukh*, ISBN 978-607-95367-0-1, pp. 21-28, SMIA, Mexico.

Pedrycz, W. and Sosnowski (2005). Genetically optimized fuzzy decision trees. *IEEE Transactions on Systems, Man and Cybernetics - Part B: Cybernetics*. pp. 633- 641.

Perez, J.; Muguerza, J.; Arbelaitz, O.; Gurrutxaga, I. and Martin, J. (2007). Combining multiple class distribution modified subsampled in a single tree. *Pattern Recognition Letters*. pp. 414-422.

Ponce, J.; Hernández, A.; Ochoa, A.; Padilla, F.;Padilla A.; Álvarez, F. and Ponce de León, E. (2009a). *Data Mining in Web Applications. Data Mining and Knowledge Discovery in Real Life Applications book*. Edited by Julio Ponce and Adem Karahoca. ISBN 978-3-902613-53-0, 436 pages

Ponce , J.; Padilla, F.; Ochoa, A.; Padilla, A.; Ponce de León, E. and Quezada, F. (2009b). Ant Colony Algorithm for Clustering through of Cliques, *Artificial Intelligence & Applications, A. Gelbukh (Ed.)*,ISBN: 978-607-95367-0-1, pp. 29-34, November 2009, Mexico.

Quinlan, J. (1993). C4.5: Programs for Machine Learning. *Morgan Kaufmann*, San Mateo, CA.

Raidl, G. (2006). A unified view on hybrid metaheuristics. *In Proceedings of Hybrid Metaheuristics, Third International Workshop*. Berlin : Springer Verlag, pp. 1-12.

Rokach, L. and Maimon, O.(2005) Top-down induction of decision trees Classifiers - a survey. *IEEE Transactions on Systems, Man and Cybernetics*. Reviews - Vol. 35-4. pp. 476-487. ISSN: 1094-6977.

Ruiz, R.; Guzman, A. and Martinez J. (1999) Enfoque Lógico Combinatorio al Reconocimiento de Patrones. Instituto Politecnico Nacional, 1999.

Safavian, S. and Landgrebe, D. (1991) A survey of decision tree classifier methodology. *IEEE Transactions on Systems, Man and Cybernetics*. pp. 660 674.)

Sánchez, D.; Vila, M.; Cerda, L. and Serrano, J. (2009). Association rules applied to credit card fraud detection. *Expert Systems with Applications: An International Journal* – Vol. 36, pp. 3630-3640. ISSN:0957-4174.

Sayyadian, M.; Shakery, A.; Doan, A. and Zhai, C. (2004). Toward Entity Retrieval over Structured and Text Data, *In Proc. of ACM SIGIR 2004 Workshop on Information Retrieval and Databases.*

Shih, Y. and Loh, W. (1997) Split Selection Methods for Classification trees. Statistica Sinica, pp. 815-840.

Shou Chih, C., Hsing Kuo, P. and Yuh Jye, L.(2005) Model Trees for Classification of hybrid data types. *In Intelligent Data Engineering and Automated Learning - IDEAL: 6th International Conference.* pp. 32-39.

Stolfo, S.; Fan, D.; Lee, W.; Prodromidis, A. and Chan, P. (1997). Credit Card Fraud Detection Using Metalearning: *Issues and Initial Results. AAAI Workshop AI Methods in Fraund and Risk Management.* Columbia : AAAI Press, pp. 83-90.

Stolfo, S.; Fan, D.; Lee, W.; Prodromidis, A. and Chan P. (2000). Cost-Based Modeling for Fraud and Intrusion Detection: Results from the JAM Project. *DARPA Information Survivability Conference & Exposition* – Vol. 2. Hilton Head : IEEE Press, pp. 130-144. ISBN: 0-7695-0490-6.

Stützle, T. and Hoos, H. H.(1996). Improving the Ant System: A detailed report on the MAXMIN Ant System. *Technical report AIDA-96-12*, FG Intellektik, FB Informatik, TU Darmstadt.

Tempich, C.; Staab, S. and Wranik, A. (2004). REMINDIN': Semantic Query Routing in Peer-to-Peer Networks based on Social Metaphers, *In 13th World Wide Web Conference (WWW).*

Tzung–Pei, H.; Wen-Yang, L.; Shu-Min, L. and Jiann-Horng L. (2007). Dynamically Adjusting Migration Rates for Multi-Population Genetic Algorithms. *Journal of Advanced Computational and Intelligent Informatics.* Vol. 11, No. 4, pp. 410-417.

Utgoff, P. (1989) Incremental induction of decision trees. Machine Learning. pp. 161-186.

Utgoff, P.; Berkman, N. and Clouse, J. (1997). Decision tree induction based on efficient tree Restructuring. *Machine Learning.* 5-44.

Utgoff, P. and Brodley, C. (1990). An Incremental Method for Finding multivariate splits for decision trees. *In Proc.7th International Conference on Machine Learning.* pp. 58-65.

Utgoff, P. and Brodley, C. (1995). Multivariate decision trees. *Machine Learning.* pp. 45-77.

Vallez, M. and Pedraza-Jimenez, R. (2007). Natural Language Processing in Textual Information Retrieval and Related Topics, [on line]. "Hipertext.net", num. 5, 2007. <http://www.hipertext.net> [Consulted: 07/15/10]. ISSN 1695-5498

Vanichsetakul, N. and Wei-Yin, L. (1988). Tree-Structured Classification via Generalized Discriminant analysis. *Journal of the American Statistical Association,* pp. 715 728.

Wang, X.; Nauck, D. and Spott, M.(2007). Intelligent data analysis with fuzzy decision trees. Soft Computing - A Fusion of Foundations, Methodologies and Applications. pp. 439 457.

Whitley, D.; Rana, S. and Heckendorn (1998). The Island Model Genetic Algorithm: On Separability, Population Size and Convergence. *Journal of Computing and Information Technology,* Vol. 7, pp. 33-47, Colorado State University.

Whitrow, C.; Hand, D.; Juszczak, P.; Weston, D. and Adams, N. (2009). Transaction aggregation as a strategy for credit card fraud detection. *Journal of Data Mining and Knowledge Discovery.* pp. 30-55.

Wu, C.-J.; Yang, K.-H. and Ho.(2006). AntSearch: An ant search algorithm in unstructured peer-to-peer networks. *In ISCC,* pages 429–434.

3

Data Mining Techniques for Explaining Social Events

Krivec Jana and Gams Matjaž
Jožef Stefan Institute,
Slovenia

1. Introduction

When trying to discover patterns and classification models for social events, machine learning can be a powerful tool. The most common usage of data mining techniques is categorization of new examples into specific classes. Nevertheless, the simple number indicating classification accuracy, as with SVM or similar non-transparent methods, is usually not good enough for the case when we want to understand the problem and check the obtained relations with human sense and knowledge. It is not good enough because we don't know whether the relations beneath are logical to human experts of the research field or even we don't know how the relations look like. We want to check the computer-constructed relations whether already known or created anew. In many cases when dealing with social events, it is of extreme importance to combine computer and human knowledge. Classification trees or classification rules seem to be the best choice for this kind of problems. The problem that might arise in this case is in the quality of the discovered patterns, e.g. it is well known that some computer-generated relations seem to be important, but statistically do not exceed the chance of random choice. That is why the procedure of conducting the best possible classification trees or rules from the data must follow certain rules. To put it shortly, first, data has to be manipulated in various, yet systematic ways in connection with opinions of a field expert. The manipulation can be executed on the level of instances, attributes, class or parameters of the data mining algorithm. Second, the quality estimation should be calculated in various ways, thus providing possibility to choose the best tree of all. We performed demographic analysis in the proposed way, obtaining some new and confirming some already published relations.

2. What to expect

In this chapter a description of the specific problem type is presented. First, a current state of the procedure dealing with social events is described, including possible inaccuracies. In the second section, a case study showing an example of the usage of machine learning techniques for mining social events is presented, discussing possible problems and future improvements.

3. Mining social events with data mining techniques

Machine learning and lately data mining are among the most successful application areas of artificial intelligence.

Whenever there are lots of learning examples, these systems learn properties of the domain and make predictions about future cases. The most common usage of DM techniques is categorization of new examples into specific classes. However, the weakness of state-of-the-art machine learning algorithms achieving the best results in terms of accuracy (e.g. ensemble methods or SVMs) is their inability to explain their predictions. There is no guarantee that these justifications will be understood by experts and other users. The induced models are often strange to the domain experts as they present the problem in a different way. Domain experts and users often perceive these methods and their predictions as black boxes.

However, machine learning is often used to get a better understanding of the relation between inputs and outputs (Mitchell, 2006). In such cases, it is usually preferable to use methods like decision trees, rule-based models, or linear models that construct knowledge which can be presented in the form of readable, understandable trees, rules and other representations thus enabling further study and fine tuning. In this way, the causes of investigated phenomena can also be discovered and described, as we might see in the case study section.

Yet, even human-transparent models often do not provide true understanding of the constructed model and can even provide counter-intuitive solutions. The induced correlations sometimes seem illogical or simply strange to the domain experts as they would explain the same case using different terms. Pazzani (1991) showed experimentally that people will grasp a new concept more easily if the concept is consistent with their knowledge. More elaborate studies of understanding new concepts were produced by the cognitive learning community (Angehrn & Gibbert, 2008). They showed that when we learn new data, we always start with our prior knowledge and try to modify it. If the new concepts are inconsistent with our prior knowledge, the new knowledge will likely be distorted or even rejected.

Data mining method are based on human-computer interaction, where user interacts with a decision tree learner to improve the trees in performance and meaning to him/her. Knowledge acquisition should be processed in a systematic way, where humans lead the data mining by comparing multiple trees constructed on different subsets of the data set and through several forms of attribute selection. By selecting the trees that are not only consistent with the data (e.g. measured by accuracy), but also meaningful, the result of the data mining process are meaningful domain models/decision trees. Such trees, in turn, contain the relations and attributes that best describe the domain.

At the end however, quantitative measures of accuracy and quality of the conducted tree should be accessed.

3.1 Conducted tree accuracy and quality estimation

In the existing literature, many different measures for evaluating the performance of information retrieval systems have been proposed. Mostly they refer to accuracy and quality of the constructed knowledge. Detailed description is presented in the next sections.

3.1.1 Classification tree accuracy estimation

Information retrieval model should contain only meaningful relations. Most meaningful relations are often considered as those with best classification accuracy. *Accuracy* is also used as a statistical measure of how well a binary classification test correctly identifies or excludes a condition (Ivanov, 1972).

	Condition (e.g., disease) As determined by *Gold* standard			
	True		**False**	
Test outcome	**Positive**	**True positive**	**False positive**	→ Positive predictive value
	Negative	**False negative**	**True negative**	→ Negative predictive value
		↓ Sensitivity	↓ Specificity	Accuracy

Table 1. Accuracy as a measurement of positive and negative prediction values.

Accuracy can be calculated on the following way:

$$\text{accuracy} = \frac{\text{number of true positives} + \text{number of true negatives}}{\text{numbers of true positives} + \text{false positives} + \text{false negatives} + \text{true negatives}}$$

To estimate the accuracy of the trees, 10-fold cross-validation is often used. In this case, these are10 iterations each time taking a different single fold for testing and the rest 9 folds for training, averaging the error of the 10 iterations. The estimated accuracy of a classification tree corresponds to a probability that a new example will be correctly classified. As the best tree in particular experimental subgroup we choose the tree with the best classification accuracy (Kohavi, 1995).

Two other interesting measures are: F-measure and Under ROC Area estimation.

The F-measure is often used in the field of information retrieval for measuring search, document classification, and query classification performance (Beitzel, 2006).The traditional F-measure or balanced F-score (**F_1 score**) is the harmonic mean of precision and recall. The precision is defined as the fraction of retrieved documents that are relevant. Recall is defined as the fraction of relevant documents that are retrieved. The F-Measure is a combined measure for precision and recall (Khandefer ,Shapiro, 2009): 2*Precision*Recall/(Precision+Recall).

Receiver operating characteristic (ROC) analysis provides tools to select possibly optimal models and to discard suboptimal ones. The machine learning community most often uses the ROC AUC (area under ROC) statistic for model comparison (Hanley, 2008). This measure can be interpreted as the probability that when we randomly pick one positive and one negative example, the classifier will assign a higher score to the positive example than to the negative. In engineering, the area between the ROC curve and the no-discrimination line is often preferred, because of its useful mathematical properties as a non-parametric statistic (Obuchowski, 2003). This area is often simply known as the discrimination. The Mann Whitney statistic is used to calculate the AUC. There are few observations regarding AUC (Fawcet, 2006):

1. It has value between [0,1]
2. A random classifier has an AUC ~0.5
3. The higher the value of AUC the better the distinguishing capability of the classifier

3.1.2 Classification tree quality evaluation

Till now, we were dealing with performance prediction. Now, we compare algorithms to see which one did better. It is not reasonable to directly use Error rate to predict which algorithm is better as the error rate might have been calculated on different data sets. So to compare algorithms, statistical tests are needed. As indicator of tree significance we have chosen Kappa statistic, which measures the agreement of predictions with the actual class. In general, Kappa statistics are appropriate for testing whether agreement exceeds chance levels, i.e. that predictions and actual classes are correlated. The Kappa statistic measures the agreement of prediction with the true class -- 1.0 signifies complete agreement. It will usually find that predictions and actual classes are correlated and even a weak classifier will tend to show a correlation between the two (Melvile et.all, 2005). As a rule of thumb values of Kappa from 0.40 to 0.59 are considered moderate, 0.60 to 0.79 substantial, and 0.80 outstanding (Landis & Koch, 1977). Most statisticians prefer Kappa values to be at least 0.6 and most often higher than 0.7 before claiming a good level of agreement. There are also quotes that a high level of agreement occurs when Kappa values are above 0.5 and that agreement is poor when Kappa values are less than 0.3. While accuracy and AUC are correlated about 0.86, Kappa and AUC are correlated about 0.93, Kappa being the metric that is most correlated to AUC (more than MSE, Logloss/Entropy, F-measure, rank-rate or others). Kappa and accuracy, although they can give different scores, almost always make the same choices (correlation is around 0.9).

4. Case study: investigation of factors influencing country's fertility rate

For the case study we have chosen an actual problem of fertility rate being too low in some and too high in other countries. We tried to discover, which factors distinguish best the two groups of countries with different Total fertility rate (TFR). TFR is the average number of children that would be born per woman if all women lived to the end of their childbearing years and bore children according to a given set of age-specific fertility rates (Christenson et. al., 2002). If the average woman has approximately 2 children in her lifetime, this is just enough to maintain the population. Sustained low fertility rates can lead to a rapidly aging population and, in the long run, may place a burden on the economy and the social security system because the pool of younger workers responsible for supporting the dependent elderly population is getting smaller. On the other hand, too high fertility rate might cause overpopulation and other social problems. Tracking trends of fertility rates and factors that are connected with them (perhaps even influence them) helps to support effective social planning and the allocation of basic resources across generations (Gams & Krivec, 2007).
The main question of the case study is: what are the reasons for low fertility of some and high fertility of other world countries? We used data mining techniques to discover which factors differ in the countries with different TFR. Even though the idea is everything but new, the proposed approach to this problem is. So far most of the research was based on the statistical analysis. The problem is that these techniques hardly allow taking a holistic perspective (Billari et. al., 2000). Data mining techniques can overpass this deficiency.

4.1 Experimental design and procedure

We used data mining techniques as a research tool, where data were manipulated in a systematical way and results were compared with different accuracy estimation methods. Moreover, the quality of induced trees was obtained, and only the most qualitative trees were taken into further consideration.

4.1.1 Basic data description and manipulation

For machine learning and data mining, data is most commonly presented in attribute-class form, i.e. in a "learning matrix", where rows represent examples and columns attributes (Vidulin & Gams, 2006). In our case, an example corresponds to one country, and a class of the country, presented in the last column, denotes fertility rate. Altogether there are 77 basic attributes and 137 countries in our case study. There are 12 binary attributes and the rest numerical. Attributes and their values were partially obtained from the demographic sources such as UN [http://esa.un.org/unpp/] and Eurostat [http://epp.eurostat.ec.europa.eu/] databases and partially from Wikipedia.

In order to get relevant and appropriate explanations, data has to be manipulated in different ways and treated from different perspectives, with some strategic or tactical plan behind it (see Figure 1). Semantics behind the investigated phenomena should best be defined by the field expert. Data are usually manipulated on the basis of particular subgroups of learning examples, different class value arrangements or number of included attributes. In our case attributes were joined into 7 subgroups, based on different previous demographic theories: all (77), general country data (13), economical (11), social (10), educational (16), country health state (6), women's status in the country (39), and automatically selected by the Weka program (Witten & Frank, 2005). Our measurements were performed on all attributes and separately on specific groups like economical, consisting of 12 attributes such as unemployment rate, GDP ($) per habitant, GDP growth (%), etc.. For the basic class we have chosen Total Fertility Rate (TFR), discretized into two values: high (>2) and low (<2). The branching point 2 was chosen because it represents the replacement level of the population. In reality, replacement level is a bit higher, around 2.1, but this number depends on several other parameters such as mortality rate and immigrations, and furthermore only two countries have fertility rate between 2 and 2.1. Nevertheless, we also split the class into three values (high TFR: >3, middle TFR: 2<TFR<3, and low TFR: <2), but due to a lack of space only the results of the first version are presented here.

Further, we conducted our procedure separately on developed countries. Developed countries are countries with high gross domestic product (GDP); above 1000$ per habitant (38 countries). GDP is defined as the total market value of all final goods and services produced within a given country or region in a given period of time (usually a calendar year) (Sullivan & Sheffrin, 1996).

4.1.2 Data mining procedure

Our research group has decades of experience in developing and using data mining (DM) and machine learning (ML) systems such as Weka (Witten & Frank, 2005) and Orange (Demsar & Zupan, 2005), the latter being developed in our broader research group.

From the ML and DM techniques available in Weka and Orange we have chosen J48, the implementation of C4.5 (Witten & Frank, 2005), a method used for induction of classification trees. This method is most commonly used when the emphasis is on transparency of the constructed knowledge. In our case this was indeed so, since the task was to extract the most meaningful relation from hundreds of constructed trees.

The most meaningful relations are those most significant to humans with the best classification accuracy at the same time. To estimate the accuracy of the trees, we used a 10-fold cross-validation, built into the system. The estimated accuracy of a classification tree corresponds to a probability that a new example will be correctly classified.

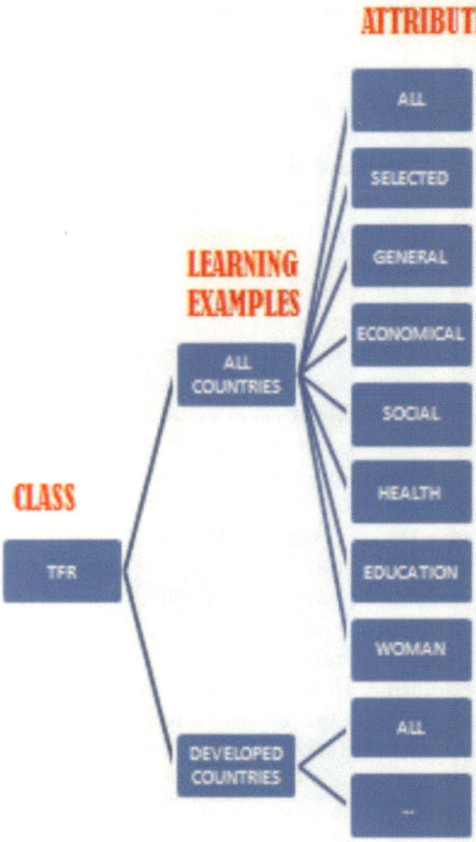

Fig. 1. The structure of the data manipulation.

We modified Weka´s J48 default parameters with the respect of the minimal number of objects in the nodes. We had long experienced the dilemma whether the constructed trees can be trusted. The standard DM approach was particularly challenged on the demographic problem since the relations are quite complex and need in-depth understanding. The decision which tree was the most useful one was based on the accuracy and quality estimations as described in the Section 3.1.2.

5. Findings and discussion

Tens of trees were created in a systematic way, as presented in Figure 1. First experiments were performed with all and then separately on the developed countries only. Finally, several selections of the attributes were tested: all, selected, general, economical, social, health, education and women. These tests resulted in 72 basic trees for all and 72 for developed countries only (8 different subgroup condition and 8 different possibilities of Minimum number of objects in the tree leafs). In addition, various further experiments with different class values were performed. In this section only the most interesting trees presented in Figure 1 were analyzed, i.e. those with most meaningful relations to humans and with best classification accuracy and quality at the same time.

		SUBGROUPS							
		All	**Selected**	**General**	**Economical**	**Social**	**Health**	**Education**	**Women**
ALL COUNTRIES	Attributes	L,Az, Ak,Ba	L,Az,Ak, 32,De	M	**Ae,Be,Di,V**	P,Ak,Ba	Az,Av	Ct,Cz,Cr	32,4,34, 37,19,6
	Min.Nr.Obj	3	4	10	3	3	8	7	**2**
	Acc (%)	81.0219	83.2117	81.7518	83.9416	81.0219	77.3723	80.292	**81.0219**
	F-measure	0.81	0.834	0.817	0.841	0.806	0.775	0.801	**0.811**
	AUC	0.817	0.875	0.793	0.791	0.809	0.836	0.803	**0.871**
	Kappa	**0.5939***	0.6505*	0.608*	0.6644*	**0.5805***	**0.5216***	**0.5697***	**0.5971***
DEVELOPED	Attributes	37,L	20	An,Ap,N, Df, Af, K	FSI,u,Bh	**Ah**	//	Ce,Cs	37,25,26
	Min.Nr.Obj	9	2	4	2	**3**	//	5	4
	Acc (%)	81.5789	84.2105	68.4211	68.4211	84.2105	//	81.5789	68.4211
	F-measure	0.795	0.79	0.663	0.663	0.831	//	0.733	0.699
	AUC	0.541	0.438	0.461	0.417	0.507	//	0.542	0.624
	Kappa	0.2652	0.2138	-0.1813	-0.1813	0.4093*		0	0.0539

* Quality of the conducted tree is acceptable

Table 1. Most relevant trees, induced from 8 different attributes subgroups, 9 different values of the parameter "Minimum number of objects in the tree leafs" processed on two different instance selections described with included attributes, minimum number of examples in the leaves and measures of accuracy and quality estimation.

Table 1 represents properties of the best trees constructed under given conditions. The attributes in the constructed tree are described here:

Ae =Human Development Index (HDI)
Af= The proportion of the adult population infected with HIV / AIDS (%) (2001-2003)
Ah = Prevalent Muslim religion
Ak = Legal abortion
An= Proportion of urban population (%)
Ap= The predominant race
Av= Prvate helath expaditure (% od BDP) (2003)
Az = The proportion of births attended by trained personnel an extensive (%) (1994-2004)
Ba= Proportion of married women (between 15 and 49 years) who use contraception
Be = GDP (Gross Domestic Product) Growth (%)
Bh= Exports of goods and services (% of GDP)
Ce= Public expenditure
Cr = Gross Enrolment Ratio. Pre-primary.
Cs= Gross Enrolment Ratio. Primary
Ct = Gross Enrolment Ratio. Secondary.
Cz = Pupil-teacher ratio. Primary
De = Internet users (per 1000 people)
Df= Personal computers (per 1000 people)
Di = GNI (Gross National Income) per capita
FSI= Failed States IndexK = Gosota (prebivalci na km^2)
L = Nr. Of stillborn children/ 1000 births
M = Literacy (%)
N= Life expectancy (male)
P = Punishable homosexuality
U = Unemployment (%) (2006)
V= GDP ($) per capita (2002-2007)
4= Percentage employees (women)
6 = Percentage employers (women)
19 = Youth (15-24) literacy rate (women)
20= Percentage of parliamentary seats in Single or Lower chamber occupied by women (2010)
25 = Women's share of tertiary enrolment (%)
26 = Female teachers, Primary education (%)
32 = Net enrolment ratio in secondary education (girls)
34 = Girls' share of secondary enrolment (%)
37 = Girls' share of primary enrolment (%)on education as percentage of GDP

In the case where all countries were taken into consideration, all groups of attributes provided trees of good quality, while when the experiment was processed only on developed countries, only the tree conducted from the social attributes seems to be significant. This means, that there are many factors or combination of them, that distinguish among countries with different TFR, while among developed countries, it is not clear, what is really connected with TFR of particular country.

5.1 All countries

What distinguish countries with lower TFR from the countries with higher TFR most, will be described with the following classification trees. The numbers in the leaf of the trees denote: class, the numbers of objects of the majority and minority class. Most representative classes are marked with a bolded frame.

The first obvious factor connected with TFR is economical situation and policy. From the tree on the Figure 2 we can see that countries with low HDI (lower than 0.771) usually has high TFR. On the other side, countries with high HDI mostly have low TFR, except if their GNI per capita is middle, GDP Growth (%) is low and BDP ($) per capita (2002-2007) is low. In the former case, the TFR is low as well. Over all we might conclude that developed countries have lower TFR in comparison with countries in development.

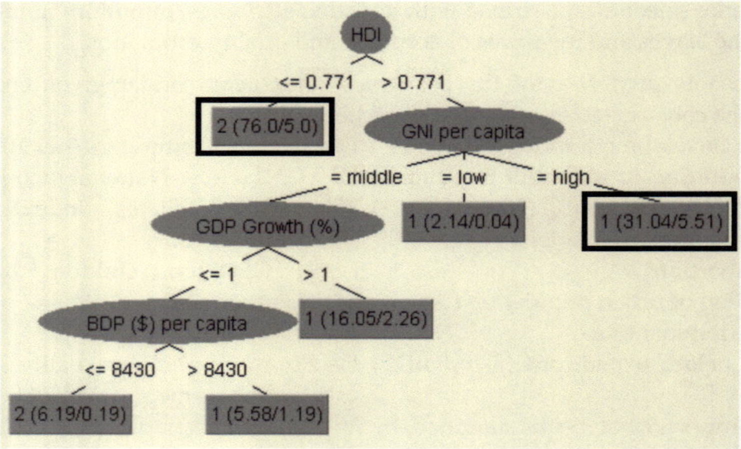

Fig. 2. Classification tree, induced from the economical attributes. Its classification accuracy is 83.9416 (F-measure: 0.841, ROC Area: 0.791, Kappa: 0.6644), the highest of the trees constructed on all countries.

Subgroup of general attributes also shows that countries development in terms of literacy is an indicator of TFR. As shown in the Figure 3, higher percentage of literacy is connected with lower TFR.

The tree constructed from social attributes also turned out to be of good quality (see Figure 4). It states, that TFR is low in the countries where abortion and contraception are allowed. The exceptions are the countries with illegal homosexuality. Whereas where abortion is not legal, high TFR is in the countries that also have high proportion of married women (between 15 and 49 years) who use contraception. Suggestions also appeared in the direction that Anti discrimination law is an indicator of low TFR countries. Overall impression is that more conservative countries have higher TFR.

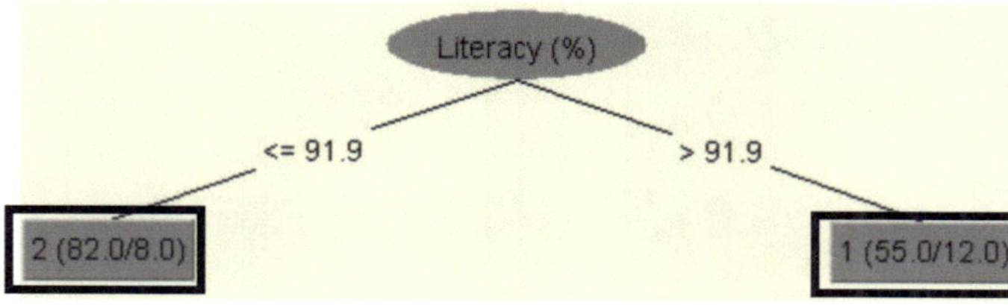

Fig. 3. Classification tree, induced from the general attributes. Its classification accuracy is 81.7518 (F-measure: 0.817, ROC Area: 0.793, Kappa: 0.608).

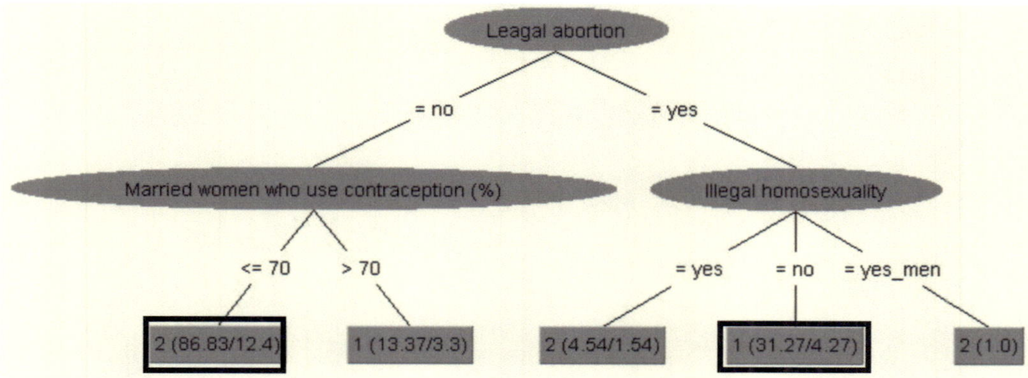

Fig. 4. Tree conducted from social attributes with the classification accuracy 81.0219 % (F-measure: 0.806, AUC: 0.809 and Kappa: 0.5805).

Among the most informative trees is the tree conducted from the attributes, automatically selected with Weka algorithm (see Figure 5).

What we see is that small number of stillborn children per 1000 births is an important indicator of lower TFR of the country. On the other hand, TFR is low when the proportion of births attended by trained personnel is extensive (more than 84%) and when abortion is legal. If abortion is not legal, than country will likely have low TFR when Net enrolment ratio of girls in secondary education is high (more than 74.5%) and internet users (per 1000 people) is more than 360. In general, one may say that where the countries health care is good, abortion is allowed, or at least where the country encourage women at their education and many citizens have an access to the internet, the TFR is lower than in the countries, which act in the opposite way. In comparison to the economic attributes, again the general impression is that the more one country is developed, the lower is TFR.

The status of the women in the country revealed a great importance of it. The most accurate tree that appeared from this iteration is the following one in Figure 6:

The tree shows us, that lower net enrolment ratio of girls in secondary education manly leads to higher TFR. Net enrollment ratio is the ratio of children of official school age based on the International Standard Classification of Education 1997 who are enrolled in school to the population of the corresponding official school age. The exceptions are the countries with high percentage of women employees. If on the other hand, net enrolment ratio of girls in secondary education is low, TFR is most of the times high. The biggest exception is the case, when Girls' share of secondary enrolment is high (more than 46.7%) and Girls' share of primary enrolment is low (less than 48.78%). The overall impression is that lower TFR is connected with higher involvement of women in education, especially in the higher education (on the secondary level or higher).

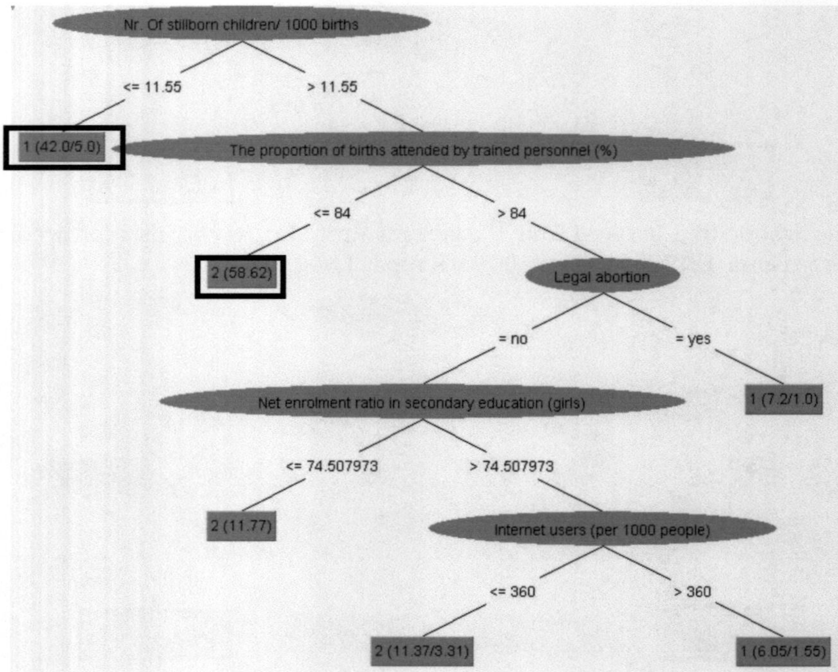

Fig. 5. Tree derived from Weka CfSSubsetEvaluation algorithm, with the accuracy 83.2117 (F-measure: 0.834 , AUC: 0.875 and Kappa: 0.6505).

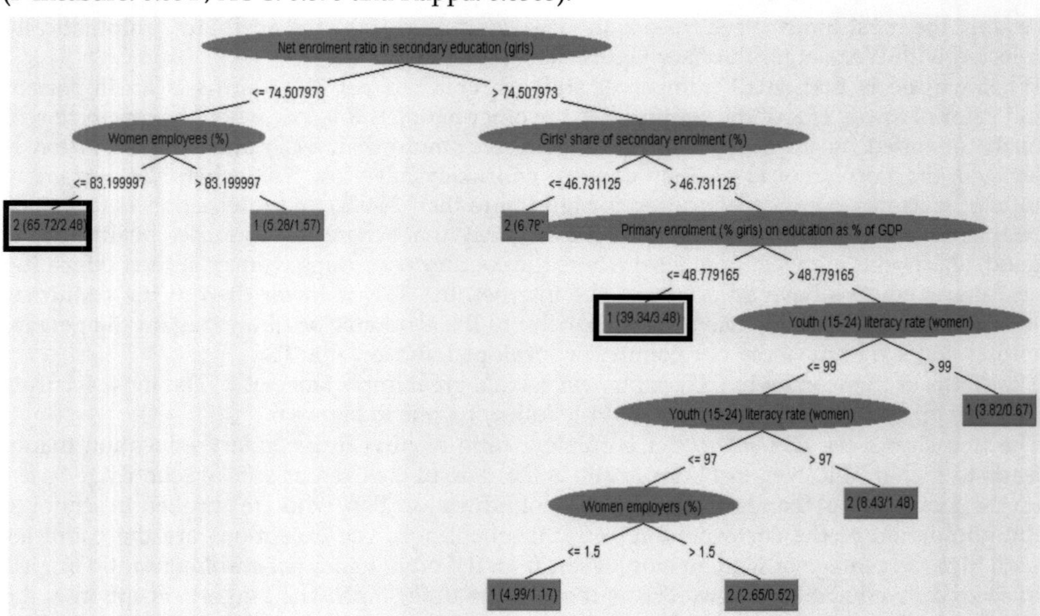

Fig. 6. Classification tree, induced from the attributes showing women status in the country. Its classification accuracy was 81.0219 (F-measure: 0.811, ROC Area: 0.871 and Kappa: 0.5971).

Are our latest findings indicator, that women career doesn't go hand in hand with family formation? Hakim proposes a theory, named Preference theory (Hakim, 2000). Preference theory seeks both to explain and predict women's choices regarding investment in productive or reproductive contributions to society. Preference theory is a historically-informed, empirically-based, multidisciplinary and predictive theory about women's choices between market work and family work. It proposes that there are three "qualitatively" different types of women, who differ among one another in their preferences about work and home: (a) the home-centred, who prefer a home life to labor market work, (b) the work-centred, of whom many are childless and all have strong commitment in their employment careers, and (c) the adaptive, who want to do some labor market work but do not commit themselves to their careers. She maintains that most women in modern affluent countries have genuine and unconstrained choices to choose between a home-career and a work-career according to their preferences, and therefore their preferences determine their home life and career. This has to do with changing gender roles. Now, young women wish to have other roles in life than that just be a mother. They seek a social status based on jobs they themselves hold and on the related financial rewards such jobs provide. Education has made them conscious of their capability; they want a just return from their years of schooling; and they wish to be considered as a autonomous individuals (Vitalli et. al., 2007) Although some authors claim that coinciding with the sharp reduction in fertility across the OECD (Organization for Economic Co-operation and Development), the correlation between fertility and female participation (and employment), which was negative during the 1960s and 1970s, became positive after 1986. From that year onward, fertility rates indeed slightly recovered in those countries with higher female participation rates whereas they suffered a sharp decline in those with low participation (Adsera, 2004).

5.2 Developed countries

As countries developmental status seems to be an important factor correlating TFR, we further took into consideration only developed countries. When doing this, economical factors lost their power of TFR prediction (tree accuracy is the lowest among all: 68.4211, F-measure, 0.663 and ROC Area: 0.417). The only statistically meaningful trees were those obtained from social attributes (See Figure 7).

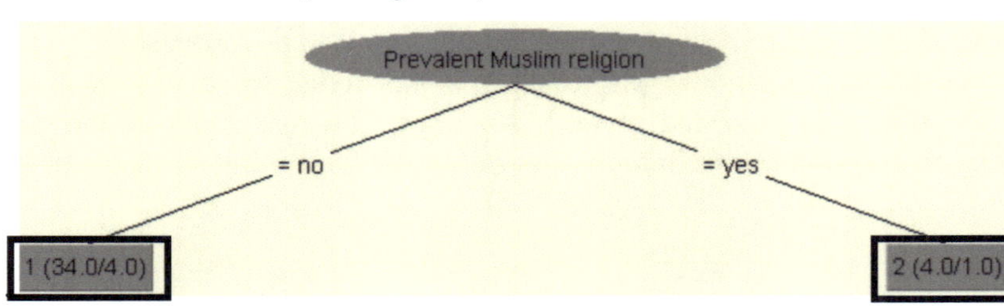

Fig. 7. Classification tree obtained from social attributes. (Accuracy: 84.2105%, F-measure: 0.831, ROC Area: 0.507 and Kappa: 0.4093).

The tree shows that prevalent Muslim religion is present in the developed countries with higher TFR. Further analysis should follow, investigating what the distinctive properties of developed Muslim countries are.

When removing the attribute showing prevalent Muslim religion in the country from the data the DM still produced a qualitative and interesting tree. Again it considers the religion;

if the prevalent religion is Christian, the TFR is low. If not, then the TFR is low if the religion is not official.

We can conclude that in developed countries religion is an important factor connected with TFR (Christianity with low TFR and Muslim with high).

5.3 General findings

We have found that the global population trends are rather uneven, as in the developed world population is now more or less stagnant and still under the regeneration limit, while in the less developed coutries population grows. The results confirmed the assumptions of the demographers; fertility is heavily influenced by the development stage of the country. As a developmental issue the literacy rate, contraception and health care situation are the pointers of fertility rate as well. The worse health care, no contraception and lower percentage of the literacy accompany high TFR. Furthermore, fertility rate is also connected with social policy of the county; namely, more conservative countries (illegal abortion, not allowed homosexuality, no antidiscrimination law) tend to have higher fertility rate than more liberal countries. Besides, an important aspect of fertility is situation of women in the country. It seems like the education of the women (specially the secondary and tertiary enrolment) and higher percentage of employment of the women is in connection with lower fertility. These results suggest that women's career doesn't goes hand in hand with establishing a family. Last but not least, religion turned out to be an important factor when considering fertility of the developed countries. The prevalent Muslim religion is connected with higher fertility, while Christianity with lower fertility rate.

When speaking broader than just about pure content of the trees, the following observations may be pointed out:

- Firstly, different measures of accuracy highly correlate among themselves. However, the measure of the tree significance is important. Namely, the relations in the conducted tree might easily be due to the coincidence – e.g. these with Kappa less than 0.5.
- After, subgroups that provided the most qualitative patterns discriminating countries with low from those of high fertility rate were examined further in order to establish that the appeared attributes are indeed the most valuable ones.
- Finally, it should be necessary to provide a detailed study of each particular attribute. Especially if the cause or a consequence relationship is to be discovered.

Regarding the fertility relations, ML tools enabled rediscovery of major well-known properties and they also provided several new ones. The case study of the demographic domain again proved that ML techniques are useful tool for mining social events.

6. Conclusion

The fertility analysis is just another field where data mining tools again proved their major asset: the constructed knowledge is in a transparent form, enabling human comprehension of relevant relations in complex forms and getting a holistic view of particular problem. In this way, an interactive and interaction process is enabled between computers and humans, exploiting the best properties of the two most advanced information machines. Regarding the fertility relations, the ML tools enabled rediscovery of major properties and provide several new comprehensions, sometimes even confronting general demographic knowledge. The case study demonstrated major advantages, threats and dilemmas:

- The new ML techniques enable exploiting several viewpoints thus enabling advanced understanding of the relations, their contexts and the actual weight instead of just getting transparent decision trees.
- When working with ML techniques we must be cautious on the quality of the results (rules, trees, etc.). Namely, not every tree or rule one get is significant enough. There is always a possibility of coincidence effect, which we check with the quality measures such as Kappa statistic.
- Is it indeed possible that there is a gap between the expert knowledge and the relations provided using ML techniques as showed with some contra intuitive relations provided by ML techniques?

At this point, it seems that the new methods might indeed be valid and that their "cold engineering" logic without social interplay can point out demographic relations in a new light, while we humans are so involved in subjective beliefs and wishes that might mislead us. Further analyses are needed to improve confidence in these tentative conclusions.

Once again, when using ML techniques for mining social events, these are the tree things one has to have in mind: meaning, accuracy and significance of the results.

New promising and extensive methods appear lately. One of them is Argument based machine learning (ABML) (Mozina et. al., 2007). It is a novel approach to machine learning, where classical machine learning is extended with concepts from the field of argumentation. This approach combines machine learning with explanations provided by domain experts. ABML is machine learning extended with certain concepts from argumentation. Arguments in ABML are a way to enable domain experts (in our case demographers) to provide their prior knowledge about a specific learning example that seems relevant for this case. In this case an experts' knowledge is not useful only for the explanation when the results are already obtained, but with the help of arguments and explanation it actually guides the procedure of building decision trees. The gained results are thus even more informative in the sense of explanation. It has already been successfully used in many domains such as chess, law and medicine (ABML) (Mozina et. al., 2006).

7. References

Adsera, A. (2004). Changing Fertility Rates in Developed Markets. The Impact of Labor Market Institutions. *Journal of Population Economics*,Vol.No.17:, January 2004, 1-27.

Angehrn, A. A. & Gibbert, M. (2008). *Learning Networks - Introduction, Background, Shift from bureaucracies to networks, Shift from training and development to learning, Shift from competitive to collaborative thinking, The three key challenges in learning networks.* The 1911 Encyclopedia Britannica.

Beitzel. S. M. (2006). *On Understanding and Classifying Web Queries. Phd Thesis.* http://ir.iit.edu/~steve/beitzel_phd_thesis.pdf.

Billari, F.C.; Furnkrantz, J. & Pskawetz A. (2000). Timing, sequencing, and quantum of life course events: a machine learning approach. Working paper 010, Max-Plank-Institute for Demographic Research, Rostock.

Christenson, M.; McDevitt, T.,; & Stanecki, K. (2004). *Global Population Profile: 2002. International Population Reports.* Health Studies Branch, International Programs Center, Washington Plaza II, Room 313A U.S. Census Bureau, Washington, DC 20233-8860.

Demsar, J. & Zupan B. (2005). From Experimental Machine Learning to Interactive Data Mining, White Paper (www.ailab.si/orange), Faculty of Computer and Information science, University of Ljubljana.

Fawcett , T (2006). An introduction to ROC analysis. *Pattern Recognit Lett,* Vol.No.27:861–874.

Gams, M. & Krivec J. (2007). Analiza vplivov na rodnost (Analysis of Impacts on Fertility). In J. Malačič, M. Gams (Eds.), *Proceedings of the 10th International Multi-conference Information Society (volume B) Slovenian Demographic Challenges of the 21st Century,* pp. 35-37. Ljubljana: Jožef Stefan Institute

Hakim, C. (2000). *Work-Lifestyle Choices in the 21st Century: Preference Theory,* Oxford Universit yPress

Hanley, J.A. & McNeil, B.J. (1983). "A method of comparing the areas under receiver operating characteristic curves derived from the same cases". *Radiology* 148 (3) 1983-09-01: 839–843. PMID 6878708.

Ivanov, K. (1972). *Quality-control of information: On the concept of accuracy of information in data banks and in management information systems.* The University of Stockholm and The Royal Institute of Technology. Doctoral dissertation.

Kohavi, R. (1995). A study of cross-validation and bootstrap for accuracy estimation and model selection, *Proceedings of the Fourteenth International Joint Conference on Artificial Intelligence* 2 (12): 1137–1143.

Kandefer, M. & Shapiro, S. C. (2009). An f-measure for context-based information retrieval. In G. Lake- meyer, L. *Morgenstern, and M.-A. Williams, editors, Commonsense 2009: Proceedings of the Ninth International Symposium on Logical Formaliza- tions of Commonsense Reasoning,* pages 79–84, Toronto, CA. The Fields Institute, Toronto,CA

Landis, J.R.; & Koch, G.G. (1977). The measurement of observer agreement for categorical data. *Biometrics* 33: 159–174.

Melville, P.; Yang, S.M.; Saar-Tsechansky, M. & Mooney R. Active learning for probability estimation using Jensen-Shannon divergence. *In Proceedings of the European Conference on Machine Learning (ECML),* pages 268–279. Springer, 2005.

Mitchell, T. (2006). *The discipline of machine learning* (Technical Report CMUML-06-108). Carnegie Mellon University.

Mozina,M.; Zabkar, J.; & Bratko,I. (2004). Implementation of and experiments with ABML and MLBA. ASPIC deliverable D3.4.

Mozina,M.; Zabkar, J.; & Bratko,I. (2007). Argument Based Machine Learning. *AI Journal.* Vol.171, No.10-15, July-October 2007, Pages 922-937

Obuchowski N.A. (2003). "Receiver operating characteristic curves and their use in radiology". Radiology 229 (1): 3–8. PMID 14519861.

Pazzani, M. (1991). The influence of prior knowledge on concept acquisition: Experimental and computational results. *Journal of Experimental Psychology: Learning, Memory & Cognition,* Vol. 17, 416–432

Sullivan, A. & Sheffrin S. M. (1996). *Economics: Principles in action.* Upper Saddle River, New Jersey 074589: Pearson Prentice Hall. pp. 57, 305. ISBN 0-13-063085-3.

Vidulin, V. & Gams M. (2006). Vpliv investicij v izobraževanje in R&R na gospodarsko rast, *Elektroteh. vestn.,* Vol. 73, No.. 5, pp. 285-290.

Vitali, A.; Billari, F.; Prskawetz, A. & Testa, M. (2007). Preference Theory and Low Fertility:A Comparative Perspektive, *European Demographic Research Papers,* No. 2, Vienna, Institute of Demography

Witten, I. H. & Frank E. (2005). Data Mining - Practical Machine Learning Tools and Techniques (sec. ed.), Morgan Kaufmann.

4

Mining Enrolment Data Using Predictive and Descriptive Approaches

Fadzilah Siraj and Mansour Ali Abdoulha
Applied Sciences, College of Arts & Sciences, Universiti Utara Malaysia
Malaysia

1. Introduction

In recent years, the technology of database has become more advanced where huge amount of data is required to be stored in the databases, and the wealth of information hidden in those datasets has been realized by business people as a useful tool for making business strategic decisions. Data mining then attract more attention as it promises to extract valuable information from the raw data that businesses can use to increase their profitability through a profitable decision-making process.

Data mining is used to describe knowledge in databases; it is a process of extracting and identifying useful information and subsequent knowledge from databases using statistical, mathematical, artificial intelligence and machine learning technique (Efraim *et al.*, 2007). Data mining applies modern statistical and computational technologies in its quest to expose useful pattern hidden within the large databases. It has proved itself as a powerful tool, capable of providing highly targeted information to support decision-making and forecasting for scientific, physiological, sociological, the military and business decision making. The predictive power of data mining comes from its unique design by combining techniques from machine learning, pattern recognition, and statistics to automatically extract concepts, and to determine the interrelations and patterns of interest from large databases (Edelstein, 1997).

To date, higher educational organizations are placed in a very high competitive environment and are aiming to get more competitive advantages over the other business competitors. These organizations should improve the quality of their services and satisfy their customers such as industries and government agencies. To remain competitiveness among educational field, these organizations need deep and enough knowledge for a better assessment, evaluation, planning, and decision-making. Majority of the required knowledge that has been stored in the educational organization's database can be extracted from the historical and operational data. Therefore, one approach to effectively tackle the student and administration challenges is through the analysis and presentation of data, or data mining.

Data mining helps organizations to use their current reporting capabilities to discover and identify the hidden patterns in databases. The extracted patterns are then used to build data mining models, and hence can be used to predict performance and behaviour with high accuracy. As a result of this insight, universities are able to allocate resources more effectively. Data mining may, for example, give a university the information necessary to take action before students quit their study, or to efficiently assign resources with an accurate estimate of how many male or female will register in a particular program (Luan, 2004).

University has collected large amounts of student data for years; however this data is typically not put in a form of improving its use. To date, universities are data-rich but information poor. Many of them did not take the advantage of data mining in analyzing and uncovering the hidden information within the student enrolment data. An attempt to uncover the hidden information will inevitably useful to produce knowledge that in effect improves management decision-making.

This study addresses usage and usefulness of data mining and its applications on higher education databases particularly for understanding undergraduate's student enrolment data at Sebha University in Libya. It utilizes ***Descriptive*** and ***Predictive*** data mining approaches in order to discover hidden information. ***Cluster analysis*** was performed to group the data into clusters based on its similarities. The clusters were also used as targets for prediction experiment. For ***Predictive Analysis***, three techniques have been used namely, ***Neural Network***, ***Logistic Regression*** and the ***Decision Tree***. The study shows that ***Neural Network*** obtains the highest results accuracy among the three techniques.

2. Data mining tasks

The objective of data mining is to identify valid novel, potentially useful, and understandable correlations and patterns in existing data (Chang & Hsu, 2005). The tasks of data mining can be modeled as either ***Predictive*** or ***Descriptive*** in nature (Dunham, 2003). A ***Predictive*** model makes a prediction about values of data using known results found from different data while the ***Descriptive*** model identifies patterns or relationships in data. Unlike the predictive model, a descriptive model serves as a way to explore the properties of the data examined, not to predict new properties. ***Predictive*** model data mining tasks include classification, prediction, regression and time series analysis. The ***Descriptive*** task encompases methods such as Clustering, Summarizations, Association Rules, and Sequence analysis (Fig. 1).

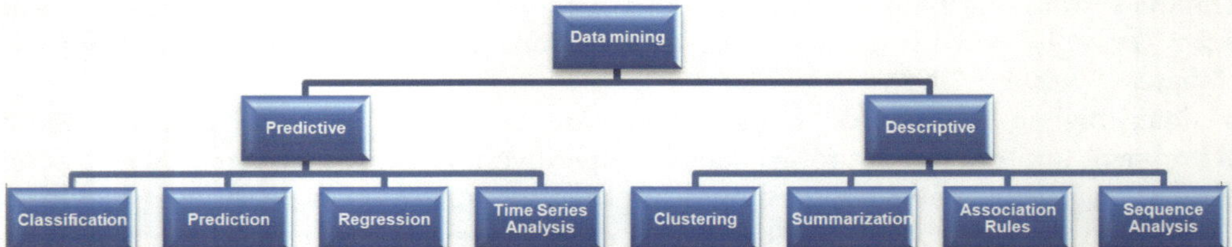

Fig. 1. Data mining tasks and models

Among ***Predictive*** models, Classification is probably the best understood of all data mining approaches. Three common characteristics of classification tasks are

- Learning is supervised
- The dependent variable is categorical
- The model built is able to assign new data to one of a set of well-defined classes.

For example, given classes of patients that corresponds to medical treatment responses; the form of treatment to which a new patient is most likely to respond to is identified (Stephens & Pablo, 2003). Unlike a classification model, the purpose of Prediction model is to determine the future outcome rather than current behaviour. Its output can be categorical or numeric value. For example, given a prediction model of credit card transactions, the likelihood that a specific transaction is fraudulent can be predicted.

Another ***Predictive*** model known as statistical Regression is a supervised learnng technique that involves analysis of the dependency of some attribute values upon the values of other attributes in the same item, and the development of a model that can predict these attribute values for new cases. For example, given a data set of credit card transactions, a model that can predict the likelihood of fraudulence for new transactions can be built. Prediction applications with one or more time-dependent attribures are called time-series problems. ***Time series analysis*** usually involves predicting numeric outcomes such as the future price of individual stock (Roiger & Geatz, 2003).

The second approach of data mining is known as ***Descriptive*** method. Descriptive data mining is normally used to generate frequency, cross tabulation and correlation. ***Descriptive*** method can be defined to discover interesting regularities in the data, to uncover patterns and find interesting subgroups in the bulk of data (Marco & Gianluca, 2005). In education, studies McNamarah (2005) used ***Descriptive*** to determine the demographic influence on particular factors. ***Summarization*** maps data into subsets with associated simple descriptions (Dunham, 2003). Basic statistics such as Mean, Standard Deviation, Variance, Mode and Median can be used as ***Summarization*** approach.

In ***Clustering***, a set of data items is partitioned into a set of classes such that items with similar characteristics are grouped together. ***Clustering*** is best used for finding groups of items that are similar. For example, given a data set of customers, subgroups of customers that have a similar buying behaviour can be identified.

Associations or *Link Analysis* are used to discover relationships between attributes and items such as the presence of one pattern implies the presence of another pattern. i.e. to what extent one item is related to another in terms of cause-and-effect. This is common in establishing a form of statistical relationships among different interdependent variables of a model. These relations may be associations between attributes within the same data item like ('Out of the shoppers who bought milk, 64% also purchased bread') or associations between different data items like ('Every time a certain stock drops 5%, it causes a resultant 13% in another stock between 2 and 6 weeks later'). ***Association Rules*** is a popular technique for market basket analysis because all possible combinations of potentially interesting product groupings can be explored (Roiger & Geatz, 2003).

The investigation of relationships between items over a period of time is also often referred to as ***Sequence Analysis*** (Han & Kamber, 2001). ***Sequence Analysis*** is used to determine sequential patterns in data (Dunham, 2003). The patterns in the dataset are based on time sequence of actions, and they are similar to association data, however the relationship is based on time. In Market Basket analysis, the items are to be purchased at the same time, on the other hand, for ***Sequence Analysis*** the items are purchased over time in some order.

3. Data mining in education

It is highly necessary to determine that data mining techniques are applicable in higher education environment. In fact, there are many algorithms that are similar in concept to stored procedures of object-oriented programming in that they are universally applicable. Almost all algorithms or models currently used in the business sectors are directly usable for research in higher education, especially in institutional researches except for ***Association Rules*** or ***Link Analysis*** which mostly used in telecommunication companies to understand groupings associated with starting points (Luan, 2001). Furthermore, prediction from Data Mining offers the university an opportunity to act before a student drops out or to plan for resource allocation with confidence gained from having complete records of all students reflecting their tracks of activities. Through data mining, a university could, for example, predict with 85 percent accuracy which students will or will not graduate. The university could use this information to plan required academic activities on those students projected to experience such graduating difficulties.

The university's data can be used to suggest solutions to a wide range of educational challenges. Seifert (2004) indicated that Data Mining can be used to explore differences, explore growth over time, evaluate programs, and to identify the root causes of problems in education as one of the many ways data can be used. A study by Chrispeels, Brown and Castillo (2000) revealed that data is a strong predictor of the efficiency in the activities of school teams. The use of data is not only increased efficiency but also, to serve as a mediator for the positive effect of other factors. Kennedy (2003) considered the use of data as a central component of its business model to increase the achievement of the set objectives.

The data can also have a positive effect on people involved in the educational process. Feldman and Tung (2001) observed that frequent usage of data in schools has metamorphosized into a more professional culture. Educators in their study have become greater collaborators during decision-making process, and school business consequently has become a less "privatized" one. Wayman, Stringfield and Yakimowski (2004) noted that school leaders who were involved in the use of data often developed a mindset of being responsible for their own destiny, increasingly able to find and use information to inform the school improvement. Armstrong and Anthes (2001) noticed that the use of data has helped in raising expectations of teachers on their students.

The applications of DM in education sector is one of the most challenging tasks, this notwithstanding, its ability to offer a unique educational decision-making process is a good justification for the required stress involved. With the introduction of Data Mining concept, decision makers (management) in the educational sectors will definitely find their jobs easier.

Although computers supporting knowledge management have been widely used in fields such as business, Thorn (2001) observed that schools presented difficult technical problems due to the variety of data needs and usage at schools. School data is always found to be in different forms and places, making it more difficult to organize the databases effectivively. In addition, Thorn described a case study where a particu;ar district was ready to implement data that has to do with decision-making, however some technological barriers served as an hindrance to the process. Recent technological advances inevitably helps schools to overcome problems resulting from such technological barriers.

Data mining techniques, for example have been used to predict student performance in certain courses, to forecast the lecturer performance at the university and others. Indirectly these techniques contribute towards a better quality education management as well as assisting the education institution managing the administrative task effectively. Schools for example will soon have a variety of affordable, efficient computing tools to aid in the data mining process (Wayman & Stringfield, 2006).

4. Methodology

The CRISP-DM methodology suggested by Chapman *et al.* (2000) was utilized in this study. This methodology involves six phases, namely Business Understanding, Data Understanding, Data Preparation, Modeling, Evaluation and Deployment as shown in Fig. 2.

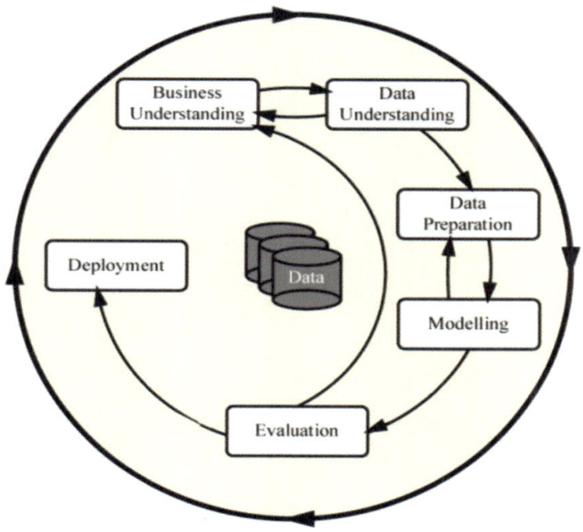

Fig. 2. Steps of CRISP-DM Methodology (Adopted from Chapman *et al.*, 2000).

In this study, as the possible areas of tests depends on the data available, and the detailed business objective cannot be identified until the data was studied. Consequently, this phase has to be performed in parallel with the data understanding and data preparation phase. The initial phase of Data Understanding focuses on understanding the study objectives and requirements from the student registrar office. The data understanding phase starts with an initial data collection and proceeds with actions in order to get familiar with the data.

4.1 Business understanding

The first phase of CRISP-DM is business understanding which focuses on project objectives and requirement from a business perspective, and converting this knowledge into a data mining problem definition as well as designing a preliminary plan to achieve the objectives. To identify the research gap and the potential problems, literature study was carried out and relevant works have been identified. In this study, research related to educational data and factors affecting students' enrollment were sought and suitable mining algorithms for ***Predictive*** and ***Descriptive*** purposes were also selected.

4.2 Data understanding

The second phase is data understanding which begins with initial data collection. At this point, the data collected from the respondents needs to be checked and understood. In order to be familiar with the data, the next step in data understanding is to identify data quality problem, get some insights about the data and detect interesting subsets to form hypotheses so as to uncover the hidden information within the data collected for this study.

A total of 8510 students' enrollment from 1998 to 2006 was collected. An original student's main table includes 38 attributes with 8 numerical attributes and the others were of categorical type. Part of the original data is shown in Table 1.

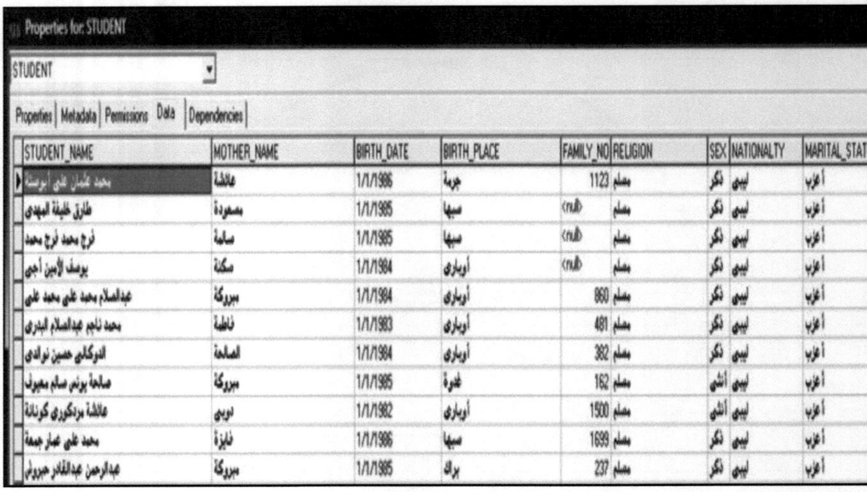

Properties for: STUDENT

STUDENT

Properties | Metadata | Permissions | Data | Dependencies

STUDENT_NAME	MOTHER_NAME	BIRTH_DATE	BIRTH_PLACE	FAMILY_NO	RELIGION	SEX	NATIONALTY	MARITAL_STATUS
محمد عثمان علي أبوستة	عائشة	1/1/1986	جرمة	1123	مسلم	ذكر	ليبي	أعزب
طارق خليفة المهدي	مسعودة	1/1/1985	سبها	<null>	مسلم	ذكر	ليبي	أعزب
فرج محمد فرج محمد	سالمة	1/1/1985	سبها	<null>	مسلم	ذكر	ليبي	أعزب
يوسف الأمين أجي	مكة	1/1/1984	أوباري	<null>	مسلم	ذكر	ليبي	أعزب
عبدالسلام محمد علي محمد علي	مبروكة	1/1/1984	أوباري	860	مسلم	ذكر	ليبي	أعزب
محمد ناجم عبدالسلام البدري	فاطمة	1/1/1983	أوباري	481	مسلم	ذكر	ليبي	أعزب
الدوكالي حسين نوادي	الصالحة	1/1/1984	أوباري	382	مسلم	ذكر	ليبي	أعزب
صالحة يونس سالم معيوف	مبروكة	1/1/1985	غدوة	162	مسلم	أنثى	ليبي	أعزب
عائشة بردكوري كرنانة	دوبي	1/1/1982	أوباري	1500	مسلم	أنثى	ليبي	أعزب
محمد علي عمار جمعة	فايزة	1/1/1986	سبها	1699	مسلم	ذكر	ليبي	أعزب
عبدالرحمن عبدالقادر حبروش	مبروكة	1/1/1985	براك	237	مسلم	ذكر	ليبي	أعزب

Table 1. Sample of Student Data

As a result of preprocessing phase, the total number of data was reduced to 6830. In this phase, the data quality problem has been identified. The data were loaded into SAS version 9.13, checking for attributes to be analyzed and it was further processed in the next phase.

4.3 Data preparation

Data preparation concerns all activities needed to construct the final dataset for modeling purposes. The tasks are most likely to be carried out multiple times and may not be in any prescribed manner. Different datasets tend to expose new issues and challenges. With the goals in mind, it is important to choose the right data mining algorithms, techniques and tools which are expected to give best results with the provided data. Dependencies among different subsets of attributes are expected to be exhibited by different subsets of data. Most often, not all variables are used in analyzing and modelling process. This phase was conducted repetitively for determining suitable attributes to be used as predictors and target (output).

To get full insight of data distribution and in identifying outliers, descriptive analysis was conducted for exploratory purposes. In this study, the Cluster number was assumed as a target and other attributes such as demographics information, qualification upon entry and examination results were considered as predictor variables.

4.4 Modeling

During the modeling phase, modeling techniques were selected and applied to the dataset used in the study. This phase include selecting an appropriate modeling technique, building the models and followed by assessment of model. Subsequently, the model selection involves selecting appropriate techniques for the problem, refine the models whenever is necessary in order to meet the requirements and other constraints. After reviewing data

mining techniques, the ***Descriptive*** approaches employed in the study were identified, namely the ***Summarization*** and ***Clustering*** methods. Since the aim of the experiment was to study the patterns and getting some information within the enrollment data, no specific target has been identified. To this end, clusters were generated by ***Clustering*** method, and later used as target or output for ***Predictive*** approach.
Once the ***Descriptive*** methods has been identified, the next step was to identify the ***Predictive*** methods to be utilized in the next phase of empirical study. The identified approaches include ***Regression, Decision Trees and Neural Network.*** In addition, comparison between these supervised approaches was also conducted to get some insight about the strength and weaknesses of each approach since one of the aims of the study was to determine whether these methods were well suited for extracting the required knowledge. As a result, the predictive method will be able to predict in which cluster does the future student will fall into based on the enrollment information.

4.4.1 Descriptive

Initially, ***Descriptive Statistics*** was carried out to investigate the nature of the dataset and the distribution of each attribute. Frequency tables were generated and the correlation analysis was also conducted to determine the relationship among the attributes, including Cross Tabulation Analysis (contingency tables). Cross Tabulation Analysis displays the relationship between two or more categorical (nominal or ordinal) variables.
Clustering Analysis was performed based on 4 clusters and the analysis conducted at this stage was based on the results obtained from Neural Connection software. For ***Clustering Analysis***, Kohonen network was used (Fig. 3) assuming the clusters, or classes, were formed from patterns that share common features and similar patterns have been grouped together. Kohonen networks are usually one or two dimensional grids of artificial neurons, or nodes, where every node in the grid is connected to all the inputs. As the output comes directly from the grid of neurons (known as the Kohonen layer), Kohonen networks have no separate output layer. Each artificial neuron is linked to each input with a weight, and can be thought of as being at a point in the input data space.

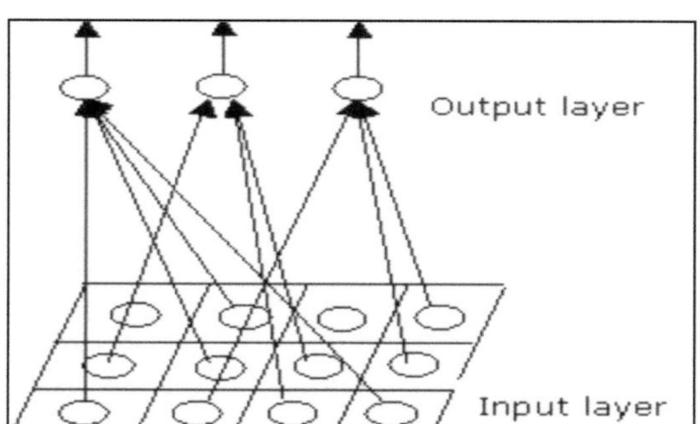

Fig. 3. Kohonen Network

Prior to training, these weights are set to initial values. Each output node at the output layer has an activation function and the output node with the best output wins the competition. The output node is identified as the output (or cluster) for that particular pattern. To enable the Kohonen layer to group similar patterns, a neighbourhood of artificial neurons around the winning artificial neuron is also altered to be more like the input pattern. This is equivalent of moving the node towards the position of a pattern in the input data space. After a number of passes through the Kohonen layer, different areas of the Kohonen layer will respond to different types of patterns within the dataset (Everitt, 1993).

4.4.2 Predictive

As the clusters were generated through Kohonen networks, these clusters were then used as output for the predictive methods. Three predictive techniques, viz. ***Regression, Decision Tree,*** and ***Neural Network*** were employed to test the accuracies of the predictive models based on clusters.

The ***Regression*** analysis model is also known as one of the most useful tools in quantitative analysis phase of the decision-making process (Marquez *et al*, 1991). It is generally used to predict future values based on past values by fitting a set of points to a curve (Dunham, 2003). The simplest form of a regression model contains a dependent variable called outcome variable and single independent variable call factor. Logistic Regression is part of a category of statistical models called generalized linear model. This model includes ordinary regression and ANOVA as well as multivariate statistics such as ANOVA and loglinear regression. Logistic Regression allows one to predict a discrete outcome, such as group membership from set of variable that may be continuous discrete or a mix of any of this.

Decision Tree is a predictive model with tree or hierarchical structure, and commonly used in classification and prediction methods. It consists of nodes, which contained classification questions, and branches, or the results of the questions. At the lowest level of the tree - leave nodes - the label of each classification is identified. Typically, like other classification and prediction techniques, the ***Decision Tree*** begins with exploratory phase. Its algorithm will try to find the best-fit criteria to distinguish one class from another. The major concerns of this techiques are the quality of the classification problems as well as the appropriate number of levels of the tree. Some leaves and branches need to be removed in order to improve the performance of the decision tree. This step is also called tree pruning. The experiments using ***Decision Tree*** were conducted in parallel with the ***Regression Analysis*** and ***Neural Network*** modelling, and the algorithm used in ***Decision Tree*** is C4.5. Standard decision tree learners such as C4.5 increase the nodes in depth-first order (Quinlan, 1993) while in best-first decision tree the "best" node is expanded first. The "best" node is the node whose split leads to maximum reduction of impurity (e.g. Gini index) among all nodes available for splitting (Shi, 2006).

Neural Network model known as multi layer perceptron with back propagation algorithm was used to establish a prediction model (Fig. 4). The distribution of data for training, validation and test set were evaluated to determine the suitable composition for obtaining a good prediction model. Some back propagation parameters were also investigated to obtain a suitable Neural Network prediction model (Sirikulvadhana, 2002). In general, there are three types of activation functions that are commonly used in neural network, namely Threshold function, Piecewise-linear function and Sigmoid function. Different from other learning algorithms, backpropagation algorithm works, or learns and adjusts the weights backward, which simply mean that it predicts the weighted algorithms by the input from the output.

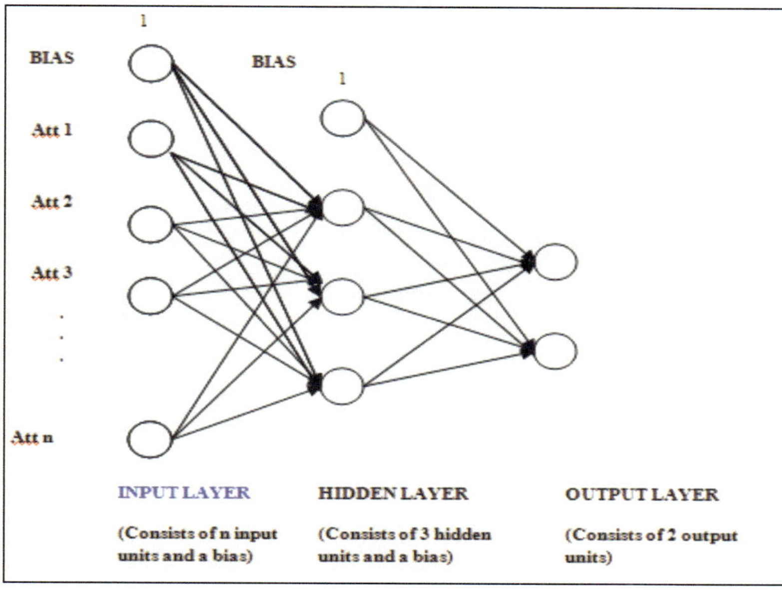

Fig. 4. The architecture of Multilayer Perceptron

4.5 Evaluation

In this phase, models were evaluated to assess the degree to which the model meets the business objectives and quality requirements. The steps involved include evaluating the results, reviewing the processes and determining the next steps. The evaluation for ***Regression, Neural Networks and Decision Tree*** was based on the classification accuracy, confusion matrix table, and classification table respectively.

Deployment

The last phase in CRISP-DM was the deployment. The knowledge from the model acquired from the experimental study were to be transferred for implementaion purposes.

5. Results

Sebha University has been established in the year 1983. To date, Sebha University has several branches, they are located at Sebha, Ghat, Tragen, Brak, Morzoq, and Obari cities. Based on the information of all the faculties of Sebha University, the distribution of students enrollment is shown in Fig. 5. Programs such as Dentistry (Sebha), Sport (Ghat), Arts (Tragen) and Sciences (Tragen) have small enrollment figures, ranging from 1% to 4% with number of students less than 350 over 8510 of all university students' population. This indicates that the university should put this fact in consideration in coming years as to which location has low students' population. However, if the faculties are grouped by the cities, Sebha faculties (Sciences, Arts, Medicine, Dentistry, Law and Agronomy) contributed to 55% of university population.

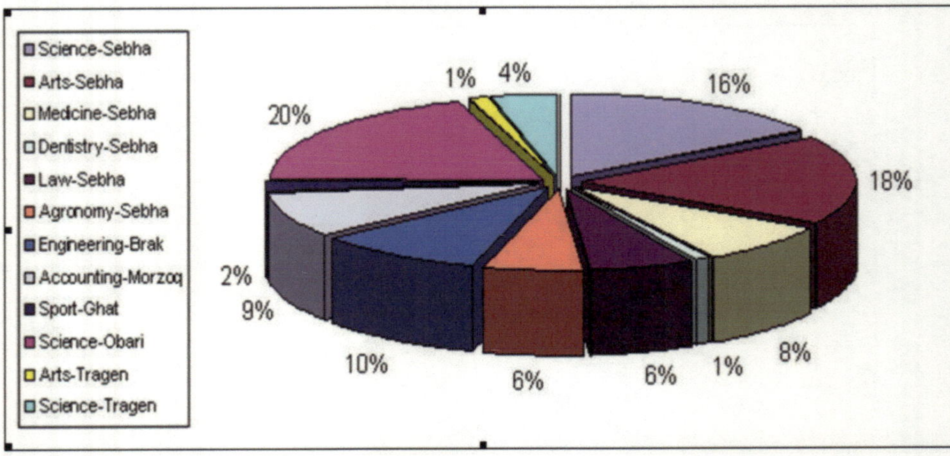

Fig. 5. Distribution of Student Population

The ***Descriptive*** statistics, particularly ***Cross Tabulation Analysis*** was carried out to discover the relationship between the attributes (Fig. 6). Based on the results shown in Fig. 5, majority of the registered students were female with ratio of 58% in all university population and almost 42% were male. Program such as Sciences (Sebha, Obari and Tragen), Arts (Sebha and Tragen), Medicine (Sebha) and Dentistry (Sebha) were more popular to female students, with ratio of 80% in some faculties, and ranging from 65% to 80%. In contrast, other degree programs such as Law (Sebha), Agronomy (Sebha), Engineering (Brak), Accounting (Morzoq) and Sport (Ghat) have more male students than female ranging from 50% to 75%.

Further analysis was carried out to determine the relationship between faculty, gender and student status. The student status was classified into ***Enroll, Move, Expel, Quit*** and ***Completed the Study***. From the analysis, it is observed that higher percentage of female students ***Completed the Study*** compared to male students undertaking Science (Obari and Sebha), Arts (Sebha) and Medicine (Sebha). On the other hand, higher percentage of male students undertaking Sport (Ghat) and Law (Sebha) completed their studies as shown in Fig. 7.

Based on results exhibited in Fig. 8 and 9, more male compared to female students have been expelled from the university. When Gender is cross tabulated with Student Status, most of the students who quitted Arts program (Sebha) are male (Fig. 8). In addition, Agronomy (Sebha) program was not preferred by female students. Fig. 9 indicates students that have been expelled from continuing Engineering (Brak) and Sciences (Sebha) programs Arts (Sebha) degree program.

The results shown in Fig. 10 indicate that more female (63%) enrolled at the university compared to male (37%). In other words, the male enrollment rate was almost half of the female rate. Most of female students (69% to 81%) undertook Arts (Sebha and Tragen), Science (Tragen, Obari and Sebha), Dentistry (Sebha), and Medicine (Sebha). The least number of female students undertook Sport (Ghat), Accounting (Morzoq) and Agronomy Sebha. On the other hand, majority of the male students were enrolled in the programmes such as Sport (Ghat), Accounting (Morzoq) and Agronomy (Sebha).

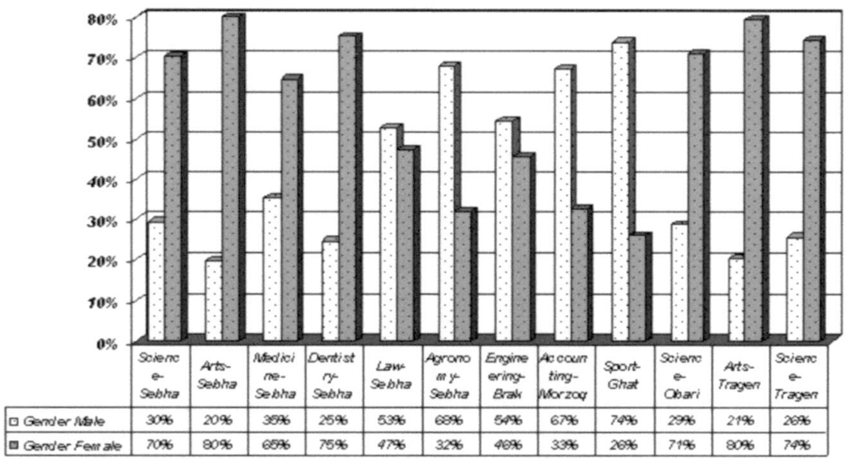

Fig. 6. Faculty with Respect to Gender

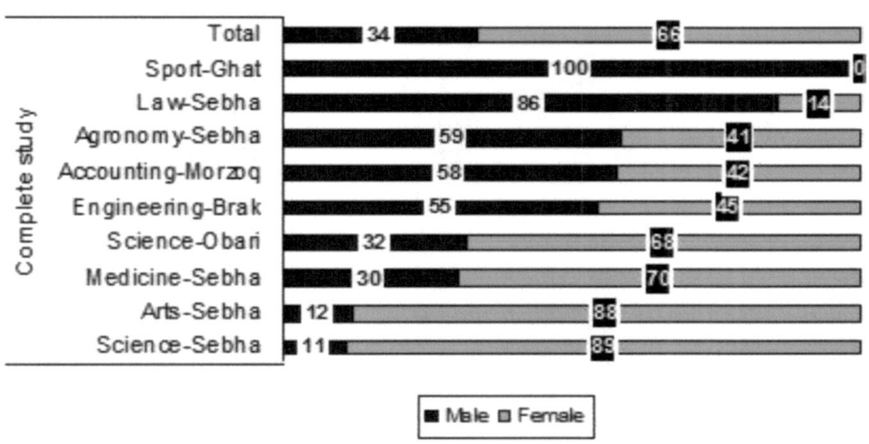

Fig. 7. Faculty with Respect to Student Status (*Complete Study)* and Gender

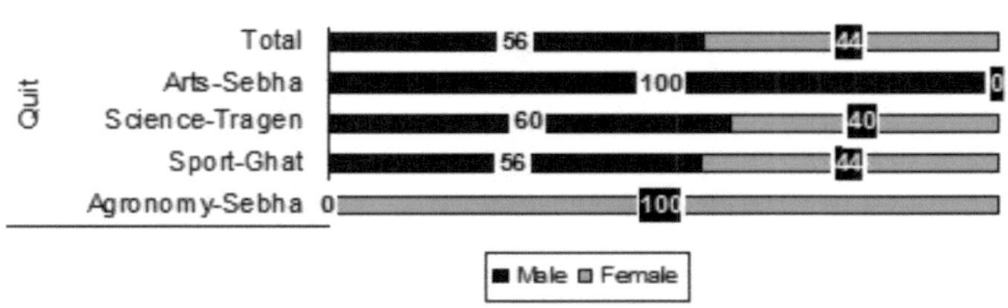

Fig. 8. Faculty with Respect to Student Status (*Quit*) and Gender

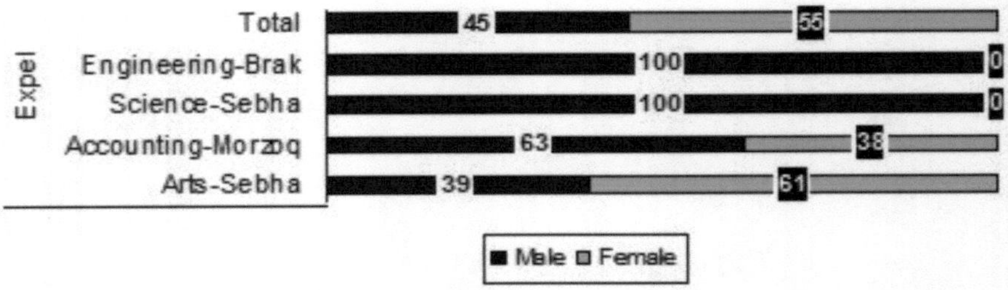

Fig. 9. Faculty with Respect to Student Status (*Expel*) and Gender

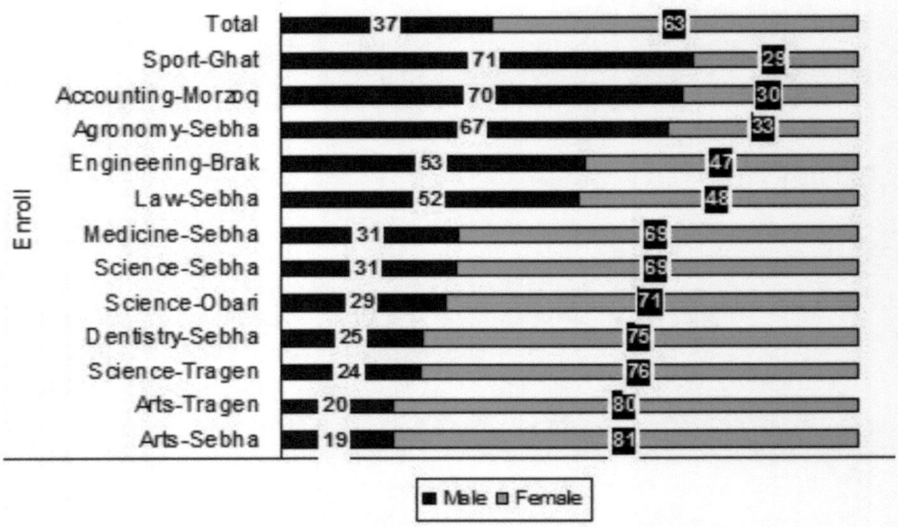

Fig. 10. Faculty with Respect to Student Status (*Enroll*) and Gender

Having performed ***Cross Tabulation Analysis***, the clustering network using Kohonen network has been carried out. As a result, 3 clusters have been identified (***Cluster 0, 1*** and 2). Further investigation was performed to carry out in order to determine the relationship between variables such as ***Religion, Gender, Nationality, State, Degree Owned, Faculty, Student Status, Admission Type, Housing Status*** and ***Register Type*** with Clusters (Table 2).

	Degree Owned	Faculty	Housing Status	Nationality
Correlation Coefficient	.156(**)	-.760(**)	-.287(**)	.332(**)
Sig. (2-tailed)	.000	.000	.000	.000

*	Correlation is significant at the 0.05 level (2-tailed).
**	Correlation is significant at the 0.01 level (2-tailed).

Table 2. The correlation between enrollment attributes and clusters

The main aim of clustering is to group cases based on its similarities. In addition, each ***Cluster*** has its own characteristic, which can be analyzed based on faculties using statistical approach. In order to determine the meaning of each ***Cluster***, cross tabulation analysis was carried out, and the ***Clusters*** analyzed based on faculties are shown in Fig. 11. Results in Fig. 11 indicates that more male in ***Cluster 0*** and **2**. On the other hand, female students has the tendency to fall into ***Cluster 1***.

Clearly, the correlation between variables ***Cluster*** and ***Faculty*** is significantly strong (p=0.00, r = -0.760) while between ***Cluster*** and ***Nationality*** is medium (p = 0.00, r = 0.332).

The relationship between the clusters based on Faculty and Gender are shown in Table 3. As for the faculty with respect to gender and cluster, clearly ***Cluster 1*** comprises of female students undertaking Arts, Sciences, Dentistry and Medicine. Male students who undertook Sports were most likely to fall into ***Cluster 3*** rather than 0. ***Cluster 3*** is more inclined to male students who undertook Law, Sport, and Sciences(Tragen). ***Cluster 0*** does not show any clear pattern.

When further analysis was performed on the clusters, it is intersting to note that the cluster is able to distinguish between Libyan and non-Libyan students. In addition, some rules with regard to faculty and nationality can also be extracted.

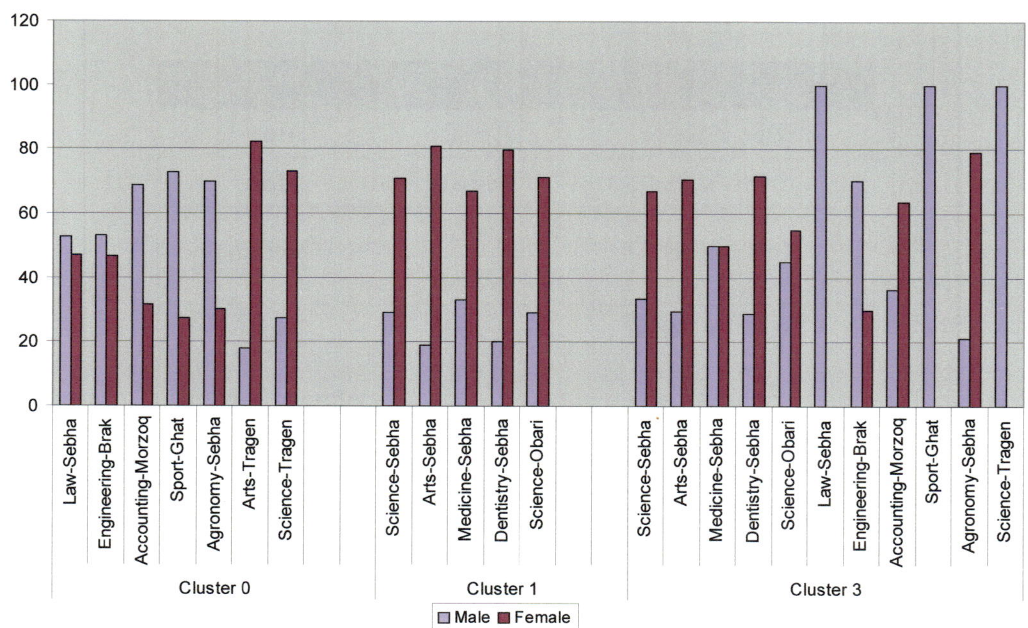

Fig. 11. Faculties with Respect to Gender for Each Cluster

Cluster 1		
Law-Sebha	Male	Almost the same
	Female	
Engineering-Brak	Male	Almost the same
	Female	
Accounting-Morzoq	Male	More
Sport-Ghat	Male	More
Agronomy-Sebha	Male	More
Arts-Tragen	Female	More
Science-Tragen	Female	More
Cluster 2		
Science-Sebha	Female	More
Arts-Sebha	Female	More
Medicine-Sebha	Female	
Dentistry-Sebha	Female	More
Science-Obari	Female	More
Cluster 3		
Science-Sebha	Female	More
Arts-Sebha	Female	More
Medicine-Sebha	Male	The Same
	Female	
Dentistry-Sebha	Female	More
Science-Obari	Male	Almost the same
	Female	
Law-Sebha	Male	All
Engineering-Brak	Male	More
Accounting-Morzoq	Female	More
Sport-Ghat	Male	All
Agronomy-Sebha	Female	More
Science-Tragen	Male	All

Table 3. The Relationship between the Cluster with Respect to Faculty and Gender

Cluster 0		
Law-Sebha	Libyan	All
Engineering-Brak	Libyan	Almost All
Accounting-Morzoq	Libyan	All
Sport-Ghat	Libyan	Almost All
Agronomy-Sebha	Libyan	Almost All
Arts-Tragen	Libyan	All
Science-Tragen	Libyan	Almost All

Cluster 1		
Science-Sebha	Libyan	Almost All
Arts-Sebha	Libyan	Almost All
Medicine-Sebha	Libyan	Almost All
Dentistry-Sebha	Libyan	All
Science-Obari	Libyan	All

<table>
<tr><th colspan="3">Cluster 2</th></tr>
<tr><td>Science-Sebha</td><td>Lebanese</td><td>More</td></tr>
<tr><td rowspan="2">Arts-Sebha</td><td>Palestinian</td><td rowspan="2">Almost the same</td></tr>
<tr><td>Sudanese</td></tr>
<tr><td>Medicine-Sebha</td><td>Palestinian</td><td>More</td></tr>
<tr><td rowspan="2">Dentistry-Sebha</td><td>Palestinian</td><td rowspan="2">Almost the same</td></tr>
<tr><td>Iraqi</td></tr>
<tr><td>Science-Obari</td><td>Palestinian</td><td>More</td></tr>
<tr><td rowspan="2">Law-Sebha</td><td>Syrian</td><td rowspan="2">Almost the same</td></tr>
<tr><td>Chadian</td></tr>
<tr><td>Engineering-Brak</td><td>Sudanese</td><td>More</td></tr>
<tr><td>Accounting-Morzoq</td><td>Sudanese</td><td>Almost all</td></tr>
<tr><td>Sport-Ghat</td><td>Tunisian</td><td>All</td></tr>
<tr><td>Agronomy-Sebha</td><td>Sudanese</td><td>Almost all</td></tr>
<tr><td>Science-Tragen</td><td>Sudanese</td><td>All</td></tr>
</table>

Table 4. The Relationship between the Cluster with Respect to Faculty and Citizenship

If the student is Libyan, and undertaking Law, he/she falls under ***Cluster 0***. This is also true for Accounting-Morzoq, Sport-Ghat, Agronomy-Sebha, Art-Tragen, and Science-Tragen. If the student is Libyan and taking Arts at Sebha, he/she falls in ***Cluster 2.*** This is also true for Libyan students at Sebha who undertook Medicine and Dentistry. However, those undertook Sciences program are from Obari and Sebha. Other international students fall into ***Cluster 3***. The relationship between the clusters based on faculty and citizenship are shown in Table 4. It is very obvious that Libyan students mostly fall into ***Cluster 0*** or ***1***.
The overall result of determining the characteristics of each ***Cluster*** and comparison between all clusters is shown in Table 5. The results exhibited in Table 3 indicate that some faculties are common to all clusters (for example Faculty of Sciences and Arts) whereas some have unique characteristics. For example, if the students undertake Arts at Tragen, the students fall into ***Cluster 0***, otherwise they fall into etiher ***Cluster 1*** or ***Cluster 2***. Students who undertook Medicine and Dentistry fall either into ***Cluster 1*** or ***Cluster 2***. On the other hand, students who undertook degree programs such as Law, Engineering, Accounting, Sport and Agronomy falls into ***Cluster 0*** or ***Cluster 2***. The proportion of male to female students in ***Cluster 0*** is nearly the same (52% and 48%), most of them stayed in University's residence and also 90% of them were admitted through government's process. As for the faculty with respect to ***Gender*** and ***Cluster***, higher percentage of female students compared to male in ***Cluster 1*** (74% versus 26%). These female students undertook programs such as Science (Sebha and Obari), Arts, Medicine and Dentistry at Sebha. This also implies that females students prefer to undertake programs at Sebha. Further observation on the results also indicate that Non-residence students were selected through university selection process.

Variables	*Cluster 0*		*Cluster 1*		*Cluster 2*	
FACULTY	**Degree**	**Place**	**Degree**	**Place**	**Degree**	**Place**
	Sciences	Tragen	Sciences	Sebha	Sciences	Sebha
			Sciences	Obari	Sciences	Obari
					Sciences	Tragen
	Arts	Tragen	Arts	Sebha	Arts	Sebha
			Medicine	Sebha	Medicine	Sebha
			Dentistry	Sebha	Dentistry	Sebha
	Law	Sebha			Law	Sebha
	Engineering	Brak			Engineering	Brak
	Accounting	Morzoq			Accounting	Morzoq
	Sport	Ghat			Sport	Ghat
	Agronomy	Sebha			Agronomy	Sebha
GENDER	**Male**	**Female**	**Male**	**Female**	**Male**	**Female**
	52%	48%	26%	74%	44%	56%
HOUSING STATUS	University Residence	Non-Residence	University Residence	Non-Residence	University Residence	Non-Residence
	66%	34%	41%	59%	41%	59%
ADMISSION CANDIDATOR FOR STUDENTS	Government	University	Government	University	Government	University
	90%	10%	5%	95%	2%	98%

Table 5. Clusters characteristic with respect to predictors' variables

For predictive analysis, three techniques have been used, namely the ***Logistic Regression***, the ***Decision Tree*** and ***Neural Networks***. For ***Regression Analysis***, only independent variables ***Faculty*** and ***Nationality*** are significant to the regression prediction model with accuracy of 99.44%. In addition, these variables also have strong significant correlation with the dependent variable (***Cluster***).

Decision Tree analysis was performed by partitioning the data into training (70%), validation (15%) and testing (15%). After the ***Decision Tree*** analysis was performed, the accuracy for training and validation is high, for training is 99.77% and validation is also 99.77%. Like ***Regression Analysis*** results, ***Faculty*** and ***Nationality*** are two important variables in ***Decision Tree*** analysis with respect to ***Cluster***. Similar partitioning of data has been applied to ***Neural Network*** and the results show that the accuracy using ***Neural Network*** is 99.98 percent (versus ***Logistic Regression*** is 99.44 percent and the ***Decision Tree*** is 99.77 percent). Fig. 12 illustrates the lift chart for the three prediction models based on clustering results as the target.

The lift chart also indicates that between 10-90% percentiles, both ***Neural Network*** and ***Decision Tree*** obtained the same accuracy. However, between 90-100% percentiles, ***Neural Network*** degrades slowly compared to ***Decision Tree***. Hence, ***Neural Network*** is the better model among the three. The empirical results and the analysis indicate that the ***Descriptive*** and ***Predictive*** methods based on clusters have revealed some characteristics and also uncover more hidden information within Sebha University enrollment data.

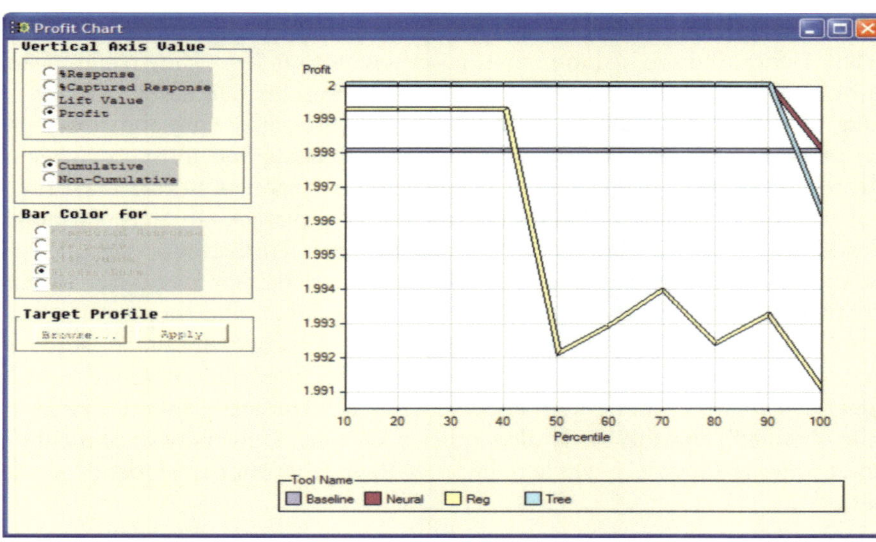

Fig. 12. Comparison of Accuracies Between Regression, Neural Network and Decision Tree Predicton Techniques

6. Conclusion

The ***Descriptive Statistics***, particularly cross tabulation analysis presents a lot of useful information about the university data. In addition, it has been concluded that more female

(63%) enrolled at the university compared to male (37%). In fact, female students tend to undertake Arts (Sebha and Tragen), Science (Tragen, Obari and Sebha) Dentistry (Sebha) and Medicine (Sebha). On the other hand, more male students tend to undertake several programs such as Sport (Ghat), Agronomy (Sebha) and Accounting (Morzoq). This may be due the fact that Sport (Ghat) and Accounting (Morzoq) is located in low population area (Ghat and Morzoq). Furthermore, Agronomy (Sebha) is far from the city of Sebha, it is around 15 kilometre. Descriptive statistics and correlation analysis defined two attributes as the most importantly attributes, they are ***Faculties*** and ***Nationalities*** with respect to ***Clusters***. Those attributes can significantly affect the student enrolment data among all other attributes.

The analysis conducted on the students that have been expelled from the university indicates that more male students are being expelled from the university compared to female students. In fact, 100% of the students that have been expelled from Engineering (Brak) and Science (Sebha) were male students. This matter is rather serious since the ratio of male to female total enrolment is about 1: 3. If this matter is not considered seriously by the university, this could lead to shortage of male students graduated with Science and Engineering degrees in future.

Cluster Analysis was performed to group the data into clusters based on its similarities. In effect, the cluster results are used also as targets for prediction experiment. For predictive analysis, three techniques have been used: they are ***Neural Network*** (NN), ***Logistic Regression*** (LR) and the ***Decision Tree***. The accuracy achieved more than 99% for ***Neural Network***, ***Regression*** and ***Decision Tree***. When further analysis was performed on the cluster, it is interesting to note that the cluster is able to distinguish between Libyan and non-Libyan students. In addition, some rule with regard to faculty and nationality can also be extracted. Hence, the prediction models based on clusters have shown significant result in exploring hidden information with Sebha University enrolment dataset.

The results of this study could be useful for those associated with the registration and education process of students in Sebha University in general, and in the registrar office in particular. Moreover, the results could assist registration planners to formulate proper and suitable plans for the university. The results will also help planners to revise for example the criteria for admission to the various student qualifications. Furthermore, the rules extracted from this study can help registrar office and university administrator to organize or restructure in order to plan necessary enhancement and improvement for enrollment purposes.

To improve the model, more attributes such as students year/semester of study and the academic achievement could be included to deliver other prediction models. In addition, it is recommended that the information and the delivered knowledge should be automated. The results obtained from this study also indicate to Sebha University in particular and all public universities in Libya as a whole to improve their proportion of students' intake based on gender.

7. References

Armstrong, J. & Anthes, K. (2001). How data can help, *American School Board Journal*, Vol. 188, No. 11, pp. 38-41.

Brown, J. D. (2007) Neural Network Prediction of Math and Reading Proficiency as Reported in the Educational Longitudinal Study 2002 Based on Non- Curricular Variables, Ph.D Dissertation, Duquesne University.

Chang, H. C. & Hsu, C.C. (2005). Using Topic Keyword Clusters for automatic Document Clustering. *Proceedings of the Third International Conference on Information Technology and Applications (ICITA'05)*, Kota Kinabalu, Sabah.

Chapman, P.; Clinton, J.; Kerber, R.; Khabaza, T.; Thomas, R.; Shearer, C. & Wirth, R. (2000). CRISP-DM 1.0 Step-by-step data mining guide, *SPSS White paper technical report*, CRISPWP-0800.

Chrispeels, J. H.; Brown, J. H. & Castillo, S. (2000). School Leadership Teams: Factors that influence their development and effectiveness, *Understanding Schools as Intelligent Systems*, Vol. 4, pp. 39-73, JAI Press.

Dunham, M. H. (2003). *Data mining introductory and advanced topics*. Upper Saddle River, NJ: Pearson Education, Inc.

Earl, L. & Katz, S. (2002). Leading School in a data-rich world, In: *Second International Handbook of Leadership and Administration*, Leithwood, K & Hallinger, P., pp. 653-696, Kluwer, Dordrecht.

Edelstein, H. (1997). Data mining: Exploring the hidden trends in your data. *DB2 Online Magazine*. Available: http:.//www.db2mag.com (URL)

Efraim, T.; Jay, E. A.; Tin-Peng, L. & Ramesh, S. (2007). *Decision Support and Business Intelligent Systems*, Pearson Education.

Everitt, B. S. (1993). Cluster analysis (2nd Ed.), Edward Arnold, London.

Feldman, J. & Tung, R. (2001). Using data-based inquiry and decision making to improve instruction, *ERS Spectrum*, Vol. 19, No. 3, pp. 10-19.

Golding, P. & McNamarah, S. (2005). Predicting academic performance in the school of computing & information technology (SCIT). *35th ASEE/IEEE Frontiers in Education Conference*. Indianapolis.

Han, J. & Kamber, M. (2001). Data mining: concepts and techniques (Morgan-Kaufman Series of Data Management Systems), Academic Press, San Diego

Kennedy, E. (2003). *Raising test scores for all students: An administrator's guide to improving standardized test performance*. Thousand Oaks, CA: Corwin Press. Available at: http://findarticles.com/p/articles/mi_m0JSD/is_8_61/ai_n6191437.

Luan, J. (2001). Data Mining as Driven by Knowledge Management in Higher Education-Persistence Clustering and Prediction, presented at 2001 SPSS Public Conference, UCSF.

Luan, J. (2004). Data Mining and Knowledge Management in higher Education Potential Application, *Proceedings of Air Forum*, Toronto, Canada.

Marco, R. & Gianluca, C. (2005). Data Mining Applied to Validation of Agent Based Models, *Proceedings of Ninteenth European Conference on Modelling and Simulation*, RIFA.

Marquez, L.; Hill, T.; Worthley, R. & Remus, W. (1991). Neural network models as an alternative to regression, Proceedings of the Twenty-Fourth Annual Hawaii International Conference on System Sciences, Vol. iv, pp. 129 - 135.

Ogor, E. N. (2007). Student academic performance monitoring and evaluation using data mining techniques. *Electronics, Robotics and Automotive Mechanics Conference (CERMA 2007)*, pp. 354-359.

Quinlan, J. R. (1993). *C4.5: Programs for Machine Learning*, Morgan Kaufmann Publisher, New York.

Roiger, R. J. & Geatz, M. W. (2003). Data Mining: A Tutorial-Based Primer, Addison-Wesley, ISBN 0-201-74128-8, Boston.

Seifert, J. W. (2004). *Data mining: An overview.* Proceeding of CRS Report for Congress, Library of Congress, pp. 1-16.

Shi, J. (2006). Best-first Decision Tree Learning, *MSc. Thesis*, University of Waikato, New Zealand.

Sirikulvadhana, S. (2002). Data mining as a financial auditing tool. *MSc. Thesis in Accounting*, The Swedish School of Economics and Business Administration, retrieved on September, 12, 2008 from www.pafis.shh.fi/graduates/supsir01.pdf.

Stephens, S. & Pablo, T. (2003). Supervised and unsupervised data mining techniques for the life sciences. *Technical Report*, Oracle and Whitehead Institute, MIT, USA.Thorn, C. A. (2001). Knowledge Management for Educational Information Systems: What is the State in the Field?, *Eucation Policy Analysis Archieves*, Vol 9, Issu 47, retrieved July 22, 2008, from http://epaa.asu.edu/epaa/v9n47/.

Wayman, J. C.; Stringfield, S. (2006). Technology-Supported Involvement of Entire Faculties in Examination of Student Data for Instructional Improvement, *American Journal of Education*, Vol. 112, pp. 1-23.

Wayman, J. C.; Stringfield, S. & Yakimowski, M. (2004). Software Enabling School Improvement Through Analysis of Student Data (Report style), Report No. 67, John Hopkins University, United States.

5

Online Insurance Consumer Targeting and Lifetime Value Evaluation - A Mathematics and Data Mining Approach

Yuanya Li[1,2], Gail Cook[3] and Oliver Wreford[3]
[1]*River and Harbor Department, Nanjing Hydraulic Research Institute, Nanjing, 210024,*
[2]*Key Laboratory of Port, waterway & sediment engineering, Ministry of Communications,*
[3]*InsWeb Corp, 11290 Pyrites Way, Suite 200, Gold River, CA95670,*
[1,2]*China*
[3]*USA*

1. Introduction

InsWeb Corporation provides an online insurance marketplace for consumer and insurance companies. The provided insurance products for shopping include automobile, term life and homeowners insurance, as well as annuities. The company business can be classified as two categories: lead purchase and policy purchase. In lead purchase consumer comes to InsWeb insurance online marketplace, compares quotes based on his/her personal information and products provided by insurance carriers, and submits lead to carriers. After that as a marketplace provider InsWeb doesn't involve in following purchase process. It is the issue between consumer and insurance carriers. In this case InsWeb involving the purchase process time is in minutes. In policy purchase category, after consumer submitting lead, the agent of InsWeb will contact the consumer and make the effort to sell the policy to the consumer. After the consumer purchase the policy, InsWeb has the opportunities to renew the policy in annual or half year period each time. For policy purchase consumer, InsWeb has the chance to involve the purchase process from year to decades. Therefore InsWeb tries to improve service for consumer policy purchase and convert more insurance lead to policy to generate more revenue. Since the revenue generating from a policy purchase is much higher than lead purchase from a lead shopping session, InsWeb has to find out the space to improve the lead close rate and retention rate.

For the quarter ended March 31, 2001, InsWeb"records more than 3.5 million unique user sessions and approximately 660,000 completed shopping sessions during the first quarter"[1]. And "InsWeb's insurance agency sold nearly 3,000 new policies during the quarter"[1]. Now "the Company's agency will expand to five additional heavily populated states with existing and new insurance companies. Further expansions are planned for the remainder of the year"[1]. To convert more shopping session into the policies sold by InsWeb insurance agency, adopt the expansion of InsWeb Corporation business, satisfy the immediate auto policy insurance purchase requirement of the internet consumers, provide high quality service to consumers and increase the policy sold number of The InsWeb's agency, the data warehouse group try to find out the internet consumer behavior and direct InsWeb agency to targeted consumers at proper time and in proper way.

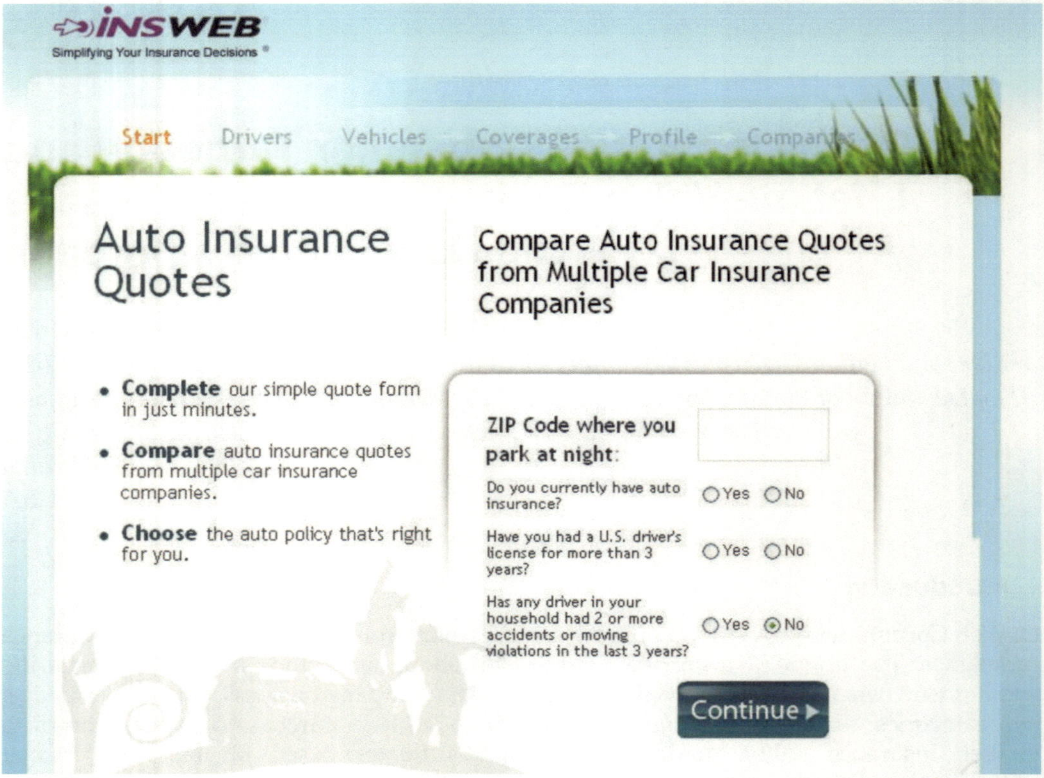

Fig. 1. The start internet page of online Auto insurance

2. The consumer information and its internet behavior collection

As an example, Figure 1 shows a leal shopping session flow chart consisted with different web pages named as Start, Drivers, Vehicles, Coverages, Profile and Companies. The work flow is that online consumers put in information of start, drivers, cars, coverage. The thirty party databases will provide consumer credit history and auto insurance history record through internet simultaneously with consumer personal information put in. With the data, the auto insurance evaluation agents of insurance companies will provide the quotes for the consumer. All the quotes from different insurance companies will listed on profile page. When consumer can choice a quote, a lead is generated. The leads has two way to go: an insurance agent of Insweb or an insurance company. If the lead is sent to an insurance company, a lead shopping session is completed. If the lead is sent to an insurance agent of Insweb, the agent will contact the consumer with phone in proper time, confirm some information and purchase purpose, then an auto insurance shopping session is completed.

All the information consumer put in and third parties provide will be stored in Insweb Data Warehouse. To record consumer behavior, InsWeb Data Warehouse invented the event log technology and got patent in 1999, by which consumer behavior on website like turning back page, jumping from one page to other page and timestamp for each step will be recorded in Data Warehouse. Each year more than ten millions of internet consumer information have been accumulated into Insweb Data Warehouse. Those data includes the detail of consumer personal information, such as age, gender, marriage, marriage history, job type, number of children, owner of house, house type, car owner, and car information like maker, car model so on.. All the static data of consumers and cars with dynamic data of consumer web behavior provide the base for the statistics analysis in data mining.

3. Tables, columns and random variables

The tables used in this analysis are Agency_leads, Agency_policy, Auto_Consumers, Auto_Drivers, Auto_quotes and other tables with Auto prefix in data warehouse. In the tables, Agency_leads table recods daily the information of consumers who submitted the leads and the leads select the quots from carriers which InsWeb E_agency coves. All the consumers in Agency_Leads are the potential InsWeb E_agency policy buyer.

InsWeb agency will contact the consumer in the table and hope to sell the auto insurance policy to them. Agency_policy table records the information of consumers who purchased the auto insurance policy from InsWeb agency. Of course only part of consumers record in Agency_Leads would buy auto policy from InsWeb agency, otherwise this analysis isn't necessary. Therefore, the number of consumer in Agency_Policy is always less than the number of consumer in Agency_Leads.

Auto_Consumers, Auto_Drivers, Auto_Quots and other tables with auto as prefix contain all the information of consumer who got to InsWeb web page and put in some personal information such as age, gender, birthday, old auto insurance policy expiration day, new auto insurance effective day, so on......By joining Agency_policy table with Auto_Consumers, Auto_Drivers, Auto_Quots, and other tables with Auto as prefix, we can get the background information of consumers who purchased Auto policy from InsWeb agency. All the background information will be used to determine the consumer motivation to purchase auto policy.

As the comparison, the Agency_Leads table will be used to join with the same tables as Agency_Policy does to get the same information. The relative information will be used as comparison stadium.

In InsWeb data warehouse, all information is saved into tables. Each table has columns which number varies from two to more than one hundred. Each column records one attribute of consumer. From analysis and mathematics view, each column is a random variable. As a random variable, each column has its value region. Due to the data types of columns are different, from integer, varchar, numerical, ..., to date, the value regions of random variables are complicate, from simple (YES,NO), a list like Carrier (Travelers, Hartfor Agency, Atanta Casualty, CSE, Explorer, FIC, GMAC, Great American, Infinity,...), age (16, 17, 18, 19,...,65) and some theoretical continuous distribute value region like old_policy_expiration_days $(-\infty,+\infty)$ (Notes: human being life is very limited, but the data consumer input would be arbitrarily distributed, not always be reasonable).

4. How to evaluate the potential auto policy purchase consumers

Some facts to determining lead closure rate are presented below in the curve figure. Psychologically, the human behavior vary with age, gender, house owner, and so on, therefore, the correlation coefficients are the functions of these facts. For the comparison purpose, the Agency_Lead and Agency_Policy tables will join with other auto tables. The all background attributes of each auto lead consumer and auto policy consumer will be listed in a big table for analysis purpose. For more than 10,000,000 auto consumer session, the statistic results are listed bellow:

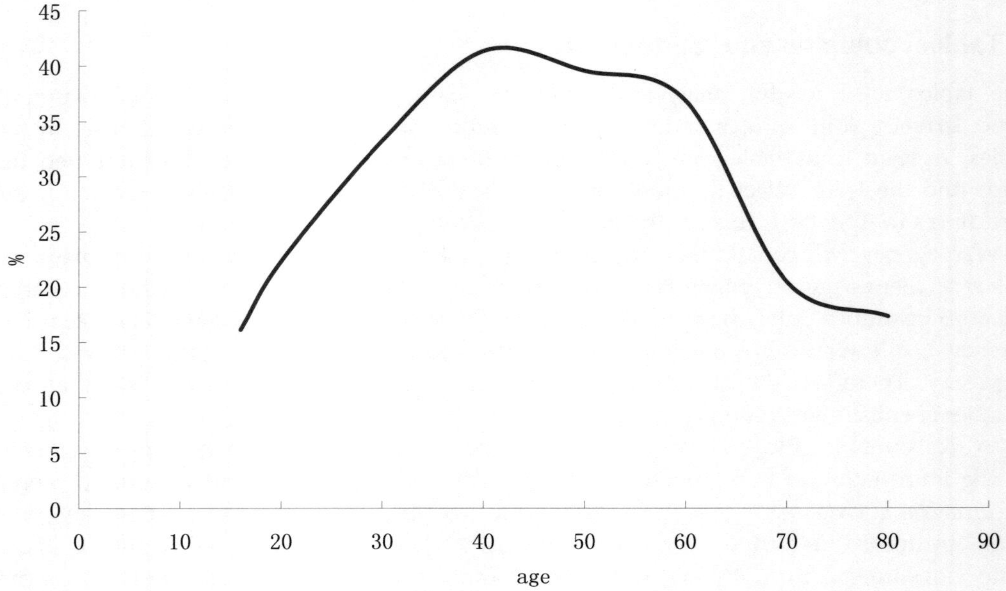

Fig. 2. The variation of consumer lead closure rate with age for female

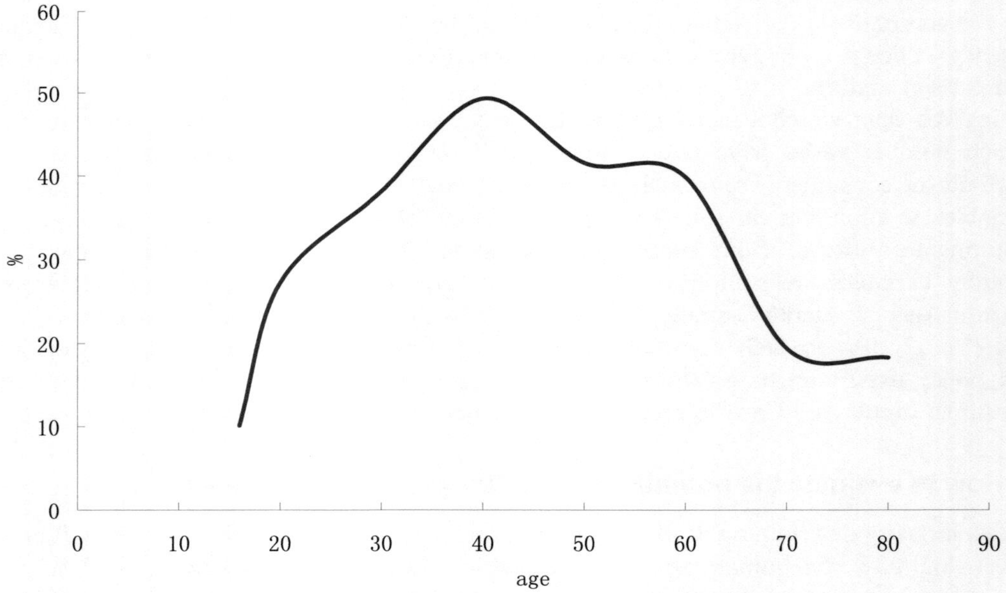

Fig. 3. The variation of consumer lead closure rate with age for male

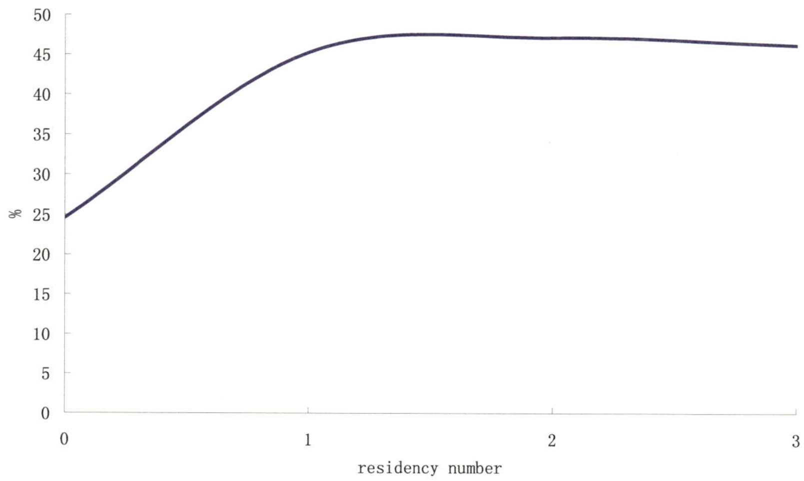

Fig. 4. The variation of consumer lead closure rate with residence_own number

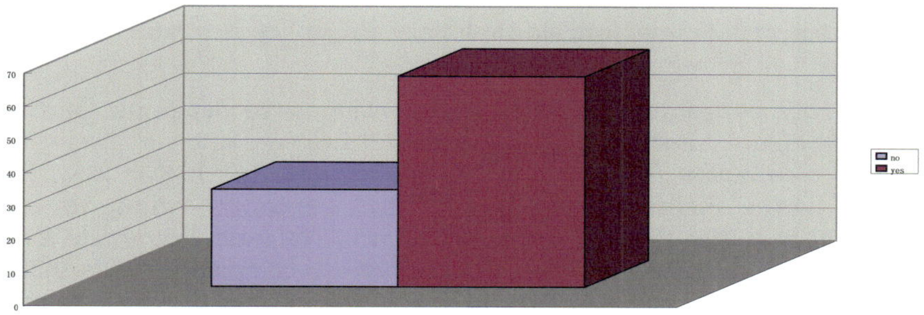

Fig. 5. The variation of consumer lead closure rate of new_policy_effective within3day random variable

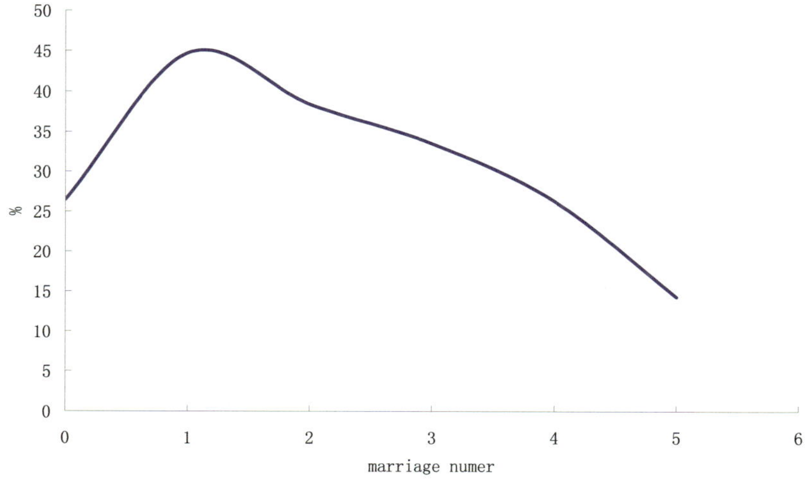

Fig. 6. The variation of consumer lead closure rate of married random variable

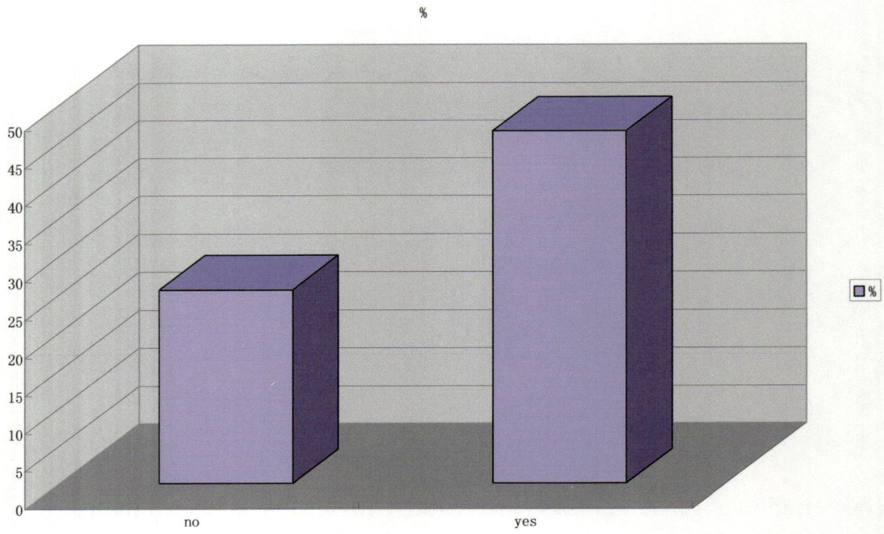

Fig. 7. The variation of consumer lead closure rate of old_policy_expiration_within_3day random variable

Figure 2 to 7 outlines the main fact for lead consumers to determine purchasing the insurance policy. Figure 2 and 3 indicates that the lead closure rate variation with age has the same trend distribution for male and female, but male has higher lead closure rate compared with female. Figure 4 shows that the lead consumers owning residencies has more lead closure rate than that not owning residency. The lead closure rate for marriage status is the person with one marriage. The consumers, completing leads that old auto insurance would be expired and new have to be effective in three day, have more potential to purchase auto insurance policy. The analysis will help auto insurance agency to identify the auto insurance lead consumer with most like hood to purchase the auto insurance policy from the huge insurance lead submitted through internet.

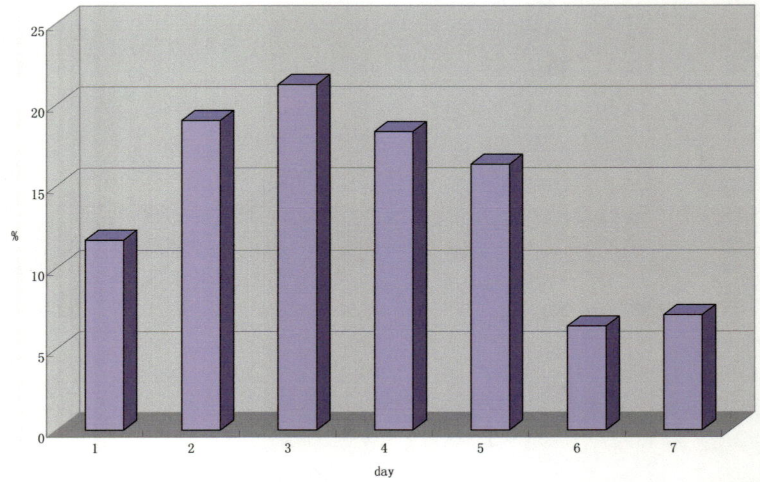

Fig. 8. The consumer internet session distribution in a week

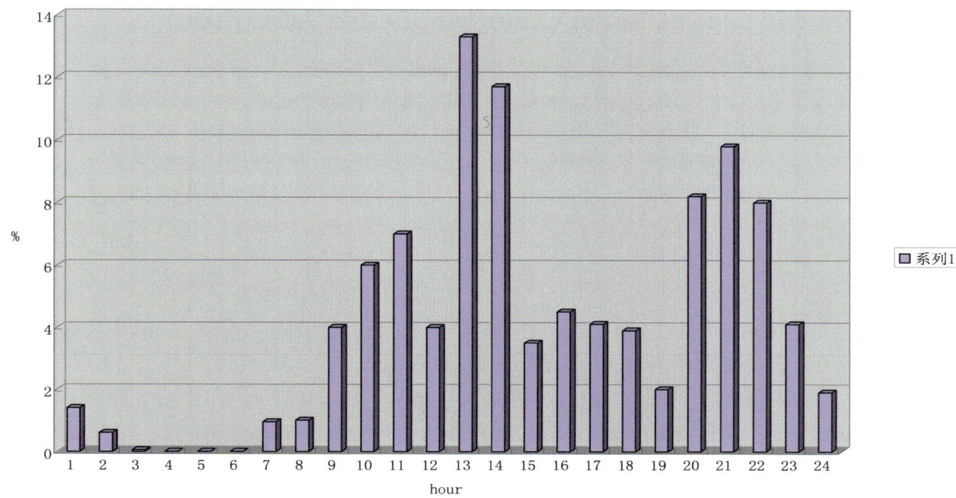

Fig. 9. The auto insurance consumer lead closure rate vary with time in week day

5. The consumer behavior variation on internet with time

Other interesting issue is that consumer session distribution on internet varies with time in week period from Monday to Sunday. When is the good time for effective consumer to submit lead, and the auto insurance policy purchaser to go to the website.
Figure 8 is the auto insurance internet session distribution in a week. From the figure, the consumers internet session is higher in week day and lower in weekend. The Monday is lowest in week day and the Friday is the second lowest in week day. The possible reason for this kind of distribution is that in weekend more people does outdoor activities and has less time going to internet, and in Monday the potential consumers have to pay more attention for the work and spend more time for weekend plan in Friday. Figure 9 is the lead closure rate distribution with a day time which is accounted in hours. The figure shows that there are two peak time for auto insurance consumers to submit the lead, one is the lunch time and other period is from 20:00 to 22:00 in the nigh.

6. Fuzzy theory for determine online auto insurance consumers

Based on the analysis above, a fuzzy formula is obtained to determine the possibility for online auto insurance consumers who would buy the auto insurance policy. The fuzzy function for all auto insurance leads is:

$$P = \sum_{1}^{7} w_i p_i \tag{1}$$

In the formula above, p_i is the value for each random variable for figure 2,3,4,5,6,7,8, and 9. Its value is simulated by y / y_{peak}, the weighting value w_i is determined by data mining and auto insurance agent feeling. In this way, all the online auto insurance session is evaluated automatically and the insurance agents can contact the consumers in the order the fuzzy formula provides. The experience shows that the fuzzy formula works well.

7. The mathematic expression of customer lifetime value (lead)

Each time a customer comes to InsWeb website, put its personal information and wonders in the website, all the personal information and customer behavior will be recorded in InsWeb data warehouse. Different customers have different lifetime value for InsWeb. InsWeb needs to determine each customer commercial from customer personal information and her/his behavior on website by data mining. A customer lifetime value for a lead can be written as

$$S = P * V \tag{2}$$

Where S is the customer lifetime value (Lead); P is the likelihood of a lead becoming a policy and V is the customer lifetime value of the policy.
To make the mathematic formula developing process clearly, this situation can be considered: number of M customers with the same personal information and background come to InsWeb website and submit agent leads. Since the decision to purchase policy from InsWeb or not is random variable for each customer, assume M_0 purchasing policy from InsWeb and $(M - M_0)$ customers don't. After half or one year, M_1 customers renew the policy and $(M_0 - M_1)$ customers don't. When the policies expiration, M_2 customers renew their policies and $(M_1 - M_2)$ customers don't. Assuming the current age of those customers is T_1 and the age those customers give up to purchase auto insurance policy is T_2, the possible time period for those customers to purchase auto insurance policy from InsWeb is

$$T = T_2 - T_1 \tag{3}$$

In T years the consumers renew their policies N times. So the process for consumers to make decision to renew their policies or not will continue N times. It is a typical N steps random walk problem. Therefore in the final step, there M_n customers will renew their policies and $(M_{n-1} - M_n)$ don't. The revenue InsWeb obtained from those M customers in their lifetime will be

$$S_{total} = C(M_0Q_0 + M_1Q_1 + M_2Q_2 + \ldots + M_nQ_n) \tag{4}$$

In which C is the commission rate, and Q_i is the auto insurance quote. Since the income and spending would change for the customers with age, the car type and insurance quote would also change with age. To each customer in the whole purchase and renew process, the revenue InsWeb obtained would be

$$S = \frac{S_{total}}{M} = C\left(\frac{M_0}{M}Q_0 + \frac{M_1}{M}Q_1 + \frac{M_2}{M}Q_2 + \ldots + \frac{M_n}{M}Q_n\right) \tag{5}$$

To make equation 4 more meaningful, it can be rewritten as

$$S = C\left(\begin{array}{l} \frac{M_0}{M}Q_0 + \frac{M_0}{M}\frac{M_1}{M_0}Q_1 + \frac{M_0}{M}\frac{M_1}{M_0}\frac{M_2}{M_1}Q_2 + \ldots \\ + \frac{M_0}{M}\frac{M_1}{M_0}\frac{M_2}{M_1}\cdots\frac{M_n}{M_{n-1}}Q_n \end{array}\right) \tag{6}$$

let

$$P = \frac{M_0}{M} \tag{7}$$

$$R_1 = \frac{M_1}{M_0} \tag{8}$$

$$R_2 = \frac{M_2}{M_1} \tag{9}$$

......

$$R_n = \frac{M_n}{M_{n-1}} \tag{10}$$

Obviously P is the probability that customer purchases the auto insurance from InsWeb agent; R_1 is the first year retention rate; R_2 is the second year retention rate and R_n is N year retention rate. Therefore the equation (6) can be written as

$$S = P * C * \begin{pmatrix} Q_0 + R_1 Q_1 + R_1 R_2 Q_2 + \\ R_1 R_2 R_3 Q_3 + \ldots + R_1 R_2 R_3 \ldots R_n Q_n \end{pmatrix} \tag{11}$$

By using the mathematics notation, equation (11) can be written as

$$S = P * C * \sum_{i=0}^{n} \left[Q_i \prod_{j=0}^{i} R_j \right] \tag{12}$$

In which R_0 is 1.0. Equation (12) is the general equation to evaluate auto insurance customer Value.

8. The simplified evaluating function for lifetime online insurance consumer policy value

In equation (12), commission rate C is constant which is determined by the deal between InsWeb and auto insurance carriers and can be considered as constant in the analysis process. Q_0 is the quote from carrier based on the consumer personal information. Therefore, the variables needed to be determined by analysis and data mining analysis are $P, R_1, R_2, \ldots, R_n,$ and $Q_1, Q_2,, Q_n$ .Due to the short history of data record in InsWeb data warehouse, no enough data to determine $R_2, R_3,, R_n,$ and $Q_2, Q_3,, Q_n$ currently. Some assumptions are taken as below:

$$R_2 = R_3 = R_4 \ldots = R_n = R_1 \tag{13}$$

and

$$Q_i = (1 + r)^i Q_0 \tag{14}$$

In which r is the quote increasing rate annually. Therefore equation (11) can be rewritten as

$$S = P * C\begin{pmatrix} Q_0 + R_1 Q_0 (1+r) + \\ R_1^2 Q_0 (1+r)^2 + \ldots + R_1^n Q_0 (1+r)^n \end{pmatrix} \tag{15}$$

When $R_1(1+r) = 1.0$, obviously

$$S = N * P * C * Q_0 \tag{16}$$

Multiply both sides of equation (15) with $R_1(1+r)$ and obtain

$$R_1 S(1+r) = P * C * Q_0 \begin{pmatrix} R_1(1+r) + R_1^2 (1+r)^2 \\ +R_1^3 (1+r)^3 + \ldots + \\ R_1^{n+1} (1+r)^{n+1} \end{pmatrix} \tag{17}$$

Equation (15) minuses equation (16), the result is

$$S - R_1 S(1+r) = P * C * Q_0 \left(1 - R_1^{n+1} (1+r)^{n+1}\right) \tag{18}$$

When $R_1(1+r) \neq 1.0$, finally, the simplified estimating function for insurance policy value is

$$S = \frac{P * C * Q_0 \left(1 - R_1^{n+1} (1+r)^{n+1}\right)}{1 - R_1(1+r)} \tag{19}$$

Equation combining (16) and (19) is the simplified lifetime value evaluation function for InsWeb online insurance policy consumer.

9. Data mining result for evaluating function of auto insurance customer value

In equation (19), r is considered as independent from consumer personal information. It is increased by insurance carriers annually. For example. State Farm and All State just increased the quote for auto insurance 2.7 last year 8.3% this year[1][2]. Based on that,

$$r = 2\% \tag{20}$$

is assumed for long time period for all quotes. For all consumers, the lead close rate P is the function of quote Q_0 and consumer personal information such as prior policy expiration day, residence year, residence month, homeownership, gender, marital status, source, state and others, P its can be written as

$$P = f_1\left(\begin{array}{l} Q_0, age, gender, expiration\_day, \\ resident\_year, resident\_month, \\ marital\_status, state, source, \\ homeownership, \ldots\ldots \end{array}\right) \tag{21}$$

In the same way, R_0 is

$$R_0 = f\left(\begin{array}{l} Q_2, age, gender, marital\_status, \\ state, source, homeowner, \ldots\ldots \end{array}\right) \tag{22}$$

P and R_0 can be determined by decision tree technology of data mining from InsWeb data warehouse data.

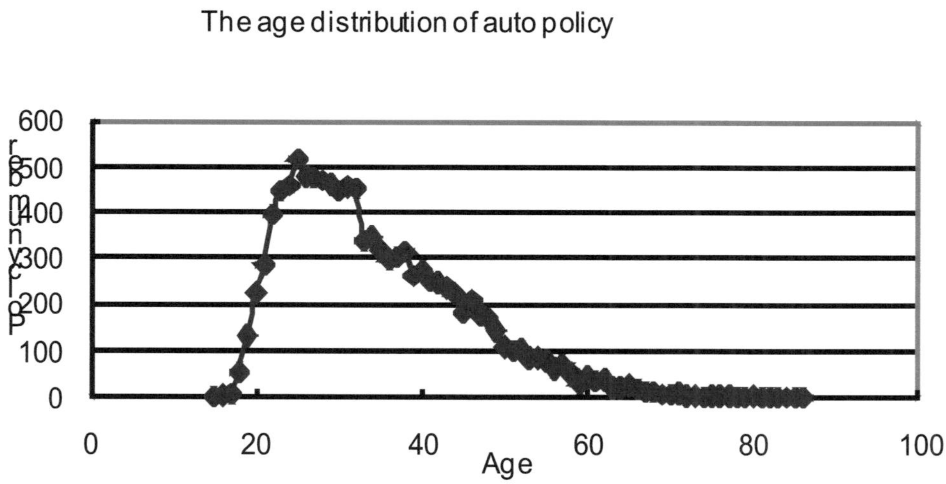

Fig. 10. The age distribution of auto policy

Another variable is N ,the total times of retention for a consumer. It is the function of consumer age. To simplify the analysis, all are adjusted to annual based and the total policy renew number is the difference the consumer age to give up driving and current age, so the N can be reasonably written,

$$N = age_s - age \tag{23}$$

In which age_s is the age for consumer to stop driving and purchasing auto insurance age and age is the current age .

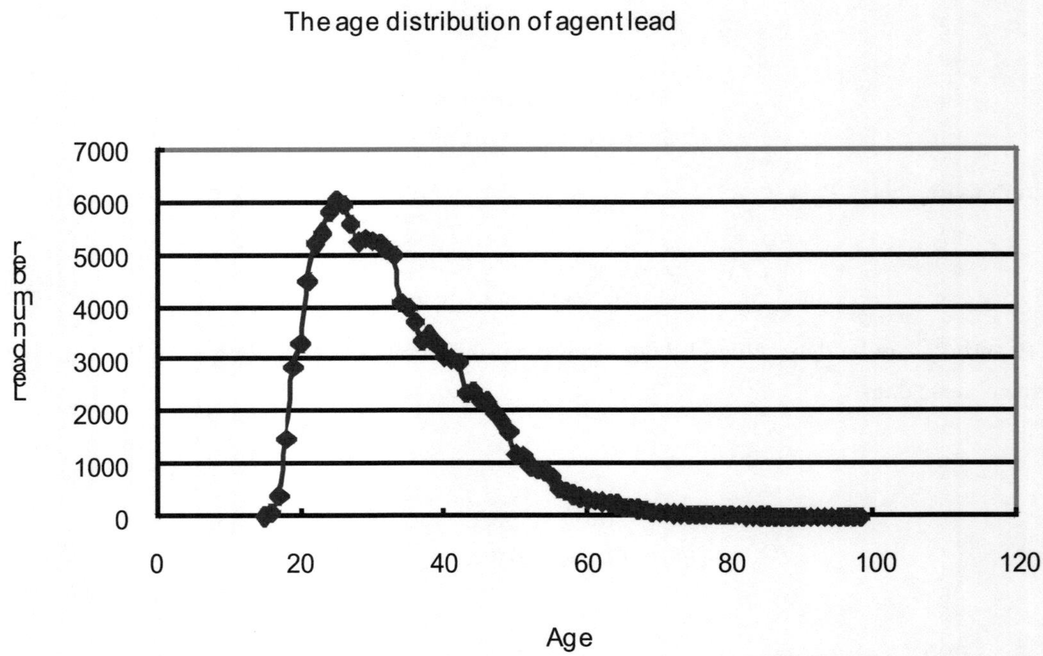

Fig. 11. The age distribution of auto agent leads

From statistic data of www.census.gov[3], the expectation of life for USA citizen is about 71 for male and 78 for female. From Figure 1 and Figure 2,there is deeply decreasing from age 62 to age. Therefore,

$$age_s = 63 \tag{24}$$

For the consumer who age is larger than 63, N is considered as zero. The average age for all policies is 34 year. The average age for population in U.S.A is 36 year [2]. It indicates that young persons trend to purchase online policy. The N can be calculated out as

$$N = 63 - 34 = 29 \tag{25}$$

It is a big task to determine equations (21) and (22). From data mining, the average lead close rate is

$$\bar{P} = 10\% \tag{26}$$

and the average retention rate is

$$\bar{R}_o = 75\% \tag{27}$$

All is based on data of 2001 year.

10. The sensitivity analysis of evaluating function of online insurance policy

From "InsWeb Reports Fourth Quarter and Year End Financial results" for 2001[4], the auto insurance agency revenue for 2001 is \$1634000. That means

$$\sum\left(N_{2001} * \bar{P} * C * \bar{Q}_{2001}\right) = \$1634000 \tag{28}$$

The total revenue generated from those policies is

$$\begin{aligned} S_{total} = \sum & \frac{P * C * Q_0\left(1 - R_1^{\,n+1}(1+r)^{n+1}\right)}{1 - R_1(1+r)} \\ & = \$1634000 \times \frac{\left(1 - (0.75 \times 1.02)^{30}\right)}{1 - 0.75 \times 1.02} \\ & = \$1634000 \times 4.254 = \$6950942 \end{aligned} \tag{29}$$

Equation (28) indicate that with renewing the policies, InsWeb would get additional 3.254 times revenue that is obtained from first policy purchase from InsWeb agent.
To analysis which direction is the best direction to increase InsWeb revenue, the parameters sensitive analysis is made as below:

$$\frac{\partial S_{total}}{\partial P} = \frac{C * Q_0\left(1 - R^{n+1}{}_1(1+r)^{n+1}\right)}{1 - R_1(1+r)} \tag{30}$$

$$\frac{\partial S_{total}}{\partial R_1} = \frac{P * C * Q_0\left(1 - R_1^{\,n}(1+r)^{n+1}\right)}{1 - R_1(1+r)} \tag{31}$$

$$\frac{\partial S_{total}}{\partial n} = \frac{P * C * Q_0(n+1)R_1^{\,n}(1+r)^{n}}{1 - R_1(1+r)} \tag{32}$$

$$\frac{\frac{\partial S_{total}}{\partial P}}{S_{total}} = \frac{1}{P} \tag{33}$$

$$\frac{\frac{\partial S_{total}}{\partial R_1}}{S_{total}} = \frac{1 - R_1^{\,n}(1+r)^{n+1}}{1 - R_1^{\,n+1}(1+r)^{n+1}} \tag{34}$$

$$\frac{\frac{\partial S_{total}}{\partial n}}{S_{total}} = \frac{(n+1)R_1^{\,n}(1+r)^{n+1}}{1 - R_1^{\,n+1}(1+r)^{n+1}} \tag{35}$$

Calculating equation (33), (34) and (35), the corresponding results are shown in tables (1), (2) and (3)

P	0.1	0.15	0.2	0.25	0.3	0.35	0.4	0.45	0.5
$\frac{1}{P}$	10	6.7	5	4	3.33	2.86	2.5	2.22	2

Table 1. The sensitivity analysis for lead close rate P

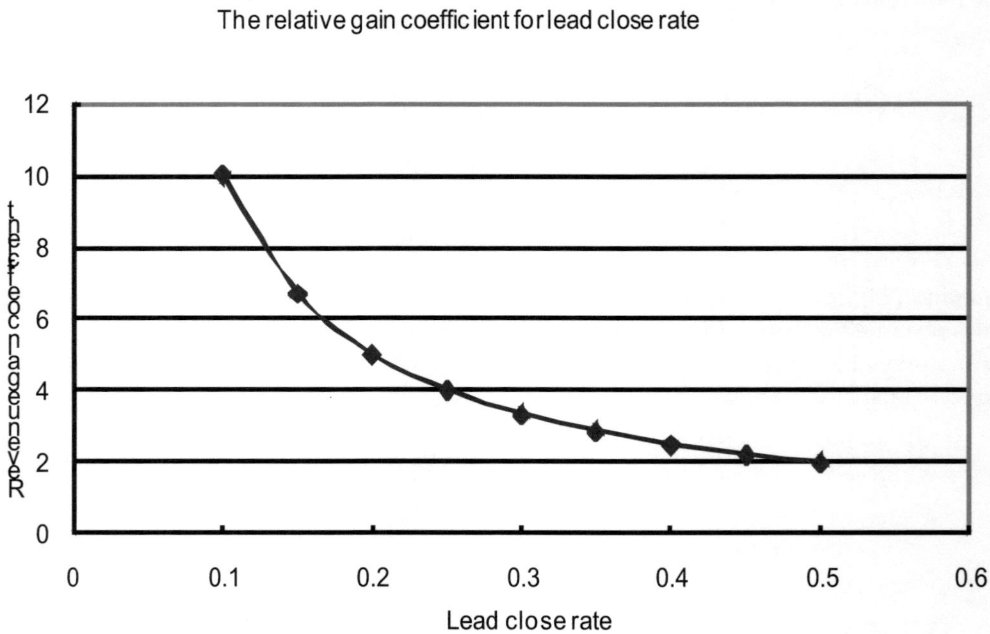

Fig. 12. The relative gain coefficient for lead close rate

R_1	0.75	0.8	0.85	0.9	0.95	1.0
$\frac{1-R_1^{n}(1+r)^{n+1}}{1-R_1^{n+1}(1+r)^{n}}$	1.0	1.0	1.0	1.0	1.0	1.0

Table 2. The sensitivity analysis for lead close rate R_1

n	29	30	31	32	33	34	35
$\frac{(n+1)R_1^{n}(1+r)^{n}}{1-R_1^{n+1}(1+r)^{n+1}}$	0.012	0.01	0.0079	0.0062	0.0049	0.0039	0.003

Table 3. The sensitivity analysis for policy renew number N

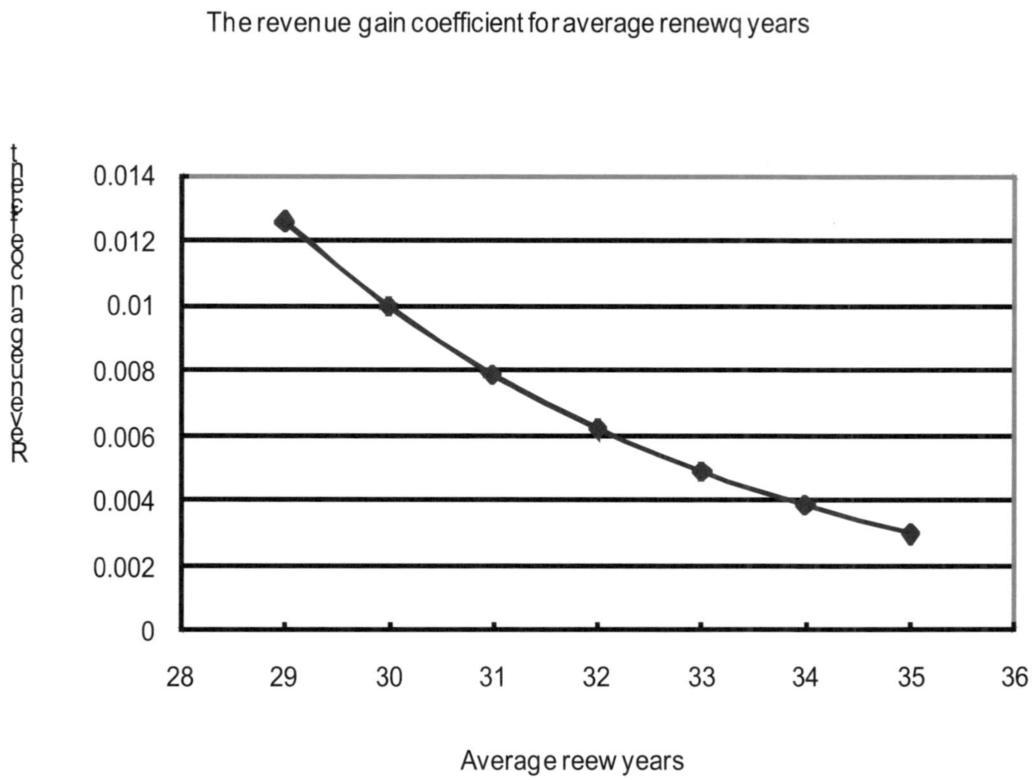

Fig. 13. The revenue gain coefficient for average renew years

Summarizing tables 1,2,3 and figures 2,2,3, the conclusions can be obtained:

1. The lead close rate is the most important parameter to determine the InsWeb online policy revenue. The revenue gain from lead close rate increasing will generate 10 times revenue obtained from retention rate increasing in the same percentage based on currently close rate and retention rate.
2. The relative revenue gain coefficient will decreasing with the close rate increasing, the theoretical minimum value is 1 when lead close rate reach 100%.
3. The retention rate is the second important parameter to affect the InsWeb online insurance policy revenue increasing. It almost keeps constant, 1.0, to the relative online policy revenue gain coefficient.
4. The parameter of average policy renew years is less important for InsWeb online policy revenue on current data mining results.

11. The maximum revenue increasing direction and revenue potential

The online policy revenue for year i can be written as

$$T_{2000+i} = \sum_{j+1}^{M_{2001+i}} \left(C * Q_j * R_j\right) + \sum_{j=1}^{N_{2001+iii}} \left(P_j * C * Q_j\right) \quad (36)$$

By introducing the average values, the equation (35) can be written as

$$T_{2001+i} = M_{2001+i-1} * C * \overline{Q}_{2001+i} * \overline{R}_{2001+i} + N_{2001+i} * \overline{P}_{2001+i} * C * \overline{Q}_{2001+i} \tag{37}$$

In equation (36), $\overline{R}_{2001+i}$ and $\overline{P}_{2001+i}$ will be considered as non-history related; M_{2001+i} is strongly history related, N_{2001+i} and $\overline{Q}_{2001+i}$ can be considered as changing history related trends (this research will be done later).

$$M_{2001+i-1} = \sum_{j=1}^{i-1} N_{2001+j} * \overline{P}_{2001+j} * \overline{R}^{i-j} \tag{38}$$

Therefore, equation (26) can be written as

$$T_{2001+i} = \sum_{j=1}^{i-1} N_{2001+j} * \overline{P}_{2001+j} * \overline{R}^{i-j} * C * \overline{Q}_{2001+i} + N_{2001+i} * \overline{P}_{2001+i} * C * \overline{Q}_{2001+i} \tag{39}$$

Moreover, equation (39) can be written as

$$T_{2001+i} = \sum_{j=1}^{i} N_{2001+j} * \overline{P}_{2001+j} * \overline{R}^{i-j} * C * \overline{Q}_{2001+i} \tag{40}$$

Considering the nature increasing process of online insurance shopping consumer number and auto insurance quote premium with time going, so

$$N_{2001+j} = N_{2001} * (1 + r_1)^j \tag{41}$$

and

$$\overline{Q}_{2001+j} = \overline{Q}_{2001} * (1 + r_2)^j \tag{42}$$

so equation (40) can be written as

$$T_{2001+i} = \sum_{j=1}^{i} N_{2001} * (1 + r)^j * \overline{P}^{i-j} * C * \overline{Q}_{2001} * (1 + r_2)^i \tag{43}$$

Generally, $\overline{P}_{2001+j}$ can be assumed as constant, so

$$T_{201+i} = N_{2001} * \overline{P}_{2001} * C * (1 + r_2)^i \sum_{j=1}^{i} (1 + r_1)^j * \overline{R}^{i-j} \tag{44}$$

Since

$$\sum_{j=1}^{i}(1+r_1)^j * \overline{R}^{i-j} = \frac{(1+r_1)\left(\overline{R}^{i+1}-(1+r_1)^i\right)}{R-1-r_1} \quad (45)$$

Therefore, equation (44) can be written as

$$\begin{aligned} T_{2001+i} &= N_{2001} * \overline{P}_{2001} * \overline{Q}_{2001} * \\ & C\frac{(1+r_2)^i(1+r_1)\left(\overline{R}^{i+1}-(1+r_1)^i\right)}{R-1-r_1} \\ & + T_{2000} * \overline{R}^{i+1} * (1+r_2)^{i+1} \end{aligned} \quad (46)$$

Since there was relocation even in the end of year 2000, we have to consider year 2000 online auto policy revenue separately. Now we can predict the InsWeb online agent policy revenue based on analysis above:

year	2001	2002	2003	2004	2005	2006	2007	2008	2009	2010
T_{2001+i}	1.634	2.354	2.973	3.522	4.024	4.498	4.957	5.412	5.872	6.343

Table 4. The InsWeb online agent policy revenue prediction

Unit: million

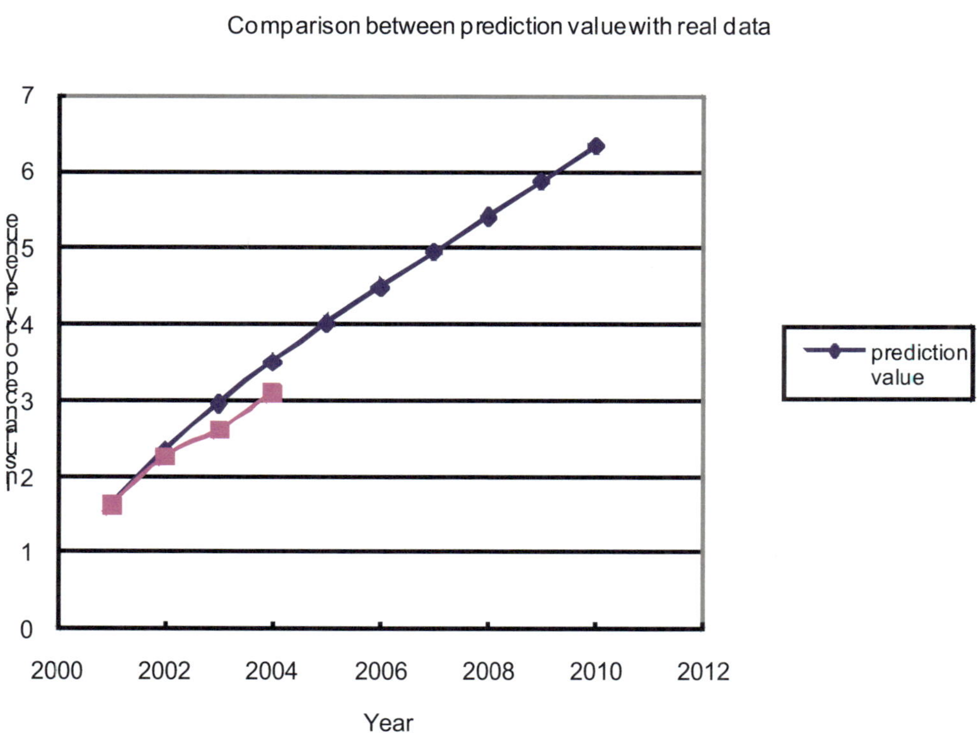

Fig. 14. The InsWeb online agent policy revenue prediction

The result in figure (4) is based on the assumptions of 2001 year carrier-state combination number, auto online auto online agent coverage and lead close rate. The whole research and prediction mentioned above was done in 2001. After 3 years some validation data is available now. The validation data is put on figure (4) for comparison. The reason that real business data is somehow lower than prediction value is that carrier-state combination number has some decrease with time going, but the trend is fellow the prediction and the comparison is acceptable.

12. Conclusion

1. The paper presents a formula to score online insurance consumer to help insurance agents.
2. The report derived a formula to estimate lifetime value of online auto insurance consumer based on probability analysis and data mining of consumer information. The formula can be written as

$$S = P * C \sum_{i=0}^{n} \left[Q_i \prod_{j=0}^{i} R_j \right] \tag{47}$$

3. After assumption of same retention rate, the simplified formula to evaluate lifetime value of online auto insurance consumer is

$$S = \frac{P * C * Q_0 \left(1 - R_1^{\,n+1} (1+r)^{n+1}\right)}{1 - R_1 (1+r)} \tag{48}$$

4. According to data analysis, retention rate is 0.75, average possible renew year is 29 and the total revenue generating from a new sold auto online policy is 4.25 time its first commission revenue.
5. This report makes the sensitive analysis to different parameters. The result shows that increasing lead close rate is most priority. It will obtain 7~10 time gain for the same revenue gain from the retention rate increasing.
6. A formula to estimate Insweb auto insurance online policy revenue is developed and 2002 to 2010 revenue prediction is given out based on this formula.
7. The comparison between predicted business revenue and real data from 2002 to 2004 is acceptable. Therefore the model and the data mining are successful.

13. Acknowledgment

The publication of the chapter is supported financially by Nanjing hydraulic Research Institute, China.

14. Reference

[1]http://more.abcnews.go.com/sections/business/dailynews/auto_insurance_rates_010607.html
[2]http://more.abcnews.go.com/sections/wnt/dailynews/healthcarecosts_wnt010725.html
[3] http://www.census.gov/prod/2002pubs/01statab/vitstat.pdf
[4] http;//biz.yahoo.com/prnews/020131/sfth063_1.html

6

Data Mining Using RFM Analysis

Derya Birant
Dokuz Eylul University
Turkey

1. Introduction

RFM stands for Recency, Frequency and Monetary value. RFM analysis is a marketing technique used for analyzing customer behavior such as how recently a customer has purchased (recency), how often the customer purchases (frequency), and how much the customer spends (monetary). It is a useful method to improve customer segmentation by dividing customers into various groups for future personalization services and to identify customers who are more likely to respond to promotions.

In recent years, data mining applications based on RFM concepts have also been proposed for different areas such as for the computer security (Kim et al., 2010), for automobile industry (Chan, 2008) and for the electronics industry (Chiu et al., 2009). Research cases of data mining with RFM variables include different data mining techniques such as neural network and decision tree (Olson et al., 2009), rough set theory (Cheng & Chen, 2009), self organizing map (Li et al., 2008), CHAID (McCarty and Hastak, 2007), genetic algorithm (Chan, 2008) and sequential pattern mining (Chen et al., 2009; Liu et al., 2009).

Integration of RFM analysis and data mining techniques provides useful information for current and new customers. *Clustering* based on RFM attributes provides more behavioral knowledge of customers' actual marketing levels than other cluster analyses. *Classification* rules discovered from customer demographic variables and RFM variables provides useful knowledge for managers to predict future customer behavior such as how recently the customer will probably purchase, how often the customer will purchase, and what will the value of his/her purchases. *Association rule mining* based on RFM measures analyzes the relationships of product properties and customers' contributions / loyalties to provide a better recommendation to satisfy customers' needs.

This chapter presents incorporating RFM analysis into data mining techniques to provide market intelligence. It proposes a new three-step approach which uses RFM analysis in data mining tasks, including clustering, classification and association rule mining, to provide market intelligence and to assist market managers in developing better marketing strategies. In our model, (i) once clustering task is used to find customer segments with similar RFM values, (ii) then, using customer segments and customer demographic variables, classification rules are discovered to predict future customer behaviors, (iii) finally; association rule mining is carried out for product recommendation. The proposed model depends on the sentence "the best predictor of future customer behavior is past customer behavior". (Swearingen, 2009)

The purpose of this study is to provide better product recommendations than simple recommendations, by considering several parameters together: customer's segment, the current RFM values of the customer, potential future customer behavior and products frequently purchased together. To the best of our knowledge, this chapter is the first in applying the RFM criterion in three data mining tasks, applied one after another, using customer demographic data, customer transaction data, and product properties. Experiments, which were carried out using the datasets collected by a sports store in Turkey through its e-commerce website, empirically demonstrate the benefits of using our model in direct marketing.

The rest of the chapter is organized as follows. Section 2 introduces the basics of RFM analysis and explains the recency, frequency and monetary concepts in detail. Section 3 reviews the literature and describes how data mining and RFM analysis are combined in the previous studies. Section 4 presents our proposed model and describes its architecture in detail. Section 5 demonstrates how the proposed model can be used to analyze a real world data, as a case study, including data preprocessing, RFM analysis, customer segmentation, customer behavior prediction and product recommendation. Finally, Section 6 concludes the chapter.

2. RFM analysis

The concept of RFM was introduced by Bult and Wansbeek (1995) and has proven very effective (Blattberg et al., 2008) when applied to marketing databases. RFM analysis depends on Recency (R), Frequency (F), and Monetary (M) measures which are three important purchase-related variables that influence the future purchase possibilities of the customers.

Recency refers to the interval between the time, that the latest consuming behavior happens, and present. Many direct marketers believe that most-recent purchasers are more likely to purchase again than less-recent purchasers. *Frequency* is the number of transactions that a customer has made within a certain period. This measure is used based on the assumption that customers with more purchases are more likely to buy products than customers with fewer purchases. *Monetary* refers to the cumulative total of money spent by a particular customer.

In order to demonstrate RFM analysis, an example dataset (customer transaction data) is given in Table 1. Table 2 shows the steps of RFM analysis, which involves scaling customers based on each RFM factor separately. The segmentation starts with recency, then frequency, and finally monetary value. It begins with sorting customers based on recency, i.e. period since last purchase, in order of lowest to highest (most recent purchasers at the top). The customers are then split into quintiles (five equal groups), and given the top 20% a recency score of 5, the next 20% a score of 4 and so on. Customers are then sorted and scored for frequency - from the most to least frequent, coding the top 20% as 5, and the less frequent quintiles as 4, 3, 2, and 1. This process is then undertaken for monetary as well. Finally, all customers are ranked by concatenating R, F, and M values. This example shows that RFM analysis can be useful even if database is small of only 15 transactions whereas it would be more powerful when the database grows.

RFM analysis assigns value-scores to each customer on the basis of her past behavior. Using the quintile system explained above, at the most, 125 different scores (5x5x5) can be assigned. These cells differ in size from one another. A customer's score can range from 555 being the highest, to 111 being the lowest. The best customers are in quintile 5 for each factor (555) that have purchased most recently, most frequently and have spent the most money.

CustomerID	Recency (Day)	Frequency (Number)	Monetary (TL)
1	3	6	540
2	6	10	940
3	45	1	30
4	21	2	64
5	14	4	169
6	32	2	55
7	5	3	130
8	50	1	950
9	33	15	2430
10	10	5	190
11	5	8	840
12	1	9	1410
13	24	3	54
14	17	2	44
15	4	1	32

Table 1. An example dataset: customer transactions

CID	Rec.	R		CID	Freq.	F		CID	Mon.	M		CID	RFM
12	1	**5**		9	15	**5**		9	2430	**5**		1	544
1	3	**5**		2	10	**5**		12	1410	**5**		2	454
15	4	**5**		12	9	**5**		8	950	**5**		3	111
7	5	4		11	8	4		2	940	4		4	222
11	5	4		1	6	4		11	840	4		5	333
2	6	4		10	5	4		1	540	4		6	222
10	10	**3**		5	4	**3**		10	190	**3**		7	433
5	14	**3**		7	3	**3**		5	169	**3**		8	115
14	17	**3**		13	3	**3**		7	130	**3**		9	155
4	21	2		14	2	2		4	64	2		10	343
13	24	2		4	2	2		6	55	2		11	444
6	32	2		6	2	2		13	54	2		12	555
9	33	**1**		15	1	**1**		14	44	**1**		13	232
3	45	**1**		3	1	**1**		15	32	**1**		14	321
8	50	**1**		8	1	**1**		3	30	**1**		15	511

Table 2. Customer quintiles and RFM values of customers

RFM provides a simple framework for quantifying customer behavior. For example, it is possible to infer from Table 2 that customer with id 9, which has RFM score 155, has made a high number of purchases with high monetary values but not for a long time. Something might have gone wrong with this customer, for example, he/she has most likely defected to a competitor's products and services or has found an alternate source and that is why his/her recency score is low. At this situation, marketers can contact with this customer and get feedbacks about how to do it better because he/she is one of the valuable customers according to his frequency and monetary values. Moreover, it is possible to plan a customer reactivation program and send him/her an extreme promotion in an effort to get his/her attention. While customers with score 155 need a reminder, 551's need to be upsold, and 515's need a sticky recurring relationship. For example, if the RFM score of a customer is identified as 515, marketers can prepare a special customer packet that includes a thank-you letter, a list of company benefits, and an incentive to make another purchase from the online store within the next 30 days.

Several studies have discussed the different versions of RFM analysis. For example, in Weighted RFM (WRFM) version, each R,F,M value is multiplied by a weight value, w_R, w_F and w_M according to its relative importance to make intuitive judgments about ranking ordering. Another version, Timely RFM (TRFM) was proposed to deal with the product periodicity i.e. to analyze different product demands in different times. RFD (Recency, Frequency, Duration) version was proposed for the web site visitors to consider the duration i.e. how long someone spends on a website. RML (Recency, Monetary and Loyalty) is an adaptation of RFM, for annual transaction environments. Loyalty is typically a normalized form of Frequency in an annual period. RFR (Recency, Frequency, Reach) was proposed for social graph, i.e. Recency - last post, Frequency - total number of posts, Reach - networks, friends. FRAT (Frequency, Recency, Amount and Type of goods) is an extended version of RFM. It induces an improvement of the segmentation by way of taking into account the categories of bought products, for example, 0 - no buy, 1 - buy a compact car, 2 - buy an economy car, 3- buy a midsize car, 4 - buy a luxury car, where the order is defined in increasing order of size.

3. Data mining + RFM

3.1 Clustering using RFM

In recent years, several researchers have considered RFM variables in developing clustering models. For example, Hosseini et al. (2010) combined weighted RFM model into K-Means algorithm to improve Customer Relationship Management (CRM) for enterprises. Wu et al. (2009) applied RFM model and K-Means method in the value analysis of the customer database of an outfitter in Taiwan to establish strong relationship and eventually consolidate customer loyalty for high profitable long-term customers. Chuang and Shen (2008) first assessed the weights of R, F, M in order to know their relative importance by Analytical Hierarchy Process method, then evaluated Customer Lifetime Values (CLV) by clustering analysis and finally, sorted customers by self-organizing map method to recognize high value customer groups.

Differently from the previous Clustering+RFM studies, this chapter proposes using K-Means++ (Arthur & Vassilvitskii, 2007) algorithm to find customer segments with similar RFM values. We propose K-Means++ algorithm instead of other clustering algorithms such as K-Means, self-organizing map because of its advantages in terms of runtime and clustering quality.

K-Means++ was proposed as a specific way of choosing centers for the K-Means algorithm, instead of generating randomly. It determines the initial center points by calculating their squared distance from the closest center already chosen. Through new seeding method, K-Means++ consistently finds better clusters than K-Means and yields a much faster because the initialization procedure that ultimately determines the number of iterations to run before stopping. For example, on a small dataset, K-Means++ terminates almost twice as fast while achieving potential function values about 20% better, on the larger dataset, it is obtained up to 70% faster and the potential value is better by factors of 10 to 1000. (Arthur &

Vassilvitskii, 2007) For these reasons, we propose K-Means++ algorithm in this chapter, instead of K-Means or other clustering algorithms.

K-Means++ is a partitioning cluster algorithm by grouping *n* vectors based on attributes into *k* partitions, where k < n, according to some measure. The name comes from the fact that *k* clusters are determined and the centre of a cluster is the *mean* of all vectors within this cluster. The algorithm starts with determining *k* appropriate initial centroids, then assigns vectors to the nearest centroid using Euclidean distance and re-computes the new centroids as means of the assigned data vectors. This process is repeated over and over again until vectors no longer changed clusters between iterations.

3.2 Classification using RFM

Recently, integration of classification techniques and RFM was studied by Olson et al. (2009) to analyze customers' response possibilities to a specific product promotion. They compared three data mining techniques: logistic regression, decision trees and neural networks, and discussed the relative tradeoffs among these data mining algorithms in the context of customer segmentation. Cheng and Chen (2009) also combined RFM attributes and rough set theory (the LEM2 algorithm) to mine classification rules that help enterprises finding out the characteristics of customers in order to strengthen CRM. Furthermore, in order to evaluate the accuracy rate of the generated classification rules, they compared their approach with different three methods: Decision Tree, Artificial Neural Networks and Naive Bayes. According to the empirical results, their procedure outperforms the other methods listed in terms of accuracy rate. Ha (2007) used decision tree technique to track changes in RFM values of customers over time, to discover classification rules related to transition paths and thus to predict the next customers' RFM values from the current customers' RFM values.

Differently from the previous Classification+RFM studies, we apply a classification algorithm using customer segments discovered by a clustering algorithm and propose the discovery of classification rules by considering customers' demographic variables such as their ages, genders, occupations, and marital statuses.

3.3 Association rule mining using RFM

In data mining, association rules are descriptive patterns of the form X→Y, where X is termed the left-hand-side, and is the conditional part of an association rule; meanwhile, Y is called the right-hand-side, and is the consequent part. Association rule mining (ARM) is a task for discovering the hidden, interesting association rules, between items in the database, having support ≥ minsup threshold. The support of an association rule indicates how frequently that rule occurs in the data. Higher support corresponds to a stronger correlation between the items in the database.

Several studies applied ARM using RFM variables to analyze customer behaviors. For example, Chen et al. (2005) recorded all customer behavior patterns (emerging patterns, added patterns, perished patterns and unexpected patterns) generated by ARM for tracking changes in customer behaviors at different time snapshots. Liu and Shih (2005) proposed an approach depending on the idea is that if customers have had similar behavior, then they are very likely also to have similar RFM values. They firstly applied two hybrid methods (Weighted RFM-based method and the preference-based Collaborative Filtering method), and then extracted frequent patterns to represent the common behavior of customers with similar purchases. Niyagas et al. (2006) used association rule mining technique and marketing techniques (RFM analysis) together to analyze historical data of e-banking usages from a commercial bank in Thailand. They applied Apriori algorithm to detect the relationships within the features of e-banking services.

Sequential Pattern Mining (SPM) is the extended version of the ARM. While ARM does not consider the order of transactions, SPM extracts frequent sequences while maintaining their order. SPM is more complicated than ARM because not only the frequent itemsets but also the temporal relationships must be found. Recently, SPM and RFM model were studied together. Chen et al. (2009) developed a novel algorithm for generating all RFM sequential patterns from customers' purchasing data. Liu et al. (2009) proposed a novel hybrid recommendation method that combines the segmentation-based sequential rule method with the segmentation-based K-Nearest Neighbors-Collaborative Filtering (KNN-CF) method. In their proposed method, sequential rules are extracted using customers' RFM values from the purchase sequences in the database.

Differently from the previous ARM+RFM and SPM+RFM studies, this chapter proposes the application of ARM after clustering and classification tasks to provide better product recommendations to customers i.e. according to their segments, RFM values and demographic variables.

4. Integrated approach

This section presents a new three-step approach which uses RFM analysis in data mining tasks. In our approach, (i) once *clustering* task is used to find customer segments with similar RFM values, (ii) then, *classification* rules are discovered using demographic variables (age, gender, education level etc.) and RFM values of customer segments to predict future customer behaviors, (iii) finally; *association rule mining* is carried out for product recommendation.

The proposed model can assist managers in developing better marketing strategies that fully utilize the knowledge resulting from data mining and RFM analysis. It is useful for predicting customer behaviors according to their demographic variables, because not all customers have purchased identical amounts, some have ordered more often, and some have ordered more recently. In addition, it provides better product recommendations than simple recommendations, by considering several parameters together: customer's segment, the current RFM values of the customer, potential future customer behavior and products frequently purchased together.

Figure 1 shows the IPO (Input, Process and Output) diagram of the proposed model. The model consists of five major parts: data preprocessing, RFM analysis, customer segmentation, prediction, and product recommendation with their evaluation processes. Each part of the approach is applied one after another. The output of each part becomes the input of the next part(s). The detail processes of each part are expressed as follows.

Step 1. Data Preprocessing

Data preprocessing step is needed to make knowledge discovery easier and correctly. Data preparation operations such as reduction in number of attributes, outlier detection, normalization, discretization, concept hierarch generation significantly improve the model; in fact a further increasing the prediction accuracy and saving in elapsed time.

In this step, the following operations should be made:

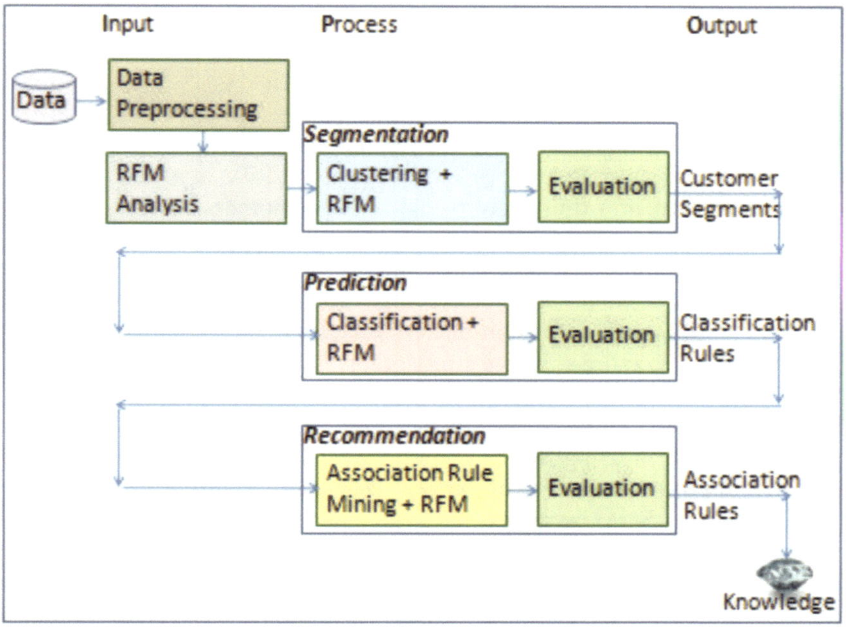

Fig. 1. IPO (Input, Process, Output) diagram of the proposed model

Dimensionality Reduction: Unnecessary attributes should be deleted, such as attributes that have only a few values (the others are null) or have only single value.

1.1 *Filling*: Missing values should be filled in using an appropriate approach.

1.2 *Handling*: Outliers and inaccurate values should be handled and removed from the dataset.

1.3 *Transformation*: Data should be transformed into an appropriate format.

1.4 *Discretization*: Before association rule mining task, continuous attributes should be encoded by discretizing the original values into a small number of value ranges. Because they have nearly a different value for every case; with such a high cardinality they provide little meaning to the association rule mining process. One common example of this phenomenon is the attribute that stores age values. The age attribute can be grouped into four ranges such as child (0-12), teenager (13-19), adult (20-59) and senior (60+).

1.5 *Concept Hierarchy Generation*: This method can be used to replace low level concepts (such as cities Istanbul, Ankara, or Izmir) by higher level concepts (such as states Marmara, Central Anatolia or Aegean).

Step 2. RFM Analysis

In this step, RFM analysis is applied by defining the scaling of R–F–M attributes. This process is divided into four parts introduced in the following:

2.1 Sort the data of three R–F–M attributes by descending or ascending order.

2.2 Partition the three R–F–M attributes respectively into 5 equal parts and each part is equal to 20% of all. The five parts are assigned 5, 4, 3, 2 and 1 score that refer to the customer contributions. The '5' refers to the most customer contribution, while '1' refers to the least contribution to revenue.

2.3 Repeat the previous sub-processes (2.1 and 2.2) for each R-F-M attribute individually. There are total 125 (5 x 5 x 5) combinations since each attribute in R–F–M attributes has 5 scaling (5, 4, 3, 2 and 1).

Step 3. Customer Segmentation

This step divides customers into numerous groups with similar RFM values, and assigns each customer to an appropriate segment. RFM analysis is used to evaluate customer loyalty, and thus identify the target customers with high RFM values by clustering analysis. The main advantage of this process is to be able to adopt different marketing strategies for different customer segments. Moreover, clustering customers into different groups improves the quality of recommendation, helps decision-makers identify market segments more clearly and therefore develop more effective strategies.

The detail process of this stage is expressed into two sub-steps.

3.1 *Clustering*: According to R–F–M attributes for each customer, data is partitioned into k clusters using the K-Means++ algorithm. (Arthur & Vassilvitskii, 2007) We propose K-Means++ algorithm instead of other clustering algorithms such as K-Means, SOM because of its advantages explained in Section 3.1.

Let D be a dataset expressed in terms of p attributes from the set $A = \{A_1, A_2,...,A_p\}$, and $A_r \in A$, which contains the intervals since last transactions, $A_f \in A$, which contains the number of transactions within a certain period, and $A_m \in A$, which contains the amount of money spent within a certain period. Each tuple $t \in D$ has p tuples $t = (CustomerID, r_i, f_i, m_i, \ldots)$, where $r_i \in \text{Range}(A_r)$ is a value in the range of the attribute A_r, $f_i \in \text{Range}(A_f)$ is a value in the range of the attribute A_f, $m_i \in \text{Range}(A_m)$ is a value in the range of the attribute A_m. Dataset D expressed as $D=<(1,r_1, f_1,m_1,\ldots), (2,r_2, f_2,m_2,\ldots),\ldots>$ is partitioned into k clusters $C = (C_1, C_2,..., C_k\}$.

3.2 *Evaluation of Clustering Results*: The purpose of this step is to evaluate the quality of the clusters, to ensure compact clusters with little deviation from the cluster centroids and while to ensure larger separation between different clusters. Different methods can be used for evaluating the efficiency of data segmentation such as Standard Deviation (σ) defined in Eq. 1, Sum of Squared Error (SSE) defined in Eq.2.

$$\sigma=\sqrt{\frac{1}{N-1}\sum_{i=1}^{N}(x_i-c)^2} \tag{1}$$

where x_i (i=1,2,..*N)* is an element in the cluster with N objects and c is the center of the cluster.

$$SSE=\sum_{i=1}^{K}\sum_{x\in c_i} dist(c_i,x)^2 \tag{2}$$

where k is the number of clusters and c_i is the center of ith cluster.

Step 4. Prediction

In this step, classification rules are discovered using demographic variables (age, gender, education level etc.) and RFM values of customer segments to predict future customer behaviors. For example, if *age = teenager* and *gender = male* and *state = Aegean* then $R\uparrow F\uparrow M\downarrow$, where the sign $\uparrow$ denotes that the value is greater than an average and sign $\downarrow$ denotes that the value is smaller than an average.

The rationale of this step is that if customers have similar demographic values, then they are very likely also to have similar RFM values. In fiercely competitive environments, discovering classification rules using customer demographic values is important for helping decision makers to target customer profiles more clearly. Additionally, the effect of classification rules on recommendations should be investigated to make more effective marketing strategies.

The detail process of this stage is expressed into two sub-steps.

4.1 *Classification:* Using customer demographic variables and R–F–M attributes, classification rules are discovered by C4.5 Decision Tree (Quinlan, 1993) algorithm. In data analysis techniques, the capabilities of C4.5 for classifying large datasets have already been confirmed in many studies.

C4.5 algorithm first grows an initial tree using the divide-and-conquer strategy and then prunes the tree to avoid overfitting problem. It calculates overall entropy and information gains of all attributes. The attribute with the highest information gain is chosen to make the decision. So, at each node of tree, C4.5 chooses one attribute that most effectively splits the training data into subsets with the best cut point, according to the entropy and information gain.

Let D be a dataset expressed in terms of p attributes from the set $A = \{A_1, A_2,...,A_p\}$, and k classes from the set $C = (C_1, C_2,..., C_k\}$. Thus each sample $d \in D$ has $p+1$ tuples $d = <V_1, V_2,.., V_p; C_j>$, where $V_i \in$ Range(A_i) is a value in the range of the attribute $A_i \in A$ and $C_j \in C$. A decision tree is constructed using C4.5 algorithm that selects an attribute A_i and a subset of its values V_i to branch on.

4.2 *Evaluation of Classification Accuracy*: Commonly used validation techniques for classification are simple validation, cross validation, n-fold cross validation, and bootstrap method. In our model, we propose n-fold cross validation technique because it matters less how the data gets divided. In this technique, dataset is divided into n subsets and the method is repeated n times. Each time, one of the n subsets is used as the test set and the other $n-1$ subsets are put together to form a training set. Then the average error across all n trials is computed.

Step 5. Product Recommendation

The core concept of this work is to extract recommendation rules from each customer group by considering classification rules and using FP-Growth Algorithm (Han et al., 2000). So, the purpose of this step is to identify the associations between customer segments, customer profiles and product items purchased together. By applying such an algorithm, it is possible to recommend products with associated rankings, which results in better customer satisfaction and cross selling.

The detail process of this stage is expressed into two sub-steps.

5.1 *ARM*: FP-Growth (Frequent Pattern Growth) is one of the Association Rule Mining (ARM) algorithms. Among the other ARM algorithms such as Apriori, Eclat, Mafia, it extracts the rules very fast from data by constructing a prefix tree and traversing this tree to generate rules. The algorithm scans the database two times only. Because of these reasons, FP-Growth algorithm is preferred in this study.

FP-Growth starts with compressing the database into a frequent-pattern tree (FP-Tree). During this process, it also constructs a header table which lists all frequent 1-itemsets to improve the performance of the tree traversal. Each item in the header table consists of two fields: item name and head of node link, which points to its first occurrence in the tree. After constructing FP-Tree and header table, the algorithm starts to mine the FP-tree by considering the items from the bottom of the header table and by recursively building conditional FP-Trees.

5.2 *Evaluation of Association Rules*: ARM algorithms use support and confidence thresholds and usually produce a large number of association rules which may not be interesting. An association rule is valid if it satisfies some evaluation measures. Evaluation process is needed to handle a measure in order to evaluate its interestingness.

In our approach, we propose to evaluate interestingness of mined rules and to express the relevance of rules with two descriptive criteria: Lift and Loevinger. These two criteria are defined on itemsets *X*, *Y* and rule *R: X→Y* as follows:

$$\text{Lift(R)}=\frac{\text{P(XY)}}{\text{P(X)P(Y)}} \tag{3}$$

$$\text{Loevinger(R)}=1-\frac{P(X)P(-Y)}{P(X-Y)} \tag{4}$$

Lift criterion represents the probability scale coefficient of having *Y* when *X* occurs. Loevinger criterion normalizes the centered confidence of a rule according to the probability of not satisfying its consequent part Y. In general, greater Lift and Loevinge values indicate stronger associations.

5. Case study

This section presents a case study which demonstrates how our proposed model was applied on the real-world data collected by a sports store. All steps of proposed model using a real world data is expressed in detail.

5.1 Data preprocessing

Dataset used in this case study was provided by a sports store in Turkey and collected through its e-commerce website within two years period. The complete dataset included 1584 different product demands in 54 sub-groups and 6149 purchase orders of 2666 individual customers. The purchase orders included many columns such as transaction id, product id, customer id, ordering date, quantity, ordering amount (price), sales type, discount and whether or not promotion was involved. While customer table included demographic variables such as age, gender, marital status, education level and geographic region; product table included attributes such as barcode, brand, color, category, sub-category, usage type and season.

Data preprocessing step handles outliers, fills missing values and makes dimensionally reduction, transformation, concept hierarchy generation, normalization and discretization. From the sport dataset, unnecessary attributes like e-mail addresses, telephone number were obviously inappropriate to be used in data mining and were discarded. Continuous attributes were encoded by discretizing the original values into a small number of value ranges. For example, the age attribute was grouped into four ranges: child (0-12), teenager (13-19), adult (20-59) and senior (60+); the number of children attribute was replaced with four groups: 0, 1, 2 and 3+. In addition, gender attribute was encoded as *m* and *f* instead of *male* and *female*. Furthermore, concept hierarchy generation method was used to replace low level concepts (city) by higher level concepts (state). Recency attribute was constructed by calculating time interval between the last transaction date and present for each customer. Frequency attribute was constructed by finding the number of transactions that each customer has made within the certain period. Monetary attribute was constructed by calculating the cumulative total of money spent by each customer. Table 3 shows the partial data from customers, products and orders tables.

Customers

CID	Age	Sex	State	Education	Marital S.	Child	Year	...
5	Teenager	M	Aegean	Middle	NeverM	0	4	...
8	Adult	M	Marmara	HighSchool	Married	0	3	...
19	Adult	F	BlackSea	HighSchool	Married	3+	4	...
...	...	...	...	...	...	...	...	...

Products

PID	PName	Price	Brand	Group	Type	Color	Sex	...
100	NK DRI FIT PO	42	Nike	TShirt	Running	NK10	Male	...
106	PM AIKI JR	81	Puma	Sneaker	Soccer	PM03	Child	...
110	AD MALV OH	125	Adidas	Jersey	Soccer	AD05	Male	...
...	...	...	...	...	...	...	...	...

Orders

TID	PID	CID	Date	Quantity	Discount	Total	Type	...
T1	106	19	2008.12.2	1	0	81	SS	...
T2	100	8	2008.12.2	1	0	42	YS	...
T3	110	5	2008.12.3	1	0	125	SS	...
...	...	...	...	...	...	...	...	...

Table 3. An example data from customers, products and orders tables

5.2 RFM model

All customers were ranked by considering their recency, frequency and monetary values and they were represented by R-F-M codes. Table 4 shows example R-F-M values of some customers after RFM analysis. For example, it is possible to infer from the first row in Table 4 that customer with id 5 has R-F-M values 4-3-4 respectively. This customer has made a high number of purchases with high monetary values, not long ago.

Figure 2 shows the distribution of the number of customers with respect to their RFM values. The distribution of RFM values varies within the limits of 0 - 4.6%. At the most, the customers have the RFM value 555 (125 customers), followed by RFM value 113 (108 customers), and next, 107 customers have the RFM value 321. Some RFM values such as 121, 125, 231, 311 etc. were not assigned to any customer.

CID	Recency (Day)	Frequency (Number)	Monetary (TL)	R	F	M	RFM
5	95	4	237	4	3	4	434
8	269	10	790	5	5	5	555
19	321	1	81	1	1	2	112
...	...	...	...	...	...	...	...

Table 4. Example R-F-M values of some customers after RFM analysis

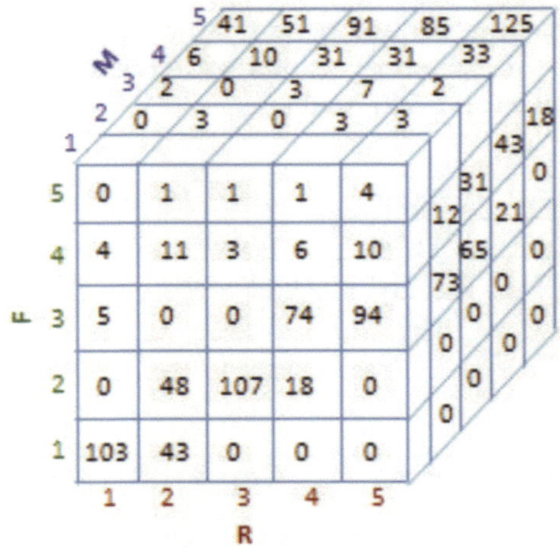

Fig. 2. RFM distribution: 125 possible RFM values and the number of customers

5.3 Customer segmentation

K-Means++ clustering was employed to group customers with similar RFM values. Customers were segmented into eight target markets in terms of the period since the last transaction (recency), purchase frequency and total purchase expenditure (monetary). The *k* parameter was set to 8, since eight (2x2x2) possible combinations of inputs (RFM) can be obtained by assigning ↑ or ↓, according to the average to R,F,M values of a cluster being less than or greater than the overall average. If the average R (F, M) value of a cluster exceeded the overall average R (F, M), then an upward arrow ↑ was included, otherwise and downward arrow ↓ was included. For example, R↑F↓M↓ represents that the average recency value of a customer segment is greater than overall average, while frequency and monetary average values are smaller than overall averages. These eight customer groups include best customers (most valuable), valuable customers, shoppers, first-time customers, churn customers, frequent customers, spenders, and uncertain customers (least valuable).

Table 5 presents the result, listing eight clusters, each with the corresponding number of customers, their average actual and scaled R, F and M values. The last row also shows the overall average for all customers. The last two columns of Table 5 show the RFM pattern for each cluster and corresponding customer type. While cluster C5 contains the maximum number of customers (425 customers, 16%), C6 includes the minimum, only 135 customers (5%).

Customer segment C1 contains the most valuable customers, because it consists of customers who have recently made regular purchases, and also have higher average purchase frequency and purchase expenditure. It is followed by cluster C2, and next cluster C3. Cluster C4 (R↑F↓M↓) may include first-time customers, who have recently visited the company, with higher recency and lower purchase frequency and monetary expenditure. Customers in C5 have made a high number of purchases with high monetary values but not for a long time. Something might have gone wrong with these customers, and therefore, it seems to be an indicator of churn likelihood. It is needed to contact with these customers i.e. sending an e-mail, and to plan a customer reactivation program i.e. promotion suggestion. Cluster 8 is concluded to be the least valuable for the business, because customers coded as 111, 112, 121 are generally the least likely to buy again.

Cluster	Size	Recency (Avg.)		Frequency (Avg.)		Monetary (Avg.)		RFM Pattern	Customer Type
		Day	R	#	F	TL	M		
C1	309	65.4	4.57	6.28	4.89	485.1	4.79	R↑F↑M↑	Best
C2	392	83.5	4.32	1.52	3.44	146.8	3.42	R↑F↑M↑	Valuable
C3	415	75.1	4.44	1.18	3.05	70.1	1.49	R↑F↑M↓	Shopper
C4	300	202.4	2.86	1.01	2.02	69.5	1.47	R↑F↓M↓	FirstTime
C5	425	247.8	2.22	4.27	4.51	387.4	4.67	R↓F↑M↑	Churn
C6	135	325.8	1.38	2.26	3.76	137.5	2.94	R↓F↑M↓	Frequent
C7	381	290.1	1.86	1.00	1.41	138.1	3.33	R↓F↓M↑	Spenders
C8	309	339.1	1.35	1.00	1.00	69.5	1.53	R↓F↓M↓	Uncertain
Overall	2666		2.85		3.01		2.95		

Table 5. The customer segments generated by K-Means++ clustering based on RFM values

The clusters that have RFM values with at least two upper arrow (↑) can be selected as target ones, all customers who belong to these clusters become candidates for conducting suitable marketing strategies, which attract the most attention.
After customer segmentation, standard deviation and SSE metrics were used to evaluate clustering results. All clusters had a lower standard deviation and SSE values. The result, as shown in Figure 3, confirmed that these eight clusters were significantly distinguished by recency, frequency, and monetary. Standard deviation values ranges from 0.67 being the highest, to 0.33 being the lowest. In the experiments, K-Means++ algorithm was run 10 times with different initial center values and the clustering result with minimum SSE was selected as final result.

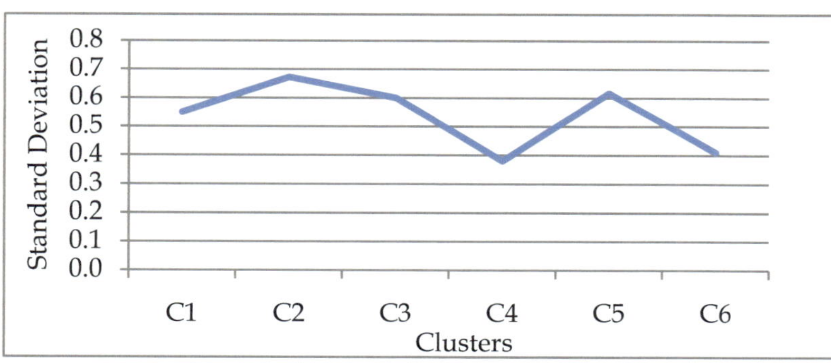

Fig. 3. Standard deviations of clusters (customer segments)

5.4. Customer behavior prediction

A customer segment is not as enough to identify, and then to predict customer's behavior. Many direct marketers believe that the RFM variables of customers are generally associated with customer profiling. For example, customers with profiles *age = teenager* and *gender = female* and *state = Aegean* can generally have *R↑F↑M↓* pattern, while customers with profiles *age = senior* and *gender = male* and *state = EasternAnatolia* can generally have *R↓F↑M↓* pattern. For this reason, in this step, classification rules were discovered using demographic variables (age, gender, education level etc.) and RFM values of customer segments.

Figure 4 shows a part of classification rules, found in the case study, that identify customer profiles and the associated RFM values. For example, rule 1 shows that customer profile with (State=Aegean, EducationLevel=Bachelors, MaritalStatus=Married, Gender=M) is highly related to R↑F↑M↑ pattern. Similarly, classification rule 5 represents that a customer profile (State=EasternAnatolia, Gender=F) is dominant or most strongly associated with R↑F↓M↓ pattern.

Rule 1: **if** *State*=Aegean **and** *EducationLevel*=Bachelors **and** *MaritalStatus*=Married **and** *Gender*=M **then** R↑F↑M↑
Rule 2: **if** *State*=Aegean **and** *MaritalStatus*=Married **and** *Gender*=M **and** *Age*=Adult **then** R↑F↑M↑
Rule 3: **if** *State*=Marmara **and** *Membership*=3 **and** *EducationLevel*=HighSchool **and** *Children*=0 **then** R↓F↑M↑
Rule 4: **if** *State*=CentralAnatolia **and** *Age*=Teenager **and** *MaritalStatus*=NeverMarried **and** *Membership*=3 **then** R↑F↑M↓
Rule 5: **if** *State*=SouthEasternAnatolia **and** *Children*=3+ **and** *Gender*=M **then** R↓F↑M↓
Rule 6: **if** *State*=Mediterranean **and** *EducationLevel*=Middle **then** R↓F↓M↑
Rule 7: **if** *State*=EasternAnatolia **and** *Gender*=F **then** R↑F↓M↓
Rule 8: **if** *State*=BlackSea **and** *Children*=3+ **and** *Gender*=F **then** R↓F↓M↓

Fig. 4. A part of classification rules found in the case study

In our experiments, classification accuracy was observed by using 5-fold cross validation technique. The highest classification accuracy 81% is obtained when different values were given to parameters (confidence factor, minimum number of objects, number of folds etc.) as inputs.

5.5 Product recommendation

In the proposed approach, after generating classification rules, association rule mining was applied to extract recommendation rules, namely, frequent purchase patterns from each group of customers. The extracted frequent purchase patterns represent the common purchasing behavior of customers with similar RFM values and with similar demographic variables. For example, not all women age 45-54 have the same tendency to purchase a product; so we should also consider their RFM values, customer segments and the other products frequently purchased together with that product.

After customers were classified by demographic variables, the recommendation list was generated by feature attributes determined using a classification rule inducer. Parameters were set up to identify association rules that had at least 40% confidence and 2% support imposed on the FP-Growth association rule algorithm. Figure 5 shows a part of association rules, found in the case study. For example, if a customer in segment C3 (R↑F↑M↓) buys a soccer ball, then marketers should recommend backpack and water bottles products. However, if a customer in segment C4 (R↑F↓M↓) buys a soccer ball, then marketers should recommend of-kick product. Other rules (Rule 7 and Rule 8) denote that marketers should recommend two different products (Reebok Sneakers or Converse Shoes) to customers according to their different RFM values.

Rule 1: {C1, Adidas soccer jersey (man), Adidas soccer jersey (woman)} → {Adidas soccer jersey (child)}
Rule 2: {M>3, Adidas Sneaker (child)} → {Adidas Socks, Adidas Equipment Bag}
Rule 3: {C3, Adidas Soccer ball} → {Adidas Backpack (unisex), Adidas Water Bottles}
Rule 4: {C4, Adidas Soccer ball} → {Nike of-kick}
Rule 5: {C5, Converse Sneaker (woman), Puma Sneaker (man)} → {Nike Cap (unisex)}
Rule 6: {C6, Adidas T-Shirt (male)} → {Adidas Short (male), Adidas Training Bag}
Rule 7: {R<=3, F<=3, M>3} → {Reebok Sneakers}
Rule 8: {R<=3, F<=3, M<=3} → {Converse Shoes}

Fig. 5. A part of association rule set on support 2% and confidence 40% for each customer segment

In the evaluation process, association rules were reduced by more than 50% to the set of potentially interesting and valuable rules. For example, the number of association rules related to C4 customer segment was reduced from 67 to 42. These reduction percentages also give weight to the need of taking into consideration the information brought by the confirmation property.

In the proposed approach, it is possible to predict the customer segment of a new customer from classification rules, according to her/his profile, and then a recommendation list can be generated according to his/her predicted segment.

6. Conclusion

This chapter proposes a novel three-step approach which uses RFM analysis in three data mining tasks: clustering, classification and association rule mining, applied one after another. Firstly, customer segments with similar RFM values are identified to be able to adopt different marketing strategies for different customer segments. Secondly, classification rules are discovered using demographic variables (age, gender, education level etc.) and RFM values of customer segments to predict future customer behaviors and to target customer profiles more clearly. Thirdly, association rules are discovered to identify the associations between customer segments, customer profiles and product items purchased, and therefore to recommend products with associated rankings, which results in better customer satisfaction and cross selling.

This chapter presents incorporating RFM analysis into data mining techniques to provide market intelligence. It aims to bring attention of data miners and marketers to the importance and advantages of using RFM analysis in data mining. In order to evaluate the proposed model and empirically demonstrate the benefits of using this model in direct marketing, a case study was carried out using the datasets collected within two years period by a sports store in Turkey through its e-commerce website. According to experimental study results, proposed approach provides better product recommendations than simple recommendations, by considering several parameters together: customer's segment, the current RFM values of the customer, potential future customer behavior and products frequently purchased together.

Future research can focus in the followings: First, the proposed approach can be tested for different versions of RFM such as Weighted RFM (WRFM), Timely RFM (TRFM), FRAT (Frequency, Recency, Amount and Type of goods). As the number of additional variables increases, the number of cells will geometrically increase. For example, if we add two types of product parameter, the number of FRAT cells becomes $2 \times 5 \times 5 \times 5 = 500$. Thus, it is unrealistic to estimate RFM model with more than two additional variables. Second, the effectiveness of the proposed approach can be evaluated for different application domains such as for the web site visitors (RFD), for annual transaction environments (RML), and for social graphs (RFR).

7. References

Arthur, D. & Vassilvitskii, S. (2007). K-Means++ The advantages of careful seeding, *Proceedings of ACM-SIAM Symposium on Discrete Algorithms*, pp. 1027-1035, ISBN:978-0898716245, New Orleans, January 2007, Society for Industrial and Applied Mathematics, USA.

Blattberg, R.C.; Kim, B-D. & Neslin, S.A. (2008). *Database Marketing: Analyzing and Managing Customers*, Chapter 12, pp. 323-337, Springer, ISBN: 978-0387725789, New York, USA.

Bult, J. R. & Wansbeek, T. (1995). Optimal selection for direct mail, *Marketing Science*, Vol. 14, No. 4, (Fall 1995) 378-394, ISSN:0732-2399.

Chan, C.C.H. (2008). Intelligent value-based customer segmentation method for campaign management: A case study of automobile retailer, *Expert Systems with Applications*, Vol. 34, No. 4, (May 2008) 2754-2762, ISSN:0957-4174.

Chen, M.; Chiu, A. & Chang, H. (2005). Mining changes in customer behavior in retail marketing, *Expert Systems with Applications*, Vol. 28, No. 4, (May 2005) 773-781, ISSN:0957-4174.

Chen, Y-L.; Kuo, M-H.; Wu, S-Y. & Tang, K. (2009). Discovering recency, frequency, and monetary (RFM) sequential patterns from customers' purchasing data, *Electronic Commerce Research and Applications*, Vol. 8, No. 5, (October 2009) 241-251, ISSN: 1567-4223.

Cheng, C-H. & Chen, Y-S. (2009). Classifying the segmentation of customer value via RFM model and RS theory, *Expert Systems with Applications*, Vol. 36, No. 3, (April 2009) 4176-4184, ISSN: 0957-4174.

Chiu, C-Y.; Kuo, I-T. & Chen, P-C. (2009). A market segmentation system for consumer electronics industry using particle swarm optimization and honey bee mating optimization, *Global Perspective for Competitive Enterprise, Economy and Ecology*, Springer London, pp. 681- 689.

Chuang, H. & Shen, C. (2008). A study on the applications of data mining techniques to enhance customer lifetime value - based on the department store industry, *Proceedings of the 7th International Conference on Machine Learning and Cybernetics*, pp. 168-173, ISBN: 978-1424420964, Kunming, China, July 2008, IEEE.

Ha, S.H. (2007). Applying knowledge engineering techniques to customer analysis in the service industry, *Advanced Engineering Informatics*, Vol. 21, No. 3, (July 2007) 293–301, ISSN:1474-0346.

Han, J.; Pei, H.& Yin. Y. (2000). Mining Frequent Patterns without Candidate Generation. *Proceedings of Conference on the Management of Data (SIGMOD'00)*, pp. 1-12, ISBN:1581132174, Dallas, Texas, United States, May 2000, ACM New York, NY, USA.

Hosseini, S.M.; Maleki, A. & Gholamian, M.R. (2010). Cluster analysis using data mining approach to develop CRM methodology to assess the customer loyalty, *Expert Systems with Applications*, Vol. 37, No. 7, (July 2010) 5259–5264, ISSN:0957-4174.

Kim, H. K.; Im, K. H. & Park, S. C. (2010). DSS for computer security incident response applying CBR and collaborative response, *Expert Systems with Applications*, Vol. 37, No. 1, (January 2010) 852-870, ISSN:0957-4174.

Li, S-T.; Shue, L-Y. & Lee, S-F. (2008). Business intelligence approach to supporting strategy-making of ISP service management, *Expert Systems with Applications* ,Vol. 35, No. 3, (October 2008) 739–754, ISSN:0957-4174.

Liu, D-R. & Shih, Y-Y. (2005). Integrating AHP and data mining for product recommendation based on customer lifetime value, *Information & Management*, Vol. 42, No. 3, (March 2005) 387-400, ISSN:0378-7206.

Liu, D-R.; Lai, C-H. & Lee, W-J. (2009). A hybrid of sequential rules and collaborative filtering for product recommendation, *Information Sciences*, Vol. 179, No. 20, (September 2009) 3505-3519, ISSN:0020-0255.

McCarty, J. A. & Hastak, M. (2007). Segmentation approaches in data-mining: A comparison of RFM, CHAID, and logistic regression, *Journal of Business Research*, Vol. 60, No. 6, (June 2007) 656-662, ISSN:0148-2963.

Niyagas, W.; Srivihok, A. & Kitisin, S. (2006). Clustering e-banking customer using data mining and marketing segmentation, *ECTI Transaction CIT*, Vol. 2, No. 1, (2006) 63-69.

Olson, D.L.; Cao, Q.; Gu, C. & Lee, D. (2009). Comparison of customer response models, *Service Business*, Vol. 3, No. 2, (June 2009) 117-130, ISSN: 1862-8516.

Quinlan, J. R. (1993). *C4.5 Programs for Machine Learning*, Morgan Kaufmann Publishers. 302 pages.

Swearingen, C. (2009). *101 Powerful Marketing Strategies for Growing Your Business Now!*, SmallBiz Marketing Services, pp. 24-27.

Wu, H-H.; Chang, E-C. & Lo, C-F. (2009). Applying RFM model and K-Means method in customer value analysis of an outfitter, *Global Perspective for Competitive Enterprise, Economy and Ecology*, ISSN: 1865-5440, Part 12, pp. 665-672, ISBN:978-1848827615, Springer London.

7

Seasonal Climate Prediction for the Australian Sugar Industry Using Data Mining Techniques

Lachlan McKinna and Yvette Everingham
James Cook University, Australia

1. Introduction

The ability to predict rainfall with adequate certainty and lead time is beneficial to both industry and public. Periods of high or low seasonal rainfall can have many follow on effects to agriculture, industry, public health and, water supply and management. In order to implement decisions, planning and management strategies to contend with these issues, the ability to predict seasonal rainfall quantities is of great importance (Klopper et al., 2006). Climate conditions are known to influence the cultivation of Sugarcane influencing planting, harvesting and milling (Muchow and Wood, 1996; Everingham et al., 2002; Jones and Everingham, 2005). Unforeseen climate events such as excessive rainfall, can adversely effect the agricultural practices related to Sugarcane cultivation. The Australian Sugarcane harvest period commences in May/June and aims to finish by November/December before the start of the rainy season (Everingham et al., 2002). The risk of excessive rainfall disrupting harvest operations is greatest towards the end of the sugarcane harvest period (Muchow and Wood, 1996; Everingham et al., 2002). Therefore, improved seasonal rainfall prediction during the October-December period is beneficial.

Statistical prediction of seasonal rainfall can be performed using a variety of techniques including: regression (Singhrattna et al., 2005), classification methods (Drosdowsky and Chambers, 2001), canonical correlation analysis (Landman and Mason, 1999) and neural networks (Mason, 1998). All statistical models require predictor variables which act as proxies for describing the behaviour of response variables (Hastie et al., 2001). When considering a seasonal forecast model, it is useful to draw predictor variables from a climate data set that is both historically and spatially complete (Washington and Downing, 1999). One of the most temporally and spatially resolute climate parameters is sea surface temperature (SST) data. Consequently, SST data are often used as an empirical measure of the ocean-atmosphere interaction in statistical climate models. However, a vast proportion of potential SST predictors may be redundant. Therefore employing data mining methods for the purpose of feature extraction and data reduction is advantageous.

Principal component analysis (PCA) is a commonly used feature extraction method that reduces data dimensionality whilst retaining the majority of the variability (Jolliffe, 1986). As sea surface temperature data sets are large, it is useful to perform PCA data reduction such that the bulk of the variability is contained in a small subset of variables (Wilks, 1995). PCA also referred to as empirical orthogonal function (EOF) analysis is commonly used throughout climate research (Wilks, 1995). PCA is popular because it is available in most statistical software packages; is easy to self-program and can be applied to a variety of multivariate data from many disciplines. However, there are some disadvantages to PCA. In situations where there is ordering associated with the independent variables, then this ordering is ignored by PCA. This is pertinent when considering application of PCA to SST data where the variables are ordered in both a latitudinal and longitudinal direction. In order to perform PCA on a SST dataset, the spatial structure is reduced by "stringing-out" each 2D monthly piece of SST data into a one dimensional (1D) vector whose element order has no significance (Wilks, 1995). The 1-D vector then becomes a row in a large matrix to which the PCA is applied as illustrated in Fig. 1.

When analysing image type data, methods that extract information whilst maintaining the spatial structure are favourable. A method of image analysis known as the 2D discrete wavelet transform (DWT) has the ability to extract high and low frequency information from the image, and can perform dimension reduction whilst maintaining the spatial structure of data (Mallat, 1989a; Mallat, 1989b; Antonini et al., 1992). Within this chapter it is proposed that SST data be considered an image and analysed using a 2D DWT to maintain the spatial integrity of the dastaset. However, the literature involving the application of 2-D DWT methods to spatial climate data for the purpose of extracting useful features is scant.

Although feature extraction methods assist in mining useful features from data, they can still output high dimensional and collinear datasets. For the purposes of statistical modelling, a larger number of predictor variables than observations results in an ill-posed situation. A large number of variables can also have practical implications upon computational speed. Therefore, it is useful to employ data mining techniques to produce a smaller sub-set of predictor variables. Random forests (RF) analysis is a non-parametric approach which has emerged from classification and regression tree theory (Brieman, 2001). The RF method is robust to outliers, noise and is ideal for datasets of large dimension. The RF method is also useful for identifying variables of importance and hence can be used for data reduction. Firth et al. (2005) found RF to be a useful method for predicting the onset of the winter rain season for the wheat growing region of southwest Western Australia using climate indices including: SST data, mean sea level pressure (MSLP) and the southern oscillation index (SOI). Furthermore, Firth et al. (2005) found the RF method was able to locate regions of SST which were deemed to be important predictor variables.

Within this chapter we have developed a statistical model for the prediction of above median rainfall for Tully, in the northern part of the Australian sugarcane growing region. Data mining methods were explored for the purposes of feature extraction and variable reduction of SST data. The 2D DWT and PCA were both used for comparitive purposes of feature extraction upon SST data. We examined the RF algorithm for the purposes of variable reduction. Classification was performed using regularised discriminant analysis (RDA) and model performance was assessed based upon a 10-fold cross validated (CV) correct classification rate (CCR).

2. Principal component analysis

PCA performs a linear transform on an n-by-d data matrix $\mathbf{X}$ to produce a matrix $\mathbf{P}$ containing a set of d uncorrelated, independent variables of which the first few will contain the bulk of the variability exhibited in the original data (Jolliffe, 1986).

The complete n by d matrix of principal components $\mathbf{P}$ is given by

$$\mathbf{P} = \mathbf{X}^T \mathbf{A} \quad (1)$$

where $\mathbf{A}$ is a d-by-d matrix with columns being eigenvectors obtained by performing an eigenvalue decomposition (Jolliffe, 1986) on the covariance matrix $\mathbf{\Sigma}$ of $\mathbf{X}$, on the case of standardized variables, the eigen-decomposition will be on the correlation matrix. The columns of $\mathbf{A}$ are arranged such that the corresponding set of eigenvalues are in descending order (Jolliffe, 1986). As a consequence of arranging the columns of $\mathbf{A}$, the first principal component retains the largest amount of variability from the original data with the second principal component containing the next largest proportion of variability and so on (Jolliffe, 1986). Thus the bulk of the variance contained in the untransformed data comes to be contained in the first few PCs (Jolliffe, 1986).

In order to perform a PCA on a time series of 2D grided data, the dataset must be restructured into a single matrix (Wilks, 1995). For example, a time series of j 2D SST data observations must be rearranged into a single matrix $\mathbf{X}$ in order to perform a PCA. Typically the first 2D SST matrix of size *n-by-d* is reshaped into a single row vector which has the size *1-by-(nxd)*. The same method is followed for the jth 2D SST data within the time series. The newly created row vectors are arranged to form the matrix $\mathbf{X}$ with the dimensions *j-by-(nxd)*. Thus, a single row reprents all the SST data from a point in time. Whereas, a column represents a time series of SST observations for a single geogrpahical location (see Fig. 1).

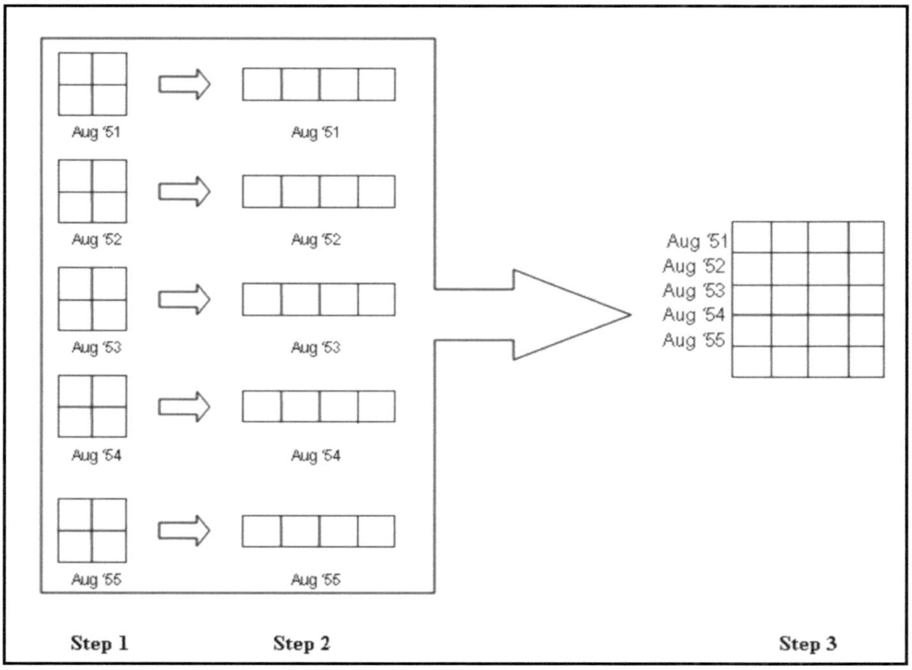

Fig. 1. A schematic diagram indicating the steps in preparing monthly 2-D spatial data for analysis in principal component analysis (PCA). Step 1 monthly spatial data matrices are arranged then in Step 2 are disassembled or "strung out" in the same manner to produce a 1-D vector. These vectors representing monthly data are then arranged as the rows of a large matrix as illustrated in Step 3.

3. 2-D discrete wavelet transform

An image can be considered a finite energy/intensity matrix of components *I(x,y)*, where *x* and *y* represent the horizontal and vertical directions respectively (Mallat, 1989a; Mallat, 1989b). The theory of the 2-D discrete wavelet transform closely follows the formulation of 1-D discrete wavelet transforms using multiresolution analysis (Mallat, 1989a; Mallat, 1989b).

A 1-D wavelet transform is similar to a Fourier transform, enabling the underlying frequencies within a signal to be identified. The Fourier transforms treats a signal as a whole or *globally* which can often cause small perturbations in the signal to be overlooked (Mallet et al., 2000). A 1-D wavelet transform allows a *localised* analysis of the signal using a *window function* which *translates* across the signal analysing discrete sections (Mallet et al., 2000). The continuous wavelet transform performed on a signal *f(t)* can be given as

$$S_{CWT}(a,b) = |a|^{-1/2} \int_{-\infty}^{\infty} f(t)\psi_{a,b}(t)dt \tag{2}$$

where $\psi_{a,b}(t)$ is the window analysing function and *a* and *b* are the *dilation* and *translation* parameters, respectively. The window function is referred to as the *mother* wavelet and has the form $\psi_{a,b}(t) = \psi\left(\frac{t-b}{a}\right)$ (Antonini et al., 1992). The wavelet transform is unique because the mother wavelet function has the ability to contract and dilate, allowing high and low frequencies in the signal to be well represented (Mallet et al., 2000). There are a number of families of wavelet functions including: Daubechies, coiflets and symlets each having its optimum use upon different signal types (Mallet et al., 2000). The symlet family however, has properties which lend themselves ideally to image analysis (Mallet et al., 2000).

An image *I(x,y)*, can be decomposed using a 2-D discrete wavelet transform (DWT) similar to how a 1-D signal *f(t)* can be analysed using a 1-D wavelet transform. The 2-D DWT analysis decomposes the image *I(x,y)* into four sub images, one *smooth* image and the three *detailed* images (Mallat, 1989a; Antonini et al., 1992; Mallet et al., 2000). The smooth image is representative of low frequency information and the three detailed images represent high frequency information from the original image (Mallat, 1989a; Antonini et al., 1992). The smooth image created is denoted as $S_j I$ and the three remaining detailed images $D_j^h I$, $D_j^v I$ and $D_j^d I$ capture high frequencies in the horizontal, vertical and diagonal directions respectively (Mallat, 1989a; Antonini et al., 1992). A 2-D wavelet transform also performs dimension reduction, with each sub-image being one quarter the size of the size of *I(x,y)*.

For further extraction of information, the smooth image $S_j I$ undergoes a successive transform, yielding another set of four sub images. The method of applying successive transforms is known as *multiscale pyramidal decomposition* (Mallat, 1989a; Antonini et al., 1992). We can consider the transform in a series of stages or levels. The original image is considered to be at the zeroth level of the transform denoted as $j = 0$. The first transform upon *I(x,y)* producing four sub-images is referred to as the first level transform (*j=1*) with sub images denoted as $S_1 I$, $D_1^h I$, $D_1^v I$ and $D_1^d I$ (Mallat, 1989a; Antonini et al., 1992). At each *level* of the multiscale pyramidal transform, further information about the horizontal, diagonal and vertical components is extracted, the dimensionality of the data is reduced and the spatial structure is maintained (Antonini et al., 1992). Figure 2 illustrates schematically the process of a multiscale transform.

An example of an image decomposition using the discrete 2-D DWT is shown in Fig. 3. The original image *I(x,y)* is a *Mandrill face* from the Matlab® Image Processing Toolbox to which 2D DWT was applied using a symlet wavelet to the first level (*j=1*) of a multiscale pyramidal decomposition. The first sub-image $S_1 I$ is the *low-pass* image and represents the low frequencies or *smooth* details from the original image. The three remaining sub-images are the *detailed* images $D_1^h I$, $D_1^v I$ and $D_1^d I$. The high frequency horizontal and vertical features of the Madrill face such as the whiskers and nose ridges are well represented in the images $D_1^h I$ and $D_1^v I$ respectively. Image $D_1^h I$ represents the horizontal features of the Mandrill face whiskers and nose ridges.

From a climatology perspective, it is useful to locate regions of high frequencies in sea surface temperature anomaly data because temporal changes of frequencies in these regions may indicate the onset of a certain meteorological event. A useful tool for the analysis of sea surface temperature anomalies is then the 2-D discrete wavelet transform as it will detect high frequencies laterally, longitudinally and obliquely. An example of a 2D DWT decomposion of an SSTA image is given in Fig. 4.

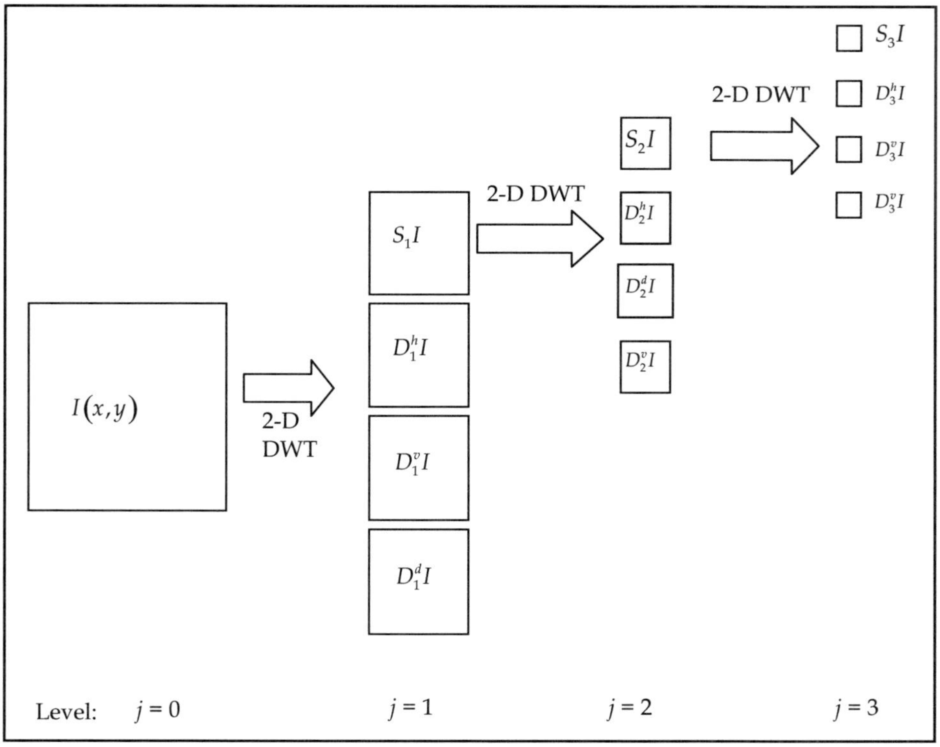

Fig. 2. A flow chart indicating a pyramidal, multiscale 2-D Wavelet transform. From the original image *I(x,y)*, four sub-images are produced one smooth image $S_1 I$ and three detailed images $D_1^h I$, $D_1^v I$ and $D_1^d I$ at level *j=1*. Successive transforms are performed upon the smooth image at each level *j* = 2, 3 in order to produce the multiscale pyramidal transform.

(A.) Original Image

(B.) Wavelet Transformed Sub-Images

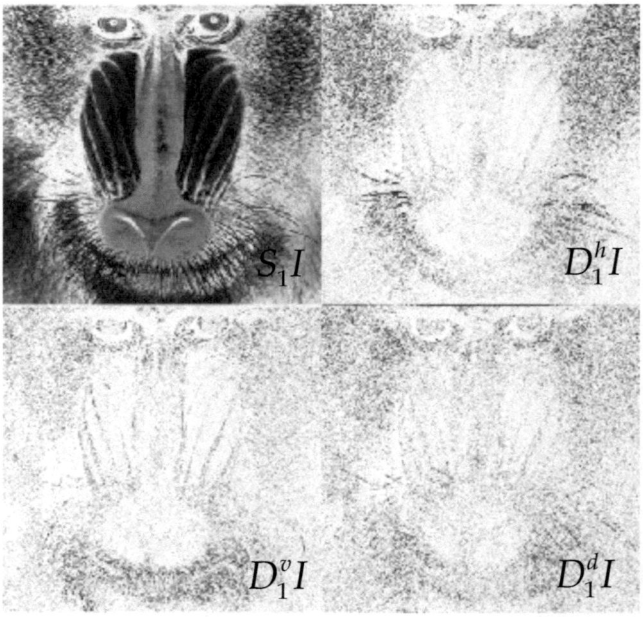

Fig. 3. (A.) Original image of a *Mandrill Face.* (B.) A first level, 2-D DWT representation of the *Mandrill* image using the Symlet wavelet with produced four sub-images S_1I, D_1^hI, D_1^vI and D_1^dI . Notice the horizontal, vertical and diagonal features extracted from the original image are emphasised in the sub-images D_1^hI, D_1^vI and D_1^dI respectively.

(A.) Original SSTA Image

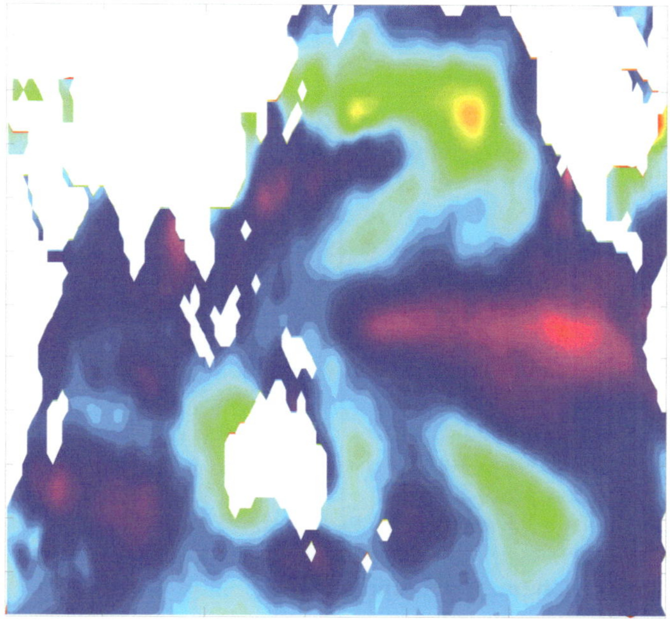

(B.) Wavelet Transformed Sub-images

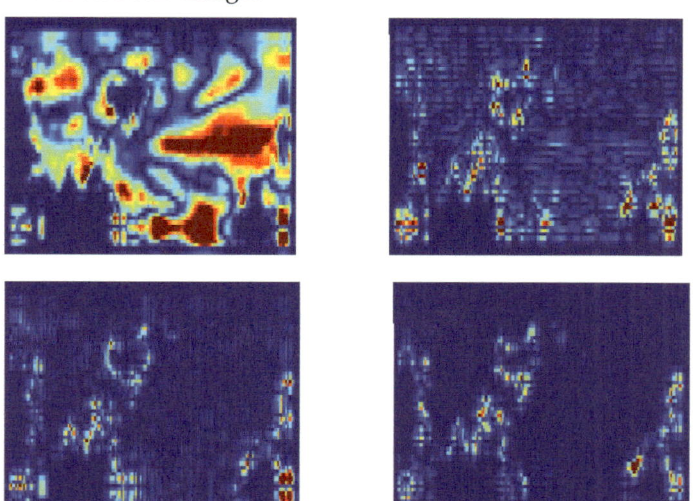

S_1I D_1^hI D_1^vI D_1^dI

Fig. 4. (A.) An example image of a single SSTA map from the Indian and Pacific Oceans surrounding the Australian continent. (B.) A first level 2-D DWT representation of the SSTA map using a Symlet wavelet. Four sub-images S_1I, D_1^hI, D_1^vI and D_1^dI were produced. Low frequency or *smooth* features are emphasised in the sub-image S_1I whereas high frequency features in the horizontal, vertical and diagonal directions are emphasised in the sub-images D_1^hI, D_1^vI and D_1^dI respectively.

4. Random forests and classification and regression trees

Feature extraction methods do not necessarily reduce the dimensionality of the data. In high dimensional and low observational settings, model performance can be adversely affected. Therefore, following feature extraction, a feature selection method which reduces the dimensionality of the data can be applied (Svetnik et al., 2004). Svetnik et al. (2004) investigated a feature selection method based upon the random forest (Brieman, 2001) technique. Random forests (Brieman, 2001) are often used as a method for classifying data into groups for the situation where there exists many predictor variables. A favourable attribute of the random forest technique is its ability to identify a subset of variables that best classify objects into groups (Brieman, 2001). The variable selection algorithm performs a random forest analysis which is indicative of the feature variables most important for classifying an observation (Svetnik et al. 2004). A fraction of the least important variables are then removed and the random forest is re-implemented. This routine is continued until an assessment criteria called the *out-of-bag error rate* (Brieman, 2001) is minimized, at which point the variables of most importance for classification are determined. This process of variable selection using random forests is contained in a package called varSelRF which performs variable selection procedure using R statistical software (Diaz-Uriarte and Alvarez de Andres, 2006). This is a very useful tool for dimension reduction in the situation where there exists many predictor variables (Svetnik et al., 2004). We will now briefly overview classification and regression trees, and random forests.

4.1 Decision trees

Classification and regression trees (Hastie et al., 2001) are collectively known as decision trees and can be used both for classification and prediction. The benefit of decision trees is that they are a non-linear method and have the ability to handle different types of data. An added benefit of classification and regression trees is their ability to handle missing data within predictor variables (Hastie et al., 2001).

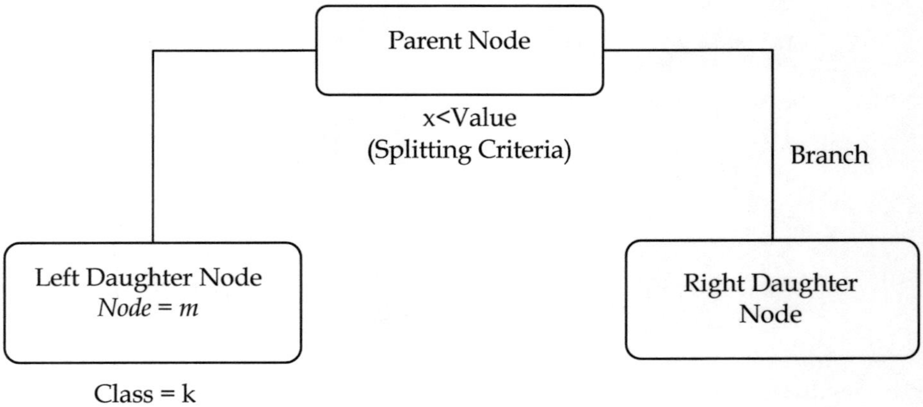

Fig. 5. Decision tree terminology: A *parent node* in a decision tree is split due to some splitting criteria into *left and right daughter nodes* which are connected to the mother node via *branches*. Eventually splitting will continue until the *terminal nodes* are reached, at which point the data should be split into distinct classes.

Decision tree methodology can be summarised into three steps; (i) splitting criteria, (ii) pruning and (iii) tree Selecting (Hastie et al., 2001).

i. The splitting criterion dictates how data is to be partitioned into new groups at each node. Splitting is performed in a *greedy* fashion at a *parent node* from which data is split into two *daughter* groups (Hastie et al., 2001). Splitting in this manner continues until *terminal* nodes are reached where only a small number of observations of the same distinct class reside (Hastie et al., 2001).
ii. *Pruning* is carried out to reduce the number of nodes in the large tree that has been created (Hastie et al., 2001). Pruning ensures the tree is not overfitted, whilst ensuring the tree is large enough to avoid biases occurring when used to make predictions (Hastie et al., 2001).
iii. Tree selection finds the optimum tree model which is often determined by examining the cross-validated error rate (Hastie et al., 2001). The tree that presents the lowest cross-validated error rate is often chosen as optimal (Hastie et al., 2001).

4.2 Tree splitting criteria

The difference between *classification* and *regression* trees is the splitting criteria used for each. For *classification trees* there are several splitting criteria, of which the most commonly used is the known as the *Gini* split criteria and is defined as

$$i(k) = \sum_{k \neq k'} \hat{p}_{mk} \hat{p}_{mk'} = \sum_{k=1}^{K} \hat{p}_{mk} \left(1 - \hat{p}_{mk}\right) \tag{3}$$

Where $\hat{p}_{mk}$ is the probability that an item in node m is of class k. The impurity measure *i(k)* is also known as the misclassification error (Hastie et al., 2001). The optimum split of the data from the parent (P) node to the left (L) and right (R) child nodes is based upon the impurity measures at each node. The change in the impurity Δ, is calculated as

$$\Delta = i(k)_P - \left[p_L i(k)_L + p_R i(k)_R\right] \tag{4}$$

where, $i(k)_P$, $i(k)_R$ and $i(k)_L$ are the impurities at the parent node and the right and left child nodes respectively (Hastie et al., 2001). The proportions of data in the left and right child nodes are denoted as p_L and p_R (Hastie et al., 2001). The split that produces the greatest change in impurity is ultimately chosen ensuring that the impurity at the child nodes is much less than that of the parent node (Hastie et al., 2001).

The splitting criteria in *regression trees* depends upon the residual sum of squares (Hastie et al., 2001). The split considers all the possible variables as predictors for the split and chooses the one which minimises the residual sum of squares error at the child nodes. The impurity measure *i(t)* for a variable y in a regression tree is given by:

$$i(t) = \sum \left\{y_j - \bar{y}(t)\right\}^2 \tag{5}$$

Where, $\bar{y}(t)$ is the mean of an observation in node t and y_j represents j^{th} observation of variable y in node t (Hastie et al., 2001). The best split at a parent node for a regression tree is determined by examining the change in impurity Δ in terms of residual sum of squares error as below

$$\Delta = SSE_P - [P_L \cdot SSE_L + P_R \cdot SSE_R] \tag{6}$$

where SSE_P is the within groups sum of squares of the parent node and SSE_L, SSE_R are the residual sum of squares error of the left and right child nodes respectively (Hastie et al., 2001). The best split occurs when the change in impurity is maximised, which means that we desire the residual sum of squares error in the child nodes to be minimised for an optimal split (Hastie et al., 2001).

4.3 Random forests

One way to improve the decision tree method is by creating an ensemble of n decision trees. An ensemble classification can then be determined by a majority vote amongst the n trees created. This is the basis for random forests, a technique that can greatly improve data classification, does not overfit and is relatively robust to noise and outliers (Brieman, 2001). The nth tree within the random forest is unpruned and grown from the nth bootstrap (Hastie et al., 2001) sample of the data. At each node of the nth tree, a sub-set of all variables *mtry* is selected randomly to determine the splitting criteria. The parameters n, *mtry* and number of nodes within each tree *nodesize* are user inputs.

Random forest performance is assessed using a measure known as the out-of-bag error rate (OOB). The OOB is a form of cross validation. OOB of the nth tree is determined when those data left out of the nth bootstrap are passed down the tree and classification is performed. The proportion of times that observations are not allocated to their true groups forms the OOB.

4.4 Variable selection using random forests

Svetnik et al. (2004) developed a method for feature selection based upon the RF technique. The method performs random forest upon the data set $(\mathbf{x}_1,...,\mathbf{x}_p\ ;\ \mathrm{y})$ and indicates which of variables $\mathbf{x}_1,...,\mathbf{x}_p$ are of most importance for classifying an observation $\mathbf{y}$ (Svetnik et al., 2004). A fraction of the least important variables are then removed and the random forest is re-implemented. This routine is continued until the OOB is minimized. The result is then a reduced subset of predictor variables (Svetnik et al., 2004; Diaz-Uriarte, 2005). A R statstical package known as varSelRF has been developed which determines variables of most importance using RF (Diaz-Uriarte, 2005). Within the package varSelRF, the user must define the fraction of least important variables dropped at each iteration.

5. Discriminant analysis

Discriminant analysis is a statistical technique used to classify observed data into one of two or more discrete, uniquely defined groups using an allocation rule (Duda and Hart, 1973; Johnson and Wichern, 2002). Allocation or discriminant rules are developed from randomly sampled "learning" or "training" data drawn from k known populations, $\pi_1,...,\pi_K$ and based upon the allocation rules, future observations are placed into groups $\omega_1,...,\omega_K$ (Johnson and Wichern, 2002; Rencher, 2002; Afifi and Clark?et al., 2004).

The Regularised Discriminant Analysis (RDA) algorithm formulates a classification score $cf(x_i)$, for allocation of a test object $\mathbf{x}_i = \left(x_{i1},...,x_{ip}\right)^T$ to class ω_k based upon the training data set (Wu et al., 1996; Johnson and Wichern, 2002; Afiti et al., 2004). The observed object x_i is assigned to the class ω_k which produces the lowest classification score (Wu et al., 1996). The classification score for RDA is given by

$$cf(\mathbf{x}_i) = (\mathbf{x}_i - \boldsymbol{\mu}_k)^T \hat{\boldsymbol{\Sigma}}_k^{-1}(\lambda,\gamma)(\mathbf{x}_i - \boldsymbol{\mu}_k) + \ln\left|\hat{\boldsymbol{\Sigma}}_k(\lambda,\gamma)\right| - 2\ln P(\omega_k) \quad (7)$$

where $\boldsymbol{\mu}_k$ is the class mean vector and $P(\omega_k)$ is the prior probability of an object belonging to class k, and $\hat{\Sigma}_k(\lambda,\gamma)$ is the regularised class covariance matrix which is a function of two regularisation parameters are introduced λ and γ (Friedman, 1989).

As the prior values of λ and γ are unknown, a training set is required such that optimum values of the regularisation parameters can be obtained (Friedman, 1989). A grid spanning $0 \le \lambda \le 1$ and $0 \le \gamma \le 1$ is formulated creating a two-parameter optimisation problem whereby a search for the best values of λ and γ is performed (Friedman, 1989). The best regularisation parameters are obtained by minimizing the misclassification risk associated with cross-validation (Hastie et al., 2001) of the training data (Friedman, 1989). Regularisation parameters of $\lambda = 0$ and $\gamma = 0$ represent quadratic discriminant analysis (QDA), $\lambda = 1$ and $\gamma = 0$ represent linear discriminant analysis (LDA), and $\lambda = 1$ and $\gamma = 1$ represents a nearest mean classifier which assigns an observation to a class with the nearest (Euclidean distance) mean (Duda and Hart, 1973; Friedman, 1989).

6. Data

6.1 Rainfall data

Sugarcane cultivation is prevalent along the east coast of Australia between the latitudes of 16° S and 25° S. We have selected Tully (17.56° S, 146.56° E) as a case study location (Fig. 6.). Tully is a very wet sugarcane growing region with an annual median rainfall total of 4000 mm. Tully was selected as a case study location because the authors have engaged participatively with industry consultative groups within this region. Monthly rainfall data was obtained from the Australian Bureau of Meteorology (BOM) for the Tully Sugar Mill, BOM station number 32042. Total October-November-December (OND) rainfall between 1950 and 1999 inclusively was calculated and converted into categories of either (i) below median rainfall or (ii) above median, rainfall after the rainfall data was median filtered to remove any long term trends.

6.2 Sea surface temperature data

The sea surface temperature (SST) data used in this investigation was the Extended Reconstructed SST dataset (ERSST version 2.0) (Smith and Reynolds, 2004) for the years 1950 - 1999. Given that the objective was to predict rainfall for the October-December period, sea surface temperatures prior to October are needed if the model is to be temporally predictive. We decided to use August sea surface temperatures so that industry would have approximately a one month lead-time to react to the prediction. Following Drosdowsky and Chambers (2000), a subset of ocean covering 60°N - 55°S and 30°E - 70°W was selected which encompassed the Indian and Pacific Oceans adjacent to the Australian Continent. The temporal and spatial resolution of the ERSST dataset is monthly, with 2° by 2° grid spacing. A median filter was passed over the data to remove any long term trends. August Sea surface temperature anomalies (SSTA) were calculated for a given SST grid point by subtracting the long term August SST average of that grid point. To ensure SSTA at higher latitudes were not overemphasised, SSTA data were scaled by the cosine of latitude.

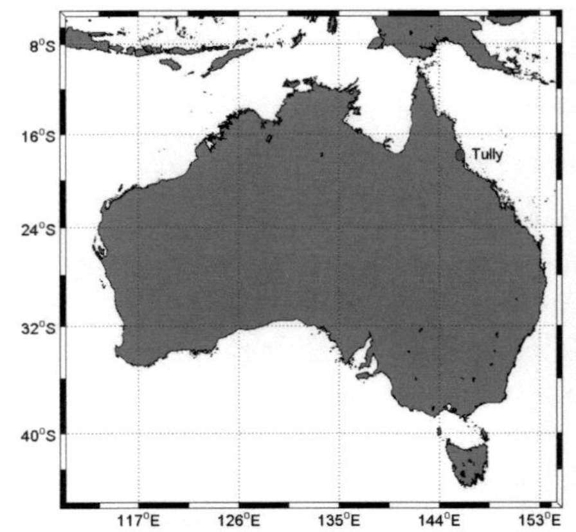

Fig. 6. Study location Tully is located on the north east coast of Australia.

7. Data mining and modelling approach

A model for the prediction of October-November-December (OND) seasonal rainfall for Tully was developed. The variables used to predict above median rainfall were data mined from August SSTA data. Two models were formulated to assess the performance of the PCA relative to the 2D DWT as a feature extraction method. Model development followed five stages as outlined in Fig. 7.: (1) rainfall and SSTA data input, (2) feature extraction, (3) feature selection, (4) discriminant analysis and (5) model validatation.

The data mining approach comprised feature extraction and feature selection steps. Feature selection was performed using the random forest variable selection technique outlined by Svetnik et al (2004). Prior to feature selection, both PCA and 2D DWT were separately performed on the August SSTA data from 1950 - 1999. Whilst there exists many types of wavelet analysing functions, a *symlet* with four vanishing moments was chosen as it had symmetrical properties which are considered suitable for image analysis (Mallet et al., 2000). The multiscale 2D DWT was then computed to the 4th level yielding the sub-images (matrices): $S_4 I$, $D_4^h I$, $D_4^v I$ and $D_4^d I$. The feature selection step was performed using the RF variable selection algorithm: varSelRF. This process identified the optimum variables for the PCA and 2D DWT feature extracted SSTA data sets respectively. The varSelRF model parameters used are outlined in Table 1. The feature extracted subset of SSTA variables that best predicted above median rainfall were chosen to train the classification rules for RDA.

varSelRF Parameter	Value
n	5000
ntree.iterate	2000
mtry	$\sqrt{\text{number of variables}}$
vars.frac.dropped	0.02

Table 1. Parameters set for varSelRF variable selection algorithm where, *n* is the number of trees in the original random forest, *ntree.iterate*, is the number of trees to use for all additional forests, *mtry* is the number of variables to randomly select at each node split and, *vars.frac.dropped* is the fraction of least important variables dropped at each iteration.

The final step of model development was model validation. This was performed using a 10-fold cross validation approach. After the feature extraction step of model development, the PCA and 2D DWT data were randomised and split into ten equal sized groups for the purpose of cross validation. A single group representing 10% of all data was isolated and kept aside as test data. The remaining 90% of data became the training data set and was used in the feature selection and discriminant analysis steps of model development. After model training was complete, the test data set was input to assess predictive skill. Model predictive skill was quantified using the percentage of observations that were correctly classified, referred to as the correct classification rate (CCR). The process of cross validation was repeated 10 times (10-fold cross validation) and predictive skill was assessed based upon the overall average CCR. Whilst there exist many measures for comparing forecasting performance we elected to use an accuracy measure based on the CCR as it provided a direct and intuitive way to compare the data mining approaches.

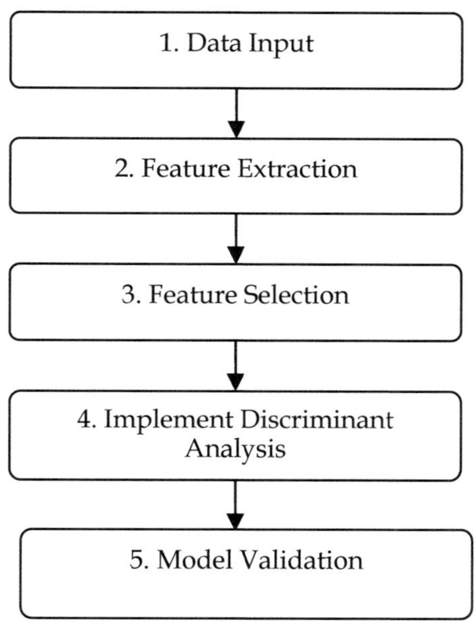

Fig. 7. A schematic diagram showing the steps for the construction of a seasonal rainfall forecast model. Data is first collected and processed with useful features/information extracted in step 2. A feature selection method is then implemented in step 3 to reduce the dimensionality of the data set. Step 5 implements a statistical learning model establish rules from previous data allowing for future prediction. Finally the model is validated to assess its performance in step 5 and feedback loop indicates the modelling process is repeated and augmented if model is deemed unskilful.

8. Results and discussion

Results displayed in Table 2 detail the 10-fold CCR for predicting above median rainfall during OND for Tully. Two different methods of feature extraction: PCA and 2-D DWT were used, whilst the best predictor variables were selected using a RF algorithm: varSelRF.

The model developed using 2D DWT feature extraction produced a 10-fold CCR of 82 % whereas, the the model developed using PCA feature extraction yielded a 10-fold CCR of 67 %. Therefore, the combined data mining approach of using 2D DWT and RF was found to give a predictive skill 20% higher than the the combined PCA and RF data mining approach. Table 2 also details the average number of variables selected using the varSelRF algorithm from each cross validation training set. The number of PCs selected was significantly less than the subset of wavelet coefficients selected. On average, only 3 PCs were selected as best predictor variables. Conversely, the the average number of wavelet coefficients selected as best predictors was 46. This may explain, in part, the improved predictive skill of the 2D DWT – RF method relative to the PC – RF method.

Feature Extraction Method	PCA	2D-DWT
10-Fold Cross-Validated CCR	67 %	82 %
AverageNo.of RF-Slected Variables	3	46

Table 2. Correct classification rates (CCR) indicating predictive skill of two of the model contrasting the feature extraction methods of PCA and 2D-DWT. The average number of variables selected from each cross validation training set using varSelRF method is also detailed.

For data reduction purposes, the number of PCs selected is usually determined by examining a scree plot. The first few PCs that explain the largest proportion of the total variance are typically selected. However, within this investigation we allowed the RF algorithm varSelRF to select the PCs of most importance for prediction from each cross validation set. It was found that during the cross validation process, PCs 4 and 8 were consistently among the set of best predictor variables. PCs 4 and 8 explained 5.7 and 3.9 % of the total variance respectively. Noteworthy was that the PCs that exlained more of the total variance (ie. PCs 1 – 3) were never selected using varSelRF. The number of PCs selected from each cross validation training set using varSelRF is shown in a bar chart (Fig. 8). The bar chart also indicates that the cummulative amount of the total variance explained by the selected subset of PCs. In a previous model for the prediction of Australian seasonal rainfall (Drosdowsky and Chambers, 2000) used PCs of SSTA data computed over the same geographical domain as we have used in this chapter. Drosdowsky and Chambers (2000), used the first two variamax rotated SSTA PCs as predictor variables which explained 11.5 and 4.3 % of the total vriability respectively. Spatial loadings plots of the first two PCs indicated they were related to the El Nino – Souther Oscillation (ENSO) and Indian Ocean SST patterns respectively (Drosdowsky and Chambers, 2000). To give some climatological understanding to the variables slected using varSelRF, we have examined the spatial loadings of PCs 4 and 8.

Spatial loadings plots of PCs 4 and 8 and are presented in Fig. 9A and 9B respectively. The loading plots indicated that PC 4 explains variability in the central-equatorial and northern Pacific Ocean, the equatorial and southwestern Indian Ocean, and the west coast of Central America. The loadings plot of PC 8 indicated it explains variability in the Southern Ocean to the east and west of the Australian contient, and also the western Pacific Ocean. From this we can assume that these regions are likely to be of importance to OND seasonal rainfall in Tully. In contrast, a spatial loadings plot of PC 1 has been included (Fig. 9C). Although PC 1 was never selected by the varSelRF algorithm, we see it strongly related to variability in the ENSO region which agrees with results of Drosdowsky and Chambers (2000). These results thus, suggest that SST variability wihin the ENSO region of the eastern tropical Pacific Ocean may not be strongly related to OND season rainfall in Tully.

It was also of interest to investigate the spatial significance of each 2D DWT coefficient selected using varSelRF. In order to do this, an inverse wavelet transform was performed. Binary matrices (0,1) of equal size to the fourth level, 2D DWT coefficient matrices S_4I, D_4^hI, D_4^vI and D_4^dI were constructed. Wavelet coefficients identified as best predictors were given a value unity, an all other coefficients were set to zero. The inverse 2D wavelet transform was then performed upon the binary wavelet coefficient matrices to derive an image *I(x,y)* with the same dimensions as the original SSTA data. The inverse wavelet derived image (Fig. 10.), revealed regions of importance lay in: the central Indian Ocean, Southern Ocean, the Coral Sea adjacent to Papua New Guinea, the Northern Pacific Ocean, and the west coast of the Central America. A region of most of importance was also identified in the equatorial eastern Pacific Ocean. Strikingly, the regions identfied as best predictors from 2D DWT coefficients were very similar to the spatial loading plots of PC 4 and PC 8.

These results suggest that the combined 2D DWT and RF approach was a useful tool for data mining teleconnections between seasonal rainfall and SST data. The results also suggest that the PCs that explain most variance in the data may not necessarily form the best set of predictor variables. As, such a variable selection method such as the RF or similar may be of benefit when choosing a sub-se tof PCs.

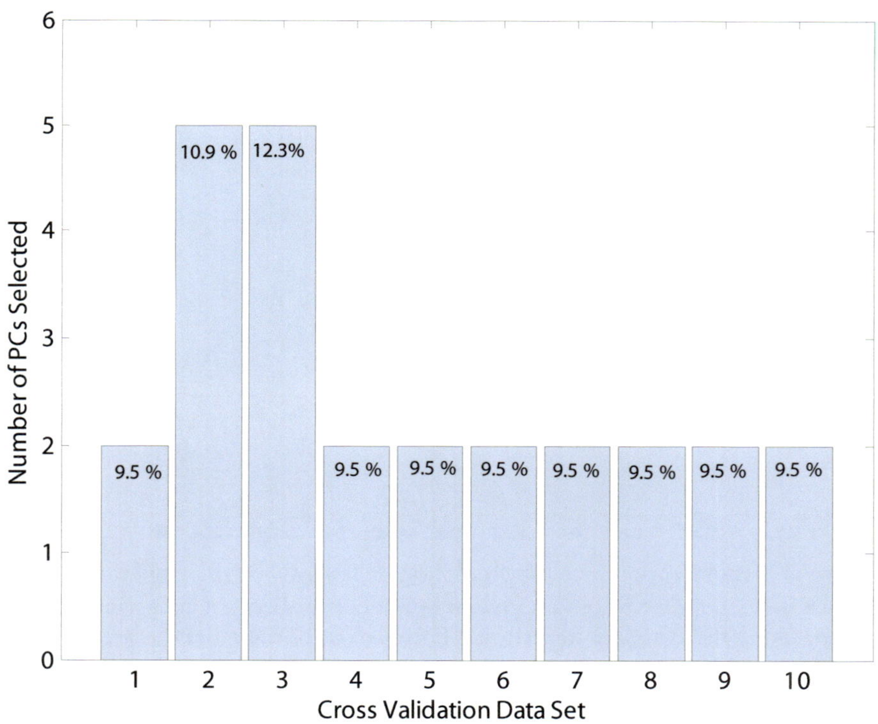

Fig. 8. Number of PCs selected using varSelRF algorithm for each cross validation set of August SSTA PCs. The cumulative percentage of total variance explained by each set of PCs is also given.

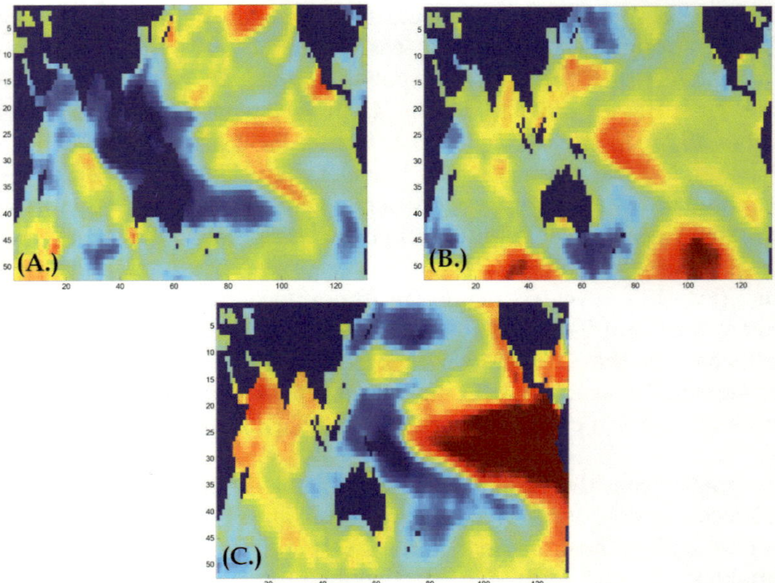

Fig. 9. Loadings plots of (A.) PC 4 and (B.) PC 8 which explained 5.7 and 3.9 % of the total variance respectively. (C.) The loadings plot of PC 1, which explained 18.2 % of the total variance respectively. Within the spatial loadings plots, warm colours indicate regions of high positive loading. Cool colours indicate regions of negative loadings.

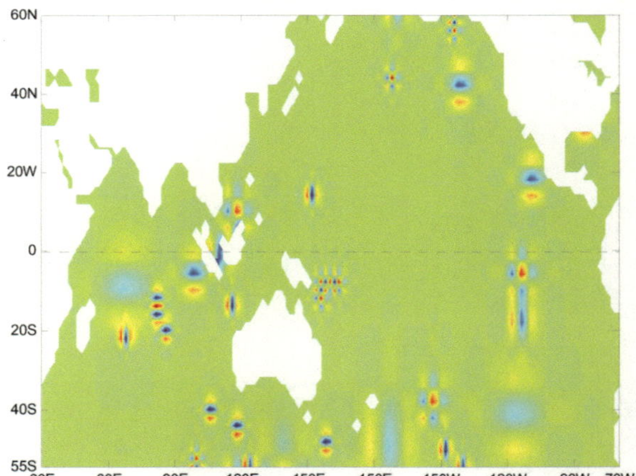

Fig. 10. Regions of most importance for prediction of Tully OND seasonal rainfall. Regions of importance were identified from an inverse wavelet transform of coefficients identified as of importance using the varSelRF algorithm. Points of colour against the green background indicate predictor locations.

9. Conclusion

The purpose of this chapter was to investigate methods of data mining sutiable for developing a seasoanl rainfall predictive model for Tully, Australia. Two data mining approaches were used to determine a subset of predictor variables from SSTA data: (i) PCA feature extraction with RF variable selection and, (ii) 2D DWT feature extraction with RF variables selection. Two separate models were then developed to predict above median OND rainfall for Tully, Australia using RDA. A 10-fold cross validation was performed upon each model to assess performance. The CCR scores were 67 % and 82 % for the PCA - RF, and 2D DWT - RF data models resepectively. The results indicated that 2D DWT -RF data mining approach typically produced a larger subset of predictor variables than the PCA - RF method. This extra degree of information may explain the enhanced predictive skill of the 2D DWT - RF predictor data set.

The RF algorithm consistently chose PC 4 and PC 8 as predictor variables, which together explained 9.5 % of total variance. Typically, variable selection is performed by selecting the first few PCs which explain the largest proportion of total variance. However, within this study PCs 1 - 3 were never selected using RF variable selection. This suggested that the spatial loadings of the PCs may have been of greater importance than the proportion of variance explained by the PC. Inverse 2D DWT allowed the wavelet variables of most importance to be spatially mapped. Interestingly, the spatial loadings of PC 4 and PC 8 were very similar to the spatial locations identified from the inverse 2D DWT. This provided further evidence to suggest that the spatial location of predictors was of greater importance than the amount of variance explained.

This research concerned constructing forecast models for the prediction of above median rainfall for OND seasonal rainfall for a single case study location: Tully, with a lead time of one month. It would be useful to extend the modelling and data mining methods of this work to other sugar growing regions across Australia and assess predictive skill. Moreover, the technique outlined in this paper need not be limited to sugarcane growing regions, but may be applicable to other locations and agricultural industries where knowledge about the future climate is paramount for enhancing forward planning activities.

10. References

Afifi, A., V. A. Clark, et al. (2004). *Computer Aided Multivariate Analysis* Chapman and Hall/CRC. USA

Antonini, M., M. Barlaud, et al. (1992). Image Coding Using Wavelet Transform. *IEEE Transactions on Image Processing* 1(2): 205-220.

Brieman, L. (2001). Random Forests. *Machine Learning* 45(1): 5-32.

Dash, M. and H. Liu (1997). Feature Selection for Intelligent Data Analysis. 1: 131-156.

Diaz-Uriarte, R. and S. Alvarez de Andres (2006). Gene selection and classification of microarray data using random forest. *BMC Bioinformatics* 7(1): 3.

Drosdowsky, W. and L. E. Chambers (2001). Near-Global Sea Surface Temperature Anomalies as Predictors of Australian Seasonal Rainfall. *Journal of Climate* 14(7): 1677-1687.

Duda, R. O. and P. E. Hart (1973). *Pattern Classification and Scene Analysis*, John Wiley and Sons. Canada

Everingham, Y. L., R. C. Muchow, et al. (2002). Enhanced risk management and decision-making capability across the sugarcane industry value chain based on seasonal climate forecasts. *Agricultural Systems* 74: 459-477.

Firth, L. and M.L. Hazelton et al. (2005). Predicting the Onset of Australian Winter Rainfall by Nonlinear Classification. *Journal of Climate*, 18(6), 772 - 781

Friedman, J. H. (1989). Regularized Discriminant Analysis. *Journal of the American Statistical Society* 84(405): 165-175.
George, E. I. (2000). The Variable Selection Problem. *Journal of the American Statistical Society* 95(452): 165 - 175.
Hastie, T., R. Tribshirani, et al. (2001). *The Elements of Statistical Learning: Data Mining, Interference and Prediction*, Springer-Verlag. New York, USA
Johnson, R. A. and D. W. Wichern (2002). *Applied Multivariate Statistical Analysis* Prentice Hall. Upper Saddle River
Jolliffe, I. T. (1986). *Principal Component Analysis*, Springer-Verlag. New York, USA
Jones, K. and Y. L. Everingham (2005). Can ENSO combined with Low-Frequency SST signals enhance or suppress rainfall in Australian sugar growing areas? MODSIM 2005 International Congress on Modelling and Simulation, Melbounre, Modelling and Simulation Society of Australia.
Klopper, E., C. Vogel, et al. (2006). Seasonal Climate Forecasts - Potential Agricultural-Risk Management Tools? *Climatic Change* 76(1): 73-90.
Kumar, P. and E. Foufoula-Georgiou (1997). Wavelet Analysis for Geophysical Applications. *Reviews of Geophysics* 35(4): 385–412.
Landman, W. A. and S. J. Mason (1999). Operational long-lead prediction of South African rainfall using canonical correlation analysis. *International Journal of Climatology* 19(10): 1073-1090.
Mallat, S. G. (1989a). A Theory for Multiresolution Signal Decomposition: The Wavelet Representation. *Pattern Analysis and Machine Intelligence, IEEE Transactions on* 11(7): 674-693.
Mallat, S. G. (1989b). Multiresolution Approximations and Wavelet Orthonormal Bases of $L^2(R)$. *Transactions of the American Mathematical Society* 315(1): 69-87.
Mallet, Y., O. de Vel, et al. (2000). Fundamentals of Wavelet Transforms. In. *Wavelets in Chemistry*, B. Walczak (Eds), Elselvier: Netherlands: 57-79.
Mason, S. J. (1998). Seasonal forecasting of South African rainfall using a non-linear discriminant analysis model. *International Journal of Climatology* 18(2): 147-164.
Muchow, R. C. and A. W. Wood (1996). Rainfall Risk and Scheduling the Harvest of Sugarcane. In. *Sugarcane: Research Towards Efficient and Sustainable Production*, J. R. Wilson, D. M. Hagarth, J. A. Campbell and A. L. Garside (Eds), CSIRO: Brisbane, Australia.
Rencher, A. C. (2002). *Methods of Multivariate Analysis*, John Wiley and Sons. Canada
Singhrattna, N., B. Rajagopalan, et al. (2005). Seasonal forecasting of Thailand summer monsoon rainfall. *International Journal of Climatology* 25(5): 649-664.
Smith, T. M. and R. W. Reynolds (2004). Improved Extended Reconstruction of SST (1854–1997). *Journal of Climate* 17(12): 2466–2477.
Svetnik, V., A. Liaw, et al. (2004). Application of Breiman's Random Forest to Modeling Structure-Activity Relationships of Pharmaceutical Molecules. In. *Multiple Classifier Systems*(Eds): 334-343.
Washington, R. and T. E. Downing (1999). Seasonal Forecasting of African Rainfall: Prediction, Responses and Household Food Security. *The Geographical Journal* 165(3): 255-274.
Wilks, D. S. (1995). *Statistical Methods in the Atmospheric Sciences*, Academic Press Inc. San Diego, USA
Wu, W., Y. Mallet, et al. (1996). Comparison of regularized discriminant analysis linear discriminant analysis and quadratic discriminant analysis applied to NIR data. *Analytica Chimica Acta* 329(3): 257-265.

8

Monthly River Flow Forecasting by Data Mining Process

Özlem Terzi
Suleyman Demirel University
Turkey

1. Introduction

In design, plan, project, construction, maintenance, and especially management of water resources, surface water input and output must be calculated based on measurements. One of the priority parameter is surface flow in the studies. The flow data measured in the past is required for design of the water structure be built in the future and calculation of natural disasters such as flood and drought according to the pre-specified risk level (Şen, 2003).

Stochastic models and artificial intelligence techniques (artificial neural networks, fuzzy logic and adaptive neuro fuzzy inference systems etc.) on flow predicting are commonly used by many researchers while data mining (DM) process is not yet widely used in the hydrology area. Russo et al. (2006) fitted a stochastic rainfall model to rainfall radar data in order to produce a realistic representation of the distribution of rainfall in space and time. The results show that the model, calibrated on the study area, is able to forecast satisfactorily the rain field in space and time. Archer & Fowler (2008) investigated the links between climate and runoff for eight gauging stations in the Jhelum catchment but then concentrated on seasonal forecasting of spring and summer inflows to Mangla Dam. They are used precipitation and temperature variables to forecast summer season flows at stations upstream from the reservoir with a lead time of up to three months based on multiple linear regression models. The analysis demonstrates that good forecasts within 15% of observed flows for 92% of years can be achieved for summer season flows from April to September. For spring flows from April to June, excellent forecasts can be provided within 15% of observed flows for 83% of years. Lin & Chen (2004) used the radial basis function network (RBFN) to construct a rainfall-runoff model, and presented the fully supervised learning algorithm for the parametric estimation of the network. The proposed methodology has been applied to an actual reservoir watershed to forecast the one- to three-hour ahead runoff. The result shows that the RBFN can be successfully applied to build the relation of rainfall and runoff. Rajurkar et al. (2004) presented an approach for modeling daily flows during flood events using ANN. They showed that the approach produces reasonably satisfactory results for data of catchments from different geographical locations. Nayak et al. (2004) suggested that performance of ANFIS model is capable of preserving the statistical properties of the time series and it is viable for modeling river flow series. Keskin et al. (2006) developed a flow prediction model, based on the adaptive neural-based fuzzy inference system (ANFIS) coupled with stochastic hydrological models. An ANFIS is applied to river flow prediction in Dim Stream in the southern part of Turkey. Synthetic series, generated through autoregressive moving-average models, are then used to train data sets of the ANFIS. They showed that the extension of input and output data sets in the training stage improves the accuracy of forecasting by using ANFIS. Jacquin & Shamseldin (2006) explored the application of Takagi–Sugeno fuzzy inference systems to rainfall–runoff modeling. The models developed intend to describe the non-linear relationship between rainfall as input and runoff as output to the real system using a system based approach. They showed that fuzzy inference systems are a suitable alternative to the traditional methods for modeling the non-linear relationship between rainfall and runoff.

Knowledge discovery uses data mining and machine learning techniques that have evolved through a synergy in artificial intelligence, computer science, statistics, and other related fields. Although there are technical differences, the terms 'machine learning', 'data mining', and 'knowledge discovery and data mining (KDD)' are often used interchangeably (Goodwin et al., 2003).

Data mining is often defined as the process of extracting valid, previously unknown, comprehensible information from large databases in order to improve and optimize decisions (Braha & Shmilovici, 2002). In another way, data mining is defined as the identification of interesting structure, where structure designates patterns, statistical or predictive models of the data, and relationships among parts of the data (Fayyad & Uthurusamy, 2002). Data mining is applied in a wide variety of fields for prediction. In addition, data mining has also been applied to other types of scientific data such as bioinformatical, astronomical, and medical (Li & Shue, 2004). Keskin et al. (2009) developed pan evaporation models using data mining process for Lakes Eğirdir, Kovada, and Karacaören Dam and formed an integrated evaporation model by aggregation of daily pan evaporation of these lakes for the Lakes District in the southern part of Turkey. They showed that the REP tree model has better agreement with measured daily pan evaporation than other models.

This chapter is organized as follows: Section 2 briefly defines the DM process. Section 3 describes to construct a model to forecast river flow using data mining process. This model is developed to be accomplished in Kızılırmak River which is longest river in Turkey. Section 4 includes conclusions of the chapter.

2. Data Mining process

Data mining (DM) process generally involves phases of data understanding, data preparation, modeling, evaluation and knowledge as shown in Figure 1. DM process is a hybrid disciplinary that integrates technologies of databases, statistics, machine learning, signal processing, and high performance computing. This rapidly emerging technology is motivated by the need for new techniques to help analyze, understand or even visualize the huge amounts of stored data gathered from scientific applications. The major data mining functions that are developed in research communities include summarization, association, classification, prediction and clustering (Zhou, 2003).

Data understanding starts with an initial data collection and proceeds with activities to get familiar with the data, to identify data quality problems and to discover first insights into the data. Data preparation covers all activities that construct the final dataset to be modeled from the initial raw data. The tasks of this phase may include data cleaning for removing noise and inconsistent data, and data transformation for extracting the embedded features (Li & Shue, 2004). Successful mining of data relies on refining tools and techniques capable of rendering large quantities of data understandable and meaningful (Mattison, 2000). The

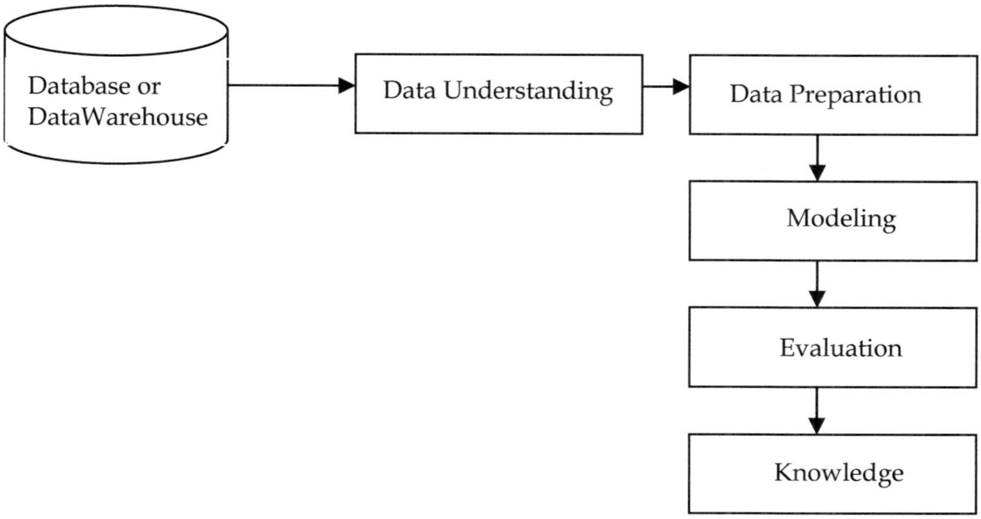

Fig. 1. Data mining process

modeling phase applies various modeling techniques, determines the optimal values for parameters in models, and finds the one most suitable to meet the objectives. The evaluation phase evaluates the model found in the last stage to confirm its validity to fit the problem requirements. No matter which areas data mining is applied to, most of the efforts are directed toward the data preparation phase (Li & Shue, 2004).

A good relational database management system will form the core of the data repository, and adequately reflect both the data structure and the process flow, and the database design will anticipate the kind of analysis and data mining to be performed. The data repository should also support access to existing databases allowing retrieval of supporting information that can be used at various levels in the decision making process (Rupp & Wang, 2004).

Data mining is a powerful technique for extracting predictive information from large databases. The automated analysis offered by data mining goes beyond the retrospective analysis of data. Data mining tools can answer questions that are too time-consuming to resolve with methods based on first principles. In data mining, databases are searched for hidden patterns to reveal predictive information in patterns that are too complicated for human experts to identify (Hoffmann & Apostolakis, 2003).

3. River flow models

A data mining process generally has five phases. In this chapter, these phases were considered as follows.

3.1 Data understanding

The DM process is applied to the Kızılırmak River in northern part of Turkey to forecast river flow. The length of the Kızılırmak River which is longest river in Turkey is 1355 km. The area of the watershed is 78 646 km^2. The average flow and rainfall are about 184 m^3/s and 446.1 mm, respectively.

The data used to develop model includes the monthly flow and rainfall observations between 1975 and 2005 years i.e. a total of 322 months in this chapter. The monthly flow data were obtained from the General Directorate of Electrical Power Resources Survey and Development Administration for Yamula (1501), Söğütlühan (1535) ve Bulakbaşı (1539) stations. The monthly rainfall data were obtained from Turkish State Meteorological Service for Kayseri, Sivas and Zara stations.

3.2 Data preparation

In some months between 1975 and 2005 years, missing rainfall and flow data are determined. Therefore, the months of missing data are not used for modeling. Hence, the models are developed according to 322 monthly data for 1975-2005 years. It is used 80% of the data for training set and 20% of the data for testing set.

3.3 Modeling

In order to develop river flow model, multilinear regression, multilayer perceptron, radial basis function (RBF) network, decision table, REP tree and KStar algorithms are used in data mining process in Weka. Detailed explanations of these algorithms are given in the following.

Multilinear Regression

The general purpose of multiple regression is to learn more about the relationship between several independent or predictor variables and a dependent or criterion variable (http://www. statsoft.com/textbook/stathome.html). Linear regression is based on the assumption of a linear relationship between the dependent variable Y and its predictors X1, X2, …, Xn. Linear regression offers simple and easily interpretable models. However, it can result in inaccurate models that predict poorly in the presence of a nonlinear or nonadditive relationship. Due to the complexity of microarchitectural event interaction and varying event performance penalties, however, it is common for a nonlinear relationship to exist. In the linear case, the functional relationship between Y and its predictors is estimated by minimizing the residual sum of squares
(http://homepages.inf.ed.ac.uk/jcavazos/SMART07/paper_9_9.pdf).

Multilayer Perceptron

The back-propagation learning algorithm is one of the most important historical developments in neural networks. It has reawakened the scientific and engineering community to the modeling and processing of many quantitative phenomena using neural networks. This learning algorithm is applied to multilayer feed-forward networks consisting of processing elements with continuous and differentiable activation functions. Such networks associated with the back-propagation learning algorithm are also called back-propagation networks. Given a training set of input-output pairs, the algorithm provides a procedure for changing the weights in a back-propagation network to classify the given input patterns correctly. For a given input-output pair, the back-propagation algorithm performs two phases of data flow. First, the input pattern is propagated from the input layer to the output layer and, as a result of this forward flow of data, it produces an actual output. Then the error signals resulting from the difference between output pattern and an actual output are back-propagated from the output layer to the previous layers for them to update their weights (Lin & Lee, 1995).

Radial Basis Function Network

A radial basis function network is a two-layer network whose output neurons form a linear combination of the basis functions computed by the hidden neurons. The basis functions in the hidden layer produce a localized response to the input. That is, each hidden neuron has a localized receptive field. The basis function can be viewed as the activation function in the hidden layer. The basis function used is a Gaussian function (Fu, 1994).

Decision Table

Decision table summarizes the data set with a "decision table." In its simplest state, a decision table contains the same number of attributes as the original data set, and a new data item is assigned a category by finding the line in the decision table that matches the nonclass values of the data item. This implementation employs the wrapper method to find a good subset of attributes for inclusion in the table. By eliminating attributes that contribute little or nothing to a model of the data set, the algorithm reduces the likelihood of overfitting and creates a smaller, more condensed decision table (Cunningham & Holmes, 1999).

REP Tree

The decision tree tool of REP tree in Weka was employed for formulating the resource access patterns for the considered applications that are common in the target execution environment. The REP tree procedure builds a decision tree using information gain as the splitting criterion, and uses reduced-error pruning for pruning. This procedure is also characterized by lower computational overhead compared to other decision-tree-based classification methods as a result of its efficient pruning mechanism (Rajan et al., 2006).

KStar

A nearest-neighbor classifier, this algorithm is highly effective in situations with noisy training data, provided it is supplied with a large enough training set. An important note to consider is that the algorithm calculates the distance between instances on all attributes, unlike some other methods. If only a few of the features of the given vector are relevant, then two instances with two identical values for the relevant features may find themselves spaced far apart by this algorithm (Young, 2004).

3.4 Evaluation

The monthly flow data of Yamula (1501) and Bulakbaşı (1539) station and monthly rainfall data of Kayseri, Sivas and Zara rainfall measurement stations are used to forecast monthly flow for Söğütlühan (1535) station. The cross-correlations between input and output parameters are calculated for the selection of the input parameters. According to cross-correlations, three different models have been developed to forecast for flow values of Söğütlühan station (Table 1). In the first model (M1), rainfall data of Kayseri, Sivas and Zara stations and flow data of Yamula and Bulakbaşı stations are used as input parameters.

Model	Input parameters
M1	Flow (1501, 1539), Rainfall (Kayseri, Sivas, Zara)
M2	Flow (1501, 1539), Rainfall (Sivas, Zara)
M3	Flow (1501, 1539)

Table 1. Construction of the developed river flow models

While input parameters of second model (M2) are rainfall data of Sivas and Zara stations and flow data of Yamula and Bulakbaşı stations, them of other model (M3) are only flow data of Yamula and Bulakbaşı stations.

Two criteria are used to evaluate the adequacy of each model: the coefficient of determination (R^2) and the root mean square error (RMSE).

The coefficient of determination based on the flow forecasting errors is calculated as,

$$R^2 = 1 - \frac{\sum_{i=1}^{n}(F_{i(flow)} - F_{i(model)})^2}{\sum_{i=1}^{n}(F_{i(flow)} - F_{mean})^2} \quad (1)$$

where n is the number of observed data, $F_{i(\text{flow})}$, $F_{i(\text{model})}$ and F_{mean} are monthly flow measurement, the results of developed flow model and mean flow measurements, respectively

The root mean square error represents the error of model and defined as,

$$RMSE = \sqrt{\frac{1}{n}\sum_{i=1}^{n}(F_{i(flow)} - F_{i(model)})^2} \quad (2)$$

where parameters have been defined above.

3.5 Knowledge

The best-fit DM algorithm is determined according to coefficients of determination (R^2) using Eq. (1) and RMSE values using Eq. (2) for testing data set. The results of statistical analyses of the models are given in Table 2. As seen from Table 2, the best-fit DM algorithm is determined as multilinear regression algorithm for M1, M2 and M3 models. Although M1, M2 and M3 models has same the R^2 values (0.981) using multilinear regression algorithm for testing data set, M3 model has the lowest RMSE among all models. The M3 models based on flow data gives generally best R^2 values. In case of a limited parameter, the M3 model based on only flow data has advantage because it uses fewer input parameters. Hence, the M3 model developed by using multilinear regression algorithm is selected for flow forecasting of Kızılırmak River among the developed models. The results of the developed model are also indistinguishable (mean, standard deviation etc.) from measured flow values.

Figure 2 shows comparison plot of flow values forecasted with M3 model and measured for testing data set. The comparison plot of the model is around 45° straight lines which imply that there are no bias effects. It is apparent a close relationship between forecasted and measured flow values. The results suggest that the monthly flow could be easily forecasted from flow and rainfall data using DM algorithms.

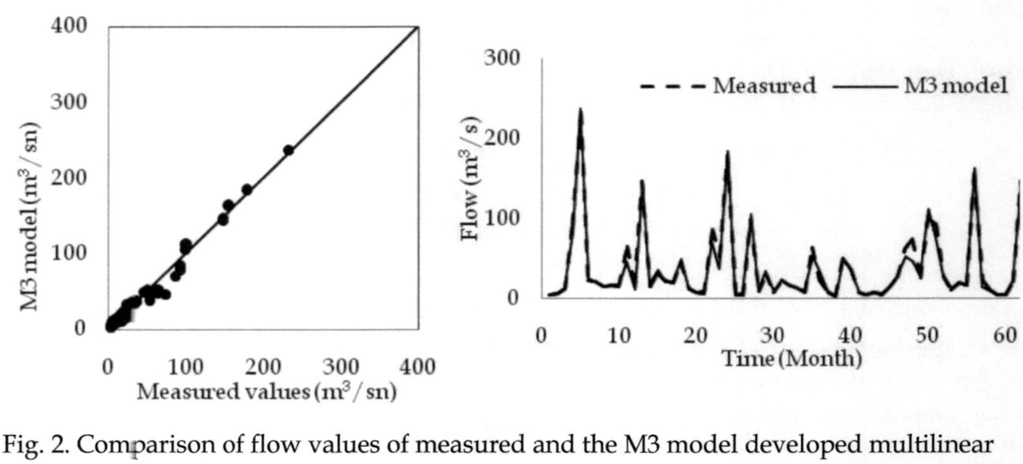

Fig. 2. Comparison of flow values of measured and the M3 model developed multilinear regression algorithm

Models	Algorithms	Testing data set					
		Mean (m^3/sn)	Std. Devia.	Skewness	Kurtosis	RMSE	R^2
M1 (rainfall data of Kayseri, Sivas and Zara stations- flow data of Yamula and Bulakbaşı stations)	Measured flow	38.59	47.18	2.20	4.93	-	-
	Multilinear Regression	38.09	47.08	2.41	5.95	6.53	0.981
	Multilayer Perceptron	41.11	47.04	2.70	9.01	8.85	0.964
	RBF Network	39.19	34.40	0.79	-1.37	36.37	0.397
	Decision Table	34.91	38.20	2.17	4.74	27.11	0.665
	REP tree	38.35	45.85	2.42	6.81	12.08	0.933
	KStar	31.69	36.79	1.96	3.07	18.41	0.845
M2 (rainfall data of Sivas and Zara stations- flow data of Yamula and Bulakbaşı stations)	Multilinear Regression	38.09	47.08	2.41	5.95	6.53	0.981
	Multilayer Perceptron	42.06	48.16	2.78	9.44	9.77	0.956
	RBF Network	40.74	37.52	0.95	-1.08	34.89	0.445
	Decision Table	34.91	38.20	2.17	4.74	27.11	0.665
	REP tree	38.28	45.89	2.42	6.79	12.09	0.933
	KStar	32.72	37.82	1.99	3.49	17.80	0.855
M3 (flow data of Yamula and Bulakbaşı stations)	Multilinear Regression	37.81	46.94	2.44	6.10	6.51	0.981
	Multilayer Perceptron	40.45	45.93	2.56	6.66	7.68	0.973
	RBF Network	34.46	39.84	2.00	2.17	22.05	0.778
	Decision Table	34.91	38.20	2.17	4.74	27.11	0.665
	REP tree	38.30	45.87	2.42	6.80	12.09	0.933
	KStar	33.22	39.49	2.12	4.21	12.23	0.932

Table 2. The descriptive statistics of developed models

4. Conclusions

Determination of the flow is of great importance especially in many issues such as flood control, use and operation of water, determination of settlement and energy production. This chapter indicates the ability of data mining (DM) process to forecast monthly flow data. The DM process has been applied to Kızılırmak River which meets vital components such as irrigation, drinking water and power generation. The various models based on rainfall and flow data are developed and compared to measurement flow data. The most appropriate algorithm is determined according to the model performance criteria for testing data set. The comparisons show that there is a better agreement between monthly flow data and the results of the multilinear regression algorithm in data mining process than others for M1, M2 and M3 models. The M3 model based on only flow data gives better performance than M1 and M2 models. It is shown that the M3 model is superior among all models. The performance of the developed models suggests that the flow could be successfully forecasted from available flow and rainfall data using DM process, and the models are used in water resources planning and management. Finally, DM process can be used for forecasting flow in which measurement system has failed or to forecast missing monthly flow data in hydrological modeling studies.

5. References

Archer, D.R. & Fowler, H.J. (2008). Using meteorological data to forecast seasonal runoff on the River Jhelum, Pakistan. *Journal of Hydrology*, 361, 10-23

Braha, D. & Shmilovici, A. (2002). Data mining for improving a cleaning process in the semiconductor industry. *IEEE Transactions on Semiconductor Manufacturing*, 15, 1

Cunningham, S. J. & Holmes, G. (1999). Developing innovative applications in agriculture using data mining. *Proc. Southeast Asia Regional Computer Confederation Conf.*, Singapore, Dept. of Computer Science, Univ. of Waikato, Hamilton, New Zealand

Fayyad, U.M. & Uthurusamy, R. (2002). Evolving data mining into solutions for insights. *Communications of the ACM*, 45, 8, 28-31

Fu, L. (1994). *Neural Networks in Computer Intelligence*. McGraw-Hill International Editions.

Goodwin, L.; VanDyne, M.; Lin, S. & Talbert, S. (2003). Data mining issues and opportunities for building nursing knowledge. *Journal of Biomedical Informatics*, 36, 379-388

Hoffmann, D. & Apostolakis, J. (2003). Crystal structure prediction by data mining. *J. Mol. Struct.*, 647,1–3, 17–39

Jacquin, A.P. & Shamseldin, A.Y. (2006). Development of rainfall–runoff models using Takagi–Sugeno fuzzy inference systems. *Journal of Hydrology*, 329, 154–173

Keskin, M.E.; Taylan, D. & Terzi, Ö. (2006). Adaptive neural-based fuzzy inference system (ANFIS) approach for modelling hydrological time series. *Hydrological Sciences–Journal–des Sciences Hydrologiques*, 51, 4, 588-598

Keskin, M.E.; Terzi, Ö. & Küçüksille, E.U. (2009). Data mining process for integrated evaporation model. *Journal of Irrigation and Drainage Engineering*, 135, 1, 39-43

Li, S.T. & Shue, L.Y. (2004). Data mining to aid policy making in air pollution management. *Expert System and Applications*, 27, 331-340

Lin, C.T. & Lee, C.S.G. (1995). *Neural fuzzy systems*. Prentice Hall.

Lin, G.F. & Chen, L.H. (2004). A non-linear rainfall-runoff model using radial basis function network. *Journal of Hydrology*, 289, 1–8

Nayak, P.C.; Sudheer, K.P.; Rangan, D.M. & Ramasastri, K.S. (2004). A neuro-fuzzy computing technique for modeling hydrological time series. *Journal of Hydrology*, 291, 1-2, 52-66

Mattison, R. (2000). *Data Warehousing: Strategies, Technologies and Techniques Statistical Analysis*, SPSS Inc. White Papers

Rajan, D.; Poellabauer, C. & Chawla, N.(2006). Resource Access pattern mining for dynamic energy management. *Proc. Workshop on Autonomic Computing: A New Challenge for Machine Learning*, Berlin, Germany

Rajurkar, M.P.; Kothyari, U.C. & Chaube, U.C. (2004). Modeling of the daily rainfall-runoff relationship with artificial neural network. *Journal of Hydrology*, 285, 96–113

Rupp, B. & Wang, J. (2004). Predictive models for protein crystallization. *Methods*, 34, 3, 390-407

Russo, F.; Lombardo, F.; Napolitano, F. & Gorgucci, E. (2006). Rainfall stochastic modeling for runoff forecasting. *Physics and Chemistry of the Earth*, 31, 1252–1261

Şen, Z. (2003). *Water Science and Methods*. Water Foundation Publications, ISBN:975-6455-02-0, İstanbul

Young, A. (2004). *Automatic acronym identification and the creation of an acronym database*. Technical Rep., Univ. of Sheffield, Sheffield, U.K.

Zhou, Z.H. (2003). Three perspectives of data mining. *Artif. Intell.*, 143, 1, 139–146

9

Monitoring of Water Quality Using Remote Sensing Data Mining

Xing-Ping Wen[1] and Xiao-Feng Yang[2]
[1]*Faculty of Land Resource Engineering, Kunming University of science and technology,*
[2]*Research Center for Analysis and Measurement, Kunming University of Science and Technology*
China

1. Introduction

Remote sensing techniques play increasingly important role over recent decades in both problems of global climate change and frequent deterioration of the status of aquatic ecology, driven by the ever-increasing needs of growing populations for drinking water, polluted by overland runoff from point and non-point sources, as well as fish and other seafood (Pozdnyakov et al., 2005). With the advent of new sensor technologies, it is possible to monitor land cover / land change in large area simultaneously and quickly (Wen and Yang, 2009a, Wen and Yang, 2009b). Remote sensing techniques have been widely used in water quality assessment (Alparslan et al., 2007, Brando and Dekker, 2003, Chen et al., 2007, Giardino et al., 2007, Hadjimitsis and Clayton, Kondratye et al., 1998, Koponen et al., 2002, Pozdnyakov et al., 2005, Ritchie et al., 2003, Seyhan and Dekker, 1986, Wang and Ma, 2001). Many documents describe water quality monitoring using different satellite sensor (Maillard and Pinheiro Santos, 2008, Giardino et al., 2007, He et al., 2008, Alparslan et al., 2007, Verma et al., 2008, Wang and Ma, 2001, Zhang et al., 2003, Martinez et al., 2007, Boken, 2007, Wang et al., 2004). The spectrum characteristics of water and pollutants are essential to water quality monitoring and assessment. The spectral characteristics of the signal received from water are a function of hydrological, biological and chemical characteristics of water, and other interference factor (Seyhan and Dekker, 1986). Suspended sediments increase the radiance emergent from surface waters in the visible and near infrared proportion of the electromagnetic spectrum(Ritchie et al., 1976), so it is promising and feasible to detect water pollutants using spectral signatures in the visible and near infrared band. Wang assessed the water quality of Taihu lake using Landsat TM imagery (Wang and Ma, 2001), and the result indicated that three visible bands of TM1, TM2 and TM3 were correlated with some water quality parameters from the lake. Alparslan (Alparslan et al., 2007) assessed water quality at Ömerli Dam using the first four bands of Landsat 7 ETM +satellite data. Hadjimitsis (Hadjimitsis and Clayton, 2009) assessed temporal variations of water quality in inland water bodies using atmospheric corrected satellite remotely sensed image data. It found that atmospheric correction was essential to water quality assessment using satellite remotely sensed imagery because it improved significantly the water reflectance. In this paper, atmospherically corrected Landsat ETM+ imagery is used to monitors water quality using stepwise multiple linear regression analysis, southwest China. Five over 30 square kilometers lakes which are Dianchi, Fuxian, Yangzong, Qilu and Xingyun Lake near Kunming city in Yunnan province are investigated. It concludes that ETM+ 1, ETM+ 2 and ETM+ 3 are important bands to monitor water quality.

2. The study area

The study area is located at Kunming city, the capital of Yunnan provinces, in southwest China (fig. 1). Yunnan literally means "south of the clouds" in Chinese. Proud to be one of five lake-rich regions in China, Yunnan Province alone had nine lakes with areas of over 30 square kilometers. They include: Dianchi Lake, Fuxian Lake, Qilu Lake, Yangzong Lake, Xingyun Lake, Erhai Lake, Lugu Lake, Yilong Lake and Chenghai Lake. Dianchi Lake nicknamed "Sparkling Pearl Embedded in the Plateau" is a large inter-land freshwater fault lake located on the Yunnan-Guizhou Plateau close to Kunming. It covers about 300 km^2 with about 39 km long from north to south, and it is the sixth largest freshwater lake in China and the largest in Yunnan Province. However, until the first wastewater plant was built in 1990, 90 percent of Kunming's wastewater was pumped untreated into Dianchi Lake. Pollution was a major problem for the lake (Zhang et al., 1996, Liu and Zhang, 1996). According to recent reports, water quality across Yunnan's network of rivers and lakes had been deteriorating steadily over the last several years. Among them, Dianchi Lake was one of the most serious pollution lakes in Yunnan province. Although water from Lake Dianchi at one point made up 40% of the drinking water for Kunming City several years ago, nowadays the city had had to shift to other sources of water due to the lake's severe algal blooms. Dianchi Lake is rated grade V (the worst grade) which makes the water unfit for agricultural or industrial uses.

In this paper, five over 30 square kilometers lakes near Kunming city in Yunnan province were investigated. There are Dianchi, Fuxian, Yangzong, Qilu and Xingyun Lake (fig. 2).

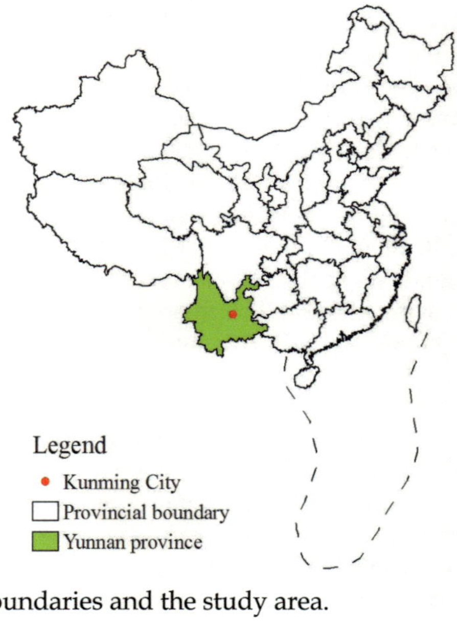

Fig. 1. China provincial boundaries and the study area.

Fig. 2. The color composite ETM+ image of band 3 (Red), band 2 (Green) and band 1 (Blue) after atmospheric correction acquired in November 2, 2000.

3. Remote sensing data

3.1 Radiometric and atmospheric correction of Landsat ETM+ imagery

This paper uses Landsat ETM+ imagery acquired in November 2, 2000 to monitor water quality near Kunming city. The Landsat 7 satellite was successfully launched from Vandenburg Air Force Base on April 15, 1999. It is a near polar-orbiting, earth mapping orbit with a 16-day repeat cycle, sun-synchronous satellite at an altitude of 705 km above the Earth. Its payload is a single nadir-pointing instrument, the Enhanced Thematic Mapper Plus (ETM+). The ETM+ sensor provides for a nadir-viewing, eight-band multispectral scanning radiometer capable of providing high-resolution image information of the Earth's surface. It detects spectrally-filtered radiation in VNIR, SWIR, LWIR and panchromatic bands from the sunlit Earth in a 185 km wide swath. In order to retrieve the ground object spectra, the radiometric and atmospheric correction is the necessary step. The following equation referred to NASA website is used to convert digital number (DN) to radiance units:

$$L_{\lambda} = \text{Grescale} * \text{QCAL} + \text{Brescale} \quad (1)$$

where:

L_{λ} = Spectral radiance at the sensor's aperture in watts/ (meter squared * ster * μm)

Grescale = Rescaled gain (the data product "gain" contained in the Level 1 product header or ancillary data record) in watts/(meter squared * ster * μm)/DN

Brescale = Rescaled bias (the data product "offset" contained in the Level 1 product header or ancillary data record) in watts/(meter squared * ster * μm)

QCAL = the quantized calibrated pixel value in DN

The imagery is atmospherically corrected using FLAASH model (Cooley et al., 2002). Fig. 3 is the comparison of four different target curves before and after atmospheric correction. Spectral reflectance curves of four different targets are similar to spectral reflectance curves of corresponging standard targets after atmospheric correction. The atmospherically corrected image is shown in fig. 2

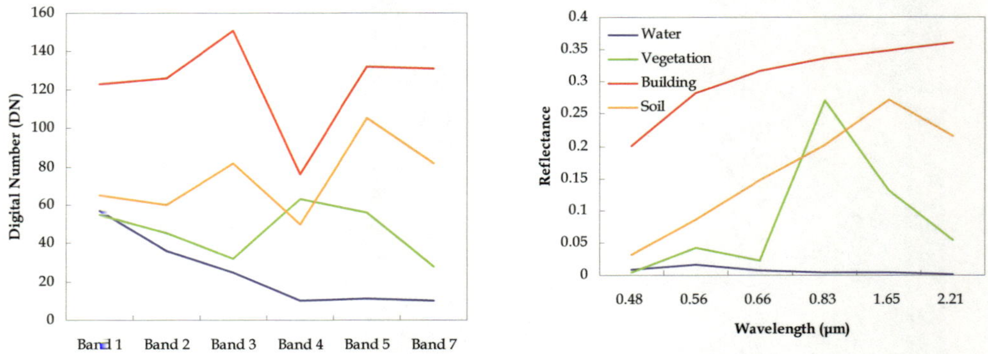

Fig. 3. Digital number curves of four different targets before atmospheric correction (left). Spectral reflectance curves of corresponding four different targets after atmospheric correction (right).

3.2 The classification of image and identification of five lakes

Five lakes are identified from the ETM+ image using classification method for avoiding effects of other pixels. Firstly, the Maximum Likelihood Classification (MLC) method

(Richards, 1999) is applied to extract water areas from the imagery. Then, the classification result is covert into vector file and polygon areas lower 30 square kilometers are removed using Geographic Information System (GIS) software. Finally, the ETM+ imagery is applied mask using the processed vector file, and only five lakes image was obtained (fig. 4).

Fig. 4. Five lakes in the study area.

4. Methodology

4.1 Optimum index factor of lakes image

Statistics is the science of making effective use of numerical data. In this paper, mean, standard deviation and correlation coefficient of reflectance values from lakes are calculated (table 1, table 2). Due to the influence of algas in lakes, the mean value of band 4 is higher. The standard deviation is widely used to measure the variability or dispersion. A low standard deviation indicates that the data value tend to be very close to the mean, whereas the high standard deviation indicates that the data is spread out over a large range of values. The band with the higher standard deviation contains the higher amount of 'information' than other bands. The correlation coefficient of different bands represents duplication among band pairs. The Optimum Index Factor (OIF) developed by (Chavez et al., 1982) is a statistic value that can be used to select the optimum combination of three bands in a satellite image with which a color composite image is created. The optimum combination is the one with the highest sum of standard deviations and the least amount of duplication (lowest correlation coefficient).

Statistic value	Band 1	Band 2	Band 3	Band 4	Band 5	Band 7
Mean	0.02238	0.05448	0.03518	0.05247	0.01207	0.00649
Standard deviation	0.01360	0.03064	0.02159	0.09680	0.02020	0.00845

Table 1. Mean and standard deviation of pixel values from lakes in different bands

Correlation	Band 1	Band 2	Band 3	Band 4	Band 5	Band 7
Band 1	1.000000	0.727497	0.738473	0.682501	0.627298	0.496868
Band 2	0.727497	1.000000	0.956101	0.540135	0.448750	0.368707
Band 3	0.738473	0.956101	1.000000	0.523605	0.454983	0.392675
Band 4	0.682501	0.540135	0.523605	1.000000	0.933209	0.689372
Band 5	0.627298	0.448750	0.454983	0.933209	1.000000	0.793760
Band 7	0.496868	0.368707	0.392675	0.689372	0.793760	1.000000

Table 2. Correlation coefficient of different bands

OIF is calculated using the formula as follows:

$$OIF = \frac{Std_i + Std_j + Std_k}{|Cor_{i,j}| + |Cor_{i,k}| + |Cor_{j,k}|} \qquad (2)$$

OIF = The optimum combination of three bands.
Std_i = The standard deviation of band i.
$|Cor_{i,j}|$ = The absolute value of the correlation coefficient of band i and band j.
Firstly, the number of possible combinations of three bands is determined, for 6 bands there are 20 combinations. Then, for each combination of three bands, the OIF is calculated. Finally, the OIF values are ranked and band 7, band 4 and band 3 with the highest *OIF* is the optimum combination. Band 4 and band 3 usually used to calculate Normalized Difference Vegetation Index (NDVI) indicates live green plants in lakes. The color composite image of band 7, band4 and band 3 is shown in fig. 5. Comparing with the fig. 2, it provides a contrast to different water quality.

4.2 Spectra of different water quality

In order to compare spectra of different water quality, typical water pixels are selected from five lakes respectively using regions of interest tools (ROIs) and the average spectra of different water quality from five lakes are calculate and illustrated (fig. 6). As shown from fig. 6, the reflectance value of band 2, band 3 and band 1 change dramaticlly according to different water quality, which are relate to the water pollutant of different lakes.

Fig. 5. The color composite image of band 7 (Red), band 4 (Green) and band 3 (Blue).

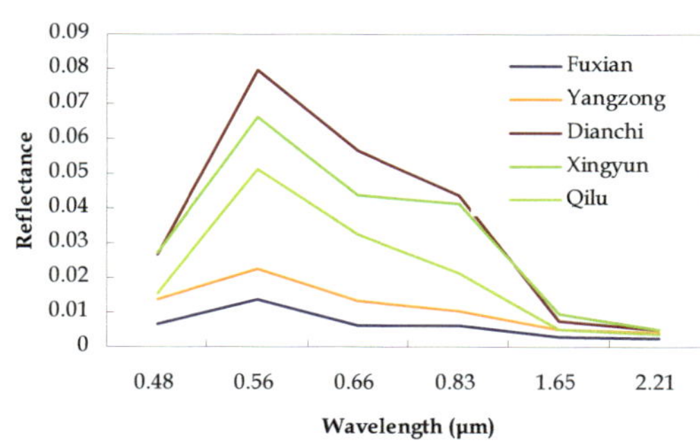

Fig. 6. Average spectra of different water quality from five lakes.

4.3 Stepwise multiple linear regression analysis of water quality level

Water quality is physical, chemical and biological characteristics of water. Water quality standards vary significantly due to different environmental conditions, ecosystems, and intended human uses. Due to the complexity of water quality, there are many types of measurements of water quality indicators. In this paper, according to spectra of different water quality, the water quality is classfied into six level. Typical sample training data are selected based on their spectra from five lakes using regions of interest tools (ROIs). Average spectra of training data in different level are shown in fig. 7. The sixth level is the average spectrum of alga in lakes. As shown from fig. 7, with the increase of pollutant, the reflectance of bands increases. The average spectrum of level 1 is similar to the spectrum of distilled water.

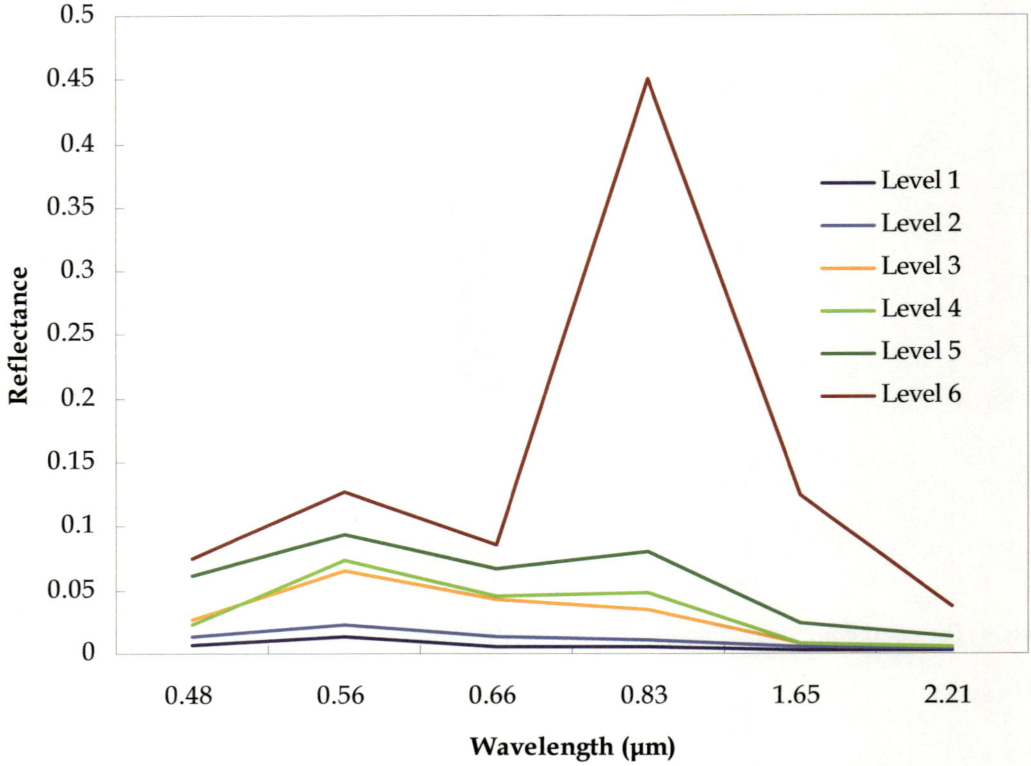

Fig. 7. Average spectra of sample training data in different water quality level.

The relationship between water quality and the reflectance is analyzed using stepwise multiple linear regression analysis (Hocking, 1976). Water quality level fitting formula using all sample training data is as follows:

$$\text{Water quality level} = \rho_1 * 7.26 + \rho_2 * 25.75 + \rho_3 * 17.14 + 0.80 \qquad (3)$$

Where:

ρ_i = The reflectance of ETM+ band *i*.

In the automatic procedure of stepwise multiple linear regression analysis, the important variables are band 2, band 3, band 1, band 7, band 5 and band 4 in sequence. The variance contributions of band 7, band 5 and band4 are less, so only band 1, band 2 and band3 are preserved in the formula. The correlation coefficient between sample data outcomes and predictive values calculated by formula (3) is 0.98. Therefore, the formula (3) is used to assess water quality. Firstly, the reflectance of bands is calculated using band math algorithm and the grey sum image is obtained. Secondly, the density slice method is applied to the processed grey imagery and the water quality level image is outputed. Finally, the result image is projected and outputed (fig. 8).

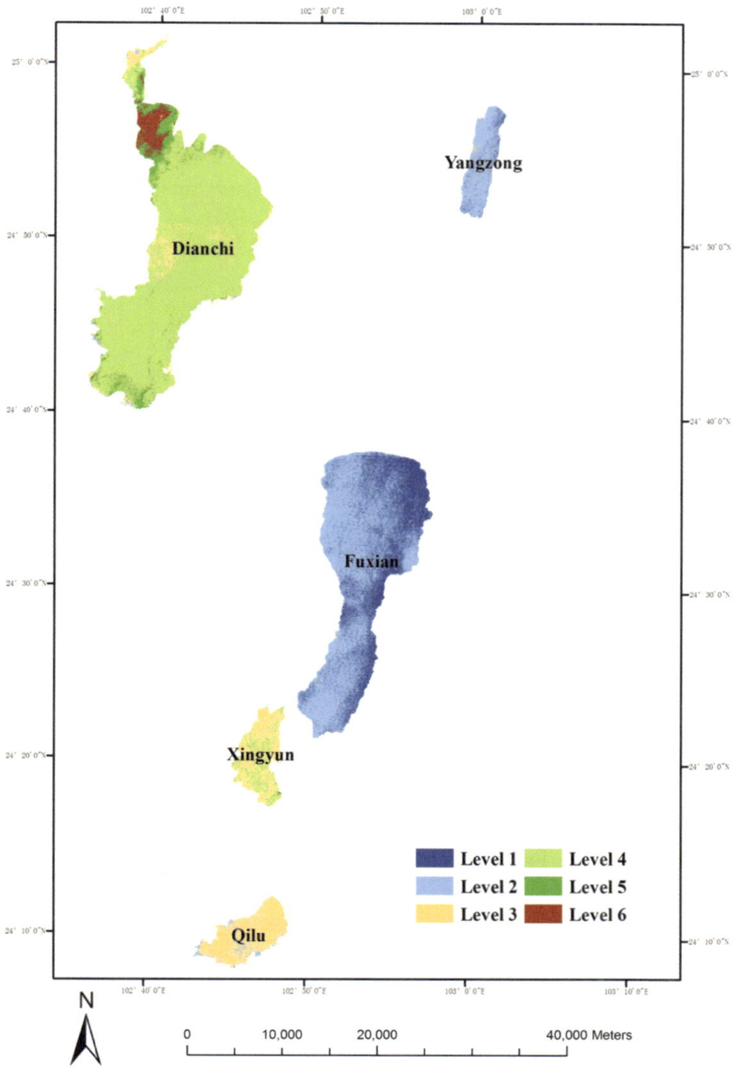

Fig. 8. The water quality monitoring image of lakes.

5. Results and discussions

In this paper, Landsat ETM+ imagery was used to monitors water quality of lakes near Kunming city in the southwest China. The water quality is distinguished with six levels from no pollution to contamination seriously. According to the stepwise multiple linear regression analysis formula, ETM+ band 1, band 2 and band 3 are close correlated with water quality. As shown from fig. 8, the water quality of Fuxian and Yangzong lakes are the best, and Dianchi and Xingyun lake are the worst, Qilu lake is in the middle. They are consistent with average spectra of five lakes water. The water quality level of Dianchi and Xingyun lakes are greater than 5, which has become highly polluted and eutrophic with serious algae problems. The pollution of Qilu lake is to some degree. Suitable water pollution controls and provention for lakes will be needed.

6. Acknowledgment

This study was jointly supported by the NSFC of Yunnan province, China (KKSA200921019), Scientific Research Foundation of Kunming University of Science and Technology (KKZ3200821048), China Postdoctoral Science Foundation (20100471687) and the innovation team of ore-forming dynamics and prediction of concealed deposits, Kunming University of Science and Technology, Kunming, China.

7. References

Alparslan, E., Aydöner, C., Tufekci, V. & Tüfekci, H. (2007). Water quality assessment at Ömerli Dam using remote sensing techniques. *Environmental Monitoring and Assessment,* Vol. 135, No. 1, 391-398.

Boken, V. K (2007). Linking landuse and groundwater quality in the Mississippi delta Using MODIS satellite data. *IEEE International Geoscience and Remote Sensing Symposium,* 5025-5027,

Brando, V. E. & Dekker, A. G. (2003). Satellite hyperspectral remote sensing for estimating estuarine and coastal water quality. *Geoscience and Remote Sensing, IEEE Transactions on,* Vol. 41, No. 6, 1378-1387.

Chavez, P. S.; Berlin, G. L. & Sowers, L. B. (1982). Statistical method for selecting Landsat MSS ratios. *Journal of Applied Photographic Engineering,* Vol. 8, No. 1, 22-30.

Chen, Q.; Zhang, Y. & Hallikainen, M. (2007). Water quality monitoring using remote sensing in support of the EU water framework directive (WFD): A case study in the Gulf of Finland. *Environmental Monitoring and Assessment,* Vol. 124, No. 1, 157-166.

Cooley, T., Anderson, G. P., Felde, G. W., Hoke, M. L., Ratkowski, A. J., Chetwynd, J. H., Gardner, J. A., Adler-Golden, S. M., Matthew, M. W., Berk, A., Bernstein, L. S., Acharya, P. K., Miller, D. & Lewis, P. (2002). FLAASH, a MODTRAN4-based atmospheric correction algorithm, its application and validation. *Geoscience and Remote Sensing Symposium,* 1414-1418,

Giardino, C., Brando, V. E., Dekker, A. G., Strömbeck, N. & Candiani, G. (2007). Assessment of water quality in Lake Garda (Italy) using Hyperion. *Remote Sensing of Environment,* Vol. 109, No. 2, 183-195.

Hadjimitsis D. & Clayton, C. (2009). Assessment of temporal variations of water quality in inland water bodies using atmospheric corrected satellite remotely sensed image data. *Environmental Monitoring and Assessment,* Vol. 159, No. 1-4, 281-292.

He, W., Chen, S., Liu, X. & Chen, J. (2008). Water quality monitoring in a slightly-polluted inland water body through remote sensing — Case study of the Guanting Reservoir in Beijing, China. *Frontiers of Environmental Science & Engineering in China,* Vol. 2, No. 2, 163-171.

Hocking, R. R. (1976). The Analysis and Selection of Variables in Linear Regression. *Biometrics,* Vol. 32, No. 1, 1-49.

Kondratye, K. Y.; Pozdnyakov, D. V. & Pettersson, L. H. (1998). Water quality remote sensing in the visible spectrum. *International Journal of Remote Sensing,* Vol. 19, No. 5, 957-979.

Koponen, S., Pulliainen, J., Kallio, K. & Hallikainen, M. (2002). Lake water quality classification with airborne hyperspectral spectrometer and simulated MERIS data. *Remote Sensing of Environment,* Vol. 79, No. 1, 51-59.

Liu, J. Q. & Zhang, Y. X. (1996). Distribution and degradation of Alkyl benzene sodium sulfonate, and its harmful effect on carp in Dianchi Lake. *GeoJournal,* Vol. 40, No. 1, 219-227.

Maillard, P. & Pinheiro Santos, N. A. (2008). A spatial-statistical approach for modeling the effect of non-point source pollution on different water quality parameters in the Velhas river watershed - Brazil. *Journal of Environmental Management,* Vol. 86, No. 1, 158-170.

Martinez, J. M., Guyot, J. L., Cochonneau, G. & Seyler, F. (2007). Surface water quality monitoring in large rivers with MODIS data application to the amazon basin. *IEEE International Geoscience and Remote Sensing Symposium,* 4566-4569,

Pozdnyakov, D., Shuchman, R., Korosov, A. & Hatt, C. (2005). Operational algorithm for the retrieval of water quality in the Great Lakes. *Remote Sensing of Environment,* Vol. 97, No. 3, 352-370.

Richards, J. A. (1999). *Remote Sensing Digital Image Analysis,* Springer-Verlag. Berlin

Ritchie, J.; Zimba, P. & Everitt, J. (2003). Remote sensing techniques to assess water quality. *Photogrammetric Engineering and Remote Sensing,* Vol. 69, No. 6, 695-704.

Ritchie, J. C.; Schiebe, F. R. & McHenry, J. R. (1976). Remote sensing of suspended sediment in surface water. *Photogrammetric Engineering & Remote Sensing,* Vol. 42, No. 1539-1545.

Seyhan, E. & Dekker, A. (1986). Application of remote sensing techniques for water quality monitoring. *Aquatic Ecology,* Vol. 20, No. 1, 41-50.

Verma, V., Setia, R., Sharma, P. & Singh, H. (2008). Geoinformatics as a tool for the assessment of the impact of ground water quality for irrigation on soil health. *Journal of the Indian Society of Remote Sensing,* Vol. 36, No. 3, 273-281.

Wang, X. J. & Ma, T. (2001). Application of Remote Sensing Techniques in Monitoring and Assessing the Water Quality of Taihu Lake. *Bulletin of Environmental Contamination and Toxicology,* Vol. 67, No. 6, 863-870.

Wang, Y., Xia, H., Fu, J. & Sheng, G. (2004). Water quality change in reservoirs of Shenzhen, China: detection using LANDSAT/TM data. *Science of the Total Environment,* Vol. 328, No. 1, 195-206.

Wen, X. & Yang, X. (2009a). Change detection from remote sensing imageries using spectral change vector analysis. *Asia-Pacific Conference on Information Processing (APCIP 2009),* 189-192, IEEE Computer Society, Shenzhen, China

Wen, X. & Yang, X. (2009b). A new change detection method for two remote sensing images based on spectral matching. *International Conference on Industrial Mechatronics and Automation (ICIMA 2009),* 89-92, IEEE Computer Society, Chengdu, China

Zhang, X., Zhang, S., Ying, W., Ren, T., Xu, C., Zhong, Z. & Zhang, S. (1996). Heavy metals pollution on the sediments in lakes Dianchi, Erhai and Poyanghu and historical records. *GeoJournal,* Vol. 40, No. 1, 201-208.

Zhang, Y. Z., Pulliainen, J. T., Koponen, S. S. & Hallikainen, M. T. (2003). Water quality retrievals from combined Landsat TM data and ERS-2 SAR data, in the Gulf of Finland. *IEEE Transactions on Geoscience and Remote Sensing,* Vol. 41, No. 3, 622-629.

10

Applications of Data Mining to Diagnosis and Control of Manufacturing Processes

Marcin Perzyk, Robert Biernacki, Andrzej Kochanski,
Jacek Kozlowski and Artur Soroczynski
Warsaw University of Technology
Poland

1. Introduction

In the majority of manufacturing companies large amounts of data are collected and stored, related to designs, products, equipment, materials, manufacturing processes etc. Utilization of that data for the improvement of product quality and lowering manufacturing costs requires extraction of knowledge from the data, in the form of conclusions, rules, relationships and procedures. Consequently, a rapidly growing interest in DM applications in manufacturing organizations, including the development of complex DM systems, can be observed in recent years (Chen et al. 2004; Chen et al. 2005; Dagli & Lee, 2001; Hur et al., 2006; Malh & Krikler, 2007; Tsang et al., 2007). A comprehensive and insightful characterization of the problems in manufacturing enterprises, as well as the potential benefits from the application of data mining (DM) in this area was presented in (Shahbaz et al., 2006). Examples and general characteristics of problems related to the usage of data mining techniques and systems in a manufacturing environment can be found in several review papers (Harding et al., 2006; Kusiak, 2006; Wang, 2007).

Application of DM techniques can bring valuable information, both for designing new processes and for control of currently running ones. Designing the processes and tooling can be assisted by varied computer tools, including simulation software, expert systems based on knowledge acquired from human experts, as well as the knowledge extracted semi automatically by DM methods. The proper choice of the manufacturing process version and its parameters allows to reduce the number of necessary corrections resulting from simulation and/or floor tests. The knowledge obtained by DM methods can significantly contribute to the right decision making and optimum settings of the process parameters. In the design phase two main forms of knowledge may be particularly useful: the decision logic rules in the form: 'IF (conditions) THEN (decision class)' and the regression-type relationships. Although the latter have been widely utilized before the emergence of DM methods (e.g. in the form of empirical formulas) and the rules created by the human experts were also in use, the computational intelligence (CI) methods (learning systems) have remarkably enhanced possibilities of the knowledge extraction and its quality.

For the manufacturing process control many varied methods are used, ranging from paper Statistical Process Control (SPC) charts to automated closed loop systems. In spite of the degree of automation of the control system it is always essential to identify the input process parameters that can be effectively used to control the process, to develop the appropriate relationships between process parameters as inputs and process results as outputs, as well as to understand and diagnose manufacturing process problems. Just like in the design stage, the input-output dependencies can be of various types, including classification and regression models. A more specific task is prediction of process parameters or product characteristics on the basis of current and past values recorded as a sequence type data, i.e. the time–series analysis.

It should be noticed that for diagnosis and control of manufacturing processes a particular type of information is extremely important: relative significances of process variables, including possible interactions existing among them. In particular, determination of the most significant process parameters can help to detect root causes of deteriorating product quality. The idea is that the process variables which are found to be the most significant for a given quality parameter, e.g. percent of defective parts, should be regarded as potential causes of the quality decline. It is important to point out that statistical methods which have been used extensively in manufacturing industry for many years, such as the SPC tools, are not capable of providing that kind of knowledge. They are useful in detecting the appearance of abnormalities of the process in the form of excessive variations of process parameters, but they are not capable of indicating their causes. Finding the most important process parameters can also be useful in prediction of break-downs of machines, equipment etc., as well as in prediction of results of manufacturing process changes, including indication of optimal or critical process parameters that can be used for the process control. Also, finding the least significant process variables can be valuable. Variations of such variables can be allowed without consequences in product quality, which can lead to remarkable savings due to reduction of time and costs of the inspections.

DM includes various types of tools of which the CI methods are certainly best suited for the tasks described above. There is a variety of learning systems available, based on different principles, e.g. artificial neural networks (ANNs), support vector machines (SVMs), prediction or decision trees (DTs), including classification trees (CTs) and regression tress (RTs), as well as the systems dedicated to classification only, such as naïve Bayesian classifier (NBC) and those based on the rough sets theory (RST).

Models used in DM can be parametric or non-parametric. Non-parametric models differ from parametric ones in that the model structure is not specified a priori but is instead determined from data, e.g. in decision trees. The non-parametric models are essentially more suitable for knowledge discovery as the nature of the relationships hidden in the data is usually not known.

Making a right choice of a CI model is important, particularly in the construction of DM systems. However, there are few comparative studies available in the literature, addressing the above discussed issues, which could show the advantages and weakness of individual tools. The purpose of the present paper is to make an appraisal of several DM methods from the standpoint of their performances in the extraction of knowledge appropriate for diagnosis and control of manufacturing processes, including some new developments made by the present authors. The research was focused on the two main tasks appearing in the application of DM in manufacturing: determination of relative significances of input process variables and logic rules extraction.

2. General methodology

Selected methods discussed in the previous chapter were assessed with the use of simulated and industrial data sets. The synthetic data were obtained by assuming analytical formulas of the type Y=f(X1, X2, ...), from which, for random values of continuous-type input variables X1, X2, ..., the continuous-type dependent variable Y was calculated. Thus, the relationships hidden in the data are assumed and can be compared to those predicted by the models. A Gaussian-type noise was imposed on the input variables, with maximum deviation ±20%; that value was found to be characteristic of many real processes. For the classification models all the continuous values were converted to categorical ones, assuming the equal intervals method. Two numbers of categories were assumed: 5 and 10. In most cases, the sets comprising 1000 records were generated in this way. Three basic formulas were used, giving simulated data sets of the characteristics described below.

Sim 1, obtained from the basic formula: $Y=X1+2\cdot X2+3\cdot X3+4\cdot X4+5\cdot X5$; linearly increasing significances of variables, in additive manner, without interactions.

Sim 2, obtained from the basic formula: $Y=X1\cdot X2+X3+X4+X5$; strong interactions between two variables of equal significances, the remaining variables have significances equal to the joint significance of the first two, without interactions among them.

Sim 3, obtained from the basic formula: $Y=\tanh(0.1\cdot X1+0.2\cdot X2+0.4\cdot X3+0.8\cdot X4+1.6.X5)$; increasing significances of variables, an additive model with asymptotic output limit (saturation value) resulting in a specific form of interaction between all input variables.

Situations similar to those represented in the above relationships often appear in practice. For example, Sim 3 may reflect simultaneous action of several chemical elements, which change the alloy microstructure and properties in the same manner. These cannot exceed certain physical limits and the actual effect of each variable depends on the structure and properties produced by the other elements.

All the industrial data sets were related to metal casting processes. Ind 1, Ind 2 and Ind 3 data sets were collected in a regular production of ductile cast iron in a cooperating foundry; the numbers of records were 861.

Ind 1 correlates chemical composition of ductile cast iron, defined by 5 elements, often considered as most important for its microstructure and mechanical properties (Mn, Si, Cr, Ni and Cu), with the material tensile strength.

Ind 2 correlates chemical composition of ductile cast iron, defined by all 9 elements controlled in the foundry (C, Mn, Si, P, S, Cr, Ni, Cu and Mg), with its tensile strength.

Ind 3 correlates chemical composition of ductile cast iron, defined by 5 elements, as in Ind 1, with its grade, assumed as the output class variable with the following four values: '400/18', '500/07', 'special 500/07 with increased hardness' and 'not classified'.

The remaining two data sets: Ind 4 and Ind 5 were obtained as readouts from a semi-empirical nomograph, which permits to calculate solidification shrinkage of grey cast iron as a function of four variables: carbon contents C (5 different values - categories), sum of silicon and phosphorus content Si+P (4 values), casting modulus M (4 values) and pouring temperature Tpor (4 values). The outputs were the decisions concerning necessity and size of application of feeders to avoid the shrinkage defects. In Ind 4 data set the output, named 'Feeder', had 2 classes ('No' - when the volume change between pouring and the end of solidification was zero or positive and 'Yes' - when the overall volume change was negative). In the Ind 5 data set the output had 3 classes ('No', 'Small' and 'Large', dependent on the magnitude of the shrinkage). The numbers of records in these data sets was 190. The discretisation of the continuous - by nature - input variables was not required, as the readouts were made for selected, fixed values of these variables.

It is worth noticing that, unlike the previously described simulated and industrial data sets, Ind 4 and Ind 5 have an important feature: a very low level of noise, which could be only a result of inaccuracies in the readouts of the nomograph. Generally, the noise existing in typical production data, as well as the simulated data generated as described above, may result in their inconsistency, defined as the occurrence of different output variable values (decision classes) for an identical combination of input values. In Ind 4 and Ind 5 data sets such inconsistencies were absent.

The appropriate computations were partly made with the use of Statistica DataMiner commercial software (StatSoft, 2008). For the ANNs and RST-related computations the software developed by the present authors' was utilized.

The other methodology issues assumed in the present research are strongly problem-dependent and will be described in the following sections.

3. Relative significances of process input variables

Several approaches to the extraction of useful information from CI models have been proposed. Most of them utilize input - output type models, however, the association rules can also be used (e.g. Chen et al., 2005; Shahbaz et al., 2006). In the first case two basic approaches can be applied: 'decompositional', which is based on an analysis of the model's parameters, and 'pedagogical', which treats the model as a black-box, i.e. uses a specially designed interrogation procedure to obtain the desired information. In finding the relative importances of input variables based on interrogation of the model, the variable significance is usually defined as the degree in which its removal from the input variables, or setting its value at a constant level, increases the model's prediction error.

It is important that a significance definition used for the problems characterised in Section 1 should reflect the overall influence of an input variable on the output rather then the sensitivity of the output to that input. The sensitivity analysis returns the output changes due to small variations of input at particular levels of the input. In the opinion of the authors the approach assumed in the present work better meets the expectations of industrial practitioners, who would be interested in finding potentially the greatest overall effect of a process variable (or group of variables) on the process results.

Two basic types of the output variables can appear: numerical continuous, represented by real numbers (regression problem) and categorical, with values represented by classes expressed verbally or by integral numbers (classification problem). In the manufacturing environment the first type seems to occur more commonly and will be treated here in a more complex way, including the approach proposed by the present authors.

Output class variables can be of two types: nominal and ordinal. In many industrial applications the ordinal type variables are of particular interest as they can be used for expressing some uncertainties and approximations of the quantities involved. It is worth noticing that the widespread approach, especially in process control applications, is based on fuzzy logic, utilizing linguistic variables. However, utilization of the fuzzy calculus requires that the input - output relationships are assumed, based on human's knowledge or intuition, whereas the CI methods are capable of semi-automated finding such dependencies, using data collected in the normal production (Czogala et al., 1995).

3.1 Advanced significance analysis of input variables for regression-type tasks

Algorithms for finding relative significances of input variables and possible interactions among them, based on a direct understanding of variable importance, have been developed by the present authors. The significance factor for a single input or for a group of inputs is defined as the maximum difference of the output, which can be obtained by changing the value of the analysed input (or inputs). The two extremes of the output are found by the conjugate gradient method, with the starting points found by a specially developed procedure, permitting to avoid local minima in most cases. All the significances thus obtained are normalised by dividing them by the value obtained for the most significant variable (or group of variables).

The definition of interaction coefficient between variables in a selected group is expressed as the ratio of the significance factor of the group to the arithmetic mean of significances of all the single variables from the group. However, the latter are taken as their minimum values with respect to the rest of the variables in the group, thus eliminating the 'assistance' of the other variables in the group. The synergy coefficient is defined as the ratio of the significance factor of the group to the sum of the above defined significances of all the single variables from the group, minus 1. It expresses (in percents) the degree in which simultaneous action of several inputs are larger than the sum of actions of the individual inputs working independently. Similarly like in the algorithms used for the relative significance factors, the significances of the single input signals within the group used for interaction and synergy computations are determined from the two extremes of the output found by the conjugate gradient method. The minima of these significances with respect to the rest of the variables in the group are found, in external computation loops, by the simulated annealing method.

The significance factors of a single input variable or a selected group of variables, as well as the interaction factors between variables within the group, are calculated repeatedly a number of times for the other variables set at random levels. The final values of significance or interaction factors are calculated as their arithmetic averages. The magnitude of the scatter of the significance factor of a given input resulting from the other inputs' levels can be a measure of the possible interactions with the other input variables.

The above algorithms were implemented using MLP-type ANNs, with one hidden layer with the number of neurons equal to the number of the network's inputs in most cases. That type of ANN architecture was found to be effective and accurate in a number of preliminary tests. The significance factors of single variables were also calculated using SVM and RT models. Some results were also compared to those obtained from one--way ANOVA, in which the significance factor was defined as the normalised F statistics values calculated for dependency between a considered independent variable and the dependent variable. The definition of interaction coefficient between two variables tested in the present work is based on the test statistics F for the interaction of the two variables in the two--way ANOVA. Further details concerning the above presented definitions and methodology can be found in (Perzyk et al., 2008).

In Fig. 1 comparisons of the relative significance factors of single variables, obtained from various regression models and ANOVA for simulated data sets, are presented. These results generally agree with the expectations, i.e. the assumed, hidden relationships in the data. The most accurate values were obtained form ANNs and SVMs. The predictions of RTs and ANOVA are much less accurate and tend to remarkably underestimate significances of the less important variables. Dispersions of relative significance factors, expressed by their average deviations resulting from randomly set values of other variables, can be observed for all models. However, negligible scatters for variables with no interactions (all variables in Sim 1 and X3, X4 and X5 in Sim 2) are observed for ANNs and SVMs only, while RTs evidently revealed non-existent interactions between input variables. It is worth noticing that the observed differences between the relative significances of the equally strong variables (such as X1 and X2 or X3, X4 and X5 in Sim 2) are mainly a result of variations which appear in the training data set due to the artificial noise imposed on the data. It was found that different training sessions of ANNs or different settings for RTS induction (for a given generation) lead to much smaller discrepancies of the significance factors.

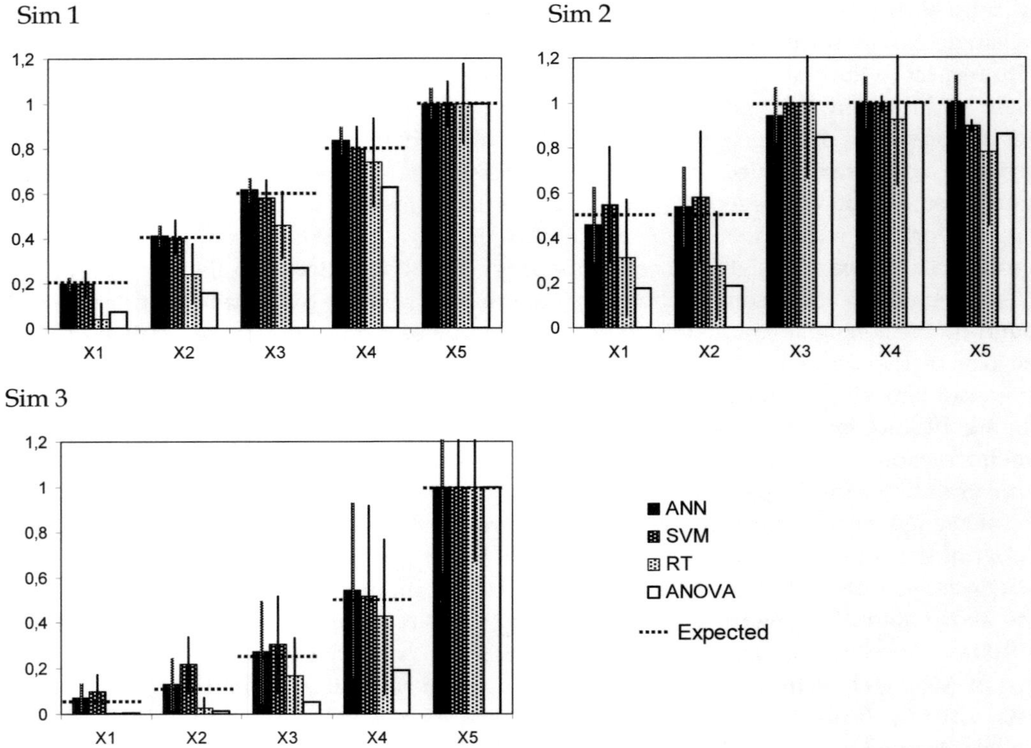

Fig. 1. Relative significance factors obtained from CI regression models and ANOVA for the simulated data sets; the scatter bars are calculated as average deviations resulting from randomly set values of the other variables

For the real, industrial data the expected values of relative significances, hidden in the data, are often not known or can be evaluated only in a qualitative manner. The data sets related to ductile cast iron production (Ind 1, Ind 2 and Ind 3) were collected in a particular plant, where some of the chemical elements could be kept at the levels which do not allow them to exhibit their full effect on the mechanical properties of the alloy. The only important information obtained from that foundry was that copper was the main element used for control of the microstructure and, consequently, the tensile strength of the alloy, and that it can be expected to have the largest significance. For Ind 2 all the models shown in Fig. 2

pointed at copper as the most significant alloying element. Different predictions from different models were obtained for the other elements, however, in the case of the probably least significant variables, such as C, P, S and Mg, all models were also fairly conformable. The control of these elements could be possibly limited or even eliminated in that particular plant.

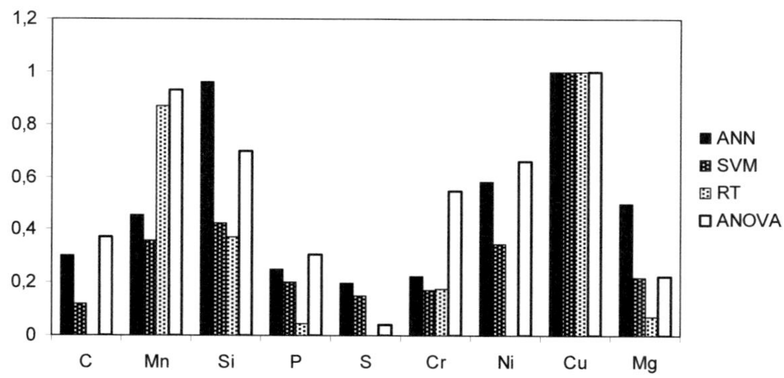

Fig. 2. Relative significance factors for the Ind 1 data set (tensile strength of ductile cast iron vs its chemical composition defined by 9 elements)

The above presented results, especially for the simulated data sets, indicated that performance of ANN and SVM models is remarkably better compared to RT and ANOVA. Further tests, concerning significances of groups of variables and interactions among them were made using the neural models only. It was found that the adjustment of appropriate settings for SVM models can be troublesome and sometimes may lead to wrong results. Despite the fact that neural models are in principle ambiguous models, in the sense that a change of the network architecture or each training session may lead to different results, they seem to be more predictable compared to SVM.

The significance factors for groups of variables were calculated for all possible combinations of the variables appearing in the simulated data sets. The tendencies of the predictions agree well with expectations in all cases. Exemplary results are shown in Fig. 3. The positive deviations, appearing for most of the variable combinations, result from the fact that all the calculated values were normalised in relation to the most significant group, which is clearly the group including all the variables. It was found that the extreme responses of the neural model, which are used for the significance computations of that group, are attenuated, i.e. the maximum response is lesser and the minimum response is larger then expected. Thus, the incompatible values, such as observed in Fig. 3, result only from the inaccuracies of the maximum significances. This behaviour of the trained network is a result of the structure of the training data: it is very unlikely that the extreme values of all five inputs, necessary to obtain the extreme value of the output, will be represented in the data set. The graphs presented in Fig. 3 also illustrate typical scatter resulting from different training sessions of ANNs.

The interaction and synergy coefficients obtained from ANNs for pairs of variables were correct in all cases (selected results are presented in Fig. 4). It should also be noticed that the proposed method offers an easy way for the estimation of interactions and synergies among larger number of variables.

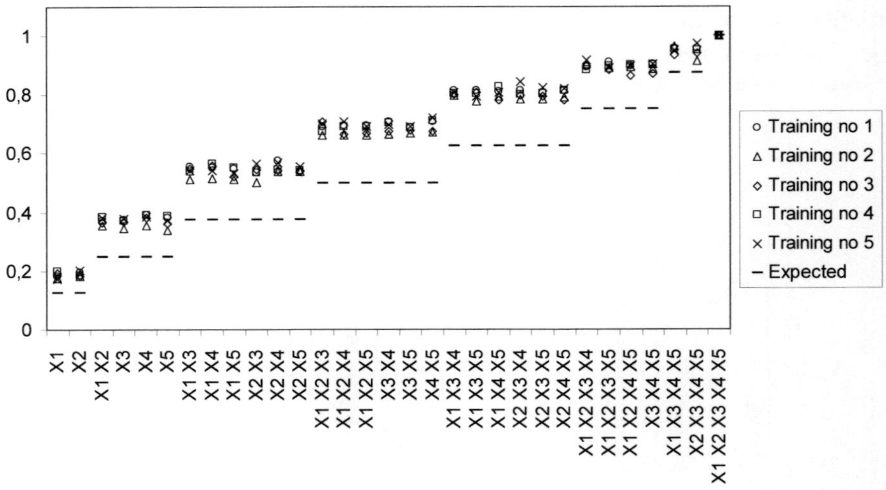

Fig. 3. Comparison of relative significance factors for all possible groups (combinations) of input variables obtained from ANNs for Sim 2 synthetic data

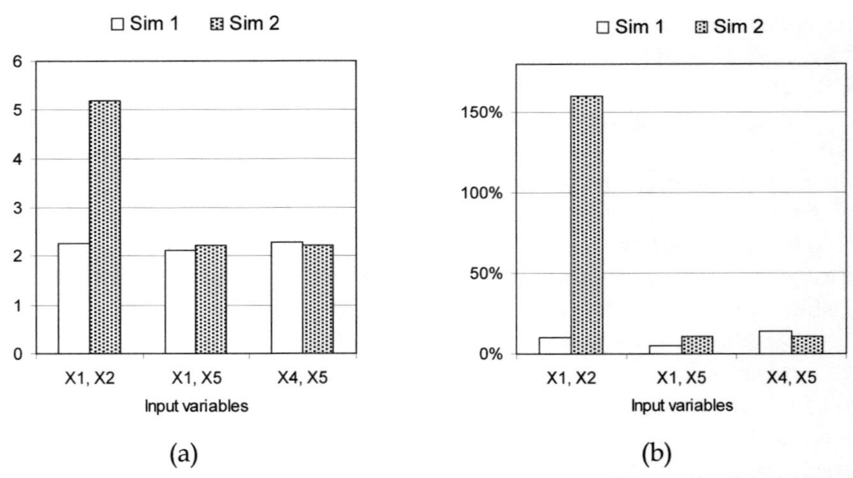

Fig. 4. Assessment of the interaction and synergy coefficients obtained from a trained ANN by the developed methodology: (a) – interaction coefficients, (b) – corresponding synergy coefficients

Results obtained from the two-factor ANOVA for Sim 2 data sets, also used for the ANNs-based computations, are presented in Table 1. It can be seen that the p-value does not indicate the existence of any interactions. Just like in the single variable analysis, this is probably a result of larger error variance appearing in the denominator of the expression for F, leading to the high p-value. This observation means that evident interactions between selected variables in the presence of other variables may not be detected by the ANOVA-based method even when the potential significance of the interacting variables is comparable to the other variables.

Input variables	F statistics value	p-value	Interaction detected	Interaction expected
X1, X2	1.221	0.1013	**No**	**Yes**
X4, X5	0.947	0.6038	No	No

Table 1. Interactions-related parameters obtained from two-factor ANOVA for Sim 2 data set

The above presented results have proved that the proposed methodology of finding relative significances of input variables is not only accurate and reflects the preferred understanding of the variable importance, but also offers additional features related to interactions and synergies. It is worth adding that the decompositional approach, based on the weight values of ANNs, e.g. the Garson's proposal, turned out to be decidedly unsatisfactory (Perzyk et al., 2008). The network learns in a different way during each training session and large differences in the network weights are the source of large differences in significance factors based solely on their values. Factors based on the present algorithm (specific interrogations of the network) give stable and accurate values, though the weights are naturally also used in the calculations of the network responses.
In Fig. 5 comparisons between various definitions of variable significance are presented, using RT models.

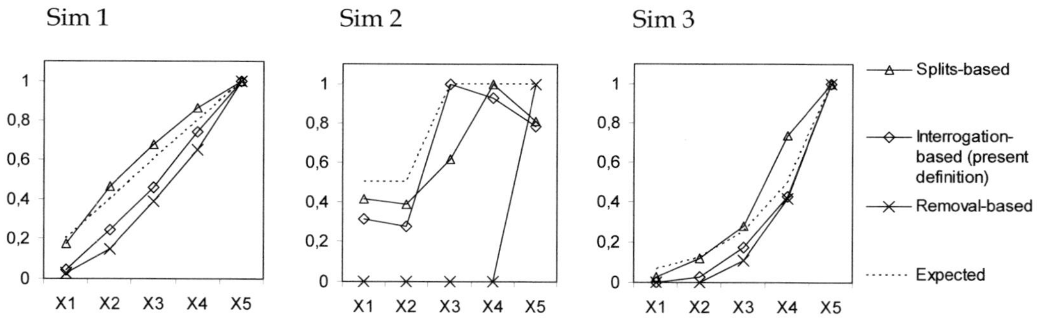

Fig. 5. Relative significances obtained for their various definitions from RT models

The RTs (and CTs, utilised in the next section) were created and evaluated with a use of the well known C&RT algorithm (Breiman et al., 1984), included in the commercial software Statistica; details of the computational procedures can also be found in the software manual (StatSoft, 2008). For the purpose of computing the relative significances of input variables, two different stopping criteria were tried out: the Statistica's default, giving relatively 'small' trees, and the user criterion of minimum records in leaves equal to 5, leading to relatively 'large' trees. It was found that for significances based on drop in node impurity in potential splits (details can be found in (StatSoft, 2008)), which is a widely used method for the estimation of the variable importances from decision trees, better results were obtained for 'small' trees. In contrast, for the significance based on classification error increase due to removal of a given variable, the 'large' trees turned out to be generally better. For all the results presented further, the settings giving better accuracies were used.
The results obtained from RTs show that the method based on the increase of the prediction error due to the removal of a given input variable may lead to very poor results. The best

accuracies of the variable significances were obtained from the approach based on split quality. However, these results are still worse, compared to the methodology proposed by the present authors and implemented with ANNs or SVMs.
The successful application of advanced regression models to finding the most significant process variables requires some additional comments. First, the computation times are long for the proposed algorithm, resulting from necessity of finding extremes of multivariable functions. Second, in some situations, only small data sets, i.e. sets including a very limited number of training examples, are available. This situation is typical for many machine break-down problems where failures are rare but costly. ANNs are demanding from the point of view of the amount of training data as the number of the model parameters (network's weights) are large and the number of training examples should be at least two times greater then the number of weights to obtain reliable results, without overfitting. The other types of models could be more suitable in such cases.

3.2 Assessment of significances of process input variables for classification tasks

For manufacturing-related problems, CTs are probably the most frequently used tools for knowledge extraction from data (e.g. (Chen et al., 2005; Huang & Wu, 2006; Hur et al., 2006; Koonce et al., 1997; Rokach & Maimon, 2006; Wang, 2007)), whereas the RST-based methods seem to be their newer alternative (e.g. (Kusiak & Kurasek, 2001; Sadoyan et al., 2006; Shen et al., 2000; Tseng et al., 2004)). Both algorithms are relative simple, especially compared to neural or fuzzy-neural systems, and easy to interpret by the users. Both of them treat the data in a natural way, however, they are based on completely different principles and algorithms.
The practical aspects of application of these tools are also different. The computation times necessary for CTs are generally short and the interpretation of rules obtained from CT can be facilitated by the graphical representation of the trees. The RST theory may require long computational times and may lead to much larger number of rules constituting the model, compared to CTs. It should be noticed, that whereas CTs are widely spread both in handbooks and in commercially available software, the RST can be rather seldom found, except for scientific literature.
A RST-based procedure, oriented at generation of full set of logic rules, was written by the present authors with a somewhat similar approach as used in the 'Explore' algorithm (Stefanowski & Vanderpooten, 2001). First, all the combinations of single input variables appearing in the data are placed in the rules (i.e. rules including only one condition are generated) and their confidences are calculated. Then the further conditions are added, providing the confidence of a rule thus obtained is increased, compared to the rule with shorter conditional part. The relative significances of input variables were calculated in a typical way, i.e. on the basis of the reduction of the so called positive region of data (i.e. giving rules of 100% confidence) resulting from removing a given variable. More details concerning RST computations can be found in (Polkowski, 2002). Details of methodology applied for CTs were presented in the previous section.
The relative significances of input variables were also calculated using the statistical method appropriate for discrete type variables, based on contingency tables. The Cramer's V statistics was used as a measure of significance.
In Fig. 6 comparisons of the calculated relative significances with the expected ones are shown and in Fig. 7 the average errors, defined as absolute differences between calculated

and expected values, are presented for several cases. It can be seen that for all the simulated data sets with 1000 records the CT predictions are very poor, compared to RST and the statistic method: not only the errors are much higher but it is also important that CTs often do not reflect the expected tendencies of the variable significances. However, the good performance of RST and statistical method is not confirmed for small data sets.

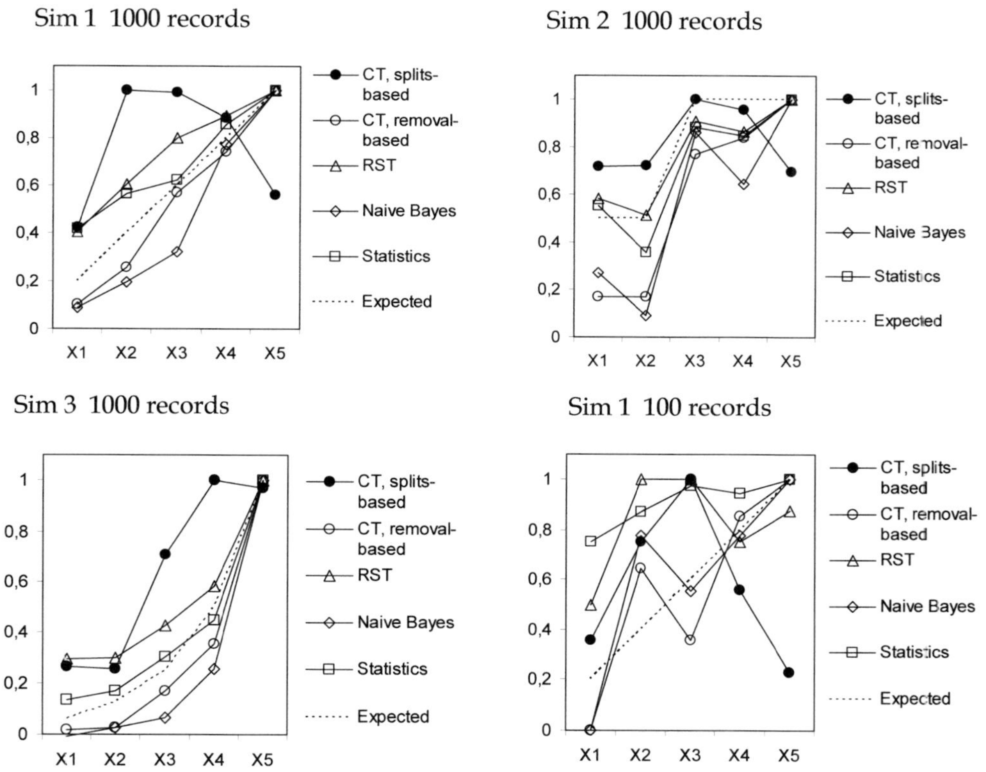

Fig. 6. Relative significances of input variables, obtained by various methods and expected, for simulated data sets with the assumed number of categories equal 5

As mentioned earlier, for the industrial data the expected values of relative significances are generally not known. The expected largest significance of copper was confirmed by more precise regression modelling presented in Fig. 2, which allowed to avoid conversion of the real numbers to categories. In Fig. 8 the results obtained for categorical type variables are presented (assuming 5 input variables) and in Fig. 9 the results for 9 chemical elements are shown, together with the above mentioned results obtained from the neural regression model - for comparison purposes.

It can be seen that for the case of 5 elements assumed as inputs and tensile strength as output (Fig. 8 left) the three methods brought generally divergent results and only the statistical approach pointed at copper contents as the most significant variable. When the ductile iron grade was assumed as the output (Fig. 8 right) the results obtained by the three methods are fairly similar and indicate copper as a significant element.

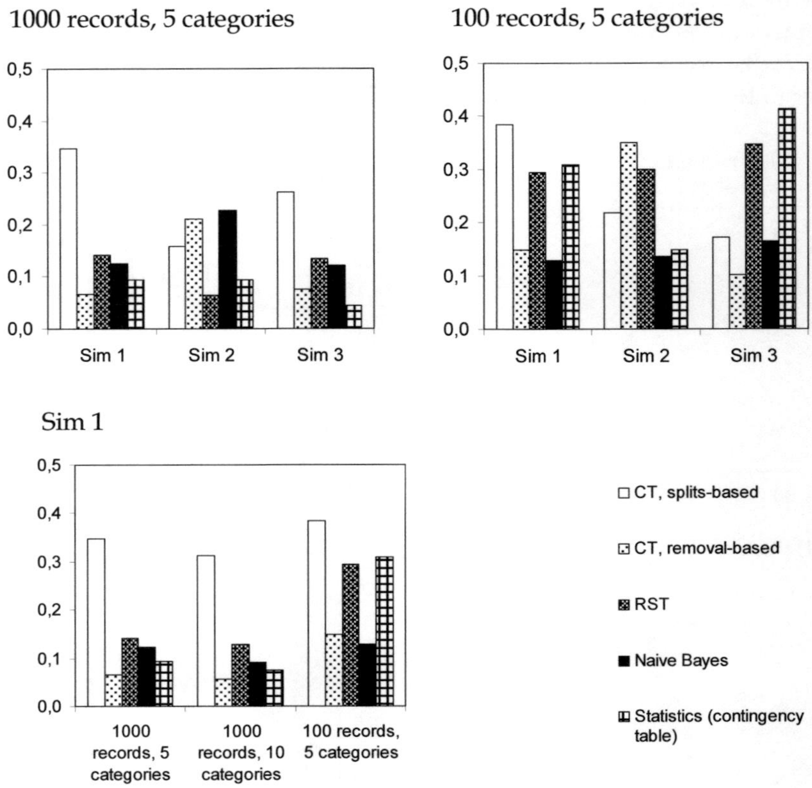

Fig. 7. Average errors of relative significances obtained by various methods and different numbers of records and categories

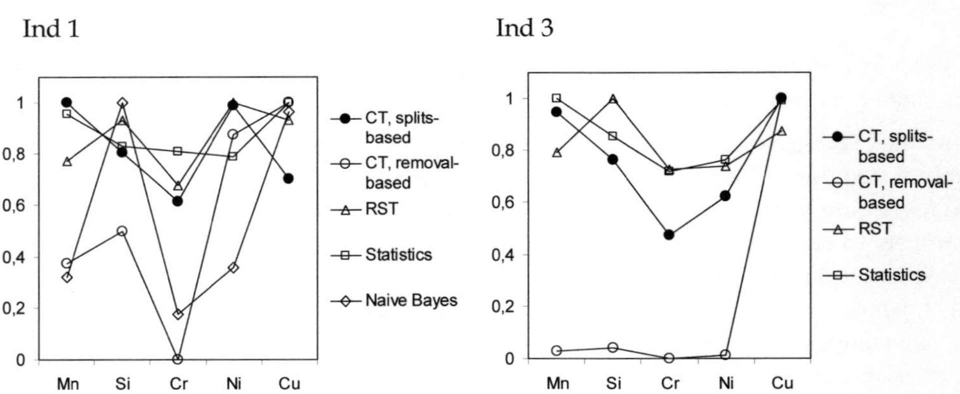

Fig. 8. Relative significances of input variables, obtained by various methods for two industrial data sets related to ductile iron production: Ind 1 – tensile strength assumed as the output (5 categories), Ind 3 – alloy grade assumed as the output (4 classes)

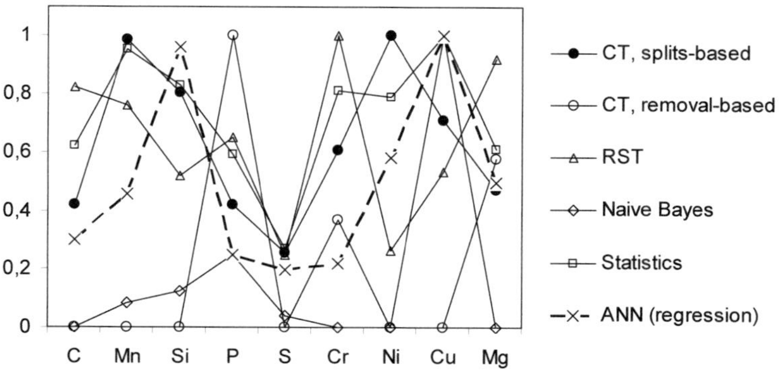

Fig. 9. Relative significances of input variables, obtained by various methods for Ind 2 data set - ductile iron tensile strength assumed as the output (5 categories, solid lines) and obtained from regression neural model for all continuous variables (dotted line)

For the case of 9 elements assumed as inputs and tensile strength as output (Fig. 9) the three methods studied in the present work give differentiated predictions for most of the input variables (except sulphur as the least significant element and manganese as a very important one). None of the present methods pointed at copper as the most significant element, as indicated by the regression analysis (Fig. 2). It is important to notice, that the latter have also shown divergent results for some variables, e.g. Mn and Si.

Ind 4 Ind 5

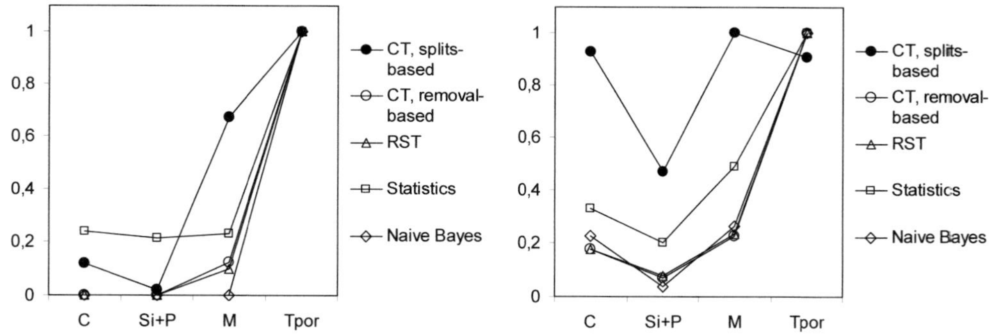

Fig. 10. Relative significances of input variables, obtained by various methods for two industrial data sets related to the feeding of grey cast iron castings: Ind 4 - requirement of feeder application assumed as the output (2 categories), Ind 5 - requirement and size of feeder assumed as the output (3 classes)

In Fig. 10 the results for two data sets related to feeding of grey cast iron castings (Ind 4 and Ind 5) are shown. The industrial experience indicates that the alloy chemical composition, commonly expressed by its carbon content and the sum of silicon and phosphorus contents, has a minor effect on shrinkage and, consequently, feeding requirements. The main influencing factors should be the pouring temperature, which directly determines the magnitude of volume change from pouring to the solidification onset, and the casting modulus which expresses the casting cooling rate, affecting kinetics of the volume changes during solidification. The results obtained by all the three methods fully confirmed these expectations for the case of two output classes (Fig. 5a). However, for the more complex output (Fig. 5b), the CTs predictions based on drop in node impurity in potential splits appeared to be very far from the expectations.

The results presented in this section indicate that for the simulated, categorical-type data, identification of significances of process parameters by the RST–based systems generally appeared to be much more precise and reliable, compared to CTs. The widely used statistical method, based on contingency tables, also demonstrated a good performance and turned out to be the best in most cases. This substantial advantage of RST–based and statistical methods was partly confirmed by the real data, related to foundry production. However, this general observation does not concern small data sets, for which the errors of those two methods increased 2 to 3 times, compared to the corresponding large sets. These errors were comparable to those obtained from CTs and may be regarded as non–acceptable for many applications.

4. Assessment of knowledge rule systems obtained from RST and CTs

4.1 Requirements for knowledge rules applicable to manufacturing processes

General requirements for knowledge rules which could be useful in manufacturing industry are rather obvious and similar to those for other areas of applications. First, the rules should be reliable, which means that there is a real chance that an application of the rule will bring the predicted result. This can be expressed by the rule quality parameters: confidence and support. Second, the rules should not be unnecessarily demanding, i.e. they should not comprise conditions which are not important, particularly redundant. Most algorithms used for knowledge extraction are first of all oriented at generation of a set of rules which best characterize the problem, i.e. the most reliable ones. However, in many industrial appliactions, particularly in manufacturing, some more specific requirements are relevant, related to design and development of new processes or control of currently running ones. Typical questions to be answered by using the rules can be formulated as follows:

- What are the most effective and reliable ways (i.e. process parameters – input values) to achieve an assumed result (class variable)?
- What would happen if we were not able to apply certain input values, i.e. what would we get if we use different ones? Do we still have a chance (and how big) to get the required result?
- What will be the predictions (and how reliable) in the case when some input variables cannot be specified, e.g. they may be out of control?
- What are all alternative ways to achieve our goal and how reliable are they?

Answering some of the above questions may result in the necessity of predictions for combination of parameters (input variables values) which have never appeared in the past (i.e. are not present in the data). It should be noticed that a user may be interested not only in obtaining a one-time prediction for such input values but also in having an appropriate rule or rules with estimated quality parameters.

The requirements for rule system and the knowledge extraction tools, suitable for manufacturing industry applications, are not only a consequence of the issues described above, but also the specificity of the available data. Typically, the number of independent variables (i.e. problem dimensionality) is not large, it seldom exceeds 10. The number of available records can vary within broad ranges, from only a few to many thousands, especially when the automatic data acquisition system is utilized. Typical industrial data are noisy, which results in their inconsistency, i.e. an occurrence of different output variable values for an identical combination of input values (conditions in a rule).

The characteristics of industrial process problems presented above imply that the following requirements for rule systems are essential or at least important:

- The rules should make use of all information in the data. This means, for example, that all output values (classes) must be represented. Even single cases can be valuable and therefore they should be reflected in the rule system.
- The rules should not contain redundant conditions as they can be misleading for the user.
- It should be possible to find a rule 'tailored' to the user specifications, including combinations of input variable values which are not represented in the data.
- Reliability of all rules should be evaluated, using the confidence and support as the primary parameters.

4.2 Characteristic behaviour of CTs and RST in rules extraction

A structure of a CT model is uniquely defined by a set of the logic expressions, corresponding to the knowledge rules. The nature of CT models, based on recursive partitioning of the data records, results in a set of conditions, which may be different from the combinations of input variables in the training data records. Some of the combinations appearing in the data set may be absent in the tree and vice versa, also some sequences of conditions occurring in the data may be abbreviated in the tree. The lack of some combinations of input values in CTs which are present in the training data, may result in the rule system in which some important rules are missing.

Another consequence is that CTs can give wrong predictions for training data. In the case of consistent data, this may be a result of improper tree structure, i.e. one in which the given combination of input values (attributes) is connected with a class of the output variable which is different from that which appears in the data. Partly incorrect predictions may be a consequence of the fact that CTs are able to give only one prediction for a given combination of input variables values. For noisy, inconsistent data it must always lead to a fraction of false predictions. Considering a CT as a knowledge rule system means that for that type of data CTs must omit some rules, potentially also important for a user. In particular, those omitted rules can be the only ones which give a certain output.

Rules obtained from CTs may include redundant conditions as the splitting variable used in the core must appear in all rules (generally, the splitting variable in a node must appear in all rules resulting from subsequent splits). In contrast, RST provides 'fitted' rules, i.e. without unnecessary conditions. That type of behaviour of both algorithms was commented in detail in (Kusiak & Kurasek, 2001).

It is essential that all of the above discussed drawbacks of the rule systems obtained from CTs are absent in the RST-based systems. Below, some results of numerical tests are presented, which demonstrate to what extent this fundamental difference may be significant. More details can be found in (Perzyk & Soroczynski, 2010).

Most of the methodology issues concerning CTs and RST computations were described at the beginning of Section 3.2. Slightly different settings were assumed here for CTs: in order to obtain possibly the largest choice of logic rules from the data, comparable to that available from RST, various splitting conditions, stopping criteria and pruning parameters were tried. The smallest trees which ensured the smallest fraction of false predictions for training sets were chosen.

In Fig. 11 the fractions of wrong predictions obtained from CTs for all consistent data subsets (i.e. all the discernible input values combinations pointing at one output value only) are shown, for selected data sets.

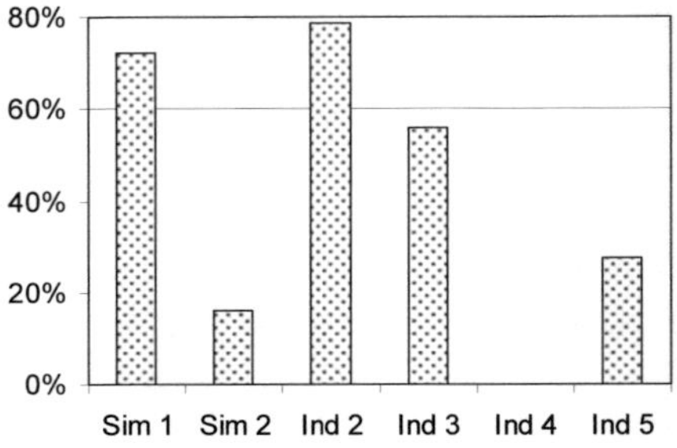

Fig. 11. Average fractions of false predictions obtained from CTs for consistent data subsets (including single records)

The general level of false predictions for the real data is much lower, compared to simulated data. An interpretation of this observation would require a deeper analysis of the data sets structures, e.g. representativeness of the classes of input and output variables.

In Fig. 12 some statistical information obtained for inconsistent data subsets is shown. It is interesting to note that in several cases CTs have pointed at the decision classes which are not predominant for the given combination of input values.

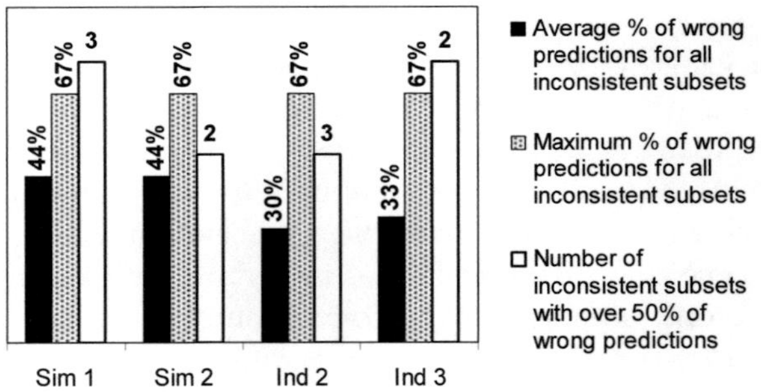

Fig. 12. Statistics of false predictions obtained from CTs for inconsistent data subsets

In Fig. 13 the fractions of rules included in CTs, which are not supported by the data, are shown, exhibiting quite large values in several cases. In principle, this can be a positive feature of CTs as such rules may be desired by a user. However, the usefulness of such rules may be questionable. First, because they do not necessarily meet the user's specific needs and second, because their reliability, defined by confidence and support, is not determined.

In Fig. 14 the numbers of rules absent in CTs, but extracted by RST, are presented, together with the total numbers of rules in CTs and from RST. The missing rules may be valuable for a user, as it was found that their confidences are relatively high and comparable with those

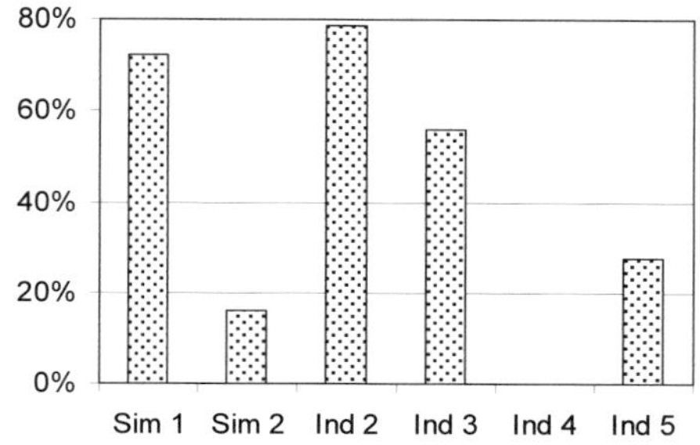

Fig. 13. Fractions of rules in CTs not supported by data

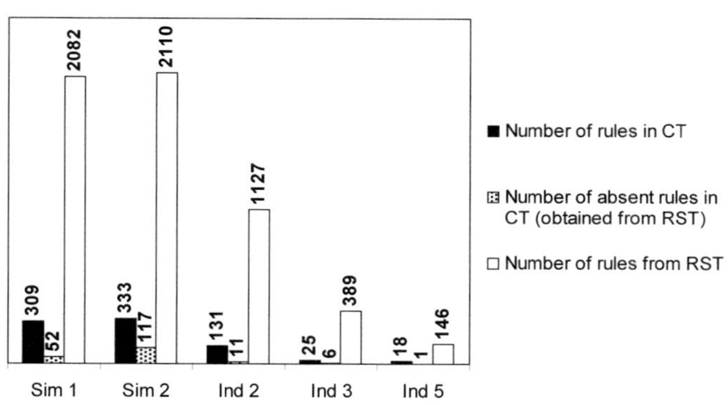

Fig. 14. Numbers of CTs rules and obtained from RST - total and missing in CTs systems obtained for the rules which are included in CTs. It is worth noticing that for some of the simulated data sets, some of the missing rules had 100% confidences.

In Fig. 15 fractions of CT rules with redundant conditions are shown. Obviously, the RST rules, taken as reference, had the same confidence values. It was also found that the average number of redundant conditions was similar to the number of important conditions. The conclusion is that the presence of redundant conditions in rules obtained from CTs, being a result of the nature of that type of models, may be their significant disadvantage.

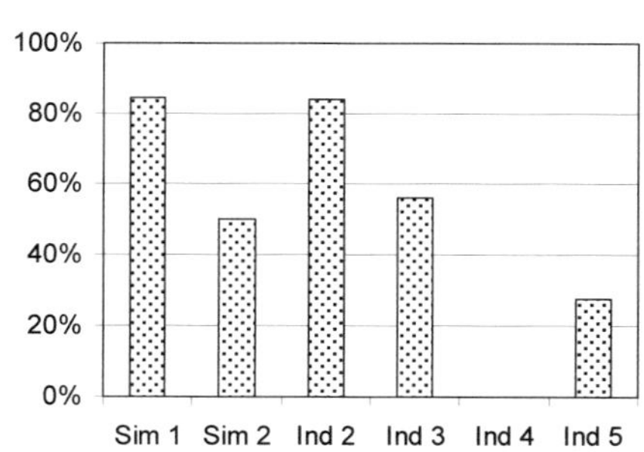

Fig. 15. Fractions of CTs rules with redundant conditions

An important feature of a rule system is its predictive capability for new data, i.e. combinations of the input variable values which have not appeared in the past. Some preliminary simple tests confirmed that for some cases CTs are unable to give predictions for the desired new input value combinations, as discussed earlier. Also, relatively large fractions of false predictions by RST-based rule systems were found; this requires treating this problem in more detail in a separate study.

In spite of that last finding, RST-based rule systems seem to be fundamentally better in almost every respect, compared to those obtained from CTs, including completeness, reliability and lack of redundant conditions of the rules.

5. Conclusion

This chapter reviews characteristic problems related to manufacturing and points out potential benefits from applications of DM in this area. Research results in two aspects of those applications are presented.

The first topic is determination of relative significances of process input variables and possible interactions among them, particularly helpful in finding root causes of product defects and optimum control of the manufacturing processes. A few different approaches and methods are discussed and evaluated, including various computational intelligence and statistical methods. Two types of data were used for testing: simulated, with assumed hidden relationships, and real, collected in manufacturing industry. For the regression-type tasks, the methodology proposed by the present authors, based on an interrogation algorithm of advanced models, in particular artificial neural networks, appeared to be fully successful. Some limitations of that approach are also discussed. For the classification-type tasks, the rough sets theory approach was found to be superior, however a simple statistical method, based on contingency tables, also demonstrated a good performance. Remarkable inaccuracies of relative significances obtained from decision trees, both in regression and classification tasks, have been shown.

The second topic of the research was knowledge rules extraction from recorded data, meeting the requirements related to control and diagnosis of manufacturing processes. The issues emphasized in the study covered completeness of the information included in the rule systems, avoidance of redundant conditions appearing in the rules and possibility of creation reliable rules for combinations of conditions absent in the training data. Two types of classification systems frequently used for knowledge extraction are compared: based on classification trees and rough sets theory. Decision trees have revealed several disadvantages as knowledge extraction tools for the applications where not only a characterization of a problem is required, but also detailed and precise rules are needed, according to actual, specific problems to be solved. For such applications the rules obtainable from RST turned out to be fundamentally better.

The study presented in this chapter pointed out at needs for further research in several areas. The methods of finding the relative significances of input variables for small data sets, both in regression and classification type tasks, require further analyses and improvements. Research aimed at development of the control systems for production processes, involving combinations of approaches utilizing rough sets theory and fuzzy sets, as suggested in (Czogala et al., 1995) would also be desirable.

Although the present paper is focused on industrial manufacturing processes, it can be expected that the obtained results, particularly those related to the significance analysis of input variables, can be useful also in other application areas.

6. Acknowledgment

This work was partly supported by grant N R07 0015 04 from Ministry of Science and Higher Education, Poland.

7. References

Breiman, L.; Friedman, J. H.; Olshen, R. A. & Stone. C. J. (1984). *Classification and regression trees*, Chapman & Hall/CRC, ISBN 0412048418, Boca Raton, Florida, USA

Chen, R. S.; Wu, R. C. & Chang, C. C. (2005). Using data mining technology to design an intelligent CIM system for IC manufacturing. in Proc. *Networking and Parallel/Distributed Computing and 1st ACIS International Workshop on Self-Assembling Wireless Networks*, pp. 70-75, ISBN 0769522947, United States, Towson

Chen, W. C.; Tseng, S. S.; Hsiao, K. R. & Liu, C. C. (2004). A data mining project for solving low-yield situations of semiconductor manufacturing. *IEEE Int Symp Semicond Manuf Conf Proc*, 129-134, ISSN 1523553X

Chen, W.C.; Tseng, S. S. & Wang, C. Y. (2005). A novel manufacturing defect detection method using association rule mining techniques. *Expert Systems with Applications*, Vol. 29, No. 4, 807-815, ISSN 09574174

Czogala, E.; Mrozek, A.; Pawlak, Z. (1995). The idea of a rough fuzzy controller and its application to the stabilization of a pendulum-car system. *Fuzzy Sets and Systems*, Vol. 72, No. 1, 61-73, ISSN 01650114

Dagli, C. H. & Lee, H. C. (2001). Engineering smart data mining systems for internet aided design and manufacturing. *International Journal of Smart Engineering System Design*, Vol. 3, No. 4, 217-225, ISSN 10255818

Harding, J. A.; Shahbaz, M.; Srinivas, M.; Kusiak, A. (2006) Data mining in manufacturing: A review. *Journal of Manufacturing Science and Engineering, Transactions of the ASME*, Vol. 128, No. 4, 969-976, ISSN 10871357

Huang, H.; Wu, D. (2006). Product quality improvement analysis using data mining: A case study in ultra-precision manufacturing industry. *Lect. Notes Comput. Sci*, 577-580, ISSN 03029743

Hur, J.; Lee, H.; Baek, F. G. (2006). An intelligent manufacturing process diagnosis system using hybrid data mining. *Lect. Notes Comput. Sci.*, Vol. 4065 LNAI, 561-575, ISSN 03029743

Koonce, D.; Fang, C. H.; Tsai, S. C. (1977) Data mining tool for learning from manufacturing systems. *Computers and Industrial Engineering*, Vol. 33, No. 1-2, 27-30, ISSN 03608352

Kusiak, A. (2006) Data mining: manufacturing and service applications. *International Journal of Production Research*, Vol. 44, No. 18-19, 4175-4191, ISSN 00207543

Kusiak, A.; Kurasek, C. (2001). Data mining of printed-circuit board defects. *IEEE Transactions on Robotics and Automation*, Vol. 17, No. 2, Apr 2001, 191-196, 1042296X

Mahl, A. & Krikler, R. (2007). Approach for a rule based system for capturing and usage of knowledge in the manufacturing industry. *Journal of Intelligent Manufacturing*, Vol. 18, No. 4, 519-526, ISSN 09565515

Perzyk, M.; Biernacki, R.; Kozlowski, J. (2008). Data mining in manufacturing: Significance analysis of process parameters. *Proc.Inst.Mech.Eng.Pt.B: J.Eng.Manuf*, Vol. 222, No. 12, 1503-1516, ISSN 09544054

Perzyk, M.; Soroczynski, A. (2010). Comparative Study of Decision Trees and Rough Sets Theory as Knowledge Extraction Tools for Design and Control of Industrial Processes. *Proceedings of World Academy of Science, Engineering and Technology,* Vol. 61, 234–239, ISSN 20703740

Polkowski, L. (2002). *Rough Sets: mathematical Foundations.* Physica-Verlag, ISBN 390815101, Heidelberg New York

Rokach, L.; Maimon, O. (2006). Data mining for improving the quality of manufacturing: A feature set decomposition approach. *Journal of Intelligent Manufacturing,*Vol. 17, No. 3, 285–299, ISSN 09565515

Sadoyan, H.; Zakarian, A.; Mohanty, P. (2006). Data mining algorithm for manufacturing process control. *International Journal of Advanced Manufacturing Technology,* Vol. 28, No. 3-4, 342–350, ISSN 02683768

Shahbaz, M.; Srinivas, M.; Harding, J. A. & Turner, M. (2006). Product design and manufacturing process improvement using association rules. *Proceedings of the Institution of Mechanical Engineers, Part B: Journal of Engineering Manufacture,* Vol. 220, No. 2, 243–254, ISSN 09544054

Shen, L.; Tay, F. E. H.; Qu, L.; Shen, Y. (2000). Fault diagnosis using Rough Sets Theory. *Computers in Industry,* Vol. 43, No. 1, August 2000, 61–72, ISSN 01663615

StatSoft, Inc. (2008). STATISTICA (data analysis software system), version 8.0. www.statsoft.com

Stefanowski, J. & Vanderpooten, D. (2001). Induction of decision rules in classification and discovery-oriented perspectives. *International Journal of Intelligent Systems,* Vol. 16, No. 1, 13–27, ISSN 08848173

Tsang, K. F.; W.Lau, W. Kwok, S. K. (2007). Development of a data mining system for continual process quality improvement. *Proceedings of the Institution of Mechanical Engineers, Part B: Journal of Engineering Manufacture,* Vol. 221, No. 2, 179–193, ISSN 09544054

Tseng, T. L.; Jothishankar, M. C.; Wu, T.; Xing, G.; Jiang, F. (2004). Applying data mining approaches for defect diagnosis in manufacturing industry. *IIE Annual Conference and Exhibition*, pp. 1441-1447, Houston, May 2004, Institute of Industrial Engineers

Wang, K. (2007). Applying data mining to manufacturing: The nature and implications. *Journal of Intelligent Manufacturing,* Vol. 18, No. 4, 487–495, ISSN 09565515

11

Atom Coloring for Chemical Interpretation and *De Novo* Design for Molecular Design

Kiyoshi Hasegawa[1], Keiya Migita[2] and Kimito Funatsu[2]
[1]*Chugai Pharmaceutical Company, Kamakura Research Laboratories,*
[2]*The University of Tokyo, Department of Chemical System Engineering,*
Japan

1. Introduction

Prediction of biological activities is valuable for finding active compounds in an effective manner, and a considerable amount of attentions has been devoted to *in silico* predictions in drug discovery process. For *in silico* predictions, quantitative structure-activity relationship (QSAR) has been widely known to be useful [1, 2]. The basic purpose of QSAR is to construct a statistical model to reveal the relationship between chemical structures and their biological activities. For the statistical analysis, chemical structures are usually represented by several kinds of chemical descriptors. The QSAR model successfully trained and scientifically validated is used for predicting the biological activities of any molecules. In addition, a physicochemical and/or mechanistic interpretation can be expected from the selected chemical descriptors in the QSAR model.

As a multivariate statistical method, partial least square (PLS) is of particular interest in QSAR study [3]. PLS can analyze data with strongly collinear, noisy and numerous descriptors, and also simultaneously model several biological activities. It can also provide us several application domains and diagnostic plots as the statistical measures. We can extract the complex patterns embedded in the data set. Recently, PLS has evolved or changed for copying with sever demands from the complex data structure [4, 5].

PLS has its major restriction that only linear relationship can be extracted from data [3]. Since many structure-activity data sets are inherently nonlinear in nature, it is desirable to have a flexible method, which can model any nonlinear relationships. Recently, there has been a considerable interest in machine learning methods (ML) such as Bayesian approach [6, 7] and support vector regression (SVR) [8, 9] for nonlinear modeling. In general, since ML employs a sort of mathematical transformations of chemical descriptors, they have drawback that any correlations between the biological activity and the original descriptors should be lost. This means that a direct interpretation of the model is not easy task. A lot of papers studying ML have reported their high performances for classification and regression rates, but unfortunately they have not referred to the aspect of chemical interpretation [10].

For chemical interpretation, we employed the extended connectivity fingerprint (ECFP) as the chemical descriptor for a statistical model. ECFP can facilitate to understand what substructures are correlated with a specific biological activity. An atom score was calculated from the degree of contribution of each substructure to the model. By visualizing the atom scores with the graded-colors, an atom color mapping onto each compound was performed.

The atom coloring is helpful as a starting point for further molecular design with the guidence of atom colors. We described herein two representative examples for application of atom colors. (classifiaction of cytochrome P450 substrates and non-substrates, and visualization of molecular selectivity in dopamine family)
After establishing a solid model, *de novo* design is available for exploring new chemical structures in computer-aided molecular design. Structure generator intended for *de novo* design generates any chemical structures that are expected to have desired biological activities. This study has been known as inverse QSAR [11, 12].
In our approach, EA-Inventor (Evolutional Algorithm-Inventor) was used as structure generator. In EA-Inventor, initial structures represented by SMILES string are modified using several mutation operations in the framework of evolutionary algorithm (EA). Biological activities of compounds are predicted by the prepared QSAR model, and their values are used as the score values in EA. After the EA cycles, i.e. prediction of biological activities and generation of new chemical structures, chemical structures that have the highest scores are obtained. We applied our *de novo* design method to two molecular design projects and demonstrated its utility. (*de novo* design using ligand-based descriptors, and protein-ligand interaction descriptors)

2. Examples of atom coloring

2.1 Classification of CYP 3A4 substrates and non-substrates

Besides an optimization of biological activity, we have to consider to avoid poor ADMET (absorption, distribution, metabolism, excretion, and toxicity) properties of molecules. ADMET processes often involve interaction with the associated proteins [13]. For example, the cytochrome P450 (CYP) isoenzymes, such as CYP 3A4, 2D6, and 2C9, are responsible proteins for the metabolism of most drug molecules. Among them, CYP 3A4 is the most important metabolism protein in human because it metabolizes the majority of commercially available drug molecules. Therefore, prediction of CYP 3A4 substrates is a key task to be solved in molecular design [14].
We employed the Bayesian approach to classify CYP 3A4 substrates and non-substrates. Large public data set comprising of 600 data points was used to develop the Bayesian model. The extended connectivity fingerprint (ECFP) was used as chemical descriptor. ECFP can facilitate to understand what substructures are correlated with substrates or non-substrates. An atom score in molecule was calculated from the Bayesian score of each ECFP descriptor. By coloring the atom scores with the five graded-colors, an atom color mapping onto each molecule was performed. The atom coloring is an effective tool for chemical interpretaion why a specific compound becomes a CYP 3A4 substrate and what chemical parts are responsible causing CYP 3A4 metabolism.

2.1.1 Bayesian model

The data set of CYP 3A4 substrates and non-substrates was taken from a public literature [15]. According to the literature, we divided whole data set into the training and test sets. The separation was performed taking considerations of their distribution in chemical space. The total number of substrates and non-substrates are 311 and 289 in the training set, respectively. The total number of substrates and non-substrates are 56 and 44 in the test set, respectively. Also, we made further external validation experiment to our prediction model of CYP 3A4 oxidation sites [16]. All of these molecules are known to be CYP 3A4 substrates. The number of molecules in the external validation set is 61

Bayesian model was constructed through the Pipeline Pilot module in Accelrys [17]. Bayesian approach compares the frequency of occurrences of chemical descriptors that are found in two groups that discriminate best between these groups (CYP 3A4 substrates versus non-substrates) [6, 7]. ECFP_6 (ECFP with path-lengths of six) was calculated in the Pipeline Pilot module and it was used as chemical descriptor. ECFP is a novel class of topological fingerprints for molecular characterization [18]. The Bayesian model for CYP3A4 classification provided us 12595 unique bins in ECFP_6. The base-line value separating between substrates and non-substrates is -0.819. Therefore, if the score of a compound is greater than this value, the compound is predicted to be substrate. Otherwise, the compound is predicted to be non-substrate. The classification rates of substrates and non-substrates in the training set are 285/311 (92%) and 280/289 (97%), respectively. The prediction rates of substrates and non-substrates in the test set are 47/56 (84%) and 37/44 (84%), respectively. The performance of the Bayesian model is well tolerated for further prediction. The established Bayesian model was applied to the CYP 3A4 substrates in the external validation set from our prediction model of CYP 3A4 oxidation sites [16]. The prediction rate is 53/61 (87%). The prediction rates from two external validation experiments are high enough to use as a prediction filter in early stage of molecular design.

2.1.2 Atom colorings

An atom scoring is a method to calculate a score value of each atom in molecule based on the Bayesian score [19]. First, a Bayesian model is built and the corresponding ECFP_6 descriptors are scored and categorized as substrate or non-substrate features. The score value of each ECFP substructure is divided by the number of heavy atoms consisting of the substructure and the calculated score value is assigned on each atom. Then, substructures of test molecule are identified, and the respective scores of atoms in the substructure are summed up and divided by the number of frequency occurrence to calculate their averaged atom scores. The schematic illustration for calculating atom scores is shown in Figure 1. An example in Figure 1 is 'Dutasteride' containing the amide substructure. The amide substructure is mapped on 'Dutasteride' and the corresponding atom scores (C4, C8, N13, and O14) are summed up.

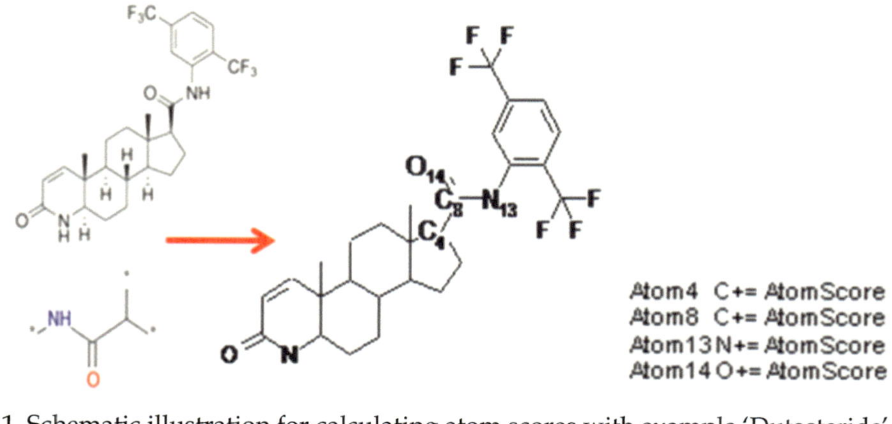

Fig. 1. Schematic illustration for calculating atom scores with example 'Dutasteride'

Four thresholds were used to color atoms in the five graded-colors (0.02, 0.01, -0.01, and -0.02). Because a higher score means a highly likelihood of CYP 3A4 substrate, the atom coloring is blue for higher, and red for lower susceptible to the CYP 3A4 metabolism. The representative examples of atom coloring are shown in Figure 2. In this figure, blue colors mean the liable atoms against CYP 3A4 metabolism. As for 'Adinazolam', tertiary N atom is identified to be liable atom. As for 'Clarithromycin', both of tertiary N atom and ethyl substituent on the macrocyclic ring are identified to be liable atoms. These predictions exactly match with the experimental results. Medicinal chemists can think any new ideas how to avoid the risk factors with the guidance of the atom coloring map.

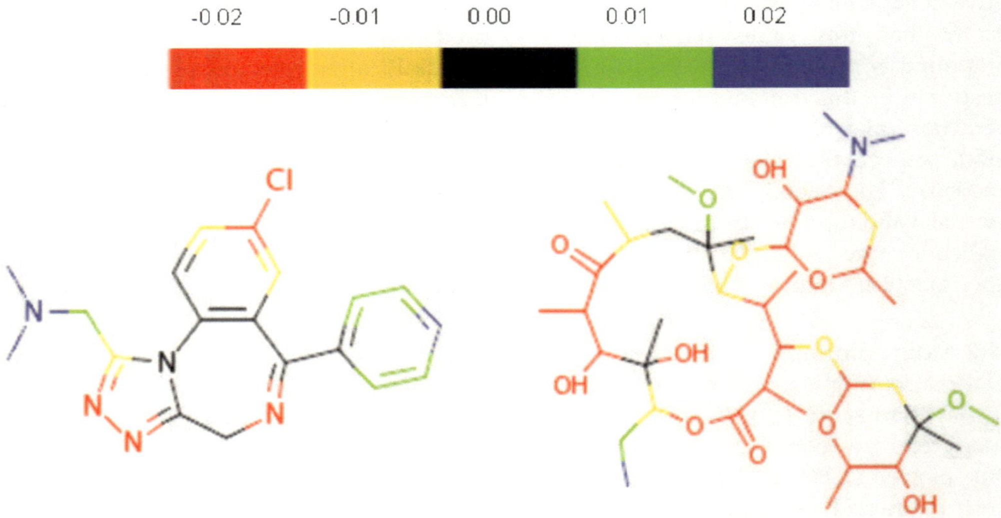

Adinazolam Clarithromycin

Fig. 2. The representative examples of atom coloring ('Adinazolam' and 'Clarithromycin')

Our approach is quite simple and it can be extended to other ADMET issues than CYP metabolism. The classification category between good and bad ADMET properties is prepared in advance and the Bayesian approach and the associated atom colorings are subsequently applied. From the atom colorings, we can easily identify unfavorable atoms in chemical structure for each ADMET property.

3. Visualization of molecular selectivity in dopamine family

In molecular design, computational methods that are capable of analyzing and predicting ligand selectivity profiles within target families are highly attractive [20]. This is the reason why molecules having activities against multi-target proteins cause many unfavorable side effects and toxicities. From the point of safety, data mining such as visualization of molecular selectivity against multi-target proteins cannot be ignored in molecular design [20].

Molecular selectivity was visualized using the combination of activity landscapes and atom colorings. The multiple inhibitory activites in dopamine family were selected to derive its molecular selectivity. At first, all of 390 molecular structures were mapped on 2D chemical space by preserving distance between any pairs of molecules using multi-dimensional scaling (MDS). The inhibitory activity values against each dopamine isoenzyme (D2, D3, and D4) were added independently to the data points in 2D chemical space. Activity landscapes were generated after making the color-graded interpolation between the data points. We can easily identify three specific active regions and the corresponding representative molecules for D2, D3, and D4 isoenzymes. Next, three support vector regression (SVR) models were separately built up using the above-mentioned ECFP descriptors and each inhibitory data set. By applying an atom coloring method to the representative molecules, the molecular selectivity differentiating each dopamine isoenzyme can be visually understood. Finally, the obtained molecular selectivity was validated from 3D homology structures.

3.1 Activity landscapes

Activity landscapes are defined by distance between any pairs of molecules and their biological activities [21]. If we envision a 2D projection of chemical space with the graded coloring of biological activity, this representation becomes reminiscent of geographical map that can readily be interpreted. The distance of two molecules is calculated as the Euclidean distance between their ECFP_6 descriptors. The Euclidean distance is defined according to the following equation [21]:

$$\delta_{ij} = \sqrt{N_i + N_j - 2N_{ij}} \tag{1}$$

where N_i and N_j denote the number of ECFP_6 binary bins present in molecules i and j, respectively. N_{ij} denotes the number of binary bins shared by both molecules. To map multi-dimensional data into 2D chemical space, MDS is employed. MDS aims at preserving relative similarity relationships between input data points by minimizing the deviation from the ideal relationships [22].

Biological activity values are then added to the data points in 2D chemical space for creating activity landscape. In general, however, the data points are sparse and unevenly distributed and must be interpolated to obtain coherent chemical space. For this purpose, a geostatistical technique termed Kringing is applied. Based on the expected value and a covariance function that describe the spatial dependence of the given data points, the Kringing method calculates the best linear unbiased estimator by minimizing the variance of the prediction error. We utilize the Kringing function as implemented in the 'fields' package of R [23]. After finishing the interpolation, 2D map is colored according to the predicted activity values. Areas with a value below a lower threshold are colored in blue, and areas with a value above an upper threshold are colored in red. Intermediate values are colored using a continuous gradient from blue via yellow to red.

We collected three inhibitory data sets of D2, D3, and D4 from GVK data base [24]. The logarithm of reciprocal value of Ki in the micro molar unit (log(-Ki)) was used as the inhibitory activity. We selected 390 molecular data points for filling all elements in three inhibitory data matrices. Three activity landscapes of D2, D3, and D4 are shown in Figure 3. In Figure 3, the region showing both high inhibitory activity and high specificity toward each dopamine isoenzyme was highlighted by the dashed circle. The representative molecules are shown beside each activity landscape. Three molecules have the common tertiary N atoms in their chemical structures to interact with the common Asp in their target dopamine proteins [25]. However, chemical fragments at two ends in molecule significantly differ to each other. They are reflected on the molecular specificity in dopamine family.

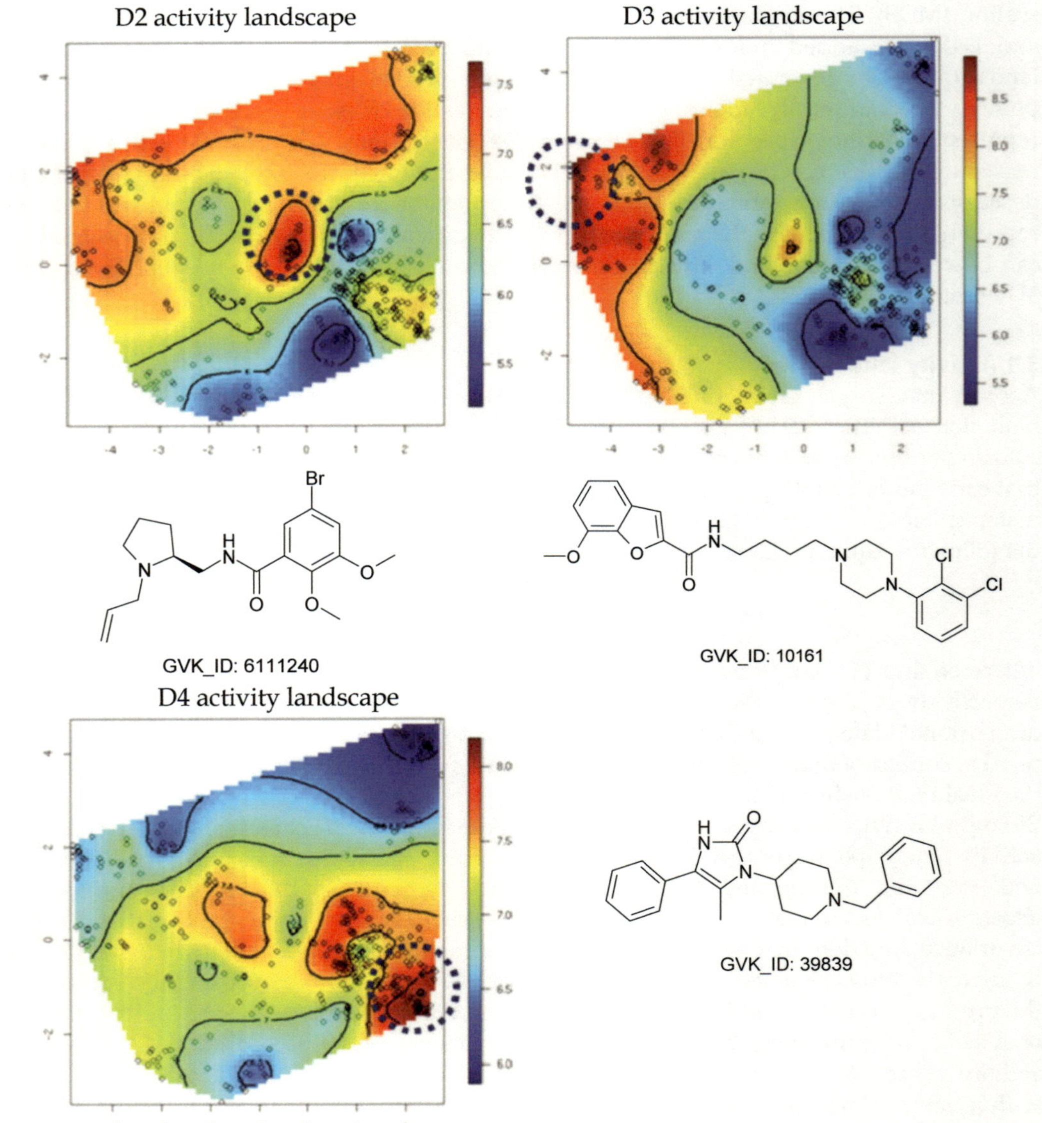

Fig. 3. Three activity landscapes and the representative molecules

3.2 SVR models

SVR was used to develop the predictive model for each dopamine isoenzyme using ECFP_6 descriptors. SVR is a regression type of support vector machine (SVM) by the introduction of a loss function comprising of the squared deviations [8-10]. The general principle of SVM is to perform a classification by constructing an n-dimensional hyper plane that optimally separates the data set into two categories.

Before SVR analysis, 3859 ECFP_6 descriptors were reduced to 82 by the filter of variance cut off of 0.1 After that, a systematic grid search was used to determine the best parameter values for D2 data set based on 10-fold cross-validation (C=2, ν=0.30, and γ=0.03125). The procedure of backward-elimination was applied to produce the final D2 model with 44 descriptors. The R^2 and Q^2 values of the final D2 model are 0.782 and 0.615, respectively. The same procedures were applied to D3 and D4 data sets. As for D3, the final model has 45 descriptor with C=2, ν=0.35, and γ=0.03125. The R^2 and Q^2 values of the final D3 model are 0.900 and 0.783, respectively. As for D4, the final model has 40 descriptor with C=1, ν=0.55, and γ=0.03125. The R^2 and Q^2 values of the final D4 model are 0.793 and 0.637, respectively. All statistical procedures were performed using the 'kernlab' package of R [26] and some written scripts in our laboratory.

3.3 Atom colorings

After building each SVR model, a local gradient was calculated according to the following formula:

$$w_{ij} = \left(\frac{\partial}{\partial x} f_j(x) \mid_{x=x_i} \right) \tag{2}$$

where i means index of compounds. J means the index of ECFP_6 descriptors. The value of local gradient indicates the descriptor importance in a specific compound. For a specific compound i, the value of descriptor j is slightly changed keeping other descriptor values to be fixed. Then, the differences of the predicted values from the SVR model are calculated. The local gradient is derived from the differences divided by the shifted values. The original idea of local gradient came from the financial study [27]. One of authors (K. Migita) has made further invention for improving the calculation efficacy and precision [28]. The value of local gradient of each substructure was used as the Bayesian score value for next atom coloring. The calculation of local gradient was performed using the written scripts in our laboratory under the R environment.

The atom colorings of each specific dopamine inhibitor are shown in Figure 4. Four thresholds were used to color atoms in the five graded-colors (0.008, 0.004, -0.004, and -0.008). The atom coloring scheme is blue for the most contributed atom to the inhibitory activity, and red for least. As shown in Figure 4, compound 6111240 is a specific inhibitor toward D2 protein and this is emphasized in the remarkable blue and green colors. Compound 6111240 has unfavorable amide part toward D4 protein, which are highlighted in red color. Other specific compounds (10161 and 39839) also show clear molecular specificity owing to the atom colorings.

These molecular specificities were validated by 3D structures of D2 and D4 proteins. The 3D structures were built by the homology modeling procedure based on the template X-ray crystal structure of β2 (PDB code: 2RH1). The 3D coordinates of homology structures of D2 and D4 proteins were cited from a recent public study [25]. In Figure 5, 3D structures of D2 and D4 proteins are shown with a specific compound 6111240. Cyan and white colors represent D2 and D4 protein structures, respectively. Compound 6111240 is shown in yellow bold color. The compound has nice polar interactions with Asp 114 and Cys 118 residues in D2 protein. However, in the case of D4 protein, due to the bulky residues (Phe 91 and Arg 186), compound cannot maintain the polar interactions in D4 protein. This could be one of reasons why compound 6111240 has high molecular specificity only toward D2 protein. Different coloring patters on amide part are nicely accordance with the differences of active site pockets between D2 and D4 proteins.

GVK_ID: 6111240

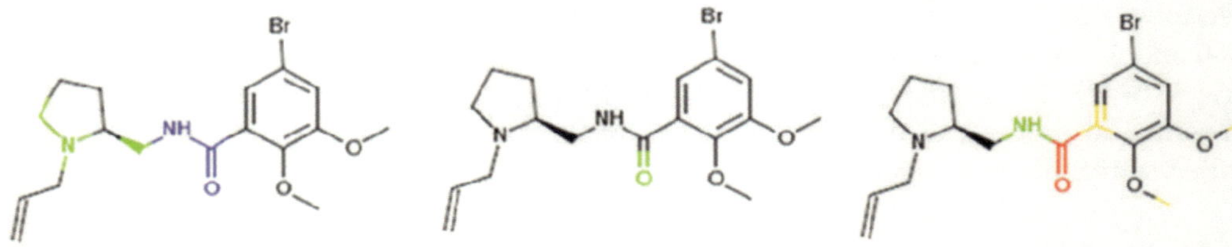

D2 = 10.07, D3 = 9.22, D4 = 6.68

GVK_ID: 10161

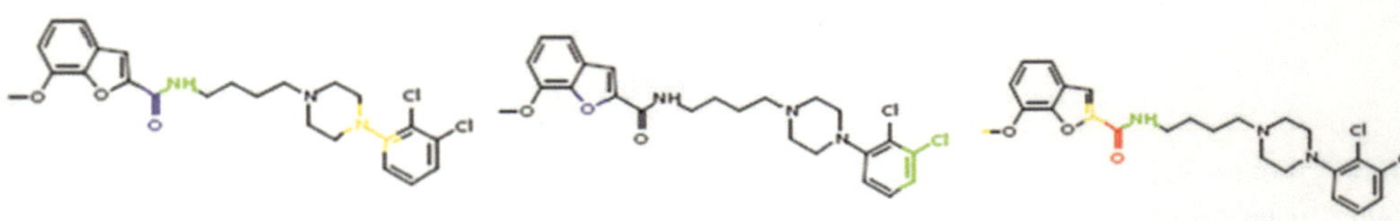

D2 = 6.43, D3 = 9.89, D4 = 6.14

GVK_ID: 39839

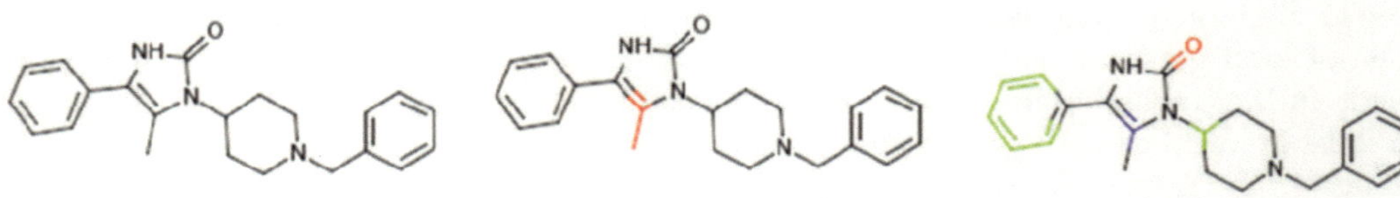

D2 = 7.25, D3 = 6.62, D4 = 9.22

Fig. 4. Atom colorings of each specific dopamine inhibitor

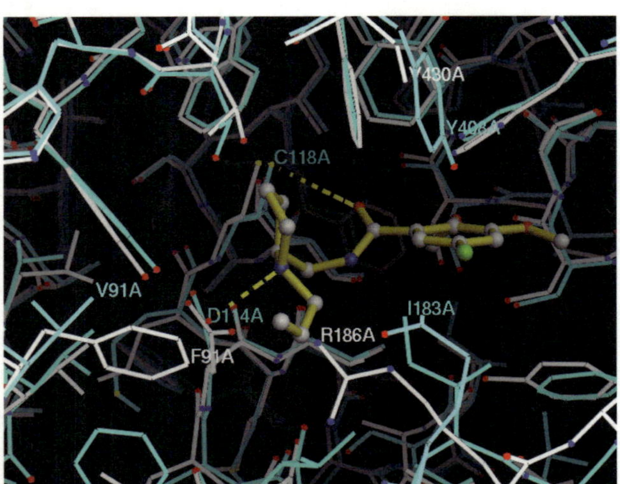

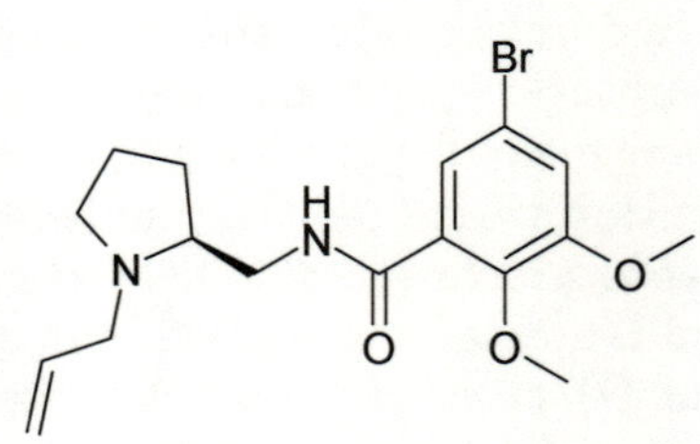

Compound 6111240

Fig. 5. Two homology models and their interactions with compound 6111240

Including biological activity, the landscape technique can be applied to multiple ADMET endpoints. This makes help us identify some interesting chemical space where compounds show high biological activity and also satisfy good ADMET properties. We are planning to construct graphical user interface (GUI) handling many landscape panels [29]. When medicinal chemists touch a data point in a specific landscape, the associated data is shown immediately with a chemical structure. This system might be a good compass to know us where synthetic compounds are in chemical space or what extent of chemical efforts is necessary to achieve chemical optimization.

4. Examples of *de novo* design

4.1 *De novo* design using ligand-based descriptors

QSAR has been successfully applied in molecular design [30]. However, when a precise QSAR model is created, chemical interpretation generally becomes difficult. In particular, in the case of a non-linear model, the relationship between chemical descriptors and biological activity cannot be described explicitly, and chemical interpretation becomes challenging [31]. In this case, an inverse QSAR approach is attractive to design practical chemical structures. Inverse QSAR is a relatively new concept that chemical structures having high biological activities are computationally generated using a structure generator [11, 12].

EA-Inventor (Evolutionary Algorithm-Inventor) was used as structure generator in our study. In EA-Inventor, chemical structures are updated using several mutation operations in an iterative manner to achieve high inhibitory activities. We applied EA-Inventor to the data set of 33 matrix metallopeptidase 2 (MMP-2) inhibitors. The scoring function for input to EA-Inventor is the prediction value derived from the SVR model. In order to prevent generated structures deviating from chemical space, the leverage value was added to the scoring function as the penalty value. The generated chemical structures are reasonable judging from 3D homology structure of MMP-2 protein as their counterparts.

4.2 EA-Inventor

EA-Inventor has been successfully applied along with the docking algorithm [32]. In our study, EA-Inventor was used in combination with prediction value derived from a specific QSAR model. Initial chemical structures are set up as a SMILE string. As mutation operations to chemical structures, 33 different transformations are available in EA-Inventor. Some typical transformations are shown in Figure 6. Transformations (i) and (ii) involve changing the atoms and bonds, respectively. Transformations (iii) and (iv) involve breaking the ring structure and changing the ring size, respectively. Transformation (v) involves the addition of the prepared chemical fragments in advance. Around 1400 libraries of fragments have been compiled by breaking down the chemical structures of drug-like molecules. Therefore, new chemical structures, including those of drug-like compounds, can be formed by combining these fragments [33]. The algorithm of EA-Inventor is schematically shown in Figure 7. The experiment of EA-Inventor was performed on the Sybyl environment [34].

4.3 SVR model

The data set of 33 MMP-2 inhibitors were collected from a literature [35] and the SVR model was developed with 496 ligand-based descriptors. These descriptors were calculated by the descriptor module in MOE [36]. After pre-processing of descriptors based on variance cut and p-values (0.1 and 0.01), 26 descriptors were selected. Then, a grid search based on leave-one-out cross-validation was performed to determine the best parameter values (C=64, ν=0.15 and γ=0.008). The procedure of backward-elimination was applied to produce the final SVR model with 15 descriptors. The R^2 and Q^2 values of the final SVR model are 0.867 and 0.795, respectively. The selected 15 descriptors have the ambiguous physicochemical meanings and their chemical interpretations are far to be ease. In this situation, an inverse QSAR becomes a powerful approach [11, 12].

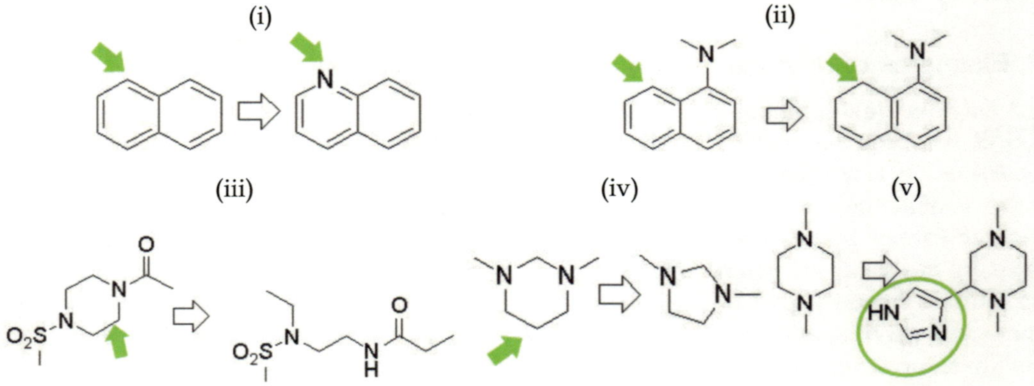

Fig. 6. Typical transformations in EA-Inventor: (i) modification of atom type, (ii) modification of bond type, (iii) breaking of ring, (iv) modification of ring size, (v) addition of fragment.

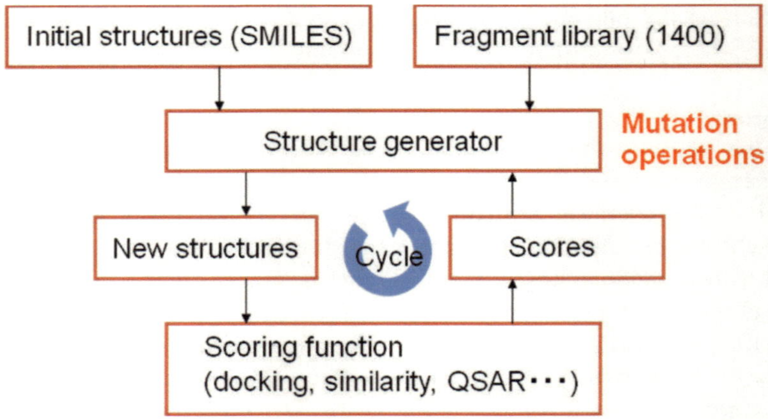

Fig. 7. Algorithm of EA-Inventor as structure generator.

4.4 *De novo* design

With fixing the core scaffold structure, EA-Inventor was performed with 100 populations and 20 generations in 10 runs. The output of generated chemical structures is shown in Figure 8. In Figure 8, symbol *a* means the predicted inhibitory activity. Symbol *b* means the leverage value. All of the generate structures have both of high predicted inhibitory activities and low values of leverage.

There are two ways for making validation about the output structure from *de novo* design: One is that actually synthesizing compounds and measuring their inhibitory activities. Other is that comparing the output structure with the target structure. Because we are not available on experimental way, we employed the latter approach for validation of our results. In Figure 9, the binding mode of one of examples (benzothiazole molecule) in the pocket of MMP-2 homology model is shown. Homology model of MMP-2 was built from a complex X-ray structure between MMP-12 and hydroxamate ligand (PDB: 1RMZ). White and orange colors represent MMP-2 protein and benzothiazole molecule, respectively. Benzothiazole molecule has the good interactions with Val 400, His 403, and Tyr 425 highlighted in red colors. Then, it is highly expected from the protein-ligand interactions that the benzothiazole molecule could show the high inhibitory activity. All of the fused 6-5 or 6-6 ring systems exemplified in Figure 8 are favorable to occupy the cavity pocket in MMP-2 protein. These results indicate that EA-Inventor can actually generate new chemical structures with the high inhibitory activities.

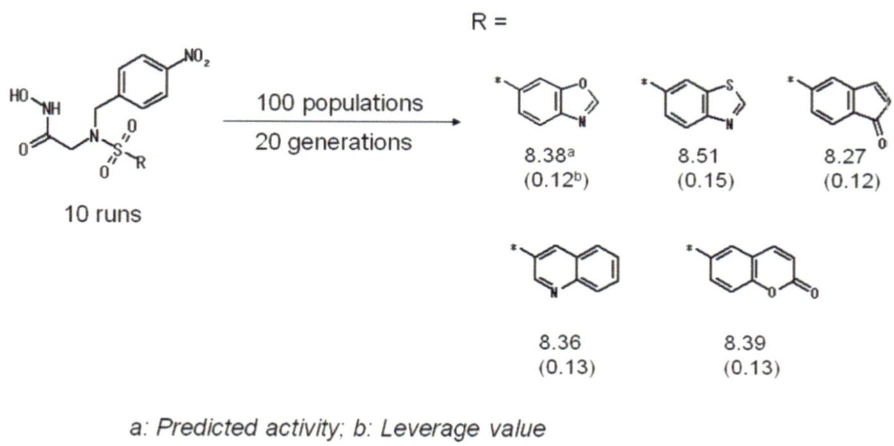

Fig. 8. Output of generated chemical structures from EA-Inventor

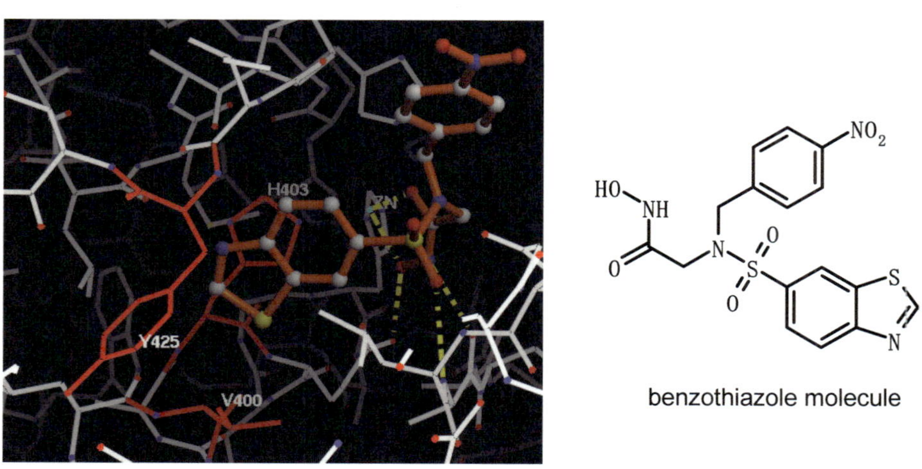

benzothiazole molecule

Fig. 9. Docking mode of benzothiazole molecule in MMP-2

We can consider the chemical structures cited in Figure 8 as the starting molecules. For example, 'benzothiazole' and 'indole' can be transformed to any aromatic rings such as benzofuran. It is rationale transformation from five member ring 'pyrolidine' to six member ring 'piperidine'. Therefore, the proposed chemical structures from EA-Inventor are good hints for further molecular design.

4.5 *De novo* design using protein-ligand interaction descriptors

Structure-based drug design (SBDD) is a technique for designing novel compounds by use of physico-chemical interactions in a complex X-ray structure between a protein and a ligand molecule [37]. The most important thing for SBDD is an accurate estimation of binding affinity of the ligand molecule against the target protein. This issue has not been solved accompanying with prediction of docking pose of molecule in the protein structure. Therefore, for a specific target protein, the scenario that the docking scoring function is customized in the framework of QSAR is highly attractive [38]. The integration of the customized docking scoring function into *de novo* design engine is interesting for designing potent molecules more accurately than those of traditional SBDD.

We customized the docking scoring function using comparative molecular binding energy (COMBINE) descriptors and SVR. COMBINE descriptors are energy terms between the ligand molecule and each amino acid residue of the target protein. The data set of 35 human caspase-3 inhibitors was used in our study. The SVR model can successfully identify important amino acid residues for explaining inhibitory activities against human caspase-3. Then, we integrated the docking scoring function into EA-Inventor. A number of molecules were virtually generated by EA-Inventor, and they were evaluated using the customized docking scoring function. EA-Inventor produced some interesting compounds and the rationale was validated using X-ray crystal structure of human caspase-3.

4.6 SVR model

The data set of 35 human caspase-3 inhibitors focusing Isatin sulfonamide analogues was taken from a literature [39]. COMBINE descriptors expressing the protein-ligand interactions were used as chemical descriptors [40, 41]. From the X-ray crystal structure of human caspase-3 (PDB code: 1GFW), total 47 amino acids were detected as the nearest amino acids forming the binding pocket. Since van der Waals, Coulomb, and hydrogen bonding interaction energies are considered, and total number of COMBINE descriptors becomes 141. All of 35 inhibitors were docked into human caspase-3 structure and COMBINE descriptors were calculated by the GLIDE docking module [42]. After pre-processing of descriptors based on variance cut of 0.05, 29 significant descriptors were selected. A grid search based on leave-one-out cross validation was used to determine the best parameter values (C=4, ν=0.95 and γ=0.03125). The procedure of backward-elimination was applied to produce the final SVR model with 13 COMBINE descriptors. The R^2 and Q^2 values of the final SVR model are 0.977 and 0.873, respectively.

The selected 13 COMBINE descriptors are as follows in the descending order of the above-mentioned local gradient values: His 121 vdw, Met 61 vdw, Ser 251 hbonds, Glu 123 coul, Phe 250 vdw, Ser 251 vdw, Asp 253 coul, Arg 207 vdw, Phe 256 vdw, Asn 208 coul, Tyr 204 coul, Tyr 204 vdw, and Lys 259 coul. Three abbreviations (vdw, coul, and hbonds) mean van der Waals, Coulombic, and hydrogen bonding interactions, respectively. Many COMBINE descriptors are derived from the van der Waals interaction. The presumed binding mode of compound 21 in human caspase-3 is shown in Figure 10. White and green present the caspase-3 protein and compound 21, respectively. The selected amino acid residues in the final SVR model are highlighted in yellow bold colors in Figure 10. They are located close to two ends of chemical structure in compound 21.

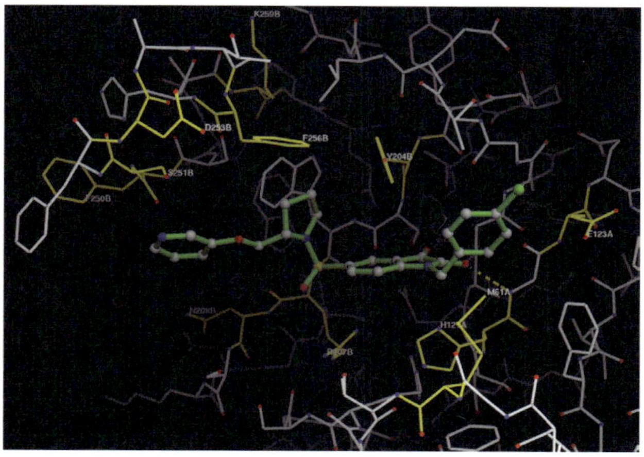

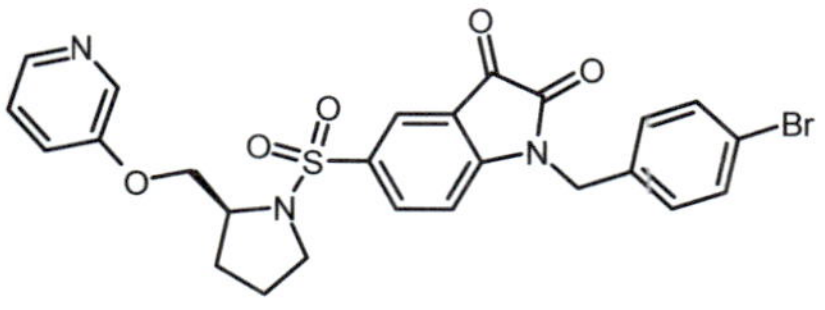

Compound 21

Fig. 10. Presumed binding mode of compound 21.

4.7 *De novo* design

With fixing the core scaffold structure, EA-Inventor was performed with 50 populations and 3 generations in 10 runs. The output of generated chemical structures from EA-Inventor is shown in Figure 11. The number below each chemical structure means the inhibitory activity predicted by the SVR model. The generated chemical structures are mainly 5 and 6-5 fused ring systems. In order to validate the output structures, they were docked into the X-ray crystal structure of human caspase-3. The presumed binding mode of indole molecule is shown in Figure 12. Three strong interactions with the indole part of molecule are highlighted in red colors: CH-π interactions of side chains of Glu 123 and Met 61, and π-π interaction of imidazole ring of His 121. These amino acid residues are included in the selected 13 COMBINE descriptors. Judging from these 3D molecular interactions, 6-5 fused ring analogues seems to be highly expected for high inhibitory activity.

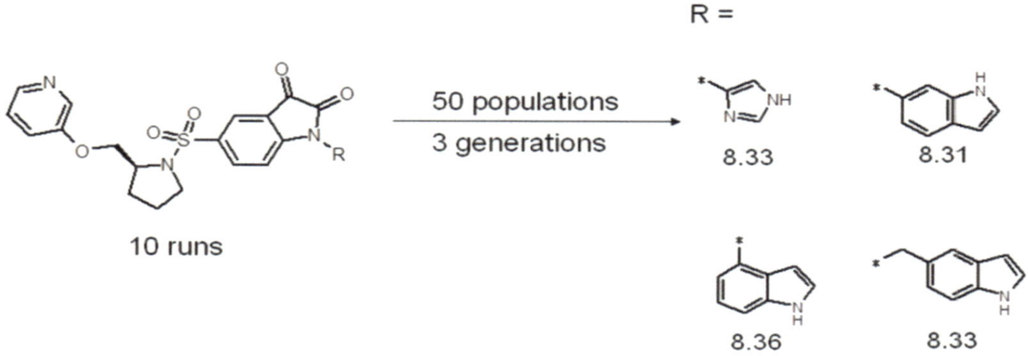

Fig. 11. EAInventor for producing chemical structures.

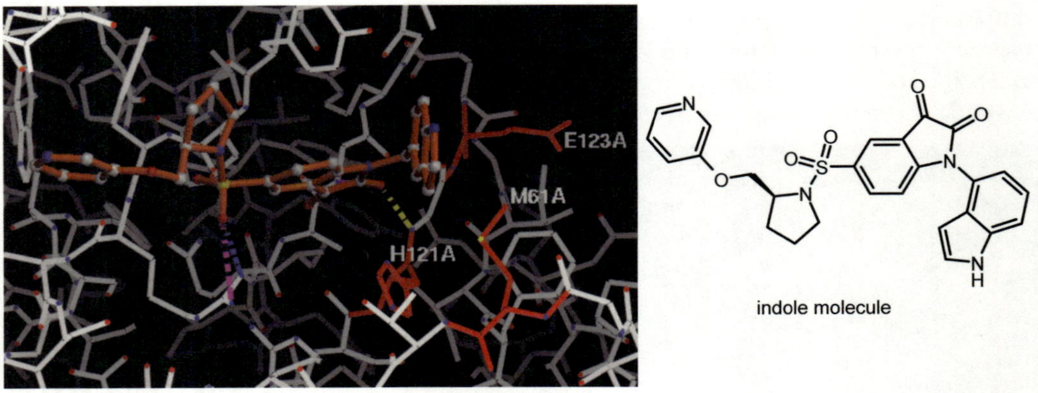

Fig. 12. Presumed binding mode of indole molecule.

Thanks to the transparent COMBINE descriptors, medicinal chemists can easily find which amino acid residues or which types of interactions are important for increasing inhibitory activity. Medicinal chemists can focus on the specific chemical parts interacting with these important amino acid residues. Their chemical parts are effectively replaced by another moiety using *de novo* design engine.

5. Conclusion

Two techniques of atom coloring and *de novo* design were introduced with their representative examples. By coloring atom scores derived from the Bayesian or SVR models with the five graded-colors, we can easily identify the key atoms in chemical structure responsible to each biological activity. The visualization encourages us to think design ideas how to modify chemical structure in next synthetic plan. *De novo* design provides us chemical structures with high inhibitory activities in the framework of QSAR. The generated chemical structures are good starting molecules for further molecular design.

As mentioned before, the landscape technique is useful to grasp rough trend in whole chemical space. The combination of landscape with *de novo* design engine is especially attractive as new strategy of molecular design. At first, we select an interesting region in chemical space. The interesting region means that it contains a chemical structure with high biological activity and good ADMET properties. Any chemical structures are virtually generated starting from the chemical structure in the region. During *de novo* simulation, the generated chemical structures are forced to stay inside the region. After that, chemical structures with same chemical profile as that of the starting molecule could be found according to this scenario. This study is in progress and the results will be disclosed in near future [43].

6. References

[1] P. Gedeck, R.A. Lewis, Exploiting QSAR models in lead optimization, *Curr.Opin.Drug Dis.Dev.*, 2008, 11, 569-575.

[2] C.W. Yap, H. Li, Z.L. Ji, Y.Z. Chen, Regression methods for developing QSAR and QSPR models to predict compounds of specific pharmacodynamic, pharmacokinetic and toxicological properties, *Mini-Rev.Med.Chem.*, 2007, 7, 1097-1107.

[3] S. Wold, M. Sjostrom, L. Eriksson, PLS-regression: a basic tool of chemometrics, *Chemom.Intell.Lab.Syst.*, 2001, 58, 109-130.
[4] K. Hasegawa, K. Funatsu, Advanced PLS Techniques in Chemometrics and Their Applications to Molecular Design. In *Chemoinformatics and Advanced Machine Learning Perspectives: Complex Computational Methods and Collaborative Techniques;* Lodhi, H.; Yamanishi, Y.; Eds., IGI publishing, 2011.
[5] K. Hasegawa, K. Funatsu, Advanced PLS Techniques in Chemoinformatics Studies, *Curr.Comput.-Aided Drug Des.*, 2010, 6, 103-127.
[6] X. Xia, E. Maliski, P. Gallant, D. Rogers, Classification of Kinase Inhibitors Using a Bayesian Model, *J.Med.Chem.*, 2004, 47, 4463-4470.
[7] P. Prathipati, N.L. Ma, T.H. Keller, Global Bayesian Models for the Prioritization of Antitubercular Agents, *J.Chem.Inf.Model.*, 2008, 17, 2362-2370.
[8] J.-P. Doucet, F. Barbault, H. Xia, A. Panaye, B. Fan, Nonlinear SVM approaches to QSPR/QSAR studies and drug design, *Curr.Comput.-Aided Drug Des.*, 2007, 3, 263-289.
[9] H. Li, Y. Liang, Q. Xu, Support vector machines and its applications in chemistry *Chemom.Intell.Lab.Syst.*, 2009, 95, 188-198.
[10] K. Hasegawa, K. Funatsu, Non-Linear Modeling and Chemical Interpretation with Aid of Support Vector Machine and Regression, *Curr.Comput.-Aided Drug Des.*, 2010, 6, 24-36.
[11] D. Hecht, G.B. Fogel, A Novel In Silico Approach to Drug Discovery via Computational Intelligence, *J.Chem.Inf.Model.*, 2009, 49, 1105–1121
[12] T. Miyao, M. Arakawa, K. Funatsu, Exhaustive Structure Generation for Inverse-QSPR/QSAR, *Mol.Inf.*, 2010, 29, 111-125.
[13] H. Li, C.W. Yap, C.Y. Ung, Y. Xue, Z.R. Li, L.Y. Han, H.H. Lin, Y.Z. Chen, Machine learning approaches for predicting compounds that interact with therapeutic and ADMET related proteins, *J.Pharm.Sci.*, 2007, 96, 2838-2860.
[14] R. Arimoto, Computational models for predicting interactions with cytochrome p450 enzyme, *Curr.Top.Med.Chem.*, 2006, 6, 1609-1618.
[15] C.W. Yap, Y.Z. Chen, Prediction of Cytochrome P450 3A4, 2D6, and 2C9 Inhibitors and Substrates by Using Support Vector Machines, *J.Chem.Inf.Model.*, 2005, 45, 982-992.
[16] K. Hasegawa, M. Koyama, K. Funatsu, Quantitative Prediction of Regioselectivity Toward Cytochrome P450/3A4 Using Machine Learning Approaches, *Mol.Inf.*, 2010, 29, 243–249.
[17] Pipeline Pilot Basic Chemistry Component Collection, Accelrys, Inc. 10188 Telesis Court, Suite 100, San Diego, CA 92121, USA.
[18] D. Rogers, M. Hahn, Extended-Connectivity Fingerprints, *J.Chem.Inf.Model.*, 2010, 50, 742–754.
[19] J.T. Metz, D.A. Stonich, D. Rogers, Visualization of Atomic Contributions to Ligand Properties, SciTegic Users Group Meeting 2007.
[20] E. Lounkine, M. Wawer, A.M. Wassermann, J. Bajorath, SARANEA – a freely available program to mine structure-activity and structure-selectivity relationship information in compound data sets, *J.Chem.Inf.Model.*, 2010, 50, 68-78.
[21] L. Peltason, P. Iyer, J. Bajorath, Rationalizing three-dimensional activity landscapes and the influence of molecular representations on landscape topology and formation of activity cliffs, *J.Chem.Inf.Model.*, 2010, 50, 1021–1033.

[22] I. Borg, P.J.F. Groenen, Modern Multidimensional Scaling. Theory and Applications, 2nd ed.; Springer: New York, NY, 2005.
[23] http://cran.r-project.org/web/packages/fields/index.html
[24] http://www.gvkbio.com/
[25] F.M. McRobb, B. Capuano, I.T. Crosby, D.K. Chalmers, E. Yuriev, Homology Modeling and Docking Evaluation of Aminergic G Protein-Coupled Receptors, *J.Chem.Inf.Model.*, 2010, 50, 626-637.
[26] http://cran.r-project.org/web/packages/kernlab/index.html
[27] L.J. CAO, F.E.H. TAY, Feature Selection for Support Vector Machines in Financial Time Series Forecasting, In Intelligent Data Engineering and Automated Learning (Lecture Notes in Computer Science), K.S. Leung, L.-W. Chan, H. Meng (Eds.), Springer Verlag, Berlin, 2009.
[28] K. Migita, personal communications.
[29] K. Hasegawa, T. Fukami, M. Ohta, Y. Shiratori, *2nd Chemoinformatics Strasbourg Summer School*, P5: Construction of ADMET local models and development of Web GUI for chemists, 2010, Obernai, France.
[30] K. Hasegawa, K. Funatsu, Data Modeling and Chemical Interpretation of ADME Properties Using Regression and Rule Mining Techniques, In Gary, W. C. (Ed.), Frontier in
Drug Design & Discovery 4. Bentham Science Publisher, 2009.
[31] R. Guha, On the interpretation and interpretability of quantitative structure-activity relationship models, *J.Comput.-Aided Mol.Des.*, 2008, 22, 857-871.
[32] L. Qian, M. Brian, S. Karl, S. Julian, Tagged Fragment Method for Evolutionary Structure-Based De Novo Lead Generation and Optimization, *J.Med.Chem.*, 2007, 50, 5392–5402.
[33] K. Hasegawa, T. Kimura, K. Funatsu, Inverse QSAR Study Using Evolutionary Algorithm *J.Comput.-Aided Chem.* , 2009, 10, 10-15.
[34] http://tripos.com/index.php
[35] D. Kumar, S.P. Gupta, A Quantitative Structure-Activity Relationship Study on Some Matrix Metalloproteinase and Collagenase Inhibitors, *Bioorg.Med.Chem.*, 2003, 11, 421-426.
[36] http://www.chemcomp.com/software-moe2009.htm
[37] I.D. Kuntz, Structure-Based Strategies for Drug Design and Discovery, *Science*, 1992, 257, 1078-1082.
[38] M. Arakawa, K. Hasegawa, K. Funatsu, Tailored scoring function of Trypsin-benzamidine complex using COMBINE descriptors and support vector regression, *Chemom.Intell.Lab.Syst.*, 2008, 92, 145-151.
[39] Q. Wang, R.H. Mach, D.E. Reichert, Docking and 3D-QSAR Studies on Isatin Sulfonamide Analogues as Caspase-3 Inhibitors, *J.Chem.Inf.Model.*, 2009, 49, 1963–1973.
[40] A.R. Ortiz, M.T. Pisabarro, F. Gago, R.C. Wade, Prediction of Drug Binding Affinities by Comparative Binding Energy Analysis, *J.Med.Chem.*, 1995, 38, 2681–2691.
[41] K. Hasegawa, T. Kimura, K. Funatsu, GA strategy for variable selection in QSAR studies. Enhancement of comparative molecular binding energy analysis by GA-based PLS method, *QSAR*, 1999, 18, 262–272.
[42] http://www.schrodinger.com/
[43] K. Hasegawa, K. Migita, K. Funatsu, in preparation of manuscript.

12

Hyperspectral Data Analysis and Visualisation

Maarten A. Hogervorst and Piet B.W. Schwering
TNO Defense & Security,
The Netherlands

1. Introduction

Electro-Optical (EO) imaging sensors are widely used for a range of tasks, e.g. for Target Acquisition (TA: detection, recognition and identification of (military) relevant objects) or visual search. These tasks can be performed by a human observer, by an algorithm (Automatic Target Recognition) or by both (Aided Target Recognition). In the past decades, the development of night vision devices in the thermal infrared and image intensifying systems has greatly extended the applicability of EO systems. Despite of these rapid developments, the current generation of sensors has important limitations. Until now, operational thermal imagers are sensitive to IR (infrared) radiation from a single spectral band in the Long Wave (8-14 µm, LWIR) or Mid Wave (3-5 µm, MWIR) infrared region. These so-called broad band sensors basically produce a monochrome (i.e. a black-and-white pan-chromatic) image that deviates considerably from a normal daylight view, and is based on temperature contrasts in a scene. With these systems, the distinction between real targets and decoys, or between military and civilian targets is often difficult to make. Also, camouflaged targets or targets that are hidden deep in the woods are difficult to detect. Recognizing different objects and materials may be difficult. Examples of misinterpretations when using an Image Intensifier system are grass that looks like snow, or trees that look like bushes, when seen from a helicopter. These misinterpretations may lead to disorientation (loss of Situational Awareness) or to a (fatal) wrong distance estimation.
Currently, multi-band and hyperspectral imaging sensors in the thermal infrared are under development. Traditionally hyperspectral imagers were developed for satellites with applications ranging from monitoring the environment, climate analysis, detection of pollution and fires. These systems also promise significant improvements in military task performance. With these new systems, targets may be distinguished not only on the basis of differences in radiation magnitude, but also on differences in spectral properties. Multi-band sensors are sensitive to several (2 to 10) sub-bands in a spectral region. Hyperspectral sensors are sensitive to many (in the order of 100) sub-bands. Hyperspectral sensors have existed for a while, and have mainly been used for remote sensing from a airborne platform or a satellite. Only recently these sensors entered the infrared spectral sensitivity regions. A recent overview on hyper spectral image technology is provided by Vagni (1990). Present-day hyperspectral sensors typically contain a very high number of spectral bands. The penalty for using such a high number of spectral bands is that for each spectral-band image the averaged signal-to-noise ratio is smaller than for a broad band sensor. Operational hyperspectral systems will be complex and expensive because of the wavelength discrimination element in the sensor. This is especially true for the infrared wavelength

range. Furthermore, the processing of this huge amount of data of a hyperspectral image cube may be troublesome. It complicates a near real-time image processing solution for automatic target detection. Band selection is therefore seen as an important step in realizing effective operational hyper/multi-spectral imaging solutions.
Hyperspectral sensors provide a large amount of information (a three-dimensional, 3-D, hypercube with the 3rd dimension coding the spectral information) at the cost of a reduced speed. The additional spectral information from multi-band or hyperspectral sensors may be used, for instance, for *automatic detection*, recognition or identification. Alternatively, the information is visualised for *human inspection*. In addition, alternative presentation methods to human observers are possible. Ergonomic presentation techniques may simplify the interpretation of the images and enhance performance, situational awareness and/or viewing comfort. Until now, the potential of the new systems is largely unknown and it is not clear how the 3-D hypercube data should be presented to the observers. Human and automatic target acquisition both have their advantages and disadvantages. In this study we focus on human target acquisition performance, although this may be supported by automatically derived information. Automatic detection processes could support the operator in a tedious task of scanning through large amounts of data, while the operator can spend his time to classifying automatically detected objects. A major advantage of the human visual system (HVS) is its superiority in pattern recognition. It is able to analyze an image at different (spatial and temporal) scales simultaneously and the interpretation is robust to spatial and temporal noise and to many types of image distortions. Humans are very flexible and able to tell which part of an image differs from the background without the need to specify what characterizes these differences. In contrast to automatic target recognition systems the number of assumptions (about signature of target and background, target shape etc.) can be small. We argue that often the final interpretation is best left to a human observer. Of course, when more knowledge about target and background (signature, shape etc.) is available this can be used to help the observer interpreting the data. A combination of automatic target recognition and presentation techniques (i.e. aided target recognition) can elevate the drawbacks of the use of human interpreters, such as limited processing capacity, processing time, memory and attention. A problem with presenting hyperspectral imagery to a human observer is the huge amount of information. The question is how the data should be made available to the human visual system, i.e. which presentation offers sufficient, or the best, information transfer. This also depends on the task at hand (e.g. detection, situational awareness, identification) and the prior information available. Several applications are available that support the processing and analysis of hyperspectral data (e.g. MicroMSI, Opticks, Envi). The emphasis in these applications lies on the processing algorithms. Here, we focus on the development and evaluation of presentation methods that optimize the information transfer to the human operator.

2. Optimal band selection

Most research involving band selection has focussed only on small bands of single or a few wavelengths. However, for a multispectral configuration narrow bands are not practical, due to the limited signal-to-noise ratio, and this would require long integration times to get a good signal-to-noise ratio. Our research therefore not only looks at the location of the bands but also at the width of the bands. In our previous research (Withagen et al., 2001) a first attempt was made by developing an algorithm that first determines the best locations, in terms of maximizing information content in a limited set of wavelengths, for the bands and than the best width of the bands. This however does not allow for a comparison between broad and narrow bands. Therefore a new algorithm has been written to find the set of bands with optimal information, given the number of bands and their width.

2.1 Band selection method

We have developed two versions of the algorithm, a fast one that can quickly find a solution but does not guarantee to find the best bands, and an optimal algorithm, which searches all possible combinations but as a consequence takes a lot longer and can only be used if the number of required bands is small. In this way information content is optimized under the set boundary conditions. Each band combination is evaluated a distance measure that quantifies the separation between classes. We use two different distance measures (Landgrebe, 2003). The Mahalonobis distance and the Bhattacharyya distance, which are both described below.
The Mahalanobis distance is defined as:

$$D = \sqrt{[\mu_1 - \mu_2]\Sigma^{-1}[\mu_1 - \mu_2]^T} \tag{1}$$

Where μ_1 and μ_2 are the class averages of the target class (class 1) and background class (class 2) and Σ is the covariance matrix of these classes.
When using the Mahalanobis distance measure one has to keep in mind that the following assumptions are made:

- The distributions of the classes are multivariate Gaussian distributions.
- The covariance matrix of these distributions is the same for all classes.
- The total number of pixels is large enough to accurately describe the covariance matrix (a rule of thumb is that the number of pixels should be at least 10 times the number of dimensions).

The distance measure is implemented by first transforming the feature-space and then calculating the Euclidian distance between the centres of the classes in this transformed feature space. The transformation makes use of the average covariance matrix of the different classes involved. The data is transformed to a different feature-space by multiplying it with the eigenvectors of this covariance matrix. The effect of this transformation is that the data is de-correlated.
The advantage of this transformation is visible in Figure 1. In the original feature-space (Figure 1a) the distance between background class BG1 (in light green) and background class BG2 (in dark green) is larger than the distance between background class BG1 (light green) and target class T1 (red), and hence the separability between classes BG1 and BG2 is better. In the transformed feature-space (Figure 1b) the classes which are most easy to separate also have the highest Euclidian distance. In the transformed feature-space the Euclidian distance is calculated between the centres of the different classes. The resulting set of distances is then stored in a distance matrix. From this matrix a final single distance value is derived in several ways depending on the experimental requirements (for example the minimum value of this matrix can be taken). Because we want to distinguish between background and target classes we choose the smallest distance between a target and a background class. This final distance value we will refer to as the quality of a band combination. In the band selection algorithm this quality is maximized.

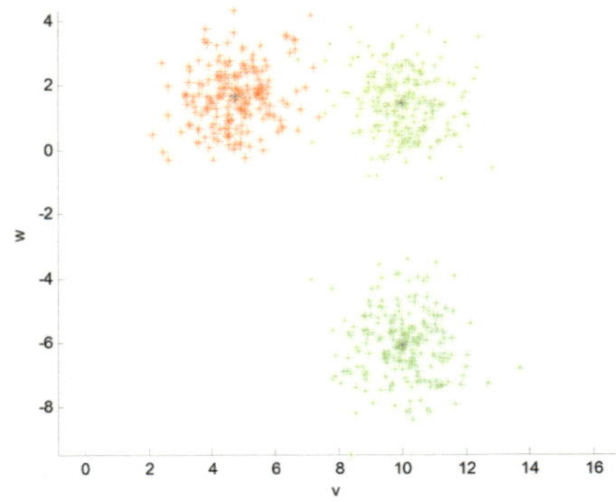

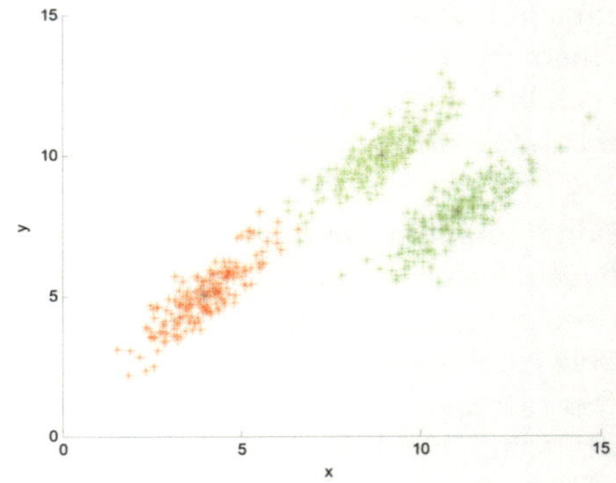

Fig. 1. Example of a 2D feature-space (a) and its transformation (b).

The Bhattacharyya distance is another distance measure that measures the distance between two multivariate Gaussian distributions. It is defined as:

$$B = \frac{1}{8}[\mu_1 - \mu_2]\left[\frac{\Sigma_1 + \Sigma_2}{2}\right]^{-1}[\mu_1 - \mu_2]^T + \frac{1}{2}\ln\frac{\left|1/2[\Sigma_1 + \Sigma_2]\right|}{\sqrt{|\Sigma_1||\Sigma_2|}} \quad (2)$$

One important difference with the Mahalanobis distance is that it does not take the average covariance matrix of the classes but keeps the class covariance matrices. The price that has to be paid in this case is that now each class has to contain enough pixels to describe its covariance matrix accurately.

2.2 Optimization of band selection

In order to find the best band combination two algorithms have been developed. The first algorithm searches all possible band combinations. This algorithm can only be used if the number of required bands is small (<4) because the calculation time increases exponentially with the number of bands. Therefore a second algorithm has been developed that searches in a more time efficient way, but as a consequence it is not guaranteed to find the optimum band combination.

The algorithms are implemented in Matlab® and make use of the toolbox PRTools, a toolbox offered for free for academic research by the University of Delft in The Netherlands. The main data-object of PRTools is called the dataset. In this dataset a large number of objects can be stored, each object consisting of a certain amount of features. We use this dataset-type to store our pixel-data. The dataset-object also makes it possible to label each object with an integer value, which can be used to divide the pixels in different classes.

We have analyzed the effects of the two algorithms:

- Algorithm 1 is the fast algorithm. The way it selects its bands is by first selecting the band with the highest quality. Then it searches for a second band that, combined with the already found band, gives the highest quality. Then it searches for a third band in the same way and this process continues way until the required number of bands are found.
- Algorithm 2 (called the optimum algorithm) searches every possible combination of bands, which guarantees that it will find the band combination with the highest quality. Because calculation times increase exponentially with the number of bands, it can only be used if the number of bands required is small. The algorithm can also be used in a sub-

optimal way, by defining a step-parameter (see below) higher than 1, in which case the algorithm gets faster. Besides a potentially better solution, Algorithm 2 has another advantage with respect to Algorithm 1: because it calculates the quality for each combination, an overview of all qualities can be made, giving extra insight in the problem.

To perform classification, the quadratic discriminant classifier (QDC) provided by PRTools is used. This is a quadratic classifier based on normal densities. For the two algorithms several inputs are needed:

- number of background classes,
- bandwidth,
- shape,
- distance type,
- overlap,
- quality criteria.

For Algorithm 2 we also set a step and time estimation parameter. For TimeEstimation, if 1, the algorithm makes an estimate of the calculation time by calculating how many combinations it will have to evaluate and multiplying this with the quality evaluation-time, which it gets by making 5 evaluations and taking the average. A Step parameter (default is 1) is defined to use the algorithm in a faster, sub-optimal way. The idea behind this parameter is that when for example a bandwidth of 30 features is used, the band consisting of features 1 through 30 will almost be exactly the same as band 2-31. By setting a step of for example 3, the algorithm will only take into account bands 1-30, 4-33, 7-36 and so on, which can greatly decrease the calculation-time without sacrificing much of the optimality of the solution.

If the overlap parameter is set to 0 (no overlap allowed), the bandwidth has also some influence on the calculation time. The larger the bandwidth the faster the algorithm will be because after the first band has been picked all features that make up this band are excluded for the following bands so effectively the total number of features decreases. Table 1 shows the calculation times of the Matlab implementation of Algorithm 1 for several numbers of bands using the Bhattacharyya or the Mahalanobis distance. The bandwidth used is 1. The number of pixels used is 1000. From this table we can conclude that the calculation of the Bhattacharyya distance takes on average about 30% less time then the calculation of the Mahalanobis distance.

number of bands	calculation time Bhattacharyya [s]	calculation time Mahalanobis [s]
2	8.5	16.0
4	19.0	31.9
6	30.9	47.7
8	43.5	63.7
10	57.3	80.3

Table 1. Band-selection calculation times for Algorithm 1 (the fast algorithm), with max_overlap = 0 and band_width = 1. The number of pixels used is 1000. Obviously calculation times are hardware dependent, but the important factor is the relative speed of the various runs.

Calculation times for Algorithm 2 are substantially longer than those of Algorithm 1. The relation between the calculation time, the number of bands and the total number of features for this algorithm is:

$$calc\_time \sim no\_pixels \cdot \frac{total\_features!}{no\_bands!(total\_features - no\_bands)!} \quad (3)$$

Depending on the value of the max_overlap parameter, the bandwidth also has a large influence on the calculation time. In Table 2 some calculation times are given for three different bandwidths and two different numbers of bands. max_overlap is set at 0 and the distance measure is Bhattacharyya. The Mahalanobis distance measure shows the same pattern but the calculation times are about 30% higher.

number of bands	Step: 1			Step: 2		
	1	10	30	1	10	30
2	00:10:03	00:07:20	00:04:58	00:02:10	00:01:50	00:00:54
3	10:33:20	07:30:00	02:08:20	01:13:20	00:48:57	00:16:10

Table 2. Band selection calculation times (hh:mm:ss) for Algorithm 2, using the Bhattacharyya distance measure, with max_overlap = 0 and band_width = 1, 10 and 30. The number of pixels used is 1000. For step parameter = 1, 2.

2.3 Results of band selection

To analyze the speed of the fast Algorithm 1 compared to slow, but optimal, Algorithm 2 a comparison has been made for a representative data set for the case that several targets are used with the following input settings:

- bandwidth = 30
- number of bands = 3
- step = 2
- overlap = 0

The data that was used consists of camouflaged military vehicles in a rural environment. Figure 3 shows an example of a typical image.

The comparison has been made for the Bhattacharyya as well as the Mahalanobis distance. Table 3 summarizes the result.

	Algorithm 1 bhattacharyya	Algorithm 2 bhattacharyya	Algorithm 1 mahalonobis	Algorithm 2 mahalonobis
Quality	0.4745	0.5450	2.3396	2.7131
QDC class. Error (miss-classified pixels)	75	76	81	78
band 1 (#features)	80 - 109	81 – 110	6 - 35	7 - 36
band 2 (#features)	114 - 143	117 – 146	110 - 139	95 -124
band 3 (#features)	168 - 197	169 – 198	169 - 198	169 -198

Table 3. Comparison of the quality between Algorithm 1 and Algorithm 2, using counting of miss-classified pixels.

Some of the bands found in the algorithm with the two classifiers are really different. Comparing band 1 for the Bhattacharyya distance and the Mahalanobis distance for Algorithm 2 shows that very different bands are selected, while the classification error is similar. This raises the question if there are more band combinations that give similar results. The differences in QDC classifier error are small and slightly in favour of the

Mahalonobis distance algorithms, and it is not known if these differences are really very significant. In view of these small QDC differences and the algorithm speeds described in the previous section, no positive choice for a preferable distance measure can be made.
To investigate this, the quality of all band combinations (34220 in total) has been plotted for the Bhattacharyya distance and the Mahalanobis distance. These plots offer a revealing view on the significance of 'best bands'. There are in fact a lot of different band combinations that have a quality close to the maximum value, especially in the case of the Bhattacharyya distance. The periodic nature of the figures arises from the systematic way in which the band combinations were chosen. Because of that, a certain band may occur more than once.
Having in mind that there is no direct translation of the distance measure into the classification result, it makes sense to not only look at the band combination with the highest distance, but also to band combinations with bands nearby those bands. If the bands are plotted that are within 10% of the maximum value for the Bhattacharyya distance, the band around 11 µm has the highest contribution to the quality, since it is always present, see Figure 2a. When this band is chosen in combination with a band between 10 and 10.5 µm, the choice of the third band does not matter anymore. It can be anywhere between 8 and 9.7 µm. Hence the contribution of this third band is minimal to the classification result. The set of the selected bands is shown in Figure 2a.
Figure 2b shows the pixel classification results. The red line in that graph represents the classification error of the band combination with the highest quality. Its classification result is average compared to the classification when the other band combinations with quality within 10% of the maximum is being used. The blue line show the classification errors for the band combinations of three bands selected from Figure 2a. The number of miss-classified pixels seems large but is considered over the entire image.

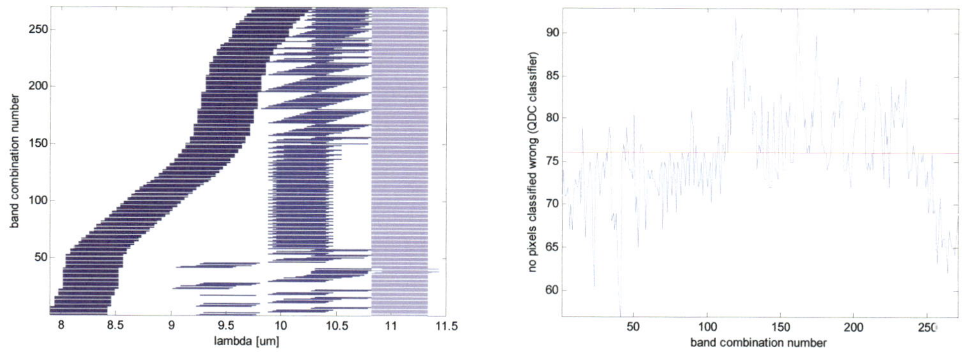

a) b)

Fig. 2. Bands that have a quality (using the Bhattacharyya distance) within 10% of the maximum quality and associated miss-classifications. Figure 2a shows the combinations of three different wavelength bands of 1 µm wide, that were selected by the algorithm. Figure 2b shows the classification errors in numbers of wrongly classified pixels for these band combinations (labelled by number).

Classification results have also been compared by using the Mahalanobis distance. This time there are only a total of 26 band combinations that are within 10% of the maximum and the bands are all around the same wavelengths. Surprisingly, these bands do not show up in the set of best bands found using the Bhattacharyya criterion. Still, the bands found with the Mahalanobis criterion give a comparable classification result. Apparently, the boundary of 10% within the maximum could be set lower to include even more band combinations.

In the application of band selection a two stage process can be applied. First, based on the distance measure a first selection of best band can be made. This results for instance in the top 10 % of bands as described in Figure 2. We can then fine-tune the band selection by calculating the number of miss-classified pixels. This process requires the use of the ground truth information or user supplied inputs. In the case of Figure 2 this would result in selecting the minimum number of miss-classified object pixels, hence the band combination 40. In this way we optimize the miss-classifications for the requested limited set of three bands.

2.4 Applications of band selection

Reasons for band selection can be processing speed, or as in our case display capability. The selection of three bands allows for easy display on the RBG channels of standard displays. In the learning phase of the band selection process of band selection, an effective visualization tool is essential to understand the steps taken by the tool. In this way the operator has a better understanding of the information content in the bands that the algorithm selects.

The number of required spectral bands is assessed with the approach described in the previous section in a number of steps in a Matlab® environment. The first requirement is that the user has to input a hyperspectral image cube in which target and background are present. Subsequently regions in the image are selected and attributed to either background or target. Target boxes are coloured in red, background boxes in white. When all relevant target and background areas are selected the spectra of all pixels inside either the target or the background boxes are plotted at the bottom panel of the graphical user interface (for this GUI see Figure 3).

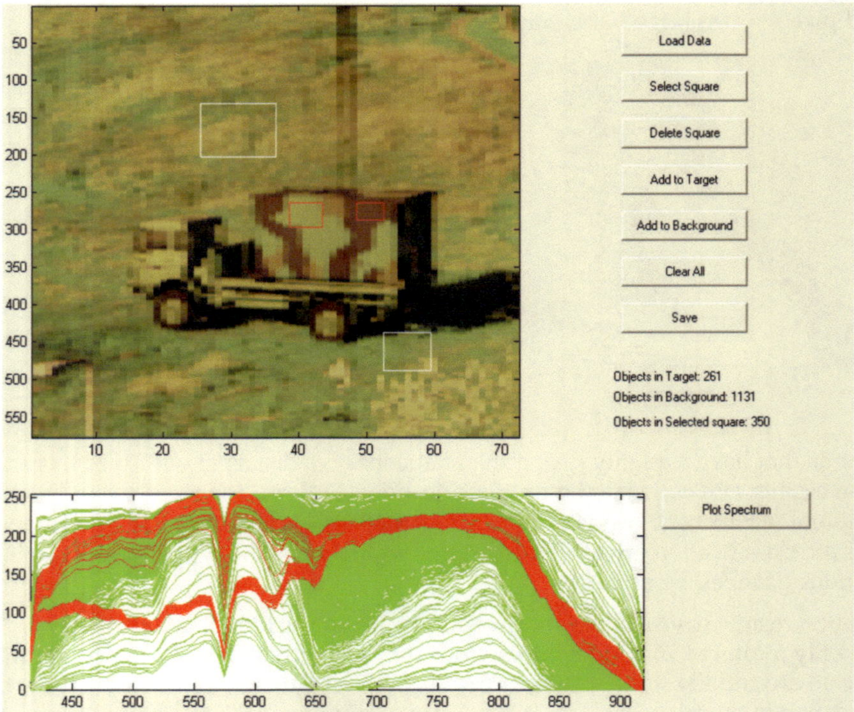

Fig. 3. Spectra from target (red lines) and background (green lines) locations in the image, and spectra of target areas and background areas are selected via this Matlab® GUI.

Within the feature (here specified as a spectral band) selection tool the feature width and the maximum allowed overlap are input. Now the optimum position of these features is calculated. The result of the optimum band positions is plotted in the top panel of the GUI (see Figure 4), by vertical lines that are drawn over the spectra. Each band starts with a blue vertical line and ends with a black vertical line. The optimum spectral band positions are also outputted to the Matlab® command line.

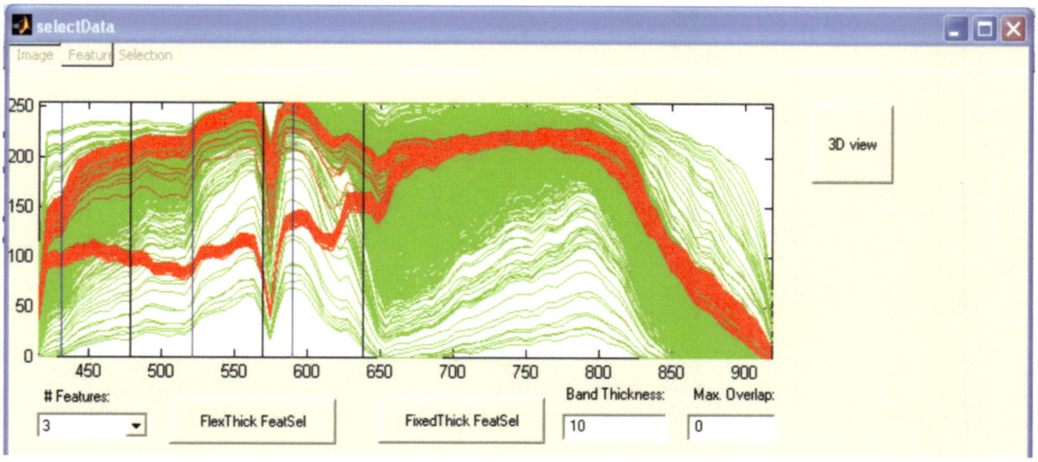

Fig. 4. Optimum position of spectral bands are indicated by vertical lines. Blue lines mark the start of the new band, black lines mark the end of the band.

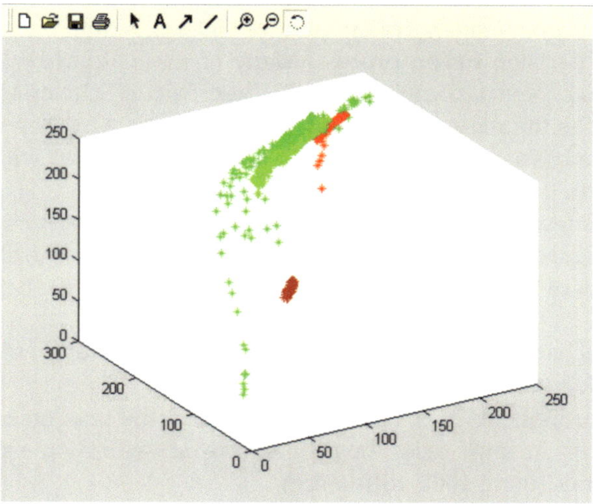

Fig. 5. Projection of pixels in 3-dimensional space spanned by three selected features (spectral bands).

If exactly three features (hence three bands) are selected the position of the pixels in 3-dimensional feature space are plotted (see Figure 5). The user can rotate the cube to inspect the separation that has been achieved between target and background pixels using the selected number of features.

2.5 Conclusions and discussion on band selection

We have presented an effective approach for optimal band selection of hyperspectral data. Our approach, named HYBASE, is typically used in a system design study and these outputs can feed operational studies. Figure 6 shows the location of the HYBASE tool in this design chain. Based on a hyperspectral data set in a relevant scenario one can make an analysis with this tool of the minimum number of required spectral bands, their widths and positions for the targets/backgrounds.

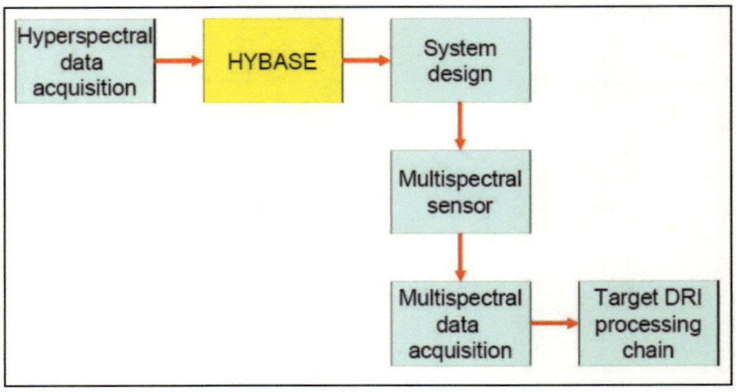

Fig. 6. Typical usage of the HYBASE base spectral band selection tool in system design.

First, the acquired hypercubes are being pre-processed using geo referencing, noise reduction, data normalization, temperature emissivity separation etc. Then, targets are being detected using anomaly and signature based detection method in combination with change detection. Spatial information is used to reduce false alarm rates. Additional sensor data from e.g. high resolution imagers, radar and/or 3D laser radar is used to classify and identify targets in a decision fusion process. Many of these algorithms run near real-time. Potential applications of sensor combinations are described in Schwering et al. (2007).

Below we will describe the main conclusions of our analysis. One has to keep in mind that these conclusions are based on an analysis using only one dataset with a frequency range from 7.7 µm to 12.1 µm (i.e. mainly emissivity is measured):

- Algorithm 1 (the fast band selection algorithm) performs good compared to Algorithm 2 (the optimal algorithm). The band combinations found by Algorithm 1 have a quality value within 15% of the quality found by Algorithm 2, while the calculation time is a lot smaller.
- Using the Bhattacharyya distance as a measure for the separation of the different classes gives comparable results as the Mahalanobis distance.
- Although no thorough study has been done between the relation of the quality and the classification error, in some cases the difference in classification error can be very large for similar qualities (up to 100% difference).
- Often, there is a whole set of different band combinations that have a comparable quality and classification result. This set is revealed by plotting the band combinations having a quality within a certain percentage of the maximum quality.
- As a consequence of the above two points, the band combination with the highest quality does not necessarily have the lowest classification error.
- The location of the best bands depends strongly on the choice of target and backgrounds.

- For a good classification result clean spectra of the targets are required. Target masks for semi-hidden targets are useless, since they contain target as well as background pixels.
- If the number of bands increases the quality increases and the classification error decreases. Although other research shows that there is an optimal number of bands for the classification error, this did not show up in our results. This optimum is due to the fact, that when the number of bands increases, statistical values used to describe the feature-space like the covariance matrix can be predicted less accurate. That this optimum did not turn up in our results is probably due to the fact that we classified areas that were also used to train the classifier.

We found no clear relationship between the bandwidth and the quality. The influence of the bandwidth on the quality is substantially less than the influence of the number of bands. This is probably because the spectra in the thermal infrared region (7.7 μm to 12.1 μm) involved did not have any sharp features.

If the complete hyperspectral image cube has to be processed the huge amount of data of a hyperspectral image cube is troublesome. This complicates a near real-time image processing solution. Band selection is an important step in realizing operational hyper/multi spectral imaging solutions. In Figure 7 we present a potential processing chain for automatic target data processing of hyperspectral image information. This describes the complete system, consisting of various real-time on-line steps, combined with supporting off-line data mining activities (represented by the history block).

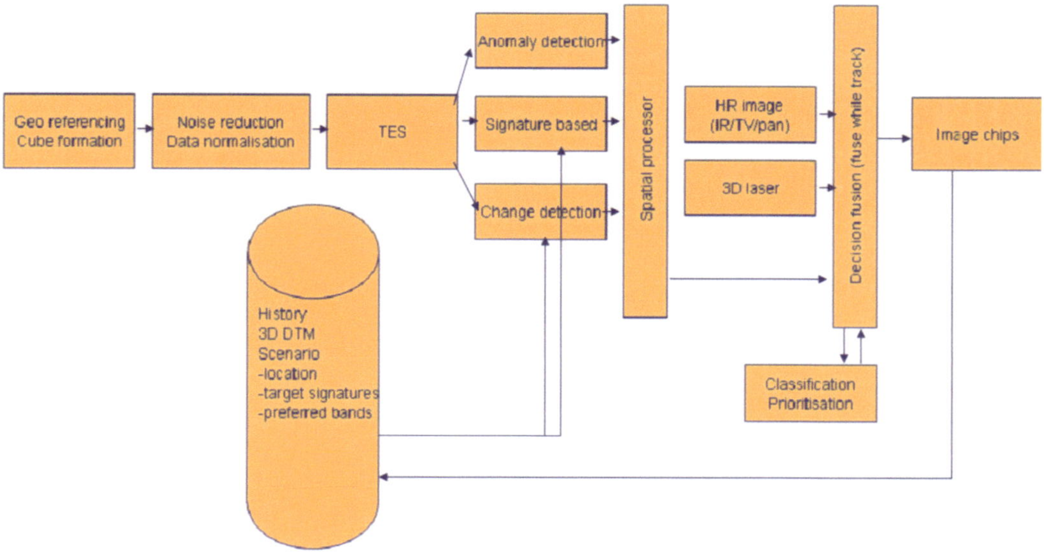

Fig. 7. A potential approach to a multi spectral image processing chain. Recorded data is put in the chain from the left, and follows each process represented in the blocks, finally resulting in image chips.

Most research involving band selection has focussed only on the location of the bands. However, for a multispectral configuration very narrow bands are not practical, because this would require large integration times to get a good signal-to-noise ratio. Our research therefore not only looked at the location of the bands but also at the width of the bands.

3. Visualisation

In automatic target detection a distinction can be made between anomaly detectors and spectral signature-based detectors. The former assume no a-priori information about the target spectral signature and simply detect those pixels that have a spectral behaviour anomalous with respect to the surrounding, global or local, background. The latter rely on the fact that the spectral reflectance of the target is known (e.g. by ground or laboratory measurements) and assume that the atmosphere can be accurately modelled in order to predict the spectral radiance expected at the sensor level. Of course, atmospheric modelling is critical and poses serious limitations to the application of this kind of algorithms in operating conditions. Nonetheless, spectral signature based detectors allow target recognition while anomaly detectors simply detect the positions of candidate targets (target cueing). In this latter case a further step is needed to mark those regions that possibly contain a true target. Furthermore, when a human observer (instead of an automatic system) interprets the data, the presentation type that suits the application best depends on prior knowledge. Our main focus is on (potential) target detection without prior knowledge. We present four new visualisation methods. These methods are evaluated in an experiment in which human observers were required to detect a number of targets.

For evaluation purposes two hyper spectral images (hyper cubes) are used obtained by an airborne hyper spectral sensor operating in the visible and NIR (near infrared) domain. It has a high spatial resolution resulting in a pixel size of approximately 0.3 meters and 160 spectral bands in the range from 0.4 μm to 1.0 μm. The targets consist of commercially available camouflage nets. The data sets were recorded in a rural environment containing mainly forest, grass and bare soil. The two hyper cubes used in this study are referred to as set A and set B. The two data sets were acquired from the same altitude (1000 m) and along the same (nominal) route. Set A was recorded in clear weather conditions around noon and set B was recorded in overcast conditions at about 6:00 pm. The datasets are 414x317 (A) and 500x307 pixels (B).

3.1 Presentation methods

We will discuss various presentation methods some of which rely on more prior information than others. The focus is on unsupervised target detection. The hyper spectral image is a 3-D data set M_{ijk}, in which i represents the (spatial) y-dimension, j the spatial x-dimension and k the index of the band (representing the wavelength dimension).

3.1.1 Broadband signal

The average over all bands can be regarded as the baseline signal. In formula (with N_k the number of bands)

$$A_{ij} = \sum_k M_{ijk} / N_k \tag{4}$$

An advantage of viewing the average signal is that the noise is low relative to the noise in the separate bands. It is therefore advisable to inspect the average signal, especially when the amount of noise in the image is relatively large. The resulting image is similar to that of a broad band sensor.

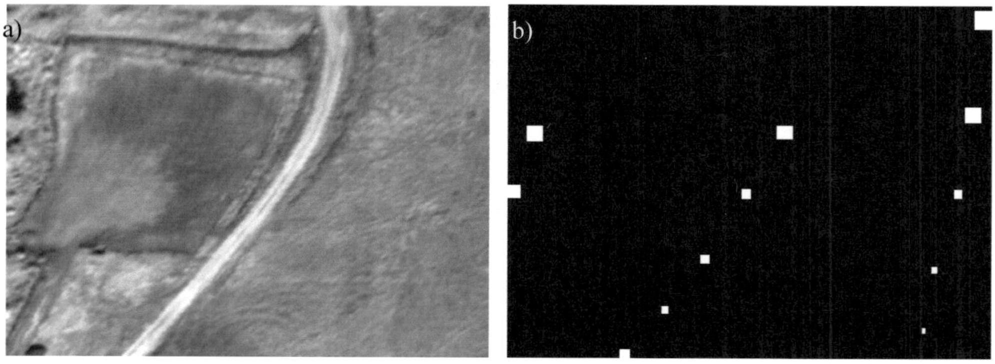

Fig. 8. Average signal of sample set A (a) and designated target locations (b).

Figure 8a shows an example of a broadband signal (set A). The designated targets are depicted in Figure 8b. In the broadband signal some targets may be visible while others may remain invisible because much of the potential target information in the data set is unavailable.

3.1.2 Movie presentations

When the hyper spectral data cube is displayed as a movie sequence all bands can be displayed. In principle there is no loss of information. In practice there are limitations to the temporal and spatial processing capabilities of the visual system which have to be taken into account when designing a good presentation form. A useful property of the data is that the (meaningful) signal varies slowly from band to band (in most cases). This means that rapid variations can be regarded as noise. When the raw data is displayed as a movie sequence the movie is almost indistinguishable from the static image of the average output. This is due to the fact that (in our case) the spatial variation between pixels is much larger than the band-to-band (wavelength dependent) variations in the output. We expect that this is a common property of hyper spectral data sets.
A solution to this problem is to subtract the average output value (of each pixel; Av_{ij}) from the output of each band and display this difference ($D_{ijk} = M_{ijk} - Av_{ij}$) as a movie sequence. In a previous study (Hogervorst & Bijl, 2006) using different hyper spectral data this method was successful in revealing many of the designated targets visible. However, with the current data this method did not work, due to the fact that pixel to pixel variations overruled the (much smaller) band-to-band variations. To make these spectral differences between pixels more visible we developed another method. We found that the difference-from-average signal D_{ijk} of each pixel is well modelled by a factor (f_{ij}) times the average profile (F_k):

$$D_{ijk} = f_{ij} \cdot F_k + \varepsilon_{ijk} \tag{5}$$

Figure 9a shows the difference-from-average (D_{ijk}, $i = 1$, $j = 1$) of the top-left pixel as a function of band index along with a scaled version of the average profile ($f_{ij}\ F_k$). The signal of the individual pixel (solid line) closely follows the scaled average profile (dashed line). Figure 9b shows the deviation (ε_{ijk}) from this model (solid line). Also shown is a version in which the band-to-band noise is reduced (dashed line). Although reduction of band-to-band noise is not strictly necessary, since the human visual system is highly robust to noise, it is more comfortable for the user. Standard noise reduction techniques can be applied to reduce the noise. We filtered the spectral signal with a Difference-of-Gaussians kernel (DOG) given by 2*Gauss(σ) - Gauss($\sigma\sqrt{2}$) (see inset Figure 9b), with $\sigma = 2$, to get rid of the high frequency modulations ($Gauss(x,\sigma)=1/\sqrt{2\pi\sigma^2}\exp[-(x^2/2/\sigma^2)]$). We used no spatial filtering to reduce the noise, since this would obscure small targets. The underlying assumption is that the fast fluctuations in the signal are due to noise. In cases in which this assumption is not appropriate information is lost by using noise reduction methods. This is the case when peaks in the signal are meaningful. In practice the width of the filter should be based on a prior analysis of the noise (preferably by inspection of a constant reference sample).

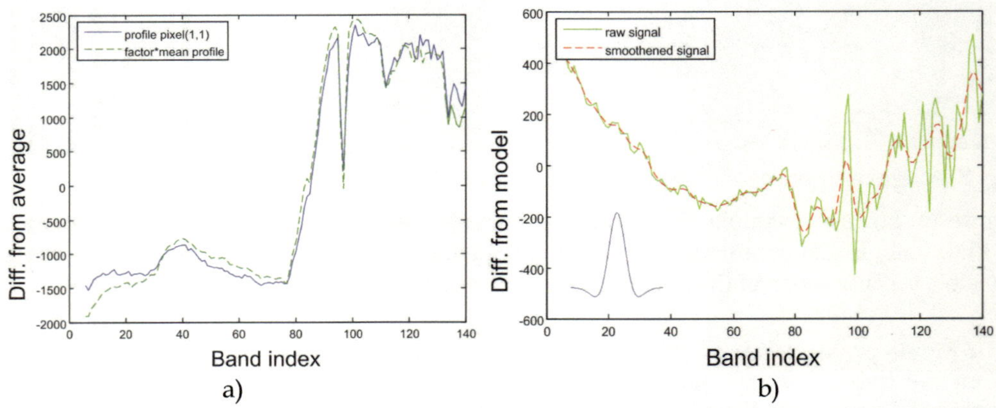

Fig. 9. a) difference-from-average output for pixel (1, 1) (top-left pixel; solid line) along with a scaled version of the mean profile (factor * mean profile; dashed line) of the difference-from-average signal. b) the deviation from the scaled average profile (solid line). This is the difference between the signals shown in Figure 9a. Also shown is a version in which the band-to-band noise is reduced (dashed line). This signal is obtained by filtering the raw signal with a Differences-of-Gaussians-kernel (see text); the filter shape is shown as an inset in Figure 9b.

Figure 10 shows three frames of a movie sequence containing the deviations from the scaled profile (see Figure 9b). In the first and last of the three example frames no targets are visible. In the middle frame most of the targets are visible. This shows the advantage of using a movie sequence as a presentation technique. Ideally, when the differences are apparent in (at least) some of the frames, this information will be picked up by the observer. Differences in spectrum between the targets and the background become apparent as a difference in the temporal profile. Furthermore, human observers take into account the fact that targets differ from elements in the background in shape and size.

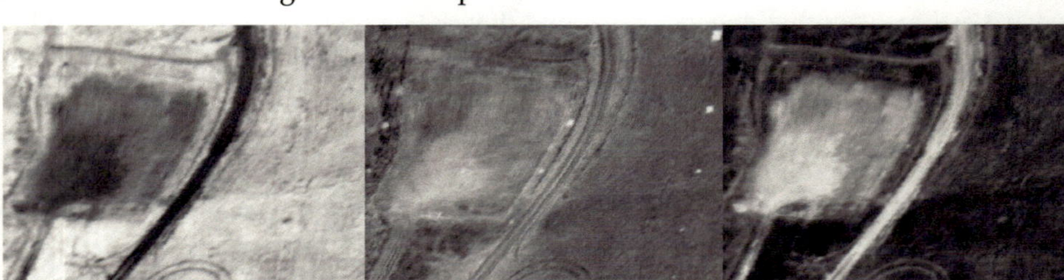

Fig. 10. Three frames of a movie sequence showing the differences from average for band indices 6, 34 and 52. The targets are invisible in bands 6 and 52 but visible in band 34. In this case we also applied dynamic noise reduction in which the temporal noise is reduced (see text). This latter transformation is not strictly necessary since the human visual system is highly robust to noise.

3.1.3 Colour schemes

The colour presentation technique produces a single image. In this case all bands of the hyper spectral signal are mapped to three independent channels. We tested several different colour schemes. In the first scheme the hyper spectral data set is divided into three broadband signals. First, the three broadband images are deduced and mapped onto the range (0, 1). Then, the average over the three images is calculated and subtracted from the broadband images. The reason for this is that (in our case) the average signal does not contain much information about the targets (see e.g. Figure 8). The difference images are then mapped onto the range (0, 1). Finally, the three (difference) images are fed into the Red, Green and Blue channels of a colour image. In a previous study (Hogervorst & Bijl, 2006) using other hyper spectral data sets this method worked quite well. However, in the current study this method did not reveal the targets. This is not surprising since a movie sequence showing the differences from the average output described in the previous section did not show the targets either. Therefore, a second data transformation was developed in which differences from the scaled average profile (see section 3.1.2 and Figure 9) are used. First we tried to apply the method described above for transforming the data into a colour image. This also did not result in an image revealing the targets. The reason for this is that this signal fluctuates rapidly from band to band from positive to negative values. So, the signal averages out in the broadband channels.

To map the signals onto a colour image we therefore resorted to a different method. We apply a principle component analysis to the (differences-from-scaled average profile) data set. The main three components are mapped into HSV-space (hue, saturation, and value components). Finally, the HSV data is transformed into an RGB-image and displayed. Figure 11a shows the result of this transformation.

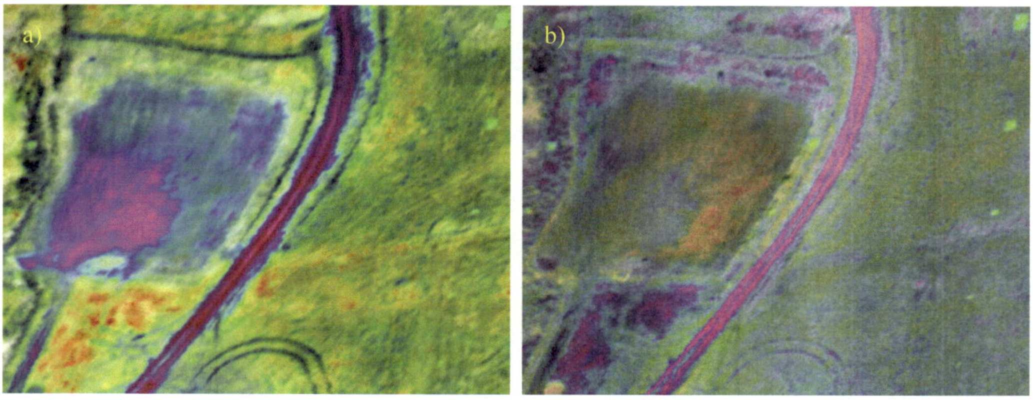

Fig. 11. a) a colour representation using the first three principal components of the differences-from-scaled average profile. The components are used as HSV-signals and converted into RGB. b) similar presentation using principal components 4, 7 and 8 (see Figure 12).

The result of the principle component analysis is interesting in its own right. Figure 12 shows the first 16 principle components. Figure 12 shows that the useful information in the hyper spectral data set (containing 160 bands) is limited to a small number of independent components (smaller than 16 in our case). With increasing component index the amount of noise increases. The targets appear in some of the components. Also visible in some of the components is fixed pattern noise with the shape of a sinusoidal corrugation (e.g. in components 5 and 6).

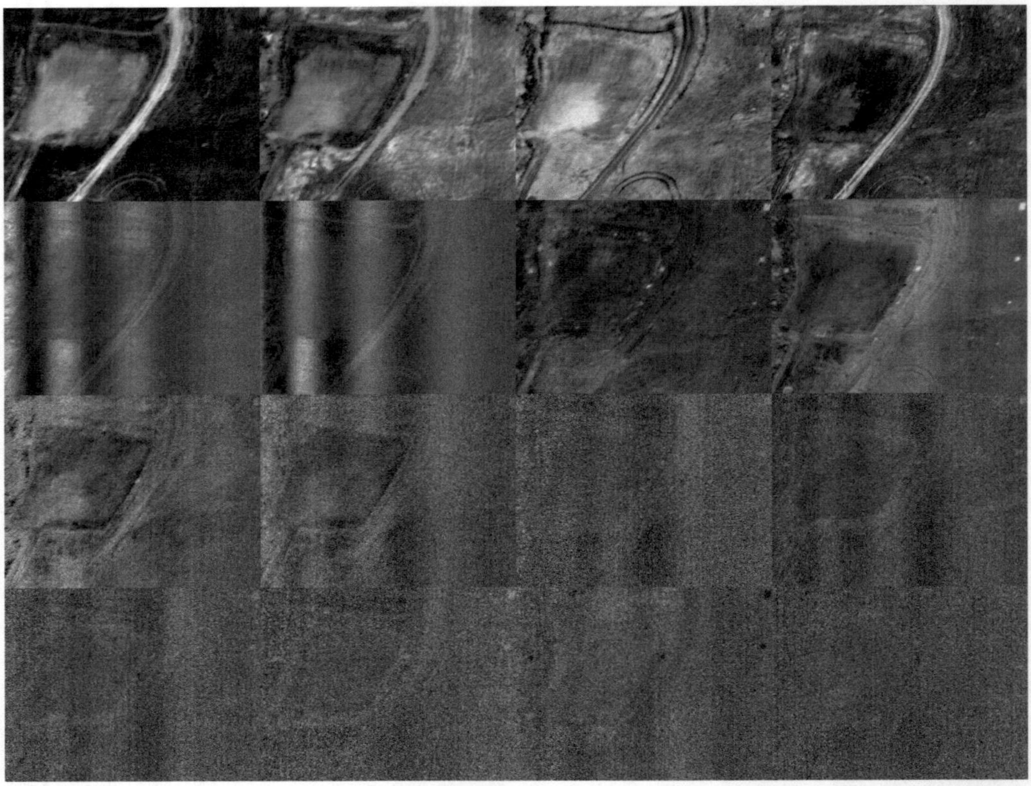

Fig. 12. First 16 principle components of difference from model (scaled average profile) data. The information content is limited to several bands: the amount of noise increases with the component index.

Which three components to combine into a colour image is difficult to decide beforehand. By default we use the first three components (Figure 11a). A more optimal combination may be found for these targets (Figure 11b). Since it is not clear from the start what the targets look like it seems reasonable to inspect all useful principle components for (potential) targets. In the evaluation experiment the default colour scheme (using the three main components) was used (assuming no prior knowledge about the targets). An alternative would be to present all informative principle components as a movie sequence, such that the loss of information is reduced.

The disadvantage of the colour scheme is that some information is lost. The advantage of this presentation type is that it can be displayed as a single image and is therefore suitable for real time presentation.

3.1.4 Signature match

When the spectral signature of the target is (reasonably) well known it can be used to highlight the target in the image. A wide range of spectral signature matching techniques exist (e.g. Green and Craig, 1985; Kruse et al., 1985; Yamaguchi and Lyon, 1986; Clark et al., 1987), which try to capture the characteristic properties of the spectral signature (e.g.

locations of steep slopes). Image spectra can be compared with individual spectra or to a spectral library (Kruse et al., 1993). This often requires calibrated hyperspectral image data in which the data is reduced to the apparent reflectance (true reflectance multiplied by some unknown gain factor).
Here, we calculate the resemblance between the signature of each pixel and that of a target. As in previous sections we use the difference-from-scaled average profile as the basic data set. We calculate the correlation between the signal of each pixel and that of the target signal. We take the average signal of the top-right target (see Figure 8b) as the target signal. The result is displayed in Figure 13a. Since (in this case) all (designated) targets have similar profiles many of the targets show up in the image. This method is well suited for finding targets with profiles similar to the one that has been identified (by inspection or prior knowledge, i.e. supervised classification). Of course, one can also look for multiple targets with different profiles simultaneously.

3.1.5 Anomaly detection

The task of the observer is to indicate (potential) targets without prior knowledge of the target or background signatures. This is similar to the task faced by an anomaly detector. We used a standard RX-detector as developed by Reed and Yu (1990) to calculate the degree of anomaly. This detector is commonly used to detect targets whose signatures are distinct from their surroundings. Instead of resorting to automatic detection, the interpretation of the data is left to a human observer.

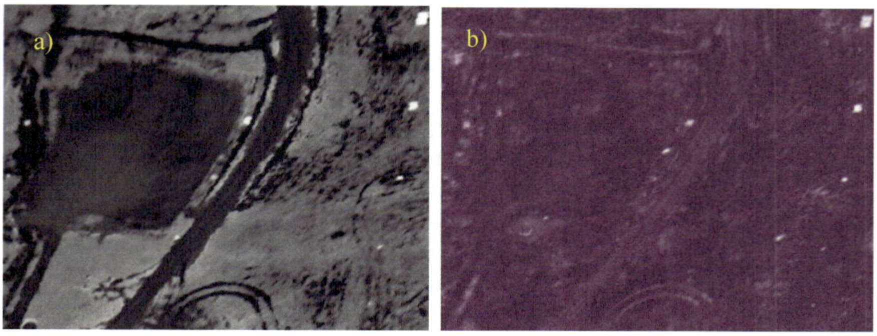

Fig. 13. a) Correlation between pixel signature and target signature (using the difference-from-scaled average profile data). b) Output of the RX-detector.

In our implementation of the RX detector a dual window was used to estimate the background mean vector and covariance matrix. It consists of a guard window that should match the size of the maximum expected target and an outer window where the training samples are collected. The following parameters were used. For data set A we used an inner window size of 71 pixels and an outer window size of 75 pixels. For data set B we used an inner window size of 80 pixels and the outer window size of 84 pixels. Figure 13b shows the output of the RX-detector for data set A.

3.2 Evaluation experiment

3.2.1 Method

Two data sets were used, referred to as set A and set B which were registered by the hyper spectral sensor described in section 3.1. We compared performance for detecting targets for 4 different presentation techniques:

- Movie
- Anomaly
- Match
- Colour

The experiments were carried out in a dimmed room. Subjects were seated in front of a 22 inch CRT-monitor (40x30 cm, 1280x1024 pixels) with a refresh rate of 75 Hz and a monitor-gamma of 2.2. Twenty four subjects participated in the experiment. Each subject was shown data sets A and B using two distinct presentation types. All combinations of presentation types and presentation order were used. The data was balanced with respect to presentation order and combination of presentation types. Each session started with an instruction showing all presentation types. In this instruction a data set was used that differed from the ones used in the experiment. The subject was told that the images represented airborne images of a natural environment containing targets. We also told the subjects that potential targets were characterized by the fact that their spectrum differs from that of the background, and that the targets differ in shape (are restricted in size) and form from background elements. They were also told that the number of targets could be anywhere between 1 and 20. The task of the subjects was to indicate potential targets by clicking the mouse in the chosen locations.

In some cases the subjects picked the same location more than once. In our analysis we treated locations less than 8 pixels apart as the same target, and the average location was used as the perceived target location.

3.2.2 Results

Figure 14 gives an overview of the performance for the different presentation types. Shown are the hit-rate and one minus the false alarm (FA) rate, in which the hit rate corresponds to the number of indicated targets divided by the total number of targets, and the false alarm rate corresponds to the number of false alarms divided by the total number of indications. Two-sided student-t tests on each of the separate data sets (A and B) were carried out (using the individual hit- and FA-rates) to determine which pairs of conditions differed significantly from each other (at a significance level of $p = 0.05$).

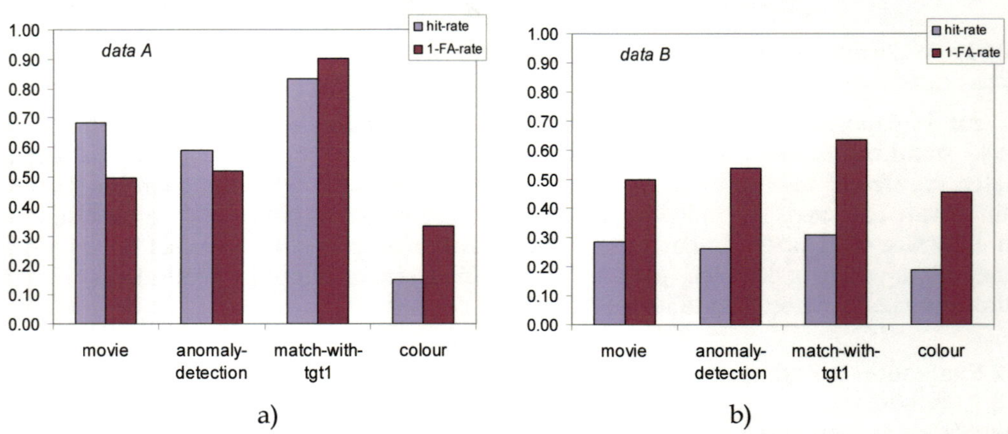

a) b)

Fig. 14. Overall performance measures HIT-rate and 1 – FA-rate (one minus false alarm rate) for the different presentation types for data sets A and B.

The best performance was found in the condition showing the match between pixel and target signature (of the top-left target), with the highest hit-rates and lowest FA-rates. Pair wise comparisons show that the hit-rate in this condition is significantly higher than the hit-rate in the "anomaly detection" and "colour" conditions in set A, while in set B the hit-rate significantly deviates from the "colour" condition. The FA-rate in this condition is significantly lower than the FA-rates of all other conditions in set A. In set B we did not find any significant differences in the FA-rates of the conditions. The "match" condition relies on prior knowledge of the target signature. This may be obtained through analysis of the data using a different presentation type. Alternatively, the target spectrum may be known from other sources of information. The results show that this information (whenever available) can be used to increase performance.

Performance in the "colour" conditions was the poorest. Pair wise comparisons reveal that the hit-rate in this condition is significantly lower than the hit-rate in all other conditions in set A, and significantly lower than the hit-rates in the "movie" and "match" conditions in set B. Also, the FA-rate is significantly higher than the FA-rate in the "match" condition in set A.

Intermediate performance was found in the "movie" and "anomaly" conditions. The hit-rate for the "movie" type is somewhat higher than that for "anomaly", but the FA-rate is also somewhat higher, although these differences are not significant. The combination of a higher hit-rate and higher FA-rate is consistent with the fact that in the "movie" condition the number of indications is higher (on average about 19%) than in the "anomaly" condition. The number of indications was found to be the largest in the "movie" condition, followed by "anomaly", "match" and "colour" conditions.

Figure 15 shows the hit-rate per target. The targets are ordered such that the average hit-rate decreases with increasing target number (set A contains 14 targets and set B contains 11 targets). Some targets are detected with (almost) all presentation types, other targets are never detected, while some targets are only detected with certain presentation types. As noticed before, hit-rate increases from "colour" to "anomaly" to "movie" to "match".

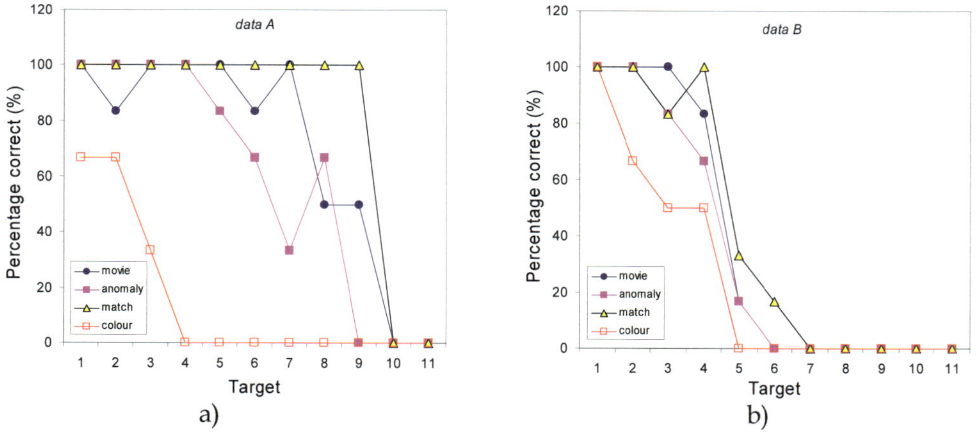

Fig. 15. Hit-rate per target for the different presentation types for data sets A and B. The targets are ordered according to difficulty of detection.

Figure 16 shows the densities of target indications for the various presentation types, along with the designated target positions for data set A. This figure shows that some areas consistently act as false targets. Also, some of the targets are missed by all of the subjects (see also Figure 15).

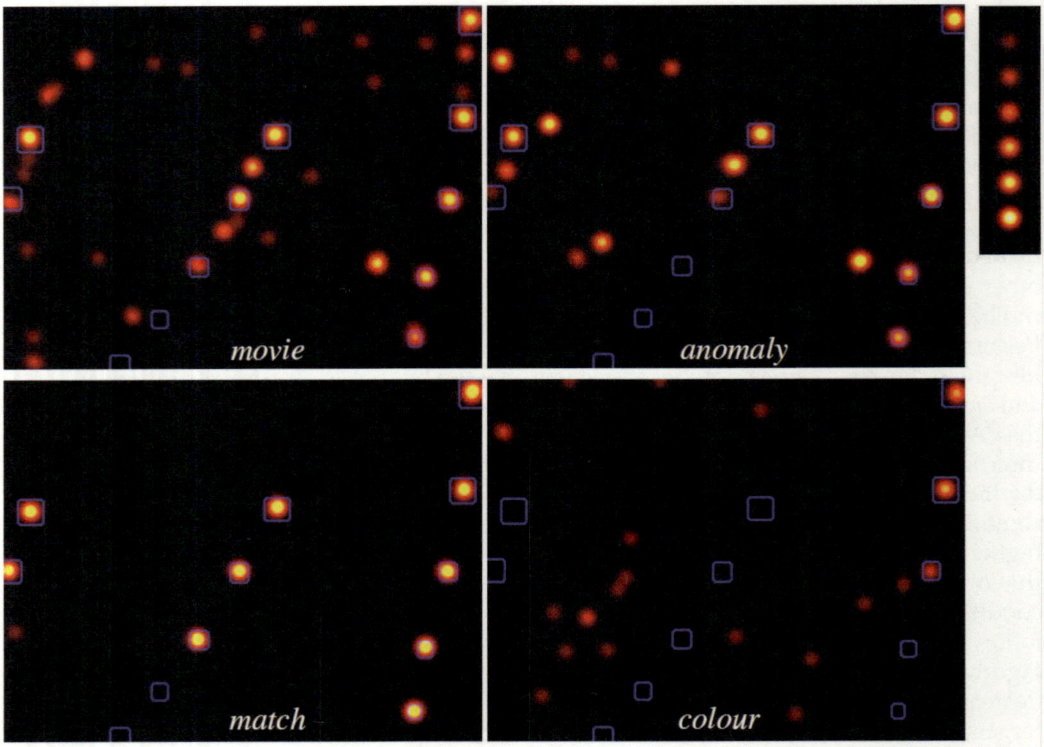

Fig. 16. Density graphs showing the density of target indications for the 4 different presentation types for data set A (for set B: see Appendix). The (blue) borders indicate the designated target positions.

3.3 Conclusion and discussion visualisation

We have presented four new methods to visualize hyper spectral data for human target detection. The human visual pattern recognition system is exploited to find potential targets and to decide whether a certain image detail is a potential target. The advantage of relying on human interpretation is that the human visual system is highly robust to noise and image transformations such as drift, translation and distortion. For instance, when the sensor (or parts of the environment) moves while the hyper spectral data is recorded, the pixels in the various bands will not be in correspondence. Automatic target recognition algorithms will have a difficult job in finding the targets in this case, while this does not represent much of a problem to the human visual system.

The first presentation type we developed is referred to as the "movie" type. In this presentation (transformed versions of) the different bands are shown in sequence. In principle no information is lost in the transformation process. The method does not rely on specific assumptions about the target signature. Its effectiveness however relies on the way the data is transformed before display. This determines whether the information in the data can be picked up by the human observer. For instance, a movie displaying the raw data looks very similar to the average broadband signal. This is due to the fact that the spatial variations are often much larger than the differences in the band-to-band variations between pixels, effectively overriding the spectral information. To overcome this problem the data was transformed (using the deviations from the scaled profile) to make the differences more visible. By applying noise reduction a clearer movie sequence can be created. This may not be strictly necessary since the visual system is well capable of discarding the noise. Even so, noise reduction can make it easier to interpret the data and may lead to faster responses, better visual comfort and less fatigue. The downside is that noise reduction removes small details from the image. In cases in which these small details contain meaningful information (this type of) noise reduction is not appropriate. For the same reason we did not use spatial averaging, since this makes it more difficult to detect small targets.

The second presentation type we investigated was the "colour" type. The advantage of such a presentation is that it results in a single image, and can therefore be used to present the data in real-time (on-the-fly). However, because a colour image contains only three independent channels, some information is lost and a suitable choice of channels has to be made. Again, the pre-processing steps in creating the colour image crucially determine whether the targets will be visible. One option is to use three broadband channels which are used as input to the RGB-channels of an image (e.g. using the result of the band selection algorithm described in section 2). As in the movie type presentation, we used the difference-from-scaled average profile as the basic data set. We applied principle component analysis to this data and used the three main components to create a colour image. This results in an image that shows only some of the targets. In general, the three (broadband) channels used for creating the colour image should be tailored to the signature of the targets and the background. The images resulting from the principle component analysis are useful for target acquisition in their own right and can be used to tailor the colour scheme to a particular set of targets. What presents the optimal colour scheme also depends on the application. Detection and identification performance depends on the distribution of noise among the different colour channels (Bijl et al., 2005). Situational Awareness benefits from naturally looking colour schemes (Toet, 2005).

The third presentation type we investigated was "anomaly detection". This method relies only on a few assumptions. The size of the targets has to be known reasonably well, although the output is not too critically dependent on this. We used the standard RX-detector (Reed & Yu, 1990). A difference with the way it is commonly used is that here the interpretation is left to a human observer (aided target detection), who can take into account the shape and size of the (potential) target. In contrast to most automatic detection algorithms the human observer does not merely analyze the output of individual pixels, but takes the context into account.

The fourth presentation type we analysed was a presentation showing the "match" between the signature of each pixel and the target signature (using the difference-from-scaled average profile data). The method relies on the fact that the target signature is known a priori. It can also be used to find targets with similar signature once one target has been identified (e.g. from using a different presentation technique). Targets with similar signature become clearly visible. The disadvantage of this method is that targets with a different signature are not revealed by this method. Of course, a match presentation can be derived for various different target signatures. These representations may be combined in a movie type presentation or by the use of colour (e.g. displaying the result for 3 target signatures).

The four presentation types were evaluated in a human observer experiment. This showed that the "match" presentation led to the best performance, with the highest hit-rate and lowest false-alarm-rate. This result was expected since all targets had similar signatures (this does not hold in general). Performance with the "colour" presentation was found to be quite poor (poorer than in a previous study: Hogervorst & Bijl, 2006). One reason for this is that the default colour scheme was used (with the three main principle components) to prevent the use of prior knowledge. A more optimal colour scheme may be determined that is geared at these targets, e.g. by using PCA (see e.g. Figure 11b). With the "movie" presentation the hit-rate was higher than in the "anomaly" presentation, but the false-alarm-rate was also somewhat higher. Which presentation type is better to use in general is difficult to decide. This will also depend on the cost associated with a hit and a false alarm. In principle, the movie sequence contains more information. However, it seems to be harder to interpret (and may be improved by training). On the other hand, the result of the anomaly detection can be displayed in a single image and is therefore more suited for real-time display.

Noise can sometimes override the signal in the separate bands of a hyper spectral sensor. In hyper spectral systems there is a trade-off between the number of bands and the noise in each band. The noise in a hyper spectral system effectively limits the useful number of bands. We have found that an indication for the number of useful independent bands can be obtained from PCA (in our case only about 10 useful independent components remain). An advantage of a hyper spectral system over a fixed broadband system is that the user can decide how to combine the information across bands (see section 2).

In order to improve search performance by prior knowledge, one may start a search by recording the signature of targets similar to the ones that one tries to find (although this may lead to a loss of targets with signatures that differ from the recorded ones). In this way, one can tune the system to the targets of interest without the need for calibrated data (which required compensation for atmosphere, etc). Similarly, it is advantageous to record the signatures of various types of background. Such information can help in tailoring the system to the interesting targets.

Some presentation types are more suitable for real-time processing (e.g. the colour scheme) and some schemes are more suitable for post-hoc analysis (e.g. the movie type). Still, schemes of the second type can be applied immediately after recording. Some of the presentation types rely more heavily on knowledge about the target than others. It is advisable to use more than one presentation type to be sure that certain information is not overlooked (e.g. in the average image) and all available information is used (and unexpected targets are not missed).

4. Overall summary

Hyperspectral sensors are used in an increasingly wide range of applications. The data contains a wealth of information. The challenge is to extract this information. Also, the question is to what extent hyperspectral data improves task performance and whether it can be approximated by a more simple multi-band sensor system. We have presented a method for choosing the bands (width and position) that result in as limited information loss as possible. Such a band selection tool is essential in the design of multispectral sensor systems, and may be used as an initial stage in data processing to reduce the amount of data. In our case, band selection optimizes the target-to-background contrast (relevant for target acquisition performance). We have described our algorithm and presented an evaluation by applying it to a representative dataset. We have also presented and evaluated different ways to visualise hyperspectral data. The various presentation types differ in the way the information is displayed and in the way information will be picked up by the observer. In a target detection experiment with human observers performance was measured and the various presentation techniques were compared. The various presentation methods vary in their optimum application, depending on the (prior) knowledge available, and whether the data is presented in real-time or used for post-hoc analysis.

We argue that often the final interpretation is best left to a (trained) human observer. Thus, the number of assumptions (signature of target and background, target shape etc.) can be restricted. Human interpretation is robust to noise and many image transformations, and can take the target background into account. Whenever knowledge about target and background (signature, shape etc.) is available this can be used to help improve the interpretation of the data by the observer (aided target detection).

5. References

Bijl, P., Lucassen,M.P. & Roelofsen,J. (2005) Identification in static luminance and color noise. *Proceedings of SPIE 5784*, 35-41.

Briottet X, Boucher, Y., Dimmeler, A., Malaplate, A., Cini, A., Diani, M., Bekman, H., Schwering, P., Skauli, T., Kasen, I., Renhorn, I., Klasen, L., Gilmore, M., Oxford, D. (2006), in *Targets and Backgrounds: XII, Characterization and Representation*, ed. W.R. Watkins, D. Clement, SPIE Vol. 6239-paper163, Orlando Florida (USA)

Clark, R. N., T. V. V. King, and N. S. Gorelick, (1987), Automatic continuum analysis of reflectance spectra: in *Proceedings, Third AIS workshop*, 2-4 June, 1987, JPL Publication 8730, Jet Propulsion Laboratory, Pasadena, California, p. 138-142.

Green, A. A., and M. D. Craig, (1985), Analysis of aircraft spectrometer data with logarithmic residuals: in *Proceedings, AIS workshop*, 8-10 April, 1985, JPL Publication 85-41, Jet Propulsion Laboratory, Pasadena, California, p. 111-119.

Hogervorst, M.A. & Bijl,P. (2006) *Visual analysis of hyperspectral images*. Report TNO-DV 2006 A338 (STG. Confidential). Soesterberg, The Netherlands, TNO Defence, Security and Safety.

Kruse, F. A., G. L. Raines, and K. Watson, (1985), Analytical techniques for extracting geologic information from multichannel airborne spectroradiometer and airborne imaging spectrometer data: in *Proceedings, International Symposium on Remote Sensing of Environment*, Thematic Conference on Remote Sensing for Exploration Geology, 4th Thematic Conference, Environmental Research Institute of Michigan, Ann Arbor, p. 309-324.

Kruse, F. A., A. B. Lefkoff, J. W. Boardman, K. B. Heidebrecht, A. T. Shapiro, J. P. Barloon, and A. F. H. Goetz, (1993), The spectral image processing system (SIPS) - Interactive visualization and analysis of imaging spectrometer data: *Remote Sensing of Environment*, v. 44, p. 145-163.

Landgrebe, D.A., (2003), *Signal Theory Methods In Multispectral Remote Sensing*, Hoboken, NJ: Wiley

Reed, I.S. & Yu, X. (1990) Adaptive multi-band CFAR Detection of an optical pattern with unknown spectral distribution parameter. *IEEE Trans. Acoustics, Speech, and Signal Processing* 38, 1760-1770.

Schwering P.B.W., van den Broek S.P., van Iersel M., (2007), in *Infrared Technology and Applications XXXIII*, eds. B.F. Andresen, SPIE Vol. 6542-100, 654230, Orlando Florida (USA), April 9-13, 2007: "EO System Concepts in the Littoral"

Seijen, H.v., Schwering,P.B.W. & Bekman,H.H.P.T. (2004) *The Kvarn campaign NL-WP4 contribution band selection algorithms application to LWIR HBA(AHI) data.* JP8.10 document Th_T_WP4_K_01. 2004. TNO.

Seijen, H.v., Schwering,P.B.W. & Bekman,H.H.P.T. (2005) *Hyper spectral Band Selection Algorithm.* Report FEL-04-A282. 2005. The Hague, TNO Physics and Electronics Laboratory.

Toet, A. (2005) Colorizing single band intensified nightvision images. *Displays*, 26, 15-21.University of Delft, www.prtools.org

Vagni, F. (2006) *Survey of Hyperspectral and Multispectral Imaging Technologies.* NATO Technical Report.

Withagen P.J., den Breejen, E., et. al. (2001), "Band selection from a hyperspectral data-cube for a real-time multispectral 3CCD camera", *Proceedings of SPIE Vol. 4381*, pp 84-93

Yamaguchi, Y., and R. J. P. Lyon, 1986, Identification of clay minerals by feature coding of nearinfrared spectra: in *Proceedings, International Symposium on Remote Sensing of Environment*, Fifth Thematic Conference, "Remote Sensing for Exploration Geology", Reno, Nevada, 29 September- 2 October, 1986, Environmental Research.

APPENDIX: Presentations and performance results of Data set B.

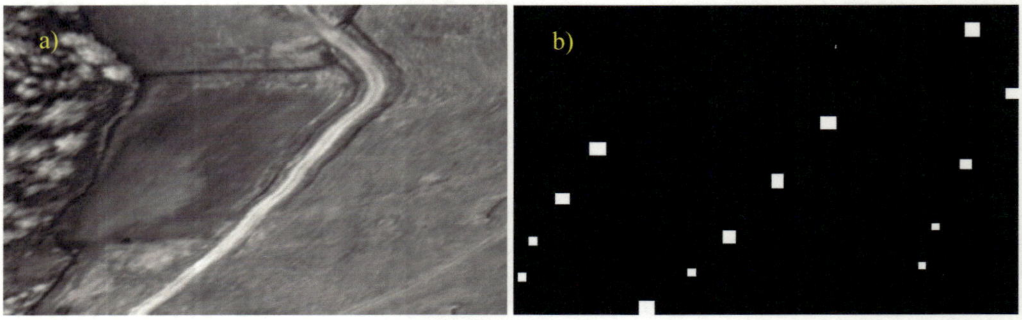

Fig. A1. Various presentation types of data set B, with a) the average, b) the designated target locations.

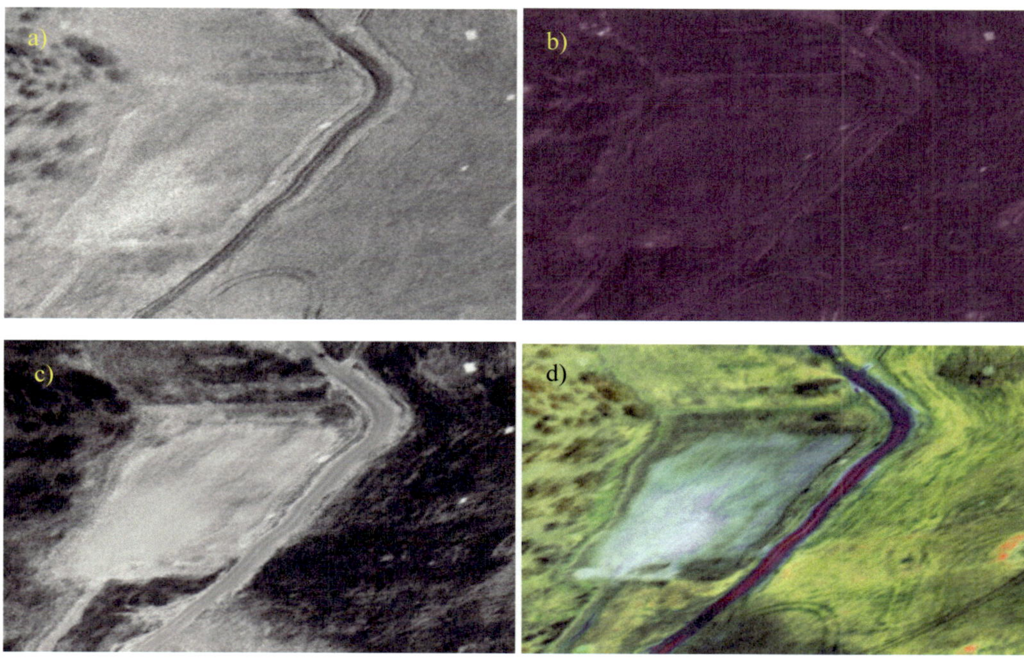

Fig. A2. Various presentation types of data set B, with a) band 37 of the movie sequence (the frame that reveals the targets best), b) anomaly, c) match with target 1 (highest target), and d) colour representation.

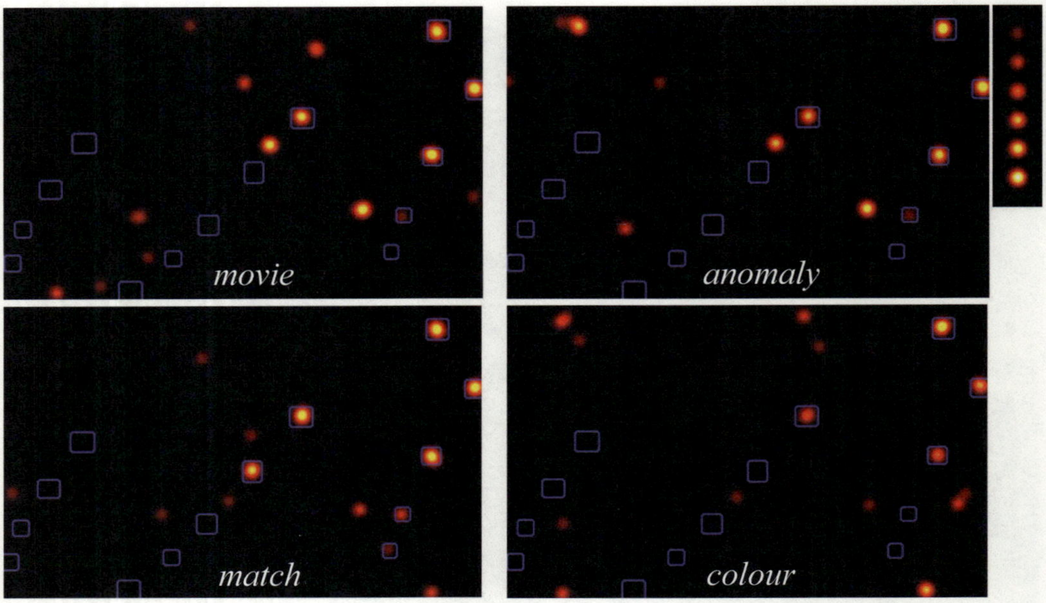

Fig. A3. Density graphs showing the density of target indications for the 4 different presentation types for data set B. The blue borders indicate the designated target positions.

13

Data Retrieval and Visualization for Setting Research Priorities in Biomedical Research

Hailin Chen and Vincent VanBuren
Texas A&M Health Science Center,
United States of America

1. Introduction

Over the past two decades, particularly after the completion of the human genome project, biomedical research has produced a huge amount of data. With the expansion of information technology, investigators have gained basic competency with integrating different resource data sets into unions. The basic principle of this integration is to use the co-occurrence of the same or similar (orthologous) elements in different data sets as links between those data sets. Increasingly more experiment-based databases have been established, which facilitates this integration of data sets. During this blooming period of biomedical research, high-throughput experimental data is fuelling systems biology research. In the pre-genomic era, researchers were only capable of conducting experiments with a single gene or a single protein at a time, which could not provide a global perspective on the molecular interactions that bridge the gap between external signal and internal response. Within the past two decades, several high-throughput technologies have been developed to address this difficulty. Expression microarrays detect the relative abundance of gene transcripts by comparing two or more biological conditions, and have become a common tool for screening thousands of genes for expression changes in response to a perturbation, or to track transcriptional changes in developmental processes. As a way of visualizing and interpreting the flood of data in recent years, the creation of biological networks from data became a prevalent target in biomedical research recently, including the construction of protein-protein interaction networks (PPN), gene regulatory networks (GRN), and metabolic and signaling networks and pathways, as well as disease-related or cell function-related networks. The integrative strategy of combining different data sets is a natural way of setting up networks. Also, based on the data obtained from high-throughput experiments, networks may be created by modeling the internal relationships of these data. Several popular analytical approaches are being utilized to model networks (Gebert, et. al., 2007; de Jong, 2002).

Boolean networks describe each element as a variable with the value 0 or 1 to represent the state of the element as 'off' or 'on', respectively. Modeling networks by means of Boolean network became popular in the wake of a groundbreaking study by Kauffman. Kauffman employed Boolean networks to model the global properties of large-scale regulatory systems, which is called Kauffman's NK Boolean networks. An NK automaton is an autonomous random network of N Boolean logic elements with each element having K inputs and one output, all taking binary (0 or 1) values. If K is large, like K=N, the network behavior is essentially stochastic. However, when K~2, the network behaves with a high degree of observed order. NK automata were thus condidered as a model of gene regulaory network. Kauffman noted that the case of K~2 was appropriate for modelling gene regulatory networks, especially in an evolutionary context (Kauffman, 1969). A Boolean network G(V,F) is defined by a set of nodes corresponding to genes $V = \{x_1,\ldots,x_n\}$ and a list of Boolean functions $F = (f_1,\ldots,f_n)$. The future state of an element is completely determined by the values of the states of other elements (regulators) by means of underlying logical Boolean functions that are defined as part of the model.

Bayesian networks model the biological network with a directed acyclic graph. For each element, a conditional distribution p(x_v | parents(x_v)) is defined, where parents(x_v) denotes the variables corresponding to the direct regulators of the element. Together defining the Bayesian network, this conditional distribution for each element uniquely specifies a joint probability distribution p(x).

$$p(x) = \prod_{v \in V} p(x_v \mid x_{pa(v)}) \tag{1}$$

Bayesian network modeling equation

Differential equations extract the network from high-throughput experimental data by considering the instantaneous concentration of each element. The instantaneous concentration of each element is completely determined by the concentration (x_n) of other elements providing a regulation function.

$$\frac{dx_i}{dt} = f_i(x_1,\ldots,x_n,t) \tag{2}$$

Differential equation modeling

Co-expression models networks from statistical analysis, and may be based on a large number of data sets collected from public repositories. Co-expression is often based on co-variance analysis. However, comparison between the co-variances among data sets having different scales would be difficult. The Pearson correlation coefficient addresses this difficulty. It measures the co-expression between every two elements with the value in the range from -1 to 1, which allows networks to be established based on some threshold value for the magnitude of the correlation.

$$corr(X,Y) = \frac{\mathrm{cov}(X,Y)}{\sigma_X \sigma_Y} = \frac{E[(X-\mu_X)(Y-\mu_Y)]}{\sigma_X \sigma_Y} \tag{3}$$

Pearson correlation coefficient equation

Combining prior knowledge into the process of network inference is often accomplished with supervised learning algorithms. The basic principle is to use natural inductive reasoning for prediction of new regulations based on the similarity of their experimental profiles to that of known regulatory elements. Knowledge-based simulation is also called rule-based simulation in the field of artificial intelligenece. Rule-based simulations contain two parts, the set of facts and the set of rules. Facts offer knowledge of each object in the network, while rules including a condition component and an action component make judgment on objects according to the conditions and operate upon the objects' behavior via actions once the conditions are satisfied. This simulation algorithm repeats the process of matching the facts in the knowledgebase against the conditions in the rule part and executes actions when the approriate conditions are satisfied (de Jong, 2002).

A variety of analytical approaches are being used to construct networks from either established databases or from high-throughput experimental data. This has led to a need for tools to visualize and analyze these networks. This need stimulated the ongoing creation of numerous algorithms and software applications for constructing, manipulating and analyzing networks. Many of those are general-purpose programs with applications to most of the commonly employed types of complex networks, including social, transportation, communication, and financial networks. Typically, transcriptional regulatory models are constructed for a particular cellular process or physiological/disease pathway of interest. The construction of networks from established databases or from high-throughput experimental data offers a visual tool for developing new hypotheses regarding underlying molecular interactions. These new well-informed hypotheses will serve as the basis for conceiving new biomedical experiments to confirm or reject these predicted interactions, and thus serve an important role in setting research priorities.

In this chapter, we are going to focus our attention on selected examples of data retrieval and visualization tools, including the **STRING** database and **Cytoscape**, and compare these popular tools with with our new web based software, **StarNet** and **Cognoscente**, for use in setting research priorities for biomedical studies.

2. Data retrieval

The **STRING** database was primarily constructed from the integration of phylogenetic profiles, a database of transcription units and a database of gene-fusion events by the Bork and Snel groups (Snel et al., 2000; von Mering et al., 2003; von Mering et al., 2005; von Mering et al., 2007, Jensen, et al., 2009). Users may infer putative protein-protein interactions with a confidence score based on the constituent relationships in this integrative database. Phylogenetic profiles are derived from an evolutionary tree. During evolution, functionally linked proteins tend to be either preserved or eliminated in new species simultaneously. This property of correlated evolution is characterized for each protein by its phylogenetic profile, and **STRING** encodes the presence or absence of an orthologous protein in every known genome. Those proteins having matching or similar profiles have a strong tendency to be functionally linked. Transcriptional units (operons) are extracted from a number of genomes by identifying the conserved gene clusters. Genes in a transcriptional unit are hypothesized to be functionally linked. Gene-fusion events can be understood by the following example. The interacting proteins GyrA and GyrB subunits of E.coli DNA gyrase are orthologs of a single fused chain (topoisomerase II) in yeast. Thus, the similarities of GyrA and GyrB to some segment of topoisomerase II might be used to predict their functional interaction in *E. coli*. **STRING** is being developed as a multi-dimensional database by combining its three original database components (phylogentics profiles, transcription units, and and gene fusions) together with known protein-protein interactions, an expression database and a database of putative protein-protein interactions found via a text-mining search in Pubmed.

Below we show an example of a **STRING** query (http://**STRING**-db.org/) of the protein-protein interactions seeded by Gata4, a well-known transcription factor in cardiac development (Figure 1).

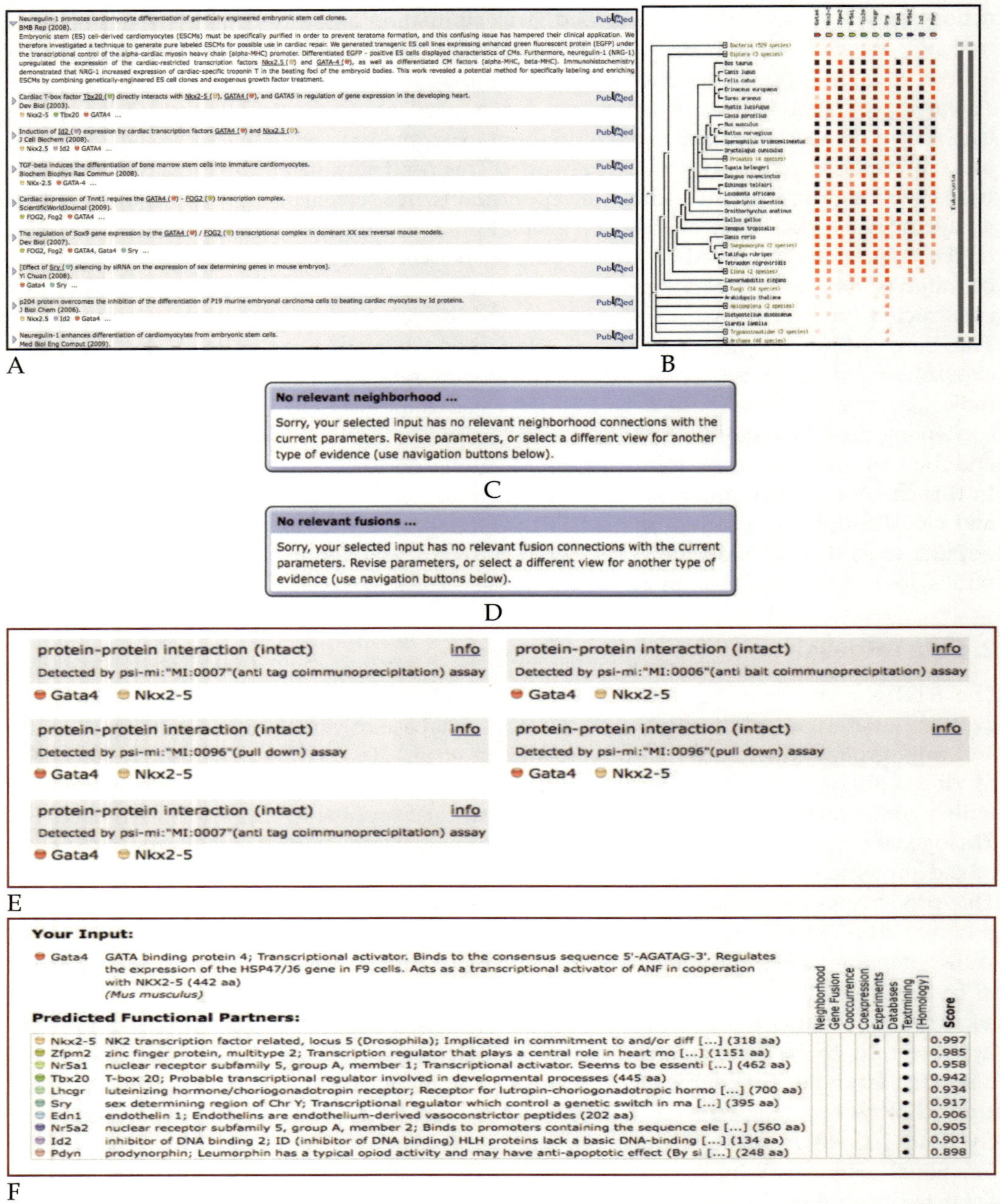

Fig. 1. **STRING** search results for Gata4 from different databases: text-mining searching database (A), phylogenetic profiles (B), transcription units database (C), gene-fusion events database (D) and known protein-protein interaction database (E). F gives a summary result of all searches, and includes a combined confidence score. Higher scores indicate greater confidence in the putative interaction. Here the highest confidence is given to NKX2-5 as an interactive partner of Gata4, as this is supported with experimental evidence.

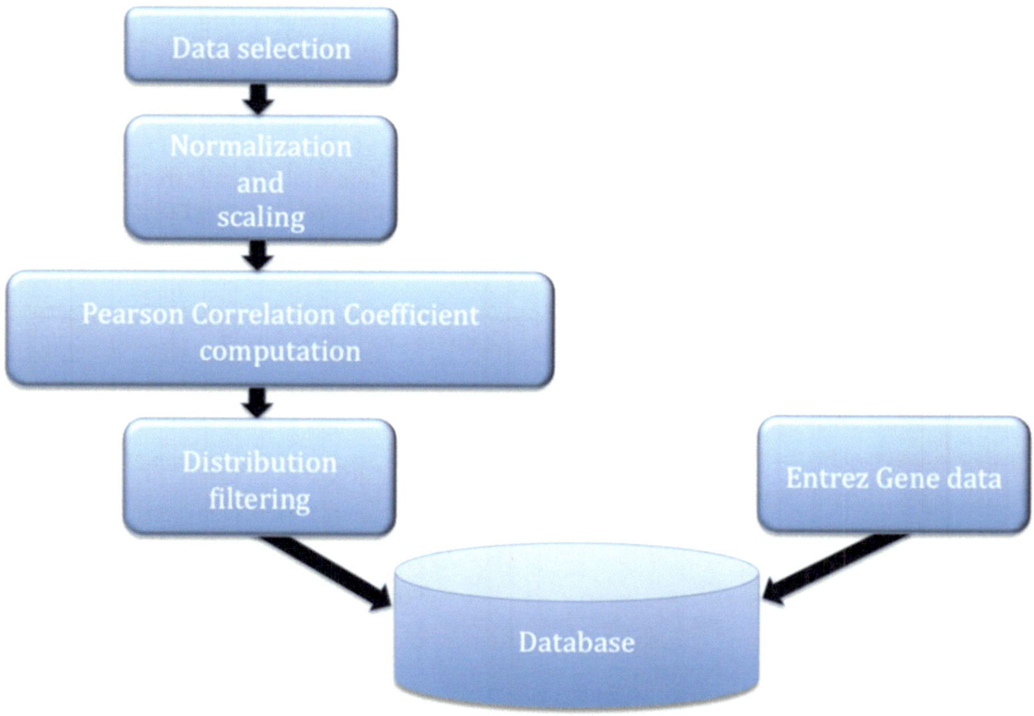

Fig. 2. Workflow of establishing the MySQL database for **StarNet**.

StarNet is a web-based interface for creating coexpression networks from correlated microarray expression profiles, where the networks radiate from a selected seed gene (Jupiter & VanBuren, 2008; Jupiter et al., 2009). To build this tool, we collected microarray data for several species from NCBI's Gene Expression Omnibus (GEO), which contains thousands of array experiments. Data was normalized and scaled using the **justRMALite** (Robust Multichip Analysis) package within the BioConductor suite of tools on the R statistical computing platform. Based on this normalized data, Pearson correlation coefficients were computed for all pairwise comparisons of genes to populate a MySQL database (Figure 2). The current version of **StarNet**, **StarNet** 2, expands the coverage from mouse to ten different species (human, rat, mouse, chicken, zebrafish, *Drosophila*, *C. elegans*, *S. cerevisiae*, *Arabidopsis* and rice) and offers two alternate data sets (Full data cohort & Development data cohort) for some of these species (human, rat, mouse and Drosophila). For each organism represented, data was collected from between 148 (rice) and 3,763 (human) Affymetrix microarray samples (Table 1). In total, 12,762 arrays were used to build our database, which is approximately 2.7% of the samples in GEO (as of August 2010). **StarNet** allows cross-species comparisons by automatically doing gene lookups across known orthologs. **StarNet** identifies gene pairs with high magnitude correlations across a large number of experiments to offer strong statistical results that include confidence intervals. To support an interpretation of the generated coexpression networks, **StarNet** offers a database search of known interactions involving genes and gene products from the prescribed networks. Thus, while tools such as **STRING** provide a data integration strategy to retrieve likely functional protein-protein interactions, **StarNet** better facilitates exploratory analysis of selected data. In comparison, **StarNet** retrieves high-ranking correlations between gene expression profiles constructed from a large collection of microarray data to iteratively build star networks around a gene of interest, while **STRING** retrieves putative relationships between elements via co-occurrence of the elements across a number of already established databases. **STRING** makes explicit predictions from multiple data sources, whereas **StarNet** provides multiple types of data that support the user's ability to make their own inferences. **StarNet** additionally supports the user's judgment by allowing greater flexibility in prescribing the relative size and topology of the networks created.

Species	Full Cohort Arrays	Development Cohort Arrays	Genes on Array
Homo sapiens	3,763	372	17,726
Mus musculus	2,145	239	16,631
Rattus norvegicus	1,982	247	11,427
Gallus gallus	164	-	12,491
Danio rerio	222	-	6,838
Drosophila melanogaster	454	195	13,060
Caenorhabditis elegans	381	-	15,015
Saccharomyces cerevisiae	254	-	5,566
Arabidopsis thaliana	3,249	-	21,281
Oryza sativa	148	-	23,419

Table 1. Expression microarray data represented in **StarNet**. The second column is the number of arrays used in the full condition, and the third is the number of arrays used in the development condition. This open-access table was reproduced from Jupiter et al., 2009.

The sets of correlation coefficients calculated as described above for the MySQL database have a relatively large memory footprint and contain a large amount of data that is of little interest from our perspective (i.e. low magnitude correlations). Thus, this collection was trimmed by selecting the 100,000 highest magnitude positive and negative correlations for each cohort. As highly correlated groups of genes in a correlation network exhibit a high amount of interconnectedness, this distribution doesn't include all genes on an array. To guarantee complete coverage for all genes on each respective platform, we constructed another sub-distribution through gene-by-gene extraction of the ten highest magnitude positive and negative correlations for the gene.

Below we used the gene Gata4, the same example used above in a **STRING** query, as our seed gene in a **StarNet** query (http://vanburenlab.medicine.tamhsc.edu/**StarNet**2.html).

On the **StarNet** query page (Figure 3), the user selects a data set cohort, which is correlation data for a collection of microarrays for a particular array platform (i.e. a particular organism), with options for ten species. There are two alternate data sets, a *Full* data set cohort and a *Development* data set cohort, available for rat, mouse, human and *Drosophila*. The *Development* data set is a subset of the *Full* data set, where the array data used in the *Development* cohort was derived from selected samples representing early embryos, embryonic heart, and adult heart. The *Full* data cohort was dervied from a heterogeneous collection of samples from a variety of tissues types. The user may also select a second cohort for pairwise comparison. The genecentric distribution, which was built by selecting high magnitude correlations on a gene-by-gene basis, is the default distribution because this distribution has complete coverage of the array platform. To create the genecentric distribution, the ten largest positive correlations to each gene were selected, where the *p*-value of the null hypothesis correlation was less than 0.05 (a two-tailed t-test was used to compute *p*-values for each correlation coefficient). This was repeated for high magnitude negative correlations, and the union of positive and negative correlations was constructed.

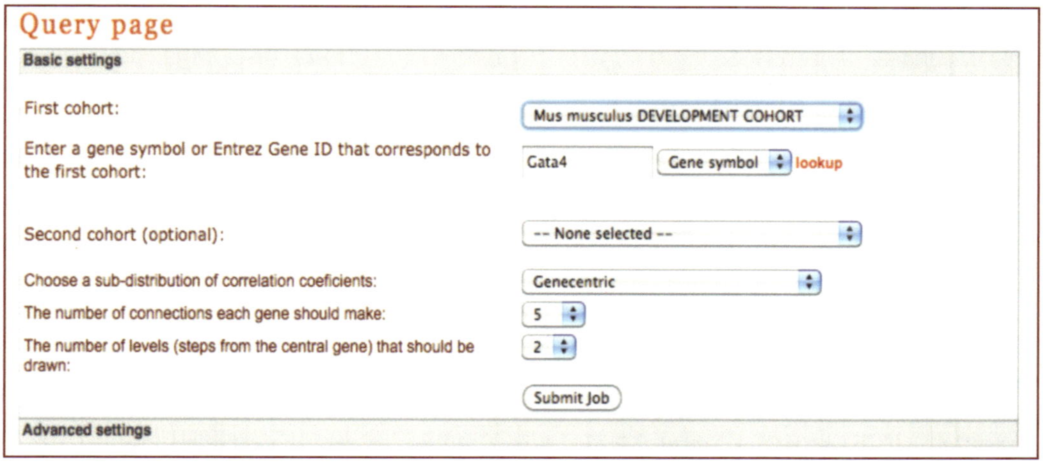

Fig. 3. Gata4 was used as the seed gene to start a search in **StarNet** of the mouse development data cohort, a set of precomputed pairwise correlations derived from selected microarray data in mouse.

There are two additional classes of correlation distribution to choose from: 1. the genecentric construction was repeated, but constrained to those genes whose GO (Ashburner, 2000) annotation contains the term "transcription"; and 2. the same strategy was repeated for those genes whose GO annotation contains either of the terms "transcription" or "signal". *The number of connections each gene should make* is specified by the user, with a default of five connections. This parameter specifies the number of highest-ranking correlations to draw as edges in the correlation network. *The number of levels* (default = two) specifies how many steps from the central node to expand the search. With Gata4 as the seed gene, the default settings will retrieve the five highest magnitude correlated genes with Gata4 (level 1, Table 2) and retrieves the five highest-magnitude correlated genes for each of those genes in the MySQL expression correletion database. The web interface of **StarNet** retrieves a table of the high magitude correlations, beginning with the high magnitude correlations with the query gene, and reports the 95%- and 99%-confidence intervals for each coefficient (Figure 4).
Although the quick pace of biomedical research is continually providing an enormous quanity of experimental data, the synthetic analysis of that data to generate informed hypotheses is progressing at a much slower rate, and building models via systematic review of the literature can be a time-consuming and inefficient process for individual investigators. **Cognoscente** is a new tool under development in our group for querying and visualizing documented biomolecular interactions (Figure 5). It is a web-based database and freely available, with no required user registration to make queries. **Cognoscente**'s knowledgebase

can be utilized as a convenient tool for collecting prior knowledge to generate new hypotheses and refine established networks using supervised learning algorithms. Moreover, it offers users the ability to directly submit new interactions so that community support can drive the completeness of the knowledgebase. For quality assurance and attribution, registration is required to make new submissions to the database.

Gene ID 1	Gene ID 2	Pearson Correlation	P-Value	Number Of Arrays
14463	14465	0.7902	~0	239
12406	14463	0.7759	~0	239
14463	241556	0.7757	~0	239
11975	14463	0.7565	~0	239
14463	23871	0.7544	~0	239
14463	21412	0.7493	~0	239
14362	14463	0.7484	~0	239
11749	14463	0.7481	~0	239
14463	54195	0.7447	~0	239

Table 2. High ranking set of correlation coefficients for GeneID 11463 (Gata4). In the coefficient database, all the genes are indexed by the Entrez GeneID. The five highest-magnitude correlated genes with 11463 (Gata4) are: 14465 (Gata6), 12406 (Serpinh1), 241556 (Tspan18), 11975 (Atp6vDa1), and 23871 (Ets1). The five top-ranking correlations are outlined by the dashed box.

3. Data visualization and analysis

Appropriate visualization of biological data can be a very powerful tool for drawing new inferences from data. When used for the standard comparison of data from two samples, visualizations showing clear differences can often obviate the need for statistical analysis. Drawing graphs or networks is a powerful way to visualize a list of documented biomolecular interactions, or for associations that are imputed from similarity metrics. These types of visualizations can offer insights and understanding of complex relationships that cannot be obtained as easily by reflecting on a pairwise list of interactions or associations.

In the previous section, we discussed how **StarNet** retrieves correlations based on a query gene of interest, and compared this functionality with how **STRING** retrieves predicted functional interactions. In this section, we focus on how **StarNet**, **Cognoscente** and **Cytoscape** may be used to powerfully visualize biological data and knowledge. We discuss how **StarNet** creates visualizations of the correlative network topologically, as well as other visualizations provided by **StarNet** that support user interpretation of the biological relevance of the correlation networks. **StarNet** allows user control over the general size and topology of the networks produced, and performs a test of GO term enrichment for those networks. The new **HeatSeeker** module in **StarNet** 2 draws false color maps comparing two selected networks from different species or conditions. **HeatSeeker** makes an unbiased comparison by combining the lists from both networks and then comparing only those genes that share orthologs on both platforms. **HeatSeeker** thus offers insight into the differential wiring of gene regulatory networks among different species or conditions (Jupiter & VanBuren, 2008; Jupiter et al., 2009).

Edge list: mouse development cohort

Gene pairs	Pearson Corr. Coefficient	95% Confidence Interval	99% Confidence Interval
Gata4 [14463] ---- Gata6 [14465]	0.78907 (n=239)	[0.7359, 0.8326]	[0.7168, 0.8446]
Gata4 [14463] ---- Serpinh1 [12406]	0.77460 (n=239)	[0.7183, 0.8208]	[0.6982, 0.8336]
Gata4 [14463] ---- Atp6v0a1 [11975]	0.75459 (n=239)	[0.6942, 0.8045]	[0.6727, 0.8182]
Gata4 [14463] ---- Ets1 [23871]	0.75407 (n=239)	[0.6935, 0.8040]	[0.6720, 0.8178]
Gata4 [14463] ---- Tspan18 [241556]	0.75401 (n=239)	[0.6935, 0.8040]	[0.6719, 0.8178]
Gata6 [14465] ---- Gata4 [14463]	0.78907 (n=239)	[0.7359, 0.8326]	[0.7168, 0.8446]
Gata6 [14465] ---- Serpinh1 [12406]	0.78420 (n=239)	[0.7299, 0.8286]	[0.7105, 0.8409]
Gata6 [14465] ---- Scarf2 [224024]	0.68336 (n=239)	[0.6093, 0.7456]	[0.5833, 0.7630]
Gata6 [14465] ---- Tcf21 [21412]	0.68105 (n=239)	[0.6066, 0.7437]	[0.5804, 0.7612]
Gata6 [14465] ---- Fzd1 [14362]	0.67788 (n=239)	[0.6028, 0.7410]	[0.5765, 0.7587]
Serpinh1 [12406] ---- Calu [12321]	0.81122 (n=239)	[0.7629, 0.8506]	[0.7455, 0.8613]
Serpinh1 [12406] ---- Gata6 [14465]	0.78420 (n=239)	[0.7299, 0.8286]	[0.7105, 0.8409]
Serpinh1 [12406] ---- Gata4 [14463]	0.77460 (n=239)	[0.7183, 0.8208]	[0.6982, 0.8336]
Serpinh1 [12406] ---- Sparc [20692]	0.77383 (n=239)	[0.7174, 0.8202]	[0.6972, 0.8330]
Serpinh1 [12406] ---- Tmem98 [103743]	0.75266 (n=239)	[0.6918, 0.8029]	[0.6702, 0.8168]
Atp6v0a1 [11975] ---- App [11820]	0.79215 (n=239)	[0.7396, 0.8351]	[0.7208, 0.8469]
Atp6v0a1 [11975] ---- Msn [17698]	0.78460 (n=239)	[0.7304, 0.8290]	[0.7110, 0.8412]
Atp6v0a1 [11975] ---- Aplp2 [11804]	0.78406 (n=239)	[0.7298, 0.8285]	[0.7103, 0.8408]
Atp6v0a1 [11975] ---- Twsg1 [65960]	0.76952 (n=239)	[0.7122, 0.8167]	[0.6917, 0.8297]
Atp6v0a1 [11975] ---- Arl2bp [107566]	0.76562 (n=239)	[0.7075, 0.8135]	[0.6867, 0.8267]
Ets1 [23871] ---- Col3a1 [12825]	0.86373 (n=239)	[0.8275, 0.8928]	[0.8144, 0.9007]
Ets1 [23871] ---- Anxa5 [11747]	0.85316 (n=239)	[0.8144, 0.8843]	[0.8004, 0.8928]
Ets1 [23871] ---- Prkar1a [19084]	0.84970 (n=239)	[0.8102, 0.8815]	[0.7958, 0.8902]
Ets1 [23871] ---- Pja2 [224938]	0.83364 (n=239)	[0.7904, 0.8686]	[0.7747, 0.8782]
Ets1 [23871] ---- Zcchc24 [71918]	0.83160 (n=239)	[0.7878, 0.8670]	[0.7720, 0.8767]
Tspan18 [241556] ---- Parva [57342]	0.89604 (n=239)	[0.8678, 0.9185]	[0.8575, 0.9246]
Tspan18 [241556] ---- Gucy1b3 [54195]	0.87850 (n=239)	[0.8459, 0.9046]	[0.8340, 0.9116]
Tspan18 [241556] ---- 9130005N14Rik [68303]	0.85826 (n=239)	[0.8208, 0.8884]	[0.8071, 0.8966]
Tspan18 [241556] ---- Tmem98 [103743]	0.84246 (n=239)	[0.8012, 0.8757]	[0.7863, 0.8848]
Tspan18 [241556] ---- Tcf21 [21412]	0.84084 (n=239)	[0.7992, 0.8744]	[0.7842, 0.8836]

Fig. 4. Query results for the star network of correlations seeded by Gata4.

INTERACTIONS

Cognoscente ID	Submitter Name	Taxonomic Name 1	Homologene Group ID 1	Entrez ID 1	Gene Symbol 1	Description 1	Taxonomic Name 2	Homologene Group ID 2	Entrez Gene ID 2	Gene Symbol 2	Gene Description 2	Interaction type	Interaction description	PubMed ID(s)	Original DB source
252192	CognoBot 1	Homo sapiens	3230	1482	NKX2-5	-	Homo sapiens	1551	2626	GATA4	-	protein - protein	Affinity Capture-Western; in vitro; in vivo	9312027, 10948187, 12845333	NCBI / BioGRID
252193	CognoBot 1	Homo sapiens	3230	1482	NKX2-5	-	Homo sapiens	1551	2626	GATA4	-	protein - protein	Affinity Capture-Western; in vitro; in vivo	9312027, 10948187, 12845333	NCBI / BioGRID
252209	CognoBot 1	Homo sapiens	3230	1482	NKX2-5	NK2 transcription factor related, locus 5	Homo sapiens	1551	2626	GATA4	GATA binding protein 4	protein - protein	-	10948187	NCBI / HPRD
252210	CognoBot 1	Homo sapiens	3230	1482	NKX2-5	NK2 transcription factor related, locus 5	Homo sapiens	1551	2626	GATA4	GATA binding protein 4	protein - protein	Nkx2.5 interacts with GATA4.	15542826	NCBI / BIND
263603	CognoBot 1	Homo sapiens	3638	2516	NR5A1	-	Homo sapiens	1551	2626	GATA4	-	protein - protein	Reconstituted Complex	10446911	NCBI / BioGRID
263604	CognoBot 1	Homo sapiens	3638	2516	NR5A1	-	Homo sapiens	1551	2626	GATA4	-	protein - protein	Reconstituted Complex	10446911	NCBI / BioGRID
264590	CognoBot 1	Homo sapiens	1551	2626	GATA4	-	Homo sapiens	3349	4776	NFATC4	-	protein - protein	in vitro; in vivo; Two-hybrid	9568714	NCBI / BioGRID
264591	CognoBot 1	Homo sapiens	1551	2626	GATA4	-	Homo sapiens	3349	4776	NFATC4	-	protein - protein	in vitro; in vivo; Two-hybrid	9568714	NCBI / BioGRID
264592	CognoBot 1	Homo sapiens	1551	2626	GATA4	-	Homo sapiens	8008	23414	ZFPM2	-	protein - protein	Affinity Capture-Western; in vitro; Reconstituted Complex; Two-hybrid	9927675, 11297508	NCBI / BioGRID
264593	CognoBot 1	Homo sapiens	1551	2626	GATA4	-	Homo sapiens	8008	23414	ZFPM2	-	protein - protein	Affinity Capture-Western; in vitro; Reconstituted Complex; Two-hybrid	9927675, 11297508	NCBI / BioGRID

Fig. 5. Screen capture of an excerpt of the documented interactions involving Gata4 reported by **Cognoscente**.

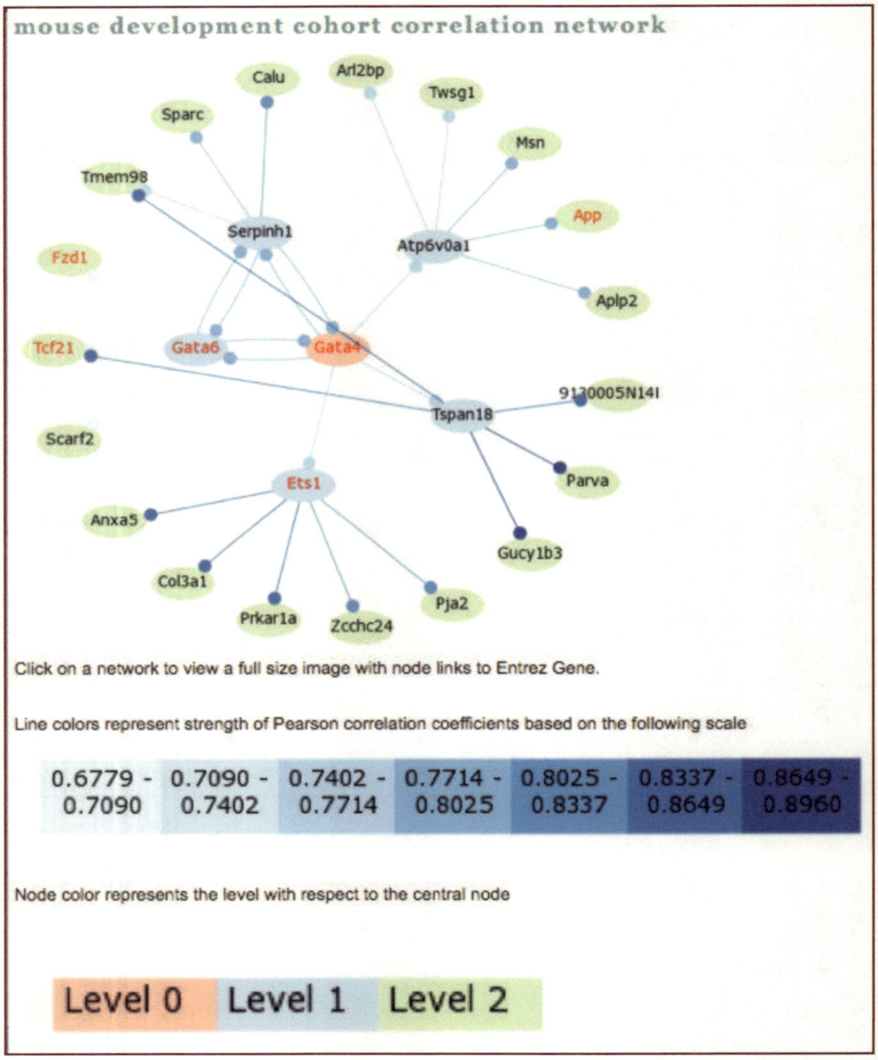

Fig. 6. Screen capture of **StarNet** result for a query with Gata4 showing the highest correlated genes with Gata4 (Level 1) and the highest correlated genes with those first order correlates (Level 2).

3.1 Visualization of correlation networks with StarNet and HeatSeeker

In StarNet, networks are constructed using a radial layout based on the highest correlations for a gene (in this case, for Gata4), and is iteratively expanded according to the specified number of levels. Graphs are drawn using AT&T's **Graphviz** drawing package (http://www.graphviz.org) using the **twopi** layout program (Figure 6). Edges standing for the correlations are colored such that darker edges represent stronger correlations. Lines connecting genes with positive correlations are drawn as shades of blue, and negative as shades of red. Gene nodes are color-coded according to their level with respect to the central node.

Matches for GO search term(s) "transcription": mouse development cohort

Official Gene Symbol	Entrez Gene ID	GO Terms
App	11820	GO:0045944
Fzd1	14362	GO:0016481
Gata4	14463	GO:0003700 GO:0003702 GO:0003704 GO:0003705 GO:0006350 GO:0006355 GO:0006357 GO:0016563 GO:0030528 GO:0043193 GO:0045893 GO:0045941 GO:0045944
Gata6	14465	GO:0003700 GO:0003705 GO:0006350 GO:0006355 GO:0016563 GO:0030528 GO:0045941 GO:0045944
Tcf21	21412	GO:0003700 GO:0006350 GO:0006355 GO:0030528 GO:0045449
Ets1	23871	GO:0003700 GO:0005667 GO:0006350 GO:0006355 GO:0006357 GO:0045944

Enriched GO terms: mouse development cohort

GO Term	GO ID	raw p-value	Bonferroni corrected p-value	Symbols (Entrez IDs)
• regulation of epidermal growth factor receptor activity	GO:0007176	6.76E-06	1.23E-03	App (11820), Aplp2 (11804)
• mating behavior	GO:0007617	1.13E-05	2.06E-03	App (11820), Aplp2 (11804)
• suckling behavior	GO:0001967	2.36E-05	4.30E-03	App (11820), Aplp2 (11804)
• cellular copper ion homeostasis	GO:0006878	3.15E-05	5.73E-03	App (11820), Aplp2 (11804)
• forebrain development	GO:0030900	4.98E-05	9.06E-03	App (11820), Aplp2 (11804), Twsg1 (65960)
• protein binding	GO:0005515	8.32E-05	1.51E-02	Gata4 (14463), Gata6 (14465), Serpinh1 (12406), Ets1 (23871), Scarf2 (224024), Tcf21 (21412), Fzd1 (14362), App (11820), Aplp2

Fig. 7. Screen capture of **StarNet** Gene Ontology analysis. The first table shows genes retrieved by **StarNet** as part of the correlation network, where the gene is annotated with a Gene Ontology (GO) term that contains the word "transcription." This default behavior alerts the user to potential directionality of regulatory influences, where such genes are typically transcription factors, and thus may have some regultory influence over genes that they are highly correlated with. The second table shows part of the GO enrichment list, which provides tentative annotation for network function as a whole. For example, the GO term *protein binding* is one of the significantly enriched terms for the Gata4 correlation network.

During the process of defining the topology of the network, two types of supporting analyses of this network are also performed. Enrichment of GO terms, which allows tentative annotation of the biological function of this network, is evaluated using the hypergeometric test (Figure 7). Orthologous genes that are on both array platforms (data cohorts) are identified for cross-cohorts analysis, then when the user clicks the '**HeatSeeker**' button on the **StarNet** result page, **HeatSeeker** will draw false color maps arranged with complete-linkage hierarchical clustering of correlation distance between genes in the super-network for each cohort (Figure 8).

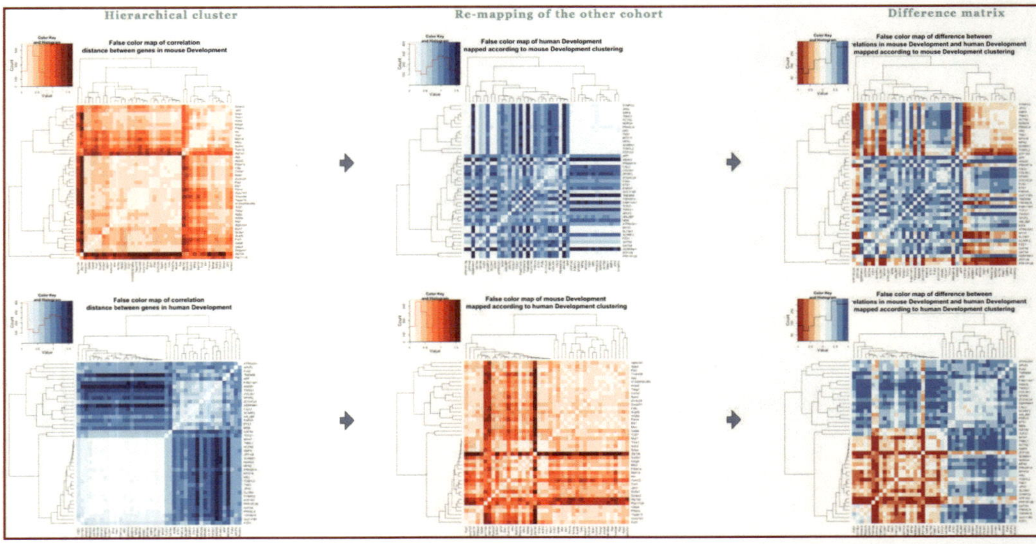

Fig. 8. Screen capture of **HeatSeeker** results for the cross-species analysis between mouse and human for the *Development* data cohort of each species. The network was seeded with Gata4 as the query gene for **StarNet** analysis and visualization. **Heatseeker** makes an unbiased comparison between correlation networks by combining the gene lists of both networks and only displaying data for genes where orthologs exist for each organism, and the gene is surveyed on both array platforms. The third column of false color maps shows the differences in correlations between the two data sets. Each of the two rows of false color maps gives an alternative clustering of the data.

3.2 Visualization of biomolecular interactions with cognoscente

Cognoscente is a querying and visualization tool for drawing biomolecular interaction networks from documented interaction knowledge, and currently holds over 300,000 unique interactions. **Cognoscente** supports any organism supported by NCBI's Entrez Gene catalog. We built **Cognoscente** as a **MySQL** database with a web-based front end. An example query with Gata4 returns all first order interactions across all known orthologs (Figure 9). **Cognoscente** addresses several specific visualization tasks for understanding and appropriatly interpreting interaction data. One of the visualization tasks that **Cognoscente** addresses is the sorting of interaction knowledge by species. Nodes in networks created by **Cognoscente** are partitioned according to the species corresponding to an ortholog for a given gene, and these partitions are color-coded by organism. Each partition is actually a hyper-node that may represent the gene, transcript, and protein corresponding to the gene symbol. These different forms are distinguished by the type of edge drawn to the node partition, which explicitly indicates protein-protein, protein-DNA, and other types of interactions (see the EDGE KEY in Figure 9). **Cognoscente** supports multiple simultaneous queries (Figure 10), multiple groups of simulataneous queries (up to three, where each group has a different color-coded box around nodes), and zeroth, first, and second order networks. Figures 9 and 10 show first order networks, where all direct interactions are identified. Zeroth order interactions are just those interactions between members of a query group, which may be useful for analyzing gene lists generated by identifying differentially expressed genes from a microarray experiment, or from gene clustering analysis. A second order network shows all direct interactions with query genes *and* all interactions with the first order interactants. Second order networks are often very large.

As more biomedical knowledge is acquired from experimentation, the inclusion of prior knowledge in the process of network inference plays an increasingly crucial role. Using correlation networks from **StarNet** and documented interaction networks from **Cognoscente**, we plan to utilize known interaction networks to trim and refine predicted network influences that arise from the correlation network, and thus provide an algorithm for defining provisional developmental and regulatory pathways by inference.

3.3 General network visualization with cytoscape

Cytoscape is a powerful, general-purposed, open-source network visualization tool that offers assistance in analyzing the networks it builds (Shannon et al., 2003; Maere et al., 2005). It was initially developed in 2001 by a small group of researchers and software engineers at the Institute for Systems Biology and has since grown into a worldwide community project. The **Cytoscape** Core handles basic features like network layout and mapping of data attributes to visual display properties. It is also designed to allow users to create plugin modules that undertake customized network analysis. Here we show an example network of yeast proteins from the galactose pathway (http://www.**Cytoscape**.org) (Figure 11).

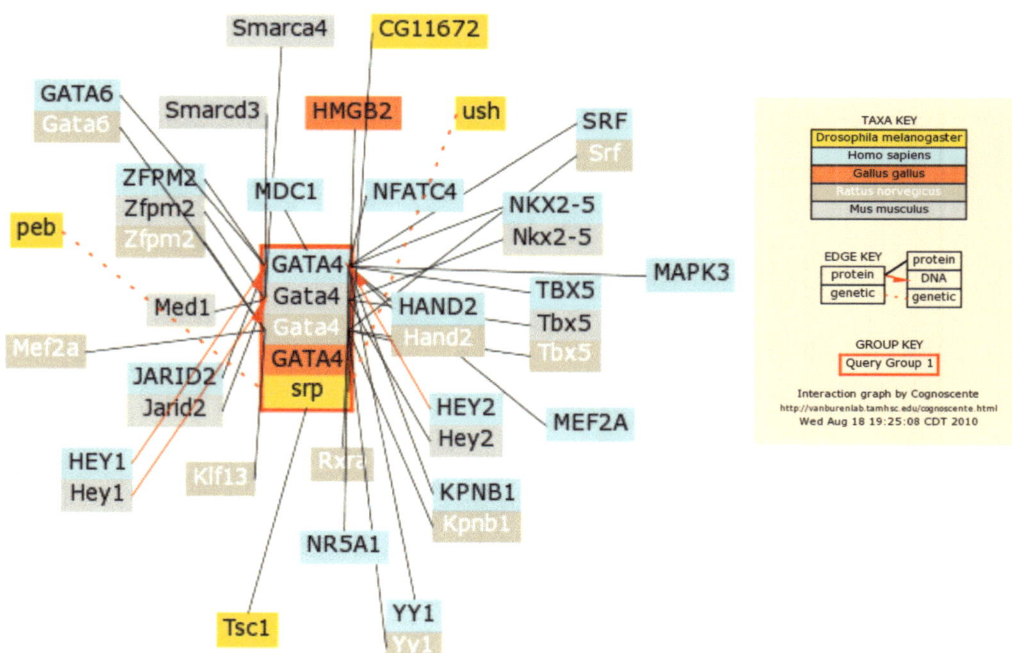

Fig. 9. Literature-based network for known biomolecular interactions, seeded by Gata4 and built with **Cognoscente**. The Gata4 gene, mRNA, and protein are all considered in this query, and different types of interactions are displayed with different types of edges. Interaction lookups are automatically performed across all known orthologs of Gata4, and the species corresponding to each documented is indicated by the node color.

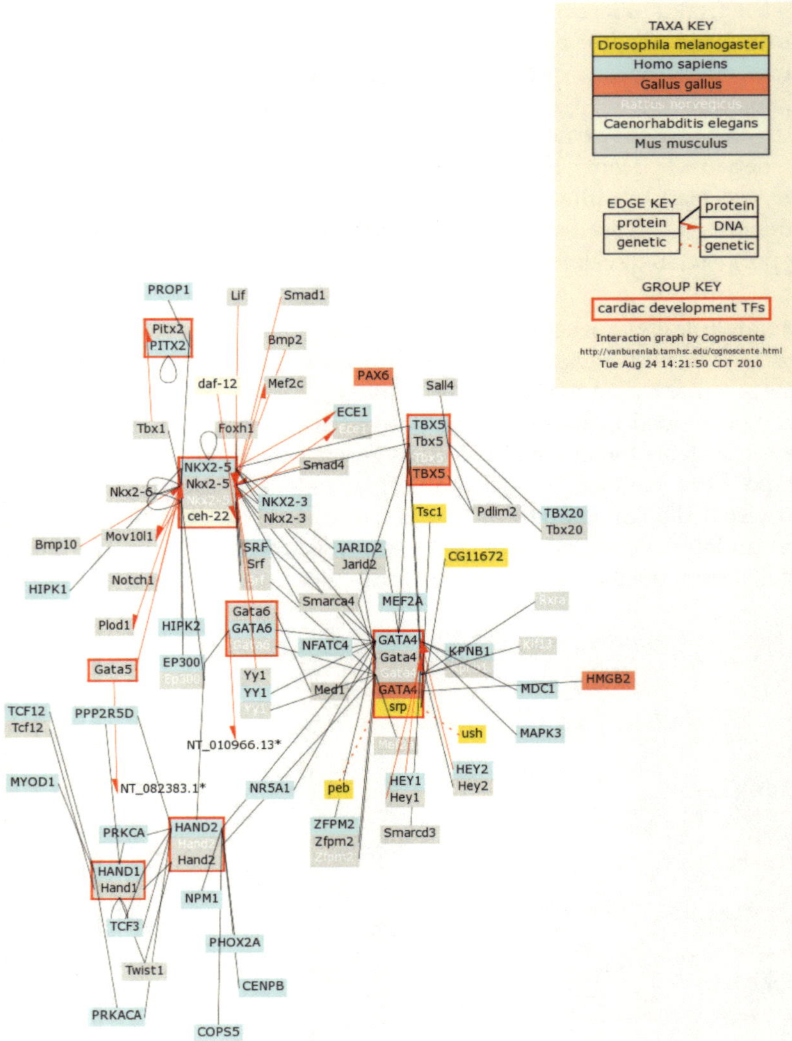

Fig. 10. **Cognoscente** has several useful capabilities, including support for multiple simultaneous queries. Here some well known transcription factors involved in cardiac development were queried as a group (red boxes) to examine documented interactions between these genes and gene products, as well all other first-order interactions with the query set.

Further analysis of this visualized network may be performed with a myriad of available plugins that provide numerous options for analytical functionality. As discussed regarding **StarNet** analysis, tests for GO term enrichment are also available in **Cytoscape**. One popular plugin, **BiNGO** (Maere et al., 2005), can be used to map functional themes of a set of elements in a network on the GO hierarchy (Figure 12). Networks built by **Cytoscape** may be partitioned into several sub-networks based on the clustering of the network elements using known functional or expressional data.

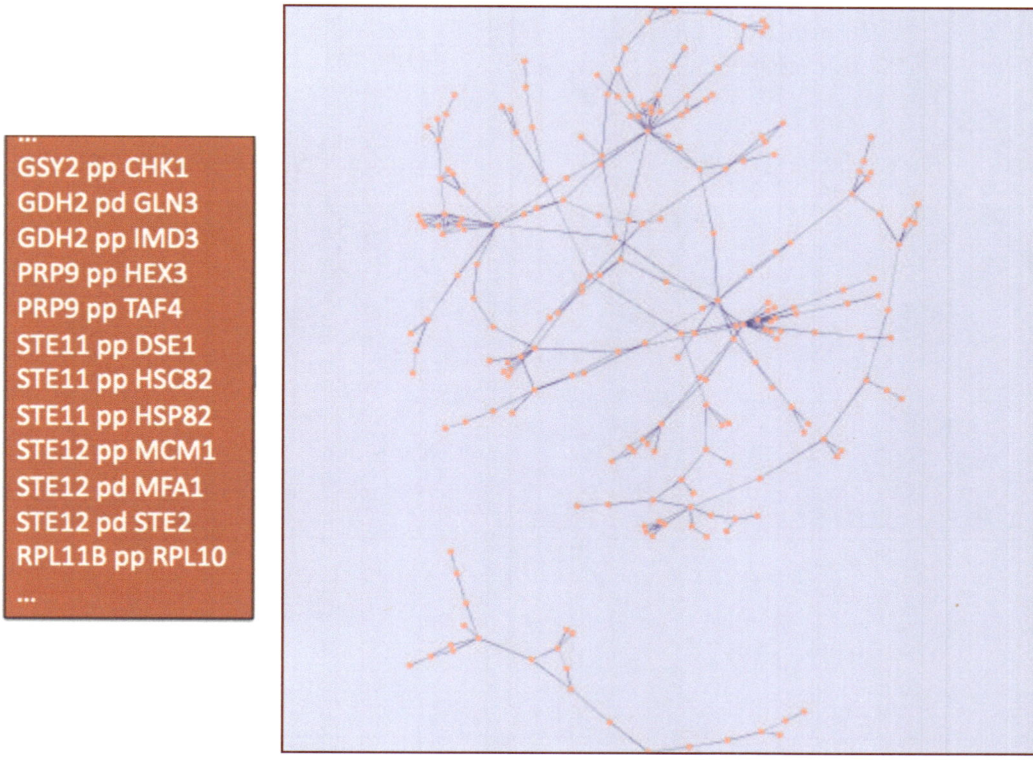

Fig. 11. A **Cytoscape** example. A known tabular network (an excerpt is shown on the left) was loaded into **Cytoscape**. Next, the topological network was generated by the software automatically (shown right). **Cytoscape** offers more than 20 layout algorithms, including standard layout algorithms such as hierarchical, edge-weighted, and spring-embedded methods. Here we used was the *spring-embedded* layout.

Cytoscape offers very diverse and flexible tools for network visualization and analysis. In comparison, **StarNet** has much more specific functionality. Except for a sample network of yeast galactose metabolism, **Cytoscape** doesn't offer precomputed networks. **Cytoscape** instead relies on the user to provide a network. So, while **StarNet** offers a mechanism for specifying and creating networks from precomputed correlation data, **Cytoscape** offers an open, flexible environment for drawing and analyzing networks created outside of Cytoscape.

4. Conclusion & discussion

Computational network analysis is increasingly used to set biomedical research priorities. In particular, functional networks of genes may incorporate literally millions of experimental observations into probabilistic networks that identify genes likely to have interactive relationships in cells. Let's look at an example to illustrate the feasibility of this strategy. The biogenesis of ribosomes is an essential cellular process conserved across all eukaryotes and is known to require >170 genes for the assembly, modification, and trafficking of ribosome components through multiple cellular compartments. Li and colleauges employed

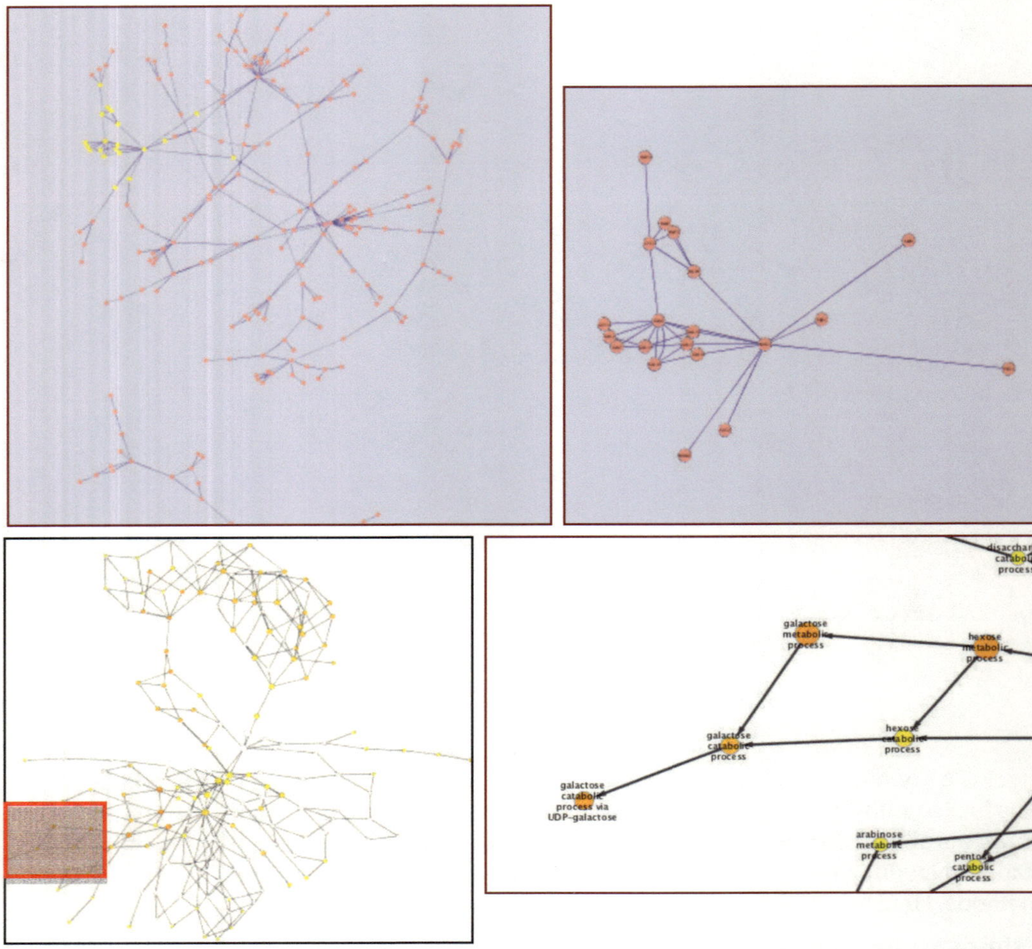

Fig. 12. The upper two panels shows the generation of the sub-network from the network of galatose pathway seeded by Gal4. In the lower two panels, the plugin **BiNGO** is used to assess GO term enrichment and build a hierarchical GO network. The lower right panel is an enlarged excerpt of the left panel (red box). The **BiNGO** network is visualized with a range of colors expressing the overrepresentation significance of the GO category represented by a node (darker nodes are more overrepresented).

network-guided genetics to set their research priorities (Li et al., 2009). They constructed computational predictor of ribosome biogenesis genes based on functional genomics and proteomics analysis, including mRNA-expression data across different conditions, protein-protein interaction datasets derived from literature, high-throughput yeast two-hybrid assays, affinity purification coupled with mass spectrometry, genetic interaction data, and in silico interaction datasets, along with analysis of comparative genomics datasets, covering 95% of yeast proteome (Figure 13). Next they calculated the naïve Bayesian probability that each yeast gene belongs to the ribosome biogenesis pathway based on gene connectivity information in the established gene networks. From the top-scoring genes, 212 candidates were manually selected based on expert knowledge for experimental validation (Table 3).

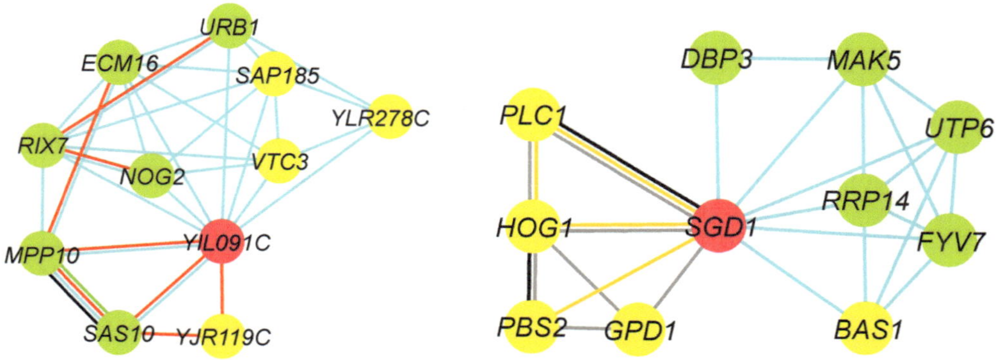

Fig. 13. Predicted ribosome biogenesis genes are labeled as red nodes. Green nodes are known ribosome biogenesis genes, and yellow nodes are genes that are not related to ribosome biogenesis. Edge color indicates how an association was established: co-expression (light blue), affinity purification (red), yeast two-hybrid assay (green), genetic interaction (yellow), co-citation (gray), and literature curation (black). This open-access figure was reproduced from Li et al., 2009.

After obtaining the 212 candidates by computational analysis, they employed different experimental methods to trim this gene group by experimental validation.

Finally, they computationally predicted and experimentally validated at least 15 previously unreported ribosome biogenesis genes (TIF4631, SUN66, YDL063C, JIL5, TOP1, SGD1, BCP1, YOR287C, BUD22, YIL091C, YOR006C/TSR3, YOL022C/TSR4, SAC3, NEW1, FUN12) which can be found in Table 3. Most of these genes have human orthologs and thus represent evolutionarily conserved components of this essential process in cells.

This is an excellent example of the integration between computational network retrieval and experimental validation to set research priorites and efficiently determine gene functions. A current goal for our group is to leverage the tools we have built to automate the prediction of functional networks, and to impute directionality of regulatory influences in these networks. Correlation doesn't imply causality, although it suggests a close relationship. Thus, the networks built by **StarNet** do not indicate that a given gene in the graph has a direct influence on any other. Moreover, edges in a **StarNet** network do not even imply a direct association between a given gene pair. High ranking correlates, however, can be judged to have a higher *probability* of a direct interaction than low-ranking correlates, so ranking the correlation of expression from numerous experimental samples remains a simple yet powerful predictive tool. Recent work has emphasized the utility of correlation as a measurement of gene co-expression relationships. For example, Reiss and colleagues (Reiss et al., 2006) discussed co-expression, noting that correlative relationships changed depending on the milieu and the similar phenomenon has also been identified by other groups. This idea provides a basis for comparing different data sets to assess differential wiring, as we have shown above with **HeatSeeker**.

Our current aim is to leverage **StarNet** data together with prior knowledge contained in **Cognoscente** as the basis for inferring complete transcriptional regulatory networks using Bayesian inference or other machine learning approaches. Although a high magnitude correlation does not imply a direct regulatory relationship, we may suspect that genes with highly correlated (or highly anti-correlated) expression have a higher probability of having a regulatory relationship than genes with lower magnitude correlations, and that ranking the magnitude of correlations will uncover gene pairs with the highest likelihood of having a regulatory relationship. Assuming that for a given gene x, that high ranking correlates have a higher probability of having a direct association than low-ranking correlates, we can begin to infer a network of the most likely direct associations. For example, where x and y are any two genes with a high correlation, potential intermediates between x and y might be identified by finding genes that have a higher magnitude correlation with x and y than x and y have with each other. Thus, for the expression profile of a given gene, a high-ranking correlation coefficient with another gene in our database may be interpreted as an assertion that the association has a relatively high likelihood of being proximal, given the available data.

ORF	Gene[a]	Human Ortholog[b]	Number of Links to Seed Genes	Network Evidence[c]	Mutant Growth	Polysome Profile Defect	Co-sedimentation[d]	Pre-rRNA Processing Defect	Ribosome Export Defect
YGR162W	*TIF4631*	*EIF4G1, EIF4G, EIF4G3*	22	MS, CX, LC	Slow	60S	Across gradient	35S, 27S, 7S, 20S	60S
YOR308C	*SNU66*	*SART1*	8	MS, CC, LC	Slow at 20°C	60S	40S	35S, 27S, 5S	No
YDL063C	—	—	5	MS, CC, YH, CX	Slow	60S	Free	35S, 27S	No
YDR412W	*RRP17*	*?NOL12*	14	CX, MS, YH	Essential	60S	Free	35S, 7S	60S
YPR169W	*JIP5*	*?AAC69625*	19	CX, MS	Essential	60S	Free, 60S	35S, 27S	No
YOL006C	*TOP1*	*TOP1*	7	CC, MS, LC, CX	Slow	60S	Across gradient	35S, 27S	No
YNL132W	*KRE33* [10]	*NAT10*	77	MS, CX, LC	Essential	40S	—	35S	40S
YDR496C	*PUF6* [21]	*KIAA0020*	94	CX, MS, LC	Slow at 20°C	60S	60S	35S, 27S, 7S	60S
YLR336C	*SGD1*	*NOM1*	31	CX, MS	Essential	40S	40S, 60S, 80S	35S	40S
YLR397C	*AFG2* [52]	*SPATA5*	7	CX, MS, CC	Essential	60S	—	35S, 7S	60S
YDR361C	*BCP1*	*BCCIP*	19	CX	Essential	60S	Free, 60S	35S	60S
YJL010C	*NOP9* [40]	*C14orf21*	56	CX, LC	Essential	40S	40S, Polysome	35S	40S
YOR287C	—	*C6orf153*	40	CX, MS	Essential	40S	—	35S	No
YDR339C	*FCF1* [41]	*CN111_HUMAN*	13	CX	Essential	40S	—	35S	40S
YMR014W	*BUD22*	—	37	CX, MS	Slow	40S	80/90S, Polysome	35S	40S
YCR047C	*BUD23* [68]	*WBSCR22*	7	MS, CX	Slow	40S	40S	35S, 20S	40S
YLR051C	*FCF2* [41]	*DNTTIP2*	13	CX	Essential	40S	—	35S	—
YGR145W	*ENP2*	*NOL10*	91	CX, MS, LC, RS	Essential	40S	—	35S	40S
YDR299W	*BFR2*	*AATF*	71	CX, MS, LC	Essential	40S	40S, 80/90S	35S	40S
YIL091C	—	*DEF*	12	CX, MS	Essential	40S	40S	35S	No
YOL022C	*TSR4*	*?PDCD2L*	30	CX	Essential	40S	Free	20S	No
YOR006C	*TSR3*	*C16orf42*	2	CX	Slow at 20°C and 30°C	40S	Free	20S	No
YGR081C	*SLX9* [43]	—	14	MS, CX, GT	Slow at 30°C	40S	40S	20S	40S
YDR159W	*SAC3*	*MCM3AP*	1	LC	Slow	40S	40S, 80/90S	35S	No
YPL226W	*NEW1*	*?ABCF1*	8	CX, MS	Slow at 20°C and 30°C	40S	Across gradient	35S	No
YJR074W	*MOG1*	*RANGRF*	3	CC, GT, MS, LC, YH	Slow	Minor	Free	35S, 27S, 20S	No
YAL035W	*FUN12*	*EIF5B*	40	MS, GN, CX	Slow	40S	Polysome	20S	No
YPR178W	*PRP4*	*PRPF4*	11	MS, LC, CC, YH	Essential	Minor	Free, 40S	35S	No
YDR378C	*LSM6* [44]	*LSM6*	7	MS, LC, CC, YH, TS	Slow	Minor	—	35S, 20S	50% cells 60S
YNL147W	*LSM7* [44]	*LSM7*	7	MS, LC, CC, YH, TS	Slow	Minor	Polysome	35S, 20S	50% cells 60S

Table 3. Some of the 212 top-scoring candidate genes for a functional role in ribosome biogenesis. This open-access table is reproduced from Li et al., 2009.

StarNet's usefulness for inference of regulatory influences is mainly limited to the domain of transcriptional regulation where the abundance of the transcript of a transcription factor is closely related to the activity of the transcription factor protein. This will be true sometimes, as indicated by a high-magnitude correlation of coexpression between a transcription factor and its target. In such cases the predictive power of **StarNet** should be good. As there are many other forms of regulation, **StarNet** will not capture all regulatory influences via co-expression correlations. For example, the activity of the transcription factor NF-kB requires the activity of IkB kinase (IKK) to phosphorylate IkB, which activates NF-kB by disassociation of IkB from NF-kB. This means that we should not expect a high-magnitude correlation between the NF-kB expression and the expression of its targets (Brasier, 2006; Gilmore, 1999; Gilmore, 2006; Perkins, 2007). Thus, incorporating proteomics data and and other types of data will be important for the inferring a complete regulatory network. One important computational approach is to discover transcription factor binding site (TFBS) by clustering genes based on their expression profiles, then search for conserved motifs in the DNA sequence upstream of these tightly clustered genes, which are then inferred to be the TFBS (Bortoluzzi et al., 2005; Pavesi et al., 2004; Roth et al., 1998). Directionality of regultory influences could be provisionally annotated using this strategy.

The most important ingredient in the process of inferring transcriptional regulatory programs and setting research priorities is the judgment of experts. That judgment is greatly enhanced by the development of effective data retrieval and visualization tools. We believe that the best tools will augment the expert's ability to make inferences and judgments, rather than attempt to replace that expert judgement. What this implies is that all predictions that are made by software should be easy to interpret, easy to trace back to the orginal data, and that the overall methodology employed in making a prediction is transparent to the expert. These principles will foster synergistic progress in biomedical research via improved communication and understanding between experimental biologists and computational biologists.

5. References

Ashburner, M., C. A. Ball, et al. (2000). "Gene ontology: tool for the unification of biology. The Gene Ontology Consortium." Nat Genet 25(1): 25-29.

Bortoluzzi, S., A. Coppe, et al. (2005). "A multistep bioinformatic approach detects putative regulatory elements in gene promoters." BMC Bioinformatics 6: 121.

Brasier, A. R. (2006). "The NF-kappaB regulatory network." Cardiovasc Toxicol 6(2): 111-130.

de Jong, H. (2002). "Modeling and simulation of genetic regulatory systems: a literature review." J Comput Biol 9(1): 67-103.

Gebert, J., Radde, N., Weber, G.W. (2007). "Modeling Gene Regulatory Networks with Piecewise Linear Differential Equations. " European Journal of Operational Research, volume 181, Issue 3, 16 September 2007.

Gilmore, T. D. (1999). "The Rel/NF-kappaB signal transduction pathway: introduction." Oncogene 18(49): 6842-6844.

Gilmore, T. D. (2006). "Introduction to NF-kappaB: players, pathways, perspectives." Oncogene 25(51): 6680-6684.

Janikow, C. Z. (1993). "A knowledge-intensive genetic algorithm for supervised learning. " Machine Learning, 13, 189-228(1993).

Jensen, L. J., M. Kuhn, et al. (2009). "STRING 8--a global view on proteins and their functional interactions in 630 organisms." Nucleic Acids Res 37(Database issue): D412-416.

Jupiter, D. C. and V. VanBuren (2008). "A visual data mining tool that facilitates reconstruction of transcription regulatory networks." PLoS One 3(3): e1717.

Jupiter, D., H. Chen, et al. (2009). "STARNET 2: a web-based tool for accelerating discovery of gene regulatory networks using microarray co-expression data." BMC Bioinformatics 10: 332.

Kauffman, S. (1969). "Homeostasis and differentiation in random genetic control networks." Nature 224(5215): 177-178.

Li, Z., I. Lee, et al. (2009). "Rational extension of the ribosome biogenesis pathway using network-guided genetics." PLoS Biol 7(10): e1000213.

Maere, S., K. Heymans, et al. (2005). "BiNGO: a Cytoscape plugin to assess overrepresentation of gene ontology categories in biological networks." Bioinformatics 21(16): 3448-3449.

Pavesi, G., P. Mereghetti, et al. (2004). "Weeder Web: discovery of transcription factor binding sites in a set of sequences from co-regulated genes." Nucleic Acids Res 32(Web Server issue): W199-203.

Perkins, N. D. (2007). "Integrating cell-signalling pathways with NF-kappaB and IKK function." Nat Rev Mol Cell Biol 8(1): 49-62

Reiss, D. J., N. S. Baliga, et al. (2006). "Integrated biclustering of heterogeneous genome-wide datasets for the inference of global regulatory networks." BMC Bioinformatics 7: 280.

Roth, F. P., J. D. Hughes, et al. (1998). "Finding DNA regulatory motifs within unaligned noncoding sequences clustered by whole-genome mRNA quantitation." Nat Biotechnol 16(10): 939-945

Shannon, P., A. Markiel, et al. (2003). "Cytoscape: a software environment for integrated models of biomolecular interaction networks." Genome Res 13(11): 2498-2504.

Snel, B., G. Lehmann, et al. (2000). "STRING: a web-server to retrieve and display the repeatedly occurring neighbourhood of a gene." Nucleic Acids Res 28(18): 3442-3444.

von Mering, C., M. Huynen, et al. (2003). "STRING: a database of predicted functional associations between proteins." Nucleic Acids Res 31(1): 258-261.

von Mering, C., L. J. Jensen, et al. (2005). "STRING: known and predicted protein-protein associations, integrated and transferred across organisms." Nucleic Acids Res 33(Database issue): D433-437.

von Mering, C., L. J. Jensen, et al. (2007). "STRING 7--recent developments in the integration and prediction of protein interactions." Nucleic Acids Res 35(Database issue): D358-362.

5.1 Websites

STRING database: http://**STRING**-db.org/

StarNet database: http://vanburenlab.medicine.tamhsc.edu/**StarNet**2.html

Graphviz graph drawing software: http://www.graphviz.org/

Cytoscape graph drawing and analysis platform: http://www.**Cytoscape**.org/

14

DNA Microarray Applied to Data Mining of *Bradyrhizobium elkanii* Genome and Prospection of Active Genes

Jackson Marcondes and Eliana G. M. Lemos
Faculdade de Ciências Agrárias e Veterinárias, Universidade Estadual Paulista
Brazil

1. Introduction

One of the factors responsible for the expansion and competitiveness of soybean crop [*Glycine max* (L.) Merrill], *Fabaceae,* is its nitrogen fixation capacity through a symbiotic association with *Bradyrhizobium japonicum* (Jordan, 1982) and *Bradyrhizobium elkanii* (Kuykendall et al., 1992) bacteria. Because of this association, N fertilization is usually not required in soybean fields. The genome of *Bradyrhizobium japonicum* USDA 110 was completely sequenced (Kaneko et al., 2002) while the genome of *Bradyrhizobium elkanii* SEMIA 587 (Rumjanek et al., 1993) is currently being sequenced at our lab. Results obtained so far allowed the selection of clones from genomic DNA libraries for the development of DNA microarray containing 2654 *B. elkanii* genes.

The potential of high-throughput DNA microarray technology applied to study the transcriptional response of many organisms to genetic and environmental changes has been clearly demonstrated in the past few years (Dhamardi & Gonzalez, 2004). Recently, the design and use of a partial-genome microarray for transcriptome analysis of *B. japonicum* was reported. This study had focused in regulatory cascade that induces nitrogen fixation (*nif*) genes (Hauser et al, 2006).

During its life cycle, rhizobia face challenges that demand gene expression regulation. The expression of specific genes is followed by the development of plant-bacteria symbiosis. In the soil, the free-living bacteria are saprophytes competing with other bacteria for subsistence. When they eventually reach a plant's rhizosphere, although rich in nutrients, bacteria must evaluate the host compatibility and compete with other rhizobia and even individuals of the same species before entering roots and establish the symbiosis through nodulation and biological nitrogen fixation. At this stage, the environment is critically altered and bacteria must adapt to a new intracellular life stile in the host plant (Oke and Long, 1999; Loh and Stacey, 2003). These successive environment changes are reflected in metabolic alterations.

Rhizobia ecological and physiological studies are important for practical research applied to the commercial inoculants industry. The competition with native bacteria for nodulation is considered the most limiting factor in the use of inoculants in agriculture (López-Garcia et al., 2002). Besides the genetic differences, the physiological status of rhizobia in the inoculant seems to be different from rhizobia in the soil, in different populations. For

instance, in high titration *B. japonicum* cultures, a *quorum-sensing* factor inhibited the expression of *nod* genes through the induction of *nolA* (Loh et al., 2001).
Since high amounts of viable cells are required in commercial rhizobia inoculants, the physiological status of inoculants is near the stationary phase and they are usually obtained through rich cultures. Because of the importance of *B. elkanii* SEMIA 587 in the composition of commercial inoculants, we studied its metabolic behavior investigating gene expression profile through DNA microarrays in two culture conditions. The response to different nutritional conditions was observed at the lag, log and stationary phases in a complex Triptone-Yeast Medium (TY) and in a Rhizobium Defined Medium (RDM).

2. Experimental design viewing microarray data

Culture conditions and growth curves. *B. elkanii* 587 cultures were kept at 28°C with aeration through an orbital stirring regime at 160 rpm. The culture media TY (Beringer, 1974) and RDM (Vincent, 1970) were used in this study. Flasks containing 100 ml of culture medium were initially inoculated with 1.5 x 10^8 cells/ml for the bacterial cells harvesting at the lag, log, and stationary phases in both media. The representative times of each phase, lag, log or stationary were, respectively: T1 (24 h), T2 (48 h) and T5 (120 h) for cultures in TY medium; and T1 (24h), T5 (120h) and T8 (192 h) for cultures in RDM.
Isolation of total RNA and cDNA labeled synthesis. Cells were collected at previously determined culture ages for total RNA extractions. The whole volume of each culture was centrifuged at 4600 x g for 10 min at 4°C. After cell lysis, extractions were performed with trizol (Invitrogen) and chloroform following the manufacturer's recommendations. ***The*** cDNA direct labeling technique was used during reverse transcription using the fluorophores Cy3 and Cy5. cDNA samples obtained from the RNA isolated from bacteria cultured in RDM were labeled with Cy3, while those produced in TY medium were labeled with Cy5. For labeling, 15 μg of total RNA of each sample was added to 15 μg of randon hexamer primers $pd(N)_6$ (Amersham Bioscience); and 1 μl of the synthetic mRNAs controls spike Ref or Test (Amershan Biosciences) for Cy3- or Cy5-labeling, respectively. The RNA mixture was joined to 2 μl of dNTP mix (dATP, dGTP, dCTP, at 5 mM each; dTTP at 2 mM), 1 μl of Cy3-dUTP or Cy5-dUTP (Amersham Pharmacia Biotech) at 25 μM, and 200 U of SuperscriptII reverse transcriptase (Invitrogen). cDNA synthesis was performed at 37°C for 3 h in the dark. The sample containing labeled cDNA was then purified in a Microcon YM-100 column (Millipore).
Common Reference RNA (CRR) for the synthesis of fluorescently labeled cDNA. In addition to the previous protocol, a bulk containing 5 μg of RNA corresponding to each culture phase in RDM was prepared. This sample, totalizing 15 μg of RNA, was named CRR and converted into Cy3-flurescently labeled cDNA. This sample was used as reference against independent samples of the phases lag, log and stationary of the medium RDM, now labeled with Cy5 from 15 μg of each RNA template. The synthesis and purification of labeled cDNAs was performed as described above.
Construction of DNA microarrays and hybrizations. Briefly, *B. elkanii* 587 genomic DNA was isolated and randomly fragmented. Fragments between 0.6 and 2.0 Kb were recovered and cloned in pUC19/*Sma*I vector (Amershan) to produce a genomic library in *Escherichia coli* DH5α. The clones selected for microarray composition were amplified independently through PCR. For each clone, PCR reactions (20 μl) were performed with 25 ng of plasmidial

DNA template, 200 μM dNTPs, 5 pmoles of the primers M13 forward and reverse (5'-CCCAGTCACGAGTTGTGTAAACG and 5'-AGCGGATAACAATTTCACAGG, respectively), $MgCl_2$ 1.5 mM, reaction buffer [1x] and 1.0 U of Taq DNA polymerase (Invitrogen). Amplification was performed with forty denaturing cycles at 96°C for 20 sec, annealing at 50°C for 30 sec and extension at 72°C for 4 min, followed by 5 min of final extension at 72°C. DNA samples were spotted in glassed slides CMT-GAPS2 (Corning) in duplicates using a GMS-417 Arrayer (Affymetrix). The resulting microarray contained 2,654 *B. elkanii* genes and 5 negative controls, human and plant genes. Hybridization was performed in the GeneTac Hybridization (Genetic Microsystems), to which microarray glass slides were attached. Each cDNA mix was distributed on the slide and hybridized at 42°C for 12 h. After the hybridization, slides were washed automatically and sequentially in 2x SSC/0.5% SDS, 0.5x SSC and 0,05x SSC, at 25°C. Each washing corresponded to a 15-min period, with 10 sec of flow and 20 sec of incubation, for 10 cycles. Slides were dried for 15 min. Three slides were used per experiment i.e., RNA extractions, labeled cDNA synthesis and hybridization were performed in triplicates in each experiment.

Microarray data validation through Quantitative Real-Time PCR. The genes *fixN* (symbiotic cytochrome oxidase) and σA (RNA polymerase primary sigma factor) were selected as target and endogenous control genes, respectively. Primers and probes were obtained through the system Assays-by-Design (Applied Biosystems). cDNAs were prepared as in the microarray experiments, except for the absence of fluorophores in the reaction. The resulting cDNAs were used in a 20 μL reaction in the presence of 1 μL of the assay (primers/probe) and 10 μL of TaqMan Universal PCR Master Mix [2x] (Applied Biosystems). The experiment was conducted in an ABI 7500 (Applied Biosystems), following the thermal cycling conditions automatically determined by the equipment. Data were analyzed by the program RQ Study (Applied Biosystems), through the algorithm $2^{-\Delta\Delta Ct}$, which calculates the fold change of gene expression of the target gene, normalized by the endogenous calibrator. The expression of the gene *fixN*, detected in *B. elkanii* during the log phase in RDM in DNA microarray experiments was confirmed by the analysis of relative quantification through Real-Time PCR. Gene expression values were coherent and very similar: 0.65 versus 0.67, for Real-Time PCR and DNA microarray, respectively.

3. Data analysis

Fluorescent signals were scanned by a GMS-418 Arrayer Scanner (Affymetrix). The location and identification of each gene in the array were defined in a text file created with the help of the program CloneTracker 2 (Biodiscovery). To adjust systematic differences in the relative intensity of each signal, quantified data were exported and transformed by the software GeneSight 5.5 (Biodiscovery). This normalization process was applied following the lowess (locally weighted linear regression) correction parameters, as a local normalization method (Quackenbush, 2002).

Three growth phases in two culture conditions were compared by the determination of the ratio (r) of median intensities of each ORF pair in the spots, in array triplicates. The ratios (Cy5/Cy3) were calculated so the Log r (base 2) of the absolute value of expression rates was positive for intensities that were higher in the medium TY, i.e., genes potentially expressed in a complex medium. On the other hand, values were negative for higher intensities in RDM, representing genes potentially expressed in a minimal medium. When

the CRR experiment data were processed, positive log r values indicated genes potentially expressed in each individual culture phase in RDM, while negative values designated the reference mixture.
Triplicate array data, which were independent in a same experiment, were processed by the statistical tool SAM (Significance Analysis of Microarrays) using Microsoft Excel. This analysis is based on a series of specific t-tests for each gene, adapted for the large-scale detection of differentially expressed genes (Tusher et al., 2001). Results were grouped functionally following the classification available on RhizoBase (www.kazusa.org.jp/ rhizobase). Furthermore, principal component analysis was performed as principal global expression patterns implemented in the Statistica data analysis software system v.7 (StatSoft Inc).

4. Global expression parameters and patterns.

The complex medium TY contained triptone and yeast extract as N, carbon and energy sources. The defined medium RDM contained glycerol as the only source of carbon and energy, and sodium glutamate as N source. Besides the metabolic differences, very distinct growth rates were observed in each medium (Fig. 1). In RDM, *B. elkanii* cells showed a growth rate nearly 4 times slower, with G = 68.2 h, in comparison to TY medium (G = 17.2 h).

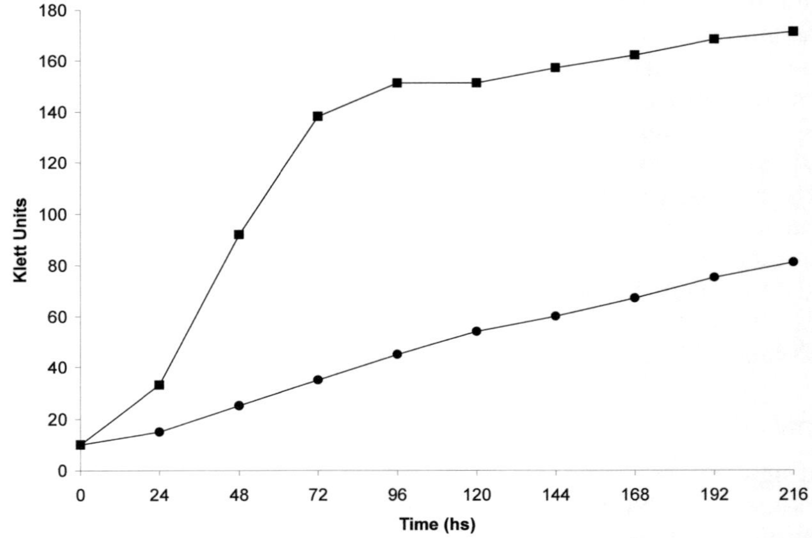

Fig. 1. Growth of *B. elkanii* SEMIA 587 on RDM medium (•) and TY medium (▪) for ten days. Cells were harvested for RNA extraction at 24, 120, and 192 hours for RDM, or 24, 48, and 120 hours for TY, meaning lag, log and stationary phases.

Based on a fold change defined as 1.5, a Log r $\geq$ 0.58 was considered as significantly higher indicator of gene expression in *B. elkanii* in our analyses (Fig. 2). The technical parameters of the SAM analysis shown in Table 1 demonstrate these data are statistically reliable. It can be observed that the highest number of significant genes was found in the log growth phase, exactly when cells present the highest metabolic activity, while no differentially expressed gene was found in RDM cultured cells at the stationary phase (Table 1). Because of the importance of this culture phase in obtaining cells for commercial inoculant production, this result led us to analyze *B. elkanii* culture in RDM in detail, applying a mix of Reference RNA (CRR). Therefore, stationary phase data in RDM were obtained from independent analyses of this curve. Lag and log results were considered more interesting for further discussion.

	Input parameters		Output parametes					
Condition	Fold Change	ΔValue	FSN	FDR	q-value (%)	Data confiability (%)	# Significant Genes	# Differentially expressed genes
Lag phase	1.5	0.13	0.87	1.06	0.2879	99.71	61	24 Cy5-TY
								37 Cy3-RDM
Log phase	1.5	0.13	0.78	0.68	0.3588	99.64	91	23 Cy5-TY
								68 Cy3-RDM
Stationary phase	1.5	0.4	0.65	0.97	0.1284	99.87	60	60 Cy5-TY
								No genes

FSN: False Significant Number.
FDR: False Discovery Rate.

Table 1. Applied parameters by SAM tool for data analysis and results.

Global gene expression patterns based on five parameters, two media and three phases, and functional categorization were analyzed (Fig. 3). The two main axes of principal component analysis accounted for 78% and 9,7% of the total variability. RDM cultures showed a higher number of differentially expressed genes in lag and log phases. This is possibly due to a more active cellular metabolism in these adaptation conditions, synthesis of enzymes and exponential growth, which requires additional gene expression for the exploration of the nutrient sources available in this medium. These results were matched with a higher amount of gene groups observed in cells grown in TY at the stationary phase, a situation in which cells were subjected to a higher stress caused by faster growth limiting available resources. The predominance of linkage protein transporters was observed in both media, while in the functional group related to transcription no differential gene expression was detected in any of the conditions. Additional data information and large tables of genes can be viewed in the supplementary material.

In general, specific genes that is going to be discussed below are categorized according to functional groups for each medium and in the different phases, respectively in the following tables (Tables 2, 3, and 4).

5. Biosynthesis of amino acids, translation apparatus and regulatory roles

Differently from cells that showed a more dynamic growth rate in TY medium, cells in RDM probably contained less ribosomes and synthesized proteins more slowly. In addition, cells grown in defined medium are more deprived of amino acids than cells grown in rich media (Tao et al., 1999). Considering the lag and log phases, these differences reflected in a higher number of differentially expressed genes and increased the expression levels related to amino acid biosynthesis and translation in RDM. A higher occurrence of genes related to the biosynthesis of amino acids of the aspartate and branched-chain families. In RDM, duringthe log phase, a *glnD* gene that encodes an uridylyltransferase was detected. This

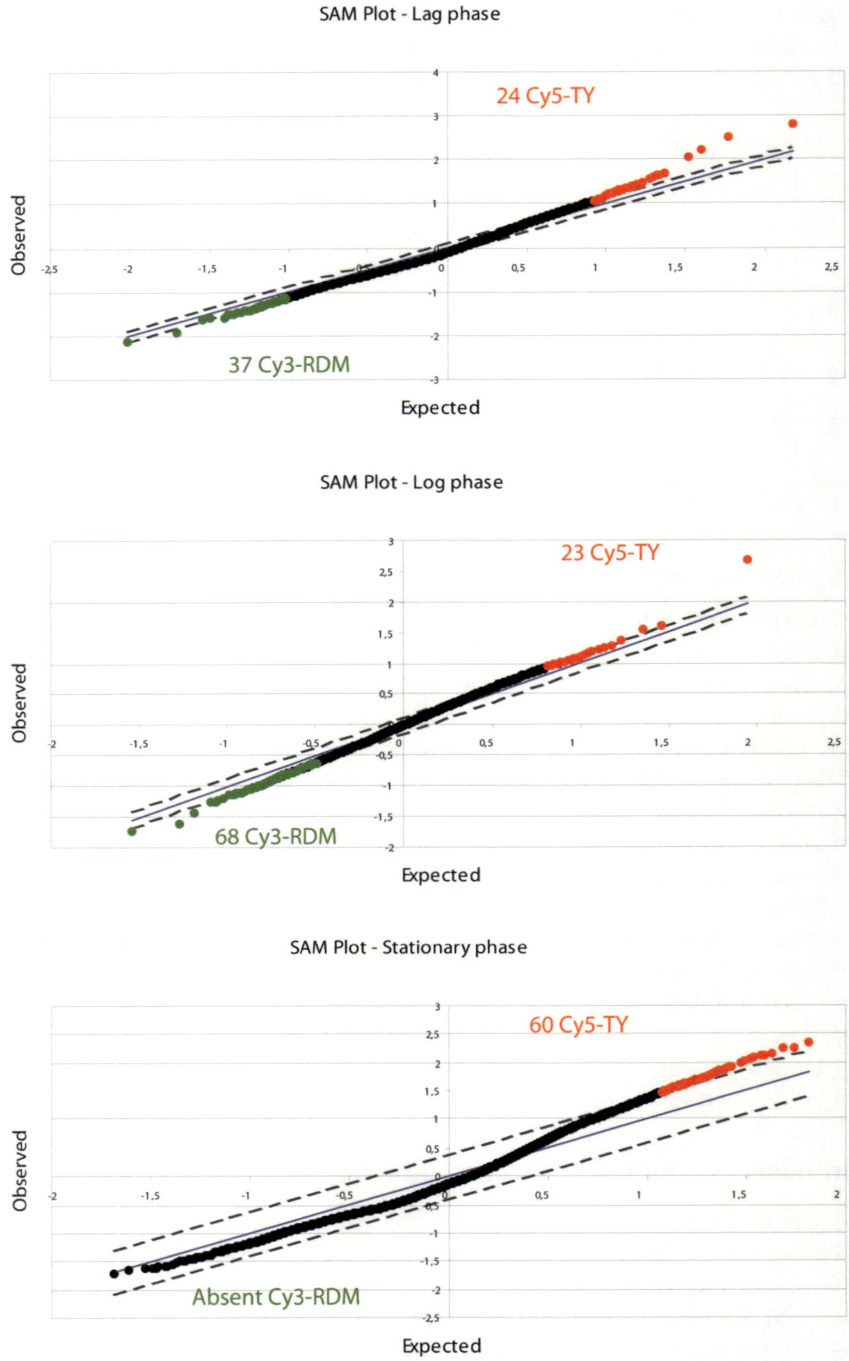

Fig. 2. Gene distribution by SAM tool. SAM plots represent the observed d(i) versus expected dE(i) relative difference of differentially expressed genes. The continuous blue line indicates when d(i) = dE(i). The dotted lines indicate the Δ distance from continuous line.

enzyme has a key role in the adenylation/deadenylation of glutamine synthetase, via uridylation/deuridylation of an adenyltransferase. Glutamine synthetase, on its turn, is involved with the production of biologically active nitrogenated compounds of and it can be considered the key enzyme in the control of N metabolism (Shatters et al., 1989).

In relation to the genes directly associated to translation roles, there was a predominance of aminoacyl-tRNA synthetase-encoding genes, e.g. *cysS*, *leuS* and *lysS*. Although no differential gene expression related to transcription was observed, several transcription regulators were observed among genes with regulatory roles. Members of the transcriptional regulation families TetR, AraC and LysR were predominant in RDM during lag and log phases, while the family Crp only predominated in TY medium. In the log phase, member of the families MarR, AsnC and AraC were found in TY.

Bacteria developed mechanisms to neutralize and expel toxic compounds from cells. Stressful conditions and nutrient source changes result in the activation and repression of genes through direct interaction of regulatory proteins with effector molecules or DNA transcriptional elements. The regulation families MerR and MarR comprise transcriptional activators and repressors, respectively. In *E. coli* these regulators control multidrug resistance pumps (Brooun et al., 1999). In rhizobia, MerR and LysR regulators also act in the repression of nodulation genes (Loh & Stacey, 2003). The regulatory protein AraC, in *E. coli* plays both positive and negative control of the arabinose operon.

Regulatory systems of two components were also detected in both culture media and in RDM only during the log phase. This system comprises the main mechanisms through

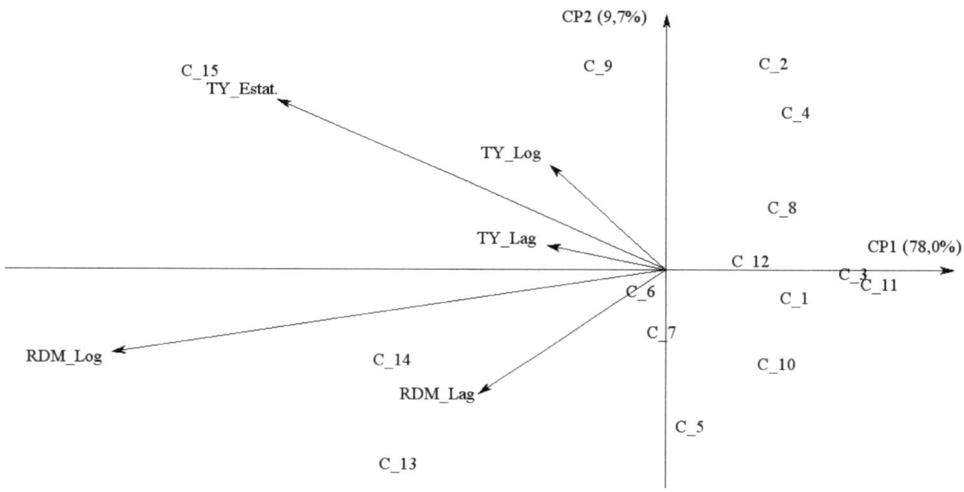

Fig. 3. Global analysis of gene expression profiles by principal component analysis showed in a bi-plot graph. It represents the projection on the two main axes of principal gene analysis based on liquid media type, growth phases, and functional groups. Vector size: number of genes. C_1 to C_15: functional categories, respectively: Amino acid biosynthesis; Biosynthesis of cofactors, prosthetic groups, and carriers; Cell envelope; Cellular processes; Central intermediary metabolism; Energy metabolism; Fatty acid, phospholipid and sterol metabolism; Purines, pyrimidines, nucleosides, and nucleotides; Regulatory functions; DNA replication, recombination, and repair; Transcription; Translation; Transport and binding proteins; Other categories; Hypothetical.

which bacteria detect environment signals and control general cellular processes; therefore it is important for environment adaptation. Typically, they consist of two individual proteins, a sensory histidine kinase and a response regulator (Pao & Saier, 1995; Stock et al., 2000).

6. Nucleotide biosynthesis, DNA replication and cell division

While genes encoding enzymes related to purine nucleotide biosynthesis were predominant in cells grown in defined medium, as *garS, KsgA* and blr7256 (adenylate cyclase), only one gene, *pyrG,* related to pyrimidines, was detected in TY medium. Ribonucleotides are later converted into deoxyribonucleotides through reduction processes. The biosynthesis of pyrimidine ribonucleotides is simpler than the biosynthesis of purine ribonucleotides, especially in the rich medium TY, when the nucleotide biosynthesis through the saving pathway is active (Tao et al., 1999). This pathway involves the use of purine and pyrimidine compounds pre-produced by biodegradation during cell nutrition. Hence, the presence of high quality nutrients in the culture medium results in high concentrations of nucleoside triphosphates (Gaal et al., 1997; Keener & Nomura, 1996).

Differentially expressed genes related to replication, recombination and DNA repair were predominant in cells grown in defined medium, especially during the log phase. The genes *topA* and *gyrA,* which encode topoisomerase I and II, respectively, were detected. DNA topoisomerases avoid DNA supercoiling during replication acting on the rotational tension of the molecule and offering a coiling support for the relaxation of the DNA helix (Zechriedrich et al., 2000). In rich medium, still during the lag phase, the cell division-related gene *ftsK* was detected. This gene seems to have a direct role in the later septation process in *E. coli* (Yu et al., 1998).

7. Biosynthesis of cofactors, prosthetic groups and carriers

Differently from the tendency observed for amino acid and nucleotides biosynthesis genes in RDM, genes associated with the biosynthesis of cofactors, prosthetic groups and carriers were predominant in the rich medium TY. This can be explained by the fact that cells grown in defined medium received most of the vitamins available in RDM, as nicotinic acid, biotin and thiamin. On the other hand, the synthesis of these vitamins must be activated in rich media. In TY, the most expressed gene in the log phase was *thiE,* which is involved in thiamin biosynthesis, followed by the genes *hemN,* and *nadD,* which are related to the biosynthesis of porphyrin and nicotinamide, respectively. The gene *pcaB,* which was also expressed in rich medium, is involved in the production of succinate and acetyl-CoA. Differentially expressed genes involved in the biosynthesis of cobalamin, *cobD,* and porphyrin, *hemE* were found in cells grown in RDM in lag and log phases, respectively.

In both media, transport and binding proteins of the family ABC (ATP Binding Cassette) were predominant. These transporters are part of a special class of membrane proteins characterized by ATP binding and the presence of large multiple transmembrane domains. Several members of this family are active transporters that act in the modulation of cellular events such as uptake, metabolism, cellular effectivity and toxicity (Glavinas et al., 2004). In RDM, other symporters and antiporters responsible for the flow of ions that regulate intracellular pH and metallic ions that work as enzyme cofactors were detected. In RDM, $FeSO_4$ was present as iron source, while TY probably contained a complex mixture of iron sources.

Access	Gene (Genic product)	Expression	Medium
	Amino acid biosynthesis		
blr6298	probable asparagine synthetase [glutamine-hydrolyzing] (*asnB*)	0.65	*TY*
blr6299	probable asparagine synthetase [glutamine-hydrolyzing] (*asnB*)	-0.79	*RDM*
	Regulatory functions		
blr4281	transcriptional regulatory	1.14	
bll5328	two-component hybrid sensor and regulator	0.96	*TY*
blr5832	transcriptional regulatory protein MarR family	0.67	
blr7984	transcriptional regulatory protein TetR family	-0.62	*RDM*
	Translation		
blr3790	cysteinyl-tRNA synthetase (*cysS*)	-0.87	*RDM*
	Purines, pyrimidines, nucleosides, and nucleotides		
blr4125	5'-phosphoribosyl-5-aminoimidazole synthetase (*garS*)	-0.86	*RDM*
bll4102	rRNA-adenine N6,N6-dimethyltransferase (*ksgA*)	-0.96	
	DNA replication, recombination, and repair		
bll0572	putative DNA topoisomerase I	0.67	*TY*
bll0875	recombinase	-0.97	*RDM*
	Cellular processes		
blr0616	cell division protein (*ftsK*)	0.89	*TY*
	Biosynthesis of cofactors, prosthetic groups, and carriers		
blr3257	cobalamin biosynthesis protein(*cobD*)	-0.87	*RDM*
	Central intermediary metabolism		
blr6768	glycogen branching enzyme (*glgB*)	-0.99	
bll2065	carbonic anhydrase (*icfA*)	-0.85	*RDM*
bll7271	carbon monoxide dehydrogenase large chain	-1.11	
	Energy metabolism		
blr3728	cytochrome D ubiquinol oxidase subunit	1.17	*TY*
blr0150	cytochrome O ubiquinol oxidase subunit I (*cyoB*)	1.15	
bll3782	cytochrome C oxidase (*coxP*)	-0.85	*RDM*
	Fatty acid, phospholipid and sterol metabolism		
blr2947	probable acyl-CoA dehydrogenase	1.19	*TY*
bll6043	enoyl-CoA hydratase/isomerase family protein	0.91	
bll3855	putative acyl-CoA dehydrogenase	-0.67	*RDM*

Table 2. Genes showing significant values for lag phases

8. Central intermediary and energy metabolism

Cells grown in rich medium did not present marked expression of genes involved in carbon, nitrogen and energy metabolism. On the other hand, following the expression tendency of genes involved in the biosynthesis of units for macromolecule production, cells grown in defined medium showed a more pronounced expression of genes related to central intermediary and energy metabolism. Glycerol was the only carbon source used for cells

Access	Gene (Genic product)	Expression	Medium
	Amino acid biosynthesis		
bll5902	threonine dehydratase	1.26	***TY***
bll7862	putative homoserine O-acetyltransferase	-0.64	***RDM***
bll6037	probable SgaA serine-glyoxylate aminotransferase	-0.61	
	Regulatory functions		
bll3466	transcriptional regulatory protein Crp family	0.70	***TY***
blr3467	two-component response regulator	-0.65	***RDM***
blr7678	transcriptional regulatory protein AraC family	-0.69	
blr5548	transcriptional regulatory protein LysR family	-0.81	
	Translation		
blr0627	leucyl-tRNA synthetase (*leuS*)	-0.68	***RDM***
blr1133	lysyl-tRNA synthetase (*lysS*)	-0.69	
blr6589	aminopeptidase P	-0.70	
	Others		
bll0916	bifunctional uridylyltransferase/uridylyl-removing enzyme (*glnD*)	-0.62	***RDM***
	Purines, pyrimidines, nucleosides, and nucleotides		
bll4805	CTP synthase (*pyrG*)	0.66	***TY***
blr7256	putative adenylate cyclase	-0.93	***RDM***
	DNA replication, recombination, and repair		
blr5111	DNA topoisomerase I (*topA*)	-0.63	***RDM***
bll4696	DNA gyrase subunit A (*gyrA*)	-0.67	
bll5057	topoisomerase II (*gyrA*)	-1.14	
	Biosynthesis of cofactors, prosthetic groups, and carriers		
bll7942	probable 3-carboxy-cis,cis-muconate cycloisomerase (*pcaB*)	0.82	***TY***
bll7086	anaerobic coproporphyrinogen III oxidase (*hemN*)	0.79	
blr0430	nicotinate-nucleotide adenylyltransferase (*nadD*)	0.60	
blr6658	thiamine-phosphate pyrophosphorylase (*thiE*)	0.90	
bll2399	uroporphyrinogen decarboxylase (*hemE*)	-0.65	***RDM***
	Transport and binding proteins		
blr0971	ABC transporter ATP-binding protein	0.60	***TY***
bll0731	glycerol-3-phosphate ABC transporter membrane spanning protein	-0.63	***RDM***
blr4039	ABC transporter substrate-binding protein	-0.64	
blr4115	putative symporter	-0.67	
blr3904	probable iron transport protein	-0.69	
bll3739	probable Na+/H+ antiporter	-0.78	
	Central intermediary metabolism		
bll0199	probable nitrile hydratase regulator	-0.62	***RDM***
blr2806	nitrite extrusion protein	-0.64	
blr0725	nitrogen regulatory IIA protein (*ptsN*)	-0.76	
bsr1750	ferredoxin (*fer3*)	-0.85	

Access	Gene (Genic product)	Expression	Medium
	Energy metabolism		
bll8141	phosphoenolpyruvate carboxykinase (*pckA)*	-0.65	***RDM***
blr4655	Phosphoenolpyruvate synthase (*ppsA*)	-0.74	
blr3958	putative acetyl-coenzyme A synthetase	-1.00	
bll4782	pyruvate dehydrogenase beta subunit (*pdhB*)	-0.64	
	Fatty acid, phospholipid and sterol metabolism		
bll6363	putative acyl-CoA dehydrogenase	0.81	***TY***
bll4711	fatty acid CoA ligase	0.81	
blr1046	long-chain-fatty-acid-CoA ligase	-0.59	***RDM***

Table 3. Genes showing significant values for log phases.

grown in defined medium, and it is used in a very efficient way. Metabolism occurs via glycerol kinase and glycerol phosphate dehydrogenase, producing glyceraldehyde-3-phosphate, which is then converted into pyruvate (Arias & Martinez, 1976). During the log phase in RDM, specifically, a gene bll0731 related to an ABC transporter for glycerol-3-phosphate was detected with higher expression level. Genes involved in pyruvate and acetyl-CoA metabolism were also differentially expressed in RDM.

In a rich medium, carbohydrate metabolism through glycolysis happens through the Entner-Doudoroff pathway with a simultaneous operation of the Embden-Meyerhof-Parnas pathway, although fructose-1,6-biphosphato aldolase is present in reduced levels and the 6-phosphogluconate dehydrogenase ($NADP^+$) is absent. However, a 6-phosphogluconate dehyidrogenase (NAD) is present in *Bradyrhizobium*, suggesting the operation of a new pathway (Kuykendall, 2005). So far, none of these enzymes was found in *B. elkanii* genome.

Still in RDM, the carbohydrate limitation may have induced the expression of genes involved in the production of energetic metabolites through lipid metabolism. In this class, some genes related to the biosynthesis of coenzyme A present in the category of fatty acid, phospholipid and sterol metabolism were detected in defined medium. On the other hand, in TY, the gene *zwf* (glucose-6-phosphate 1-dehydrogenase), which is involved in glycolysis, was detected during the stationary phase. This gene may probably have been induced in this phase for the use of poly-β- hydroxybutyrate (PHB). PHB is a carbon-storage polymer, and is production begins with the condensation of two acetyl-CoA molecules, synthesis of acetoacetyl-Coa and the reduction to produce D-β-hydroxybutyril-Coa, which is finally incorporated to a PHB molecule (Tombolini et al., 1995).

During the lag phase, the presence of the cytochromes oxidase *coxP*, detected in RDM, and *cyoB* and bll3728 in TY medium suggest that aerobic respiration increased in these culture conditions. However, since the only source of aeration of the liquid culture of both media was orbital agitation, it is likely that with time and the population density increase, a microaerobic environment was created. This oxygen limitation may have simulated a symbiotic condition inducing the expression of some symbiotic and N fixation-related genes (Table 5) at that point and upcoming phases. A symbiotic cytochrome-c oxidase, *fixN*, was detected in RDM during the log phase (Table 5). *fixNOQP* genes encode a cytochrome-c oxidase specifically required for bacteroid respiration (Fischer, 1994). This idea corroborates with the detection of genes encoding superoxide dismutase and catalase in TY medium (Table 5) in lag and stationary phases, respectively. However, these cellular detoxification genes may just be acting in the process of tolerance in the adaptation and stress period in each phase, lag and stationary.

Access	Gene (Genic product)	Expression	Medium
	Amino acid biosynthesis		
blr0650	imidazoleglycerol-phosphate dehydratase(*hisB*)	0.94	*TY*
	Regulatory functions		
bll3466	transcriptional regulatory protein Crp family	1.41	
blr1163	transcriptional regulatory protein MarR family	1.37	
blr1096	phosphate regulon, two-component response regulator (*phoB*)	1.00	*TY*
bll0904	two-component response regulator (*regR*)	0.96	
bll2814	transcriptional regulatory protein AsnC family	0.89	
blr8099	GTP-binding protein	0.78	
	Translation		
bll5087	glutamyl-tRNA (amidotransferase)	0.95	
blr1133	lysyl-tRNA synthetase (*lysS*)	0.89	*TY*
blr3130	serine protease DO-like precursor	0.88	
bll5368	serine protease	-0.69	*RDM*
	Purines, pyrimidines, nucleosides, and nucleotides		
blr7737	putative adenylate cyclase	0.92	
blr7371	carbamoylphosphate synthase small chain (*carA)*	1.07	*TY*
bll4805	CTP synthase(*pyrG*)	1.06	
	DNA replication, recombination, and repair		
bll0572	putative DNA topoisomerase I	0.93	*TY*
	Biosynthesis of cofactors, prosthetic groups, and carriers		
bll7086	anaerbic coproporphyrinogen III oxidase (*hemN*)	1.68	
blr0430	nicotinate-nucleotide adenylyltransferase (*nadD*)	1.21	*TY*
blr2404	probable gamma-glutamyltranspeptidase precursor (*ggt*)	0.77	
	Transport and binding proteins		
blr3568	ABC transporter permease protein	1.24	
bll6293	HlyB/MsbA family ABC transporter	1.08	*TY*
bll1193	integral inner membrane metabolite transport protein (*mtbA*)	0.85	
bll7341	RhtB family transporter (*rhtB*)	-0.56	*RDM*
	Energy metabolism		
blr6760	glucose-6-phosphate 1-dehydrogenase (*zwf*)	1.10	
bll0322	probable trehalose-6-phosphate synthase (*otsA*)	1.05	
bll0323	probable trehalose-phosphatase (*otsB*)	0.95	*TY*
bll5920	UDP-glucuronic acid epimerase (*lspL*)	0.93	
bll2210	multicopper oxidase (*copA*)	1.13	
	Fatty acid, phospholipid and sterol metabolism		
blr3955	acyl-CoA dehydrogenase	1.26	
blr0981	acyl-CoA dehydrogenase	1.23	*TY*
bll2948	putative long-chain-fatty-acid--CoA ligase	0.79	
blr0139	putative acyl-CoA dehydrogenase	-0.54	*RDM*

Table 4. Genes showing significant values for stationary phases.

Access	Phase	Gene (Genic product)	Expression	Medium
		Nitrogen fixation		
blr7496	*lag*	nitrogen fixation protein	0.89	TY
blr1770	*log*	Molybdenum processing protein (*nifQ*)	0.74	
blr2763		cytochrome-c oxidase (*fixN*)	-0.67	RDM
blr1756	*estat*	nitrogenase metalloclusters biosynthesis protein (*nifS*)	0.91	TY
blr1756		nitrogenase metalloclusters biosynthesis protein(*nifS*)	-0.63	RDM
		Hydrogenase		
bll6933	*estat*	HupK protein (*hupK*)	0.88	TY
		Detoxification		
bll7774	*lag*	superoxide dismutase	1.13	TY
blr0778	*estat*	catalase	1.14	
		Symbiosis		
blr2025	*lag*	acyl transferase (*nodA*)	1.00	TY
bll1631	*log*	GDP-mannose 4,6-dehydratase (*noeL)*	-0.68	RDM
blr3959		nodulation protein N (*nodN)*	-1.00	

Table 5. Genes related to symbiosis and nitrogen fixation showing significant expression ratios

An unexpected result was the expression of a *hupK* gene (Table 5) in TY medium during the stationary phase, because *B. elkanii* is classified as Hup^-, differently from *B. japonicum*, which is Hup^+ (Minamisawa, 1989). This gene is part of an operon that encodes the hydrogenase system. This hydrogen uptake system oxidizes the hydrogen produced by nitrogenase and this H_2 recycling reduces energy losses (Evans et al., 1988).

9. Conclusion

The roles of genes analyzed in this work were determined through their homology with proteins which sequences are stored in data banks. A number of genes was classified in the 'hypothetical' category, because no homology was found with known genes or roles. Data reflect the expression rates of the relative transcript levels of individual genes, with no indication of regulation mechanisms.

Cells grown in a richer medium (TY), with higher availability of carbon and energy sources, grew faster and expressed a group of genes involved in cellular processes, regulation roles and energetic metabolism-related pathways. Cells grown in defined medium (RDM) face the need of synthesizing all their building blocks (monomers) from a single carbon and energy source. This process reflected not only in the activation of biosynthesis pathways, but also in the high expression of cellular process regulators, central intermediary and energetic metabolism and the metabolism of fatty acids.

Among the genes with significant rates, *fixN* was selected for Real-Time PCR validation. The relative expression result validated DNA microarray results, demonstrating the analyses and differential expression rates are trustworthy for genes expressed in the media RDM and TY. The apparent alteration of an aerobic respiratory metabolism to anaerobic seems to be one of the most peculiar results. The respiratory chain in *B. japonicum* has several branches, synthesizing a number of terminal oxidases appropriate for different environment conditions.

The induction of genes involved in symbiosis an N fixation during *Bradyrhizobium elkanii* culture must be considered to evaluate commercial inoculants preparations. The simulation of an environment with low oxygen tension may be taking place in commercial packages during the storage of the liquid product. Thus, the same process inducing these genes observed in our cultures might happen in liquid inoculants formulas. Two hypotheses are suggested for these conditions, and both must be experimentally analyzed and studied. First, cells in the inoculants contain a group of genes readily activated for symbiosis and N fixation at the moment of inoculation, which is favorable for an interaction with plants. Second, when bacterial cells are released from the package to be inoculated in plants, they undergo a new series of gene expression induction, retarding their interaction with plants and therefore the symbiosis process itself. Although the first hypothesis is very attractive, the second seems to be more adequate.

Finally, facing the new technologies and platforms for DNA sequencing that allows the analysis of gene expression rates, DNA microarrays still seem an attractive and important option once the same array has the advantage of being applied to different biological situations not always covered in sequencing experiments.

Probably, the DNA microarray technique will remain a viable alternative for many years primarily to search for genes related to environmental and metagenomics analysis.

10. Acknowledgements

The authors are thankful to 'Fundação de Amparo à Pesquisa do Estado of São Paulo' (FAPESP) for the financial support and the fellowship granted to J. M and also to Prof. Dr. Antônio S. Ferraudo for help with statistical analysis.

11. References

Arias, A.; Martinez-de-Drets, G. (1976). Glycerol metabolism in *Rhizobium*. *Canadian Journal of Microbiology*, v. 66, pp. 150-153, ISSN: 1480-3275.

Beringer, J. E. (1974) R factor transfer in *Rhizobium leguminosarum*. *Journal of General Microbiology*, v. 84, pp. 188-198, ISSN: 0022-1287.

Brooun, A.; Tomashek, J.J.; Lewis, K. (1999). Purification and ligand binding of EmrR, a Regulator of multidrug transporter. *The Journal of Bacteriology*, v. 181, pp. 5131-5133, ISSN: 0021-9193.

Dharmadi, Y.; Gonzalez, R. (2004). DNA microarrays: Experimental issues, data analysis, and apllication to bacterial systems. *Biotechnology Progress*, v. 20, pp. 1309-1324, ISSN: 8756-7938.

Evans, H.J.; Russell, S.A.; Hanus, F.J.; Ruiz-Argéso, T. (1988). The importance of hydrogen recycling in nitrogen fixation by legumes. *In: World crops: cool season food legumes*, Summerfield, J.R. (Ed), pp. 777-791, Kluwer Academic Publishers, ISBN: 90-247-3641-2:501–511, Boston, MA.

Fischer, H.M. (1994). Genetic regulation of nitrogen fixation in rhizobia. *Microbiological Reviews*, v. 58, pp. 352-386, ISSN:0146-0749.

Gaal, T.; Bartlett, M.S.; Ross, W.; Turnbough Jr, C.L.; Gourse, R.L. (1997). Transcription regulation by initiating NTP concentration: rRNA syntesis in bacteria. *Science*, v. 278, pp. 2092-2097, ISSN: 0036-8075.

Glavinas, H.; Krajcsi, P.; Cserepes, J.; Sarkadi, B. (2004). The role of ABC transporters in drug resistance, metabolism and toxicity. *Current Drug Delivery*, v. 1, pp. 27-42, ISSN: 1567-2018.

Hauser, F.; Lindemann, A.; Vuilleumier, S.; Patrignani, A.; Schlapbach, R.; Fischer, H.M.; Hennecke, H. (2006). Design and validation of a partial-genome microarray for transcriptional profiling of the *Bradyrhizobium japonicum* symbiotic gene region. *Molecular Genetics and Genomics*, v. 275, pp. 55-67, ISSN: 1617-4615.

Jordan, D. (1982). Transfer of *Rhizobium japonicum* Buchanan 1980 to *Bradyrhizobium* gen. nov., a genus of slow growing root-nodule bacteria from leguminous plants. *International Journal of Systematic Bacteriology*, v. 32, pp. 136-139, ISSN: 0020-7713.

Kaneko, T.; Nakamura, Y.; Sato, S.; Minamisawa, K.; Uchiumi, T.; Sasamoto, S.; Watanabe, A.; Idesawa, K.; Iriguchi, M.; Kawashima, K.; Kohara, M.; Matsumoto, M.; Shimpo, S.; Tsuruoka, H.; Wada, T.; Yamada, M.; Tabata, S. (2002). Complete genomic sequence of nitrogen-fixing symbiotic bacterium *Bradyrhizobium japonicum* USDA110. *DNA research*, v. 9, pp. 189-197, ISSN, 1340-2838.

Keener, J.; Nomura, M. (1996). Regulation of ribosome synthesis. In: *Escherichia coli and Salmonella: cellular and molecular biology*, Neidbardt, F.C.; Curtiss III, R.; Ingraham, J.L.; Lin, E.C.C.; Low, K.B.; Magasanik, B.; Reznikoff, W.S.; Riley, M.; Schacchter, M.; Umbarger, H.E. (Eds), pp. 1417-1431, ASM Press, ISBN: 1555811647, Washington, DC.

Kuykendal, L.D. (2005). Genus I. *Bradyrhizobium* Jordan 1982, 137^{VP}. In: *Bergey's Manual of Systematic Bacteriology, The Proteobacteria, part C (The Alpha-, Beta-, Delta-, and Epsilonproteobacteria)*, Brenner, D.J., Krieg, N.R.; Staley, J.T.; Garrity, G.M. (Eds), pp. 438-442, Springer, ISBN: 978-0-387-24145-6, New York, NY.

Kuykendall, L.D.; Saxena, B.; Devine, T.E.; Udell, S.E. (1992). Genetic diversity in *Bradyrhizobium japonicum* Jordan 1982 and a proposal for *Bradyrhizobium elkanii* sp. *nov*. *Canadian Journal of Microbiology*, v. 38, pp. 501-505, ISSN: 1480-3275.

Loh, J.; Stacey, G. (2003). Nodulation gene regulation in *Bradyrhizobium japonicum*: a unique integration of global regulatory circuits. *Applied and Environmental Microbiology*, v. 69, pp. 10-17, ISSN: 0099-2240.

Loh, J.T.; Yuen-Tsai, J.P.Y.; Stacey, M.G.; Lohar, D.; Welborn, A.; Stacey, G. (2001). Population density-dependent regulation of the *Bradyrhizobium japonicum* nodulation genes. *Molecular Microbiology*, v. 42, pp. 37-46, ISSN: 0950-382X.

López-Garcia, S.L.; Vázquez, T.E.E.; Favelukes, G.; Lodeiro, A.R. (2002). Rhizobial position as a main determinant in the problem of competition for nodulation in soybean. *Environmental Microbiology*, v. 4, pp. 216-224, ISSN: 14622912.

Minamisawa, K. (1989). Comparison of extracellular polysaccharide composition, rhizobitoxine production and hydrogenase phenotype among various strains of *Bradyrhizobium japonicum*. *Plant and Cell Physiology*, v. 30, pp. 877-884, ISSN: 0032-0781.

Oke, V. &Long, S.R. (1999). Bacteroid formation in the *Rhizobium*-legume symbiosis. *Current Opinion in Microbiology*, v. 2, pp. 641-646, ISSN: 1369-5274.

Pao, G.M.; Saier Jr, M.H. (1995). Response regulators of bacterial signal transduction systems: selective domain shuffling during evolution. *Journal of Molecular Evolution,* v. 40, pp. 136-154, ISSN: 0022-2844.

Quackenbush, J. (2002). Microarray data normalization and transformation. *Nature Genetics,* v. 32, pp. 496-501, ISSN: 1061-4036.

Rumjanek, N.G.; Dobert, R.C.; Berkum, P.; Triplett, E.W. (1993). Common soybean inoculant strains in Brazil are members of *Brayrhizobium elkanii. Applied and Environmental Microbiology,* v. 59, pp. 4371-4373, ISSN: 0099-2240.

Shatters, R.G.; Somerville, J.E.; Kahn, M.L. (1989). Regulation of glutamine synthetase II activity in 104A14. *The Journal of Bacteriology,* v. 171, pp. 5087-5094, ISSN: 0021-9193.

Stock, A.M.; Robinson, V.L.; Goudreau, P.N. (2000). Two-component signal transduction. *Annual Review of Biochemistry, v.* 69, pp. 183-215, ISSN: 0066-4154.

Tao, H.; Bausch, C.; Richmond, C.; Blattner, F.R.; Conway, T. (1999). Functional genomics: Analysis of *Escherichia coli* growing o minimal and rich media. *The Journal of Bacteriology,* v. 181, pp. 6425-6440, ISSN: 0021-9193.

Tombolini, R.; Buson, S.; Squartini, A.; Nuti, M.P. (1995). Poly-beta-hydroxybutyrate (PHB) biosynthetic genes in *Rhizobium meliloti*-41. *Microbiology,* v. 141, pp. 2553-2559, ISSN: 1350-0872.

Tusher, V.; Tibshirani, R.; Chu, G. (2001). Significance analysis of microarrays applied to transcriptional responses to ionizing radiation. *Proceedings of the National Academy of Sciences, USA,* v. 98, pp. 5116-5121, ISSN: 0027-8424.

Vincent, J.M. (1970). *A manual for the practical study of root-nodule bacteria,* pp. 164, Blackwell Scientific, ISBN: 0632064102, Oxford, OXF.

Yu, X.; Tran, A.H.; Sun, Q.; Margolin, W. (1998). Localization of cell division protein FtsK to the *Escherichia coli* septum and identification of a potential N-terminal targetint domain. *The Journal of Bacteriology,* v. 180, pp. 1296-1304, ISSN: 0021-9193.

Zechiedrich, E.L.; Khodursky, A.B.; Bachellier, S.; Schneider, R.; Chen, D.; Lilley, D.M.J.; Cozzarelli, N.R. (2000). Roles of topoisomerases in maintaining steady-state DNA supercoiling in *Escherichia coli. The Journal of Biological Chemistry,* v. 275, pp. 8103-8113, ISSN 1083-351X.

15

Visual Gene Ontology Based Knowledge Discovery in Functional Genomics

Stefan Götz and Ana Conesa
Bioinformatics and Genomics Department,
Centro de Investigaciones Príncipe Felipe
Spain

1. Introduction

The molecular biology and the study of the genome has been transformed in the last decade by the avalanche of a conspicuous amount of data produced by high-throughput technologies. The accessibility to massive sequencing, microarrays and proteomics methods implies that studies on the genome-wide scale has become feasible for a large number of laboratories throughout the world. The great challenge in current genome research is to transform these data into knowledge, knowledge that will lead to a better understanding of the molecular processes underlying the observed biological phenomena. The discipline of functional genomics has arisen to integrate genomic sequences, experimental genome screening and novel bioinformatics methods to facilitate comprehension of genome-wide data. Within this framework, visualization appears as a helpful component to interpret results from high-throughput experiments and can be indispensable when working with large datasets. Typically, functional genomics makes use of structured functional terms like the Gene Ontology (GO) vocabulary (Ashburner M, 2000) and in this case the "natural" visualization format is a graph of a group of functionally annotated elements. In this graph, nodes represent the functional labels (the GO terms) to which genes or proteins are annotated to and arcs represent the relationships among them. Visualization of genomics data within the GO graph structure is effective in providing a rapid insight into the functional composition of a dataset and for understanding functional information within its biological context. This is of outermost importance in functional genomics research where both the overview and the detail are essential to create hypothesis over the functioning of biological systems.

However, a problem when visualizing GO functional information is that graphs can become extremely large and difficult to navigate if the number of represented elements (genes, proteins or simply GO terms) is high. Moreover, not all nodes are equally important and different kind of information might be associated to them. Therefore, the goal of a good visualization technique is to provide an informative view of the data that is efficient in generating new knowledge.

In this chapter we review current methods to visualize and perform data mining from GO contained genomic data. We start with a brief introduction to the Gene Ontology and present several third-party approaches for the visualization of GO data. The body of this document will focus on visual solutions for GO-based data mining available in the

Blast2GO suite. These include tools for zooming, filtering, highlighting, summarizing, transforming and exporting GO data. Blast2GO is freely available to the scientific community at www.blast2go.org.

2. Visualization of genomics data through the Gene Ontology

The **Gene Ontology** is a controlled vocabulary of terms for describing gene product characteristics. It is developed by the GO Consortium (http://www.geneontology.org). The project aims at the standardization of gene product attributes and terms are generally defined to be valid across species. The GO consists of three independent ontologies that describe gene and protein functions from the perspective of the **Biological Process** in which they operate, the **Molecular Function** or role they have and the **Cellular Component** they localize. The GO Consortium also maintains a database of GO term annotated gene products and many laboratories worldwide use this vocabulary to describe their genomic data.

The GO is a hierarchical vocabulary with a Directed Acyclic Graph (DAG) structure, meaning that ancestor (or parent) terms are more general concepts than descendant (or children) terms and that connections between node elements can be many to capture different relationships between biological concepts. The ontology contains more than 30.000 terms distributed in about 20 levels. Another characteristic of the GO is the consistency or "true path rule": given the annotation of a gene to a certain GO level and term, all ancestor terms up to the root must be true for that gene. The Gene Ontology is not only used to annotate gene products with functional labels[1], but also to study their activity from a functional perspective, i.e. to approach genome research as the working of functionally related groups of genes that act coordinately as a *System*.

When considering the visualization of GO contained genomics data, different levels of complexity can be envisaged. First, we can consider the visualization of a single annotated gene or a specific GO term. This typically results in simple graphs that do not pose major representation challenges apart from informing on the relationships between terms and possibly the annotation event for that gene. A more complex situation arises when the annotation of a group of genes has to be displayed. Here large DAGs are produced with many levels and connections between nodes, and information enhancing methods are highly required to identify and quantify the knowledge potential. Finally, one might want to represent a subset of selected GO terms that have been obtained by some data mining or statistical methods, for example, from a functional enrichment analysis of some gene expression data (see below). This represents normally an intermediate situation between the two previous cases with respect to graph size. The visual requirement here would be in the representation of the statistical value associated to the selected terms.

Different GO visualization, browser and query programs can be found that are freely available to the scientific community. A significant number of them are listed at the Gene Ontology website (http://www.geneontology.org/GO.tools.shtml). A common approach to browse the GO is the tree representation, such as provided by the AmiGO (Carbon S, 2009) and QuickGO (Binns D, 2009) engines. Tree browsers show the GO as an indented list, similar to file browsers, where terms can be expanded by mouse click to view their children and navigate down through the hierarchy (see Figure 1). If a term appears in multiple

[1] the terms 'functional annotation', 'functional label' and 'GO term' will be used exchangeable throughout the text

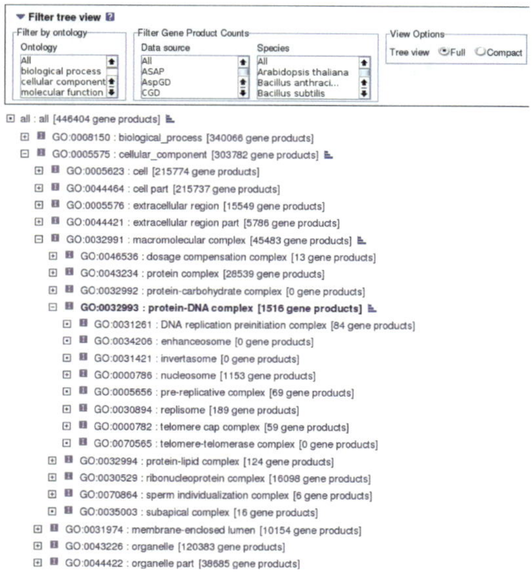

(a) AmiGO browser at the Gene Ontology site, taken from www.geneontology.org

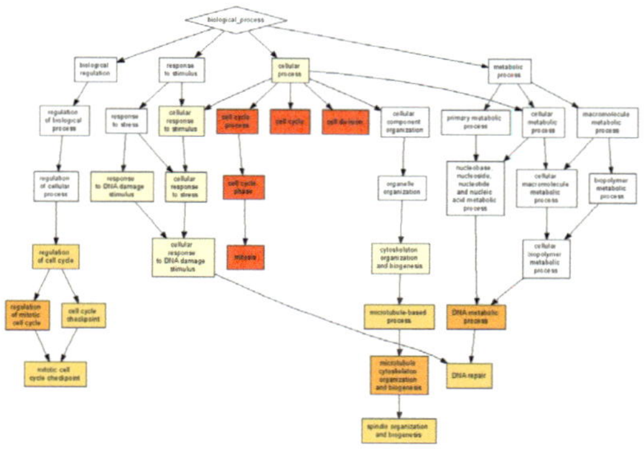

(b) Enriched GO graph by GOrilla, taken from http://cbl-gorilla.cs.technion.ac.il/example.html

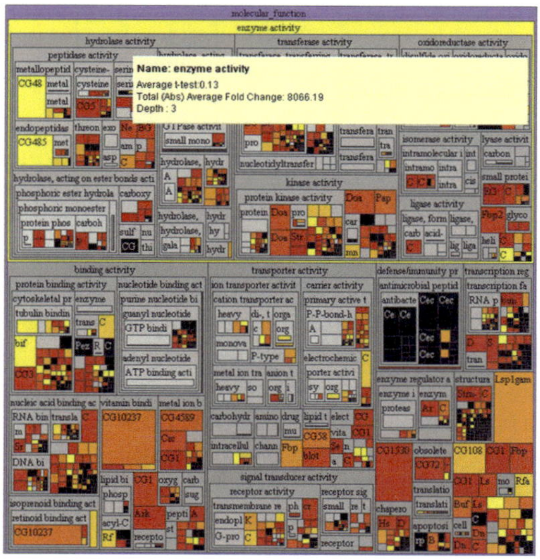

(c) TreeMap view of an annotate dataset, adapted from http://syntheti.cc/ndimensions/zb/treeviz/treemaps.html

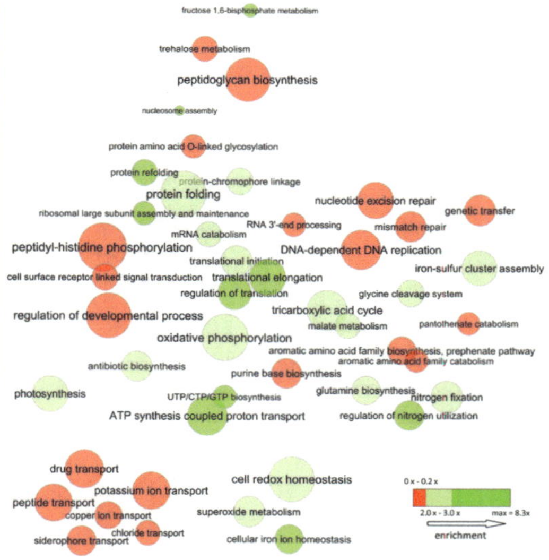

(d) REViGO plot, adapted from (Supek F, 2010)

Fig. 1. Different visualization engines for Gene Ontology data locations in the tree, all occurrences are displayed. These browsers are indicated for the visualization of single gene or term data and to recover rich information on specific elements of the GO database, but are limited to represent large annotation datasets.

A popular data mining application of the Gene Ontology is the identification of functional categories that are over or underrepresented in a subset of genes selected or ranked for their association to a given phenotype, the so called Pathway Analysis (Al-Shahrour F, 2004). Many bioinformatics tools perform these analyzes, such as Babelomics (Medina I, 2010), DAVID (Dennis G Jr, 2003) or GOrilla (Eran Eden & Yakhini, 2009), to cite a few. DAG based visualization of pathway analysis results typically goes through the display of the subgraph corresponding to the set of enriched GO terms together with a coloring scheme of nodes that indicate the significant value of the enrichment test (see Figure 1).

An interesting development for the visualization of GO based genomics data is the treemap approach (Baehrecke EH, 2004). Treemaps are a space-filling visualization technique for hierarchical structures that show attributes of leaf nodes by size and color-coding. Although, similarly to tree browsers, treemaps impose a flattening of DAG structure, the implementing software offers versatility to code different gene or GO term attributes into the elements of the treemap (see Figure 1). As disadvantage, the compartment-like display of treemaps, far from the familiar graph structure of the Gene Ontology, might be dis-appealing for untrained users and this may explain the lesser use of this solution. Finally, one of the few tools that offer functionalities for reducing the complexity of large GO graphs is REViGO (Supek F, 2010). REViGO is a web server that can take long lists of Gene Ontology terms and summarize them by removing redundant GO terms. The site provides a visualization engine that represent GO graphs by grouping GO terms based on their semantic similarity (see Figure 1).

3. GO visualization with Blast2GO

3.1 Blast2GO

Blast2GO, is a suite of tools and methods for assigning functional labels to novel genome sequences and for knowledge discovery in functional genomics research. The application has, therefore, two main aspects: (i) the generation of functionally annotated sequences according to the Gene Ontology (and other) vocabularies which is based on the similarity between the unknown sequences and known labeled genes (ii) the data-mining of genomics (experimental) datasets making use of this functional information. Blast2GO has been developed to be a user-friendly, biologist-oriented software and employs a large variety of graphical resources to present and analyze annotation data (Götz S, 2008). These features have granted the application great acceptance in the functional genomics scientific community. Blast2GO has been used in hundreds of genomics projects covering a great variety of organisms and it is today the most cited software of its kind (http://www.blast2go.org/b2g_in_papers).

The graphical functions of Blast2GO have been implemented to facilitate browsing and analysis at different levels of complexity of the functional data. In the following sections we will describe in detail all these functionalities and show examples of their application as data mining tools.

3.2 Visualization of one annotated sequence

In the process of assigning functional labels to sequence data by similarity-based automatic procedures a number of steps have to be covered. These typically include:

- comparison of un-characterized sequences to known, annotated genes deposited in public repositories
- identification of primary function candidates as the functional labels belonging to the similar genes
- transfer of selected GO terms to the novel sequences

In Blast2GO this procedure entails the computation of an annotation score (AS) for each node of the reconstructed GO sub-graph encompassed by the set of candidate terms. This annotation-score is used to select transferred labels and to control the intensity of the annotation process. The annotation-score considers the amount of similarity between novel and known sequences: greater similarity implies higher annotation-score, and the quality of the candidate functional term: those candidate terms that are not themselves the result of an automatic procedure are favoured. Additionally, the Blast2GO annotation algorithm takes into account the position of the term within the Ontology: a given term will not be transferred if a descendant is. The reader is referred to (Conesa A, 2005) for a detail explanation of the Blast2GO annotation algorithm.

Although computational annotation of high-throughput data is normally an unsupervised process, it might be sometimes convenient to check the annotation event of specific sequences to understand or modify annotation parameters. Blast2GO provides a graphical view on a single sequence annotation through the combination of color, shape and labeling formats. Given the complete set of potential GO term annotation candidates, the corresponding sub-graph is constructed. Primary candidate terms are identified by their GO code while each node in the graph is coloured according to its annotation-score. Finally, the shape of the node is indicative of the effective transference of the term: octagonal-shaped nodes are newly assigned annotations while rectangular nodes are non-transferred terms (see Figure 2). This representation has a number of advantages: on one had it permits the understanding of the relationships among candidate functions and of the potential functional diversity of the novel sequence. On the other hand, it informs on the selection procedure for transferred terms. Finally, it shows the level of specificity (ontology depth) of the novel annotations.

3.3 Combined graph

The major advantage of the GO graph visualization is when representing the information contained in a group of sequences. Two basic features are provided by graph structures: context -biological concepts are placed within the framework of a general biological sense-, and differentiation -by applying different highlighting forms to nodes according to their relevance. In Blast2GO, the graphical function to display multiple sequences is called "Combined Graph" that creates a joint DAG of a set of annotated genes. It is important to mention that Blast2GO supports the true-path consistency rule of the Gene Ontology, meaning that when a given sequence is assigned to a GO term, all parent terms become also annotated with that sequence. Different parameters are available at the Combined Graph function to enhance the visual analysis of a sequences dataset, including coloring schemes, filtering and graphical layout. In most cases, enhancing options rely on the computation of a node associated value that tells something about the relevance of the term within the dataset. These will be described in the following sections together with their use to create customized graphs.

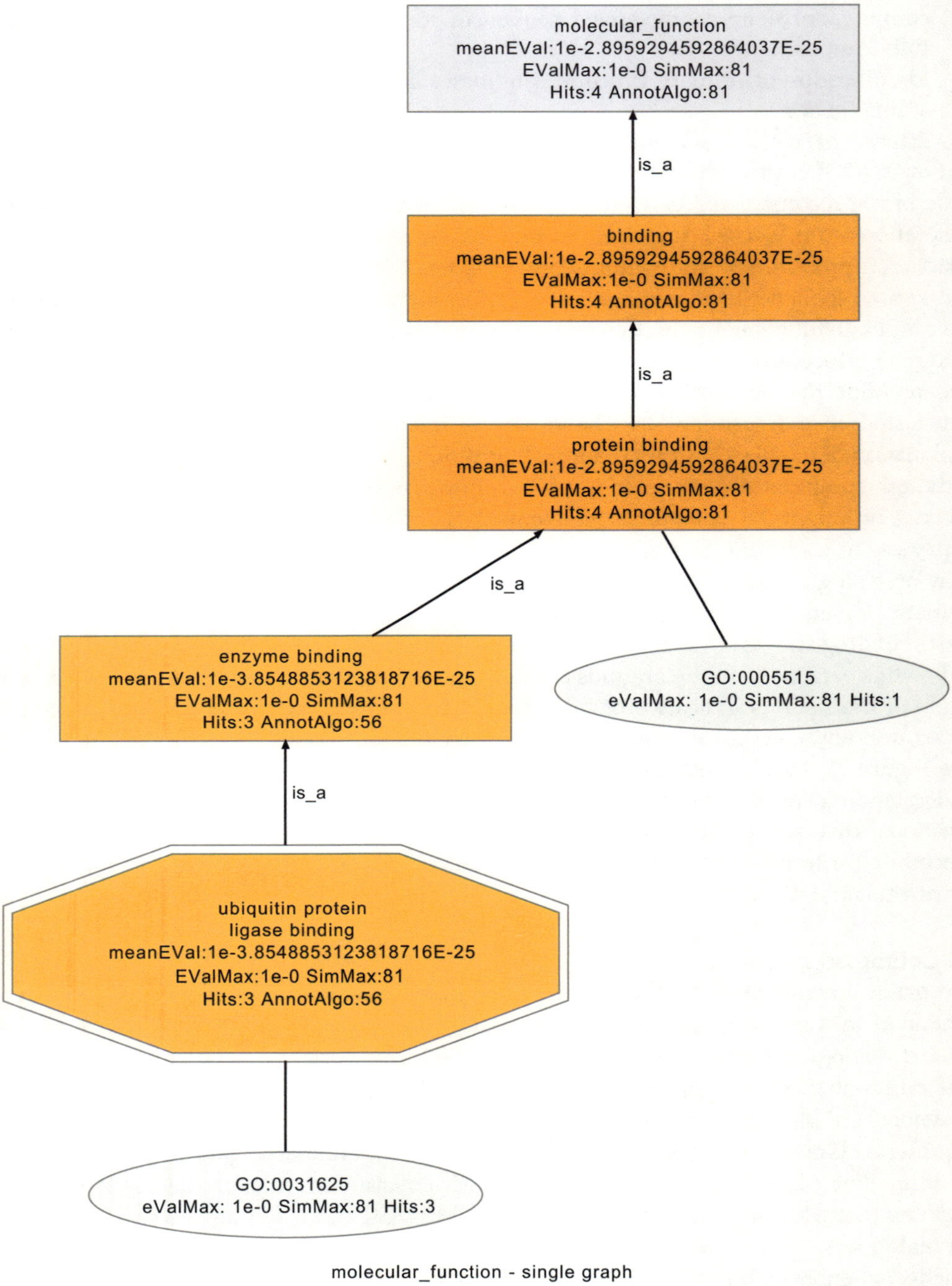

Fig. 2. A GO graph of the molecular function annotation of a single sequence. It shows to possible GO term annotations (oval nodes) for a given sequence and the finally assigned term in octagonal shape. Intermediate nodes are rectangular. Nodes are colored according the Annotation Score ("AnnotAlgo").

3.3.1 Node relevance and coloring. The Blast2GO Node-Score

A first, straight-forward approach to estimate node relevance is by counting the number of annotated sequences at each GO term and display consequently node color intensity proportionally to this value. This approach is available in Blast2GO under the Combined Graph menu and creates graphs with a gradual coloring from the bottom to the top of the graph, having parent terms darker tints that their children (see Figure 3). This strategy is useful to concentrate attention in general, high populated terms. However, due to GO true-path rule coloring by number of sequences invariably highlights high level nodes and this might not be adequate to find interesting specific terms down in the hierarchy.

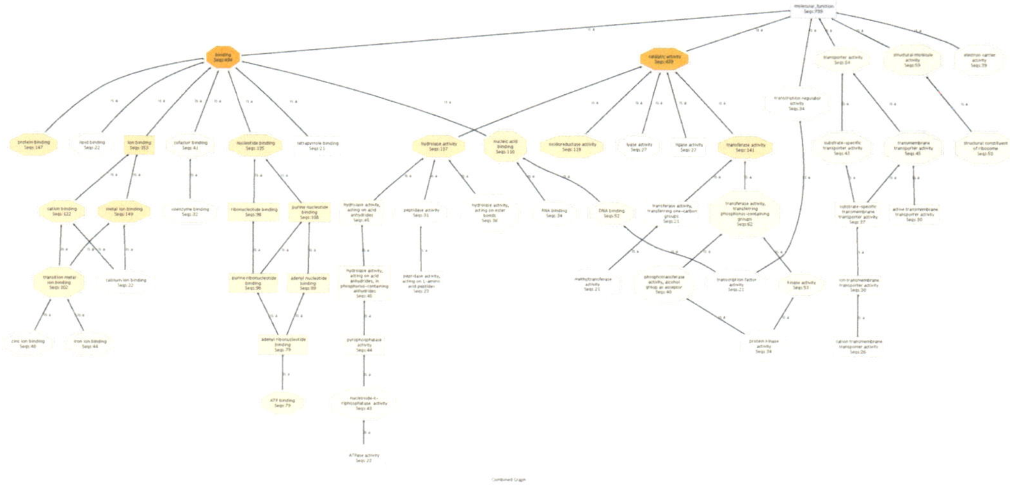

Fig. 3. A GO molecular function DAG of 1000 sequences, representing only terms with at least 20 sequences, colored by the amount of sequences for each term.

Another possibility would be to weight and color nodes by their information content. Within the GO, the information content (IC) (Resnik, 1995) of a node is defined by the inverse of the logarithm of the frequency of annotations: $IC(g) = -log_{10}p(g)$ where g is an element of the GO and GO is the overall set of all GO terms. $p(g)$ is defined as the relative frequency of the occurrence of g. The IC of terms decreases as going up in the graph reaching its minimum at the top level (root) to which all sequences are indirectly assigned ($p(root) = 1$). In a way, this parameter is the opposite at the number of annotated sequences and coloring by this metric results as well in a gradual highlighting scheme. In Blast2GO we propose a novel node metric that combines the information content of a given term and its position withing the Gene Ontology. The node-score (NS) is a trade off between functional assignment and the hierarchical topology of the GO. The node-score is defined as the sum of sequences directly or indirectly associated to a given GO term weighted by the distance between the term and the term of "direct annotation" i.e. the GO term the sequence is originally annotated to. This weighting is achieved by multiplying the sequence number by a factor $\alpha\,[0,\infty]$ to the power of the distance between the term and the term of direct annotation (see Equation 1 for a mathematical expression). In this way, the node-score is accumulative and the information of lower-level GO-terms is considered, but the influence of more distant information (i.e. annotations) is suppressed/decreased depending on the value of α. This compensates for the drawback of the earlier described method of simply counting the number of different sequences assigned to each GO-term. The α parameter allows this behaviour to be further adjusted. A value of zero means no propagation of information and can be increased by rising α. Figure 4 displays the graph shown in Figure 3 colored according to the node-score metric. Note the difference in the highlighting at the different levels of the DAG.

$$node-score(g) = \sum_{g_a \in desc(g)} gp(g_a) \cdot \alpha^{dist(g,g_a)} \tag{1}$$

where:

- desc(g) represents all the descendant terms for a given GO term g
- dist(g,g_a) is the number of edges between the GO term g and the GO term g_a
- g is an element of the GO where GO is the overall set of all GO terms
- gp(g) is the number of gene products assigned to a given GO term g

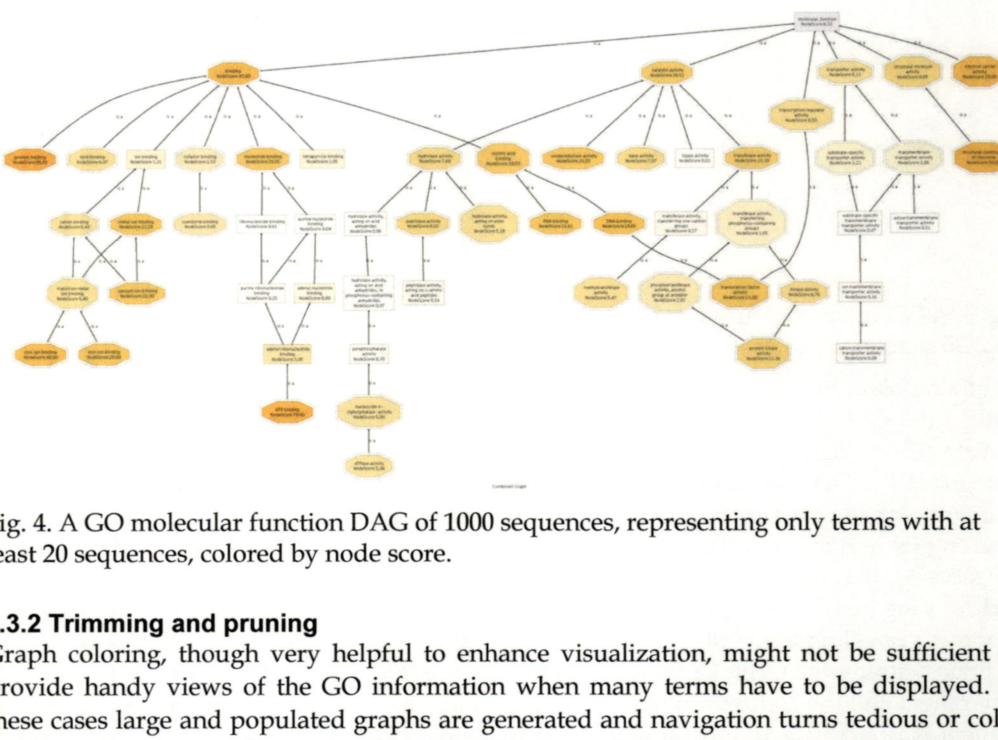

Fig. 4. A GO molecular function DAG of 1000 sequences, representing only terms with at least 20 sequences, colored by node score.

3.3.2 Trimming and pruning

Graph coloring, though very helpful to enhance visualization, might not be sufficient to provide handy views of the GO information when many terms have to be displayed. In these cases large and populated graphs are generated and navigation turns tedious or color gradients become too flat to provide clear differences between nodes. In such scenarios it seems more indicated to reduce the size of the graph in a way that relevant information is retained and unimportant terms are hidden. Blast2GO introduces two possibilities for decreasing graph size by using the two node metrics computed in combined graphs. Users can set a filter on the number of sequences annotated to a given node so that only nodes bearing more than a given threshold will be displayed. This results in a "trimming" effect on the GO DAG. The tree is reduced from the tips and only functional terms at the higher levels of the Ontology are retained. This option can be interesting to summary information and only show functionalities with a sufficient number of members, but at the cost of loosing specific, informativerich terms. Moreover, since different areas of the Gene Ontology are differently developed, trimmed graphs are often uneven in the depth of their different branches. The other option is to filter on the basis of the Blast2GO node-score hiding nodes that do not surpass a specified value. The result here is a pruning effect: the graph is diminished from intermediate nodes that carry redundant information and the resulting tree is enriched in highly informative nodes. Pruning has, however, one potential drawback: since many connecting nodes may get hidden the biological context of the ontology might be affected, having the selected terms a harder task in facilitating the biological interpretability of the genomic dataset. In practice, a balance between the two filtering options has to be achieved to obtain compact and informative graphs which are easy to interpret.

3.3.3 Summarizing, GO slims

Another widely adopted approach for making large GO graph easier to handle is summarizing by a **GO slim**. GO slims are cut-down versions of the GO ontologies containing a subset of the terms of the whole GO. They provide a broad overview of the functional content of a large dataset without the detail of the specific fine grained terms. The process of summarizing a set of GO terms by GO slim implies that terms have to be *mapped* to their corresponding GO slim counterparts and, logically, several GO terms map to the same GO slim term. The result is that a DAG of thousands of nodes can be *condensed* or *slimmed* to a few dozen of key terms, which makes the graph navigable and easy to evaluate. Different GO slim mappings are available that offer different specifications to summarize GO information. Usually these GO slim mappings are specified for organisms or biological domains, such as 'yeast', 'plant' or 'oryzae'. A list of GO slims and a Perl script for mapping can be found at the Gene Ontology site (http://www.geneontology.org/GO.slims.shtml). The **Blast2GO** software offers the functionality to map and represent GO slim summaries of an annotation dataset. Up to 8 different slims are supported and once mapping is completed the regular Blast2GO graphical and enhancing functions (Combined Graph, coloring, filtering, etc) can be applied to the new annotation dataset.

In comparison to the previous graph modification functions, GO slims represent a more static summary of the functional data, since the terms that get displayed are fixed for a giving mapping version. This, which is generally not the most desired option for data mining purposes can be handy when different datasets need to be compared or when a standard summary of the functional content of a dataset needs to be reported.

Figure 5, presents three DAGs of the Molecular Function Ontology of the same 1000 sequences. The first graph is unfiltered to show complexity of the information, the second graph shows the functional information after having applied a GO slim reduction. The third graph is filtered and thinned depending on the number of sequences belonging to each GO-term and the node-score. All GO terms with less than 10 sequences were removed (tip nodes) and all the nodes with a node-score smaller than 12 applying an alpha of 0.4 were removed (intermediate nodes).

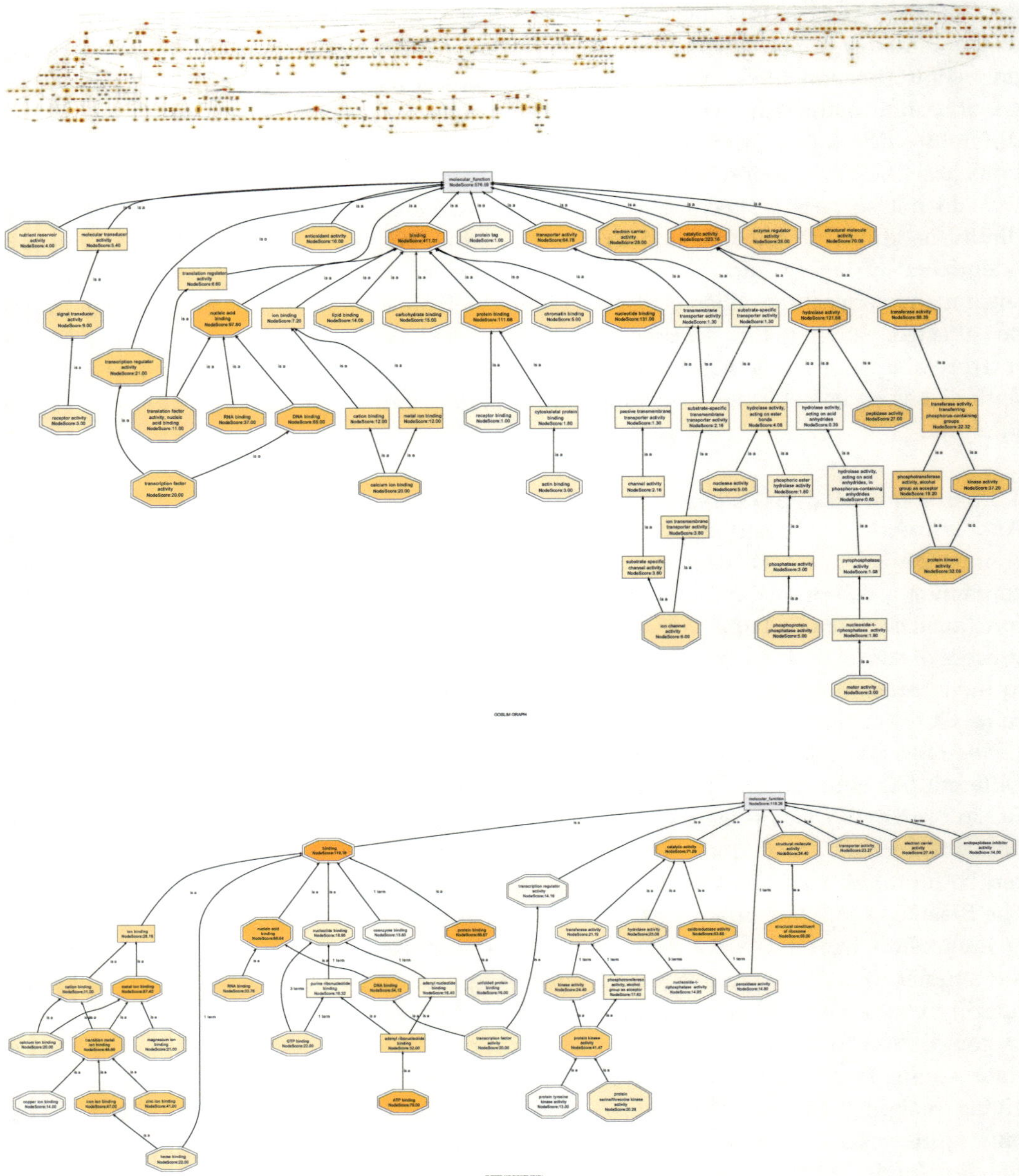

Fig. 5. The molecular functions of 1000 sequences visualized in 3 different ways: The first graph is unfiltered, the second graph shows the functional information after having applied a GO slim reduction and the third graph is filtered and thinned according to the number of sequences belonging to each GO-term and the node-score. All GO terms with less than 10 sequences (tip nodes) and all intermediate terms with a node-score smaller than 12 (with a=0.4) were removed.

3.3.4 Pie charts

Although the GO graph is the most suitable layout for analyzing the functional meaning of an annotated dataset, scientists find some times convenient other kind of representations when presenting and publishing their results. Pie- and less frequently bar-charts are commonly used. Translation of the Combined Graph of a group of sequences into a pie chart, is however, not trivial. As DAGs have multiple hierarchy levels and pies are "flat" representations, some kind of projection or term selection has to be made before creating a pie. One common option is to "cut" the DAG at a selected level and represent terms at this position as a pie chart. The size of the slides will be proportional to the number of annotated genes at each term belonging to the chosen level. This approach poses two main problems. Firstly, it generates size inconsistent diagrams: since one given sequence can be annotated to multiple terms, the sum to the sizes of the different pie slides might be different from the total number of genes in the dataset. This is in slight contradiction with the notion of pie chart (as the distribution of a whole among several classes) and therefore GO-derived pies much be considered as radial flat representations of a graph structure rather than "proper" pie charts. Secondly, the different slides of the pie may not represent terms semantically or informationally equivalent. This is due to the fact that different areas of the GO has different intensity of development. For example, on some branches third level terms may represent very specific notions since in other areas could refer to highly generic concepts. A way to circumvent this problem is to cut different branches of the GO at different levels depending on some value that is indicative of the information content of the node (see Figure 6). Blast2GO offer both options to generate pie charts from Combined Graphs: one-level pie (see Figure 7.a) where the chart contains terms of only one level of the GO and multi-level pie (Figure 7.b). For this last case two different metrics can be use in Blast2GO to indicate the

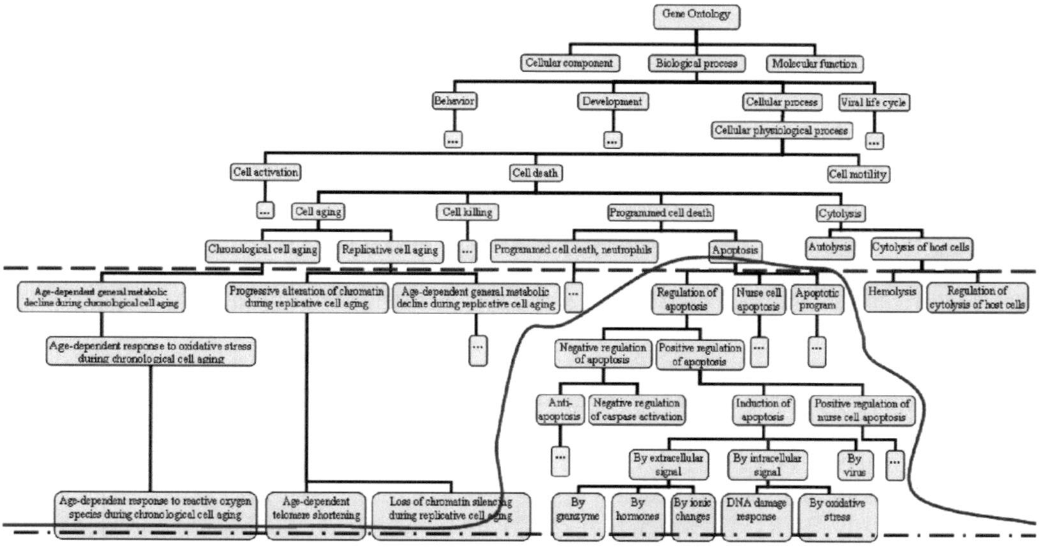

Fig. 6. The multi-level pie function allows instead of a fixed/lowest level of abstraction (dashed line/dash-and-dot line) a custom level of abstraction with different depths in various sub-trees of the GO (continuous line) depending on a user-specified weight criteria (Figure taken from: Khatri & Draghici (2005))

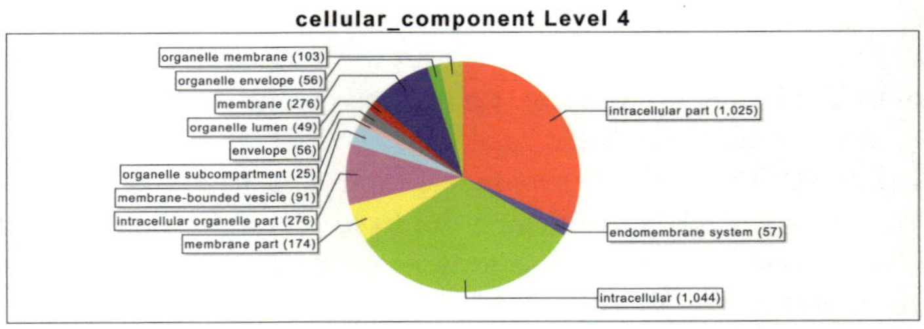

(a) cellular component GO pie at level 4

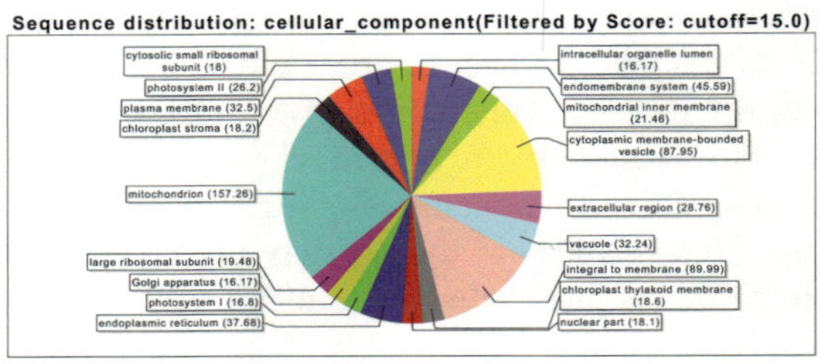

(b) multi-level pie at node-score 15

Fig. 7. Two different pie charts generated with Blast2GO. (a) shows the functional information of a given annotation set at GO level 4 while (b) shows all the GO terms which surpassed the node-score filter (cutoff=15).

"node-importance" and in this way the point of sectioning: the pie will contain the most specific node of each branch that surpass a user specified cut-off level for the number of sequences or the node-score. So generated pies show a greater diversity of functions that have more similar weights withing the dataset.

3.3.5 Visualization of statistical data

A last scenario where visualization on the DAG has gained popularity is for the display of statistical results of functional genomic data-mining approaches. In this case the relevance of a node is not in the number of annotated sequences, but because some additional experimental data has indicated the association of functions to a certain phenotype. The most popular test is the enrichment analysis of gene expression data. Functional enrichment has been made available at Blast2GO by the integration in the application of the Gossip algorithm (Blüthgen et al., 2005). Gossip computes a Fisher's Exact Test (Fisher, 1922) applying robust FDR (False Discovery Rate) correction for multiple testing and returns a list of significant GO terms ranked by their adjusted p-values. Results are represented in Blast2GO in tabular format or are directly visualized on the DAG, colouring by significance value (see 16 for an example). This kind of "enriched graphs" typically displays highlighted branches of terms semantically related. Analysis of the colored terms within branches permits to identify the level of functional specificity that associated to the phenotype, as well as the level of abstraction where this association is lost. In addition of the Fisher's Exact Test, Blast2GO supports the visualization on the DAG of any kind of statistical result or numeric value directly associated to GO functions. GO terms can be uploaded in a tab-separated format with a column containing the numerical statistical value scaled between 0 and 1. The color scale is set form dark red (0) to dark blue (1) passing through white (0.5). A good example of such a use can be found in Conesa et al. (2008). Biological functions related to several clinical measurements were identified through multivariate projection strategies and visualized by a DAG colouring the significant GO terms on a scale from red to blue depending on their significance (see Figure 8).

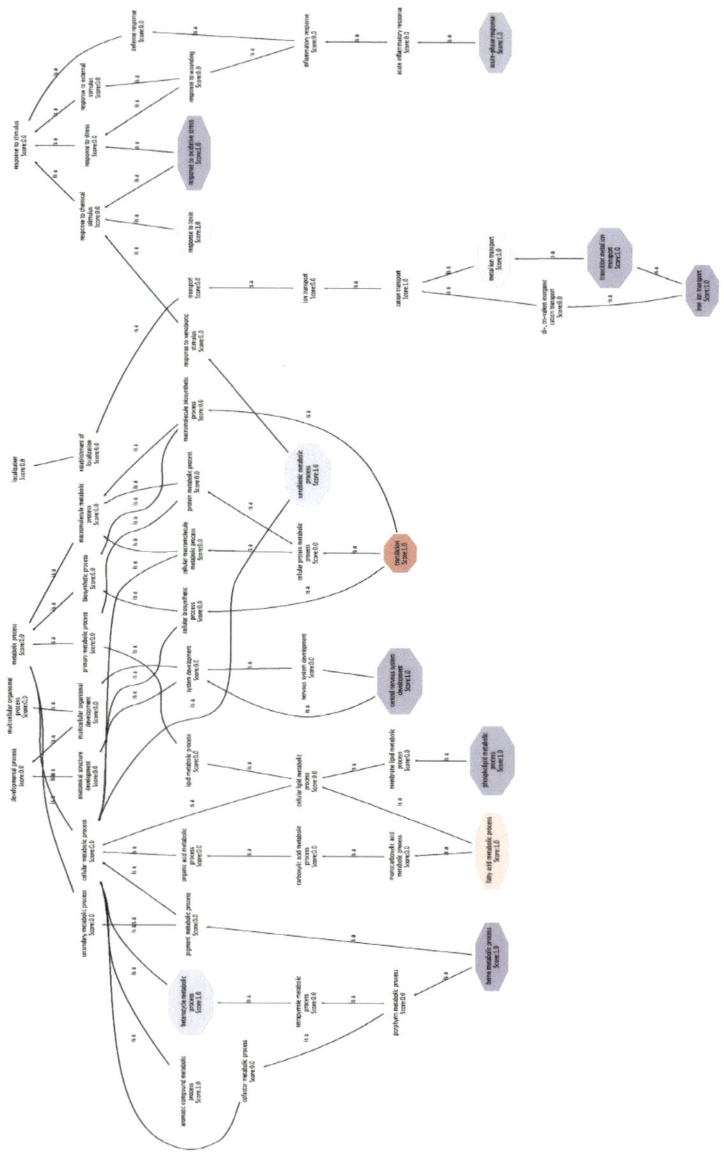

Fig. 8. GO DAG (part) of the pool of significant terms (biological processes) detected for functional variables by the statistical model. Term color intensity is proportional to the importance of the functional class in the model. Hexagonal nodes are the actual selected GO terms.

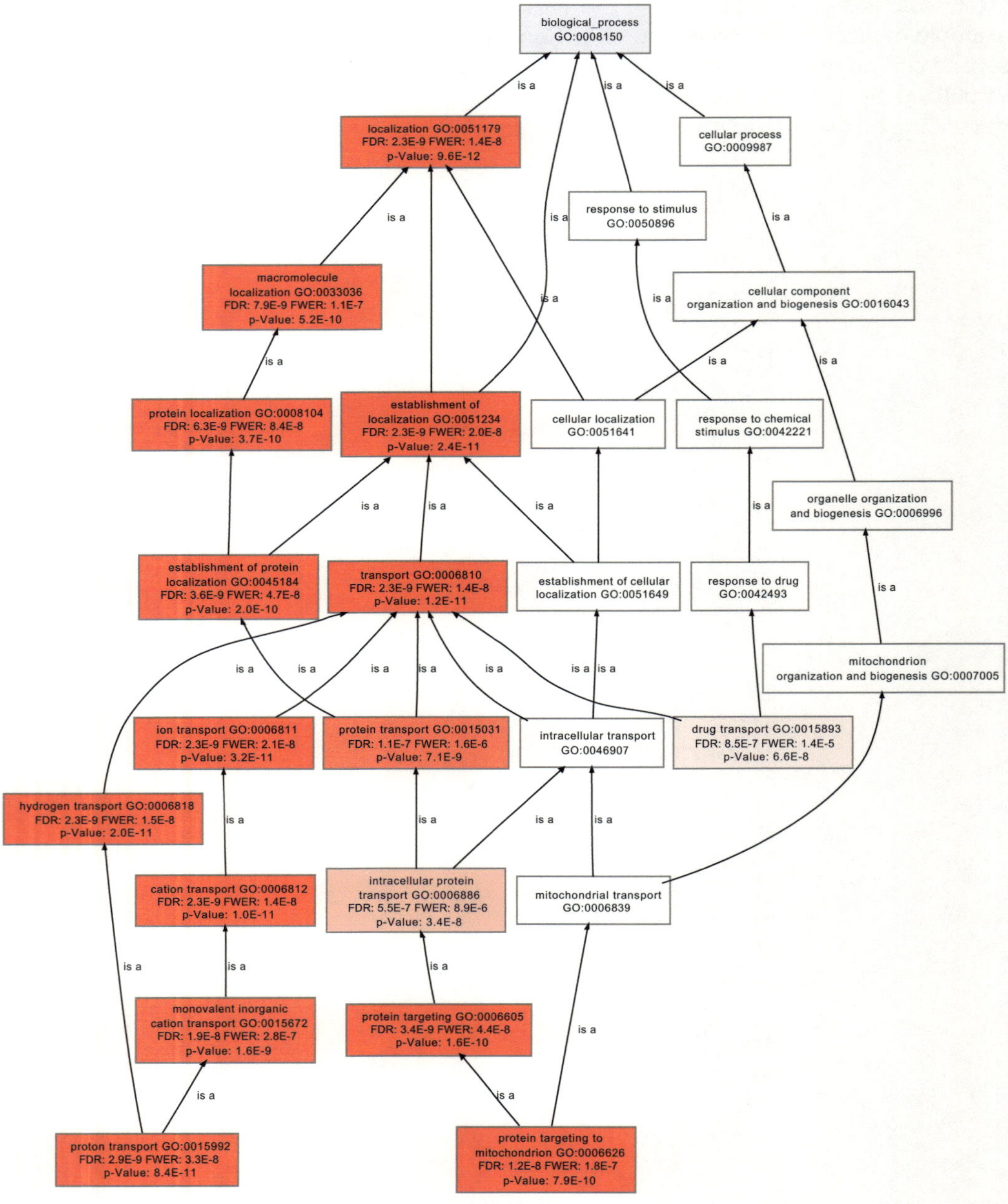

Fig. 9. Enriched graph of the subset of genes expressed in membrane in Soybean. Node filter has been set at FDR $\leq 1 \cdot 10^{-6}$. Nodes are colored accordingly to their FDR value in the Fisher's Exact Test against the whole Soybean genome array. Figure taken from (Conesa & Götz, 2008).

4. Concluding remarks

Visualization under the frame of the Gene Ontology Graph is an effective data mining approach for analyzing large functional genomics datasets as it provides functional information within a broad biological context. The different enhancing, summarizing and exploring functionalities described in this chapter are valuable for granting easy access to the most relevant functional information and facilitating the process of knowledge discovery. These options are readily available in the Blast2GO application, an up-to-date bioinformatics tool for advanced GO graph exploring. As the Gene Ontology further expands to include new relationships between terms, links among branches or richer annotation data, and novel metrics become available for assessing and comparing functional datasets, additional graphical features will need to be developed.

5. References

Al-Shahrour F, Díaz-Uriarte R, D. J. (2004). Fatigo: a web tool for finding significant associations of gene ontology terms with groups of genes, *Bioinformatics* 20: 578–580.

Ashburner M, Ball CA, B. J. B. D. B. H. C. J. D. A. D. K. D. S.-E. J. H. M. H. D. I.-T. L. K. A. L. S. M. J. R. J. R. M. R. G. S. G. (2000). Gene ontology: tool for the unification of biology. the gene ontology consortium, *Nat Genet* 25: 25–29.

Baehrecke EH, Dang N, B. K. S. B. (2004). Visualization and analysis of microarray and gene ontology data with treemaps, *BMC Bioinformatics* 5: 84.

Binns D, Dimmer E, H. R. B. D. O. C. A. R. (2009). Quickgo: a web-based tool for gene ontology searching, *Bioinformatics* 25: 3045–3046.

Blüthgen, N., Brand, K., Cajavec, B., Swat, M., Herzel, H. & Beule, D. (2005). Biological profiling of gene groups utilizing gene ontology., *Genome Informatics* 16(1): 106–115. URL: *http://view.ncbi.nlm.nih.gov/pubmed/16362912*

Carbon S, Ireland A, M. C. S. S. M. B. L. S. A. H. W. P. W. G. (2009). Amigo: online access to ontology and annotation data, *Bioinformatics* 25: 288–289.

Conesa, A., Bro, R., García-García, F., Prats, J. M. M., Götz, S., Kjeldahl, K., Montaner, D. & Dopazo, J. (2008). Direct functional assessment of the composite phenotype through multivariate projection strategies., Genomics 92(6): 373–383. URL: http://dx.doi.org/10.1016/j.ygeno.2008.05.015

Conesa, A. & Götz, S. (2008). Blast2go: A comprehensive suite for functional analysis in plant genomics, *International Journal of Plant Genomics* 2008: 1–13. URL: *http://dx.doi.org/10.1155/2008/619832*

Conesa A, Götz S, G.-G. J. T. J. T. M. R. M. (2005). Blast2go: a universal tool for annotation, visualization and analysis in functional genomics research, *Bioinformatics* 21: 3674–3676.

Dennis G Jr, Sherman BT, H. D. Y. J. G. W. L. H. L. R. (2003). David: Database for annotation, visualization, and integrated discovery, *Genome Biology* 4: P3.

Eran Eden, Roy Navon, I. S. D. L. & Yakhini, Z. (2009). Gorilla: A tool for discovery and visualization of enriched go terms in ranked gene lists, *BMC Bioinformatics* 10: 48.

Fisher, R. A. (1922). On the interpretation of "chi" from contingency tables, and the calculation of p, *Journal of the Royal Statistical Society* 85(1): 87–94.

URL: *http://dx.doi.org/10.2307/2340521*

Götz S, García-Gómez JM, T. J.W. T. N. S. N. M. R. M. T. M. D. J. C. A. (2008). High-throughput functional annotation and data mining with the blast2go suite, *Nucleic Acids Research* 36: 3420–35.

Khatri, P. & Draghici, S. (2005). Ontological analysis of gene expression data: current tools, limitations, and open problems, *Bioinformatics* 21(18): 3587–3595.
URL: *http://dx.doi.org/10.1093/bioinformatics/bti565*

Medina I, Carbonell J, P. L. M. S. G. S. C. A. T. J. P.-M. A. N.-C. R. S. J. G. F. M. M. M. D. D. J. (2010). Babelomics: an integrative platform for the analysis of transcriptomics, proteomics and genomic data with advanced functional profiling, *Nucleic Acids Research* 38 Suppl: W210–3.

Resnik, P. (1995). Using information content to evaluate semantic similarity in a taxonomy, *IJCAI 1995*, pp. 448–453.
URL: *http://citeseerx.ist.psu.edu/viewdoc/summary?doi=10.1.1.55.5277*

Supek F, Skunca N, R. J. V. K. S. T. (2010). Translational selection is ubiquitous in prokaryotes, *PLoS Genet* 6: e1001004.

16

Data Mining in Neurology

Antonio Candelieri[1,2], Giuliano Dolce[1],
Francesco Riganello[1] and Walter G Sannita[3,4]
[1]*Research in Advanced Neurorehabilitation, Intensive Care Unit S. Anna Institute,*
[2]*Laboratory of Decision Engineering for Health Care Delivery, University of Cosenza,*
[3]*Department of Motor Science and Rehabilitation, University of Genova,*
[4]*Department of Phychiatry, State University of New York,*
[1,2,3]*Italy*
[4]*USA*

1. Introduction

Data Mining intersects database technology, modelling techniques, statistical analysis, pattern recognition, and machine learning. It makes use of advanced tools for large databases management and automatic/semiautomatic analyses in order to identify significant trends and associations deemed informative because novel, implicit to the data, and of potential support in prediction and decision making.

Methodological relevance and application in healthcare and biomedicine are increasing, with implications in fields as different as information management in healthcare organisation, public health, epidemiology, patient monitoring and management, signals and images analyses. It essentially represents an effective and efficient solution providing new predictive criteria for early diagnosis and prognosis, or supporting medical staffs in patient management such as in therapy planning and personalization. Knowledge extracted from pertinent clinical databases through data mining techniques may be new or suitable of integration with consolidated knowledge and improve reliability while reducing subjectivity in decision making processes.

In this chapter we discuss about the general rationale underlying Data Mining and its peculiarities of application in the medical field, notably in the neurological domain. Relevant decision making problems, proposed solutions and open issues are summarized and the state-of-the-art of Data Mining in medicine and neurology is discussed in perspective. This review cannot and is not meant to be exhaustive, but should outline the potential use of Data Mining for supporting clinicians in their decision making.

2. Rationale and background

Data Mining was introduced in 1989 by Fayaad as a non-trivial process to identify reliable, novel, and potentially useful patterns in large data sets (Fayaad, 1996) though an iterative and multidisciplinary approach based on interaction with the application domain expert, data pre-processing, acquisition of consolidated knowledge, selection and use of the most suitable Data Mining methods, and evaluation and post-processing of the results. In this

regard, Data Mining is regarded as a step in a wider process known as Knowledge Discovery in Databases (KDD), or simply Knowledge Discovery.
Novel knowledge implicit to the dataset and of potential use can be extracted through several approaches following five different tasks or learning processes: Classification and Regression (Supervised Learning), Clustering (Unsupervised Learning), Association Rule Learning and Feature Selection. In Classification and Regression, a set of cases (instances) is available, where each case is represented by a set of variables (attributes) of varying size. One of these variables is the "target" attribute of the learning process: in classification tasks (*i.e.* diagnosis, good or poor prognosis, any rating at the outcome scales, etc.) it is a nominal variable and represents the "class" (group) to which each instance belongs. In Regression tasks the target attribute is a numeric variable (*i.e.* systolic/diastolic blood pressure, heart rate, glucose concentration, etc.). If a target (either nominal or numeric) variable exists, the learning task is "supervised" because the learning strategies try to find a reliable relationship of other attributes with the target. In this regard, supervised learning techniques may be used *e.g.* to find diagnostic/prognostic criteria or predict trends in clinical or vital factors depending on the subjects' profile (*e.g.* glucose concentrations to be expected based on genetic information, familiarity, life style, etc.).
Unlike Classification and Regression, Clustering is known as an "unsupervised" learning task, in which no target variable is identified: instances are essentially clustered at different levels, according to a predefined similarity or distance measure. Instances which are "near" may be considered similar and belonging to the same "class" or cluster according to the distance measures. Clustering algorithms may be also adopted in Classification tasks: the target attribute is in this case excluded from the analysis and instances are clustered according to a predetermined distance measure; if instances belonging to the same cluster are also attributable to the same class (target variable preliminary excluded), the adopted distance measure may be considered a reliable relationship among all the other attributes value and the target one.
Association Rule Learning is meant to identify relationship among attributes, with no reference to any particular target variable: in this procedure, the relevant relationships are ranked and presented to the analysts for their evaluation (*e.g.*, correlations among numeric variables are ranked according to their significance level).
Feature Selection approaches are adopted to identify the attributes that are more relevant for the learning goals. The selection of the most relevant attributes allows to 1) provide the analyst with a first "return of knowledge" about the main involved factors, and 2) reduce the computation time of learning tasks while improving reliability.
Several methodologies and implementations are today available for each Data Mining task; each one presents at least one parameter to be set to modify the "structure" and reliability of the extracted pattern (knowledge representation). The *a priori* identification of the most useful methodology and parameter(s) configuration is usually difficult; to test different methodologies/implementations and different parameter(s) values is a weaker, yet practicable approach.
A crucial issue in the use of any Data Mining task is the reliability evaluation of the extracted knowledge on data not used for analyses. This is more relevant in the medical field, when reliability is a predictive criterion for new individual patients.
The exploratory and confirmatory process in science provides a useful perspective on the problem of circular analysis. Hypotheses generated by exploring the dataset require

confirmation by means of independent data, because any relationship observed in a dataset will be consistent with it irrespective of a true relationship. An independent dataset for selective analyses would serve to ensure independence of the results under the null hypothesis and thus prevent circularity.
Data Mining methodologies may suffer from circularity and need independent datasets for validation. This use of the same dataset for selection and selective analysis, also known as "double-dipping" (Kriegeskorte et al., 2009) is crucial. Independent data may be unavailable, but suitable validation techniques to estimate the reliability of the predictive model "mined" from data are at hand. Cross-validation essentially works by repeatedly splitting the dataset into K smaller, independent subsets and to take advantage of a split-data analysis. A single subsample is adopted as test set and the remaining K-1 subsamples are used for training. The selection process (training) and test must be performed independently for each cross validation fold, and the procedure increases the computational demands as the independence each split-off subset needs to be guaranteed when implementing a correct cross-validation scheme.

3. Data mining in medicine

In recent years, computer technology is increasingly implemented in healthcare to meet the needs of solutions supporting clinicians in their daily decision making activities. In this regard, Data Mining tools may be useful to control for human limitations such as subjectivity or errors due to the fatigue and to provide ready indications for the decision processes (early diagnosis and prognosis, improvement or worsening, etc.).
Predictive models provide the best support to the clinicians' knowledge and experience. In order to reduce subjectivity, several (expert) systems have been proposed to codify and provide consolidated medical knowledge. Data Mining can be integrated into these systems to reduce subjectivity while providing potentially useful new medical knowledge (evidence-based medicine). For instance, Bratko and co-workers have developed a system to interpret ECGs through models extracted by Data Mining techniques (KARDIO; Bratko et al, 1989). Several techniques to analyze biomedical data from tissues or body fluids have been developed to obtain predictive models and identify small sets of relevant variables (biomarkers) to be used for validation. Schummer and colleagues, have applied cluster analysis to compare breast cancer and healthy tissues and identify markers for early diagnosis and prognosis (Schummer et al., 2010). In particular, authors identified 43 differentially expressed genes and compared them on two sets of data from breast cancer patients with good or poor outcome and from healthy women undergoing reduction surgery, respectively. The study identified three genes with high expression only in cancer with poor outcome and further research on their reliability as markers in the early detection of cancer with poor outcome is in progress. These authors also found that some histologically normal breast tissues removed from distant site in a breast with cancer displayed a cancer-like expression profile, suggesting that these regions may be predisposed to malignancy despite apparent histological normality. These findings might help in the early diagnosis and treatment.
Another relevant application is in the processing of biomedical signals expressive of internal regulation and responses to stimulus conditions, whenever detailed knowledge about interactions among different subsystems is lacking and standard analysis techniques may be ineffective, as it is often the case with non-linear associations. In this regard, Data Mining

allows identify relationships explaining continuous data, such as biomedical signals acquired on patients in the Intensive Care Units, and develop intelligent monitoring systems also sending reminders, alerts and alarms for preselected critical conditions.

A paradigmatic medical field benefitting from this approach is cardiology, where the analysis of monitored vital parameters signals the patient's worsening or alarming events. Candelieri and colleagues have proposed Data Mining in the early detection of criticalities in chronic heart failure patients monitored in remote at home, to be compensated for by prompt action avoiding hospitalization (Candelieri et al., 2008 and 2009; Candelieri & Conforti, 2010); in this project, a Classification task was performed on a limited number of vital parameters (systolic blood pressure, heart rate, body temperature, body weight) easy to be acquired in semi-automatic/automatic way. Approach proved able to reliably predict a patient's risk of heart criticality in two weeks, with reduced healthcare costs and improved quality of life. Some extracted criteria also provided the medical staff with a return of knowledge "easy-to-understand" because obtained through methodologies using understandable codification patterns such as Decision Trees and Rule Learners (Candelieri et al., 2008).

Data Mining techniques also assist clinicians in the diagnosis through computer-based systems for the interpretation of images with medical relevance (endoscopy, ecography, radiology, tomography, ultrasonography, magnetic resonance, etc.). These systems aim is usually to reproduce the specialists' expertise in the pre-identification of the affected regions (Innocent et al., 1997; Zhu and Yan, 1997; Phee et al., 1998; Veropoulos et al., 1998; Karkanis et al., 1999).

Data Mining also offers a support to identify reliable relationship between the patients' profiling or therapy and outcome. Madigan and Curet used Data Mining to predict the length of hospitalization and destination after discharge of patients with obstructive pulmonary disease, heart failure and hip replacement (Madigan & Curet, 2006) at variance with the limits and poor suitability of traditional statistical approaches (Iezzoni, 2004). Data from 580 patients living in the US were obtained though the 2000 National Home and Hospice Care Survey (NHHCS) and the survey which was conducted by the National Center for Health statistics (NCHS). CART (Classification and Regression Trees) were applied with two purposes, namely to identify the parameters predictive of the destination at discharge and length of hospitalization (home healthcare service outcome), and investigate the applicability of Data Mining in the analysis of home healthcare data. The patient's age (especially when 85 or older) was a relevant factor both in destination and length of stay, irrespectively of the disorder. Other contributions were from type of agency and payment, and ethnicity; in particular, hospitalization was shorter for hospital-based agencies.

Some caution was expressed about the relations identified by CART, which were suggested to explain the dataset without any cause-and-effect relationship been implicated; in particular, the type of agency was associated with outcome, but ranking the agencies standard on this basis would be wrong. Despite the appropriate cautions, however, the study confirmed the potentialities of Data Mining in home healthcare monitoring.

Lu and colleagues (Lu et al., 2006) ran a Data Mining study to detect impaired motility in elderly subjects and provide information about risk factors to be used when planning interventions for outcome improvement. Authors started from the prevision that by the 2030 more than 70 million of people in the US will be elderly (65 or older) and mobility will play a key role in health management (Center and Disease Control and Prevention, and Merck Institute of Aging & Health in American, 2004). The study was performed on a dataset of 8259 patients with eight demographic and patients' care attributes (age, gender, race, service, primary insurance, marital status, religion, and disease code) by means of a Decision Tree algorithm (J48) able to predict impaired mobility and a ten-fold cross validation. Feature Selection methods (Wrapper Subset Evaluator and Naïve Bayes classifier) were also applied to pre-identify relevant attributes and therefore ameliorate the Decision Tree performance. J48 provided an initial accuracy of 69.5% (specificity: 70%; sensitivity: 69%) when using all variables and a 68,5% accuracy after a Feature Selection reduction to five variables (specificity: 72%; sensitivity: 65%). (The three attributes proving useless were race, primary insurance and religion).

4. Data mining in neurology

Herskovitz and Gerring (Herskovitz & Gerring, 2003) suggested that Data Mining techniques may be applied for a better understanding of the existing relationships among variables obtained from lesion-deficit analysis (LDA). Bayesian methods proved computationally tractable, effective in representing non-linear associations among LDA variables and more sensitive and specific than methods based on Chi-square and Fisher exact statistics. LDA provides extensive information about associations between the brain structure and function, but usually generates large cohorts of variables, thus making the modelling of data relations by traditional statistical approaches difficult.

4.1 Neurological diagnosis and prognosis

Decision in the management of traumatic brain injury patients may be crucial. In particular, neurologists and neurosurgeons usually have to make decisions in a short time and on the basis of several patient's data. Several studies analyzed genomic data, clinical parameters at admission, and laboratory tests while comparing different Data Mining techniques.

Ji and colleagues proposed a Data Mining procedure to provide the clinician with useful guidelines supporting the decision making processes in the management of traumatic brain injury patients (Ji et al, 2009). They proposed a multi-level system able to give suggestions congruent to the condition in which data were acquired: on-site (data acquired at the side of accident), off-site (information acquired at admission to the hospital, such as co-morbidities and complications), and helicopter (data acquired during transportation to the hospital). The on-site and off-site dataset were used to obtain predictive models about the patients' outcomes (survival, clinical outcome with rehabilitation or at home), while the helicopter dataset was used to work out a model able to predict the length of hospitalization in intensive care unit (ICU). The days in ICU ranged between 0 and 49, but data was clustered in two groups of non-severe and severe patients' with cut-off stay in ICU at two days. The decision problems (survival and outcome predictions and estimation of ICU length of stay) were defined as classification tasks and were approached by AdaBoost, C4.5 (Decision Tree algorithm), CART, Artificial Neural Network with Radial Basis Functions (RBF-ANN), and Support Vector Machine (SVM). Authors also adopted the Feature Selection methods (specifically the Logistic Regression identifying the most significant variables prior to the training process) in order to improve the classifiers performance. All classifiers were evaluated through ten-folds cross validation techniques. A combined C4.5-CART approach using the significant variables proved the best solution for the three decision problems, with accuracy of 84% and 89.7% for survival and clinical outcome prediction, respectively. The C4.5-CART combination attained an accuracy of 93.1% in predicting ICU permanence of patients transported to hospital by helicopter.

The system proposed by Ji and colleagues can be regarded as an effective support tool improving the clinician diagnostic and prognostic accuracy of traumatic brain injury; it will be tested in all the 17 hospitals of the Carolina Healthcare system (CHS), improved and made available to the research community (as a web-based or stand-alone application) in order to receive useful feedbacks.

Important previous studies aimed at optimizing management of traumatic brain injuries by using data mining methodologies were performed by Choi and colleagues (Choi et al., 1991) used decision trees procedures to predict outcome after severe brain injuries and achieved 77.7% correct predictions. Nissen and colleagues (Nissen et al., 1999) used Bayesian networks to predict poor or good outcome (death, survival in a vegetative state or with disabilities) with 75.8% overall accuracy.

More recently, Yin and colleagues (Yin et al., 2006) carried on a pilot study on the effectiveness of different analysis strategies in the prediction of outcome after severe brain injury; they used Bayesian Networks, Decision Trees, Logistic Regression, Support Vector Machines and Artificial Neural Networks on a dataset of over seven hundred patients with severe brain injury and estimated the model performance through ten-folds cross validation. The rating at the Glasgow Outcome Scale (GOS) (Jennet and Bond, 1975) was assessed for each patient and represented the target attribute of the Data Mining analysis. Class labels were defined in six different ways and all the related classification definitions were investigated: a- five different classes corresponding to the five GOS classes (1=death; 2=vegetative state; 3=severe disability; 4=moderate disability; 5=full recovery or recovery with minor disabilities); b- three classes (obtained by clustering GOS classes 2, 3 and 4); c- two classes (obtained by clustering GOS classes 1 with 2 and classes 3, 4 and 5); d- two classes (clusering GOS classes 2, 3, 4 and 5; e- two classes clustering GOS classes 1, 2, 3 and 4; f- two classes, clustering GOS classes 5 with 4 and GOS classes 1, 2 and 3.

A reliable model predicting the outcome proved not practicable, but several aspects to be taken into account for this kind of studies were outlined. In particular, the validation techniques for evaluating the realistic prediction reliability of extracted models and then the significant influence of outcome classes aggregation on prediction performance proved crucial. No individual algorithm outperformed the others, and authors suggested to apply multiple algorithms in parallel to reduce errors.

Grzymala-Busse and colleagues confirmed these findings in a study (Grzymala-Busse et al., 2008) in which they compared the classification methods LEM2 (a rule-based learner) and BeliefSEEKER (a Bayesian network-based approach) on 42 clinical variables. Nets obtained through BeliefSEEKER were successively converted into set of rules to be compared with those obtained through LEM2 in order to discover a set of rules predicting the most probable outcome after severe brain injury. BeliefSEEKER produced simpler rules than LEM2 and proved most performing at the ten-folds cross validation. Weak rules could be removed from the LEM2 set therefore improving its performance to the same level of BeliefSEEKER. It was concluded that these Data Mining approaches are comparable, without any indication as to clinical usefulness being given.

Early prognosis is necessary for subjects in a vegetative state (a condition of severe impairment of consciousness requiring continuous care); the issue was approached via

Decision Tree (Dolce et al., 2008a) and Artificial Neural Networks (Pignolo et al., 2009) in studies analyzing the appearance/disappearance of twenty-two relevant clinical signs with respect to outcome in three hundred and thirty-three subjects in a vegetative state, whose outcome was rated according to the Glasgow Outcome Scale. Aim of studies was to identify the clinical signs observed by the medical staff at the admission and after 50, 100, and 180 days to be used as markers of good or poor outcome.

A model (Figure 1) based on CART algorithm proved reliable in predicting the outcome after identifying a limited set of significant clinical signs and the timing of observation (Dolce et al., 2008a). Performance as evaluated through cross-validation techniques ranged from 74% to 83% depending on the follow-up time point. Outcome was good (GOS classes 4 and 5; accuracy: 89-91%) when visual pursuit (or eye tracking) and spontaneous motility re-appeared and oral automatisms disappeared early during the follow-up. Absence of eye tracking and spontaneous motility at any time point and appearance of oral automatisms at 100 days after the admission indicated poor outcome (GOS classes 1 and 2) with 80-100% accuracy. Aetiology proved a relevant variable particularly at the initial phases of follow-up, with better outcome for traumatic brain injuries.

The relationship between clinical signs appearance/disappearance and outcome was investigated by same research group with Artificial Neural Networks (Pignolo et al., 2009) in a model equating a neural network to a "black box" with no return of easy-to-understand knowledge. The results were comparable, but the decision tree-based model (Dolce et al., 2008a) performed better and proved more understandable.

4.2 Therapy planning and rehabilitation

Catalano and colleagues used Data Mining analysis to investigate the interaction of demographics and parameters such as work disincentives and vocational rehabilitation services patterns with the employment outcome of traumatic brain injury patients (Catalano et al, 2007). Traumatic brain injury patients could be clustered in 29 homogeneous subgroups with different employment rates ranging from 11% to 82%, where differences were essentially explained by work disincentives, race and rehabilitation service variables. In particular, European Americans showed a higher employment rate (53%) than others ethnic groups: Native, Asian, African, and Hispanic/Latino Americans with employment rate of 50%, 44%, 42%, and 41% respectively. Furthermore, subjects without psychiatric disabilities and work disincentives had a higher employment rate than those with such characteristics (51% versus 41% and 58% versus 45%, respectively). Vocational rehabilitation service features (notably, job search and placement assistance and on-the-job support services) were relevant in predicting employment outcomes for traumatic brain injury patients.

More recently, Gibert and colleagues proposed an approach integrating Data Mining techniques, traditional statistics, and tools for interpretation to predict the evolution of life quality among patients with spinal cord injury (Gibert et al., 2009) with a life expectancy comparable to the healthy, but persistent disability.

Differing psychological responses to similar physical impairments were observed, suggesting that factors generating negative psycho-emotional responses (*i.e.* depression) and worse quality of life should be promptly identified to provide the subjects with appropriate assistance.

All studied patients were in follow-up after discharge and were periodically evaluated by the Periodic Integral Evaluation (PIE), with procedures taking into account aspects of medical, functional, neuropsychological, social, health education and health risk prevention

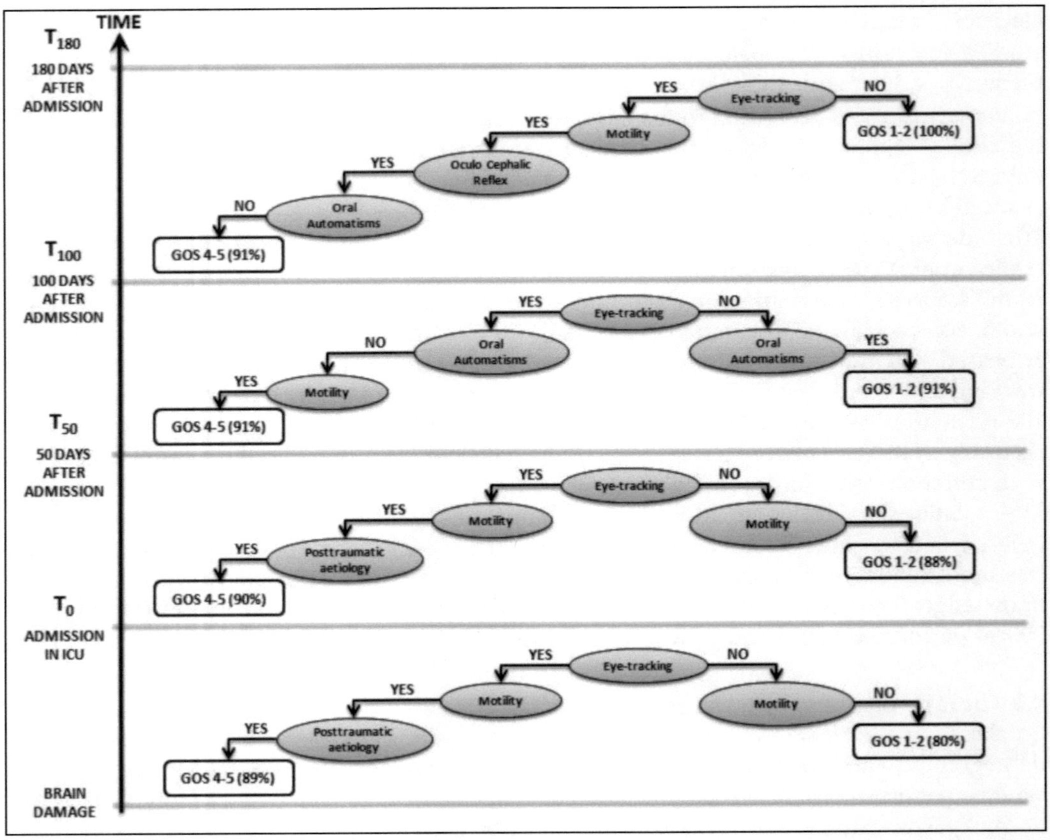

Fig. 1. Eexample of application of a CART model in the prediction of outcome of patients in vegetative state. Four major clinical signs and the timing of their observation provided the significant information accounting for the model. The overall cross-validated accuracy of prediction ranged 74-83% for each time point during the follow-up. Recovery of spontaneous motility, eye tracking and oculo-cephalic reflex not observed at admission or in early phase of clinical monitoring and the disappearance of oral automatisms correlated with a positive outcome (i.e. in classes 4 or 5 of the Glasgow Outcome Scale; correct prediction was in 89-91% of patients). Absence of eye tracking and mobility at any time point and the appearance of oral automatisms at T100 or later were indicative of poor prognosis (classes 1 or 2 of the Glasgow Outcome Scale; 80-100% accuracy depending on time of observation). Aetiology proved crucial at T0 and T50, when reappearing eye tracking and spontaneous motility allowed a favourable prediction of outcome in 89-90% of patients in VS due to traumatic head injury, to become irrelevant at T100. A retrospective cohort study in about 400 subjects in a vegetative state (Dolce et al., personal communication) confirmed the predictive power of eye tracking as indicated by the CART model. The patients' rating at the Glasgow Outcome scale after a 250-day follow-up was better in those subjects with recovered visual tracking and inversely correlated with the time of re-appearance (i.e. early recovery reliably predicted better outcome), although subjects with late recovery of eye tracking (after 230 days or more) had better outcome than those without it.

to predict asymptomatic pathologies and prevent complications, long hospitalization and survival risks. As result, PIE ratings were mainly characterized by the interaction among the patients' functionality and psychological variables, whereas demographic and social features appeared irrelevant with the exception of time from injury (that had negative effects on the quality of life), academic degree and living in couple. Psycho-emotional responses were not correlated to the severity of brain lesion, although patients with more severe impairment have a worse quality of life.

With the identification of targeted therapies remaining a critical goal, application of data mining techniques is increasing. Saatman and colleagues have outlined the needs of a new classification system for therapeutic interventions in traumatic brain injury, suggesting to adopt tools for intelligent data analysis such as Knowledge Discovery and Data Mining methods (Saatman et al., 2008).

The clinical classification systems in use can be subdivided into *etiological, symptom, prognostic* and *pathoanatomic* classification systems. Traumatic brain injuries are usually classified by one of three main systems: clinical indexes of severity, pathoanatomic classifiers, and physical mechanism evaluation schemes. Clinical indexes of severity belong to symptom classification systems and remain the major inclusion/exclusion criteria in clinical trials for traumatic brain injury. The Glasgow Coma Scale (GCS) severity scale is commonly used because of its high inter-observer and prognostic reliability (Teasdale and Bennet, 1974); it assesses the consciousness level after brain damage, is of help for early prognosis (*e.g.* at admission), has allowed develop three prognostic models of increasing complexity, and proved informative for clinical management and prognosis, but offers no information about physiopathology mechanisms of neurological deficits (Murray et al., 2007).

Several schemes were proposed and adopted to characterize the pathoanatomy of brain injury, including the Marshall score for Computerized-Tomography (CT) images (Marshall et al., 1992) and the Rotterdam score (Maas et al., 2005). The first one proved to be reliable in predicting both the risk of increased intracranial pressure and outcome in early severe and moderate traumatic brain injury adults, but presents many limitations in classifying patients with multiple brain damage types and standardization of certain CT features. On the other hand, the second score system is well standardized and able to predict outcome, but is too recent and not fully validated.

About traumatic brain injury classification by physical mechanism there is a considerable, but not perfect, correlation with pathoanatomic damage type. Under this respect, mechanistic classification may be really useful in modelling injuries and prevention, but not in clinical practice because the usually incomplete details of the traumatic event. In traumatic brain injury classification, physiopathologic mechanisms may be adopted to characterize targets for treatment. One widely accepted and used schema consists in differentiating "primary" versus "secondary" damage. The first refers to the unavoidable damage occurring at time of injury, and the second to secondary insults, such as hypoxia, hypertension, etc. However these systems are not commonly used in treatment trials because limited availability and usage of sophisticated monitoring parameters.

Saatman and colleagues suggested that improved procedures for classification would help understand pathological mechanisms in greater detail, while supporting the clinician's titration of treatment and improving outcome. Advances in diagnostic tools, technical solutions and intelligent methods for data analyses would promote the development of multidimensional classification systems for traumatic brain injury based on diagnostic, prognostic, anatomic, and pathophysiological parameters and able to select patients potentially benefitting of medical interventions and the best treatment (Saatman et al., 2008). An *ad hoc* committee would develop the multidimensional database and provide solutions for data sharing and data mining in order to facilitate collaboration and knowledge discovery (Saatman et al., 2008).

4.3 Image and signal analysis

Computer-assisted systems for images and signals interpretation support prompt decisions and reduce subjectivity of the assessment. Liao and colleagues proposed a novel method based on a combination of machine vision with Data Mining to automatically detect intracranial hematomas through the analysis of CT brain scans (Liao et al., 2007).

CT is usually preferred in the emergency room when intracranial hematomas are suspected and type, location and shape (*e.g.* epidural, subdural or intracerebral) are to be defined. However, identification following the current guidelines remains essentially qualitative. The model proposed by Liao and colleagues was able to a- identify hematomas on digital CT slices by a machine vision technique; b- assess severity by automatic labelling of pixels by depth and affected regions; and c- apply a decision tree-based algorithm to provide hematomas diagnosis independent of, and to support clinical diagnosis. Data Mining techniques (C4.5 decision tree) identified a reliable relationship between the features measured by machine vision and the clinician's diagnosis. The approach was evaluated on 48 pathological images and provided two decision rules similar to those used by medical experts and able to make correct diagnosis. The method resulted faster, less expensive and safely applicable also to patients with unstable vital signs than the magnetic resonance imaging (RMI) and was congruent with the development of a good clinical decision support system.

Application of data mining to the functional magnetic resonance imaging (fMRI) is aimed at developing paradigms for functional investigation in the absence of *a priori* hypotheses. Several approaches, such as Support Vector Machines and Fisher discriminant analysis were applied, mostly for patter recognition (Haxby et al., 2001; Haynes and Rees, 2006; Ku et al., 2008; and Hardoon et al., 2007).

Blaschko and colleagues proposed a semi-supervised regression analysis using data at rest (Blaschko et al., 2009). Resting state activity is defined as the background level of brain activation in the absence of functional tasks and is generally measured in the awake subjects by long fMRI scanning sessions where the only instructions given to subjects are to close the eyes and do nothing. The spontaneous fluctuations of neural activity in these conditions are thought to provide relevant information on brain structural and functional aspects. For example, some brain regions resulted more active at rest than while performing a task, therefore suggesting a sort of (homeostatic) default brain state (Biswal et al., 1997; Raichle et al., 2001; Raichle and Snyder, 2007), whereas spontaneous fluctuations were usually found directly correlated to metabolic activity and behavior (Biswal et al., 1997; Bianciardi et al., 2009).

However, fMRI analyses at rest are limited by the absence of time-locking to events, and traditional statistics may become useless due to noise. Blaschko and colleagues adopted semi-supervised learning techniques to improve the accuracy of a regression model based on fMRI changes in response to stimuli (viewing a movie), making use of instances with and without the related class labels in order to obtain a reliable relationship among the input and output variables. They noted that brain activity at rest is similar to that induced by stimulus conditions, allowing to augment functional data by using resting state data acquired for completely different purposes (e.g., baseline recording).

The processing of biomedical signals related to internal regulation and response to stimuli may benefit of data mining techniques whenever knowledge about (non-linear) interactions among different subsystems is lacking, *a priori* hypotheses are difficult to formulate and traditional statistics are not practicable. Signals are usually less expensive to acquire than images and can be recorded over time with negligible discomfort (as in the case of monitoring). Recording procedures are non-invasive and Data Mining techniques are powerful solutions when useful knowledge of the regulation and response mechanisms are to be investigated.

Riganello and coworkers applied several classification algorithms to detect in healthy controls, posttraumatic patients and subjects in vegetative or minimally conscious states a reliable relationship between the emotional status induced by complex sensory stimuli (symphonic music). The emotional responses were independently classified by the controls and posttraumatic patients' report and by the heart rate variability (HRV) parameters in all subjects (Riganello et al., 2008). A model based on one HRV parameter (nominally the normalized unit of low frequency band power, nu_LF, with low frequency band power ranging from 0.04 to 0.15 Hz) could classify the emotional responses in all subjects (including those in vegetative or minimally conscious state) with accuracy (evaluated via suitable cross-validation techniques) of about 70% for both healthy subjects (training set) and posttraumatic patients (independent test set).

The applicability of the knowledge acquired on healthy and traumatic subjects to investigate brain processing in patients in a vegetative state was tested (Riganello et al., 2010a; Riganello & Candelieri, 2010). A comparative analysis and validation on different data mining methods is reported elsewhere (Riganello et al., 2009).

Following a comparable approach, Dolce and coworkers identified by HRV spectral analyses the emotional response of subjects in a vegetative state patients to the presence or voice of a relative (the *mom's effect*) (Dolce et al., 2008b). Although preliminary, these findings suggest that autonomic concomitants of emotional changes can be induced by complex stimuli also in vegetative state, with implications on the residual responsiveness of these subjects.

The model used to classify the emotional response to symphonic music (Riganello et al., 2010a) was applied retrospectively, without retraining, to analyze the emotional response of 12 subjects in a vegetative state to a relative (the "mom's effect") (Dolce et al., 2008b). The emotional condition was classified as being "positive" or "negative" in an experimental paradigm including baseline, the mother's presence or voice (test condition), and the presence/voice of persons unfamiliar to the subject (control or sham condition). Data mining classified the emotional response as being "positive" in 8 subjects in the test condition and as "negative" in 11 subjects in the control condition (Riganello et al., 2010b).

5. Conclusions and discussions

Data Mining - the non-trivial process of identifying valid, novel, and potentially useful patterns in data (Fayaad, 1996) - has been applied with success to different fields, such as engineering, banking, marketing and customer relationship management, and various areas of science.

To date, application in the analyses of datasets with medical/neurological relevance is still limited. However, several approaches are suitable of use in the investigation of practical problems in medicine and the expectations are that efficient and practicable solutions will be made available in increasing number and variety of application.
The potentialities of Data Mining in clinical medicine is mainly in the identification of relations, patterns and models supporting prediction and the clinician's decision making processes, *e.g.* for diagnosis, prognosis, and treatment planning. When validated, these predictive models could be embedded in the clinical information systems as clinical decision support modules, reducing both subjectivity and time in making decisions.
Application in the medical field differs from the Data Mining use in business, marketing and economy. For instance, medical datasets and decisions are usually biased to some extent by measurement errors, missing data or miscoding the information in textual reports. In addition, some major issues concern the processes of knowledge extraction and representation: decision making should be supported by conceptually user-friendly models (*e.g.* decision tree and rule sets) rather than by "black-box" models (*e.g.* artificial neural networks and support vector machines). The reliability and wide application in fields such as images and signals interpretation notwithstanding, research on Data Mining should focus in greater detail also on the extraction of understandable rules from trained black-boxes (such as neural networks); theoretical research should provide mathematical justifications for the properties of Data Mining algorithms (Magoulas & Prentza, 2001).

6. References

Bianciardi, M., Fukunaga, M., van Gelderen, P., Horovitz, S. G., de Zwart, J. A. & Duyin, J. H. (2009). Modulation of spontaneous fMRI activity in human visual cortex by behavioral state, *Neuroimage*, 45, 1, 160-168. 1053-8119.

Biswal, B. B., Van Kylen, J. & Hyde, J. S. (1997). Simultaneous assessment of flow and bold signals in resting state functional connectivity maps, *NMR Biomed*, 10, 4-5, 165-170. 0952-3480.

Blaschko, M., Shelton, J. & Bartels, A. (2009). Augmenting feature-driven fMRI analyses: semi-supervised learning and resting state activity, *Proceedings of the 2009 Conference on Neural Information Processing Systems (NIPS 2009)*, 126-134. 01-2010.

Bratko, I., Mozetic, I. & Lavarac, N. (1989). KARDIO: a study in deep and qualitative knowledge for expert systems, *Cambridge, Massachusetts: MIT Press*. 0262022737.

Candelieri, A., Conforti, D., Perticone, F., Sciacqua, A., Kawecka-Jaszcz, K. & Styczkiewicz, K. (2008). Early detection of decompensation conditions in heart failure patients by knowledge discovery: The HEARTFAID approaches, *Procedings of Computers in Cardology 2008*, 893-896. 0276-6547.

Candelieri, A., Conforti, D., Sciacqua, A. & Perticone, F. (2009). Knowledge Discovery Approaches for Early Detection of Decompensation Conditions in Heart Failure Patients, *Proceedings of ISDA, 2009 Ninth International Conference on Intelligent Systems Design and Applications*, 357-362, 2009. 978-0-7695-3872-3.

Candelieri, A. & Conforti, D. (2010). A Hyper-Solution Framework for SVM Classification: Application for Predicting Destabilizations in Chronic Heart Failure Patients, *The Open Medical Informatics Journal*, 4, 135-139. 1874-4311.

Catalano, D., Pereira, A. P., Wu, M. Y., Ho, H. & Chan, F. (2006). Service patterns related to successful employment outcomes of persons with traumatic brain injury in vocational rehabilitation, *Neurorehabilitation*, 21, 4, 279-293. 1053-8135.

Center and Disease Control and Prevention, and Merck Institute of Aging & Health in American. (2004). The state of aging and health in american, *Washington DC: Merck Company Foundation.*

Choi, S., Muizelaar, J., Barnes, T., Marmarou, A., Brooks, D. & Young, H. (1991). Prediction tree for severely head injured patients, *Journal of Neurosurgery*, 75, 251-255. 0022-3085.

Dolce, G. & Sazbon, L. (2002). The posttraumatic vegetative state, Thiene, 1-58890-116-5.

Dolce, G., Quintieri, M., Serra, S., Lagani, V. & Pignolo, L. (2008a). Clinical signs and early prognosis in vegetative state: a decisional tree, data-mining study, *Brain Injury*. 22, 7-8, 617-623. 0269-9052.

Dolce, G., Riganello, F., Quintieri, M., Candelieri, A. & Conforti, D. (2008b). Personal interaction in vegetative state: a data-mining study, *Journal of Psychophysiology*, 22, 3, 150-156. 0269-8803.

Fayaad, U. (1996). From data mining to knowledge discovery: an overview. *American Association for Artificial Intelligence (AAAI) Press, Menlo Park*, 1-34, 0-262-56097-6.

Gibert, K., Garcia-Rudolph, A., Curcoll, L., Soler, D., Pla, L. & Tormos, J. M. (2009). Knowledge discovery about quality of life changes of spinal cord injury patients: clustering based on rules by states. *Studies in Health Technology and Informatics*, 150, 579-583. 0926-9630.

Grzymala-Busse, J. W., Hippe, Z. S., Mroczek, T., Bucinski, A., Strepikowska, A. & Tutaj, A. (2008). Prediction of severe brain damage outcome using two data mining methods, *Proceedings of Conference on Human System Interactions*, 585-590. 978-1-4244-1542-7.

Hardoon, D. R., Mourao-Miranda, J., Brammer, M. & Shawe-Taylor, J. (2007). Unsupervised analysis of fMRI data using kernel canonical correlation. *Neuroimage*, 37, 4, 1250-1259. 1053-8119.

Haxby, J. V., Gobbini, M. I., Furey, M. L., Ishai, A., Schouten, J. L. & Pietrini, P. (2001). Distributed and overlapping representations of faces and objects in ventral temporal cortex, *Science*, 293, 5539, 2425-2430. 0036-8075.

Haynes, J. & Rees, G. (2006). Decoding mental states from brain activity in humans, *Nature Reviews Neuroscience*, 7, 7, 523-534. 1471-0048.

Herskovits, E. H. & Gerring, J. P. (2003). Application of data-mining method based on Bayesian networks to lesion-deficit analysis, *Neuroimage*, 19, 4 ,1664-73. 1053-8119.

Iezzoni, L. I. (2004). Risk adjusting rehabilitation outcomes, an overview of methodologic issues, *Am J Phys Med Rehabil*, 83, 316-326. 0894-9115.

Innocent, P. R., Barnes, M. & John, R. (1997). Application of the fuzzy ART/MAP and MinMax/MAP neural network models to radiographic image classification, *Artificial Intelligence in Medicine*, 11, 241-263. 0933-3657.

Jennet, B. & Bond, B. (1975). Assessment of outcome after severe brain damage: a practical scale, *Lancet*, 1, 480-484. 0140-6736.

Ji, S., Smith, R., Huynh, T. & Najarian, K. (2009). A comparative analysis of multi-level computer-assisted decision making system for traumatic brain injuries, *BMC Medical Informatics and Decision Making*. 9, 2. 1472-6947.

Karkanis, S., Magoulas, G. D., Grigoriadou, M. & Schurr, M. (1999a). Detecting abnormalities in colonoscopic images by textural description and neural networks, *Proceedings of Workshop on Machine Learning in Medical Applications, Advanced Course in Artificial Intelligence-ACAI99*, Chania, Greece, 59-62.

Karkanis, S., Galoussi, K. & Maroulis, D. (1999b). Classification of endoscopic images based on texture spectrum, *Proceedings of Workshop on Machine Learning in Medical Applications, Advanced Course in Artificial Intelligence-ACAI99*, Chania, Greece, 63-69.

Kriegeskorte, N., Simmons, W. K., Bellgowan, P. S. F. & Baker, C. I. (2009). Circular analysis in systems neuroscience - the dangers of double dipping, *Nature Neuroscience*, 12, 535-540. 1097-6256.

Ku, S., Gretton, A., Macke, J. & Logothesis, N. K. (2008). Comparison of pattern recognition methods in classifying high-resolution bold signals obtained at high magnetic field in monkeys. *Magnetic Resonance Imaging*, 26, 7, 1007-1014. 0730-725X.

Liao, C., Xiao, F., Wong, J. & Chiang, I. (2007). A knowledge discovery approach to diagnosing intracranial haematomas on brain CT: recognition, measurement and classification, *Proceedings of the 1st international conference on Medical biometrics*, 73-82. 0302-9743.

Lu, D., Street, W. N. & Delaney, C. (2006). Knowledge discovery: detecting elderly patients with impaired mobility, *Stud Health Technol Inform*, 122, 121-3. 0926-9630.

Maas, A. I., Hukkelhoven, C. W., Marshall, L. F. & Steyeberg, E. W. (2005). Prediction of outcome in traumatic brain injury with computed tomographic characteristics: a comparison between the computed tomographic classification and combinations of computed tomographic predictors. *Neurosurgey*, 57, 1173-1182. 0148-396X.

Madigan, E. A. & Curet, O. L. (2006). A data mining approach in home healthcare: outcomes and service use, *BMC Health Services Research*, 6, 18. 1472-6963.

Magoulas, G. D. & Prentza, A. (2001). Machine Learning in medical applications. *Machine Learning and Its Applications, Lecture Notes in Computer Science*. 2049, 300-307. 3-540-42490-3.

Marshall, L. F., Marshall, S. B., Klauber, M. R., Van Brukum, C. M., Eisemberg, H., Jane, J. A., Luerssen, T. G., Marmarou, A. & Foulkes, M. A. (1992). The diagnosis of head injury requires a classification based on computed axial tomography, *Journal of Neurotrauma*, 9, Suppl. 1, 287-292. 0897-7151.

Murray, G. D., Butcher, I., McHugh, G. S., Lu, J., Mushkudiani, N. A., Maas, A. I., Marmarou, A. & Steyeberg, E. W. (2007). Multivariable prognostic analysis in traumatic brain injury: results from the IMPACT study, *Journal of Neurotrauma*, 24, 329-337. 0897-7151.

Nissen, J. J., Jones, P. A., Signorini, D. F., Murray, L. S., Teasdale, G. M. & Miller, J. D. (1999). Glasgow head injury outcome prediction program: an independent assessment, *Journal of Neurology, Neurosurgery, and Psychiatry*, 67, 769-799. 0022-3050.

Phee, S. J., Ng, W. S., Chen, I. M., Seow-Choen, F. & Davis, B. L. (1998). Automation of colonoscopy part II: visual-control aspects, *IEEE Engineering in Medicine and Biology*, May-June, 81-88. 0739-5175.

Pignolo, L., Riganello, F., Candelieri, A. & Lagani, V. (2009). Vegetative State: Early Prediction of Clinical Outcome by Artificial Neural Network, *Proceedings of The Fifth International Workshop on Artificial Neural Networks and Intelligent Information Processing (ANNIIP 2009), In conjunction with Sixth International Conference on Informatics in Control, Automation and Robotics (ICINCO 2009)*, 91-96. 978-989-674-002-3.

Raichle, M. E., MacLeod, A. M., Snyder, A. Z., Powers, W. J., Gusnard, D. A. & Shulman, G. L. (2001). A default mode of brain function, *Proc Natl Acad Sci USA*, 98, 2, 676-682. 1091-6490.

Raichle, M. E. & Snyder, A. Z. (2007). A default mode of brain function: a brief history of an evolving idea, *Neuroimage*, 37, 4, 1083-1090. 1053-8119.

Riganello, F., Quintieri, M. Candelieri, A., Conforti, D. & Dolce, G. (2008). Heart rate responses to music: an artificial intelligence study on healthy and traumatic brain-injured subjects, *Journal of Psychophysiology*, 22, 4, 166-174. 0269-8803.

Riganello, F., Lagani, V., Pignolo, L. & Candelieri, A. (2009). Data-mining approaches for the study of emotional responses in healthy controls and traumatic brain injured patients: comparative analysis and validation, *Proceedings of The Fifth International Workshop on Artificial Neural Networks and Intelligent Information Processing (ANNIIP 2009), In conjunction with Sixth International Conference on Informatics in Control, Automation and Robotics (ICINCO 2009)*, 125-133. 978-989-674-002-3.

Riganello, F. & Candelieri, A. (2010). Data Mining and the functional relationship between heart rate variability and emotional processing: comparative analyses, validation and application, *Proceedings of The Third International Conference on Health Informatics (HEALTHINF 2010)*, 159-165. 978-989-674-016-0.

Riganello, F., Candelieri, A., Quintieri, M. & Dolce, G. (2010a). Heart rate variability: an index of brain processing in vegetative state? An artificial intelligence, data mining study, *Clin Neurophysiol*, (in press). 1388-2457.

Riganello, F., Candelieri, A., Dolce, G. & Sannita, W. G. (2010b). Residual emotional processing in the vegetative state: a scientific issue?, *Clin Neurophysiol*, (in press). 1388-2457. (doi 10.1016/j.clinph.2010.09.006).

Saatman, K. E., Duhaime, A., Bullock, R., Maas, A. I. R., Valadka, A., Manley, G. T. & Workshop Scientific Team and Advisory Panel Members. (2008). Classification of traumatic brain injury for targeted therapies, *Journal of Neurotrauma*, 25, 7, 719-738. 0897-7151.

Schummer, M., Green, A., Beatty, J. D., Karlan, B. Y., Karlan, S., Gross, J., Thornton, S., McIntosh, M. & Urban, N. (2010). Comparison of breast cancer to healthy control tissue discovers novel markers with potential for prognosis and early detection. *PLoS ONE*, 5, 2, e9122. 1932-6203.

Teasdale, G. & Bennet, B. (1974). Assessment of coma and impaired consciousness. A practical scale, *Lancet*, 2, 443-448. 0140-6736.

Veropoulos, K., Campbell, C. & Learmonth, G. (1998). Image processing and neural computing used in the diagnosis of tuberculosis. Colloquium on Intelligent Methods in Healthcare and Medical Applications, York, UK.

Yin, H., Li, G., Leong, T. Y., Kuralmani, V., Pang, H., Ang, B. T., Lee, K. K. & Ng, I. (2006). Experimental Analysis on Severe Head Injury Outcome Prediction—A Preliminary Study, Technical Report TRD9/06, School of Computing, National University of Singapore.

Zhu, Y. & Yan, H. (1997). Computerized tumor boundary detection using a Hopfield neural network, *IEEE Transactions on Medical Imaging*, 16, 55-67. 0278-0062.

17

Glucose Prediction in Type 1 and Type 2 Diabetic Patients Using Data Driven Techniques

Eleni I. Georga[1,2], Vasilios C. Protopappas[2] and Dimitrios I. Fotiadis[1]
[1]*Department of Materials Science and Engineering, University of Ioannina,*
[2]*Department of Mechanical Engineering and Aeronautics, University of Patras,*
Greece

1. Introduction

Diabetes mellitus, commonly referred to as diabetes, is a group of metabolic diseases characterized by high blood glucose concentrations resulting from defects in insulin secretion, insulin action or both [American Diabetes Association, 2008[a]]. Diabetes has been classified into two major categories, namely, type 1 and type 2 diabetes. Type 1 diabetes, which accounts for only 5-10% of those with diabetes, is caused by the cell-mediated autoimmune destruction of the insulin producing β-cells in the pancreas leading to absolute insulin deficiency. On the other hand, type 2 diabetes is a more prevalent category (i.e. accounts for ~90-95% of those with diabetes) and is a combination of resistance to insulin action and an inadequate compensatory insulin secretion. The chronic hypergycemia of diabetes is associated with long-term microvascular (diabetic neuropathy, nephropathy and retinopathy) and macrovascular (coronary artery disease, peripheral arterial disease, and stroke) complications.

Diabetes treatment requires the control of clinical and non-clinical variables affecting the blood glucose metabolism [American Diabetes Association, 2008[b]]. It is widely recognized that the tight glycemic control can prevent or reduce the progress of many long-term complications of diabetes. However, a major limiting factor in the glycemic management of type 1 and insulin treated type 2 diabetes is hypoglycemia, which is the condition where the blood glucose is much lower than normal levels. Thus, for most patients with type 1 diabetes, either using multiple insulin injections or insulin pump therapy, self-monitoring of blood glucose should be carried out three or more times a day, whereas, for patients using less frequent insulin injections or non-insulin therapies, the self-monitoring of blood glucose could be useful in achieving their glycemic targets. Recently, continuous glucose monitoring (CGM) systems have been developed which provide many significant benefits in diabetes management, especially for those patients with hypoglycaemia unawareness. Moreover, diabetes control further necessitates the monitoring and analysis of patient's contextual information, such as medication, diet, physical activity and his overall lifestyle. For instance, in type 1 diabetic patients, exercise can cause hypoglycemia in the case where the medication dose or the carbohydrate consumption is not altered.

In addition to the general guidelines that the patient follows during his daily life, several diabetes management systems have been proposed to further assist the patient in the self-management of the disease. One of the most essential components of a diabetes management system concerns the predictive modelling of the glucose metabolism. It is evident that the prediction of glucose concentrations could facilitate the appropriate patient reaction in crucial situations such as hypoglycemia. Thus, several recent studies have considered advanced data-driven techniques for developing accurate predictive models of glucose metabolism. Data-driven techniques mainly depend on the input - output data from experiments and do not require any knowledge about the physiology of diabetes. These techniques exploit the information hidden in the data (e.g. medication, diet, physical activity, glucose measurements) in order to learn the glucose response to various stimuli. In this direction, the appearance of advanced continuous glucose sensing technologies as well as of activity monitoring devices could significantly enhance the prediction of glucose. CGM technology is used to aid in modelling the real-time trends in glucose data. However, the CGM systems do not measure the blood glucose but the glucose in the subcutaneous (s.c.) tissues. Finally, given the complexity of the glucoregulatory system, the data-driven techniques are considered to be beneficial compared to the contrary approach employing mathematical simulation models.

The scope of this chapter is (a) to present to the reader the current state of the art in predictive models of glucose metabolism in diabetes and (b) to describe a new approach to the problem by employing machine learning techniques using free - living data. The chapter is organised as follows. In Section 2, the related work in the field of modelling the glucose metabolism in diabetic patients is reviewed thoroughly. In Section 3, the proposed glucose prediction method and the derived results are presented. Finally, in Section 4, we discuss the achievements in the field and compare all relative works by identifying their advantages and disadvantages.

2. State of the art in glucose prediction

Several studies have been presented in the literature aiming at the prediction of glucose in diabetic patients. The reported methods can be divided into two major groups. The first one includes mathematical models that simulate the underlying physiology of the glucose - insulin regulatory system. Compartmental models, which are a class of linear dynamic models, have been widely used for studying various aspects of normal physiology and the pathophysiology of diabetes [Carson & Cobelli, 2001; Makroglou et al., 2006]. Recently, new important quantitative knowledge has been gained on glucose metabolism and control by insulin (e.g., the EGP profile during a meal, the hepatic glucose production, the muscle glucose utilization, the kinetics of regular and slowly acting insulin after a s.c. injection), which has allowed the development of new and more accurate simulation models [Dalla Man et al., 2007]. Nevertheless, they are still limited because of the inherent complexity of the glucose - insulin system. On the other hand, the second group of methods provides data-driven models which are able to predict the glucose concentration based only on existing input-output data. Several specific methods are available for formulating such data models, including methods of machine learning and time series analysis. In what follows, we will review the relevant literature on data-driven models of glucose metabolism.

2.1 Machine learning methods

The prediction of the glucose time series as a function of the input variables can be considered as a regression problem with a time component. The fact that the relationship between input variables (i.e. medication, diet, physical activity, stress etc.) and glucose levels is nonlinear, dynamic, interactive and patient-specific [Tresp et al., 1999], necessitates the application of non-linear regression models such as artificial neural networks, support vector regression and Gaussian processes. Different types of neural networks have been considered in modelling the blood glucose metabolism, such as multilayer perceptron (MLP) [Kok, 2004; Zitar & Al-Labali, 2005; Quchani & Tahami, 2007], radial basis function (RBF) [Baghdadi & Nasrabadi, 2007], wavelet [Zainuddin et al., 2009], time series convolution [Tresp et al., 1999] and recurrent neural networks (RNN) [Tresp et al., 1999; Mougiakakou et al., 2006]. Additionally, Gaussian processes have derived prominent results regarding glucose prediction [Valletta et al., 2009].

The predictive performance of MLP neural network has been compared with that of Elman RNN in [Quchani & Tahami, 2007]. The aim of this study was the prediction of the blood glucose concentration before lunch based on the following features: (a) dosage of short-acting insulin, (b) dosage of long-acting insulin, (c) amount of carbohydrates, (d) stress level (from 1 to 4 discrete levels), (d) exercise level (from 1 - 4), (e) blood glucose concentration before breakfast and (f) period of time between two consecutive measurements of glucose. The data were obtained from 10 type 1 diabetic patients treated by a conventional s.c. insulin therapeutic regimen. The results showed that the Elman RNN outperform the MLP network to a significant extent (mean absolute error 10.4 mg/dl vs. 24.15 mg/dl).

An interesting approach for the prediction of glucose in type 1 diabetes was followed by [Kok, 2004; Baghdadi & Nasrabadi, 2007; Zainuddin et al., 2009] in which the day is split into four intervals (i.e. morning, afternoon, evening, night) and a different model is built for each one based on the fact that the blood glucose concentrations for these intervals are uncorrelated. The predictions of glucose at the end of each interval were made using 19 different features regarding dosage of short-acting insulin, dosage of long-acting insulin, past blood glucose measurements, amount of carbohydrates, exercise level and stress level. The only difference between the above mentioned works concerns the feature selection technique and the neural network that is employed.

A number of prediction models specific to type 1 diabetes, including non-linear compartmental models, time series convolution neural networks and RNNs, were compared in [Tresp et al., 1999]. The combination of the RNNs with a linear error model gave the best results deriving a root mean squared error (RMSE) of 51 mg/dl. The inputs that were used for this model are the following: (a) dosage of short-acting insulin, (b) dosage of long-acting insulin, (c) amount of fast carbohydrates, (d) amount of intermediate carbohydrates, (e) amount of slow carbohydrates, (f) duration of regular exercise, (g) duration of intense exercise and (h) past blood glucose level estimates. One remarkable characteristic of this approach is that the effects of food, insulin and exercise on blood glucose were approximated by linear response functions. The efficiency of RNNs has been also demonstrated in [Mougiakakou et al., 2006] where CGM data were used for the prediction of the s.c. glucose concentration in type 1 diabetic patients. Similarly with Tresp et al., compartmental models found in the literature were employed to simulate the kinetics of insulin and the absorption of carbohydrates. They report an average RMSE of 24.08 mg/dl in case where the teacher forcing learning algorithm was applied.

The Gaussian processes have also been used successfully for the prediction of glucose. More specifically, a Gaussian processes prediction model for type 1 diabetic patients was developed in [Valletta et al., 2009] based on continuous glucose measurements, physical activity information as well as information regarding food intake and insulin injections. The prediction model was evaluated on data collected from 18 patients with type 1 diabetes. A

CGM sensor was used to gather the patient's glucose concentration every five minutes. Additionally, physical activity information was collected by a multi-sensor body monitor, the so-called SenseWear armband activity monitor (BodyMedia Inc.). Given the dynamic effects of food, insulin and physical activity on glucose levels, the authors introduced time lag variables for each input that were determined by simulations. Although no quantitative results were provided, it seems that this method can predict glucose in the short-term reasonably well and is able to follow the trends in glucose time series.

2.2 Time series analysis

Time series analysis provides methods that can be used to identify systematic patterns in time series data (such as trends and seasonalities) as well as methods for time series modelling and prediction (i.e. system identification). The autocorrelation analysis of CGM time series [Bremer and Gough, 1999] made clear that glucose dynamics have a detectable structure and, thus, the glucose can be predicted by exploiting its recent history. Since that work, several studies have considered autoregressive (AR) prediction models based on CGM data [Sparacino et al., 2007; Gani et al., 2009; Gani et al., 2010]. In addition, several multivariate time series models have been developed that are enhanced with external information regarding insulin, food and physical activity [Stahl et al., 2009; Rollins et al., 2010]. However, these approaches should take into account the non-stationary behaviour of the glucose time series.

Two simple prediction methods have been applied for the first time to real CGM time series, obtained from 28 type 1 diabetic patients over a period of 48 hours, in [Sparacino et al., 2007]. In particular, the CGM time series was described by either a first order polynomial model or a first order AR model in which the parameters were dynamically identified through weighted linear least squares. In order to remove the high frequency noise from the raw CGM signals, Sparacino et al. applied a low-pass first-order Butterworth filter. For a 30 min prediction length with weight equal to 0.8, the AR model produces a median RMSE of 20.32 mg/dl and detects the positive and negative trends with an average time lag of 3.79 min and 10.06 min, respectively. Overall, the relative performance of the polynomial and the autoregressive models is quite similar during negative trends; in contrast, the autoregressive model performs better during positive trends. In addition, AR models of higher order were found to be unstable and AR models with fixed parameters to yield unacceptable prediction lags with delays equal to the prediction length.

The use of CGM data and AR models for the prediction of glucose has been also suggested by Gani et al. [Gani et al., 2009]. They have proposed an AR model of an order of 30 with fixed coefficients which successfully predicts the s.c. glucose concentration of patients with type 1 diabetes. The s.c. glucose measurements were collected by 9 patients for approximately 5 days. Similarly with Sparacino et al., the CGM data were smoothed by applying the Tikhonov regularization approach. The construction of AR models through regularized least squares resulted in AR coefficients that reflect the temporal dependencies in the glucose signal, and in stable, accurate predictions. In particular, the AR model is able to yield 30 min glucose concentration predictions with an average RMSE of 1.8 mg/dl and a negligible prediction time lag of 0.2 min, and 60 min glucose concentration predictions with an average RMSE of 12.6 mg/dl and average prediction lag of 12.3 min. Gani et al. argue that AR models of low order, such that proposed by Sparacino et al., can produce acceptable predictions, but they introduce significant delays between predicted and measured values, because they are not sufficient to capture the temporal variations of the glucose signal. In

addition, they confirm the instability of the AR models of order higher than one, which is also reported by Sparacino et al., in the case where the AR coefficients are not regularized.
In a subsequent work [Gani et al., 2010], the authors showed that their method results in AR models in which the coefficients do not vary significantly among different individuals, suggesting the feasibility of obtaining individual-independent predictive models. For this purpose, they employed data from three separate studies, involving patients with both type 1 and type 2 diabetes, and utilizing three different CGM devices. The results of this investigation were attributed to the fact that the features of the glucose signals in the frequency domain were found common among patients. Considering that the AR models represent the signal's frequency information and are invariant with respect to the signal's amplitude and phase, the development of similar models was predictable.
Many researchers have incorporated in their time series models the influence of external input variables. Stahl et al. [Stahl et al., 2009] investigated the ability of a variety of linear and non-linear system identification methods (i.e. autoregressive moving average (ARMA) linear regression, autoregressive moving average with exogenous input (ARMAX) linear regression, Wiener model identification, subspace-based identification) to predict the blood glucose concentration for the next two hours with a reasonable accuracy. This target accuracy was defined as a standard deviation of the prediction error less than 18 mg/dl in the 95% of the cases. The identified models were fitted to real data collected during the first six months of a newly diagnosed type 1 diabetic patient who used a traditional blood glucose meter. For modelling purposes, the blood glucose samples were interpolated using a least-squares spline method to obtain a sampling rate of 15 min. In addition, the absorption of injected insulin from the s.c. tissues as well as the digestion and absorption of carbohydrates were described using compartmental models and proposed models found in the literature. The linear models (ARMAX, subspace-based and general transfer function models) were proved insufficient to predict the glucose responses. Therefore, a log-normalized linear model based on subspace-based identification and a GTFM-Wiener model was employed; nevertheless, the prediction error was rather improved.
Recently, a causation modelling methodology with the ability to infer the s.c. glucose concentration using an extensive set of highly correlated non-invasive input variables has been developed [Rollins et al., 2010]. More specifically, the inputs concerned food (i.e. carbohydrates, fats, and proteins), physical activity and stress. This study was initiated by the requirement to determine the independent, dynamic contribution of each input to the overall dynamics of glucose response. For this reason, the predicted glucose was completely determined from measured input data only and previously measured glucose levels did not used in its inference. Accordingly, the s.c glucose concentration was modelled though a block-oriented Wiener network that uses non-linear, in the parameters' space, response surfaces. The prediction method was evaluated using real data of a type 2 diabetic patient collected under free-living conditions over a period of 25 consecutive days. For 5 min predictions, they report an average absolute error of 13.3 mg/dl and a correlation coefficient of 0.7, and they argue that one critical reason for not being able to achieve better results is probably due to lack of information about insulin. However, one important characteristic of this approach is that its predictive accuracy is not limited by the size of the prediction horizon, since it does not depend on past glucose measurements. Moreover, the analysis of the independent dynamic response of each input revealed significant conclusions regarding their effect on dynamic glucose behaviour.

3. The proposed method

Prediction of glucose can be used to provide immediate feedback to the diabetic patients about how the glucose is affected by their lifestyle and treatment. In addition, it offers the means of making real-time suggestions regarding modifications to diet and activity related profile as well as diabetes medications in order to avoid critical events. This study investigates the ability to model the glucose metabolism of type 1 diabetic patients using a multi-parametric set of data recorded under free-living conditions. The proposed method considers the effect of diet, medication, and physical activity on glucose control with the aim to provide accurate glucose predictions.

3.1 Materials and methods

3.1.1 Materials

Seven patients with type 1 diabetes participated in this study who were treated with insulin injections (insulin doses and types were different for each patient). The observation period of the study was on average 10 days (range from 5 – 14 days). All patients wore the Guardian Real-Time CGM system (Medtronic Minimed) that monitors the s.c. glucose concentrations every 5 min. The glucose sensor calibration requires at least four blood glucose measurements to be made daily using a standard blood glucose meter. In addition, the glucose sensors have to be replaced every 3 days. The patients were also equipped with the SenseWear body monitoring system (BodyMedia Inc.) which monitors their daily physical activities. The SenseWear armband collects data using five sensors: heat flux, skin temperature, near body temperature, galvanic skin response and a two axis accelerometer. Finally, information regarding the food intake (i.e. type of food, serving sizes and time) and the insulin injections (type, dose and time) was recorded by the patients using a specially designed paper diary. The food composition (i.e. calories, carbohydrates, fat etc.) was postanalyzed by a dietician.

3.1.2 The method

The method for the prediction of the s.c. glucose concentration is presented schematically in Figure 1. It comprises compartmental models of the glucose – insulin regulatory system and a predictive model of glucose. The compartmental models are used to simulate (a) the ingestion and absorption of carbohydrates (the Meal Model), (b) the absorption and the pharmacokinetics / pharmacodynamics of subcutaneously administered insulin (the Insulin Model) as well as (c) the impact of exercise on glucose - insulin metabolism (the Exercise Model). In addition, support vector machines for regression (SVR) are employed to provide individualized glucose predictions. The input variables of the proposed model include the rate of glucose appearance in plasma after a meal, R_a, the plasma insulin concentration, I_p, the s.c. glucose measurements, *gl*, as well as a set of physical activity related variables. As it can be seen from Figure 1, we assume two different approaches to investigate the physical activity's effects on diabetes. In the first approach, the Metabolic Equivalent of Task (*MET*), the heat flux (*hf*) and the skin temperature (*st*) variables, which are recorded by the SenseWear armband, are used as inputs in the model. The second approach utilizes the alterations in circulating glucose and insulin concentrations (G_{exer}, I_e) during and shortly after exercise as computed by the Exercise Model. The main components of our method are presented in the following subsections.

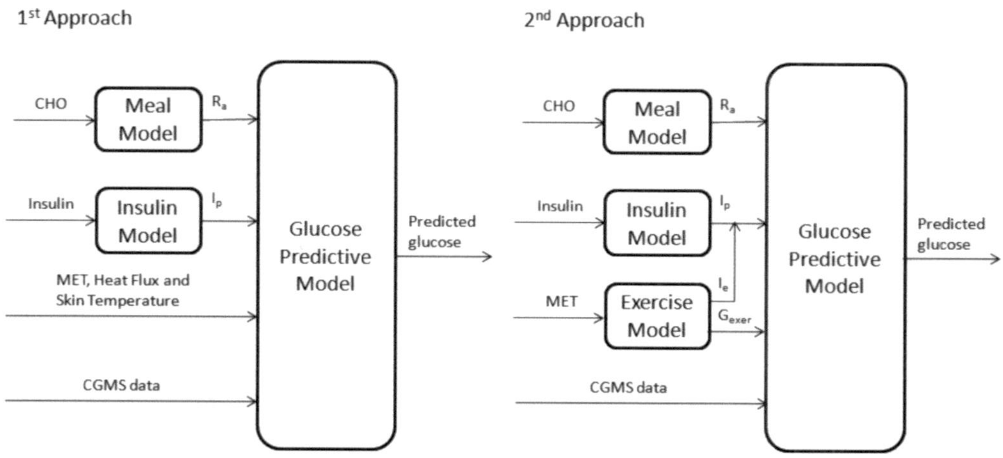

Fig. 1. Schematic representation of the proposed method

3.1.2.1 The insulin model

The absorption of subcutaneously injected insulin is described by the pharmacokinetic model proposed in [Tarin et al., 2005]. This model describes the diffusion of insulin through the s.c. depot, the molecular dissociation of insulin (hexameric/dimeric) and the absorption of insulin into the bloodstream by the following nonlinear partial differential equations:

$$\frac{\partial c_d(t,r)}{\partial t} = P\left(c_h(t,r) - Qc_d(t,r)^3\right) - B_d c_d(t,r) + D\nabla^2 c_d(t,r), \tag{1}$$

$$\frac{\partial c_h(t,r)}{\partial t} = -P\left(c_h(t,r) - Qc_d(t,r)^3\right) + \kappa c_b(t,r)\left(c_{h,\max} - c_h(t,r)\right) + D\nabla^2 c_h(t,r), \tag{2}$$

$$\frac{\partial c_b(t,r)}{\partial t} = -\kappa c_b(t,r)\left(c_{h,\max} - c_h(t,r)\right) + d_b D\nabla^2 c_b(t,r), \tag{3}$$

where c_h, c_d, c_b are the hexameric, dimeric and bound insulin concentrations in the s.c. tissue, respectively, D is the diffusion constant, d_b is a non-dimensional factor that reduces the diffusion effect, P is the dimeric-to-hexameric association rate, Q is the corresponding equilibrium constant, κ is the proportional factor of disengagement of hexameric insulin from the bound state, $c_{h,max}$ is the maximum concentration of hexameric insulin and B_d is the absorption rate constant. The bound state in this model is a virtual state introduced to model the dynamics of long-acting insulin analogues e.g. Glargine. As can be observed from these equations, the diffusion process of insulin in the s.c. tissue is considered to be isotropic i.e. homogeneous and with rotational symmetry with respect to the origin (injection site). Additionally, it is assumed that only the dimeric form of insulin can be absorbed into the plasma with a rate proportional to its concentration. Hence, the exogenous insulin flow (U/min) into the bloodstream is given by:

$$I_{ex}(t) = B_d \int_{V_{sc}} c_d(t,r) dV, \tag{4}$$

where V_{sc} is the complete s.c. volume. This model allows the description of all insulin formulations through the adequate selection of the parameters Q, D, B_d, k, $c_{h,max}$, and d_b. However, the system of partial differential equations has no closed solution and therefore, a time and space discretization is implemented for the numerical calculation of the dimeric insulin concentration.

To estimate the plasma insulin concentration, I_p (uU/ml), a compartmental modelling approach is used [Cobelli et al., 1982]. The model describes the concentration - time evolution of plasma insulin I_p, hepatic insulin I_h and interstitial insulin I_i after a s.c. injection and is given as follows:

$$\dot{I}_p = \frac{I_{ex}(t)}{V_d} - k_1 I_p(t) + k_2 I_h(t) + k_3 I_i(t), \tag{5}$$

where V_d is the plasma insulin distribution volume, and k_1, k_2, k_3 are the rate constants of plasma, hepatic and interstitial insulin elimination, respectively. The input to this physiological model is the exogenous insulin flow, $I_{ex}(t)$, and the output is the plasma insulin concentration I_p. Figure 2(a) shows the exogenous insulin flow profile of Aspart and Glargine insulin injections resulting from the insulin therapy of Patient 4 over a time horizon of two days. It can be seen that the profile varies substantially depending on the injected insulin doses and formulations, i.e. insulin Glargine has a slower onset of action and a longer duration of action than Aspart insulin, whose activity peaks rapidly. The plasma insulin concentration of the combined effect of both insulin types is depicted in Figure 2(b). The long action of Glargine insulin, which resembles the basal insulin secretion of non-diabetic individuals, as well as the effect of Aspart insulin, which is used for controlling the postprandial hyperglycemia, can be observed.

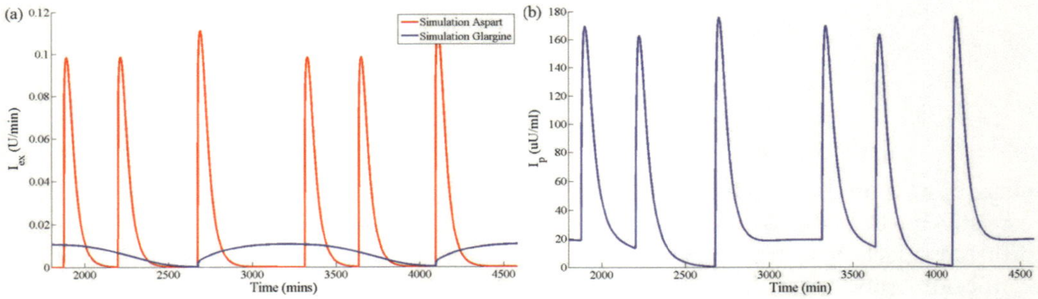

Fig. 2. (a) Exogenous insulin flow of Patient 4 as computed by the insulin compartmental model, (b) Cummulative profile of plasma insulin (Aspart and Glargine) concentration of Patient 4 as computed by the insulin compartmental model

3.1.2.2 The meal model

The model by Lehmann and Deutch [Lehmann & Deutch, 1992] is used to describe the ingestion and absorption of carbohydrates intake. This model describes the rate of appearance of glucose in plasma on the assumption that the rate of gastric emptying is a trapezoidal function and that the intestinal glucose absorption follows first order linear kinetics. The amount of glucose in the gut, q_{gut}, after the ingestion of a meal containing D grams of glucose equivalent carbohydrates is defined as:

$$\dot{q}_{gut}(t) = -k_{abs}q_{gut}(t) + G_{empt}(t,D), \tag{6}$$

where k_{abs} is the rate constant of intestinal absorption and G_{empt} (mg/min) is the gastric emptying function.

The function G_{empt} is described by:

$$G_{empt} = \begin{cases} V_{\max}/T_{asc}, & t < T_{asc} \\ V_{\max}, & T_{asc} < t \le T_{asc} + T_{\max} \\ V_{\max} - (V_{\max}/T_{des})(t - T_{asc} - T_{\max}), & T_{asc} + T_{\max} < t \le T_{asc} + T_{des} \\ 0, & \text{otherwise} \end{cases} \tag{7}$$

where

$$T_{\max} = \frac{2D - V_{\max}(T_{asc} + T_{des})}{2V_{\max}}, \tag{8}$$

corresponds to the duration of the period for which the gastric emptying function is constant and maximum (V_{max}), and T_{asc}, T_{des} are the duration of rising up and dropping periods of G_{empt}, respectively. Then, the rate of appearance of glucose in plasma (mg/min) is given as:

$$R_a(t) = k_{abs}q_{gut}(t). \tag{9}$$

The values for the model parameters have been derived from [Lehmann & Deutch, 1992] and are assumed to be patient-independent.

3.1.2.3 The exercise model

The model used to derive the exercise-induced changes on glucose – insulin metabolism is based on a recent study of Roy & Parker [Roy & Parker, 2007]. In particular, we have developed an algorithm that extracts the most significant exercise events by analyzing the measurements provided by the SenseWear armband. Then, the physiological processes, which occur during an exercise event and at the recovery period, are simulated utilizing the model presented in [Roy & Parker, 2007]. This model describes the effect of exercise on the dynamics of glucose and insulin as follows:

$$\dot{G}_{prod} = a_1 PVO_2^{\max}(t) - a_2 G_{prod}(t), \tag{10}$$

$$\dot{G}_{up} = a_3 PVO_2^{\max}(t) - a_4 G_{up}(t), \tag{11}$$

$$\dot{I}_e = a_5 PVO_2^{\max}(t) - a_6 I_e(t). \tag{12}$$

The terms G_{prod} and G_{up} represent the rates (mg/min) of hepatic glucose production (glycogenolysis) and glucose uptake induced by exercise, respectively, while the I_e (uU/(ml.min)) denotes the rate of insulin removal from the circulatory system during and after exercise. In addition, although the corresponding equation is not given here, the rate of glycogenolysis during prolonged exercise decreases by a factor of G_{gly} due to the depletion of glycogen stores in the liver. The dynamics of glycogenolysis are described in detail in [Roy & Parker, 2007]. The intensity of the exercise (intense walking) as recorded by the activity device over time for Patient 1 is shown in Figure 3(a) along with the computed metabolic response of the patient. More specifically, Figure 3(b) illustrates the glucose uptake rate (G_{up}) and the hepatic glucose production rate (G_{prod} - G_{gly}) during and after exercise, where it can be observed that the effects of exercise progressively attenuate during the recovery period. The rate of insulin removal from plasma (I_e), as shown in Figure 3(c), exhibits also similar behaviour.

As shown in the equations (10-12), the exercise intensity is quantified by the percentage of the maximum oxygen consumption ($PVO_2^{\max}$). Since the SenseWear armband does not report the oxygen uptake (VO_2) during exercise, the term $PVO_2^{\max}$ was calculated by:

$$PVO_2^{\max} = \frac{VO_2}{VO_2^{\max}} = \frac{3.5MET}{VO_2^{\max}}, \tag{13}$$

where $VO_2^{\max}$ is the maximal oxygen uptake and depends on patient's age, gender and physical status. For each patient, the $VO_2^{\max}$ value was derived from reference tables.

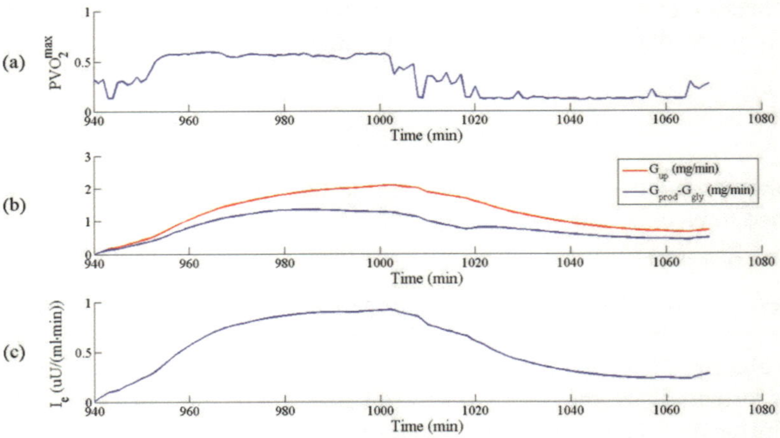

Fig. 3. The effects of an exercise event on metabolism of Patient 1. (a) Data from sensors, (b) Glucose uptake and production rate as computed by the exercise compartmental model, (c) Insulin removal rate as computed by the exercise compartmental model

The implications of exercise in the glucose – insulin regulatory system are incorporated into the proposed method by introducing an additional input variable, the G_{exer}, which describes the blood glucose variation (mg/min) during exercise and at the recovery period:

$$G_{exer} = \left(G_{prod} - G_{gly}\right) - G_{up}. \tag{14}$$

Accordingly, the insulin dynamics are modified by adding the term I_e in the equation (5), resulting in:

$$\dot{I}_p = \frac{I_{ex}(t)}{V_d} - k_1 I_p(t) + k_2 I_h(t) + k_3 I_i(t) - I_e(t). \tag{15}$$

Regarding the parameters for the exercise model, they are obtained from [Roy & Parker, 2007].

3.1.2.4 The glucose predictive model

In this study, a support vector machine for regression [Smola & Scholkopf, 2003; Bishop, 2006] is employed to predict the s.c. glucose concentrations. Let us consider that the training data set D comprises N input vectors $x^1, \dots, x^N$ ($x^i \in R^d$) with corresponding target glucose values $t^1, \dots, t^N$. In ε-SVR our goal is to find a linear model of the form:

$$y(x) = w^T \phi(x) + b, \tag{16}$$

which must satisfy the following conditions:

$$t^n \le y(x^n) + \varepsilon + \xi_n, \tag{17}$$

$$t^n \le y(x^n) - \varepsilon + \hat{\xi}_n. \tag{18}$$

The function $\phi(x)$ denotes a fixed feature-space transformation and w and b are the weights and bias parameters, respectively. The error function for ε-SVR is defined as:

$$C\sum_{n=1}^{N}\left(\xi_n + \hat{\xi}_n\right) + \frac{1}{2}\|w\|^2, \tag{19}$$

which must be minimized subject to the constraints $\xi_n, \hat{\xi}_n \ge 0$, as well as (17) and (18). This can be achieved by introducing the Lagrange multipliers $a_n, \hat{a}_n \ge 0$ and $\mu_n, \hat{\mu}_n \ge 0$ and by minimizing the Lagrangian:

$$\begin{aligned} L = C\sum_{n=1}^{N}\left(\xi_n + \hat{\xi}_n\right) + \frac{1}{2}\|w\|^2 - \sum_{n=1}^{N}\left(\mu_n\xi_n + \hat{\mu}_n\hat{\xi}_n\right) \\ - \sum_{n=1}^{N}\alpha_n\left(\varepsilon + \xi_n + y_n + t_n\right) - \sum_{n=1}^{N}\hat{\alpha}_n\left(\varepsilon + \hat{\xi}_n + y_n + t_n\right). \end{aligned} \tag{20}$$

Solving the optimization problem, it is found that the predictions for the new inputs can be made using:

$$y(x) = \sum_{n=1}^{N}\left(a_n - \hat{a}_n\right)k\left(x, x^n\right) + b, \tag{21}$$

where $k(x,x') = \phi(x)^T \phi(x')$ is the kernel function. From the corresponding Karush-Kuhn-Tucker (KKT) conditions, which state that at the solution the product of the dual variables and the constraints must vanish, results that $a_n\hat{a}_n = 0$. Therefore, the SVR provides a sparse solution, since the only terms that have to be evaluated in the predictive model are those which involve the support vectors, i.e. the data in the training set for which exactly one of the Lagrange multipliers is greater than zero.

To be more specific, given the input x, the prediction of the s.c. glucose concentration, y, at the time $t+l$, assuming that t is the current time, is given by:

$$y_{t+l}(x) = y_{t+l}(x_1,\ldots,x_d). \quad (22)$$

where $x_i = x_i(t),\ldots,x_i(t-n_i\Delta t)$, with i =1,..., d, denotes the inputs in the model, $n_i\Delta t$ is the time lag for the input x_i, Δt is the sampling time and l is the prediction length.

3.2 Model training and evaluation

The proposed method is evaluated using the dataset obtained from seven type 1 diabetic patients. The SVR is trained individually for each patient and a V-fold cross validation algorithm is used to avoid over-fitting. More specifically, V-fold cross validation splits the dataset D in k equal parts, where k is defined as the total number of days for which the patient is monitored. Thus, the value of V coincides with the value of k and each fold contains the data of the ith day, with i =1,..., k. The SVR is built using a linear kernel function and the parameter ε in the ε-insensitive loss function is set equal to 0.001. The regularization parameter C is optimized using a grid search method. Similarly, V-fold cross validation is used by the search method to calculate the optimal values for that parameter.

Time lags of 30 min are considered for the I_p, Ra and gl input variables, while the time lag for the exercise-related inputs (i.e. MET, st, hf and G_{exer}) is assumed to be 3 hours. The sampling time, Δt, was 5 min for all the above cases. Predictions are performed for four different values of prediction length l, i.e. 15, 30, 60 and 120 min.

The predictive accuracy of the proposed method is assessed by calculating the RMSE, and the correlation coefficient, r, for each patient's test set. Furthermore, the Clarke's Error Grid Analysis (EGA) [Kovatchev et al., 2004; Clarke, 2005] is used to assess the clinical significance of the errors between the predicted and the measured s.c. glucose concentrations. The Clarke's EGA method uses a Cartesian diagram, in which the predicted values are displayed on the y-axis, whereas the values from glucose sensor are displayed on the x-axis. This diagram is subdivided into 5 zones: A, B, C, D and E. The points that fall within zones A and B represent sufficiently accurate or acceptable glucose results, points in zone C may result in unnecessary corrections, points in zone D could lead to incorrect treatments, and points in zone E represent erroneous treatment.

3.3 Results

The RMSE (mg/dl) and r values obtained from the first approach are reported in Table 1. It can be observed that the short-term glucose predictions (i.e. for 15 and 30 min) present low error and high degree of correlation with the real glucose profiles. More specifically, the average value of RMSE for 15 min and 30 min predictions is equal to 9.60 mg/dl and 16.23 mg/dl, respectively. In both cases, the predicted glucose concentrations exhibit a strong correlation with the measured values (i.e. 0.95 and 0.88). However, as prediction length increases (i.e. for 60 and 120 min), the performance of the proposed method significantly decreases. Concerning the 60 min predictions, the derived results are still adequate compared to the previous values, whereas, the accuracy of the 120 min predictions is considerably lower. In addition, the predictions for some patients (i.e. Patient 2, 3, 5, 6, 7) are found systematically more accurate, in terms of RMSE, than for Patient 1 and Patient 4 which most probably resulted from better model training due to the longer follow-up period; nevertheless, slight differences are observed in the associated r values. For the second approach, the derived results, as it is shown in Table 2, are almost equal to those for the first approach.

No. of Patient	Prediction Length							
	15 min		30 min		60 min		120 min	
	RMSE (mg/dl)	r	RMSE (mg/dl)	r	RMSE (mg/dl)	r	RMSE (mg/dl)	r
Patient 1	12.57	0.96	21.36	0.90	33.06	0.75	62.29	0.28
Patient 2	9.69	0.95	16.32	0.87	24.52	0.68	31.11	0.37
Patient 3	9.33	0.95	15.85	0.87	25.77	0.67	33.91	0.46
Patient 4	11.92	0.92	19.24	0.81	29.06	0.62	39.25	0.40
Patient 5	6.45	0.91	11.04	0.91	17.89	0.70	26.22	0.48
Patient 6	10.85	0.95	18.38	0.86	24.82	0.72	34.64	0.49
Patient 7	6.42	0.98	11.45	0.93	18.84	0.82	23.48	0.70
Average (SD)	9.60 (2.45)	0.95 (0.02)	16.23 (3.87)	0.88 (0.04)	24.85 (5.33)	0.71 (0.06)	35.84 (12.81)	0.45 (0.13)

Table 1. Prediction results obtained from the first approach (exercise described only by sensor data)

No. of Patient	Prediction Length							
	15 min		30 min		60 min		120 min	
	RMSE (mg/dl)	r	RMSE (mg/dl)	r	RMSE (mg/dl)	r	RMSE (mg/dl)	r
Patient 1	12.07	0.96	19.93	0.91	30.99	0.80	55.43	0.46
Patient 2	9.58	0.96	15.91	0.88	24.06	0.69	31.24	0.42
Patient 3	9.28	0.95	15.59	0.87	25.35	0.69	33.82	0.44
Patient 4	11.73	0.92	18.97	0.82	28.70	0.63	37.99	0.35
Patient 5	6.50	0.90	11.09	0.91	16.78	0.65	23.80	0.47
Patient 6	11.18	0.95	18.95	0.86	26.58	0.70	37.18	0.46
Patient 7	6.20	0.98	11.69	0.94	21.19	0.80	33.60	0.51
Average (SD)	9.51 (2.39)	0.95 (0.03)	16.02 (3.55)	0.88 (0.04)	24.81 (4.74)	0.71 (0.07)	36.15 (9.70)	0.44 (0.05)

Table 2. Prediction results obtained from the second approach (exercise described by compartmental modelling)

Clarke's EGA clearly shows that the vast majority of the predicted-measured glucose points lay in zones A and B, which indicate clinically acceptable results. On the other hand, a small amount of points belong to the other zones (i.e. C, D and E), which indicate potentially dangerous overestimation or underestimation of the actual values. Figure 4 represents the Clarke's EGA plots for Patient 5, in the case where the first approach is followed. In this figure, it is shown that as the prediction length increases, the plots become more spread, as expected. Tables 3 and 4 report the average results obtained from the two different approaches, respectively. We observe that nearly all the points lay in zones A and B, even if a higher prediction length is considered. Occasional points belong to the C zone, whereas only a few points belong to the D zone. Finally, no points belong to the erroneous E zone. In addition, no differences are evident between the results obtained from the two approaches.

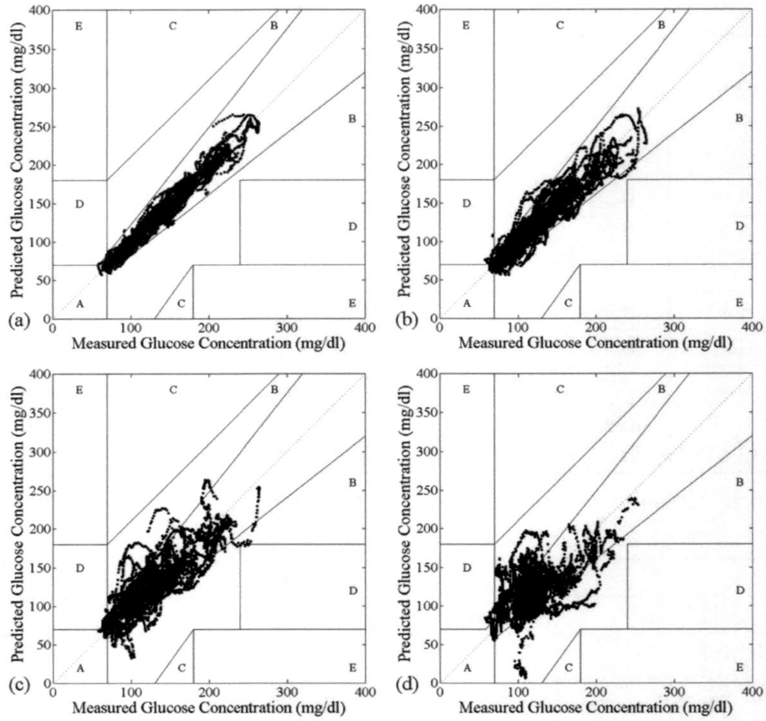

Fig. 4. Clarke's EGA diagrams for Patient 5 based on the first approach. (a) – (d) correspond to different prediction lengths (i.e. 15, 30, 60, 120 min)

Zone	Prediction Length			
	15 min	30 min	60 min	120 min
Zone A	98.86 %	92.54 %	80.02 %	62.91 %
Zone B	1.08 %	6.97 %	18.49 %	33.78 %
Zone C	0.00 %	0.02 %	0.07 %	0.37 %
Zone D	0.06 %	0.47 %	1.42 %	2.94 %
Zone E	0.00 %	0.00 %	0.00 %	0.00 %

Table 3. Average percentages of points falling into the different zones of the Clarke's EGA for the first approach (exercise described only by sensor data)

Zone	Prediction Length			
	15 min	30 min	60 min	120 min
Zone A	98.58 %	92.54 %	79.96 %	60.10 %
Zone B	1.35 %	6.89 %	18.33 %	36.84 %
Zone C	0.00 %	0.02 %	0.09 %	0.20 %
Zone D	0.07 %	0.55 %	1.62 %	2.86 %
Zone E	0.00 %	0.00 %	0.00 %	0.00 %

Table 4. Average percentages of points falling into the different zones of the Clarke's EGA for the second approach (exercise described by compartmental modelling)

4. Discussion

Glucose metabolism is a non-linear, dynamic system, the behaviour of which has been extensively modelled by data-driven methods. Table 5 provides a summary of most of the studies on glucose prediction in diabetes reported in the literature, along with a short description of methods used, input variables and patient types.

During the last decade, the application of machine learning methods in predictive modelling of glucose concentration in patients with diabetes has gained much attention. Simple feed forward neural networks [Kok, 2004; Zitar & Al-Labali, 2005; Quchani & Tahami, 2007; Baghdadi & Nasrabadi, 2007] as well as more sophisticated types such as recurrent [Tresp et al., 1999; Mougiakakou et al., 2006] and wavelet neural networks [Zainuddin et al., 2009] have been utilised up to now for the prediction of the glucose concentration in diabetic patients. The results obtained in these works show that reasonably accurate glucose predictions can be made; however, a direct comparison between them is not feasible since they refer to different prediction horizons. Furthermore, the performance of these methods highly depends on the input which is used. Firstly, the fact that the predictions are mainly based on glucose measurements recorded 3-4 times per day inevitably affects the output of the prediction. Nevertheless, the development of glucose sensors introduced the utilization of CGM data for the prediction of glucose which was a breakthrough in the field [Mougiakakou et al., 2006]. In addition, in most of these studies the physical activity is qualitatively described, except for the work of Valletta et al. [Valletta et al., 2009] which employs Gaussian processes to model the glucose variations in response to real activity data recorded continuously throughout the day. Given that activity plays an important role in glucose regulation, this consideration constitutes a substantial limitation.

The prediction of glucose in diabetic patients has also been addressed through time series analysis. The fact that glucose can be predicted by exploiting the recent history of CGM data was initially suggested by Bremer and Gough [Bremer and Gough, 1999]. This was further demonstrated by the findings of three subsequent studies [Sparacino et al., 2007; Gani et al., 2009; Gani et al., 2010] showing that AR models can provide stable, accurate predictions. One advantage of AR models consists in the interpretability of the AR coefficients, which describe the temporal dependencies in the glucose signal. In addition to this, the estimation of the model parameters involves a convex optimization problem with a unique minimum. Apart from AR models, linear and non-linear time series models with external input variables have also been developed [Stahl et al., 2009; Rollins et al., 2010]. It is noteworthy that in the study of Rollins et al. [Rollins et al., 2010] employing a block-orient Wiener network, real data from an activity device are utilised to quantify the effect of physical activity. Equally important, the authors made an attempt to examine the individual dynamic characteristics of each input regarding food, insulin, and activity in order to interpret their effects on glucose behaviour. However, much of modern theory of time series is concerned with stationary time series and, therefore, it is needed to establish some conditions, e.g. CGM data must be a first and second order stationary process.

The problem of glucose prediction in diabetic patients from a multi-parametric set of free-living data (i.e. food, insulin, physical activity and continuous glucose measurements) has been addressed in the context of Gaussian processes [Valletta et al., 2009] and Wiener networks [Rollins et al., 2010]. The same problem is treated here with the aid of support vector machines for regression. Accounting for the physiological processes related to diabetes (i.e insulin absorption, gut absorption), we employed appropriate compartmental models found in the literature. In addition, we assumed two different approaches to investigate the activity's effects on diabetes. For the first time, to the best of our knowledge, the changes on glucose - insulin levels induced by exercise are incorporated into a glucose predictive model, and, moreover, an exercise model is fed with real sensor data to indicate the exercise intensity.

Study	Diabetes Type (No of Patients)	Input Variables	Method
Zitar & Al-Labali, 2005	Type 2 (70)	BG, Insulin, Meal Announcement (1 or 0), Exercise Announcement (1, 0)	MLP Neural Network
Quchani & Tahami, 2007	Type 1 (10)	BG, Insulin, CHO, Exercise Levels, Stress Levels	Elman RNN
Kok, 2004	Type 1 (1)	BG, Insulin, CHO, Exercise Levels, Stress Levels	MLP Neural Network
Baghdadi & Nasrabadi, 2007	Type 1 (1)	BG, Insulin, CHO, Exercise Levels, Stress Levels	RBF Neural Network
Zainuddin et al., 2009	Type 1 (1)	BG, Insulin, CHO, Exercise Levels, Stress Levels	Wavelet Neural Network
Tresp et al., 1999	Type 1 (1)	BG, Insulin, CHO, Exercise Duration	RNN
Mougiakakou et al., 2006	Type 1(4)	CGM Data, Insulin, CHO	RNN
Valletta et al., 2009	Type 1 (18)	CGM Data, Insulin, CHO, Exercise Data	Gaussian Processes
Sparacino et al., 2007	Type 1 (28)	CGM Data	AR model
Gani et al., 2009	Type 1 (9)	CGM Data	AR model
Stahl et al., 2009	Type 1(1)	BG, Insulin, CHO	ARMA, ARMAX, Wiener and Subspace-Based System Identification
Rollins et al., 2010	Type 2 (1)	CGM Data, CHO, Fats, Proteins, Exercise Data	Block-Oriented Wiener Network
This work	Type 1(7)	CGM Data, Insulin, CHO, Exercise Data	SVR

Table 5. Summary of works on glucose prediction in diabetic patients using data-driven techniques (BG: blood glucose, CHO: carbohydrates)

The application of compartmental models describing the absorption of subcutaneously administered insulin and the absorption of glucose from the gut following a meal is also reported in several studies [Mougiakakou et al., 2006; Valleta et al., 2009; Stahl et al., 2009] dealing with the problem of the prediction of glucose. Compartmental analysis of these processes is necessitated because the data collected by the patients (i.e. food, insulin) are non-uniformly sampled; on the contrary most of the predictive methods require uniformly sampled data. Nevertheless, response functions can also be used for this purpose as in [Tresp et al., 1999; Rollins et al., 2010]. On the other hand, the reason why we used exercise compartmental models was to examine if accurate predictions could be achieved from simulation outputs (made from real exercise data) which model the metabolic response not only during exercise but also during the recovery period. The overall approach has the advantages of SVR. First we must consider that the optimization problem is transformed into a dual convex quadratic programming leading to a global minimum. Moreover, compared with the existing kernel regression modelling approaches (i.e. RBF), it gives significant algorithmic and representation advantages by producing sparser models. Finally, it has to be mentioned that SVR is effective even on large and high dimensional datasets, which is the case in glucose prediction problems.

The results obtained in the present study make clear that the glucose concentration in patients with type 1 diabetes can be predicted with a sufficient numerical accuracy in the short-term. The increase in the length of prediction leads to more significant deviations of the obtained predictions from the reference glucose concentrations as also reported in previous studies [Sparacino et al., 2007; Stahl et al., 2009; Gani et al., 2009]. Small differences were observed in the predictive accuracy among the patients of our study, which indicates that the proposed scheme could be applied to most of type 1 patients (given that lifestyle data are recorded in a similar way). It becomes apparent from the Clarke's EGA that the performance of the proposed prediction method is also significant from a clinical point of view since practically all of our predictions do not fall in the zones which would lead to incorrect or erroneous treatment (i.e. C - E). A direct comparison of the present study could be performed with that of Valletta et al. [Valletta et al., 2009]; however, the authors provide no quantitative results. Compared to [Rollins et al., 2010], we found more accurate predictions, but we have to consider that the model proposed by Rollins et al. does not exploit information about insulin, since it concerns type 2 diabetic patients. Although the studies employing AR models [Stahl et al., 2009; Gani et al., 2009] produced better results, they largely depend on the assumption that the CGM data are described by a stationary process.

Tables 1 and 2 show that the two approaches which were used to describe the physical activity yielded almost equal results. Since in the second approach the predictions are based only on segments containing significant (discrete) exercise events, this would imply that sufficient predictions could still be achieved without necessitating the activity monitor to be worn continuously throughout the day, but only during exercise, which practically enhances the possibilities of a predictive system to be acceptable by the patients. Moreover, this second modelling approach can accept as input descriptive exercise event announcements manually notified by the patient; however, the predictive accuracy in that case should be tested. In addition, the ability to analyse and predict the effects of exercise on glucose metabolism can be exploited for providing to the patient advices on hypothetical scenarios for forthcoming exercise events. The above advantages offered by exercise compartmental modelling are extremely useful for diabetes advisory systems.

Considering the intra- and inter-individual variability in the metabolic response to food, insulin and exercise, it could be very important to estimate the parameters involved in the compartmental models from each patient's data. However, this process would require the conduction of tracer experiments, and thus it was not included in this study. Another simplification in our study was that the influence of the fats, proteins and other food nutrients on the dynamics of the digestive and absorptive processes, as well as the effect of the glycemic index, was not considered. Also, there are factors affecting the insulin absorption and insulin kinetics (e.g. site of injection, ambient and body temperature), which have not been investigated. The introduction of these variables in our study would lead to more realistic modelling of the glucose metabolism; therefore, it will be taken into account in the future. We also intend to improve the performance of the SVR by determining the most appropriate kernel function and by estimating the parameter ε in the insensitive loss function, but our final objective is to form a generalized predictive model that can be applied to group of patients.

5. References

American Diabetes Association (2008)[a]. Diagnosis and Classification of Diabetes Mellitus. *Diabetes Care,* Vol. 31, No. 1, (January 2008) 55-60, 1935-5548

American Diabetes Association (2008)[b]. Standards of Medical Care in Diabetes. *Diabetes Care,* Vol. 31, No. 1, (January 2008) 12-54, 1935-5548

Baghdadi, G. & Nasrabadi, A. M. (2007). Controlling blood glucose levels in diabetics by neural network predictor, *Proceedings of the 29th Annual International Conference of the IEEE Engineering in Medicine and Biology Society,* pp. 3216-3219, 978-1-4244-0787-3, France, August 2007, IEEE, Lyon

Bishop, C. M. (2006). *Pattern Recognition and Machine Learning,* Springer, 0-387-31073-8, New York

Bremer, T. & Gough D. A. (1999). Is Blood Glucose Predictable From Previous Values? A Solicitation for Data. *Diabetes,* Vol. 48, (March 1999) 445-451, 1939-327X

Caumo A.; Simeoni M. & Cobelli C. (2001). Glucose Modelling, In: *Modelling Methodology for Physiology and Medicine,* Carson, E. & Cobelli C., (Ed. 2001), 337-372, Academic Press, 0-12-160245-1, San Diego

Clarke, W. L. (2005). The original clarke error grid analysis (EGA). *Diabetes Technology and Therapeutics,* Vol. 7, No. 5, (October 2005) 776-779, 1520-9156

Cobelli, C.; Federspil, G.; Pacini, G.; Salvan A. & Scandellari C. (1982). An integrated mathematical model of the dynamics of blood glucose and its hormonal control. *Mathematical Biosciences,* Vol. 58, No. 1, (February 1982) 27-60, 0025-5564

Dalla Man, C.; Rizza, R. A. & Cobelli, C. (2007). Meal Simulation Model of the Glucose-Insulin System. *IEEE Transactions on Biomedical Engineering,* Vol. 54, No. 10, (October 2007) 1740-1748, 0018-9294

Gani, A.; Gribok, A. V.; Rajaraman, S.; Ward, W. K. & Reifman, J. (2009). Predicting subcutaneous glucose concentration in humans: Data-driven glucose modelling. *IEEE Transactions on Biomedical Engineering,* Vol. 56, No. 2, (February 2009) 246-254, 0018-9294

Gani, A.; Gribok, A. V.; Lu, Y.; Ward, W. K.; Vigersky, R. A. & Reifman, J. (2010). Universal Glucose Models for Predicting Subcutaneous Glucose Concentration in Humans. *IEEE Transactions on Information Technology in Biomedicine,* Vol. 14, No. 1, (January 2010) 157-165, 1089-7771

Kok P. (2004). Predicting blood glucose levels of diabetics using artificial neural networks, *Research Assignment for Master of Science,* Delft University of Technology

Kovatchev, B.P.; Gonder-Frederick, L.A.; Cox, D.J. & Clarke, W.L. (2004). Evaluating the accuracy of continuous glucose monitoring sensors: Continuous glucose-error grid analysis illustrated by TheraSense Freestyle Navigator data. *Diabetes Care*, Vol. 27, No. 8, (August 2004) 1922-1928, 1935-5548

Lehmann E. D. & Deutsch, T. (1992). A physiological model of glucose-insulin interaction in Type 1 diabetes mellitus. *Journal of Biomedical Engineering*, Vol. 14, No. 3, (May 1992) 235-242, 0141-5425

Makroglou, A.; Li, J. & Kuang, Y. (2006). Mathematical models and software tools for the glucose-insulin regulatory system and diabetes: An overview. *Applied Numerical Mathematics*, Vol. 56, No. 3-4, (March 2006) 559-573, 0168-9274

Mougiakakou, S. G.; Prountzou, A.; Iliopoulou, D.; Nikita, K. S.; Vazeou, A. & Bartsocas, C. S. (2006). Neural network based glucose - insulin metabolism models for children with type 1 diabetes, *Proceedings of the 28th Annual International Conference of the IEEE Engineering in Medicine and Biology Society*, pp. 3545-3548, 1557-170X, USA, August 2006, IEEE, New York

Quchani, S. A. & Tahami, E. (2007). Comparison of MLP and Elman Neural Network for Blood Glucose Level Prediction in Type 1 Diabetics, *Proceedings of the 3rd Kuala Lumpur International Conference on Biomedical Engineering*, Vol. 15, pp. 54-58, 978-3-540-68016-1, Malaysia, December 2006, Springer Berlin Heidelberg, Kuala Lumpur

Rollins, D.; Bhandari, N.; Kleinedler, J.; Kotz, K.; Strohbehn, A.; Boland, L.; Murphy, M.; Andre, D.; Vyas, N.; Welk, G. & Franke, W. E. (2010). Free-living inferential modelling of blood glucose level using only noninvasive inputs. *Journal of Process Control*, Vol. 20, No. 1, (January 2010) 95-107, 0959-1524

Roy, A. & Parker, R. S. (2007). Dynamic Modelling of Exercise Effects on Plasma Glucose and Insulin Levels. *Journal of Diabetes Science and Technology*, Vol. 1, No. 3, (May 2007) 338 – 347, 1932-2968

Smola, A. J. & Scholkopf, B. (2004). A tutorial on support vector regression. *Statistics and Computing*, Vol. 14, No. 3, (August 2004), 199-222, 0960-3174

Sparacino, G.; Zanderigo, F.; Corazza, S.; Maran, A.; Facchineti, A. & Cobelli, C. (2007). Glucose Concentration can be Predicted Ahead in Time from Continuous Glucose Monitoring Sensor Time-Series. *IEEE Transactions on Biomedical Engineering*, Vol. 54, No. 5, (May 2007) 931-937, 0018-9294

Stahl, F. & Johansson, R. (2009). Diabetes mellitus modelling and short-term prediction based on blood glucose measurements. *Mathematical Biosciences*, Vol. 217, No. 2, (February 2009), 101-117, 0025-5564

Tarin, C.; Teufel, E.; Pico, J.; Bondia, J. & Pfleiderer, H. J. (2005). A Comprehensive Pharmacokinetic Model of Insulin Glargine and Other Insulin Formulations. *IEEE Transactions on Biomedical Engineering*, Vol. 52, No. 12, (December 2005) 1994 – 2005, 0018-9294

Tresp, V.; Briegel T., & Moody, J. (1999). Neural-network models for the blood glucose metabolism of a diabetic. *IEEE Transactions on Neural Networks*, Vol. 10, No. 5, (September 1999) 1204-1213, 1045-9227

Valleta, J. J.; Chipperfield, A. J. & Byrne, C. D. (2009). Gaussian process modelling of blood glucose response to free-living physical activity data in people with type 1 diabetes, *Proceedings of the 1st Annual International Conference of the IEEE Engineering in*

Medicine and Biology Society, pp. 4913-4916, 978-1-4244-3296-7, USA, September 2009, IEEE, Minneapolis

Zainuddin, Z.; Pauline O. & and Ardil C. (2009). A Neural Network Approach in Predicting the Blood Glucose Level for Diabetic Patients. *International Journal of Computational Intelligence*. Vol. 5, No. 1, (Winter 2009) 72-79, 2070-3821

Zitar, R. A. & Al-Jabali, A. (2005). Towards neural network model for insulin/glucose in diabetics-II. *Informatica*, Vol. 29, No. 2, (June 2005) 227-232, 0350-5596

18

Data Mining Based Establishment and Evaluation of Porcine Model for Syndrome in Traditional Chinese Medicine in the Context of Unstable Angina (Myocardial Ischemia)

Huihui Zhao, Jianxin Chen, Qi Shi and Wei Wang
Beijing University of Chinese Medicine
Beijing, 100029,
China

1. Introduction

Building an animal model for a disease is a better avenue not only to investigate the disease state in ways which would be inaccessible in human patients with the disease, but also to test new drug for the treatment of the disease. Unstable angina (UA) is a serious disease that causing more than 1 million deaths annually in China. It accounts for heavy burden not only on patients and their families but also on society. Therefore, an increasing number of UA patients pose a major challenge to the entire medical community. The animal model for UA is usually simulated by animal model for myocardial ischemia since the core pathology of UA is myocardial ischemia. There are three widely used methods to reproduce myocardial ischemia animal models: An occlusion of the coronary artery by microembolization, coronary artery ligation and Ameroid constrictor or coling/gelefoam [Monnet & Chachques, 2005].Among them, Ameroid constrictor is best fit to induce chronic myocardial ischemia when compared with other methods due to its progressive occlusion. Ameroid constrictors have been used in many species of animals. However, porcine hearts have a coronary anatomy most similar to the counterpart of human hearts. They seem to develop much less collateral circulation than dogs after induction of coronary occlusion, which makes them more attractive for the reproduction of chronic myocardial ischemia [Weaver et al., 1986].

1.1 Traditional Chinese medicine and western medicine

Traditional Chinese Medicine (TCM) is a medical system with its continuous practice in the past 3000 years and records thousands of herbal prescriptions, some of which are tested and validated continuously in the clinics [Li et al.,2007]. TCM is taken by most people in China as a complementary therapeutic avenue to treat UA since its herbal remedies have some advantages over western medicine, such as fewer side effects and less cost. Historically, TCM uses pattern recognition strategies to identify patients' characteristics at individual level. These patterns, or so called syndromes, are recognized by collecting patient information through questioning, inspecting, and physical examinations including pulse and tongue recognitions. It is generally acknowledged that more than one distinctive clinical pattern can usually be found within each biomedical disease or condition. The clinical patterns or syndromes under each biomedical disease therefore can be viewed as unique subsets of that patient population in question. In TCM practice, specific treatment strategies including using Chinese herbal medicine or acupuncture would be applied aiming each pattern/syndrome of a specific biomedical condition. Therefore, the research of syndromes is usually taken place in the context of a disease diagnosed by criteria established in western medicine. Thanks to clinical epidemiology and related data mining approaches, the number of syndromes and the diagnosis criteria of each syndrome in the context of many diseases have been already determined and established in China[Zheng, 2002] ;[Chen et al., 2007]. Nowadays, investigation material basis of syndromes in the context of biomedical diseases is a research focus, thus building an animal model for syndromes plays a key role in understanding nature of syndromes.

1.2 Blood stasis syndrome in TCM

In the UA patients, a syndrome named blood stasis syndrome (BSS) occupies more than 70% in the cohort [Sun et al., 2007]. It plays a key role in treating UA patients not only because it's high frequency, but because there are so many herbal remedies that have been tested effectively in clinics for treating BSS that it can help to treat UA in a personalized way.
BSS is described in TCM theory as a slowing down of the blood flow due to disruption of Heart Qi, and its main clinical manifestations in UA patients include fixed stabbing pain in the chest, aggravation of pain in the night, chest oppression and shortness of breath, palpitation, purplish tongue, thin and unsmooth pulse. BSS is considered as a special stage of UA or myocardial ischemia in TCM and has special pathological and pathophysiologic mechanisms.
BSS is also an important underlying pathology process of many other diseases according to TCM theory. It is often understood in biomedical terms in terms of hematological disorders such as hemorrhage, congestion, thrombosis, and local ischemia (microclots) and tissue changes.

1.3 State-of-art of animal models for BSS in the context of UA

Due to the significant association between BSS and UA, it is urgent for medical society to investigate material basis of BSS in the context of UA. Animal model for BSS is a better way to understand it. However, there is no available animal model with long period of stability and accurate validation for BSS since there is no widely accepted animal model for syndrome in TCM. Formally, syndrome is clinically diagnosed by mean of four traditional phenotype information gathered methods, such as questioning, inspecting, pulse and tongue recognitions, but the related phenotype information is hard to be gathered from animals since it is impossible to inquire, listen and feel the pulse of most animals. Although inspecting information could be collected from an animal, the difference between human and an animal is large, which make symptoms have different medical meaning among clinics and animal model. Therefore, a novel strategy is needed to be presented to build and evaluate syndrome in TCM for an animal in the context of UA.

1.4 A computational strategy to evaluate BSS in context of UA

The biggest obstacle of building animal model for syndrome is that it is hard to diagnose the syndrome in an animal by traditional four methods (questioning, inspecting as well as pulse and tongue recognitions) as they are performed in clinics because of the large difference of phenotype information between human and animal. However, the physical and chemical specifications of human and animal may have more similar biomedical meaning than the phenotype information. Therefore, the novel strategy to build and evaluate an animal model for BSS is performed by two sequential steps.

1. In clinics, investigation and establishment of association between BSS and related physical and chemical specifications in the context of UA by a computational way.
2. In animals, we build animal model for UA and evaluate whether an animal is BSS by the association established from clinics.

Many research efforts have been performed to investigate distinct clinical biomarkers and pathological mechanisms of BSS in the past 50 years. The research strategy places heavily on discovering some specific biomarkers for BSS. However, it is found that these detected biomarkers have none specificity for BSS. Indeed, BSS (in the context of UA) is a complex disease and the biomarker for it is not sole. As it is pointed out that, the era of one disease with one specific gene has gone[Hayden, 2008], most researchers have realized that there is no distinct single parameter of BSS caused by some kind of unbalance in regulation network and system biology is a better avenue to discover biomarkers and interaction network of them [Li et al.,2007]. Thus, statistical analysis methods to discover biomarkers for BSS in the system biology is turned from t test to data mining approaches. t test is used to discover one biomarker with significant difference between case and control groups. Beyond t test, data mining approaches can investigate significance of a pattern with more than two biomarkers between two groups. The association between BSS and physical and chemical specifications can be uncovered by data mining approaches.

In this paper, we first used data mining approaches to establish association between BSS and inflammation factors from UA data obtained by clinical epidemiology. Alternatively, we built animal model for UA and used the established association in clinics to evaluate whether an animal is with BSS.

The paper is organized as following. The section 2 is devoted to clinical epidemiology for UA patients. The data mining of association between syndrome and inflammation factors is presented in section 3. Building and validating animal model for syndrome in TCM in the context of myocardial ischemia is proposed in section 4. In Section 5 we summarize our finding and give conclusion and discussion.

2. Clinical epidemiology survey for UA in-patients

There are many evidence that inflammation system is significantly associated with Coronary Heart Disease (CHD) including UA [Gustavsson & Agardh, 2009];[Davidson et al., 2009]. Furthermore, although "golden inflammation factor" for BSS is hard to discover, it is still found that some inflammation factors, for example, Tumor necrosis factor α (TNF-α), Interleukin 6 (IL-6), Endothelin (ET) and Nitrogen monoxide (NO), are associated with the pathology of BSS in the context of UA[Mao et al., 2004]; [Yuan et al., 2006]; [Zhang et al., 2005]; [Ma et al., 2007]. Alternatively, the four factors are relatively easy to be measured from animals, which make them a better bridge to communicate between human and animal. The goal of clinical epidemiology for UA is to establish association between BSS and inflammation factors in the context of UA.

The inclusion criteria are composed of three conditions: (1) Based on diagnosis criteria of UA established in 2002 by ACC and AHA [Braunwald, 2002]; (2) patients aged between 55 and 75; (3) Patients agree to sign the informed consent. Moreover, the exclusion criteria are composed of four conditions: (1) Besides UA, a patient also suffers from other cordis disease such as acute myocardial infarction, myocarditis, and cardiac nerve functional disease; (2) A patient with angina caused by other diseases, for example, rheumatic fever, syphilis, congenital coronary anomalies, hypertrophic cardiomyopathy, cardiac mitral stenosis; (3) Besides UA, a patient also suffers from stroke, diabetes, nephritis, renal failure, pulmonary infection, urinary tract infection, rheumatism, osteoarthritis, serious disease caused by liver, renal, haematogenous system, incretion system; (4) A woman patient in gestation or lactation.

The fifty-seven UA in-patients were included in the survey in AnZhen Hospital in Beijing from September 2006 to August 2007, each of which was told to pause Resisting Platelet Acti vating drug for 24 hours. The 10 milliliter limosis vein blood of each patient was took out early morning in the next day of hospitalization. The 10 ml blood was divided into two parts. The first 2 ml was saved in the cuvette (American B-D Co.Ltd) with 2% EDTA anticoagulant and the other 8 ml was put into the counterpart with trisodium citrate anticoagulant. All samples were centrifuged with 2500 r/min for 10 minutes to separate plasma from the blood, which was kept at -80°C.

It is noted that no healthy control subjects were included since we study syndrome in the context of UA. BSS is used to divide the UA into two groups, UA with BSS and UA with none-BSS.

Each patient included is diagnosed whether is BSS by TCM experts. The difference between two groups is studied by data mining approaches, which establishes the association between syndrome and physical and chemical specifications measured in plasma.

3. Data mining approaches to establish association between BSS and inflammation factors

The response variable is a categorical variable composed of BSS and non BSS and the independent variables are the four inflammations factors. The goal of data mining for clinical data is to build association between four inflammation factors and BSS in the context of UA.

In a first step, Independent sample t test method is employed to detect factors that are significantly different between BSS and Non-BSS. Using a threshold $P < 0.01$, only TNF-α is detected that is different between the two groups. However, the student' t test statistics only measure the significance of single independent variable, it can not measure significance of a pattern composed of more than 2 factors between two categories. Data mining approaches provide a better solution to build association between a pattern and response variable. They can not only deal with data with large samples and more variables, but also for small samples. The significance of a pattern between two categories is evaluated by three performance measures of data mining approaches: Accuracy, Specificity and Sensitivity.

Generally, data mining methods are divided into two complementary parts. The one is supervised classification and the other is unsupervised cluster. Here, the association between four factors and syndrome in TCM is investigated by classification approaches, which are mainly composed of five groups [Ian & Eibe ,2005]. i.e. Neural network, Support vector machine, Decision tree, Bayes approach and Logistic approach.

The accuracy of association establishment not only affects investigation of BBS in microcosmic level in clinics, but also has impact on successful evaluation of animal model for syndrome. However, there is no evidence that what classification approach is best fit to establish association between BSS and four factors. Consequently, we carried out a comparison study to detect the best classification approach for the UA data here.

Comparison study is usually used in data mining field, especially for classification, to choose the best model for establishment of association.
We employed three hackneyed performance measures of all classification approaches: accuracy, sensitivity and specificity. A distinguished confusion matrix was obtained to calculate the three measures. Confusion matrix is a matrix representation of the classification results. the upper left cell denotes the number of samples classifies as true while they were true (i.e., true positives, TP), and lower right cell denotes the number of samples classified as false while they were actually false (i.e., true false, TF). The other two cells (lower left cell and upper right cell) denote the number of samples misclassified. Specifically, the lower left cell denotes the number of samples classified as false while they actually were true (i.e., false negatives, FN), and the upper right cell denotes the number of samples classified as true while they actually were false (i.e., false positives, FP).Once the confusion matrixes were constructed, the accuracy, sensitivity and specificity are easily calculated as: sensitivity = TP/(TP + FN); specificity = TN/(TN + FP). Accuracy = (TP + TN)/(TP + FP + TN + FN); where TP, TN, FP and FN denotes true positives, true negatives, false positives and false negatives, respectively[Delen et al., 2005].
3-fold cross validation was used here to minimize the bias produced by random sampling of the training and test data samples.

3.1 Bayes approach

Bayes classification approach originates from Bayes rules in statistics, in which Naïve Bayes and Bayesian network are two classification models that can perform the classification task[Morelande et al.,2007].We do not describe the mathematic principle of the two models in detail. Table 1 shows the results of three performance measures. The local comparison study indicates that Naïve Bayes has better performance for classification in Bayes method, so it can be taken as a 'delegate' of Bayes approach to compete with other classification approaches. However, it is found that the better model in Bayes approach has low specificity, although the sensitivity is high, therefore, Bayes approach may be not a good way to establish association between BSS and 4 factors.

Approach	Models	TP	FN	Sensitivity	Specificity	Accuracy
		FP	TN			
Bayes approache	Bayesian network	41	0	100%	0%	71.9%
		16	0			
	Naïve Bayes	40	1	97.6%	37.5%	80.7%
		10	6			

Table 1. The performance of Bayes in classifying BSS in the UA data

3.2 Neural network

With regard to neural network approach, Multilayer perceptron (MLP) with back propagation algorithm and Radial-basis Function Network (RBF) are extensively applied in various fields for classification [Lee, 2006] ;[Peng et al., 2007]. As depicted in Table 2, RBF performs better than MLP in accuracy in classifying BSS.
Both two types of neural networks have hidden layers, which make neural networks have powerful classification ability. However, as the other side of coin, the hidden layers hamper

the interpretation of neural network when applied to classification here, thus neural network remains a "Black Box" for us (Figure 1). Despite this, the powerful ability of classification by neural network still greatly helps us to establish association between BSS and inflammation factors.

Approach	Model	TP	FN	Sensitivity	Specificity	Accuracy
		FP	TN			
Neural Networks	MLP	33	8	80.5%	75%	78.9%
		4	12			
	RBFN	38	3	92.7%	75%	87.7%
		4	12			

Table 2. RBF is the best for Neural Networks

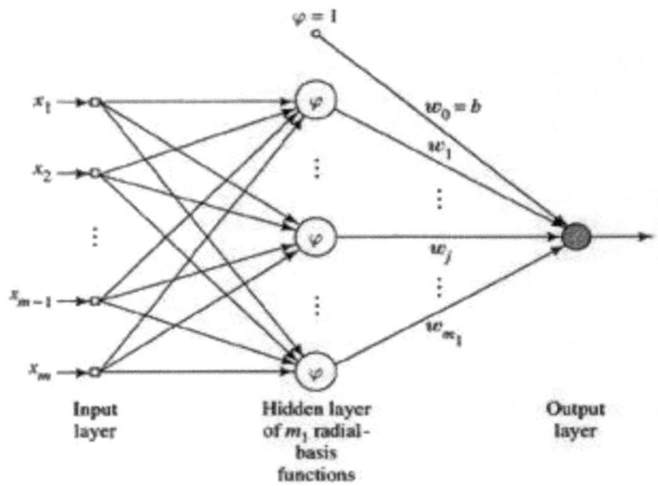

Fig. 1. The topology of MLP and RBF network

3.3 Support Vector Machine

Support Vector Machine (SVM) was a newly developed supervised learning method during last decade (Figure 2) [Vapnik, 1995]. Here, we use two most frequently applied SVM types. One is introduced in [Platt, 1980], called SMO. The other is Libsvm that can be accessed in [Chang & Lin, 2001]. Table 3 is responsible for the local comparison study results of SVM. We easily conclude that Libsvm can be considered as 'delegate' of SVM.

Approach	Model	TP	FN	Sensitivity	Specificity	Accuracy
		FP	TN			
SVM	SMO	41	0	100%	0%	71.9%
		16	0			
	Libsvm	38	3	92.7%	50%	80.7%
		8	8			

Table 3. Libsvm is slightly best in a steady way

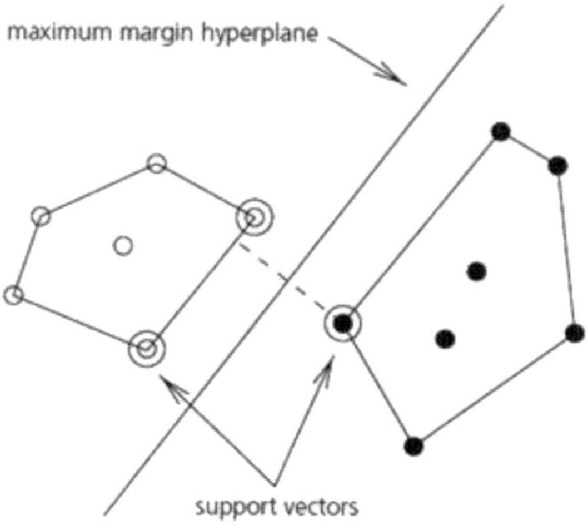

Fig. 2. The topology of support vector machine

3.4 Decision tree

As the name implies, this approach recursively separates observations in branches to construct a tree for the purpose of improving prediction accuracy [Shekhar et al., 2007]. Here we employ three kinds of decision tree classification models. J48, ADTree and Random Forest. Table 4 depicts the performance of local comparison study outcomes. The algorithm J48 is better in the decision tree methods than other two models. The tree is illustrated in Figure 3, from which we can see that Decision Tress is very intuitionistic, association between BSS and inflammation factors is clearer than other approaches. Of course, the advantage in interpretation usually goes with the slightly low accuracy in classification. It is found in Table 4 that most models in Decision Tree approach have low classification accuracy.

3.5 Logistic regression

Logistic regression is a generalization of linear regression [Hastie et al., 2001]. It is used primarily for predicting binary or multi-class dependent variables. It only contains solo model. The Table 5 is the classification result.

Approach	Model	TP / FP	FN / TN	Sensitivity	Specificity	Accuracy
Decision Tree	J48	37 / 6	4 / 10	90.2 %	62.5%	82.5%
	ADTree	36 / 11	5 / 5	87.8 %	31.3 %	71.9%
	Random Forest	36 / 11	5 / 5	87.8 %	31.3 %	71.9%

Table 4. J48 is 'delegate' of decision tree

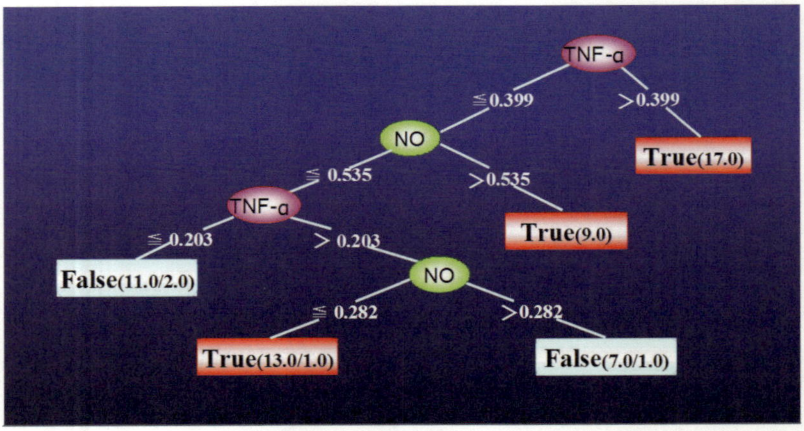

Fig. 3. The association between BSS and inflammation factors is delineated by decision tree

Approach	Model	TP	FN	Sensitivity	Specificity	Accuracy
		FP	TN			
Logistic	Logistic regression	36	5	87.8 %	37.5%	73.7%
		10	6			

Table 5. Logistic regression performs the task well

3.6 A summary of association between BSS and inflammation factors

By global comparison, we find that radial basis function network is most fit for build association between microscopic specifications and macroscopic syndrome. The second best is J48 from decision tree approach. Although till now RBF network is a kind of "Black Box" model so we could not "see" how the four factors interact with each other to behave differently between two categories, the trained RBF network is still able to predict whether an UA case is BSS.

Fortunately, the decision tree is a better approach to investigate the association. As depicted in Figure 3, the tree is composed of two factors, TNF-α and NO. True and False in the terminal of tree represent BSS and Non-BSS respectively. From it we can see that TNF-α and NO are significantly associated with BSS and they are selected from four inflammation factors. The other two factors are considered as low association with the BSS by the decision tree approach. It is important to note that TNF-α has significant difference between BSS and Non-BSS while NO has no significance between the two groups by t test in statistics, which suggests that the data mining approaches not only take the specifications with significant difference into account, but also never "give up" specifications with no significance. Furthermore, by carefully investigation of the tree, it is found that the higher the TNF-α, the more possibility to be diagnosed as BSS. Besides this, a lower concentration in TNF-α still induces the BSS if NO is high than 0.535 (after normalization), that is to say, BSS is associated with a combination of TNF and NO. Finally, some patients with high concentration in NO may have BSS while the other may with Non-BSS as we can see from the tree, this is why NO has no significant difference between the two groups. In a word, the association between two factors and BSS can be mined and uncovered by data mining approaches, which can help to investigate the inner mechanism of BSS.

4. Building and evaluating animal model for BSS in the context of myocardial ischemia

Myocardial ischemia is the nature of UA. We first built myocardial ischemia animal model and then evaluated and predicted whether an animal is BSS by established RBF network. The animal for building model was chosen as Chinese experimental minis swine since the heart of swine is most similar to the counterpart of human as we have discussed above.

4.1 Material

Healthy Chinese experimental minis swine (provided by Chinese University of Agriculture), weight was 25±4kg, aged between 6 months and 10 months. Regardless of sex of swine .The healthy animals are randomly divided into two groups: model group and sham operation group. In the former group, Each Chinese experimental mini swine was instrumented with a size-matched Ameroid constrictor (Research Instrument SW, USA, inner diameter of 2.75 mm) on the anterior descending branch under general anesthesia in sterile condition. Based on early results of dynamic observations, evaluations were performed four weeks after operation. Clinical performances of animals were collected and electrocardiogram, echocardiography, coronary angiography were detected. Meanwhile, blood was obtained from former cava vena to detect blood rheological features and the concentration of prostacyclin, thromboxane A2, endothelin-1 and calcitonin gene-related peptide. Then the diseases of model animals were diagnosed.

All animals were maintained and treated in accordance with the Principles of Laboratory Animal Care, formulated by the National Society for Medical Research, and the guide for the Care and Use of Laboratory Animals, prepared by the National Academy of Sciences and published by the National Institutes of Health (NIH Publication No. 86-23, revised 1985). The local ethics committee of Beijing University of Chinese Medicine approved all animal experiments.

General anesthesia was induced in the animals in a fasting state by intramuscular ketamine (25 mg/kg). They were intubated and anesthesia was maintained with continuous intravenous ketamine. After electrocardiogram (ECG) was performed, the heart of the animal was exposed through a left thoracotomy. A 4 to 6 mm segment of the left anterior descending coronary artery beginning at its origin was then freed by blunt dissection and an Ameroid constrictor with an internal diameter of 2.75mm was placed around the exposed segment. The Ameroid constrictor did not interrupt the blood flow initially, but by its hygroscopic nature, it gradually occluded the vessel by external compression. After placement of the constrictor, the thoracotomy was closed by layers and the electrocardiogram was performed again.

The surgery was performed under continuous monitoring of ECG. After recovered from anesthesia, animals were extubated. During the first 3 days after surgery, penicillin (4,800,000 units per day) was injected intramuscular to anti-infective.

4.2 Evaluating the MI disease of animal model

Selective coronary angiography was performed after 4 weeks and the degree of narrowing of the anterior descending branch were observed.

Echocardiography study was conducted pre and 4 weeks post surgery respectively to evaluate the degree of stenosis and myocardial function. Echocardiography studies including the images of six standard planes (parasternal long axis, short axis at bicuspid level, papillary muscle level, cardiac apex level, apical four chambers and apical two chambers), Adopting LVEDd, LVEDs, IVST, LVAW thickness (bicuspid level, papillary muscle level, cardiac apex level), EDV, ESV, Peak early diastolic velocity, Peak late diastolic velocity, etc, and calculating EF, FS, SV, $\Delta T\%$. 2-DE is introduced to visual examination the movement of the left ventricular muscles.

Once the animal model for MI is built, by using the established association, each animal can be evaluated whether is with BSS based on the "communication bridge"-the four inflammation factors. However, the difference of the four factors in concentration contained in the blood is needed to be investigated before evaluation. That is to say, the four factors should have the same scale on human and swine.

4.3 The significant difference of inflammation factors between animal and human

We found that each inflammation factor takes different concentration between animal and human. The student's t tests showed that there is significant difference between microscopic specifications of animal and human (Table 6). In order to bridge the gap, we employed normalization method for each group to scale the concentrations of each factor. The normalized method was given in equation (1):

$$\overline{X} = \frac{X - \min(A)}{\max(A) - \min(A)} \quad (1)$$

Where X represents factors, $\overline{X}$ is responsible for the normalized factors. A is the group (human or animal) where X is included. $\min(A)$ is the minimal value of X in group A while $\max(A)$ is the maximal value of X. It is easy to see that $\overline{X}$ values between 0 and 1.

	ET	TNF	IL-6	No
Human	66.611±18.576	0.68053±0.24097	68.94±47.134	82.912±54.451
Animal	137.16±24.391	1.7656±0.53346	320.39±98.939	57.747±29.497

Table 6. Mean and standard derivation of each factor for human and animal respectively.

As shown in Figure 4, after normalization with regard to each group, the concentrations of factors are in the same scale, which paves a basis for further prediction. Otherwise, the great error would be occurred during the prediction of whether an MI animal is BSS.

Figure 4 shows that the minimum of ET concentration is larger than maximal of counterpart in human, which means that the difference of four inflammation factors between animal (swine) and human is significant. After normalization with regard to each group, as depicted in nether figure, the factors are in the same scale between zero and one.

4.4 Evaluating whether an animal is BSS by RBF network in the context of MI

As shown above, human data was used to train the RBF network and animal data was used for test animal model by using the model built by RBF network. The RBF network has the ability to predict whether a new case is BSS after training by the clinical data. The parameter information for RBF network that configures the classification model is shown detailedly in Table 7. Each animal with myocardial ischemia disease can be predicted by the network. The detailed results are shown in Table 8. We can see that 10 animals from total 13 animals personalized therapy of UA should be taken into account. Furthermore, the frequency of

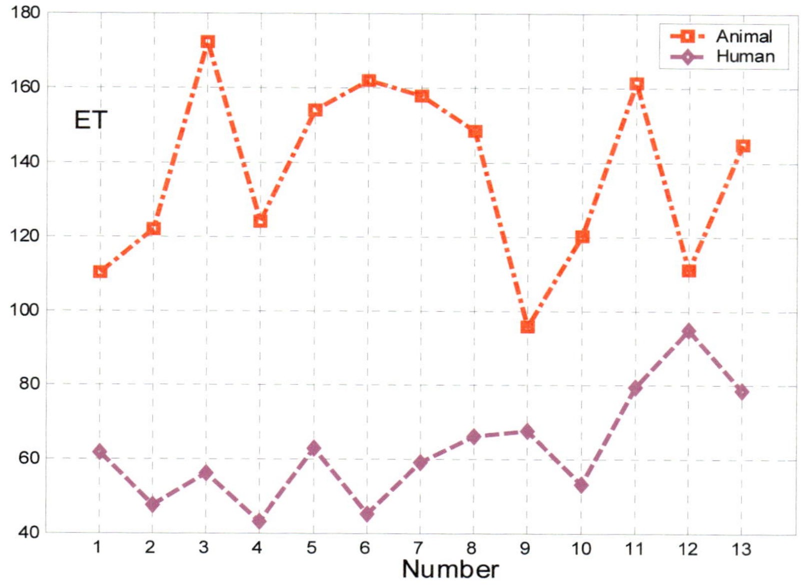

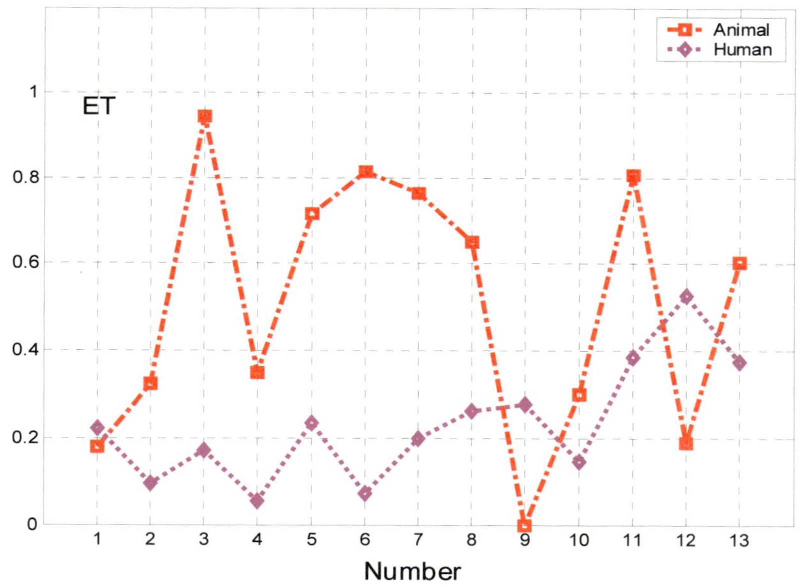

Fig. 4. 13 patients that are randomly chosen from the cohort are compared with 13 swine.

BSS in the context of animal model is nearly 77%. While in the clinics, the frequency of BSS are with BSS, the other animals are with non-BSS, which means that BSS in the context of MI is a subtype of MI (UA). By concept of syndrome in TCM, MI cohort can be divided into different groups, each of which has same phenotype that is characterized by the syndrome. Chinese herbal is prescribed in accordance with syndrome diagnosed. Therefore, in the context of UA is about 72%, the frequency error is 5%, it can be considered as sampling error since there are only 13 animals to be included here. It indicated that the evaluation of BSS in the animal model is accurate to some extent. Moreover, we used the second best classification approach (Decision tree J48) to re-evaluate again the 13 animals, we found out that most of animals are evaluated as same kind of syndrome. So the results obtained by RBF network evaluation and prediction are robust and credible.

Parameter	Description	Setting
Clustering Seed	The random seed to pass on to K-means	1
Ridge	Set the Ridge value for the logistic or linear regression	1.0E-8
Maxiam Iteration	Maximum number of iterations for the logistic regression to perform.	-1
minStdDev	Sets the minimum standard deviation for the clusters.	0.1
numClusters	The number of clusters for K-Means to generate.	2

Table 7. Parameter setting for RBF network

Animal	ET	TNF-	IL-6	NO	Prediction By RBF	Prediction By J48
1	0.17948	1	0.52407	0.11825	FALSE	TRUE
2	0.32296	0.13656	0.37839	0.38443	FALSE	FALSE
3	0.94394	0.77967	0.92968	0.49553	TRUE	TRUE
4	0.34929	0.67016	0.34369	0.68466	TRUE	TRUE
5	0.71667	0.5637	0.20881	0.36932	TRUE	TRUE
6	0.81531	0.30977	0.78601	0.30622	TRUE	FALSE
7	0.76521	0.85297	0.73035	0.43243	TRUE	TRUE
8	0.64986	0.52443	0.78601	1	TRUE	TRUE
9	0	0.51134	0.6987	0.49499	TRUE	TRUE
10	0.30225	0.66274	0.64863	0	FALSE	TRUE
11	0.80805	0.6514	0.48062	0.18028	TRUE	TRUE
12	0.1889	0.363	0.24321	0.11709	TRUE	TRUE
13	0.60479	0.45899	0.91622	0.36986	TRUE	TRUE

Table 8. The prediction of whether a disease animal is BSS or non-BSS by using two better classification approaches. It is noted that the normalization of animal model is with regard to all animals, including sham operation groups (data not shown here since they are not needed to be evaluated by the approaches).

5. Conclusion and discussion

In this paper, we proposed a novel strategy to build and evaluate an animal model for BSS in TCM in the context of UA. The work filled the blank of adequately evaluating animal

model for syndrome and solved the problem of how to diagnose syndrome in animal. We took advantage of supervised data mining approaches to establish the association between physical and chemical specifications and syndrome in the context of the disease in clinical data obtained by clinical epidemiology survey. The accuracy of classification of data mining approach guarantees the association establishment is right (higher than 87%). Then the specifications were used as "Communication Bridge" to translate the association to the animal. The prediction results showed that animal model with same disease (UA) may have different syndrome phenotypes and the association established in the clinics could be used to evaluate whether an animal is of BSS. The presented strategy here not only builds and evaluates animal for syndrome in TCM, but also paves a key basis to uncover the mechanism of syndrome and treat disease in a personalized way.
The paper only took the most important syndrome in the UA-BSS into account. So the UA cohort is divided into two subgroups: BSS and non-BSS. However, by former clinical research, it was found that there are about seven syndromes can be discovered in the context of UA. The further work will focus in the differential diagnosis of each syndrome by physical and chemical specifications in the context of UA and build animal models for them respectively.

6. Acknowledgement

This work was supported by a grant from the National Basic Research Program (973 Program) under grant No. 2011CB505106, the National Department Public Benefit Research Foundation of China under grant No. 200807007, the Creation for Significant New Drugs Project of China under grant No. 2009ZX09502-018, National Natural Science Foundation of China under grant No. 30902020.

7. References

Braunwald, ET AL.(2002). ACC/AHA 2002 Guideline Update for the Management of Patients With Unstable Angina and Non–ST-Segment Elevation Myocardial Infarction.*J Am Coll Cardiol*, 2002, 40, 1366-1374, ISSN 0002-9149

Chang, CC. & Lin, CJ.(2001). LIBSVM : a library for support vector machines, 2001. Software available at http://www.csie.ntu.edu.tw/~cjlin/libsvm.6.

Chen, JX.; Xi, GC. & Chen, J.(2007).An unsupervised pattern (syndrome in traditional Chinese medicine) discovery algorithm based on association delineated by revised mutual information in chronic renal failure data. *Journal of biological systems*, 2007, vol.15, no.4, 435-451, ISSN 0218-3390

Davidson, KW.; Schwartz, JE. & Kirkland, SA. (2009). Relation of inflammation to depression and incident coronary heart disease (from the Canadian Nova Scotia Health Survey [NSHS95] Prospective Population Study),2009, vol.103, no.6, 755-761.

Delen, D.; Walker, G. & Kadam, A.(2005). Predicting breast cancer survivability: a comparison of three data mining methods. *Artificial Intelligence in Medicine*, 2005, vol.34, no. 2, 113-127, ISSN 0999-3657

Gustavsson, CG. & Agardh, CD.(2009). Inflammatory activity increases with haemoglobin A1c in patients with acute coronary syndrome. *Scandinavian Cardiovascular Journal*, 2009, vol.99999, no.1, 1-6, ISSN 1401-7431

Hastie, T.; Tibshirani, R. & Friedman, J.(2001). *The elements of statistical learning*, Springer-Verlag, ISBN 978-0-387-84857-0, New York

Hayden, EC.(2008).Biological tools revamp disease classification. *Nature*, 2008, vol.453, no.7156, 709, ISSN 0028-0836

Ian, H.W. & Eibe , F.(2005).*Data mining: Practical machine learning tools and techniques*, Morgan, ISBN 0120884070

Lee, K. (2006).MLP-based phone boundary refining for a TTS database. *IEEE Transactions on Audio, Speech, and Language Processing*, 2006, 14, 981-989, ISSN 1558-7916

Li, S.; Zhang, X. & Li, Y.(2007) .Understanding Zheng in traditional Chinese medicinein the context of neuro-endocrine immune network. *IET System Biology*, 2007, vol.1, no.1, 51–60, ISSN 1751-8849

Ma, XJ.; Yin, HJ. & Chen, KJ.(2007). Research Progress of Correlation between Blood stasis Syndrome and Inflammation. *Chinese Journal of Integrated Traditional and Western Medicine* , 2007, Vol. 27, No.7, 669-672, ISSN 1003-5370 (PMID: 17717936) (Chinese)

Mao, YL. ; Yuan, ZK. & Huang, XP.(2004). Study on relationship between the polymorphism of angiotensin converting enzyme gene and blood stasis syndrome in patients with coronary heart disease. *Chinese Journal of Integrated Traditional and Western Medicine*, 2004, Vol. 24, No.9, 776-780, ISSN 1003-5370 (PMID: 15495818) (Chinese)

Monnet, E. & Chachques, JC. (2005) .Animal Models of Heart Failure: What Is New? *Ann Thorac Surg*, Apr 2005, 79, 1445–1453, ISSN 0003-4975

Morelande, M.; Kreucher& Kastella, K.(2007). A Bayesian Approach to Multiple Target Detection and Tracking. *IEEE Transactions on Signal Processing*, 2007, Vol.55, No.5, 1589-1604, ISSN 1053-587X

Peng, J.; Li, K. & Irwin, G.(2007). A Novel Continuous Forward Algorithm for RBF Neural Modeling. *IEEE Transactions on Automatic Control*, 2007,52, 117-122,ISSN 0018-9286

Platt, J.(1980). Training of Support Vector Machines using Sequential Minimal Optimization. *Advances in Kernel Methods - Support Vector Learning*, Schoelkopf, B. ; Burges, C. & Smola, A. , MIT Press, ISBN 0262194163

Shekhar, R.; Phoha, G. & Balagani, K.(2007). K-Means+ID3: A Novel Method for Supervised Anomaly Detection by Cascading K-Means Clustering and ID3 Decision Tree Learning Methods. *IEEE Transactions on Knowledge and Data Engineering*, 2007,19, 345-354, ISSN 1041-4347

Sun, ZQ.; Xi, GC. & Yi, JQ.(2007).Select informative symptom combination of diagnosing syndrome. *Journal of biological systems*, 2007, vol.15 no.1, 27–37, ISSN 0218-3390

Vapnik, V.(1995). *The Nature of Statisfical Learning Theory*. Springer, 0387987800, New York

Weaver, ME.; Pantely, GA. & Bristow, JD. (1986). A quantitative study of the anatomy and distribution of coronary arteries in swine in comparison with other animals and man. *Cardiovasc Res*, Dec 1986,20, 907–917,ISSN 0008-6363

Yuan, ZK. ; Huang, XP. & Tan, GB. (2006). Analysis of the Function of Vascular Endothelial Cells in Coronary Heart Disease Patients of Blood-Stasis Syndrome. *Chinese Journal of Integrated Traditional and Western Medicine* , 2006, Vol. 26, No.5, 407-410, ISSN 1003-5370 (PMID: 16883905) (Chinese)

Zhang, JG. ; Yang, N. & He, H.(2005). Effect of Astragalus Injection on Plasma Levels of Apoptosis-related Factors in Aged Patients with Chronic Heart Failure. *Chinese Journal of Integrated Traditional and Western Medicine* , 2005, Vol. 25, No.11, 187-190, ISSN 1003-5370 (PMID: 16181532) (Chinese)

Zheng, YY. (2002). *State Food and Drug Administration. Guiding principle of new drug clinical research of traditional Chinese medicine*, Medical Science Publishing House of China, ISBN 750672586x, Beijing (Chinese)

19

Results of Data Mining Technique Applied to a Home Enteral Nutrition Database

Maria Eliana M. Shieferdecker, Carlos Henrique Kuretzki, José Simão de Paula Pinto, Antônio Carlos Ligoki Campos and Osvaldo Malafaia
Universidade Federal do Paraná,Curitiba, Brasil

1. Introduction

This chapter presents the results of data mining (ID3 and A PRIORI) techniques applied to a Health (nutrition) database that was originated from a knowledge management point of view.

As participants of a Graduate Program in Surgery, we developed a knowledge management strategy and operationalized it by an information system, called SINPE, which is able to manipulate a large database (actually with 500,000+). Data items are organized into data collecting protocols that store data in a relational database. The system offers tools to retrieve and analyze data, with some basic (descriptive) statistics and graphic charts generated automatically. An interface allows to apply data mining algorithms into collected items. A main feature of the system is that it was developed from the usability point of view, because the primary users are physicians with low domain of information systems. Thus the system is very easy to manage.

The aim of this work was to apply these data mining techniques to a home enteral nutrition database in order to identify features not previously suspected.

The data mining technique was applied to a large health database protocol, with 1592 specific (nutrition) collected items. After the selection of interesting items the ID3 and APRIORI algorithms were applied to 111 patients, 58 females and 53 males, between 19 and 92 years old. These data were analyzed and presented in graphics and tables. Two questionnaires were answered by the users to validate the tool and its results. All operations were performed by physicians with low knowledge of data mining techniques, who were assisted by a BS in Computer Science professional.

After mining the database, obtained results were compared with the international literature and the overall results met our expectations. Among other results, the data mining technique applied to the home enteral nutrition database identified an unexpected high incidence of malnutrition among patients that were receiving home enteral nutrition. Readmission after treatment was also higher than expected, reaching a 50% rate. Physicians who used the system approved it. No discrepancy was observed while using the system, but there are some parameters that must be better explained.

The application of data mining techniques to a large medical (nutrition) database allowed us to identify nutrition features not previously known, which helped to improve public nutrition policies in this specific area. This user friendly system was proved useful when applied to a large nutrition database. It is necessary to improve the samples, such as confidence and support, in a way to better explain these results.

2. Data collecting protocols

To make a data protocol for a research is similar to build a large questionnaire. It is a simple but methodical task. The questions to be used are defined by a specialist, using his tacit knowledge and some medical references. Each time new research is needed a new protocol is generated. In our approach, the principal items of a health area, like gastroenterology, are first defined and stored in a database. A Master Protocol is organized. Then, when a medical research in gastroenterology is started, say Zenker's diverticulum, the necessary data collecting items are obtained from the master protocol, by choice in a knowledge tree, generating a specific protocol. Master items are never deleted, but may be inactivated. Collected data are linked to a specific protocol that will be analysed in terms of item frequency, patient's genre, age and ascendance, presence or absent of certain symptoms, and so on.
The original idea of this approach was developed over the last 15 years in a Brazilian school hospital, and for the last 10 years applied in clinical researches by graduate (master and doctorate) students while composing their theses. Over the years were organized 500,000 items, in 40 master and 234 specific data collect protocols, arranged in the following areas (Table 1):

Master protocol	# items
Diseases of the Esophagus	2656
Urological Device	1030
Anorectal Diseases	3926
Liver Transplantation	4892
Bowel	2967
Bile Ducts, Extrahepatic	1948
Diseases of the Pancreas	5059
Diseases of the Stomach	2172
Small intestine	9349

Table 1. A brief view of SINPE's database protocols

The basic problems involved with this task are to manage protocols, how to improve data quality and how to build a user friendly system for healthcare professionals that store and help analyse data.

2.1 The SINPE system

SINPE is a Brazilian Portuguese contraction for Sistema Integrado de Protocolos Eletrônicos (Integrated Electronic Protocols System). Developed by medical informatic graduate students nowadays intends by sixth version, presenting a MS-Windows Desktop, a handheld Windows Compact Edition-based (Fischer et al., 2003) and a web interface for data collect. The task of protocol building have only a desktop interface, because our experiences with handheld to large user interaction necessary to make the knowledge tree using this interface was not good; the same occurred with browsers, that forcing to develop an applet or other way for better interaction. Actually there is not a Linux version, because our physicians do not use this system yet.

In Medicine, a common approach to make a research is to build a data collect (clinical) protocol to conduce the observations. A protocol is like a structured questionnaire, consisting in information about diseases, treatments, drugs, patient data, therapies and clinical history (Sackett et al., 2000).

To make a protocol is not a simple task, since there is an extensive number of references about the theme that must be included. Common reference sources are international journals, books, congress proceedings and older studies / researches (Warren & Warren, 1993).

After obtaining the material, the method used is to select the most important and organize then in a logical sequence. This procedures result in a protocol (see Figure 1).

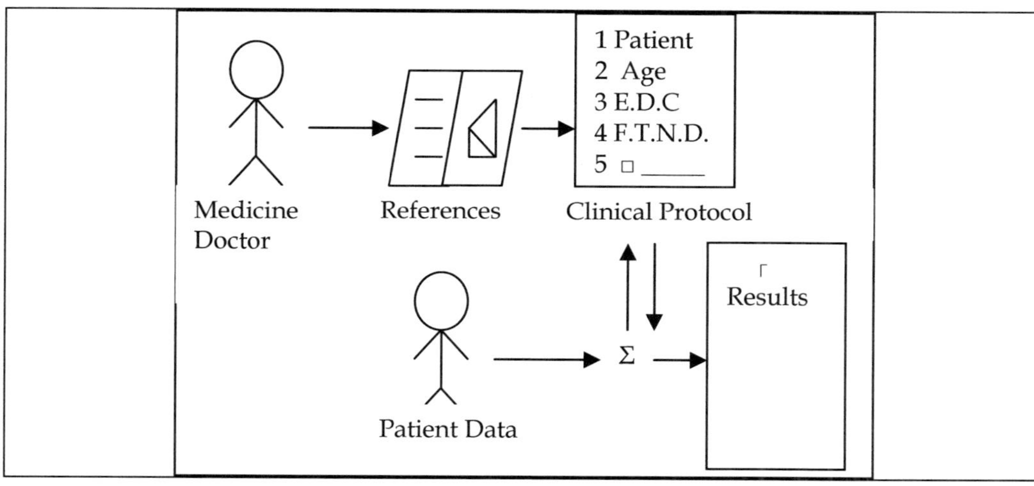

Fig. 1. The process to make a clinical protocol

A first problem related to this way to conduce researches is to make new protocols, according to the above description, because each new detail needs to be tested, and, since too many researches have overlapped metadata, like patient sex or allergy, the proposed approach results in a significant amount of work to make new protocols (see Figure 2).

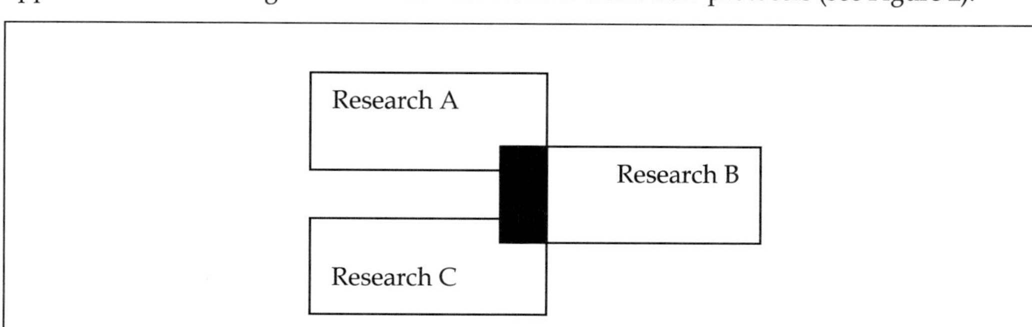

Fig. 2. Overlap of metadata in different researches

In SINPE's, our approach is to categorize the common metadata to an area, gastroenterology by example, in a master protocol, and then build specific protocols from the master. The process to relate data collected in a protocol to a unique master description, makes it easy to proceed with the same or correlated researches in different sites, which improves epidemiologic studies, and the integration process with the pre-existent hospital information systems (Afrin et al., 1997).

Earlier, when the system was idealized, the first prototype was built using object oriented paradigm (Russel, 2000) and SUN's JAVA to make an MS-Windows® stand alone application, with a centralized database and a web applet, but the final result was a problem to manage: it is difficult to physicians to control the JAVA environment variables, like "PATH", "VM Versions", and conflict with other applications (like Oracle® 8.x clients) installed in the computer. The centralized database was not over clinical research department responsibility, and there is not a DBA to manage backup, recovery and other DBMS procedures. Also, the use of JAVA technology forced us to improve the memory capacity of the microcomputers in use. This was built in 99-2000's. The actual system was developed using Microsoft dotNET framework, with C# coding and Access and SQL Server databases, since MS-Windows environment is widely used by Brazilian healthcare professionals. A reduced class diagram is showed in figure 3, in which it is possible to view the classes that define a master and a specific protocol.

A security model was developed to manage the system, producing 4 user types: an administrator, a data collector, a protocol elaborator and a viewer. Differences between them are concerned to a power to create master protocols, new users and sites, new master and specific protocols, only collect data or only view protocols and data results.

This approach was developed as a part of doctorate studies in medical informatics that resulted in an information system called SINPE. The SINPE has been used by master degree students, that build master protocols over a PhD supervision and by doctorate students that are responsible for multicentre studies.

2.2 The SINPE Process

The difficulty related to put a new system in practice is directly proportional to the operational/ behavioral changes that will be made from this application. As a way to put SINPE to work we developed a three phase process that manages activities, as showed in Figure 4.

The phase I is not different from the traditional way to build protocols, since it consists in identifying references about a theme. But here the references and the metadata (patient temperature, temperature unit and temperature limits, for example) are stored in a database and will be accessible by many researches at time. A concept may be related to metadata (like fewer) and may exist as a link to an external dictionary (like ICD-10) or metathesaurus (like UMLS) (Lindberg et al., 1993; Rocha et al., 1994). This phase is very important to insure data quality.

Once finished phase I, in phase II a specific research will be build selecting concepts from master's database. It is possible to use the same concepts (consisting in metadata, description, archives like images or sounds and references) in various protocols. Once a concept is used, it may be actualized but not removed from the database. There is a possibility to invalidate an old used concept, but never to remove it (Sacket & Straus, 1998). With this, we guarantee the knowledge management/ reuse of questionnaires.

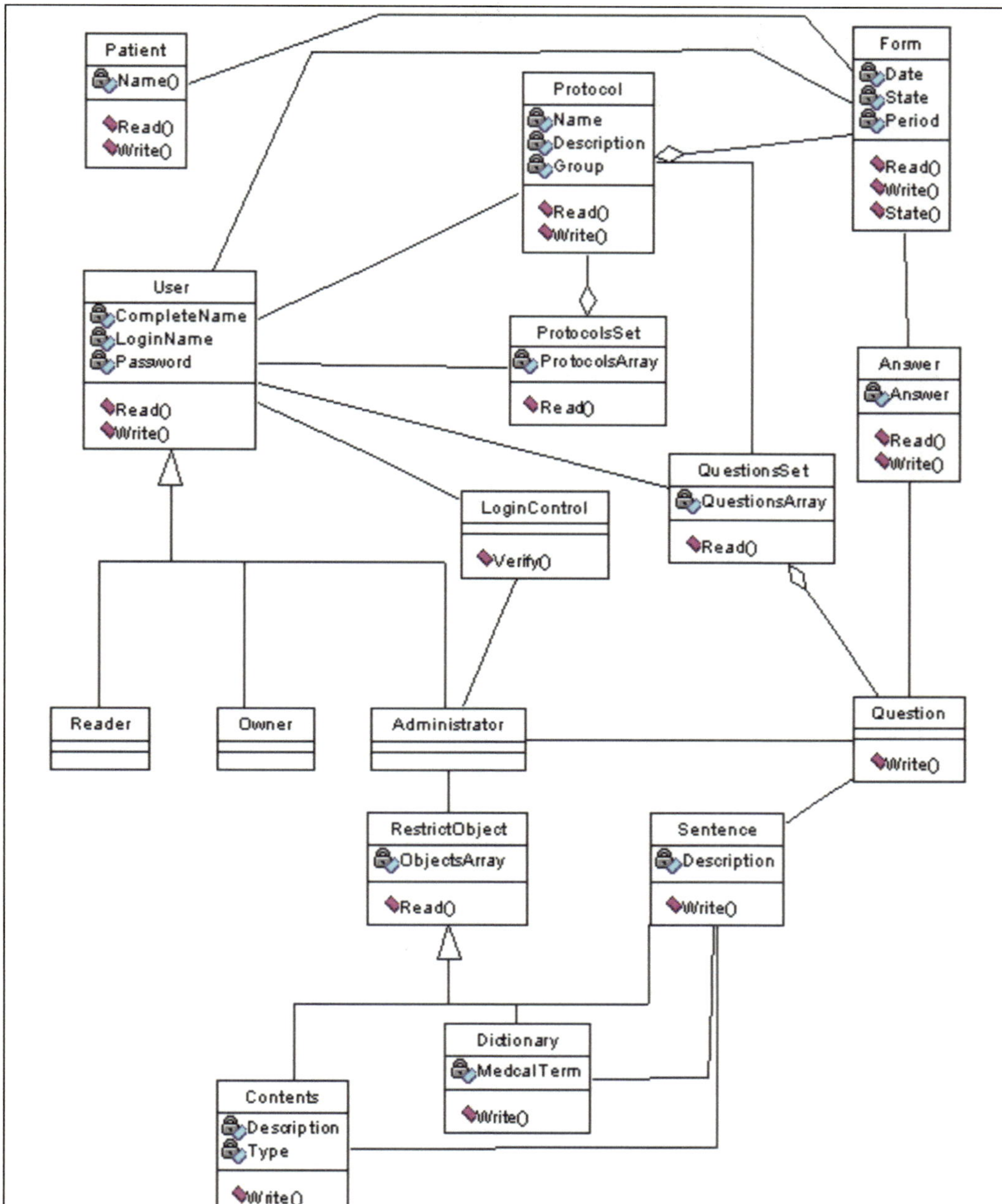

Fig. 3. SINPE's reduced class diagram

When a specific protocol is built it may be distributed for the researches or his or her co-workers that will collect the data. In this phase (phase III), the data may be collected by using a trivial MS-Windows® interface, Web-based interface or by a handheld computer simplified interface (Graham et al., 2002). The database may reside in a local copy or a remote (Internet accessible), decentralized or centralized SGBD.

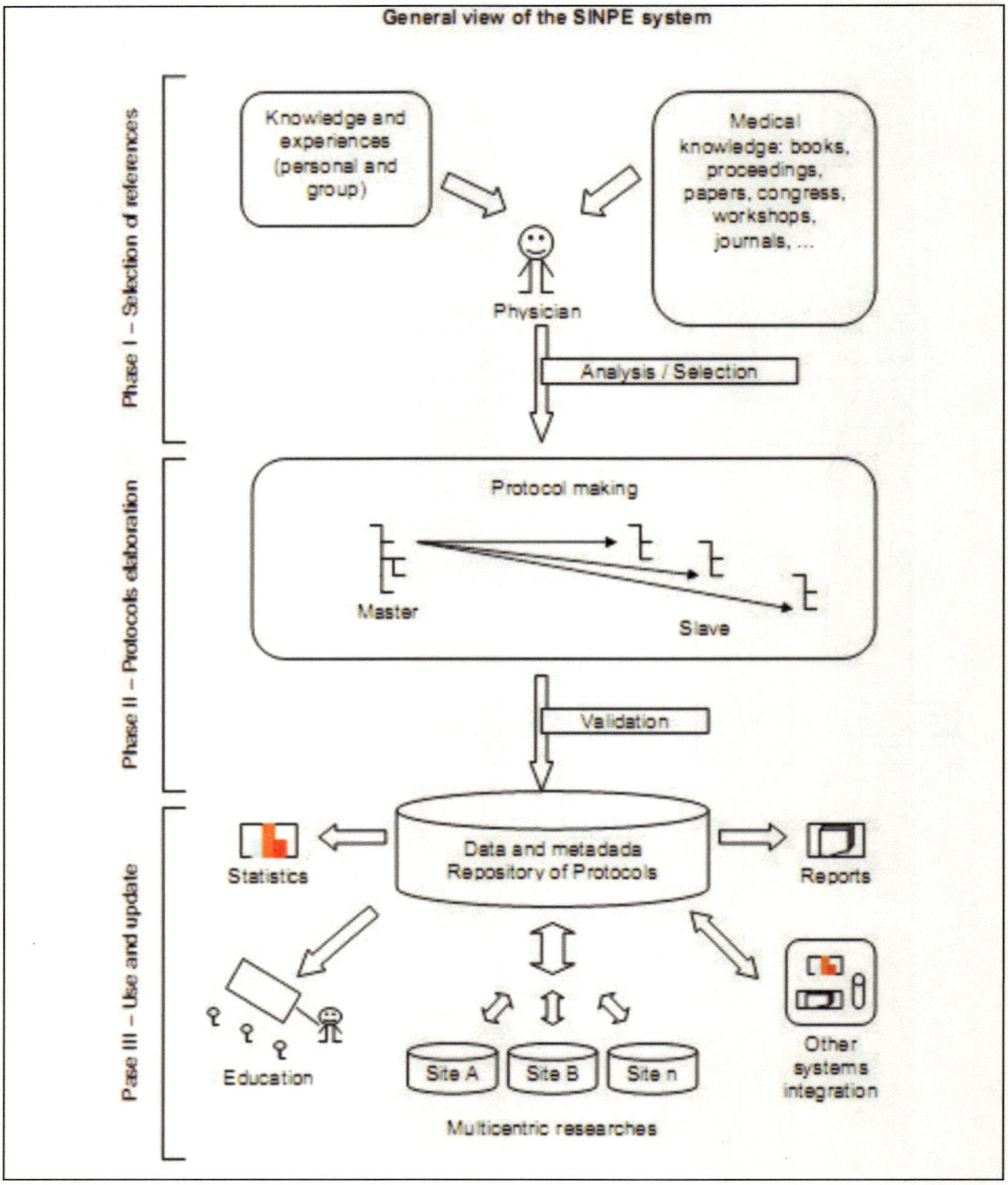

Fig. 3. SINPE's reduced class diagram

2.3 SINPE's analysis tool and use in learning/ education

Once protocols are elaborated and data are collected, SINPE's offers an analysis tool that generates descriptive statistics and some graphs automatically when a specific protocol is selected, and permits to elaborate reports, export files and print results. For each item in a protocol the analyzer will calculate its proportion related to total data collected and some

epidemiological data, like patient's gender or race. To help results evaluation we implemented a data mining tool, that permits to evaluate the collected data using a wizard interface: physicians may not know algorithms or calculus (Ingelfinger, 1993), only the hypothesis to be validated (or not).
Another use of the this system is in training areas, allowing students to access a high quality database to make "ad hoc" questions about diseases and their treatments, negative and positive responses on drug dosages, epidemiologic studies and so on. To enforce this use we are now idealizing a system to make clinical cases based on collected data by the clinical protocols system (showed in Figure 4).

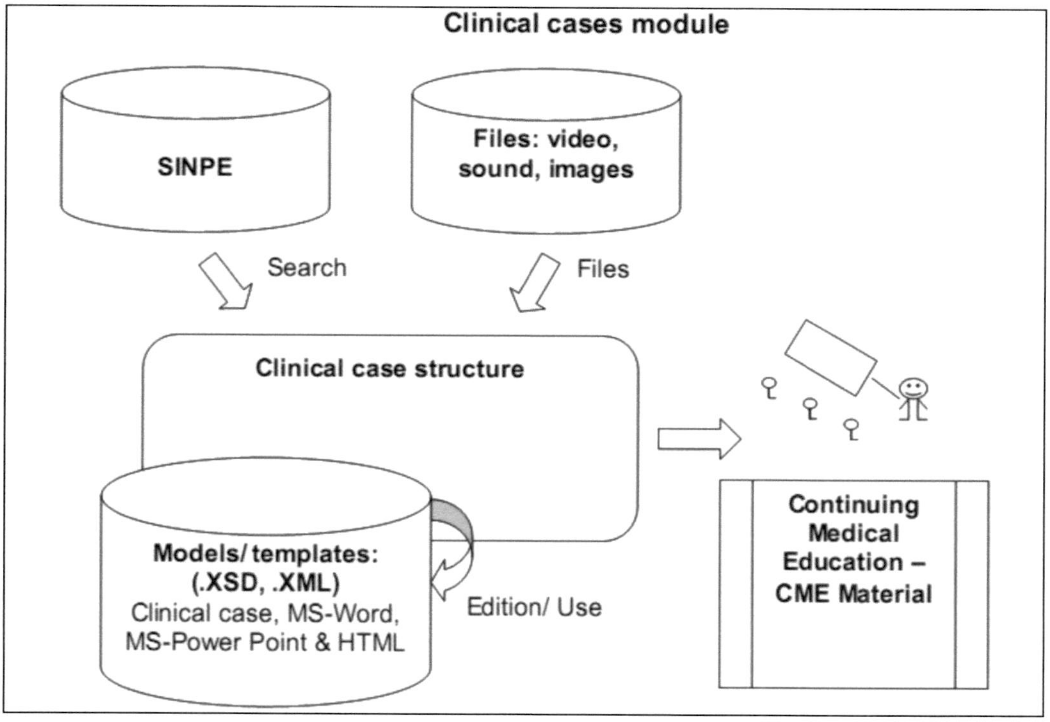

Fig. 4. SINPE's reduced class diagram

An advantage of the use of SINPE's approach is that there are high quality metadata linked with high quality collected data that will allow the use of data mining techniques with adequate precision and considerable importance in their results.

3. Home enteral nutrition

The use of computational resources, especially regarding the capture, storage and retrieval of clinical data, has been important to the production of relevant and reliable clinical studies (Haux et al., 2002; Doebbeling et al., 2006). These databases allow the collection of structured clinical information to the analysis and production of prospective studies in large series of patients. It contributes to the quality of healthcare, development and solidification of technical and scientific knowledge. The integration of technological advances in information and on health sciences allows the production of relevant and reliable clinical studies.

The home care is growing, it is applied to 460 patients per million of the United States of America's population, and in 40 patients per million habitants in Spain (Moreno Villares, 2004; Planas, et al., 2006). Having the records of patients in nutritional therapy at home is important, because this information enables the coordination of resources and improvement of health care (Planas et al., 2003).

The study "Elaboration and Validation of an Electronic Protocol for Homecare Enteral Nutritional Therapy in Patients Attended by the Municipal Health Unities of Curitiba" applies an electronic protocol for homecare enteral nutrition patients (TNED) through a research performed in 111 home visits of Curitiba´s health units users. The development of the research evolved the following stages: elaboration of an electronic protocol for TNED with 1793 sub items grouped in nine main items: identification, nutritional evaluation, diet prescription, enteral nutrition indications, enteral tube feeding access, enteral nutrition composition, administration systems, complications and re-hospitalization. This theoretical base was created as an electronic protocol called Informatized Master Protocol of TNED using the integrated System of Electronic Protocols (SINPE©). A specific electronic protocol was then created from this master protocol, which was applied for the evaluation of homecare users of the municipal health units. The demonstration of the results was produced using the visualization interface module of information. There were 58 females and 53 males, between 19 and 95 years of age, whose data were analyzed and presented using graphics. These images could be saved, copied to the computer transference area (memory), allowing their exportation to other softwares or insertion in analysis files. The Electronic Protocol creation and its application on TNED municipal health units patients was possible. A number of useful information emerged from this research, such as: most of caregivers are family members; most of the patients are malnourished; neurological diseases are those that predominates as indication for homecare enteral nutrition, and between those, stroke was the most prevalent, gastrostomy was the most used tube feeding method, the most frequent complications of the nutritional therapy were the gastrointestinal ones; more then half of the patients needed to be re-hospitalised after the beginning of home enteral nutritional therapy. The database analysis resulted in important information that contributed for research and creation of public nutrition politics.

3.1 Results on data mining in a health database in nutrition

A general view of applied data mining allowed the creation of algorithms. A critical view over results versus application versus reality was therefore possible. The Apriori method rule showed that a BMI ≤ 22 kg/m^2 implied the intake of a homemade diet. The patients with IMC ≤ 22 kg/m^2 are characterized as malnourished and were receiving a homemade enteral diet. This relation may indicate that quality of the infused diet is related with the nutritional state of the patient.

These results have a key relevance on clinical decisions and contribute to the improvement of public policies in healthcare. If the malnourished patients are those who receive the homemade diet it can indicate that this diet is not meeting the nutritional needs of the patients, and therefore the prescription must be modified.

According to Van Bemmel (VAN BEMMEL, 1997), techniques of Data Mining and Knowledge Discovery in Databases processes were originally developed for corporate sales and production data, but they are also relevant to health care settings.

To Witten and Frank (WITTEN, 2005) Data Mining is defined as the process of discovering patterns in data. These processes should be automated or semi-automatic. But the patterns discovered must be meaningful and that they lead to some benefit.

"Many times a Data Mining is a part of the discovery of knowledge as one of the most important fields on knowledge management. [...] Techniques such as Bayesian models, the decision tree, artificial neural networks, association rules and genetic algorithms are generally used in the discovery of patterns that are known or previously unknown to the system and to users. Data mining can be used: applications, marketing, customer relationship, engineering, medicine, analysis of crimes, prognosis specialist, Web mining and mobile computing, among others." (Chen, 2005).

Data mining is also used to extract rules from health care data. For example, it has been used to extract diagnostic rules from breast cancer data (Chen, 2005).

Malnutrition is associated with poor clinical outcomes such as delayed recovery from illness, longer length of hospital stay, increased occurrence of complications and reduced quality of life (RUSSELL, 2007). The data mining enables better practices by presenting the relation link between these items, allowing the identification of related factors with malnutrition.

Techniques such as data mining and text mining need to be used with great care in the biomedical applications, in view that medical data are often sensitive and involves private and confidential information. Errors and incorrect associations could be rapidly propagated through electronic media, especially when large databases and powerful computational techniques are involved (Chen, 2005).

The Apriori method of data mining has been widely used on supermarkets sales databases, but despite this application, the Apriori method can be easily applied on health areas in order to develop rules involving possible items. The application of specific databases on health care has also great commercial potential.

4. Conclusion and future works with the use of SINPE in nutrition related studies

When observing healthcare and its guidelines we have perceived the need for quality data and strong processes as a way to assure efficient guidelines. Some data mining tasks conduced over a database with high quality data are applicable to various areas of the medical sciences. This study is an adequate demonstration of that. With the SINPE we were able to obtain improvements in data organization and quality, and also usability enhancement when considering the use of statistic functions.

5. References

Afrin LB, Kuppuswamy V, Slater B, Stuart RK. Electronic Clinical Trial Protocol Distribution via the World-Wide Web: A Prototype for Reducing Costs and Errors, Improving Accrual, and Saving Trees. *JAMIA* 1997; 4(1):25-35.

Doebbeling, B. N.; Chou, A. F.; Tierney, W. M. *Priorities and strategies for the implementation of integrated informatics and communications technology to improve evidence-based practice.* Journal of General Internal Medicine, v. 21, n. 2, p. S50- S57, 2006.

Fischer S. (2003), Stewart TE, Mehta S, Wax R, Lapinsky SE. Handheld Computing in Medicine. *JAMIA* 2003; 10: 139-149.

Graham M, Chignell M, Harumi T. Design of Documentation for Handheld Ergonomics: Presenting Clinical Evidence at the Point of Care. *Proceedings of the 20th annual international conference on Computer documentation*, October, 2002.

Haux, R.; Ammenwerth E.; Herzog, W.; Knaup P. *Health care in the information society. A prognosis for the year 2013*. International Journal of Medical Informatics, v.66, p. 3 – 21, 2002.

Ingelfinger JA, Mosteller F, Thibodeau LA, Ware JH. *Biostatistics in Clinical Medicine* 3rd ed. New York: McGraw-Hill; 1993.

Lindberg DAB, Humphreys BL, McCray AT. The Unified Medical Language System. *Methods of Information in Medicine* 1993; 32(4):281-91.

Moreno Villares, J.M. *La práctica de la nutrición artificial domiciliaria en Europa.* Nutrición Hospitalaria, v.19, p. 59-67, 2004.

Planas, M.; Castellá, M.; García Luna, P.P. et al. *Nutrición enteral domiciliaria (NED): Registro Nacional del año 2000.* Nutrición Hospitalaria, v. 18(1), p. 34-38, 2003.

Planas, M.; Lecha, P. P.; García Luna, P.P. et al. *Registro Nacional de la Nutrición Enteral Domiciliaria (NED) del año 2003.* Nutrición Hospitalaria, v. 21 (1), p. 71-4, 2006.

Rocha RA, Huff SM, Haug PJ, Warner HR. Designing a Controlled Medical Vocabulary Server: The VOSER Project. *Computers and Biomedical Research* 1994; 27(6):472-507.

Russel, LT. Clinical Trial Remote Data Capture Client/Server Solution. *Addendum to the 2000 proceedings of the conference on Object-oriented programming, systems, languages, and applications,* January, 2000.

Russell CA."Impact of malnutrition on healthcare costs and economic considerations.," Clinical Nutrition Supplements, vol. 2, pp. 25–32, 2007.

Sackett DL et al.. *Evidence-Based Medicine*. How to Practice and teach. EBM. 2nd Ed., Edinburgh: Churchill Livingstone, 2000.

Sackett DL, Straus SE. Finding and appling evidence during clinical rounds: the evidence cart. *JAMA*, 1998.

Van Bemmel JH, Mussen MA. Handbook of Medical Informatics: Springer, 1997.

Warren JR, Warren DE. A knowledge-Based Patient Data Acquisition System for Primary Care Medicine. *Proceedings of the second international conference on Information and knowledge management*, December, 1993 .

Witten IH, Frank E. Data Mining: practical machine learning tools and techniques, San Francisco: Elsevier, 2005.

20

Data Mining in Personalized Speech Disorder Therapy Optimisation

Danubianu Mirela, Tobolcea Iolanda and Stefan Gheorghe Pentiuc
"Stefan cel Mare" University of Suceava,
"A.I. Cuza" University of Iasi,
"Stefan cel Mare" University of Suceava,
Romania

1. Introduction

In the context of the Sustainable Development Strategy adopted by the European Council in 2006, one of the key challenges is related to public health, whose general objective envisages a good level of public health. In order to accomplish that, one of the specific targets includes better treatments of diseases. It is true that there are affections which by their nature do not endanger the life of a person however they may have a negative impact on the quality of life. Various language or speech disorders are part of this category, because language is the most common mean of interpersonal communication. It enables the transfer content from one person to another and also performs an important cognitive function of integration, design and conceptualization of thinking. Language enables an individual to live in community, it offers them the opportunity to demonstrate their qualities and to adapt to different situations. This kind of impairments affects a considerable percentage of people, most of them being children, but if they are discovered and treated in time, they can be often corrected.

The logopaedic intervention proposes some specific objectives such as detection, complex assessment and identification of language and communication disorders of pre-school and young school children and targeting logopaedic therapy to correct, recovery, compensation, adaptation and social integration. This last goal involves the application of a personalized therapy to each child or group of children with similar characteristics, therapy adjusted according to their disease severity and directed towards eliminating the causes that has generated the speech impairment.

Information technology is used by specialists in order to assist and supervise speech disorder therapy. Consequently they have collected a considerable volume of data about the personal or familial anamnesis, regarding various disorders or regarding the process of personalized therapies. These data can be used in data mining processes that aim to discover interesting patterns which can help the design and adaptation of different therapies in order to obtain the best results in conditions of maximum efficiency.

Data mining involves the application of analysis on large volumes of data using algorithms which, at acceptable efficiency of calculation, produce a particular enumeration of patterns from such data. As an exploration and analysis technique of large amounts of data in order to detect patterns or rules with a specific meaning, from apparently unrelated data, data mining may help discover relationships that can anticipate future problems or might solve the studied problems.

According to the logopaedic activity the tasks performed by data mining can be grouped into the following categories: classification, clustering and association rules.

The aim of this chapter is to present some aspects regarding the possibility of applying data mining techniques in order to optimize the personalized therapy of speech disorders, in particular the therapy of dyslalia, and to present a data mining system designed for this purpose.

2. What are speech disorders?

2.1 Speech disorders and their implication in the individual's social life

Language is of outmost importance to each individual's mind and personality structuring, as it is a means of human communication, education and child development, of the understanding and creating of specific human relationships.

Most children have no speech difficulties; they prove fluency, expressivity and the communication is pleasant and attractive. Others, on the contrary, have difficulties when they wish to express their thoughts in words. Although they make great efforts, their speech is incorrect, altered, in more serious cases it becomes stammered or dyslalic, this creating an uncomfortable feeling, an overwhelming complex of inferiority. As a result, these children back away, "close the doors" to the ones around them, they isolate themselves from the group, as their deficient language doesn't allow them to establish good interpersonal relationships needed for good communication purposes.

So, speech disorders may be defined as a problem with fluency, voice, and/or how a person utters speech sounds. These may have different causes, from organic to functional, neurological or psycho-social causes.

Dyslalia is articulation disorder that consists in difficulties with the way sounds are formed and strung together. These are usually characterized by omitting, distorting a sound or substituting one sound for another. Dyslalia has the greatest frequency among handicaps of language for psychological normal subjects as well as for those with deficiencies of intellect and sensory.

The prevention and treatment of speech disorders is a complex issue, stirring the interest of speech therapists, as well as to those asked to contribute to the children's language education. Early treatment of speech impairments ensures improved efficiency, as psycholinguistic automatisms are not consolidated in young children, and through adequate educational interventions, they can be replaced by correct speech acts. Treating speech disorders prevents school or society failure for the child. This process also involves child therapy in his/her ordinary life style, involving family, parents and school.

Differential diagnosis will decide upon the therapy for correcting language as psycho diagnosis allows an adequate therapeutic program and the elaboration of a prognosis regarding the evolution of the child, along with the therapeutic process. The therapy has to be adapted to each language therapist, to each particular case, to the child's learning rhythm and style, as well as to the level of the impairment. Due to the complexity of the possible problems involved, the therapeutic methods will vary significantly, from analysis, synthesis to global therapeutic specific methods and techniques. This is why, a good knowledge of all these methods will allow therapists to pick the best ones for a specific case. Therapy stages are to be followed in a specific order, regardless of the methods, according to each child's psychosomatic structure. The therapy starts with the involved psychological processes (cognitive, psychometric and affective-emotional) and it is build on stages, moments and concrete objectives, materialized in specific therapeutic techniques. The techniques materialize in exercises and procedures which the child has to perform in order to achieve the final aim: a correct speech act.

2.2 Information and communication technology in speech disorders therapy practices

Information and Communication Technology (ICT) can help persons whose physical conditions make communication difficult and can be used in speech therapy as a real clinical tool. The technical means can be used in combination with the speech therapist's clinical competences in order to help their patients, orienting the evaluation, the treatment and the constant feedback in a more flexible and modern way.

Computers can help in diagnosing the speech disorders, can produce audio-visual feedback during the treatment and monitor and evaluate the therapeutic progress. Also, they provide some sets of practical exercises for the patients who are not under the direct supervision of a speech therapist.

The use of Computer Based Speech Therapy (CBST) systems for speech therapy creates a new psychological and pedagogic situation, a special learning environment, by facilitating a superior method for information recovery. The children's interest in the therapeutic activity is cultivated by the enrichment of the material resources as a support for an efficient and rapid learning by using new tools of information and communication technology. The computer supports the children's curiosity for knowledge acquisition by giving new and rich information that can be provided in their natural dynamics. This fact, also increases the children's motivation for learning.

Consequently, there are some advantages of using the CBST , such as: the possibility to detect aspects impossible or difficult to realize by other means and to separate or recompose phenomena that are imperceptible by other means; the capacity to accurately playback the content and allow immediate playback of the information or as often as necessary and last but not least the appeal it has for children due to the original aspects involved, as well as to the aesthetic way of presenting the information.

To conclude, there are more arguments supporting the use of ICT for increasing the efficiency of speech therapy. Firstly, there is the possibility to record the verbal material, in order to provide that "language immersion" necessary for acquiring correct pronunciation. These records constitute tools of self-control of the errors made and the progress achieved, enabling the child to hear and to judge himself/herself from the outside.

For the speech therapist, a CBST constitutes a tool for controlling and evaluating the efficiency of the proposed strategy, helping to adapt the therapeutic schema. It is also an important aid for the therapist in the analysis of the speech therapy steps, the responses received from the patients, managing to appreciate the efficiency of the methods, the means used in reaching the established goal.

A CBST can develop the logical thinking of the children and their affectivity, it can create a pleasant, relaxed, and attractive climate, increasing the efficiency of the therapy.

Finally, a CBST constitutes the most complex method that comprises the audio-visual techniques. Its great advantage consists in realizing some educational and instructive software programs; it helps and increases the efficiency of the didactic activity.

Recently, a therapeutic software useful for correcting various speech disorders has been elaborated. Some programs are simple and produce a single type of visual and auditory feedback, while others are extremely complex, allowing a sustained training, realized for several aspects of speech.`

There are some international projects whose priorities are represented by developing information systems that will allow the elaboration of personalized therapeutically paths.

The OLP (Ortho-Logo-Paedia) project (OLP 2002) for speech therapy started in 2002; the project is financed by the EU and it is a complex project, involving the Institute for Language and Speech Processing in Athens and seven other partners from the academia and medical domains. It aims to accomplish a three - module system (OPTACIA, GRIFOS and TELEMACHOS) capable of interactively instructing the children suffering from dysarthria (difficulty in articulating words due to disease of the central nervous system). The proposed interactive environment is a visual one and is adapted to the subjects' age (games, animations). The audio and video interface with the human subject will be the OPTACIA module, the GRIFOS module will make pronunciation recognition and the computer aided instruction will be integrated in the third module - TELEMACHOS.

An interesting project is STAR - Speech Training, Assessment, and Remediation (STAR 2002), started in 2002, a project which is still in the development phase. The members (AI. duPont Hospital for Children and The University of Delaware) aim to build a system that would initially recognize phonemes and then sentences. This research group offers a voice generation system (ModelTalker) and other open source applications for audio processing.

Speechviewer III developped by IBM (Speechviewer III) creates an interactive visual model of speech while users practice several speech aspects (e.g. the sound voice or special aspects from current speech).

The ICATIANI device developed by TLATOA Speech Processing Group, CENTIA Universidad de las Américas, Puebla Cholula, Pue. México uses sounds and graphics in order to ensure the practice of Spanish Mexican pronunciation. Each lesson explains sounds pronunciation using the facial expression with a particular accent on specifying articulation points and the position of the lips. The system includes several animated faces, each of them showing the correct method of vocal pronunciation and providing feedback to the child answers. In this case, if the child's pronunciation matches the system one, the child is rewarded by a smile or otherwise warned by a sad face.

The information systems with real time feedback that address pathological speech impairments are relatively recent due firstly to the amount of processing power they require. The progress in computer science allows at the moment for the development of such a system with low risk factors. Children pronunciation is also used to enrich the existing audio database and to improve the current diagnosis system's performances.

The personalized therapy system of dyslalia for Romanian language - TERAPERS was developed within the Center for Computer Research in the University "Stefan cel Mare" of Suceava (Danubianu & al, 2009, a). This project aims to develop a system which is able to assist teachers in their speech therapy of dyslalia and to follow how the patients respond to various personalized therapy programs.

It has reached some specific objectives (Danubianu & al 2009, a) such as: initial and ongoing therapy evaluation of children and identification of a modality for standardizing their progresses and regresses (at the level of the physiological and behavioral parameters); the development of an expert system for the personalized therapy of speech impairments that allows designing a training path for pronunciation, individualized according to the speech disorder category, the previous experience and evolution of the child's therapy; the

development of a therapeutically guide that allows mixing classical methods with the adjuvant procedures of the audio-visual system and the design and the achievement of a database that contains the child's data, the set of exercises and the results obtained by the child.
The system contains two main components as is presented in Figure 1: an intelligent system installed on each office computer of the speech therapists and a mobile system used as a friend for the child therapy. The two systems are connected (Danubianu &al, 2009, a).

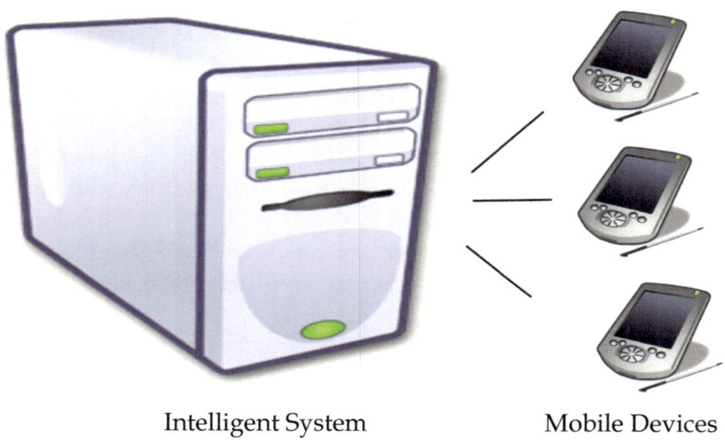

Fig. 1. TERAPERS Architecture

The intelligent system is the fix component of the system installed on each speech therapist's office computer. This system includes the following parts:
- an evaluation module of the children's progress;
- an expert system that will produce inferences based on the data presented by the evaluation module;
- a virtual module of the mouth, that would allow the presentation of every hidden move that occur in speaking,

The main stream activities of the intelligent system from TERAPERS are presented in Figure 2. All these activities are materialized in a consistent volume of data stored in a relational database (Danubianu &al, 2009, a).

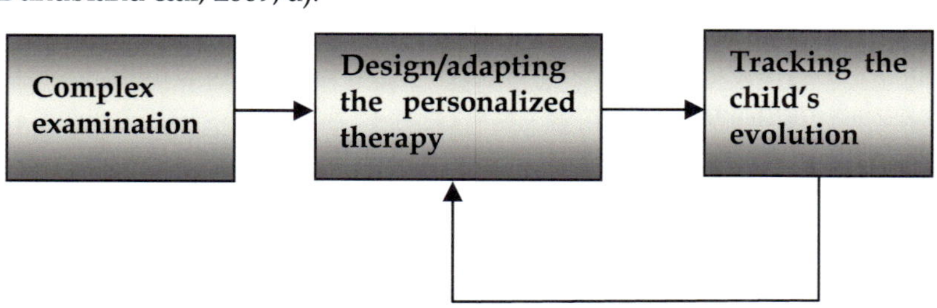

Fig. 2. The functional schema of the intelligent system of TERAPERS

Starting from a complex examination of the child, mainly related to the way he/she articulates phonemes in different construction, speech therapists can establish a diagnosis. Based on this diagnosis a personalized therapy program is designed. During the therapy the initial program can be modified and adapted to the child's current needs and evolution.

The mobile device has two main objectives. It is used by the child in order to resolve the homework prescribed by the speech therapist and delivers to the intelligent system a personalized activity report of the child.

3. Knowledge discovery in databases and data mining

3.1 Knowledge discovery in databases

Knowledge Discovery in Databases (KDD) has emerged as a consequence of the huge volumes of data, resulted from the technological progress, that we witnessed in the last years. These data collections have lead to a paradox generated by the fact that, although there was a lot of data, the information extracted from these data was poor.
The Knowledge Discovery in Databases was defined as the process of identifying valid, novel, potentially useful, and understandable patterns in data.
The process may be generalized to nondatabase sources of data, although it emphasizes databases as a primary source of data. (Cios & al. 2007)
Knowledge Discovery in Databases involves an interactive and iterative sequence of steps. An important objective, for which one spent considerable efforts was related to the establishment of a process model.
The first model for Knowledge Discovery in Databases has been developed in academia by Fayyad et al. but it was used in various domains, including engineering, medicine, e-business, or software development. It consists of nine steps, which are listed as follows: developing and understanding the application domain, creating a target data set, data cleaning and pre-processing, data reduction and projection, choosing the data mining task, choosing the data mining algorithm, data mining, interpreting mined patterns and consolidating discovered knowledge.
The academic models were quickly followed by some industrial models. The most representative is the six-step CRISP-DM model, developed by a large consortium of European companies, which has become the leading industrial model.
The CRISP-DM model, presented in Figure 3, consists of the following six steps: business understanding, data understanding, data preparation, modeling, evaluation of the model and deployment (Chapman & al, 2000).
Business understanding is the first phase of the KDD process that focuses on understanding the project objectives and requirements from the business perspective. There are some tasks to do. First the data analyst must understand, from the business perspective what the client want to realize. Even if there are many objective and constraints, they must be properly balanced. It is also important to describe the criteria for a useful outcome of the project from the business point of view. Secondly, the analyst must assess the situation regarding the resources, constraints or other facts that should be taken into consideration to make a good project plan. After that, the data mining goal must be determined. A such data mining goal might be "Find the optimal personalized therapy for the patient with the following characteristics….". The result of this phase is a project plan.
Data understanding consist of initial data collection, data describing and assessing and verifying data quality. Initial collection may include data loading where necessary, into a specific tool for data understanding. This action might require some initial data preparation operation. If the data come from multiple sources the integration must be done. In conjunction with data collection this phase offer a data description that refers to the format

of the data and its volume measured in number of records and fields for each table. Finally the data quality must be examined. To achieve this it should answer some questions such as:

- Is the data complete?
- Is the data correct or does it contain errors?
- Does the data contain any missing values?

Data preparation aims to build the final data set from the initial raw data. Tasks specific to this phase contain table, record and attribute selection and transformation and cleaning data for modelling tools. In the selection step we decide which data to use for the analysis, based on criteria such as: relevance to the data mining goals, quality and limits on data volumes or data type. The cleaning data step involves the selection of clean subsets of the data or the insertion of proper values where they are missing, and its aim is to improve the data quality to the of analysts' requirements. Other data preparation operation refers to the production of derived attributes, the transformation of values for existing attributes and data integration. Sometimes it is necessary to format data as the modeling tool requires.

The next phase, when the model is build by various modeling techniques is called modeling. This phase is the core of the knowledge discovery process. The first step in this phase select the technique to be used. Then it is necessary to generate a procedure to test the model's quality. The model is created by running the modeling tool on the prepared data set. The last step of this phase is related to the assessment of the model. Now, the data mining specialist interprets the model according to the domain of knowledge.

Evaluation of the model consists of three steps: evaluation of results, reviewing of the process and determining the next steps. In this phase, evaluation of results aims to asses if the model meets the business objectives and what are the business reasons that may explain the model's efficiency. Even if the model is satisfactory it is advisable to review the whole process in order to see if there is a task that has been overlooked. Then, according to the assessment results and process review, the expert must decide whether the project is proper for deployment or it is necessary to initiate further iterations.

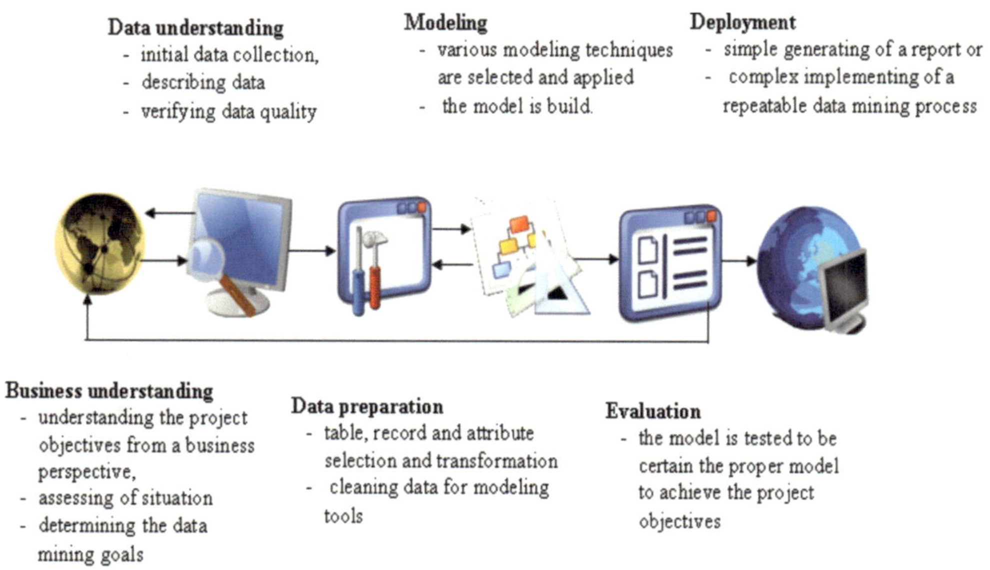

Fig. 3. CRISP-DM model for KDD process (Danubianu & al, 2010)

The last phase of the KDD process is deployment. This task considers the evaluation results in order to deploy the data mining results into the business and to establish a strategy for deployment. The first outcome of this step is a deployment plan. Then, if the model obtained from data mining phase become a part of business, it is important to design a monitoring and maintenance plan. At the end of the project, depending on the deployment plan, a final report is elaborated. This final report may be a summary of the project or a presentation of the data mining results. As part of this step may consist in assessing what was done well in the project and what needs to be improved.
Looking at the models presented above one can observe that both of them contains a step (called data mining in the Fayyad model and modeling in the CRISP-DM model) that applies different methods and algorithms in order to discover new patterns.

3.2 Data mining

Data mining involves the application of analysis on large volumes of data using algorithms which produce a particular enumeration of patterns from such data.
Data mining may facilitate the discovery from apparently unrelated data, relationships that can anticipate future problems or might solve the studied problems. So, data mining is defined as the operation of extracting the interesting and previously unknown information and represents one phase in the complex process of Knowledge Discovery in Databases.
Data mining solve problems which can be divided into two general categories: prediction and knowledge discovery (or description). Even prediction is the main goal of data mining, it is often preceeded by description. For example, in a health care application for a disease recognition, which belongs to predictive data mining, we must mine the database for a set of rules that describes the diagnosis knowledge, and this knowledge is further used for the prediction of the disease when a new patient comes in.
Each of these two problems has some associated methods. For prediction we can use classification or regression while for knowledge discovery we can use deviation detection, clustering, association rules, database segmentation or visualization.
Data classification is a supervised learning method which consists in a two-step process. First, by analyzing database tuples described by attributes a model is built. It describes a predetermined set of data classes or concepts. Each tuple is assumed to belong to a predefined class, as determined by one of the attributes, called the class label attribute. The data set analyzed to build the model form the training data set. In the second step, the model is used for classification. Before that, it is necessary to estimate the predictive accuracy. The simplest technique for this use a test set of class labelled samples, independent of the training set, and randomly selected from the whole data set. The accuracy of the model on a data test set is calculated as the percentage of test set sample that are correctly classified by the model previously build. To find this percentage, for each test sample, the known class is compared with the model's class prediction for that sample.
If the accuracy is acceptable the model can be used for classifying future data tuples for which the class label is not known. The various classification methods can be compared and evaluated according more criteria, such as: predictive accuracy, speed, robustness, scalability and interpretability. (Han & Kamber, 2000)
Whereas classification determines the set membership of the samples, the prediction of continuous values can be modeled by *regression*. In this case model design consists of finding a structure for it, on computing an optimal value for its parameters and assessing

the model quality. The model structure relates the type of mathematical formula that describes the system behavior. Depending on the model structure, regression models may be categorized as follows: simple linear regression, multiple linear regression, polynomial regression, logistic regression or nonlinear regression.

We can also distinguish between static and dynamic models. Static models produce outcomes based only on the current input, whereas dynamic models produce outcomes based on the current input and the past history of the model behavior.

Clustering, often referred to as unsupervised learning, involve a process that discovers structures in data without any supervision. As the name clustering implies, unsupervised algorithm is capable of discovering structures on its own by exploiting similarities or differences between individual data points on a data set.

There are a lot of strategies for clustering formation, and many approaches try to determine what similarities between data mean.

Clustering techniques can be divided into three main categories: partition, hierarchical clustering and model based clustering. For each of these categories, the clustering principles are different because they use different ways of processing and formatting the results.

Partition based clustering methods use objective functions whose minimisation is supposed to lead to the discovery of the structure existing in the data set. This category of methods works with a predefined number of clusters and proceeds to the optimisation of the objective function. There are some variants in which successive splits of the clusters are allowed. In this case we have a dynamically adjusted number of clusters.

The successive development of clusters is the idea of hierarchical clustering. We can start with a single cluster that is the entire data set successively divided or we can start with individual points treated as initial clusters which are merged and form new clusters. The last way of forming final clusters leads to the concept of agglomeration clustering.

In model-based clustering we assume a probabilistic model of the data and then we estimate its parameters.

Association rules mining is also an important data mining method that aims to find interesting dependencies in large sets of data items. These items are often stored in transactional databases that must have a specific format. This format can be generated by an external process or can be extracted from relational databases or data warehouses. Interesting associations between data items can often lead to information used for decision making.

The algorithms used in data mining are often well-known mathematical algorithms, but in this case they are applied to large volumes of data and to general business problems. The mostly used are: statistical algorithms, neural networks, decision trees, genetic algorithms, nearest neighbor methods, rule induction and data visualization.

Statistical algorithms have been used by analysts to detect unusual patterns and explain patterns using statistical models as linear models. Such systems cannot determine the form of dependencies hidden in data and require that the user provides his own hypotheses that will be tested by the system.

One of the main statistical concepts which can be used for data mining techniques is Bayes theorem. This can be also used for implementing of more complex Knowledge Discovery in Database techniques, such Bayesian networks.

Neural networks simulate the human brain capacity to find patterns. In our acceptation a neural network is a set of connected inputs/outputs where each connection has an

associated weight. For this reason neural network learning is also referred to as connection learning.
One of the most widespread architectures for neural network, multilayered perceptron with back propagation of errors, emulates the work of neurons incorporated in a hierarchical network. In this case the input of each neuron of the current layer is connected with the outputs of all neurons belonging to the previous layer. The data to be analyzed is treated as neuron excitation parameters and is fed to inputs of the first layer. These excitations of a layer neurons are propagated to the next layer neurons, being weakened or amplified with the weights assigned to the corresponding intraneural connection. At the end of this process a single neuron, situated at the topmost neuron layer, acquires some values considered to be a prediction.
Neural networks involve long training periods and require a number of parameters which are determined empirically. One of these parameters may be the network topology. Some of the neural network advantages include their tolerance to noisy data, as well as their ability to classify patterns on which they have not been trained, but their critics underline their poor interpretability, since it is difficult to interpret the symbolic meaning behind the learned weights. So, a major disadvantage of neural networks consists in their Knowledge representation.
Decision trees can be applied for classification or clustering tasks. If we have a heterogeneous data collection and a set of attributes that describe the data, decision trees aim to divide the data set into smaller, more homogeneous subsets, using the values of the attributes selected. There are several techniques for constructing or modeling the trees, referred to as decision-tree based algorithms which aim to minimize the size of the tree while maximizing the accuracy of the classification.
Genetic algorithms are based on the principles of natural evolution. They use terminology and concepts analogous to those used in biology. For example, genetic algorithms encode each point in a solution space into a string called chromosome. The features in this string are genes and their position in the string is called locus. During the execution of genetic algorithms samples evolve similar to the natural evolution process to provide optimal solutions. In data mining this kind of algorithms can be used for prediction, clustering and association rules inference.

4. Application of data mining techniques in speech disorders therapy area

The tasks performed by data mining and related to speech therapy activity can be grouped into the following categories:

- classification which aims to place the people with different speech impairments in predefined classes. It is a possibility of tracking the size and structure of various groups of patients. Classification is based on the information contained in many predictor variables, such as personal or familial anamnesis data or related to lifestyle, to join the patients with different classes.
- if there are no predefined classes we can group people with speech disorders on the basis of similarity of different features by clustering, It is an important task which helps the therapists understand who they patients are. Clustering aims to find subsets of a predetermined segment, with homogeneous behavior towards various methods of therapy that can be effectively targeted by a specific therapy.

- association rules which find out associations between different data which seems to have no semantic dependence. An important task of the association is to determine why a specific therapy program has been successful on a segment of patients with speech disorders while on the other it was ineffective.

From the above, we may conclude that data mining can be a useful tool. Nevertheless, there is a limitation. Data mining applications generate information by analyzing patterns of data obtained from the systems which assist and supervise the speech therapy. Such patterns can help to predict the evolution of the individuals that are currently in the process of therapy, or to design a scheme of appropriate therapy for them. However data mining technology can not provide information about impairments, people or behaviors that are not found in the databases that provide data for analysis.

5. Logo-DM system

5.1 System objectives

A considerable volume of data was collected by the researchers due to the development and use of information technology in order to assist speech disorder therapy. Increased volume of data available did not lead immediately to a similar volume of information to support the decisions of effective therapy, because the classical methods of data processing are not applicable in such cases.

We think these data can be the foundation of data mining processes that show interesting information for the design and adaptation of different therapies in order to obtain the best results in conditions of maximum efficiency.

The idea of trying to improve the quality of logopaedic therapy by applying some data mining techniques started from the TERAPERS project developed within the Center for Computer Research of "Stefan cel Mare" University of Suceava (Danubianu & al, 2009,a). The data collected in this system together with data from other sources (e.g. demographic data, medical or psychological research) may be the set of raw data that will be the subject of data mining. This is why we have proposed the development of the Logo-DM system.

Currently, economic needs require correct answers to questions such as the following

- how is the estimated duration of therapy for a particular case?,
- what is the predicted final state for a child or what will be its state at the end of various stages of therapy?,
- what are the best exercises for each case and how can they dose their effort to effectively solve these exercises?,
- how is family receptivity associated - which is an important factor for a successful of the therapy - with other aspects of family and personal anamnesis?

All this may be the subject of predictions obtained by applying data mining techniques on data collected by using TERAPERS. It is also interesting, as part of the knowledge discovered by data mining algorithms, to use it to enrich the knowledge base of the expert system embedded in TERAPERS.

Consequently, the Logo-DM system aims to optimize the personalized therapy of dyslalia for pre-school and young school children using data mining techniques. By implementing classification, clustering and association rules algorithms we can:

- group the patients in clusters with similar characteristics regarding diagnosis and its severity and anamnesis data (e.g. family and personal history);

- associate groups with general therapy schema which will then be customized for subgroups or individual;
- prediction of intermediate states and final status of new patients by placing them in a class labeled S (stationary), A (improved) or C (corrected).

5.2 Overview of the logo-DM data mining process

As we have previously mentioned, the main source of data for the Logo-DM system is the data collected in TERAPERS database. We have also presented the main stream of TERAPERS activities in Figure 2. All these activities are materialized in the data stored in a relational database.

To build personalized therapy programs speech therapists need a complex examination for the children. They should also make record of relevant data related to personal and family anamnesis. Analysis of how children articulate phonemes in various constructions allows diagnosis and classification in a certain class of severity of speech disorder. The collection of anamnesis data may provide information related to various causes that may negatively influence the normal development of the language. It contains historical data and data provided by the cognitive and personality examination.

The applied personalized therapy programs request data such as number of sessions/week, exercises for each phase of therapy and changes of the original program according to the patient's evolution. In addition, the report downloaded from the mobile device collects data on the efforts of child self-employment. These data refer to the exercises done, the number of repetitions for each of these exercises and the results obtained.

The estimation of the child's progress materializes data which indicate the moment of assessing the child and his/her status at that time.

Figure 4 partially presents the database schema which contains data collected in TERAPERS. This database, together with data from other sources (e.g. demographic data, medical or psychological research) is the set of raw data that will be the subject of data mining.

In that form, the data is not appropriate for data mining algorithms, so Figure 5 presents the complete sequence of the operations applied, according to the CRISP-DM model, in order to transform them from raw data into useful knowledge.

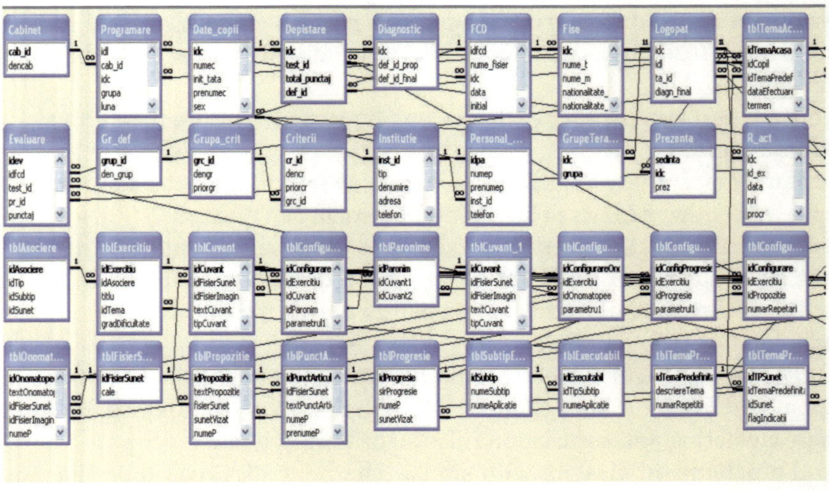

Fig. 4. The TERAPERS Database Schema

As illustrated above and according to Figure 5 the main data source for Logo-DM is a relational database. To avoid actualization anomalies, this database is characterized by a high degree of normalization so various features, potentially useful for data mining are placed in different tables

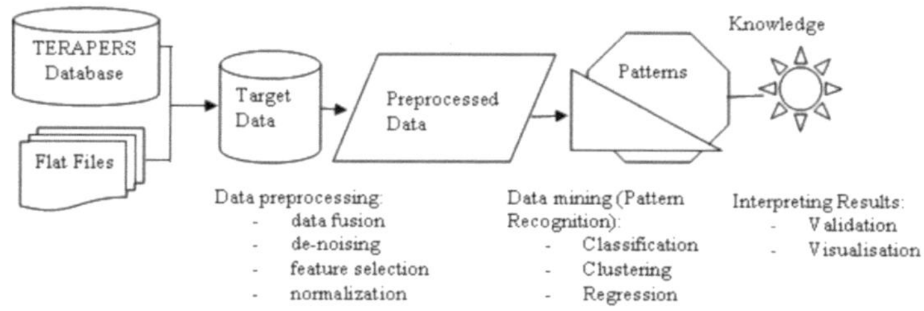

Fig. 5. LOGO-DM view of the end to end data mining process (Danubianu & al, 2009, b)

If we make a system final goals analysis combined with a data analyze we conclude that we need to work only with tables that contain data regarding the children anamnesys and complex logopaedic examination, data regarding different types of speech or language disorders, tests and assessment trials of each test, data regarding the personalized therapy content and management. So, as a first step in data preprocessing is to eliminate those tables which do not contains such data. Thus we achieve a significant decrease in the number of tales used, from 60 to 24. Here we have a superset of necessary data for data mining.

For building and managing of the TERAPERS database we have used Microsoft Access because is cheap and easy to use.

After analyzing the available technologies, it was concluded that the effective implementation of the Logo-DM system can be made with a database management system which entails multi-user, increased security and, last but not least, provide facility for analysis and implement data mining algorithms. We consider that Oracle meets these conditions.

In this context a problem which must be solved is the one concerning the migration of data from MS Access to Oracle. We have done that by using Oracle SQL Developer Migration Workbench. To migrate date it is necessary to cover four steps: capturing the database source, converting the database capture, generating the Oracle database and migrating data.

After data migration from MS Access a series of modifications were required on data types. For example, a data type subject to conversion, is "Date and Timestamp".

The analysis of the database content can reveal interesting issues related to data quality or the need for transformation. We have made a first assessment of data quality through the following measures: completeness, conformity, accuracy, consistency and redundancy. The mechanisms provided by the used database management system have imposed a minimum, controlled redundancy and have assured data consistency. The values were stored in the fields correspond to reality, but unfortunately useful data for analysis are missing from some records. Therefore it is necessary to supplement data gaps, and if this is not possible, the removal of the record for accurate results is suggested.

To obtain proper data for the analysis we should make the following types of transformation: transformations of the structure, and changes aimed at value.

Structural transformations are dictated by the fact that there are fields in the database containing data related to a complex of features to be addressed individually in the analysis.

Value transformation refers to the replacement of coded data by the rules, enabling, for example, the effective storage with descriptive values of characteristics allowing rapid interpretation of results.

An important operation required in this stage is filling the data gaps. We found that, due to the fact that in the TERAPERS database schema some fields values are not restricted to *not null*, these values are partially filled. They should be filled automatically or if this is not possible manually. It is a problem that can be solved in time by setting those fields that have relevance for analysis and by configuring them as *not null* in data sources tables.

Creating target data set is accomplished through joined tables containing useful features followed by a projection on a superset of appropriate attributes, as shown in (1)

$$\Pi_{I_i}(T_1 \rhd\lhd T_2 \rhd\lhd \ldots \rhd\lhd T_k) \tag{1}$$

where: I_i is a superset of the attributes regarding the useful characteristics

$T_1 \ldots T_k$ is the set of tables containing the attributes in the list of projection.

For example, target data set necessary to establish the profile of children with speech disorders, can be obtained by joining tables which contain: general data about children, family and personal anamnesis, data on complex evaluation and associated diagnosis. The result is a set of 129 features. The statement that performs that is presented in (2)

```
create table caract_copii as
    select f.*, l.diagn_final
        from fise f, logopat l                                    (2)
        where f.idc=l.idc;
```

Data mining techniques were not designed to process large amounts of irrelevant features. Consequently before their application, a selection of the relevant features is required (Guyon & Elisseeff 2003) (Liu & Motoda, 1998). The most important objectives of feature selection are: to avoid over fitting and improve model performance.

Concretely, in the feature selection problem, we are given a fixed set of candidate features for use for building a model, and we must select a subset that will be used to train the model that is "as good as possible" according to some criterion.

We have used for feature selection a variant of the mRMR method (Peng & al, 2005) for categorical values. It is based on mutual information criteria, formally defined, for two discrete random variables *X* and *Y*, as:

$$I(X;Y) = \sum_{y\in Y}\sum_{x\in X} p(x,y)\log\left(\frac{p(x,y)}{p_1(x)p_2(y)}\right) \tag{3}$$

where $p(x,y)$ is joint probability distribution function of X and Y, and $p_1(x)$ and $p_2(y)$ are the marginal probability distribution functions of X and Y respectively.

For discrete random variable, the joint probability mass function is:

$$p(x,y) = p(X=x, Y=y) = p(Y=y \mid X=x)^{*} p(X=x)$$

$$= p(X=x \mid Y=y)^{*} p(Y=y) \tag{4}$$

Since these are probabilities, we have

$$\sum_x \sum_y p(X = x, Y = y) = 1 \tag{5}$$

The marginal probability function, p ($X = x$) is:

$$p(X = x) = \sum_y p(X = x, Y = y) = \sum_y p(X = x \mid Y = y) p(Y = y) \tag{6}$$

The criterion used is related to minimizing redundancy and maximizing relevance for the chosen characteristics.
The result of the tests performed on data collected from TERAPERS and prepared as described in the above mentioned example revealed that for classification, the minimum error is obtained if we deal with a number ranging from 50 and 55 features selected out of 129.
The target data set, obtained after these steps, is subject to data mining algorithms. For an effective implementation of algorithms we have taken into account, and tested, two possibilities: the use of the Oracle Data Mining kernel (ODM) which offers the possibility to apply algorithms for classification, clustering and association rules and the use of some open source implementations of relevant algorithms adapted and integrated into our own system.
We took into account the types of data included in the set and we used implementations in Oracle of Adaptive Bayes Network, Seeker Model and decision trees build with CART and ID3/C4.5 for classification, in order to cluster the Oracle implementation of A-Clustering algorithm and for association rules Apriori algorithm.

5.3 System architecture

Data mining aims to derive knowledge from data. The architecture of a data mining system plays an important role in the efficiency of data mining.
Data mining systems must satisfy the following requirements:

- not limit the size of the dataset;
- performance optimization should be done for large data sets;
- architecture must serve as a flexible support for various data mining techniques and algorithms such as classification, clustering or association rules;
- they must support the specific priorities of the user or groups of users and they must have the ability to manage concurrent sessions of data mining;
- they should allow a total control of data access;
- they should provide remote administration and maintenance.

The basic components of a data mining system are: user interface, specific data mining services, access services and the data itself.
User interface allows the user to select and prepare data sets on which to apply the data mining techniques. Formatting and presentation of data mining results is also an important task for the user interface. Data mining services comprise all components of a system that processes a special algorithm for data mining, for example the discovery of association rules. These components access data through data access service and can be optimized for certain database management systems, or provide a standard interface such as ODBC. Data is the fourth component of the data mining system. These four components are present in all data

mining systems. In practice there are three different architectures, where these components are distributed on different levels. These are: the one level architecture, the two levels architecture and the most complex architecture is on three levels.
Considering the characteristic of the domain we have proposed for the system a two levels client server architecture. This architecture is presented in Figure 6.
On the client side there is the user interface (GUI) which allows the user to communicate with the system in order to select the task to perform, to select and submit the datasets on which data mining needs to be applied. Pattern evaluation and the post-processing step consisting in pattern visualization are also performed on the client. The knowledge base is the module where the background knowledge is stored.
The more difficult computational tasks of data mining operations are carried out on the server. Here, the data mining kernel contains modules able to perform classifications, clustering and association rule detection. Supplementary the pre-processing data module allows data to become suitable for applying data mining algorithms.

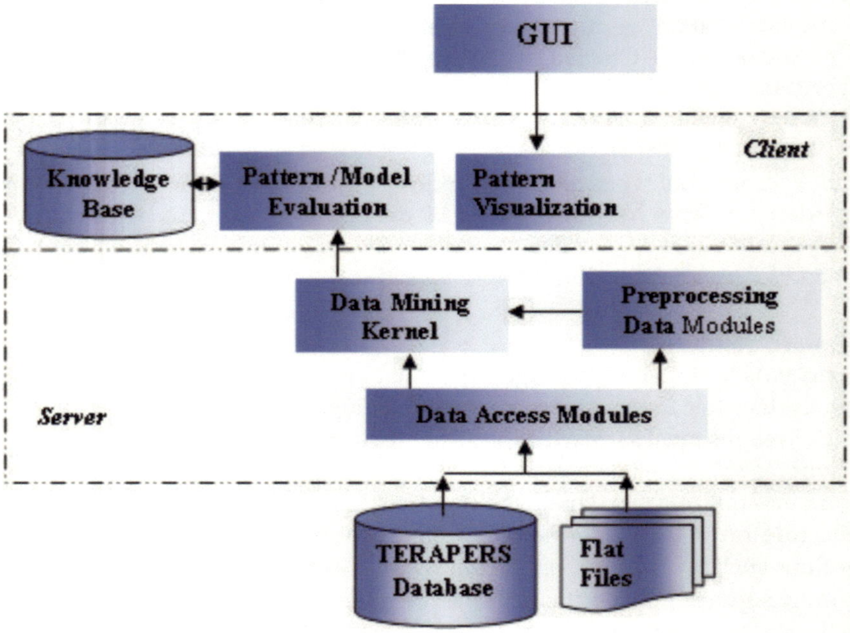

Fig. 6. Logo-DM Architecture (Danubianu &al, 2010)

6. Experimental results

Although the TERAPERS system, which is the main source of data for Logo-DM is used since September 2008, the volume of data which are available to data mining algorithms is still quite low. However we have obtained good results in predicting a patient's status, considering certain characteristics, in different phases of therapy.
Table 1 presents a comparison between the prediction obtained by using the Logo-DM system on the status of a group of 25 children with various forms of dyslalia (rhotacism, polymorphic dyslalia) and the real state of these children, assessed by the therapists at the end of the first two stages of speech therapy.

Patient's state	At the end of the first stage of therapy		At the end of the second stage of therapy	
	Predicted	Real	Predicted	Real
Stationary (S)	1	1	0	1
Improved (A)	24	23	22	23
Corrected (C)	0	1	3	1

Table 1. Results of prediction made by Logo-DM

7. Conclusion

Data mining technology can be a useful tool for the speech disorder therapy because it is able to provide information that enables the implementation of personalized therapy programs optimized and adapted to the characteristics of each child. This leads to a decreased duration of therapy, increasing the possibilities of achieving superior results and ultimately to lower cost of therapy.

Considering the opportunity of data mining techniques application on data collected in the process of speech therapy, we have concluded that methods such as classification, clustering or association rules can provide useful information for a more efficient therapy. Consequently, we have designed and we are currently implementing a data mining system that aims to use data provided by TERAPERS system, developed by the Research Center for Computer Science of "Stefan cel Mare" University of Suceava , in order to optimize the personalized therapy of dyslalia.

We have tested the modules for data pre-processing and on target data sets obtained from these modules, and we have applied more algorithms for detecting the most appropriate solutions for the data mining kernel.

We have obtained good results regarding the prediction of the future state of a new patient.

At present our efforts are directed towards the implementation of visualization modules and towards building a user friendly interface.

8. References

Chapman P., Clinton J., Kerber R., Khabaza T.,Reinartz T.,Shearer C., Wirth R.,(2000) *CRISP-DM 1.0. Step by step data mining guide*, 2000, Crisp-DM Consortium

Cios K., Pedrycz W., Swiniarski R., Kurgan L. (2007) *Data Mining. A Knowledge Discovery Approach*, Springer Science-Business Media, ISBN 978-0-387-33333-5, New York

Danubianu M., Pentiuc St.Gh., Schipor O., Nestor M., Ungurean I., Schipor D.M.,(2009), TERAPERS - Intelligent Solution for Personalized Therapy of Speech Disorders, *International Journal on Advances in Life Science*, Vol. 1, No. 1, 2009, p.26-35, ISSN: 1942-2660

Danubianu M., Pentiuc St. Gh., Socaciu T. (2009) Towards the Optimized Personalized Therapy of Speech Disorders by Data Mining Techniques, *Proceedings of The Fourth International Multi Conference on Computing in the Global Information Technology ICCGI* 2009, pp. 1-6, ISSN/ISBN 978-0-7695-3751-1, France, 23-29 August, Cannes - La Bocca, IEEE Computer Society Conference Publishing Services

Danubianu M., Pentiuc St.Gh., Tobolcea I, (2010) Advanced Information Technology-Support of Improved Personalized Therapy of Speech Disorders, *Proceedings of*

*International Conference on Computers, Communications & Control, ICCCC 2010,*Romania, May 12-16, 2008, Baile Felix

Guyon I., Elisseeff A.,(2003) *An introduction to variable and feature selection*. J. Mach Learn Res., 3, p.1157–1182, 2003

Han J, Kamber M., (2000), *Data Mining Concepts and Techniques,* Morgan Kaufmann Publishers, 2000

Liu H., Motoda H. (1998) *Feature Selection for Knowledge Discovery and Data Mining*. Kluwer Academic Publishers, Norwell, MA, 1998

OLP Ortho-Logo-Paedia (2002) Project for Speech Therapy (http://www.xanthi.ilsp.gr/olp)

Peng H, Long F, Ding C (2005) *Feature Selection Based on Mutual Information: Criteria of Max-Dependency, Max-Relevance, and Min-Redundancy IEEE Transactions on Pattern Analysis and Machine Intelligence,* Vol. 27, No. 8, p. 1226-1238, 2005

Speechviewer III (http://www.synapseadaptive.com/edmark/prod/sv3)

STAR (2002) Speech Training, Assessment, and Remediation (http://www.asel.udel.edu/speech)

21

Data Mining Method for Energy System Aplications

Reşat Selbaş, Arzu Şencan and Ecir U. Küçüksille
Department of Mechanical Education, Technical Education Faculty, Süleyman Demirel University, Turkey

1. Introduction

In recent years, data storage capacity of computers increased as well as their speeds. With these advances in the technology, millions of data can be recorded in computer memories. These data can be used for a better service to customers by companies. For example, millions of people are shopping in supermarkets everyday. These shopping data are added to companies' records every day. Information about customers' shopping habits can be obtainede by the analysis of these data and more efficient service can be offered by companies. However, companies don't use these data efficiently. Therefore, these data stay just as records in computer memories.

"Data mining process" is a term for efficient usage of data. There are many different definitions for data mining process in literature. Data mining is a step in the KDD process that consists of applying data analysis and discovery algorithms that produce a particular enumeration of patterns (or models) over the data [1]. Data mining is an interdisciplinary field bringing together techniques from machine learning, pattern recognition, statistics, databases, and visualization to address the issue of information extraction from large databases [2]. This technology is motivated by the need of new techniques to help analyze, understand or even visualize the huge amounts of stored data gathered from business and scientific applications. It is the process of discovering interesting knowledge, such as patterns, associations, changes, anomalies and significant structures from large amounts of data stored in databases, data warehouses, or other information repositories [3].

Data mining process is used in finanel, health, communication, medicine and science fields. The most vivid example is "Amazon" web site.

Many computer programs are used for data mining processes. Some are open source and some cost money. While WEKA, Rapid Miner, Pentaho, Orange, Scriptella ETL(Extract-Transform-Load), KNIME, ELKI(Environment for DeveLoping KDD-Applications Supported by Index-Structures) programs are open source, SPSS Clementine, Sql Server Business Intelligent Studio, SAS Data Mining Software, ODM(Oracle Data Mining) Softwares cost money.

In this chapter, DM process used in the energy systems is reviewed. Available literature summaries published in this area is presented.

2. Data mining process

In Table 1, side-by-side comparison of the major existing KDDM models is shown [4].

Model	Fayad et al.	Cabena et al.	Anand&Buchner	CRISP-DM	Cios et al.	Generic Model
Area	Academic	Industrial	Academic	Industrial	Academic	N/A
No of Steps	9	5	8	6	6	6
Refs	(Fayyad et al., 1996d)	(et al., 1998)	(Anand & Buchner, 1998)	(Shearer, 2000)	(Cios et al., 2000)	N/A
Steps	1 Developing and Understanding of the Application Domain 2 Creating a Target Data Set 3 Data Cleaning and Preprocessing 4 Data Reduction and Projection 5 Choosing the DM Task 6 Choosing the DM Algorithm 7 DM 8 Interpreting Mined Patterns 9 Consolidating Discovered Knowledge	1 Business Objectives Determination 2 Data Preparation 3 DM 4 Domain Knowledge Elicitation 5 Assimilation of Knowledge	1 Human Resource Identification 2 Problem Specification 3 Data Prospecting 4 Domain Knowledge Elicitation 5 Methodology Identification 6 Data Preprocessing 7 Pattern Discovery 8 Knowledge Post-processing	1 Business Understanding 2 Data Understanding 3 Data Preparation 4 Modeling 5 Evaluation 6 Deployment	1 Understanding the Problem Domain 2 Understanding the Data 3 Preparation of the Data 4 DM 5 Evaluation of The Discovered Knowledge 6 Using the Discovered Knowledge	1 Application Domain Understanding 2 Data Understanding 3 Data Preparation and Identification of DM Technology 4 DM 5 Evaluation 6 Knowledge Consolidation and Deployment

Table 1. Side-by-side comparison of the major existing KDDM models

2.1 CRISP-DM data mining process

A systematic approach is essential to obtain satisfactory results for the DM analysis. Nowadays, a number of versions of DM tools exist. The most widespread application amongst the tools is CRISP-DM. CRISP-DM was developed by a consortium which consist the firms of NCR System Engineering (USA-Denmark), Daimler-Chrysler AG (Germany), SPSS Inc. (USA) and OHRA Verzekeringen en Bank Groep B.V (Netherlands) [5,6]. CRISP-DM is a process which defines the basic stages of DM, as can be seen from Fig. 1.

Business understanding

This initial phase focuses on understanding the project objectives and requirements from a business perspective, and then converting this knowledge into a data mining problem definition, and a preliminary project plan designed to achieve the objectives. [6, 7].

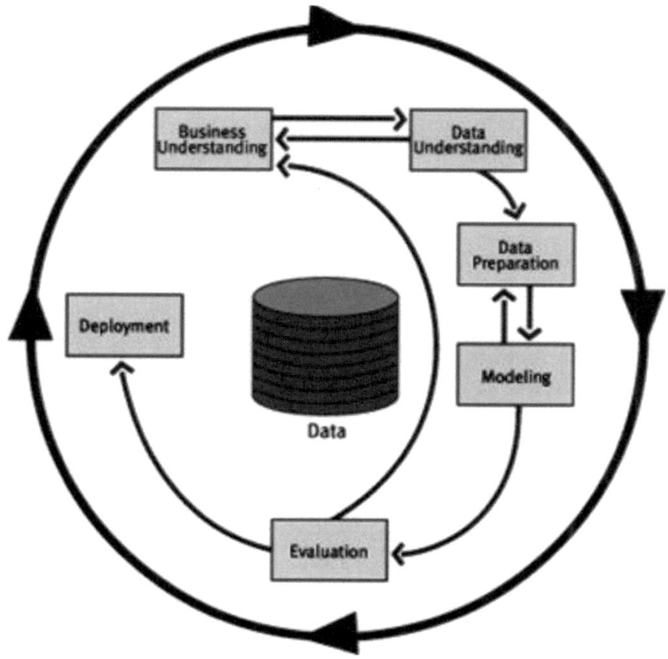

Fig. 1. CRISP-DM data mining process [5]

Data understanding

Second stage is called as the understanding of the data content. Data stored in a various environments such as Microsoft stores data in a hundred different database and 70 different data warehouses. First step is getting the meaningful data from those database or data warehouses for the selected application. In the meantime, in this phase data quality and discovering first insights into the data are seen as two important aspects.

Data preparation

The data preparation phase covers all activities to construct the final data set or the data that will be fed into the modeling tool from the initial raw data. Tasks include table, record, and attribute selection, as well as transformation and cleaning of data for modeling tools. The five steps in data preparation are the selection of data, the cleaning of data, the construction of data, the integration of data, and the formatting of data [8].

The purpose of the cleaning stage is selecting unsuitable or incorrectly entered data in the data. For example, filling the mean value for the instead of the incomplete data or erasing abnormal data records outside of the normal dispersion area assuming the meaningful data is in the normal distribution [6].

Data conversion is required for recording data in different formats or values since some data mining algorithms work only with data in digital format. In this case it needs to convert data in text format to the digital one. Purpose of the feature selection is determination of the most dominant parameters in forecasting a value. It might be assigned many features to estimate a value. However, it is not always easy to collect the determined data. For this case, by finding the effective properties data acquisition can be fast and simple. In addition, data are divided into two groups as training and testing data.

Modeling

In this phase, various modeling techniques are selected and applied and their parameters are calibrated to optimal values. Typically, several techniques exist for the same data mining problem type. Some techniques have specific requirements on the form of data. Therefore, stepping back to the data preparation phase may be necessary. Modeling steps include the selection of the modeling technique, the generation of test design, the creation of models, and the assessment of models [8]. If the task is fully accomplished, in this case, selection of the correct algorithm is much easier. Each task requires different algorithms and it is not known which one gives the best result without constructing the model. It may be only possible to guess according to the condition of the data in hand. If there is a linear relationship between whole input and estimation variables, choosing the decision tree algorithm can be good choice. If there is a complex relation among the variables, in this situation neural network algorithm can be selected [9]. Some of these algorithms are linear regression, multi layer perceptron, KStar, decision trees, K-means.

Evaluation

Before proceeding to final deployment of the model built by the data analyst, it is important to more thoroughly evaluate the model and review the model's construction to be certain it properly achieves the business objectives. Here it is critical to determine if some important business issue has not been sufficiently considered. At the end of this phase, the project leader then should decide exactly how to use the data mining results. The key steps here are the evaluation of results, the process review, and the determination of the next steps [8]. In this point, there are several tools exist. For instance, if there digital data exist for the estimation and wanted to test the accuracy of the model, RMSE (root mean square error) or $\underline{R}^2$ (correlation coefficient) can be used [6].

Deployment

Model creation is generally not the end of the project. The knowledge gained must be organized and presented in a way that the customer can use it, which often involves applying "live" models within an organization's decision-making processes [8].
Depending on the requirements, the deployment phase can be as simple as generating a report or as complex as implementing a repeatable data mining process across the enterprise. Even though it is often the customer, not the data analyst, who carries out the deployment steps, it is important for the customer to understand up front what actions must be taken in order to actually make use of the created models. The key steps here are plan deployment, plan monitoring and maintenance, the production of the final report, and review of the project [8].
Knowledge discovery uses data mining and machine learning techniques that have evolved through a synergy in artificial intelligence, computer science, statistics and other related fields [10].

3. Applications of data mining method in the energy system applications

Data mınıng method has been used by various researchers in energy system applications. This section deals with an overview of these applications. Some examples on the use of data mining method in the energy system applications are summarized in Table 2.

Area	Number of applications
Energy efficient building design	1
HVAC systems	2
Energy demand modeling	4
Electricity price forecast	1
Prediction of properties of refrigerants	3
Object tracking	2
Optimization of wind turbine	2
Cluster of load profiles	1
Modeling of absorption heat transformer	1
Analysis of fluidized-bed boiler	1

Table 2. Summary of numbers of applications presented in energy system applications

Küçüksille et al. have used data mining for the determination of thermophysical properties as the specific heat capacity, viscosity, heat conduction coefficient, density of the same refrigerants. This study presented ten modeling techniques within data mining process for the prediction of thermophysical properties of refrigerants (R134a, R404a, R407c and R410a). These are linear regression (LR), multi layer perception (MLP), pace regression (PR), simple linear regression (SLR), sequential minimal optimization (SMO), KStar, additive regression (AR), M5 model tree, decision table (DT), M5'Rules models. Relations depending on temperature and pressure were carried out for the determination of thermophysical properties as the specific heat capacity, viscosity, heat conduction coefficient, density of the refrigerants.

Obtained model results for every refrigerant were compared and the best model was investigated. Results indicate that use of derived formulations from these techniques will facilitate design and optimize of heat exchangers which is component of especially vapor compression refrigeration system [11].

Şencan has used data mining process to determine specific volume values of methanol/LiBr and methanol/LiCl used in absorption heat pump systems. Linear regression (LR), pace regression (PR), sequential minimal optimization (SMO), M5 model tree, M5'Rules and back propagation neural network (BPNN) models were applied within the data mining process. Mathematical formulations were found to be in good agreement with the experimental data [12].

Tso and Yau have used regression analysis, decision tree and neural networks models in the data mining approach for the prediction of electricity energy consumption. Model selection is based on the square root of average squared error. In an empirical application to an electricity energy consumption study, the decision tree and neural network models appear to be viable alternatives to the stepwise regression model in understanding energy consumption patterns and predicting energy consumption levels. With the emergence of the data mining approach for predictive modeling, different types of models can be built in a unified platform: to implement various modeling techniques, assess the performance of different models and select the most appropriate model for future prediction [13].

Kusiak et al. was applied data mining approach to analyze relationships among parameters of a circulating fluidized-bed boiler. The efficiency could be predicted to the same degree of accuracy with and without the data describing the fuel composition or boiler demand levels in study. Authors have determined that data mining approach is applicable to different types of burners and fuel types [14].

Figueiredo et al. have presented an electricity consumer characterization framework based on a knowledge discovery in databases procedure, supported by data mining techniques. This framework consists of two main modules: the load profiling module and the classification module. The load profiling module creates a set of consumer classes using a clustering operation and the representative load profiles for each class. The classification module uses this knowledge to build a classification model able to assign different consumers to the existing classes [15].

The electricity price forecast framework, which can predict the normal price as well as the price spikes based on data mining approach by Lu et al. has carried out. The proposed model is based on a mining database including market clearing price, trading hour, electricity demand, electricity supply and reserve. This proposed model is able to generate forecasted price spike, level of spike and associated forecast confidence level [16].

Şencan et al. used different methods such as linear regression (LR), pace regression (PR), sequential minimal optimization (SMO), M5 model tree, M50 rules, decision table and back propagation neural network (BPNN) for modelling the absorption heat transformer. A theoretical modeling of an absorption heat transformer for the temperature range obtained from an experimental solar pond with dimensions 3.5 x 3.5 x 2 m is presented. The working fluid pair in the absorption heat transformer is aqueous ternary hydroxide fluid consisting of sodium, potassium and caesium hydroxides in the proportions 40:36:24 (NaOH:KOH:CsOH). The best results were obtained by the back propagation neural network model. A new formulation based on the BPNN is presented to determine the flow ratio (FR) and the coefficient of performance (COP) of the absorption heat transformer [17].

Küçüksille et al. has applied data mining approach for the modeling of thermodynamic properties of alternative refrigerants. In addition, mathematical equations in order to calculate enthalpy, entropy and specific volume values of each refrigerant were presented.The values calculated from obtained formulations were found to be in good agreement with actual values. The results of this work show that DM can use for predicting accuracy of thermodynamic properties of refrigerants for every temperature and pressure [18].

Yu et al. used a decision tree method for building energy demand modeling. This method is applied to Japanese residential buildings for predicting and classifying building EUI levels and its basic steps, such as the generation of decision tree based on training data and the evaluation of decision tree based on test data are presented. The results have demonstrated that the use of decision tree method can classify and predict building energy demand levels accurately (93% for training data and 92% for test data), identify and rank significant factors of building EUI levels automatically, and provide the combination of significant factors as well as the threshold values that will lead to high building energy performance [19].

Kim et al. developed a process which can help project teams discover useful patterns to improve energy efficient building design. This paper utilized data mining technology, which is a data analysis process that combines different techniques from machine learning, pattern recognition, statistics, and visualization, to automatically extract concepts, interrelationships and patterns of interest from a large dataset. By applying data mining technology to the analysis of energy efficient building designs one can identify valid, useful, and previously unknown patterns out of energy simulation modeling [20].

Hou et al. used data mining (DM) method is developed to detect and diagnose sensor faults based on the past running performance data in heating, ventilating and air conditioning (HVAC) systems, combining a rough set approach and an artificial neural network (ANN). The reduced information is used to develop classification rules and train the neural network to infer appropriate parameters. The differences between measured thermodynamic states and predicted states obtained from models for normal performance (residuals) are used as performance indices for sensor fault detection and diagnosis. Real test results from a real HVAC system show that only the temperature and humidity measurements of many air handling units (AHU) can work very well as the measurements to distinguish simultaneous temperature sensor faults of the supply chilled water (SCW) and return chilled water (RCW). The logic diagram of the DM based sensor fault detection and diagnosis strategy is shown in Fig. 2 [21].

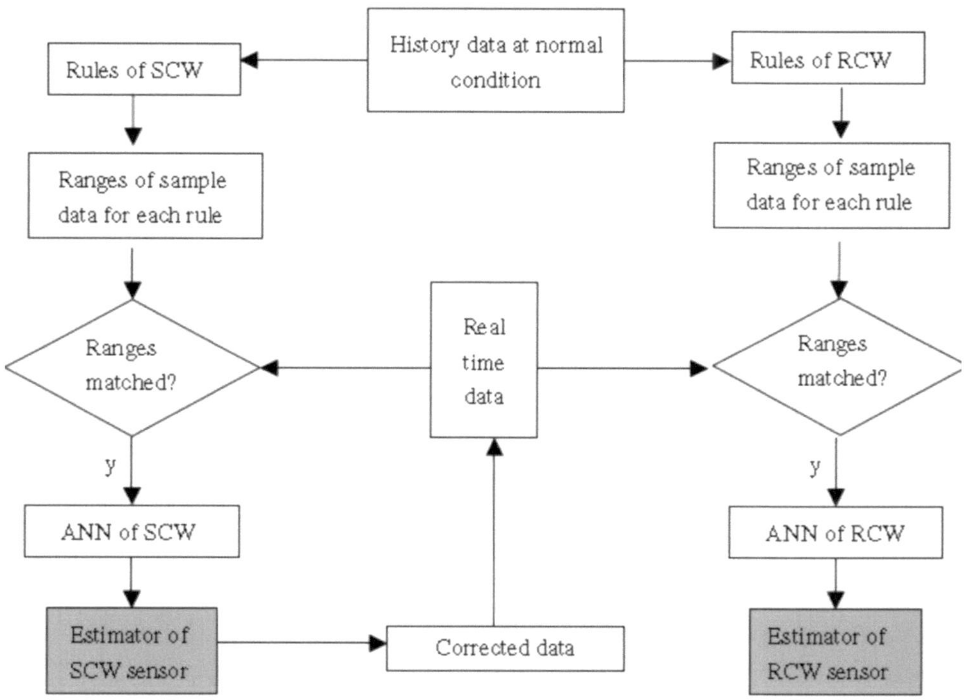

Fig. 2. Logic diagram of DM based sensor FDD strategy [21].

Dominguez-Navarro et al. used data mining to analyze the composition of the electric demand among the different consumption and the behavior of each type of load. The proposed method uses a heuristic optimization algorithm (Tabu Search) for minimizing the error between the real demand and the calculated approximation to this demand. This search is adaptative because the algorithm changes the relative weight of each load as well as the profile of each load. The obtained results show the good operation of the proposedmethodology [22].

Lu et al. used data mining based electricity price forecast framework, which can predict the normal price as well as the price spikes. The normal price can be predicted by a previously proposed wavelet and neural network based forecast model, while the spikes are forecasted based on a data mining approach. This paper focuses on the spike prediction and explores the reasons for price spikes based on the measurement of a proposed composite supply-demand balance index (SDI) and relative demand index (RDI). These indices are able to reflect the relationship among electricity demand, electricity supply and electricity reserve capacity. The proposed model is based on a mining database including market clearing price, trading hour, electricity demand, electricity supply and reserve. Bayesian classification and similarity searching techniques are used to mine the database to find out the internal relationships between electricity price spikes and these proposed. The mining results are used to form the price spike forecast model. This proposed model is able to generate forecasted price spike, level of spike and associated forecast confidence level. The model is tested with the Queensland electricity market data with promising results. Flow chart of the comprehensive electricity price forecast model in Fig. 3 were presented [23].

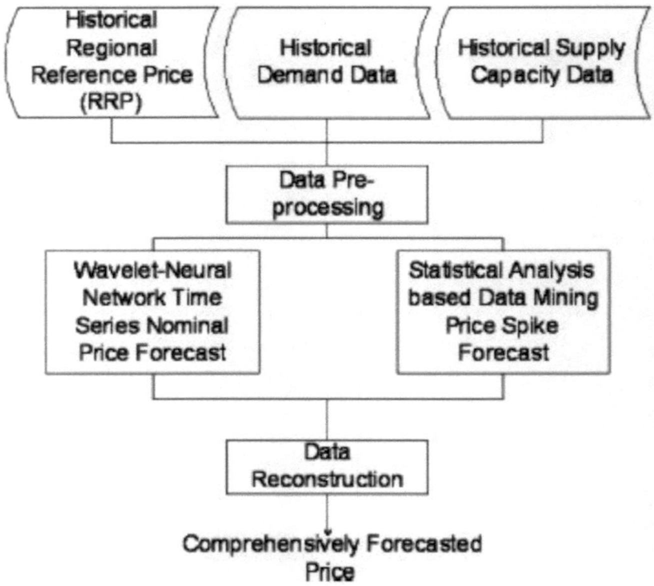

Fig. 3. Flow chart of the comprehensive electricity price forecast model [23].

Tseng and Lin proposed a novel data mining algorithm named TMP-Mine with a special data structure named TMP-Tree for efficiently discovering the temporal movement patterns of objects in sensor networks. They proposed novel location prediction strategies that utilize the discovered temporal movement patterns so as to reduce the prediction errors for energy savings. Through empirical evaluation on various simulation conditions and real dataset, TMP-Mine and the proposed prediction strategies are shown to deliver excellent performance in terms of scalability, accuracy and energy efficiency [24].

Tseng and Lu proposed a novel strategy named multi-level object tracking strategy (MLOT) for energy-efficient and real-time tracking of the moving objects in sensor networks by mining the movement log. In MLOT, they first conducted hierarchical clustering to form a hierarchical model of the sensor nodes. Second, the movement logs of the moving objects are analyzed by a data mining algorithm to obtain the movement patterns, which are then used to predict the next position of a moving object. They used the multi-level structure to represent the hierarchical relations among sensor nodes so as to achieve the goal of keeping track of moving objects in a real-time manner. Through experimental evaluation of various simulated conditions, the proposed method is shown to deliver excellent performance in terms of both energy efficiency and timeliness. Fig. 4 shows the system architecture. The

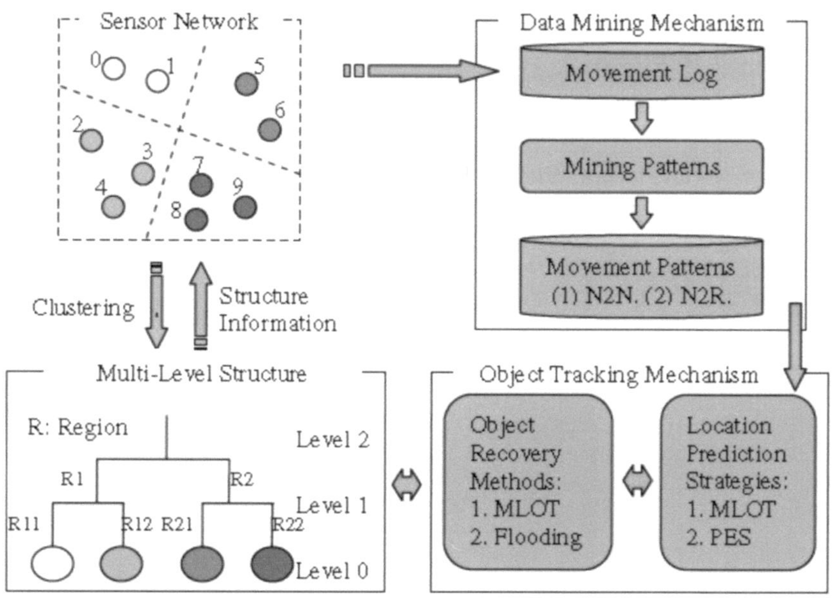

Fig. 4. System architecture [25].

system workflow consists of three main phases: (1) clustering of sensor nodes; (2) discovery of movement patterns; and (3) prediction and recovery of locations of moving objects [25].

Azadeh et al. presented an integrated fuzzy system, data mining and time series framework to estimate and predict electricity demand for seasonal and monthly changes in electricity consumption especially in developing countries such as China and Iran with non-stationary data. It is difficult to model uncertain behavior of energy consumption with only conventional fuzzy system or time series and the integrated algorithm could be an ideal substitute for such cases. To construct fuzzy systems, a rule base is needed. Because a rule base is not available, for the case of demand function, look up table which is one of the extracting rule methods is used to extract the rule base. This system is defined as FLT. Also, decision tree method which is a data mining approach is similarly utilized to extract the rule base. This system is defined as FDM. Preferred time series model is selected from linear (ARMA) and nonlinear model. For this, after selecting preferred ARMA model, McLeod–Li test is applied to determine nonlinearity condition. When, nonlinearity condition is satisfied, preferred nonlinear model is selected and compare with preferred ARMA model and finally one of this is selected as time series model. At last, ANOVA is used for selecting preferred model from fuzzy models and time series model. Also, the impact of data preprocessing and postprocessing on the fuzzy system performance is considered by the algorithm. In addition, another unique feature of the proposed algorithm is utilization of autocorrelation function (ACF) to define input variables, whereas conventional methods which use trial and error method. Monthly electricity consumption of Iran from 1995 to 2005 is considered as the case of this study. The MAPE estimation of genetic algorithm (GA), artificial neural network (ANN) versus the proposed algorithm shows the appropriateness of the proposed algorithm [26].

Kusiak et al. presented data-driven approach for minimization of the energy to air condition a typical office-type facility. Eight data-mining algorithms are applied to model the nonlinear relationship among energy consumption, control settings (supply air temperature and supply air static pressure), and a set of uncontrollable parameters. The multiple-linear perceptron (MLP) ensemble outperforms other models tested in this research, and therefore it is selected to model a chiller, a pump, a fan, and a reheat device. These four models are integrated into an energy optimization model with two decision variables, the setpoint of the supply air temperature and the static pressure in the air handling unit. The model is solved with a particle swarm optimization algorithm. The optimization results have demonstrated the total energy consumed by the heating, ventilation, and air-conditioning system is reduced by over 7%. Fig. 7 shows the flowchart of the Particle swarm optimization (PSO) algorithm [27].

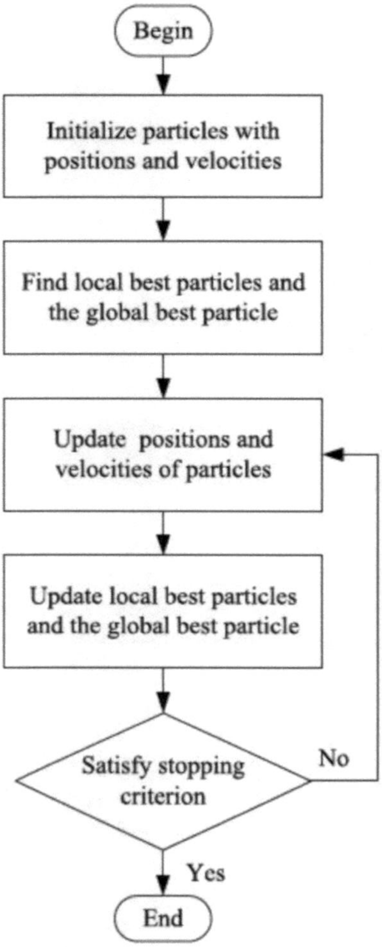

Fig. 7. Flowchart of the PSO algorithm [27].

Kusiak and Zheng presented an evolutionary computation approach for optimization of power factor and power output of wind turbines. Data-mining algorithms capture the relationships among the power output, power factor, and controllable and non-controllable variables of a 1.5 MW wind turbine. An evolutionary strategy algorithm solves the data-derived optimization model and determines optimal control settings. Computational experience has demonstrated opportunities to improve the power factor and the power output by optimizing set points of blade pitch angle and generator torque. It is shown that the pitch angle and the generator torque can be controlled to maximize the energy capture from the wind and enhance the quality of the power produced by the wind turbine with a DFIG generator. These improvements are in the presence of reactive power remedies used in modern wind turbines. The concepts proposed in this paper are illustrated with the data collected at an industrial wind farm [28].

Kusiak et al. presented a data-driven approach for maximization of the power produced by wind turbines. The power optimization objective is accomplished by computing optimal control settings of wind turbines using data mining and evolutionary strategy algorithms. Data mining algorithms identify a functional mapping between the power output and controllable and non-controllable variables of a wind turbine. An evolutionary strategy algorithm is applied to determine control settings maximizing the power output of a turbine based on the identified model. Computational studies have demonstrated meaningful opportunities to improve the turbine power output by optimizing blade pitch and yaw angle. It is shown that the pitch angle is an important variable in maximizing energy captured from the wind. Power output can be increased by optimization of the pitch angle. The concepts proposed in this paper are illustrated with industrial wind farm data. Fig. 8 show optimization framework [29].

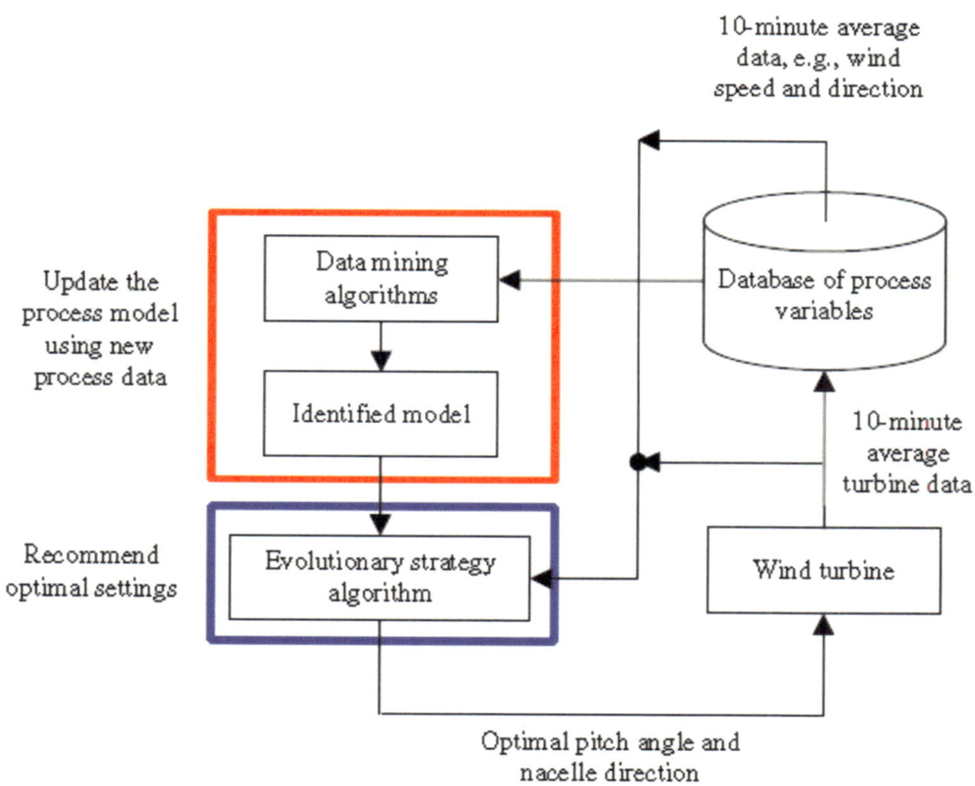

Fig. 8. Optimization framework [29].

Lin et al. applied datamining techniques to the CLP (China Light and Power) Power database in order to analyze (a) the effect of temperature and relative humidity on the peak load, (b) the cluster of load profiles in various buses in response to disturbances. The results draw attention to special phenomena associated with the particular system operation, such as that several substations whose load behavior during disturbances whenever they happened are statistically very similar to that of substation AAA are always very seriously impacted by the disturbances. Such results pinpoint these substations for further system studies, which may lead to enhanced overall performance. On the other hand, based on the limited records in the data-mining process, certain 'unexpected' findings are revealed (including in substation BBB) and closer scrutiny of future data collected in the associated buses will thus be called for [30].

4. Conclusions

From the description of the various applications presented in this paper, one can see that data mining method have been applied in many fields of energy systems. In this chapter, various applications made using data mining method have been reviewed. Available literature summaries published in this area is also presented. Data mining method is becoming useful as alternate approaches to conventional techniques. Data mining has also been applied for modeling, optimization, prediction and control of complex systems. As can be seen from the applications presented, data mining method has been applied successfully in a wide range of energy system applications.

Surely, the number of applications presented here is neither complete nor exhaustive but merely a sample of applications that demonstrate the usefulness and possible applications of data mining method. Based on the work presented here it is believed that data mining method offers an alternative method.

5. References

[1] Fayyad, U, Piatetsky-Shapiro, G and Smyth, P, 1996d, Knowledge discovery and data mining: towards a unifying framework. In Proceedings of the 2nd International Conference on Knowledge Discovery and Data Mining, Portland, OR, pp. 82–88.

[2] Cabena, P, Hadjinian, P, Stadler, R, Verhees, J and Zanasi, A, 1998, Discovering Data Mining: From Concepts to Implementation. Prentice Hall.

[3] Hui, S. C., Jha, G., "Data mining for customer service support", Information & Management, Volume 38, Issue 1,2000, pp. 1-13

[4] Kurgan, L. A., Musilek, P., "A survey of Knowledge Discovery and Data Mining process models", The Knowledge Engineering Review, 2006,21:1, pp. 1 -24.

[5] Chapman et al., 2000 Chapman, P., Clinton, J., Kerber, R., Khabaza, T., Reinartz, T., Shearar, C., et al. (2000). CRISP-DM 1.0 Step-by-Step Data Mining Guide (p. 13).

[6] Fernandez et al., 2002 I.B. Fernandez, S. H. Zanakis and S. Walczak, Knowledge discovery techniques for predicting country investment risk, Computers & Industrial Engineering (43) (2002), pp. 787–800.

[7] Wirth and Hipp, 2000 Wirth, R., & Hipp, J. (2000). CRIPS-DM: Towards a standard process model for data mining. In Proceedings of the fourth international conference on the practical applications of knowledge discovery and data mining, Manchester, UK (pp. 29–39).

[8] Shearar, 2000 C. Shearar, The CRISP-DM model: The new blueprint for data mining, Journal of Data Ware Housing 5 (4) (2000), p. 13-19.
[9] Tang and MacLennan, 2005 Z. Tang and J. MacLennan, Data mining with sql server 2005, Wiley (2005).
[10] Sencan, 2007 A. Sencan, Modeling of thermodynamic properties of refrigerant/absorbent couples using data mining process, Energy Conversion and Management 48 (2007), pp. 470–480.
[11] E. U. Küçüksille, R. Selbas, A. Şencan, Data mining techniques for thermophysical properties of refrigerants, Energy Conversion and Management 50 (2009) 399–412.
[12] A. Şencan, Modeling of thermodynamic properties of refrigerant/absorbent couples using Data Mining Process, Energy Conversion and Management, 48 (2007) 470–480.
[13] G. K. F. Tso, K. K. W. Yau, Predicting electricity energy consumption: A comparison of regression analysis, decision tree and neural Networks, Energy, 32 (2007) 1761–1768.
[14] A. Kusiak, A. Burns, F. Milster, Optimizing combustion efficiency of a circulating fluidized boiler: A data mining approach, International Journal of Knowledge Based Intelligent Engineering Systems, 9(2005) 263-274.
[15] V. Figueiredo, F. Rodrigues, J. G. Gouveia, An Electric Energy Consumer Characterization Framework Based on Data Mining Techniques, IEEE Transactions on Power Systems, 20(2005) 596-602.
[16] X. Lu, Z. Y. Dong, X. Li, Electricity market price spike forecast with data mining techniques, Electric Power Systems Research, 73 (2005) 19–29.
[17] A. Sencan, O.Kızılkan, N.C. Bezir, S.A. Kalogirou, Different methods for modeling absorption heat transformer powered by solar pond, Energy Conversion and Management 48 (2007) 724–735.
[18] E. U. Küçüksille, R. Selbas, A. Şencan, Prediction of thermodynamic properties of refrigerants using data mining, Energy Conversion and Management, In Press.
[19] Zhun Yu, Fariborz Haghighat, Benjamin C.M. Fung, Hiroshi Yoshino, Energy and Buildings 42 (2010) 1637–1646.
[20] Hyunjoo Kim, Annette Stumpf , Wooyoung Kim, Analysis of an energy efficient building design through data mining approach, Automation in Construction, In Press.
[21] Zhijian Hou, Zhiwei Lian, Ye Yao, Xinjian Yuan, Data mining based sensor fault diagnosis and validation for building air conditioning system,Energy Conversion and Management 47 (2006) 2479–2490.
[22] José A. Dominguez-Navarro, José L. Bernal-Agustín, Rodolfo Dufo-López, Data mining methodology for disaggregation of load demand, Electric Power Systems Research 79 (2009) 1393–1399.
[23] Xin Lu, Zhao Yang Dong, Xue Li, Electricity market price spike forecast with data mining techniques, Electric Power Systems Research 73 (2005) 19–29.
[24] Vincent S. Tseng, Kawuu W. Lin, Energy efficient strategies for object tracking in sensor networks: A data mining approach, The Journal of Systems and Software 80 (2007) 1678–1698.

[25] Vincent S. Tseng, Eric Hsueh-Chan Lu, Energy-efficient real-time object tracking in multi-level sensor networks by mining and predicting movement patterns, The Journal of Systems and Software 82 (2009) 697–706.

[26] A. Azadeh, M. Saberi, S. F. Ghaderi, A. Gitiforouz , V. Ebrahimipour, Improved estimation of electricity demand function by integration of fuzzy system and data mining approach, Energy Conversion and Management 49 (2008) 2165–2177.

[27] Andrew Kusiak, Mingyang Li, Fan Tang, Modeling and optimization of HVAC energy consumption, Applied Energy 87 (2010) 3092–3102.

[28] Andrew Kusiak, Haiyang Zheng, Optimization of wind turbine energy and power factor with an evolutionary computation algorithm, Energy 35 (2010) 1324–1332.

[29] Andrew Kusiak, Haiyang Zheng, Zhe Song, Power optimization of wind turbines with data mining and evolutionary computation, Renewable Energy 35 (2010) 695–702.

[30] J. K. Lin, S. K. Tso, H. K. Ho, C. M. Mak, K. M. Yung, Y. K. Ho, Study of climatic effects on peak load and regional similarity of load profiles following disturbances based on data mining, Electrical Power and Energy Systems 28 (2006) 177–185.

22

Regression

Mohsen Hajsalehi Sichani and Saeed Khalafinejad
Sharif University of Technology
Iran

1. Introduction

In recent years, data mining has been widely used in various areas of science and engineering and solved many serious problems in different areas of science such as electrical power engineering, genetics, medicine and bioinformatics. Data Mining is used to extract information from data. Data mining uses AI and Statistics in its algorithms. Information refers to patterns underlying data, and data refers to recorded facts. However, the captured data need to be converted into information and knowledge to become useful. Data mining is the entire process of applying computer-based methodology, including new techniques for knowledge conversion into data. The following example is a good motivator:
Imagine you are the owner of a big supermarket and you are asking for the convenience of customers and ease of access to stuffs for customers and a high sale. In this case, if you save all of data such as time of shopping, day of shopping, sold stuffs, name of the customers and so on for about 3 to 6 months and then use data mining you might find the following information:

1. The customers who buy cheese, they also buy bread. You can put cheeses and bread near each other.
2. During holidays customers buy more fast foods such as hamburgers, tuna fish. You can put more of these foods at your supermarket on holidays.
3. Special customers for special occasions order special kind of stuffs. By sending their desired food you can surprise them (risk is part of everything!!!).

Other important usage of data mining can be found at (Hsiang-Chuan Liu, 2008), (Peter C. Austin, 2010).
Some words are important and necessary and you should remember them such as attribute, instance, classification, association, clustering, supervised and unsupervised learning, missing value, overfitting, and target. These terms will be explained shortly during this chapter and also related terms to this chapter will be covered completely.
In this chapter we will focus on linear regression, logistic regression, and neural network (Perceptron) and we will provide sufficient practical examples to make this concept easier to understand. In this way, we will use some free data mining software such as WEKA(www.cs.waikato.ac.nz) and RapidMiner(www.rapidminer.com) which are written by Waikato and Yale University, respectively.
At the end, we will focus on one the important area of regression method which is not well known. This part of the book has a wide variety of use in security such as breaking some patterns of serial numbers, wireless security keys, and so on.

2. Basic concepts of data mining

In data mining, data can be divided into five groups. In other words, attributes can be categorized into five groups: nominal (categorical), numeric (integer, continuous), ordinal, interval and ratio. These terms will be explained in the next paragraphs.

For enlightening, consider weather attribute. The values of the weather attribute can be sunny, rainy, or cloudy. Definitely these values are not comparable or multipliable or not appropriate for mathematical operations. These values are nominal. But, the length attribute can be assigned any numeric value within the range of Natural numbers.

Numeric attributes measure numbers, whether integer or real. Nominal attributes have values that are distinct or can be considered just a label or name. Nominal is the Latin word for name. Consider these two values: hot and cold, you can arrange them but you cannot define any instances. For example you can say, hot is warmer than cold but you do not know how much the difference in degree is. These kinds of attributes are ordinal. The comparison is logical but subtract or add is not acceptable. It might be a little hard sometimes to distinct nominal and ordinal quantities. It depends on user.

Consider the year, for example 2010 and 2012. You cannot add them or subtract them because it does not make sense. You can say 2012 is 2 years greater than 2010, but you cannot say 1.0009 times the year 2010 because year 0 is totally arbitrary and historians chose it. These kinds of attributes are interval.

But if you consider the distance between the object and itself, that is zero, thus distance is a ratio quantity. Mathematical operation is logical and for example it makes sense to multiply 3.14 times a distance to get an circle's area. Instances make dataset. Every single piece of data is an instance. Instances some times are called examples. Each instance is useful and is a part of learning.

Instances are categorized based on the values of features; attributes; that measure different aspects of instances.

Target is an attribute that the instances want to be classified into.

If the target be one and after doing data mining we got rules such as this:

If weather be sunny then the temperature is around 40.

Then this is classification. In other words, classification predicts the value of a given attribute. If these rules are used to predict the value of any attribute then it is association rules. In other words, an association predicts the value of arbitrary an attribute(s).

If temperature = cool then humidity = normal

If temperature = high and temperature $\geq$ *60 then humidity = high*

In Clustering, the groups of examples that belong together are sought.

If the input(s) are assigned to at least one output, and the learning uses the outputs, then this is supervised learning. The unsupervised learning is totally opposite.

If there is no output(s) or the output(s) does not used during learning, then it is unsupervised learning. Please be aware of this matter that the output during the supervised learning is the same as target. Simply, if there is a target and that target is used for learning, then it is supervised learning, else it is unsupervised learning. Classification learning sometimes is called supervised learning because the attributes or the target acts as an input. Missing values are missed values! If you are collecting data, it might be impossible for you to find some data, and then these data are missing data and they will be replace by a question mark "?" like below.

Overfitting is a concept that will occur on following condition:

Weather	*Sunny*	*Rainy*
Temperature	30	?
Play	No	Yes

Table 1. Missing values.

Overfitting might happen when training data are finite and if the learning model cover all of the data. In the following figure, fig 1, the concept of overfitting is totally obvious. Although for the training data the error is minimum, for the testing data, the error will be very high (Kantardzic, 2003), (Witten & Frank, 2005).

3. Regression concept

If you start with regression, you might find it a little confusing. So it is better to forget the meaning of regression in your literature readings.
In statistics, regression analysis is the concept of understanding the relation between independent and dependent variables. Precisely, it tries to understand how the value of dependent variable changes while one of the independent variable is varying when the other independent variables are fixed.
One of the main job of regression is forecasting and predicting. Another job is helping to find out which of independent variables has the most or less (or no) effect on the dependent variable.
There are lots of developed algorithms and functions that are for regression analysis such as linear regression or logistic regression. In the following pages, we make you familiar with linear regression,multilayer perceptron,logistic regression. Then, two of data mining tools will be introduced and two practical examples will be shown. At last, we will focus on one of the most important but less famous usage of data mining which is security. And we provide some useful example of using regression analysis in cracking and breaking serial numbers (Kantardzic, 2003), (Witten & Frank, 2005).

4. Linear regression

Linear regression analyses the relationship between two variables (X, Y) and tries to model the relationship by fitting a linear equation to the observed data. These two variables should be numeric. The linear regression line as a standard curve tries to find new values of X from

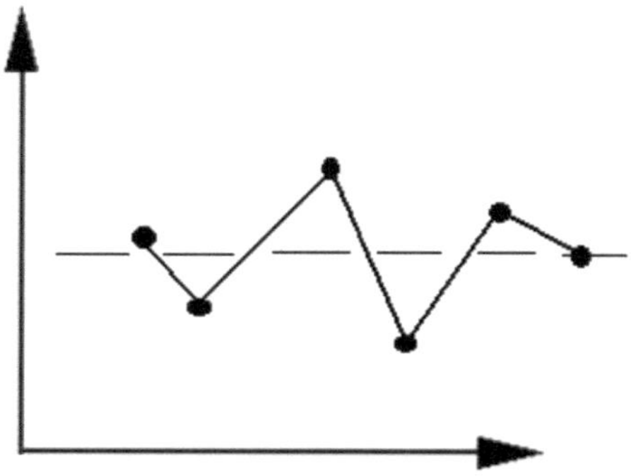

Fig. 1. Overfitting.

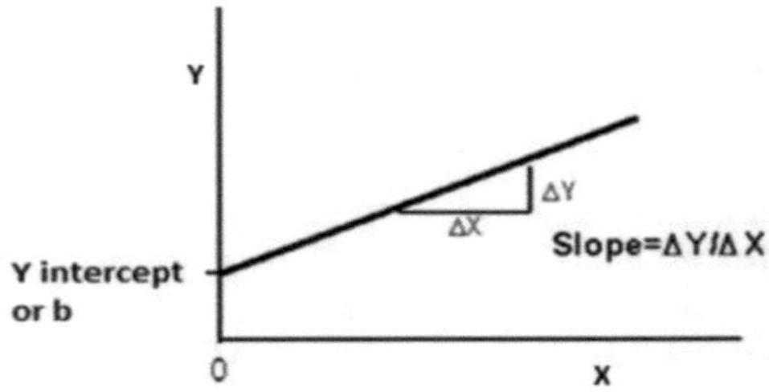

Fig. 2. Intercept and slope.

Y, or Y from X. A linear regression line has an equation like $Y = a + bX$, where X is the explanatory variable and Y is the dependent variable. The slope of the line is b, and a is the intercept (the value of y when $x = 0$.)
In data mining form, expressing the class as a linear combination of the attributes, with predetermined weights is linear regression.

$$x = w_0 + w_1 a_1 + w_2 a_2 + \ldots + w_k a_k \tag{1}$$

x is the class; $a_1, a_2, \ldots$ are the attribute values; and $w_0, w_1, \ldots$ are weights.
$x^{(1)}$ is the class of the first instance and the superscript above the attribute values denotes that it is the first example.

$a_1^{(1)}$,
$a_2^{(1)}$,
$\vdots$
$a_k^{(1)}$,

$$w_0 a_0^{(1)} + w_1 a_1^{(1)} + w_2 a_2^{(1)} + + w_k a_k^{(1)} = \sum_{j=0}^{k} w_j a_j^{(1)} \tag{2}$$

The next part is choosing the coefficients w_j—there are $k + 1$ of them-to minimize the sum of the squares of these differences over all the training instances. n is number of training instances. Then the sum of the squares of the differences is shown in the following formula (Witten & Frank, 2005).

$$\sum_{i=1}^{n} (x^{(i)} - \sum_{j=0}^{k} w_j a_j^{(i)}) \tag{3}$$

The expression inside the parentheses is the difference between the ith instance's actual class and its predicted class.
The most common method for finding the regression line is the least-squares.
This method calculates the best-fitting line for the observed data by minimizing the sum of the squares. This method is shown in the following example.
The mathematical form of least square is summarized as follows:

$$b = (\sum y - m \sum x)/n \tag{4}$$

$$r = (n\sum(xy) - \sum x \sum y)/(\sqrt{([n\sum x^2 - \sum x)^2][n\sum(y^2) - (\sum y)^2]} \quad (5)$$

$$m = n\sum(xy) - \sum x \sum y / n\sum(x^2) - (\sum x)^2 \quad (6)$$

"m" is slope, "b" is intercept and "r" is correlation coefficient. Linear correlation coefficient, measures the strength and the direction of a linear relationship between two variables. Look at the following example:

Xvalues	*Yvalues*
40	4
41	6
42	5
43	8
44	7

Table 2. Finding linear regression between two variables.

Now, we will find slope and intercept. Afterward, we use them to form regression equation.

1. Find the number of values N=5
2. Find XY, X^2 as below

Xvalues	*Yvalues*	*XY*	X^2
40	4	160	1600
41	6	246	1681
42	5	210	1764
43	8	344	1649
44	7	308	1936

Table 3. Find the linear regression between two variables.

3. Find $\sum X$,$\sum Y$,$\sum XY$, $\sum X^2$.
   $\sum X = 210$
   $\sum Y = 30$
   $\sum XY = 1286$
   $\sum X^2 = 8830$
4. Substitute in (6),Slope will be 0.8.
5. Substitute in (4),intercept will be -27.6.
6. Substitute these values in regression equation formula
   Regression Equation: $y = a + bx, y = -27.6 + 0.8x$

Suppose, we want to know the approximate y value for the variable $x = 10$. So, we can substitute the value in the above equation.The result is:

Regression Equation:

$$y = a + bx$$
$$y = -27.6 + 0.8 * x$$
$$y = -27.6 + 0.8 * 10 = -19.6$$

5. Neural network

Neural Network (NN) is a simulated neural cell by hardware or software. In this section, terms like neuron, learning, and experience are referring to the concepts of neural networking in a computer system.
Neural networks have the ability to learn by examples. We will discuss neurons, NNs in general, Multilayer Perceptron, and Back Propagation networks. Multilayer Perceptron networks are popular types of network that can be trained to recognize different patterns including images, signals, and texts (M.K. Alsmadi, 2009), (Nirkhi, 2010), (Peter Auer, 2008).

5.1 History

The history of some of the NN algorithms is summarized as follows:

- 1943 McCulloch-Pitts neuron model
- 1949 Hebbian Network
- 1958 Single Layer Perceptron
- 1982 Hopfield Network
- 1982 Kohonen Self Organization Map(SOM)
- 1986 Back Propagation(BP)
- 1990's Radial Basis Function Network
- 2000's Support Vector Machine(SVM)

5.2 Important functions of NNs

There are four main functions in NNs that are shown below.

1. Identity (Linear) Function
2. Binary Step Function With Threshold θ(Heaviside)[threshold OR hard limit if $\theta = 0$]
3. Bipolar Step Function With Threshold θ [Sign OR symmetrical hard limit if $\theta = 0$]
4. Sigmoid Function (S-shaped Curves)
    a. Binary Sigmoid(Logistic OR Log-Sigmoid)
    b. Bipolar Sigmoid
    c. Hyperbolic Tangent
    d. ArcTan

Fig 3 is linear function, Fig. 4 is Binary Step Function and the two equations under it are its equations, Fig. 5 is Bipolar Step Function and the two equations under it are its equations, and at last Fig. 6 is Binary Sigmoid Function.
The function which is shown in Fig. 6 is Sigmoid function. The coefficient "a" is a number constant and can be chosen between 0.5 and 2.
σ stepness usually $\sigma > 0$
$F(x) = 1/(1 + exp(-\sigma x)) = 1/(1 + e^{(-\sigma x)})$
$f'(x) = dx/dy = \sigma f(x)[1 - f(x)]$

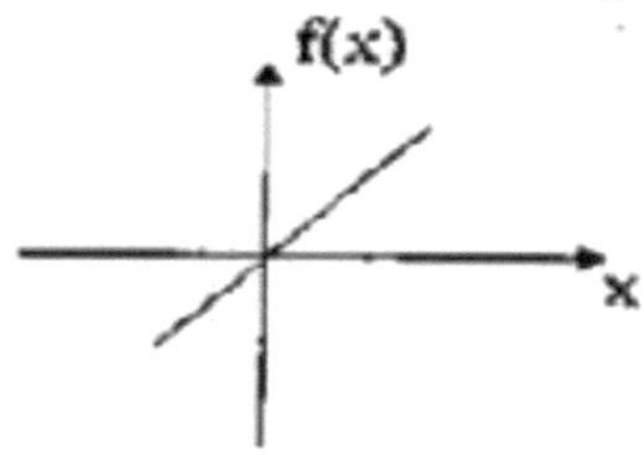

Fig. 3. Identity (Linear) Function $f(x) = x, forallx$

5.3 Neuron

The neuron can be thought as a program, or process that has one or more inputs and produces an output. The inputs simulate what a neuron gets, while the output is what a neuron generates. The following figures can clarify this concept more, fig 7.

5.4 Neural networks definition

A neural network is a group of neurons connected together. Connecting neurons together to form a neural net can be done in different ways such as SOM or Multilayer Perceptron.

5.5 Multilayer pereceptron

Multilayer perceptron (MLP) is a function that learns through back propagation algorithm. Back propagation pseudo-code $(http : //scialert.net/fulltext/?doi = ajsr.2008.146.152$ $\&org = 11)$. is explained below

The following steps show a Back Propagation NN:

Step 0. Initialize weights and biases.

Step 1. While stopping condition is false, do steps 2-9.

Step 2. For each training pair, do steps 3-8.
Feedforward:

Step 3. Each input unit $(X_i, i = 1, \ldots, _m)$ receives input signal x_i

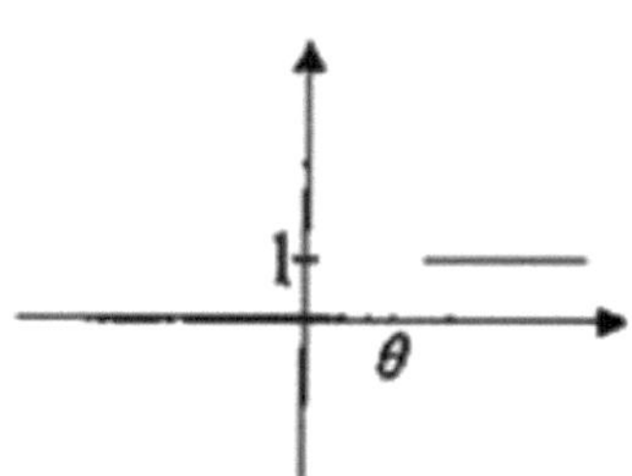

Fig. 4. Binary Step Function with Threshold θ.

$f(x) = 1$ if $x => \theta$
$f(x) = 0$ if $x < \theta$

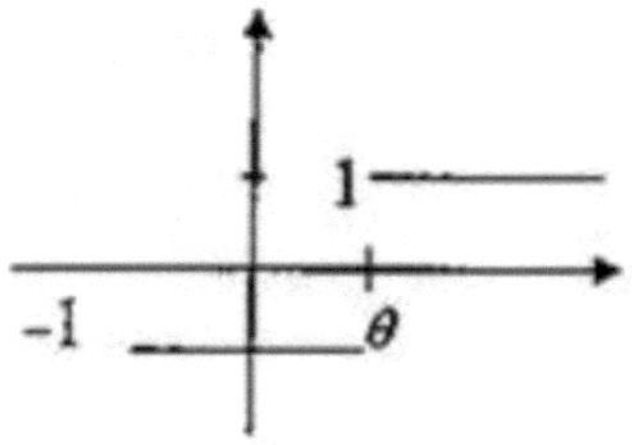

Fig. 5. Bipolar Step Function with Thresholdθ.

$f(x) = 1$ if $x => \theta$
$f(x) = -1$ if $x < \theta$

and broadcasts this signal to all units in hidden layer.

Step 4. Each hidden unit ($Z_j, j = 1, \ldots, p$) sums its weighted input signals,
$Z_{inj} = v_{0j} + \sum_{i=1}^{n} x_i v_i j$
And applies its activation function to compute its output signal,
$Z_j = f(Z_{inj})$
And sends this signal to all units in the output layer.

Step 5. Each output unit ($Y_k, K = 1, \ldots, m$) sums its weighted input signals,
$y_{ink} = w_{0k} + \sum_{j=1}^{n} z_j w_{jk}$
And applies its activation function to compute its output signal,
$y_k = f(y_{ink})$
Backprpagation of error:

Step 6. Each output unit ($Y_k, K = 1, \ldots, m$) receives a target
pattern corresponding to input training pattern, computes its error information term,
$\delta_K = (t_k - y_k) f'(y_{ink})$
Calculates its weight correction term,
$\Delta w_{jk} = \alpha \delta_k z_j$
And calculate its bias correction term,
$\Delta w_{0k} = \alpha \delta_k$
And sends δ_K to units in hidden layer.

Step 7. Each hidden unit ($Z_j, j = 1, \ldots, p$) sums its delta inputs

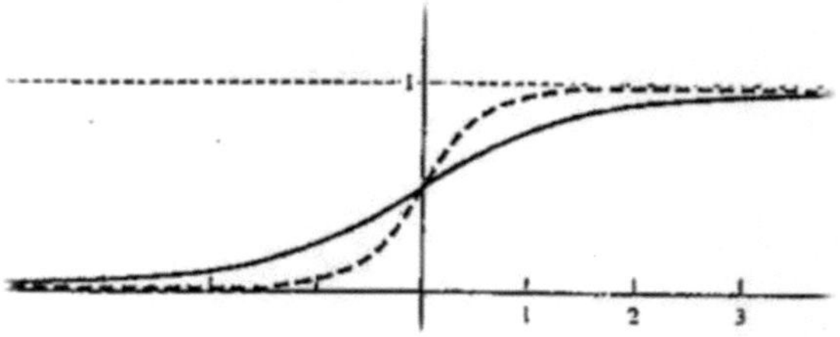

Fig. 6. Binary Sigmoid Function.

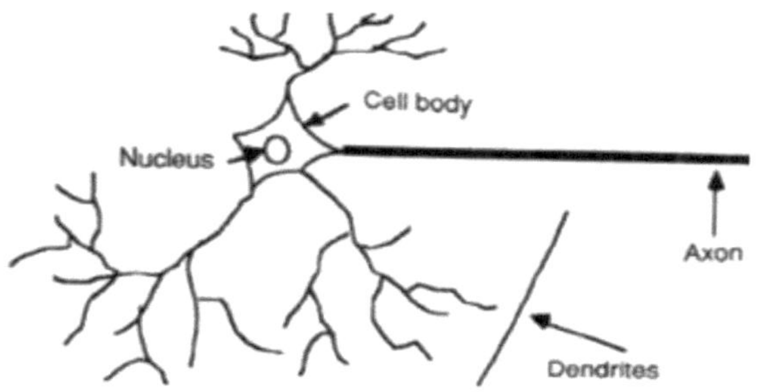

Fig. 7. Natural neuron.

from units in the output layer,
$\delta_{inj} = \sum_{(k=1)}^{m} \delta_K w_{jk}$
And multiplies by derivative of its activation function to calculate its error information term,
$\delta_j = \delta_{inj} f'(z_{inj})$
Calculates its weight correction term,
$\Delta v_{ij} = \alpha \delta_i x_i$
And calculates its bias correction term,
$\Delta v_{0j} = \alpha \delta_j$
Updates weights and biases:

Step 8. Each output unit $(Y_k, K = 1, \ldots, m)$ updates its weights and bias (j=0,. . . ,p):
$W_{jk}(new) = W_{jk}(old) + \Delta w_{jk}$
Each hidden unit $(Z_j, j = 1, \ldots, p)$ updates its weights and bias (i=0,. . . ,n):
$V_{ij}(new) = v_{ij}(old) + \Delta v_{ij}$
Step 9. Test stopping condition.

Two of the most important functions of MLP are Bipolar Sigmoid and Binary Sigmoid. Please consider the next example:
input vector is (0,1)
target is 1
learning rate (α) is 0.25
n=2
p=2
activity function is Binary Sigmoid and slope (m) is 1
$\sigma = 1$

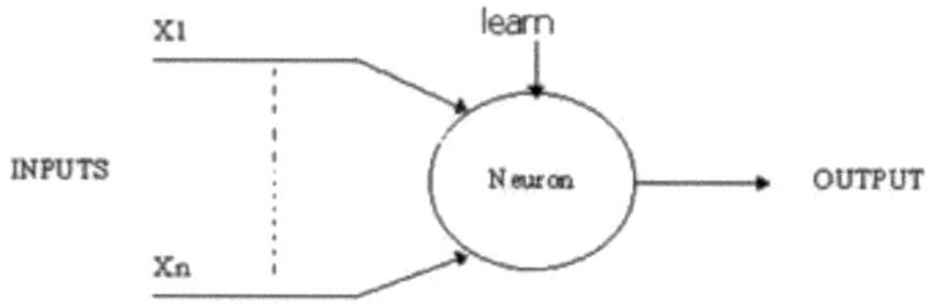

Fig. 8. Computer neuron (simulated).

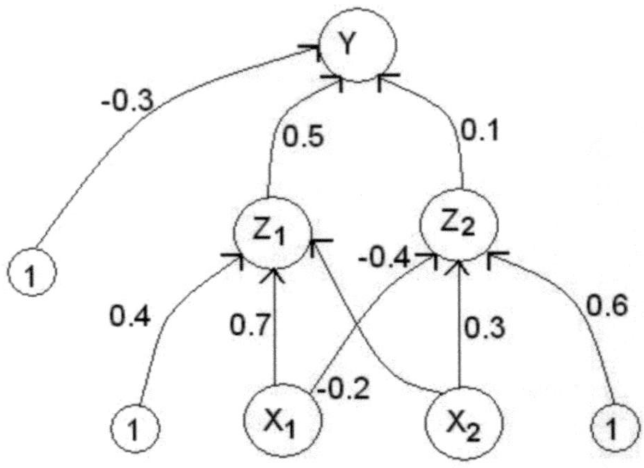

Fig. 9. MLP.

find weights and biases for MLP with above information, and continue until you reach the floating-point with three digits.
$f(x) = 1/1 + e^{-x}$
$f'(x) = f(x)[1 - f(x)]$

Step 0.Initialize weights and biases

Step 1.Begin training:

Step 2.For input vector $X = (0,1)$ with $t_1 = 1$,do steps 3-8.

Feedforward:

Step 3.$x_1 = 0, x_2 = 1$

Step 4.For j=1, 2:

$Z_{inj} = v_{0j} + \sum_{i=1}^{n} x_i v_i j$

$z_{in1} = 0.4 + 0 * 0.7 + 1 * (-0.2) = 0.2$

$z_{in2} = 0.6 + 0 * (-0.4) + 1 * 0.3 = 0.9$

$z_j = f(z_{inj})$

$z_1 = 0.550$

$z_2 = 0.711$

Step 5.For k=1:

$y_{ink} = w_{0k} + \sum_{j=1}^{p} z_j w_{jk}$

$y_{in1} = -0.3 + 0.550 * 0.5 + 0.711 * 0.1 = 0.046$

$y_k = f(y_{ink})$

$y_1 = 0.512$

Backpropagation of error

Step 6.For k=1:

$\delta_K = (t_k - y_k) f'(y_{ink})$

$\delta_{k=1} = (1 - 0.512) * f'(0.046) = 0.122$

and for j=1,2:

$\Delta w_{jk} = \alpha \delta_k z_j$

$\Delta w_{11} = 0.25 * 0.122 * 0.550 = 0.017$

$\Delta w_{21} = 0.25 * 0.122 * 0.711 = 0.022$

$\Delta w_{0k} = \alpha \delta_k$

$\Delta w_{01} = 0.25 * 0.122 = 0.031$

Step 7.For j=1,2:

$\delta_{inj} = \sum_{k=1}^{m} \delta_K w_{jk}$

$\delta_{in1} = 0.122 * 0.5 = 0.061$

$\delta_{in2} = 0.122 * 0.1 = 0.012$

$\delta_j = \delta_{inj} f'(z_{inj})$

$\delta_{j=1} = 0.061 * f'(0.2) = 0.015$

$\delta_{j=2} = 0.012 * f'(0.9) = 0.002$

and for i=1,2:

$\Delta v_{ij} = \alpha \delta_i x_i$

$\Delta v_{11} = 0.25 * 0.015 * 0 = 0.000$

$\Delta v_{21} = 0.25 * 0.015 * 1 = 0.004$

$\Delta v_{12} = 0.25 * 0.002 * 0 = 0.000$

$\Delta v_{22} = 0.25 * 0.002 * 1 = 0.001$

$\Delta v_{0j} = \alpha \delta_j$

$\Delta v_{01} = 0.25 * 0.015 = 0.004$

$\Delta v_{02} = 0.25 * 0.002 = 0.001$

Update weights and biases

Step 8. For k=1 and j=0,1,2:

$W_{jk}(new) = W_{jk}(old) + \Delta w_{jk}$

$W_{11}(new) = 0.517$

$W_{21}(new) = 0.122$

$W_{01}(new) = -0.269$

for j=1,2 and i=0,1,2:

$V_{ij}(new) = v_{ij}(old) + \Delta v_{ij}$

$V_{11}(new) = 0.700$

$V_{21}(new) = -0.196$

$V_{12}(new) = -0.400$

$V_{22}(new) = 0.301$

$V_{01}(new) = 0.404$

$V_{02}(new) = 0.601$

Step 9.Test stopping condition.

6. Logistic regression

Logistic regression is part of regression model called generalized linear models (Kantardzic, 2003), (Witten & Frank, 2005), (Handan Ankarali Camdeviren, 2007), (Hsiang-Chuan Liu,

2008). A logistic regression example is shown in the Fig. 10.
The Fig. 10 can be written as the following formula:

$$f(z) = e^z / e^z + 1 = 1/1 + e^{-z} \tag{7}$$

The most important thing about the logistic regression is that the input value can be any value from negative infinity to positive infinity. But the output value only can be between zero and one. The variable z is usually defined as

$$z = B_0 + B_1 x_1 + B_2 x_2 + \ldots + B_k x_k \tag{8}$$

where B_0 is called the intercept and B_1, B_2, B_3, and so on, are called the regression coefficients of x_1, x_2, x_3 respectively.
The two main formulas in statistics which are used in logistic regression are shown below, more information available at (*http : //luna.cas.usf.edu/ mbrannic/files/regression/Logistic.html*):

$$Odds(x) = Pr(x)/[1 - Pr(x)] \tag{9}$$

$$Prob = Odds/(1 + Odds) \tag{10}$$

The application of logistic regression may be illustrated by using a fictitious example of death from diabet disease. This simplified model uses only three risk factors (age, sex, and blood Glucose level) to predict the 20-year risk of death from diabet disease. This is the model:

B_0 = - 7.0 (the intercept)
B_1 = + 2.2
B_2 = - 2.0
B_3 = + 1.2
x_1 = age in years, less than 50
x_2 = sex, where 0 is male and 1 is female
x_3 = Glucose level, in $mmol/L$ above 200
Which means the model is
risk of death is:$= 1/1 + e^{-z}$, where $z = -7 + 2.2x_1 - 2x_2 + 1.2x_3$

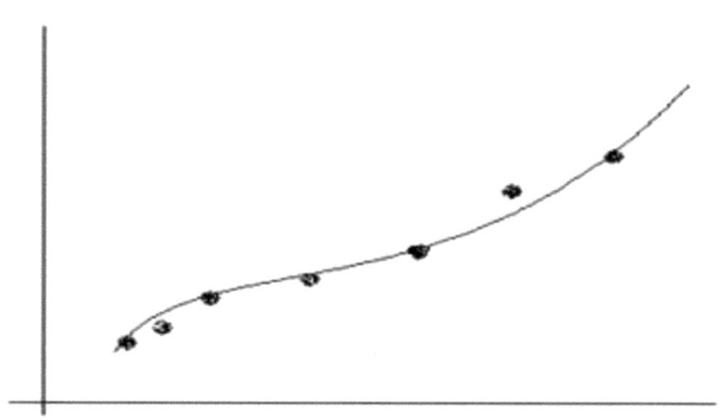

Fig. 10. Logistic regression.

In this model, increasing age is associated with an increase in risk of death from diabet disease (z goes up by 2.2 for every year over the age of 50), female sex is associated with a decrease in risk of death from diabet disease (z goes down by 2.0 if the patient is female), and increasing Glucose is associated with an increase risk of death (z goes up by 1.2 for each 1 $mmol/L$ increase in Glucose above 200). This model will be used to predict Mohsen's risk of death from diabet disease: he is 50 years old and his glucose level is 205. Mohsen's risk of death is therefore
$1/1 + e^{-z}$,where $z = -7 + 2.2 * (50 - 50) - 2 * (0) + 1.2 * (205 - 200)$
This means that by this model, Mohsen's risk of dying from diabet disease in the next 20 years is 0.26.

7. Practical example

Now let's us start some practical examples. The first one will be done by WEKA and the second one by RapidMiner. First of all, we need a data set. Data set is a collection of recorded data in a specific format that you will be familiar with in the next few lines. Our data set name is cmc and its extension is "arff". If you search "cmc.arff" in google you can find and download it easily. When you download it, right click on it and chose "open with" and then open it with "notepad". Better software is "Notepad++" which is free to download and can be easily found through the web. As soon as you open it you will see some things like this:

%1.*Title* : *ContraceptiveMethodChoice*
%2.*Sources* :
%(*a*)*Origin* : *Thisdatasetisasubsetofthe*1987*NationalIndonesia*
%*ContraceptivePrevalenceSurvey*
%......

@*relationcmc*
@*attribute Wifes* − *age INTEGER*
@*attribute Wifes* − *education* 1,2,3,4
@*attribute Husbands* − *education* 1,2,3,4
@*attribute Number* − *of* − *children* − *ever* − *born INTEGER*
@.............................

@*data*

24,2,3,3,1,1,2,3,0,1
45,1,3,10,1,1,3,4,0,1
....
As you can see it is composed of 5 groups.
First group is: %. Whatever line started with this is a comment for user.
Second group is: '@*relationcmc*'. This is the name of dataset.
Third group is: '@*attributeWifes* − *ageINTEGER*'. This line says that Wifes-age is an attribute and its type is Integer. Integer and Real belongs to Numeric types. The next line of this group says that *Wifes* − *education* is an attribute which it has just four values as 1,2,3,4. These numbers can be interpreted as labels. By reading the **first group** you can find out that these number are referring to what. For example 1 means low education(1 = *low*,2,3,4 = *high*).
Fourth group is: '@*data*'. This means that the data is started from the next line.

Fifth group is: $'24,2,3,3,1,1,2,3,0,1'$. This line is start of data. This can be interpreted like this: The attribute which is Wifes-age has value 24, the second attribute which is Wifes-education has value 2, and so far. There are some important rules here such as the number of attributes should be the same as number of values in data part. For example, if we have 10 value in each line of data which are separated by $','$ and we should have 10 attributes.
If you read more and do more practice you can find out more rules. One of the best resources is chapter 7 to 14 of (Witten & Frank, 2005)
Let's go and execute linear regression algorithm on this data set. For executing linear regression the target should be numeric and it is better that other attributes be numeric but it is depend on the usage and aim of linear regression. Without any purpose but only making familiar reader with linear regression we change all attributes to numeric by just renaming the type of attributes.
At the end it is like this:
$@attribute\ Wifes - age$ numeric
$@attribute\ Wifes - education$ numeric
$@attribute\ Husbands - education$ numeric
$@attribute\ Number - of - children - ever - born$ numeric
$@attribute\ Wifes - religion$ numeric
$@attribute\ Wifes - now - working$ numeric
$@attribute\ Husbands - occupation$ numeric
$@attribute\ Standard - of - living - index$ numeric
$@attribute\ Media - exposure$ numeric
$@attribute\ Contraceptive - method - used$ numeric

Sometimes for some purposes you can execute filter on your data such as converting numeric data to nominal or removing some attributes. The following figure,fig 11, shows the place of filters in Weka.

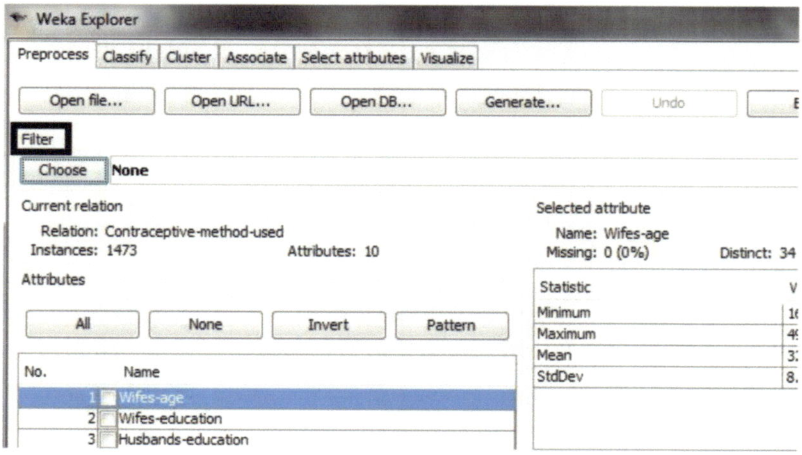

Fig. 11. Filter.

For executing linear regression, we chose "classify" from top tab (as shown in the above picture, fig 12). Then we chose "linear regression" from functions and leave other setting unchanged. Afterwards, we chose the last attribute as the target as shown in the below image, fig 13, and click on start to execute the algorithm.

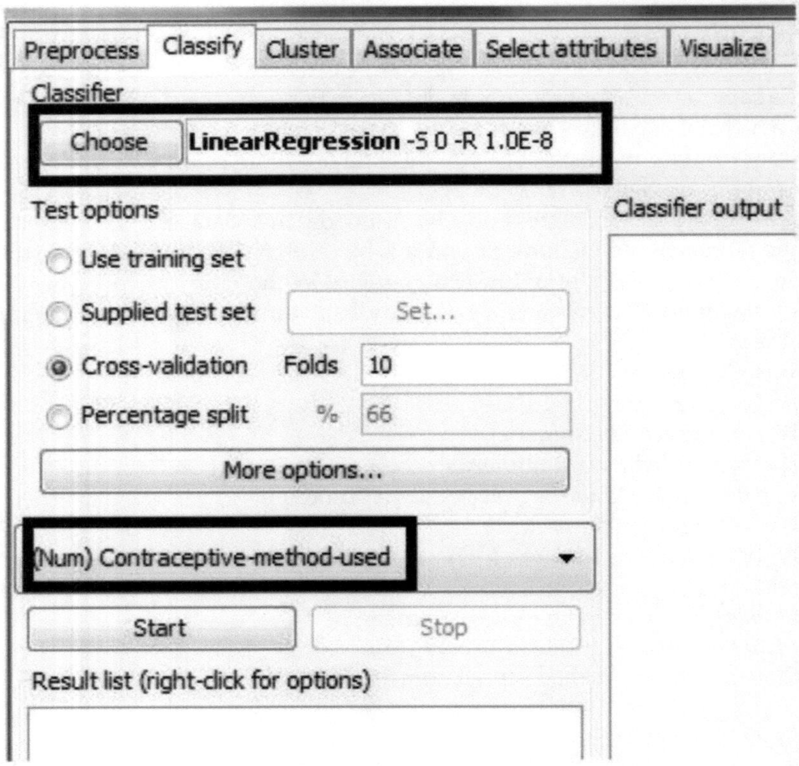

Fig. 12. Classify.

Output is shown in the following image, fig 13.
As you can see in figure 13, the regression equation based on the target $('contraceptive - method - used')$ is found and also some other values such as correlation coefficient are also found.
Enough is enough. Let's go to a very simple security example. A good example is in (M. Hajsalehi Sichani, 2009). Imagine you are a programmer and you have created software and you have designed a system for entering activation code. Its algorithm is like this:

1. Get the CPU id, like 2300
2. Multiply it by 3 and give it back to user as given-number, $2300 * 3 = 6900$
3. User must call you and tell you his given number (6900) and you put this number in the following equation:
   $3 * x + 5$
   and you give him 23705 $(3 * 6900 + 5 = 20705)$.
4. Now the user enters 20705 in the software as activation code.
5. Your program will substitute the given number in the equation $3 * x + 5$, and if the activating number is equal to the result then it let the user to use your software.

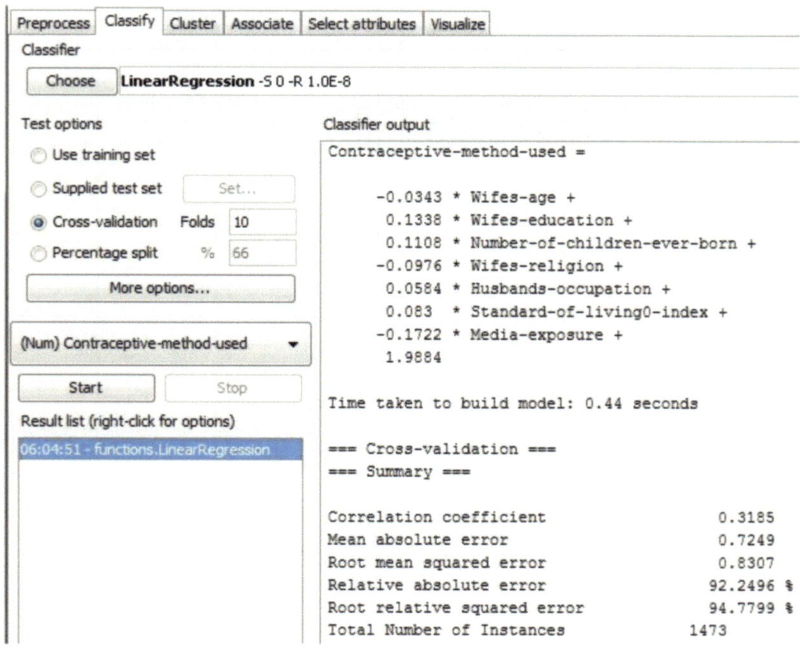

Fig. 13. Output of Weka.

Notice that instead of CPU id you can get his name and convert it to Ascii codes which are also integers number. Remember that in reality these kinds of algorithms are much more complicated than here.
Now as a cracker, Saeed, calls you and wants to activate the following numbers (left column) and you gave him the activation numbers (right column). Then he changes the data to an acceptable format (arff). The following lines are content of arff file.

@relationcrack
@attribute given − number numeric
@attribute activation − code numeric

@data

6900,20705
6903,20714
6906,20723
6909,20732
6912,20741
6915,20750
6918,20759
6921,20768
6927,20786
6930,20759

6936,20813
Then will start his work with RapidMiner. We will persuade him from now in figure 14 through 18, respectively.

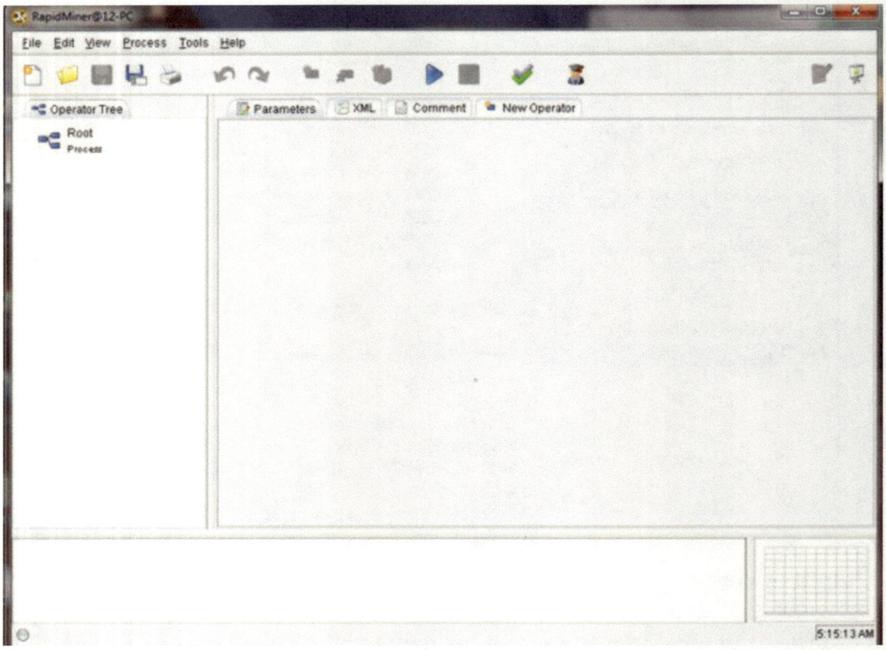

Fig. 14. Rapidminer enviroment.

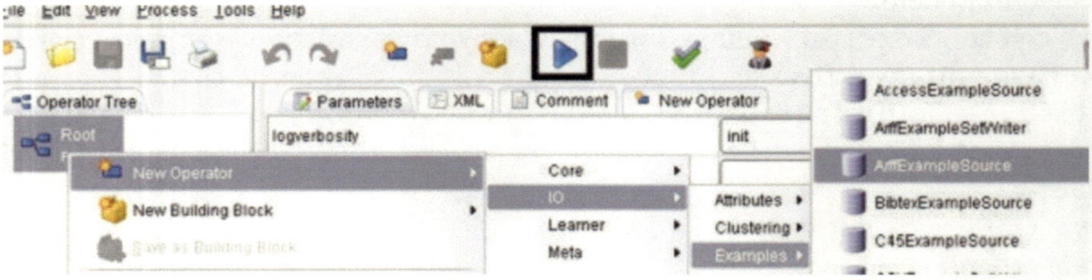

Fig. 15. Rapidminer first step.

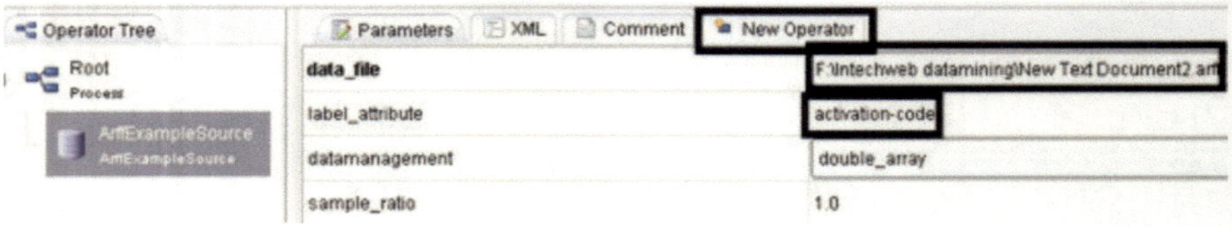

Fig. 16. Rapidminer second step.

As you can see in fig 18, the RapidMiner found the equation and the pattern behind the data.

8. Conclusion

We hope, in this chapter, you became familiar with the basic concept of data mining, linear regression, logistic regression, and neural network.

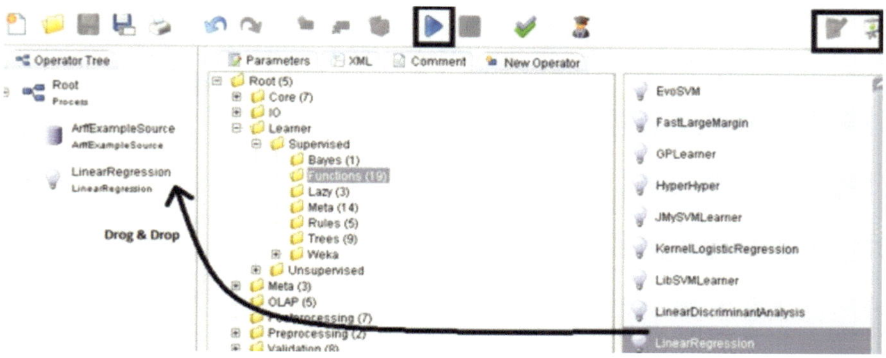

Fig. 17. Rapidminer 3rd step.

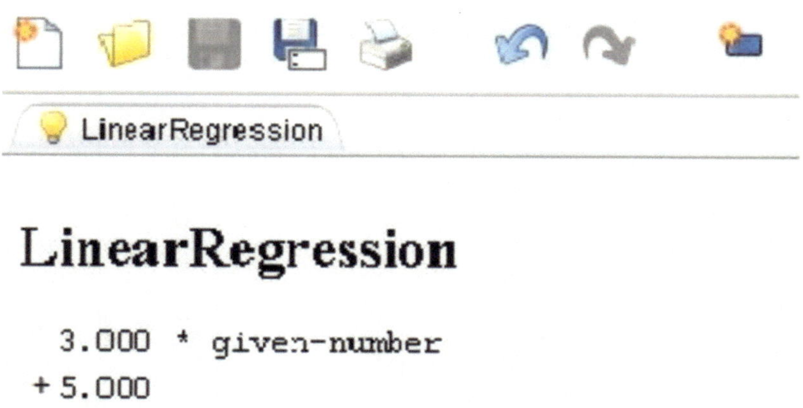

Fig. 18. Rapidminer found equation!.

At the end of this chapter, we focus on two of the data mining tools, Weka and RapidMiner, and show one practical example by each of them, individually. The second practical example was a security example which was a simplified one. Other data mining software are exists but may not be free like SPSS. The similar logic is behind them and if you know how to work with one of them, you can work with the rest of them. Just install them and start working.
At last, we hope you have found this ability to go and study data mining by your-self and use different resources such as google, sciencedirect, and IEEE.
We would announce a great thanks to H. Ghominejad for her technical support and also a great thanks to *Intechweb.org* team for their support.

9. References

Handan Ankarali Camdeviren, Ayse Canan Yazici, Z. A. R. B.-M. A. S. (2007). Comparison of logistic regression model and classification tree: An application to postpartum depression data, *Expert Systems with Applications* vol. 32: 987–994. www.sciencedirect.com.

Hsiang-Chuan Liu, Shin-Wu Liu, P.-C. C. W.-C. H. C.-H. L. (2008). A novel classifier for influenza a viruses based on svm and logistic regression, *International Conference on Wavelet Analysis and Pattern Recognition, ICWAPR '08* Vol. 1: 287–291. www.IEEE.org.

Kantardzic, M. (2003). *Data Mining: Concepts, Models, Methods, and Algorithms*, John Wiley & Sons.

M. Hajsalehi Sichani, A. M. (2009). A new analysis of rc4: A data mining approach (j48). www.secrypt.com.

M.K. Alsmadi, K. Bin Omar, S. N.-I. A. (2009). Performance comparison of multi-layer perceptron (back propagation, delta rule and perceptron) algorithms in neural networks, *IEEE International Advance Computing Conference, IACC 2009* pp. 296–299. www.IEEE.org.

Nirkhi, S. (2010). Potential use of artificial neural network in data mining, *The 2nd International Conference on Computer and Automation Engineering (ICCAE)* Vol. 2: 339–343. www.IEEE.org.

Peter Auer, Harald Burgsteiner, W. M. (2008). A learning rule for very simple universal approximators consisting of a single layer of perceptrons, *Neural Networks* vol. 21: 786–795. www.sciencedirect.com.

Peter C. Austin, Jack V. Tu, D. S. L. (2010). Logistic regression had superior performance compared with regression trees for predicting in-hospital mortality in patients hospitalized with heart failure, *Journal of Clinical Epidemiology, In Press, Corrected Proof, Available online 21 March 2010* . www.sciencedirect.com.

Witten, I. H. & Frank, E. (2005). *Data Mining : Practical machine learning tools and techniques*, 2nd edn, Morgan Kaufmann series in data management systems, UNITED STATES OF AMERICA.

Data Mining: Machine Learning and Statistical Techniques

Alfonso Palmer, Rafael Jiménez and Elena Gervilla
University of the Balearic Islands
Spain

1. Introduction

The interdisciplinary field of *Data Mining* (DM) arises from the confluence of statistics and machine learning (artificial intelligence). It provides a technology that helps to analyze and understand the information contained in a database, and it has been used in a large number of fields or applications. Specifically, the concept DM derives from the similarity between the search for valuable information in databases and mining valuable minerals in a mountain. The idea is that the raw material is the data to analyse, and we use a set of learning algorithms acting as diggers to search for valuable nuggets of information (Bigus, 1996).

We offer an applied vision of DM techniques, in order to provide a didactic perspective of the data analysis process of these techniques. We analyze and compare the results from applying machine learning algorithms and statistical techniques, under DM methodology, in searching for knowledge models that show the structures and regularities underlying the data analysed. In this sense, some authors have pointed out that DM consists of "the analysis of (often large) observational datasets to find unsuspected relationships and to summarize the data in novel ways that are both understandable and useful to the data owner" (Hand, Mannila & Smyth, 2001), or, more simply, "the search for valuable information in large volumes of data" (Weiss & Indurkhya, 1998), or "the discovery of interesting, unexpected or valuable structures in large databases" (Hand, 2007). Other authors define DM as "the exploration and analysis of large quantities of data in order to discover meaningful patterns and rules" (Berry & Linoff, 2004).

These definitions make it clear that DM is an appropriate process for detecting relationships and patterns in large databases (although we point out that it can also be applied in relatively small databases). In this sense, the concept of Knowledge Discovery in Databases (KDD) has been frequently used in the literature to define this process (Han & Kamber, 2000, 2006; Hand et al., 2001), specifying that DM is a stage of the process, and highlighting the need for a previous stage of integration and collection of data (if we start with large raw databases), and also the stage of cleaning and preparing data (data pre-processing) before building descriptive/predictive models in the DM stage (applying suitable techniques to the analysis requirements). On the other hand, several authors have used the concept of DM (instead of KDD) to refer to the complete process (Bigus, 1996; Two Crows, 1999; Paul, Guatam & Balint, 2002; Kantardzic, 2003; Ye, 2003; Larose, 2005).

In our work, we focus on the DM stage; i.e., the phase of application of suitable modelling techniques according to analysis needs. We show the analysis and comparison of several techniques to obtain knowledge models (predictive models) - we start from a pre-processed, relatively small volume of data (as we have said before, handling large databases is not a necessary requirement to apply data mining techniques). We analyze several machine learning and statistical (classical and modern) techniques. In order to choose these techniques, we took as a reference the work of the editors Michie et al. (1994), in which they review the wide repertory of classification techniques. In particular, we chose two classical machine learning techniques, Artificial Neural Networks (ANN) and Decision Trees (DT), two modern statistical techniques, k-Nearest Neighbor (k-NN) and Naive Bayes (NB), and a classical statistical technique, Logistic Regression (LR). Recently, Nisbet et al. (2009) have presented a work in which they explain and exemplify the use of these classification techniques with the *Statistica* platform, although they also use (to a lesser extent) the *SPSS Clementine* and *SAS Enterprise Miner* platforms. In our work, we exemplify the use of these techniques with the non commercial *Weka* platform.

The aim of the work that we are presenting is double. On the one hand, we present a comparison of the five aforementioned techniques, from a theoretical (methodological) and applied perspective. The applied perspective is covered from a case study, with the intention of comparing the performance of the models obtained with these techniques from one and the same database; with this applied aim, we use the Weka platform, an open code, freely distributed, *data mining* platform (developed in Java), in order to cover the second of the aims proposed in this work, which is to exemplify the advantages of Weka in order to carry out the comparative performance study from its *Explorer* and *Experimenter* modules.

2. Methodology

In this section we aim to offer an integrating view of the use of *Data Mining* (DM) methodology and techniques through a presentation of the procedures common to these techniques in the process of obtaining predictive models, and through a description of the methodological peculiarities associated to them. Specifically, we focus on a description of techniques which allow us to generate categorical response predictive models (classification models).

Table 1 presents a classification of some techniques included in DM according to the nature of the data analyzed. In this sense, we present the techniques available depending on the nature of the predictor variables and the output variable. If the output variable is continuous or categorical we find ourselves dealing with supervised learning models, whereas if there is no output variable we are dealing with unsupervised learning models.

Specifically, we will deal with the techniques of *Neural networks*, *Classification trees*, *k-Nearest Neighbor*, *Naive Bayes* and *Logistic regression*, since they make it possible to analyze categorical output variables in order to generate classification models.

Classification is a task that belongs to the category of supervised learning and it refers to the task of analyzing a set of pre-classified objects in order to learn a model (or function) which can be used to classify unknown data in one of several predefined classes (An, 2006).

From the perspective of supervised learning, the analysis technique estimates the model from the knowledge that it has of the behaviour of each of the entries in the selected output variable, in such a way that the supervised techniques itself supervises whether or not the model it is building adjusts to the knowledge it has of the reality. In this sense, the aim of

	Continuous response	Categorical response	No response
Continuous predictors	Linear regression Neural networks k-Nearest Neighbor	Logistic regression Neural networks Discriminant analysis k-Nearest Neighbor	Principal components Cluster analysis
Categorical predictors	Linear regression Neural networks Regression trees	Neural networks Classification trees Logistic regression Naive Bayes	Association rules

Table 1. Data mining techniques according to the nature of the data (Shmueli et al., 2007)

supervised learning is to generate knowledge based models which will help in predicting the behaviour of new data.

A common requirement in predictive modelling techniques is the use of a data sample (test data) which is independent of the one used in the construction of the model (training data), with the intention of assessing the model's generalization capacity (assessment of the model).

On the other hand, in unsupervised learning there are no known results to guide the algorithm in obtaining the model, but rather this explores the properties of the data with the aim of identifying behaviour patterns with no knowledge of these "a priori". In this way, the aim of unsupervised learning is to generate knowledge based models with a descriptive, not predictive, intention.

2.1 Artificial Neural Networks

Artificial Neural Networks (ANN) are data processing systems whose structure and functioning are inspired by biological neural networks. ANN were developed based on the following guidelines:

- Information processing occurs in simple elements called neurons.
- The neurons transmit signals through established connections.
- Each connection (communication link) has an associated weight.
- Each neuron applies an activation function (usually non linear) to the total entry of connected neurons received (sum of entries weighted according to the connection weights), thus obtaining an output value which will act as the entry value which will be transmitted to the rest of the network.

The fundamental characteristics of ANN are parallel processing, distributed memory and adaptability to the surroundings.

The processing unit is the artificial neuron, which receives the entries from the neighbouring neurons and calculates an output value, which is sent to all the remaining neurons.

As far as the representation of input and output information is concerned, we can find networks with continuous input and output data, networks with discrete or binary input and output data and networks with continuous input data and discrete output data.

An ANN is made up of the sequential order of three basic types of nodes or layers: input nodes, output nodes and intermediate nodes (hidden layer) (Figure 1). The input nodes are in charge of receiving the initial values of the data from each case in order to transmit them to the network. The output nodes receive input and calculate the output value.

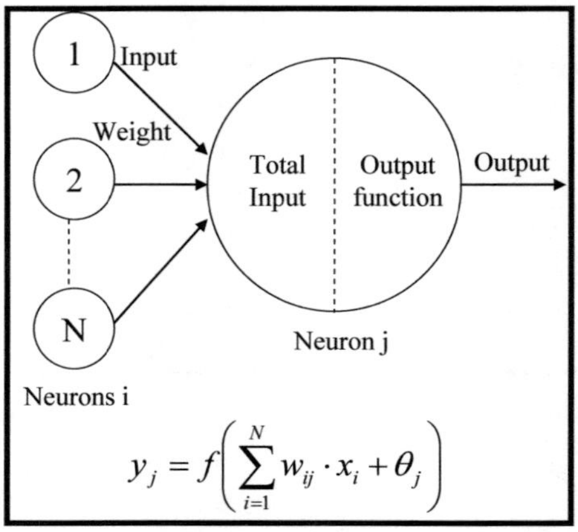

Fig. 1. Generic working of an artificial neuron and its output mathematical representation

This set of nodes used by the ANN, together with the activation function, makes it possible for the ANN to easily represent non-linear relationships, which are the most difficult as far as multivariate techniques are concerned.

The most used activation functions are: the step function, identity function, sigmoid or logistic function and the hyperbolic tangent.

There is a large selection of ANN models. A combination of the topology (number of neurons and hidden layers, and how they are connected), the learning paradigm and the learning algorithm define an ANN model (Bigus, 1996).

It can be said that an ANN has three advantages which makes it very attractive in data handling: adaptive learning through examples, robustness in handling redundant and inaccurate information and massive parallelism.

The most used method in the practical applications of ANN is the *multilayer perceptron,* which was made popular by Rumelhart et al. (1986).

A multilayer perceptron type of ANN starts with an input layer in which each node or neuron corresponds to a predictor variable. These input neurons connect with each of the neurons making up the hidden layer. The nodes in the hidden layer in turn connect with the neurons in another hidden layer. The output layer is made up of one (binary prediction) or more output neurons. In this sort of architecture, the information is always transmitted from the input layer towards the output layer.

The popularity of the multilayer perceptron is mainly due to the fact that it is capable of acting as a universal function approximator. More specifically, a "backpropagation" network which contains at least one hidden layer with enough non-linear units can learn any sort of function or continuous relationship between a group of input variables (discrete and/or continuous) and an output variable (discrete or continuous). This property makes multilayer perceptron networks general, flexible and non-linear tools. A complete description of the mathematical foundations associated with the training stage and the functioning stage of the *backpropagation* algorithm in multilayer perceptron architecture can be found in Rumelhart et al. (1986).

The usefulness of the multilayer perceptron, lies in its ability to learn virtually any relationship between a set of input and output variables. On the other hand, if we use techniques derived from classical statistics such as linear discriminant analysis, this does not have the capacity of calculating non-linear functions and, therefore, will show a lower performance compared to the multilayer perceptron in classification tasks that involve complex non-linear relationships.

When the network is used to classify normally the output layer has as many nodes as the number of classes and the node of the output layer with the highest value offers the estimate of the class which the network makes for a certain input. In the special case of two classes it is common to have a node in the output layer, and the classification between the two classes is carried out by applying a cut off point to the node value.

If one of the virtues of ANN is that they allow modelling any sort of functional relationship (linear or non linear) between variables and, therefore, act as universal function approximators, another of the outstanding advantages of this technique, compared to classical modelling techniques, is that it does not impose any sort of restriction with respect to the starting data (type of functional relationship between variables), neither does it usually start from specific assumptions (like the type of distribution the data follow). Another virtue of the technique lies in its capacity to estimate good models even despite the existence of noise in the information analyzed, as occurs when there is a presence of omitted values or outlier values in the distribution of the variables. Hence, it is a robust technique when dealing with problems of noise in the information presented; however, this does not mean that the cleaning criteria of the data matrix should be relaxed.

Nevertheless, its extreme flexibility lies in the need to have sufficient training data and that it requires more time for its execution than other techniques (Shmueli et al., 2007). It is worth pointing out that in ANN, as well as the set of training data to build the model and the set of independent data (test data) in order to assess its generalization capacity, a third set of independent data (validation set) is used to avoid overfitting the model (during the learning process) which can cause an excessive number of parameters or weights regarding the problem (Hastie et al., 2001, p. 356).

Despite the advantages presented concerning the technique, on the other hand, one of the most important criticisms that have been raised against the use of ANN focuses on the fact that a knowledge of the weights within the network does not in general help the interpretation of the underlying process that the prediction of a certain output value generates. To put it another way, the reproaches against the use of this technique are limited to the difficulty in understanding the nature of the internal representations generated by the network in response to a certain problem. Despite this, this perception of ANN as a complex "black box" is not completely true. In this sense, different attempts at interpreting the weights of the neuronal network have arisen, of which the most widely used is the so-called sensitivity analysis (Montaño & Palmer, 2003), implemented in ANN programmes as recently presented by Palmer et al. (2001), under the name of *Sensitivity Neural Network 1.0.*

2.2 Decision Trees

Decision trees (DT) are sequential partitions of a set of data that maximise the differences of a dependent variable (response or output variable). They offer a concise way of defining groups that are consistent in their attributes but which vary in terms of the dependent variable.

DT are made up of nodes (input variables), branches (groups of entries in the input variables) and leaves or leaf nodes (values of the output variable).

The construction of a DT is based on the principle of "divide and conquer": through a supervised learning algorithm, successive divisions of the multivariable space are carried out in order to maximise the distance between groups in each division (that is, carry out partitions that discriminate). The division process finalizes when all the entries of a branch have the same value in the output variable (pure leaf node), giving rise to the complete model (maximum specified). The further down the input variables are in the tree, the less important they are in the output classification (and the less generalization they allow, due to the decrease in the number of inputs in the descending branches).

To avoid overfitting the model, the tree can be pruned by eliminating the branches with few or scarcely significant entries. As a result, if we start from the complete model, after the tree pruning this will gain in generalization capacity (assessed with test data), at the expense of reducing the degree of purity of its leaves (Larose, 2005).

There are different learning algorithms designed to obtain DT models (see Table 2). The learning algorithm determines the following aspects:

- Specific compatibility with the type of variables: nature of the input variables and the output variable.
- Assessment procedure of the distance between groups in each division: division criteria.
- Restrictions can be placed on the number of branches each node can be divided into.
- Pruning parameters [pre-pruning / post-pruning]: minimum number of entries per node or branch, critical value of the division, performance difference between the extended and reduced tree. Pre-pruning implies using stopping criteria during the construction of the tree, whereas post-pruning applies the pruning parameters to the whole tree.

The most used algorithms (Table 2) are CART (*Classification And Regression Trees*), CHAID (*Chi-Squared Automatic Interaction Detection*), QUEST (*Quick, Unbiased, Efficient Statistical Tree*) and C4.5 / C5.0.

The CART algorithm was designed by Breiman et al. (1984) and it generates binary decision trees, where each node is divided exactly into two branches. In this way, if the input variable is nominal and has more than two categories, it groups different categories in one branch. If the input variable is nominal or continuous, it still generates two branches, associating a set of values limited by the operators to each one of them "less than or equal to" or "greater" than a certain value. The CART algorithm makes it possible to introduce nominal, ordinal and continuous input data into the model. The output variable of the model may likewise be nominal, ordinal or continuous.

The CHAID algorithm (Kass, 1980) was originally designed to handle only categorical variables. Nevertheless, nowadays it makes it possible to handle nominal and ordinal categorical output data and continuous variables. The tree construction process is based on the calculation of the significance of a statistical contrast as a criterion in order to decide the hierarchy of importance of the predictor variables, and to establish clusters of similar values (statistically homogeneous) with respect to the output variable, keeping all the values that turn out to be heterogeneous (distinct) unaltered. Similar values are melted in one category, forming part of one branch of the tree. The statistical test used depends on the level of measurement of the output variable. If the aforementioned variable is continuous, the F test is used. If the output variable is categorical, the Chi-square test is used.

A differential characteristic between the CART and CHAID algorithms is that the latter allows the division of each node into more than one branch; therefore it tends to create much wider trees than the binary development methods.
The QUEST algorithm (Loh & Shih, 1997) can be used if the output is nominal-categorical (allows the creation of classification trees). The tree construction process is also based on the calculation of the significance of a statistical contrast. For each input variable, if this is a nominal categorical variable, it calculates the critical level of a Pearson Chi-square independence contrast between the input variable and the output variable. If the input variable is ordinal or continuous, it uses the F test.
The C5.0 algorithm (Quinlan, 1997) only admits categorical output variables. Input variables may be categorical or continuous. This algorithm is the result of the evolution of algorithm C4.5 (Quinlan, 1993) designed by the same author and which has as a nucleus the ID3 version (Quinlan, 1986). The ID3 algorithm is based on the concept of *information gain* to select the best attribute.

ALGORITHMS	Input variables	Output variable	Type of prediction	Splitting branches	Splitting criterion
CHAID	categorical / numerical	categorical / numerical	classification / regression	≥2	Chi-square / F
QUEST	categorical / numerical	categorical	classification	=2	Chi-square / F
CART	categorical / numerical	categorical / numerical	classification / regression	=2	GINI / Least squared deviation
C4.5 / C5.0	categorical / numerical	categorical	classification	≥2	Gain Ratio

Table 2. Comparative between learning algorithms for decision trees (amplified version of Gervilla et al., 2009)

One of the most outstanding advantages of DT is their descriptive nature, which allows us to easily understand and interpret the decisions made by the model, as we have access to the rules that are used in the predictive task (an aspect that is not taken into consideration in other machine learning techniques, such as ANN). Thus, DT allow the graphic representation of a series of rules concerning the decision that must be made in the assignment of an output value for a certain entry, offering a friendly, intuitive explanation of the results.
On the other hand, the decision rules provided by a tree model have a predictive value (not only descriptive) from the moment in which their accuracy is assessed from independent data (test data) to the ones used in the construction of the model (training data).
Another attractive characteristic of DT is that they are intrinsically robust to missing values, as they handle them without having to impute values or eliminate observations.
Nevertheless, DT do have some weaknesses (Shmueli et al., 2007): they are sensitive to small changes in the data and, unlike the models that assume a particular relationship between the response and the prediction (e.g. a linear relationships like a linear regression), DT are

not linear and are not parametrical. This allows for a wide range of relationships between the predictors and the response, but it can be a weakness: given the fact that the partitions are carried out on unique predictors rather than on combinations of predictors, DT probably omit relationships between predictors, particularly linear structures such as linear or logistic regression models.

Another drawback in the construction of DT is the problem of overfitting the model, that is to say, the DT includes not only the real patterns or structures present in the data, but also part of the "noise". To reduce this problem as much as possible there are several strategies:

- Strategies that slow down the growth of the tree before it reaches the perfect classification of the examples in the training set (for instance, the CHAID algorithm).
- Strategies that make it possible for the tree to grow completely and afterwards carry out some pruning (for instance, the CART and C4.5 algorithms). These latter have been shown to be more efficient than the former.

One final disadvantage of DT is that they need a large set of data in order to build a good classifier. Nevertheless, Breiman & Cutler (2004) have introduced "Random Forests", which deal with these limitations. The basic idea is to create multiple DT from the data (and thus obtain the "forest") and to combine their result to obtain a better classifier (see Breiman, 2001).

2.3 k-Nearest Neighbor

When we run into new situations, we human beings are guided by memories of similar situations we have experienced in the past. This is the basis of the k-Nearest Neighbor (k-NN) technique. That is, the k-NN technique is based on the concept of similarity. Moreover, this technique constructs a classification method without making assumptions concerning the shape of the function that relates the dependent variable with the independent variables. The aim is to identify in a dynamic way *k* observations in the training data that are similar to a new observation that we want to classify. In this way, *k* similar (neighbouring) observations are used to classify the observation specifically in a class (see Figure 2). More specifically, k-NN looks for observations in the training data that are similar or near to the observation that has to be classified, based on the values of the independent variables (attributes). Then, depending on the classes of these nearby observations, it assigns a class to the observation that it wishes to classify, taking the majority vote of the neighbours to determine the class. In other words, it counts the number of cases in each class and assigns the new case to the one that most of its neighbours belongs to (Two Crows, 1999).

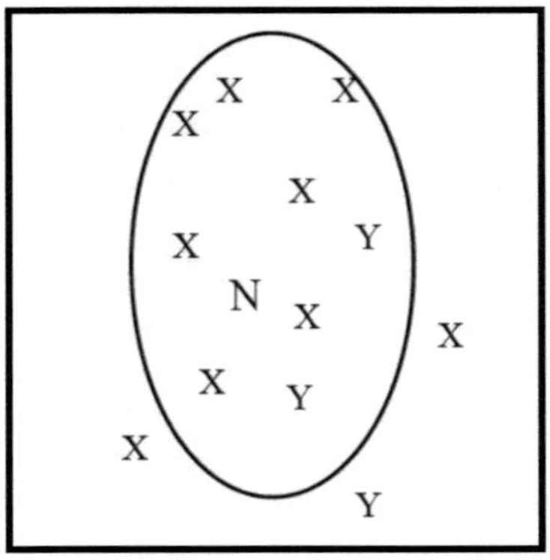

Fig. 2. Graphical representation of k-NN classification (Two Crows, 1999)

Even though the method may appear "naive", it is capable of competing with the other more sophisticated classification methods. Hence, where the linear model is rigid, k-NN is extremely flexible. The performance of this technique for data of the same size depends on *k*, and on the measurement used to determine which observations are nearby.

As a result, in the application of the technique we must take into account how many neighbours are to be considered (*k* value), how we measure the distance, how we combine the information for more than one observation and whether all the neighbours should bear the same weight (see Berry & Linoff, 2004).

As has been said, the k-NN technique classifies an unknown example in the most common class by using its *k* nearby neighbours. It assumes that all the examples correspond to points in an *n*-dimensional space. A neighbour is considered nearby if it has the least distance in the *n*-dimensional space of attributes (An, 2006). If we set *k*=1, the unknown example is classified in the class of the nearest neighbour in the training data.

Although there is no formula to choose the *k* number, it is worth noting that if we choose a small *k* value, the classification may possibly be too affected by outlier values or unusual observations. On the other hand, choosing a not very small *k* value will tend to damp any idiosyncratic behaviour learnt from the training data. Nevertheless, if we choose a *k* value that is too large, locally interesting behaviour will be overlooked.

You can let the data help to solve this problem by following a procedure of cross validation. That is, we can try several *k* values with different training sets chosen at random and choose the *k* value that minimizes the classification error.

With respect to the way of measuring the distance, the most common distance function is the Euclidean distance (1), where x and y represent the *m* values of the attributes of two cases.

$$d_{\text{Euclidean}}(x, y) = \sqrt{(x_i - y_i)^2} \quad (1)$$

Although, alternatively, the Manhattan distance may also be used (2)

$$d_{\text{Manhattan}}(x, y) = | x_1 - x_2 | + | y_1 - y_2 | \quad (2)$$

The Euclidean distance has three drawbacks:

- The distance depends on the units chosen to measure the variables.
- It does not take into account the variability of the different variables.
- It ignores the correlation between variables.

One solution is to use a measurement called statistical distance (or *Mahalanobis* distance).

By way of advantages of the k-NN technique we can highlight (An, 2006; Mitchell, 1997; Nisbet et al., 2009): first of all, it does not simplify the distribution of objects in space in a set of comprehensible characteristics; instead, the training set is stored completely as a description of this distribution. Furthermore, the k-NN method is intuitive, easy to implement and effective in practice. It can construct a different approximation to the target function for each new example to be classified, which is advantageous when the target function is very complex, but it can be described by a collection of less complex local approximations. Finally, this technique builds a classification method without carrying out assumptions concerning the shape of the function that relates the dependent variable (classification variable) with the independent variables (attributes).

On the other hand, the most important disadvantage is that k-NN is very sensitive to the presence of irrelevant parameters. Other disadvantages:

- The time to find nearby neighbours in a large training set may be very high.
- The number of observations that are needed in the training data increases exponentially with the number of dimensions (variables).

2.4 Naive Bayes

Bayesian methods use the Bayes rule or formula (3) (based on Bayes' theorem), which expresses a very powerful framework to combine information from the sample with expert opinion (prior probability) so as to produce an up-dated expert opinion (posterior probability) (Giudici, 2003).

Specifically, the Naive Bayes technique (NB) is a very powerful classification technique and is one of the most widely used ones, due to its computationally simple process (Hand & Yu, 2001). As it is based on Bayes' theorem, it can predict the probability of a given case belonging to a certain class. Its computational simplicity is due to the assumption known as class *conditional independence* (this assumes that the effect of an attribute value on a certain class is independent of the values of the other attributes), and in this sense it is considered a "naive" classifier (Han & Kamber, 2000, 2006).

This classifier predicts that a case A will belong to class C_i which has the highest X conditioned posterior probability (set of attributes of the case in the predictor variables). Bayes' theorem allows us to define the Bayes' formula (3) that this posterior probability provides; and since P(X) is constant for all the classes, we only need to maximize $P(X \mid C_i)P(C_i)$ in the classification process.

$$P(C_i \mid X) = \frac{P(X \mid C_i)P(C_i)}{P(X)} \tag{3}$$

From a set of training data, $P(C_i)$ how many times each class C_i occurs in these data can be estimated. To reduce the computational cost of estimating $P(X \mid C_i)$ for all possible x_k (predictor variables), the classifier uses precisely the "naive" assumption that the attributes used to describe X are conditionally independent from each other given class C_i. This conditional independence can be found in the expression (4), where the *m* value indicates the number of predictor variables that participate in the classification.

$$P(X \mid C_i) = \prod_{k=1}^{m} P\left(x_k \mid C_i\right) \tag{4}$$

The studies that compare classification algorithms (e.g. Michie et al., 1994) have often shown that NB is comparable in its working with ANN and DT, and in fact exceeds these sophisticated classifiers if the attributes are conditionally independent given the class. Recent theoretical analyses have shown why NB is so robust (Domingos & Pazzani, 1997; Rish, 2001).

The appeal of NB classifiers lies in their simplicity, computational efficiency and good performance in classification. What is more, NB can easily handle unknown values or missing values. Nevertheless, it has three important drawbacks (Shmueli et al., 2007): first of all, it requires a large number of cases in order to obtain good results; secondly, if a prediction category is not present in the training data, the technique assumes that a new case with this category in the predictor has zero probability; finally, even though we obtain a good performance if the aim is to classify or order cases according to their probability of belonging to a certain class, this method offers very biased results when the aim is to estimate the probability of belonging to a class.

Above and beyond these drawbacks, the NB technique is straightforward to use, it adjusts to the data and is easy to interpret. In addition, it requires only one exploration of the data. This simplicity, parsimony and interpretability has led it to enjoy widespread popularity, especially in the literature of machine learning (Hand et al., 2001).

2.5 Logistic Regression

Linear regression is used to approach the relationship between a continuous response variable and a set of predictor variables. However, when the response variable is categorical, linear regression is not appropriate.

Logistic regression (LR) is a generalized linear model. It is used mainly to predict binary variables (with values like yes/no or 0/1). Thus, LR techniques may be used to classify a new observation, whose group is unknown, in one of the groups, based on the values of the predictor variables.

As with linear regression, the classification depends on the linear combination of the attributes. The logistic function (5) transforms the linear combination into an interval [0,1] (Ye, 2003). Thus, in order to use LR, the dependent variable is transformed into a continuous value which is a function of the probability of the event happening (Parr-Rud, 2001; Witten & Frank, 2005).

$$p = \frac{1}{1 + \exp^{-(\beta_0 + \beta_1 x_1 + \beta_2 x_2 + \ldots + \beta_k x_k)}} \tag{5}$$

In LR we follow two steps: the first step consists of estimating the probability of belonging to each group and in the second step we use a cut off point with these probabilities to classify each case in one of the groups. The parameters of the model are estimated with the method of maximum likelihood through a process of successive iterations. For a more detailed explanation of the LR technique, consult Larose (2006).

Lastly, it is worth commenting that LR can produce stable results with relatively few data (Harris-Jones & Haines, 1998). On the other hand, the fact that traditional regression is so widely accepted, easily implemented and generally understood makes it even more attractive (Hill et al., 2004). What is more, LR shows behaviour analogous to a diagnostic test.

3. Applying data mining techniques

In this section we go further, from the applied point of view, into the integration within DM methodology of the techniques described in the previous section. We use the *Weka* platform to meet this aim. In the first section, we give a brief description of the functionalities integrated in the Weka interface, with the aim of providing the reader with a presentation of the tool and to specify its virtues. In the second section, we propose a case study in order to compare with Weka the performance of predictive models obtained with the techniques indicated.

3.1 Weka interface

Weka (Waikato Environment for Knowledge Analysis) is a data mining platform distributed under public license GNU-GPL: it is free software that can be freely used, copied, studied, modified and distributed and it is protected from appropriation attempts that would restrict these user liberties.

Bearing in mind its characteristics, we find that it is a tool which, first of all, has an interactive interface which contains four user-machine interaction modalities (Fig. 3):

- **Explorer:** is the most used mode and the most descriptive.
- **Experimenter:** useful mode to compare the performance of different predictive models (experiments).
- **KnowledgeFlow:** allows the visual programming of modelling design through connected object modules.
- **Simple CLI (Simple Client):** provides a console to execute the functionality of the system through commands; it makes it possible to carry out any operation supported by Weka directly, although it does demand a comprehensive command of the application.

Fig. 3. Applications of the Weka interface

Within the **Explorer** modality, it provides extensive support to the overall process of data mining (Fig. 4):

1. Access to databases, exploration and selection of data and data processing:
   - **Preprocess**: functionality aimed at importation, transformation (application of filters) and data extraction.
   - **Visualize**: functionality aimed at the visualization of data using graphic techniques.
2. Predictive and descriptive modelling. Compiles a wide range of data mining procedures for the obtention of knowledge models:
   - **Classify** (classification and regression): predictive modelling (supervised learning).
   - **Cluster** (grouping) and **Associate** (association rules): descriptive modelling (unsupervised learning).
   - **Select attributes**: selection of predictive attributes.

Lastly, it is worth highlighting the possibility of **system extensibility**: it allows the user to modify Weka by integrating new functionality developed in Java code, using its structure and object oriented functional design. This represents the main advantage as opposed to other closed code data mining platforms (commercial programmes).

In Witten & Frank (2005) you can find a detailed description of the different modalities of interaction with Weka.

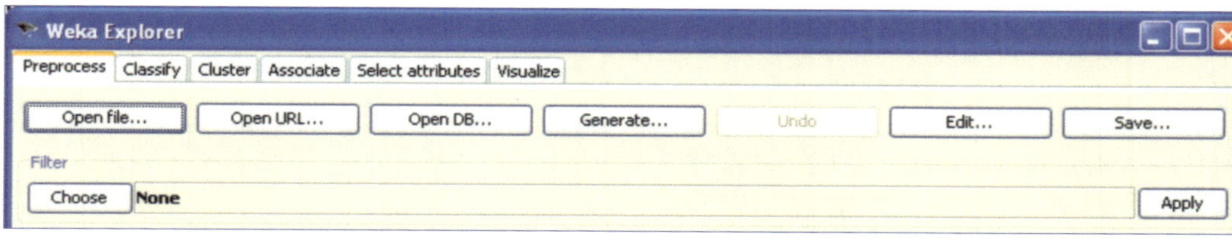

Fig. 4. Weka Explorer interface

3.2 Case study

Once we have presented the methodological basis of the techniques involved in this work, in this section we aim to contribute comparative elements of the information provided by these techniques in an applied context. These comparative elements refer to the predictive power (accuracy) of the knowledge models generated and the descriptive components that add informative value to the decision making processes (classifications). Thus we aim to provide a more integrating view, if possible, of DM methodology, since we provide common assessment parameters in order to compare the results obtained.

Nevertheless, from the analysis of these results we do not aim to reach substantial conclusions related to the context from which the data used comes, but rather our intention is to divulge to the readers a series of methodological tools that allow us to detect knowledge patterns in a way that is practically automatic and, on the other hand, to make it easier to interpret the descriptive elements associated with the assessment of the models obtained.

From an initial sample of 9300 young people aged between 14 and 18 years, in which information concerning variables intervening in the consumption of addictive substances was collected, we selected a sub-sample of 2526 young people. We are interested in studying the relationship between the consumption / non consumption of cannabis (output variable) among the people surveyed and the reasons the subjects surveyed have for consuming or not consuming drugs (input variables). Specifically, we collected fifteen possible reasons (variables) for consuming drugs and eleven reasons (variables) for not consuming; the possible response to each of these variables is dichotomous (yes/no). On the other hand, if in the initial sample (complete) the percentage of consumers of cannabis is nearly 18%, as opposed to 78% of non consumers, the sub-sample selected shows a greater balance between consumers/non consumers (44.4%/55.6%); this equilibrium (or balancing) is justified by methodological motives, as there must be a similar number of entries in each of the output categories (consumes/does not consume), so that they can be equally represented in the modelling stage (detection of classificatory patterns).

In a session with **Explorer**, first of all we loaded (Open file...) in the **Preprocess** section the data to be analyzed, whose structure (database) has been adapted to the Weka format: Arff file. Once the data file is open, it is possible to explore the variables they contain (Fig. 5). It is also possible to read data in the CSV (comma delimited) format from Weka, although it is not possible to import databases in the more widely used formats such as Excel, Access, SPSS, etc. However, there is the possibility of converting these other more common formats into the native Arff format from the data mining platform *RapidMiner* (free, open code software, which also allows the use of the algorithms included in Weka). For instance, if the data source is in SPSS format, we can indicate whether we are interested in extracting the names of the variables and/or their labels in another format (Arff, in this case), and whether we are interested in using the labels of the values (option be default) instead of the numerical values.

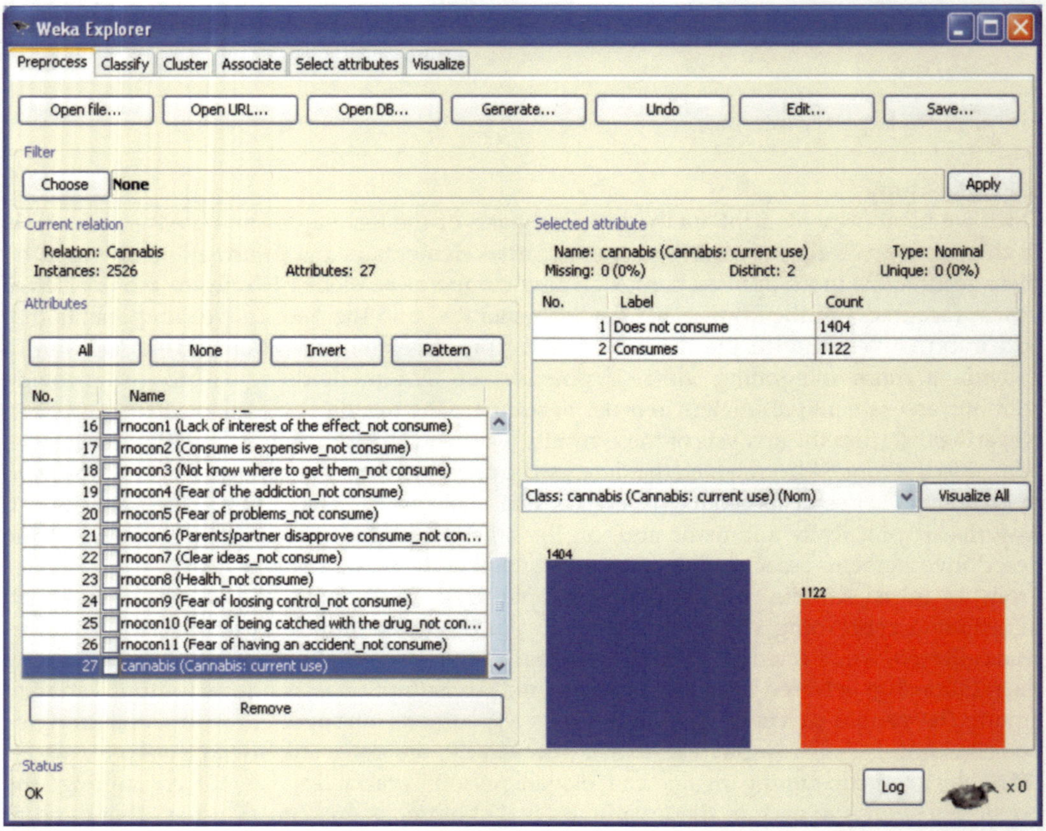

Fig. 5. Weka Explorer interface: exploring variables

From the section **Classify**, we access the different modelling techniques integrated in Weka (Fig. 6). For instance, we can select the *J48* classifier (weka.classifiers.trees.J48); this classifier uses the C4.5 algorithm (Quinlan, 1993) to generate a classification tree which is in agreement with a series of parameters determined by the algorithm (to edit them, click on the classifier) and other parameters determined by data mining methodology (in *Test options*). In the example (Fig. 6) we have indicated that the J48 classifier uses 70%of the sample (training data) to create the model, and the rest as test data. The output variable is also indicated (predicted variable), which by default is the last variable in the database. The *Start* button allows us to generate the model and access (in *Classifier output*) the model's assessment results. It can be observed that the model has correctly classified 599 of the 758 test patterns (79%), with a larger percentage of hits in the category *Does not consume* (83.4%) than in the category *Consumes* (73.9%).

It is possible to access the graphic representation of the classification tree (Fig. 7) through the options of the contextual menu (*Visualize tree*) of the model generated (in the *Result list*).

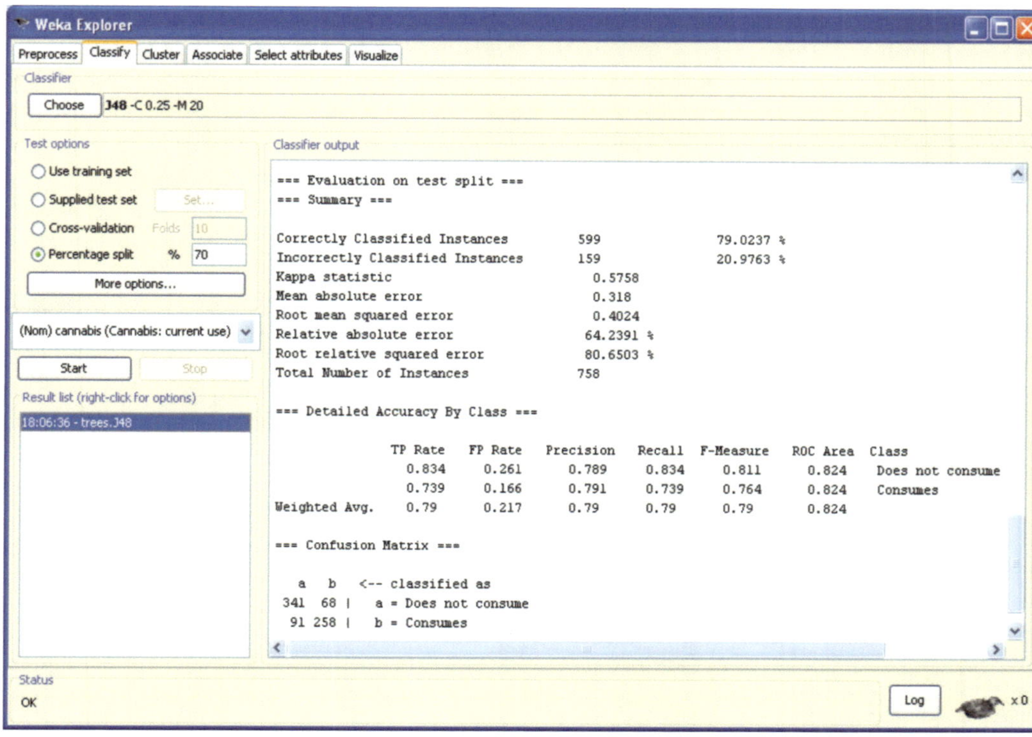

Fig. 6. Evaluation of the selected decision tree model on test data

What is more, the descriptive nature of decision trees allows us to easily derive the *classification rules* used by the model, with information from their **support** (percentage of cases in which the antecedent and consequent of the rule - correct prediction - are found with respect to the total subjects) and their **confidence** (percentage of cases in which the antecedent and consequent of the rule are found with respect to the number of subjects in which the antecedent of the rule is found). In Table 3 we show some examples. If we focus on the rule associated to leaf 1 (*Leaf1* in Fig. 7), it can be seen that out of the 1768 subjects who took part in the generation of the model (training stage), 550 (31.3%) of them consider - antecedents of the rule - their pleasurable nature a reason for consuming drugs (rcons3) and do not consider the fact that their friends consume a reason for consuming (rcons9) and at the same time -consequent of the rule - they are consumers of cannabis. Hence, if we want to classify new subjects in the output variable (consumes / does not consume), in the case in which their values in the output variables coincide with the model's rule, this would indicate that they are consumers of cannabis, with a confidence of 82.3% in the decision adopted. The confidence of the rule indicates to us, therefore, that there are 17.7% of subjects (118 cases) who fulfil the antecedent of the rule, but not the consequent (they are not consumers of cannabis).

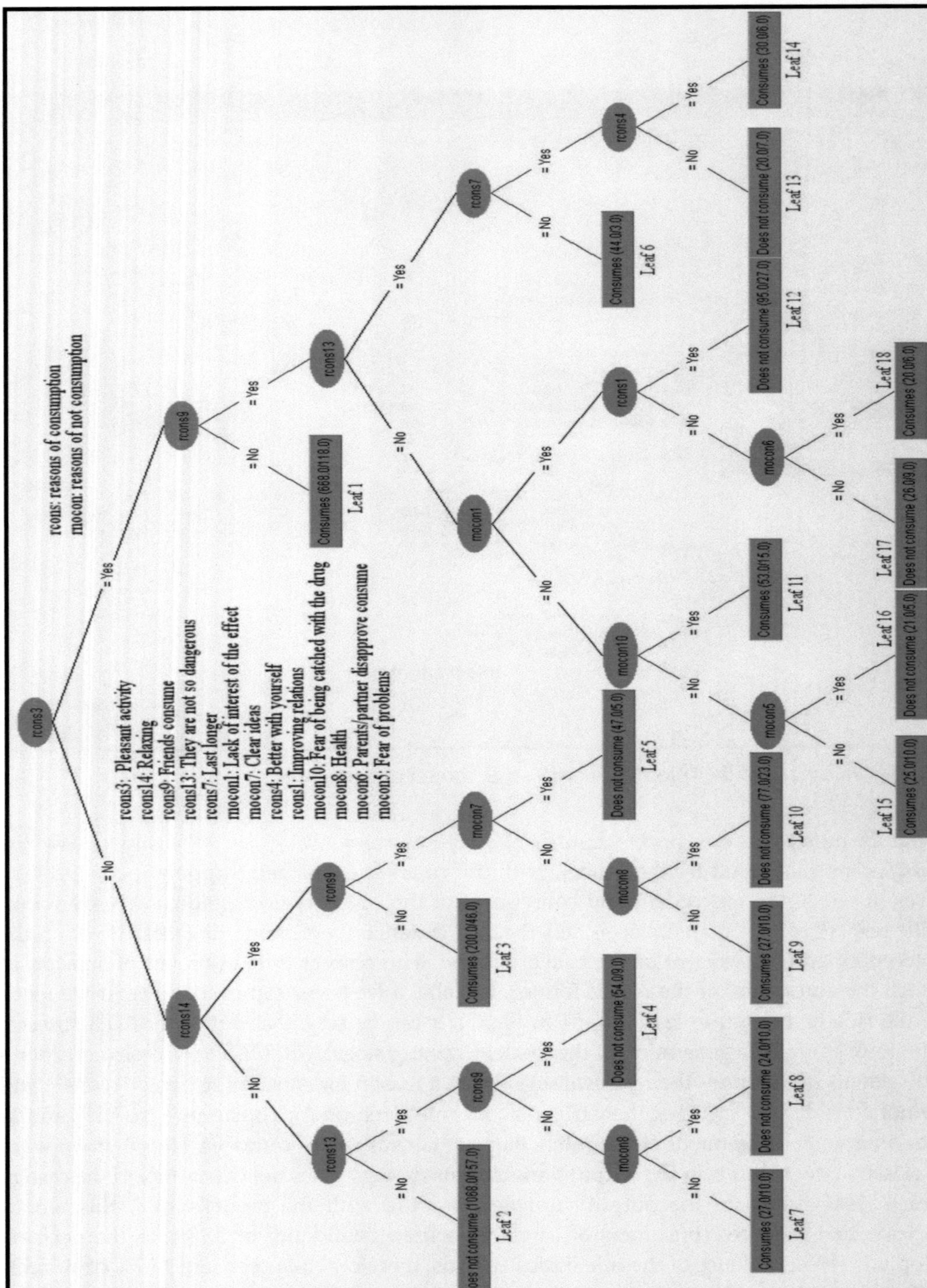

Fig. 7. Decision tree to classify subjects in "consumes" or "does not consume" cannabis

Leaf 1 **Rule:** IF (rcons3 = Yes) & (rcons9 = No) THEN (Consumes) **Cases:** 668; **Correctly classified:** 550 → **Rule support:** 31.1% (550/1768) **Rule confidence:** 82.3% (550/668)
Leaf 2 **Rule:** IF (rcons3 = No) & (rcons14 = No) & (rcons13 = No) THEN (Does not consume) **Cases:** 1068; **Correctly classified:** 911 → **Rule support:** 51.5% (911/1768) **Rule confidence:** 85.3% (911/1068)
Leaf 5 **Rule:** IF (rcons3 = No) & (rcons14 = Yes) & (rcons9 = Yes) & (rnocon7 = Yes) THEN (Does not consume) **Cases:** 47; **Correctly classified:** 42 → **Rule support:** 2.4% (42/1768) **Rule confidence:** 89.4% (42/47)
Leaf 14 **Rule:** IF (rcons3 = Yes) & (rcons9 = Yes) & (rcons13 = Yes) & (rcons7 = Yes) & (rcons4 = Yes) THEN (Consumes) **Cases:** 30; **Correctly classified:** 24 → **Rule support:** 1.4% (24/1768) **Rule confidence:** 80% (24/30)

Table 3. Some classification rules from the selected decision tree

As mentioned above, with Weka we have generated other classifying models from the techniques described in the previous section, using the same training (70%) and test (30%) sub-samples in all of them.

Specifically, to generate a neural network we used the *MultilayerPerceptron* classifier (weka.classifiers.functions.MultilayerPerceptron) (it uses the *backpropagation* algorithm), keeping 20% of the training data as validation data (*validationSetSize* parameter of the classifier).

In order to obtain the k-Nearest Neighbor model, we used the *IBk* classifier (weka.classifiers.lazy.IBk), with the Euclidean distance function.

Lastly, we generated a Naive Bayes model (weka.classifiers.bayes.NaiveBayes) and a logistic regression model (weka.classifiers.functions.Logistic).

Table 4 shows the comparison of the correct classifications (accuracy) between models, through the respective confusion matrices (bivariate contingency tables in which the real classification categories are crossed with the entries in the categories estimated by the model). It is shown that in all the models selected there is a relatively high accuracy (ranging between 76.6% for the *IBk* model and 80.1% for the *Logistic* model). If we analyze the accuracy according to the classificatory category, in all the models the percentage of correct classifications in the category *Does not consume* is greater (ranging between 81.4% for the *NaiveBayes* model and 90.5% for the *IBk* model), whereas in the *Consumes* category the range of correct classifications moves between 60.5% for the *IBk* model and 75.9% for the *Logistic* model.

Since the same test sub-sample was used in all the models selected, it is possible to carry out a comparison of the coincidences in the classification of the cases (Table 5). The condition of coincidence was established in those cases in which all the models converge on the same

		Actual category		
Decision Tree		Does not consume	Consumes	Total
Predicted category	Does not consume	**341**	91	432
	Consumes	68	**258**	326
J48	Total	409	349	**758**
	Accuracy	83.4%	73.9%	**79.0%**
Artificial Neural Network		Does not consume	Consumes	Total
Predicted category	Does not consume	**358**	111	469
	Consumes	51	**238**	289
MultilayerPerceptron	Total	409	349	**758**
	Accuracy	87.5%	68.2%	**78.6%**
k-Nearest Neighbor		Does not consume	Consumes	Total
Predicted category	Does not consume	**370**	138	508
	Consumes	39	**211**	250
IBk	Total	409	349	**758**
	Accuracy	90.5%	60.5%	**76.6%**
Naive Bayes		Does not consume	Consumes	Total
Predicted category	Does not consume	**333**	96	429
	Consumes	76	**253**	329
NaiveBayes	Total	409	349	**758**
	Accuracy	81.4%	72.5%	**77.3%**
Logistic Regression		Does not consume	Consumes	Total
Predicted category	Does not consume	**342**	84	426
	Consumes	67	**265**	332
Logistic	Total	409	349	**758**
	Accuracy	83.6%	75.9%	**80.1%**

Table 4. Confusion matrix and model performance with test data

classification, whereas the condition of non coincidence is given when at least one model classifies in a different way to the rest. It can be seen that there are 76% of cases in which all the models converge on the same classification, with the greater agreement found in the category *does not consume*.

	Prediction agreement			
	Does not consume	Consumes	Not agreement	Total
Cases	367	209	182	758
Percent	48.4%	27.6%	24%	
	Agreement: 76% (576 cases)			

Table 5. Prediction agreement between models

We can also analyze the confusion matrix between the cases that converge on the classification predicted by the five models (576 subjects) and the real classification category (Table 6). We found that the percentage of correct classifications is 84.9%, with greater accuracy (91.9%) in the category *does not consume.*

		Actual category		
Agreement		Does not consume	Consumes	Total
Predicted category	Does not consume	**307**	60	367
	Consumes	27	**182**	209
	Total	334	242	**576**
	Accuracy	91.9%	75.2%	**84.9%**

Table 6. Confusion matrix between prediction agreement and actual classification

Weka also allows us to access the individual prediction data if the option *Output predictions* is activated using the button *More options…* (see Fig. 6); these predictions are included in the window of results (*Classifier output*) together with the model's assessment information. In this way, we can compare the predicted classification and confidence level (probability) in this classification, case by case and for each model.

We extracted the individual predictions obtained in each of the five models to a data base outside Weka (Fig. 8), so as to be able to compare the degree of agreement and the confidence level in the joint classificatory decision (0: does not consume; 1: consumes) for a certain case. For instance, we can compare the predicted classification in cases 1 and 6; in both cases, the five models converge on the classification (*consumes*), even though the confidence level for this decision is lower (on average) in subject 1 (p=0.805) than in subject 6 (p=0.925).

Weka also allows us to reassess a given model with a new set of data independent from the one used in its construction. Through the contextual menu of the *Result list* section of Explorer (see Fig. 6), the model can be loaded in memory (*Load model* option) if it had been saved (*Save model* option) before closing the Weka session in which it was built. Once the model has been loaded in the memory, a new set of data must be chosen through the

Supplied test set option, and finally select *Re-evaluate model on current test set* in the contextual menu of the model. This option can also serve in new cases to find out the classification proposal of already validated predictive models (by activating the *Output predictions* option).

Finally, it is possible to access the Weka *Experimenter* model in order to configure experiments (simulations) with different predictive model techniques applied to the same set of data (Fig. 9), and thus be able to assess and compare the capacity of the techniques to generate good predictive models.

	actual	predictedJ48	predictedMLP	predictedKNN	predictedNB	predictedLog	predictionJ48	predictionMLP	predictionKNN	predictionNB	predictionLog
1	1	1	1	1	1	1	,816	,903	,636	,868	,803
2	0	0	0	0	0	0	,731	,733	,687	,583	,500
3	1	0	0	0	0	0	,835	,867	,565	,646	,820
4	0	0	0	0	0	0	,835	,889	1,000	,835	,819
5	1	0	0	1	0	0	,835	,902	,600	,793	,841
6	1	1	1	1	1	1	,816	,963	,857	,996	,993
7	0	0	0	0	0	0	,835	,890	,700	,925	,850
8	1	0	0	0	0	0	,835	,942	,722	,911	,914
9	1	1	0	0	0	0	,774	,687	,600	,537	,533
10	0	0	0	0	0	0	,835	,936	,818	,962	,962
11	0	1	0	0	1	1	,816	,689	,680	,558	,542
12	1	0	1	1	1	1	,835	,765	,545	,889	,792

Fig. 8. Comparative according to cases (test data) of the degree of agreement between models

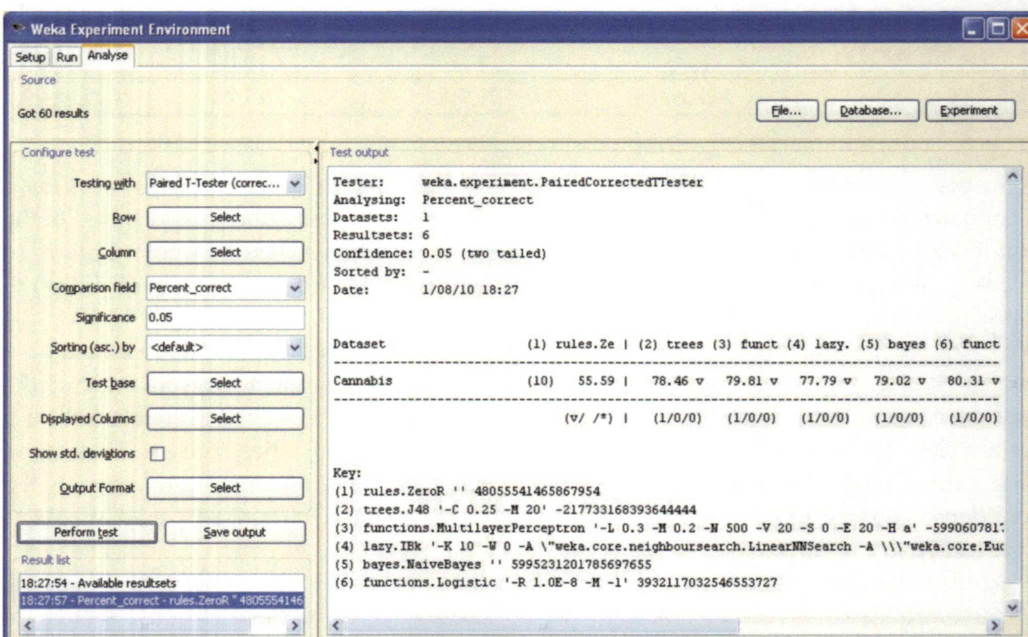

Fig. 9. Comparison of the accuracy (percent correct) between techniques

We proposed an experiment to compare the five classificatory techniques under study in relation to the ZeroR classifier (weka.classifiers.rules.ZeroR). This is the simplest classifier, which predicts the mode (the most repeated value) for a categorical output variable (and the mean for a numerical output variable). In the experiment, we indicate the division of the sample into training (70%) and test (30%) data and 10 repetitions (models) were specified for each technique.

The comparison was carried out from the mean percentage values of the cases correctly classified in the ten models generated for each technique and their standard deviations (hidden by default, but which can be shown if the corresponding option is chosen). As well as the percentage of correct cases (*Percent_correct*) it is possible to choose other indices of interest in the *Comparison field* (see Fig. 9), such as the area under ROC curve (*Area_under_ROC*). The values of these indices for each of the specified repetitions are stored in an Arff data file, whose variables can be analyzed in Weka itself or in other data analysis programmes (with prior extraction to a compatible data format).

By pressing the button *Experiment* (Fig. 9), the mean values and standard deviations of the chosen comparison index are used to study (from a statistical t test) whether there are significant differences between the classificatory accuracy of the models obtained from the first of the techniques defined in the experiment (in this case, ZeroR) and the classificatory accuracy of each of the remaining techniques used.

As can be observed, the ZeroR classifier indicates us that the mean percentage of correct classifications (with test data) is 55.6%, which obviously corresponds to the percentage of subjects in the sample who are non consumers (most frequent category). The rest of the classifiers show a much higher mean percentage of classifications, whose difference with respect to this reference value is, in all cases, statistically significant.

4. Discussion

When faced with the question, *what is the best algorithm for classification?* There is evidently no general answer that can help us to know prior to an analysis of the data which technique or algorithm I should apply in order to obtain the best classificatory model. In this sense, Nisbet et al. (2009, p. 256) indicate us that if different classificatory algorithms are used, we will discover that the best algorithm for classifying a set of data may not work well in another set of data; in other words, different techniques or algorithms have a better functioning in different data sets, and in this sense, they claim that "*using a diversity of algorithms is best*". They even establish an analogy between the process of creation of knowledge models and the process of sculpting a statue, which they call "*the art of data mining*" (Nisbet et al., 2009, p. 46). In the literature you can find DM definitions which point in this same direction, for instance: "data mining is the art of discovering meaningful patterns in data" (Pyle, 2003). Weiss & Indurkhya (1998, p. 21), reflect on this question and ask the question, "*Data Mining: Art or Science?*", which they answer, "no universal best approach is describable for data mining; making good decisions is part art, part science"; in this sense, these authors combine the art and science of DM in their work: they use science when it is known and effective, and offer guidance in practical issues that are not easily quantifiable.

Our scientific contribution to DM has been precisely to present arguments that point in the direction of convincing applied researchers of the usefulness of using different techniques or algorithms in the search for knowledge models that will help in decision making concerning a given problem. Researchers should take on the role of designer in this task: they should design the data selection, cleaning and preparation processes, as well as the model obtention and validation processes through the wide repertory of associated techniques, algorithms and parameters that are at their disposal. Precisely, the Weka platform offers an ideal space to combine the art and science of DM in an effective way, as demonstrated in the previous section of the chapter.

5. References

An, A. (2006). Classification Methods. In J. Wang (Ed.), *Encyclopedia of Data Warehousing and Mining* (pp. 144-149). Hershey, PA: Idea Group Inc.

Berry, M. & Linoff, G. (2004). *Data Mining Techniques. For marketing, sales, and customer relationship management* (2nd ed.). Indianapolis: Wiley.

Bigus, J.P. (1996). *Data Mining with neural networks: solving business problems from application development to decision support*. New York: McGraw-Hill.

Breiman, L. & Cutler, A. (2004). *Random Forests.* Retrieved from http://stat-www.berkeley.edu/users/breiman/RandomForests/cc_home.htm

Breiman, L. (2001). Random Forests. *Machine Learning,* 45, 1, 5-32.

Breiman, L., Friedman, J.H., Olshen, R.A. & Stone, C.J. (1984). *Classification And Regression Trees.* Monterey, CA: Wadsworth & Brooks/Cole Advanced Books & Software.

Domingos, P. & Pazzani, M. (1997). On the optimality of the simple Bayesian classifier under zero-one loss. *Machine Learning,* 29, 103-130.

Gervilla, E., Jiménez, R., Montaño, J.J., Sesé, A., Cajal, B. & Palmer, A. (2009). The methodology of *Data Mining*. An application to alcohol consumption in teenagers. *Adicciones,* 21, 1, 65-80.

Giudici, P. (2003). *Applied Data Mining. Statistical Methods for Business and Industry*. England: John Wiley & Sons.

Han, J. & Kamber, M. (2000). *Data Mining: Concepts and Techniques*. San Francisco: Morgan Kaufmann.

Han, J. & Kamber, M. (2006). *Data Mining: Concepts and Techniques* (2nd ed.). San Francisco: Morgan Kaufmann.

Hand, D.J. (2007). Principles of Data Mining. *Drug Safety,* 30, 7, 621-622.

Hand, D.J., Mannila, H. & Smith, P. (2001). *Principles of Data Mining*. London: The MIT Press.

Hand, D.J. & Yu, K. (2001). Idiot's Bayes - not so stupid after all? *International Statistical Review,* 69, 3, 385-398.

Harris-Jones, C. & Haines, T.L. (1998). Sample Size and Misclassification: Is More Always Better? In *Proceedings of the Second International Conference On the Practical Application of Knowledge Discovery and Data Mining*, London, U.K., 301-312.

Hastie, T., Tibshirani, R. & Friedman, J. (2001). *The Elements of Statistical Learning: Data Mining, Inference, and Prediction.* New York: Springer.

Hill, C.M., Malone, L.C. & Trocine, L. (2004). Data Mining and Traditional Regression. In H. Bozdogan (Ed.), *Statistical Data Mining and Knowledge Discovery* (pp. 259-275). Boca Raton, FL: Chapman & Hall.

Kantardzic, M. (2003). *Data Mining: Concepts, Models, Methods, and Algorithms.* New York: Wiley.

Kass, G.V. (1980). An exploratory technique for investigating large quantities of categorical data. *Applied Statistics,* 29, 2, 119-127.

Larose, D.T. (2005). *Discovering Knowledge in Data : An Introduction to Data Mining.* Hoboken, NJ: Wiley.

Larose, D.T. (2006). *Data Mining Methods and Models.* Hoboken, NJ: Wiley.

Loh, W. & Shih, Y. (1997). Split selection methods for classification trees. *Statistica Sinica,* 7, 815-840.

Michie, D., Spiegelhalter, D.J. & Taylor, C.C. (Eds.) (1994). *Machine Learning, Neural and Statistical Classification.* New York: Ellis Horwood Ltd.

Mitchell, T.M. (1997). *Machine Learning.* New York: McGraw-Hill.

Montaño, J.J. & Palmer, A. (2003). Numeric sensitivity analysis applied to feedforward neural networks. *Neural Computing and Applications,* 12, 2, 119-125.

Nisbet, R., Elder, J. & Miner, G. (2009). *Handbook of Statistical Analysis & Data Mining Applications.* San Diego, CA: Academic Press.

Palmer, A., Fernández, C. & Montaño, J.J. (2001). Sensitivity Neural Network 1.0 [Computer program]. Available at mailto: alfonso.palmer@uib.es

Parr-Rud, O. (2001). *Data Mining Cookbook. Modeling Data for Marketing, Risk, and Customer Relationship Management.* New York: John Wiley & Sons.

Paul, S., Guatam, N. & Balint, R. (2002). *Preparing and Mining Data with Microsoft SQL Server 2000.* Online Books: Microsoft.

Pyle, D. (2003). Data Collection, Preparation, Quality, and Visualization. In N. Ye (Ed.), *The handbook of Data Mining* (pp. 365-391). New Jersey: Lawrence Erlbaum Associates.

Quinlan, J.R. (1986). Induction of Decision Trees. *Machine Learning,* 1, 1, 81-106.

Quinlan, J.R. (1993). *C4.5: Programs for Machine Learning.* San Mateo, CA: Morgan Kaufmann.

Quinlan, J.R. (1997). *C5.0 Data Mining Tool.* Rule Quest Research. Avalaible from http://www.rulequest.com

Rish, I. (2001). An empirical study of the naive Bayes classifier. *Proceedings of IJCAI 2001 Workshop on Empirical Methods in Artificial Intelligence.*

Rumelhart, D.E., Hinton, G.E. y Williams, R.J. (1986). Learning internal representations by error propagation. In D.E. Rumelhart & J.L. McClelland (Eds.), *Parallel distributed processing* (pp. 318-162). Cambridge, MA: MIT Press.

Shmueli, G., Patel, N.R. & Bruce, P.C. (2007). *Data Mining for Business Intelligence. Concepts, Techniques, and Applications in Microsoft Office Excel with XLMiner.* New Jersey: John Wiley & Sons.

Two Crows Corporation (1999). *Introduction to Data Mining and Knowledge Discovery* (3rd ed.). Maryland: Two Crows Corporation.

Weiss, S.M. & Indurkhya, N. (1998). *Predictive Data Mining. A Practical Guide*. San Francisco, CA: Morgan Kauffman.

Witten, I.H. & Frank, E. (2005). *Data Mining. Practical Machine Learning Tools and Techniques* (2nd ed.). San Francisco, CA: Morgan Kauffman.

Ye, N. (Ed.) (2003). *The handbook of Data Mining*. New Jersey: Lawrence Erlbaum Associates.

24

Dynamic Data Mining: Synergy of Bio-Inspired Clustering Methods

Elena N. Benderskaya[1] and Sofya V. Zhukova[2]
[1]*St.Petersburg State Politechnical University,*
[2]*Graduate School of Management,*
Russia

1. Introduction

Dynamic data mining (DDM) comprises advantages of static methods used to reveal implicit structure of classes and at the same time benefits from high quality results obtained in the field of time series analysis. Clustering problem is recognized to be the most crucial in almost any knowledge domain: telecommunications and networking, nanotechnology, physics, chemistry, biology, health care, sociology, economics, etc (Aliev & et. al., 2008; Ceylan & et. al., 2009; Chee & Schatz, 2007; Ghosh & et. al.; 2008; Pedrycz & Weber, 2008; Xu & et. al., 2010). Scientists are in chase of new materials and new decision making techniques that manage data, information, devices or people on the fly. Centralized management techniques are mainly ineffective if we need to operate heaps of redundant information under uncertainty in real time. Decentralized control of interconnected elements, called networks, collectives, colonies, ensembles, maps is based on self-organization and bio-inspired principals that underlie amazing effects applied in highly interdisciplinary environment.

In the paper we extend the thorough comparative analysis of bio-inspired methods provided in resent research (Blum & Merkle, 2009; Budyan & et. al., 2009; Dressler & Akan, 2010) for benefit of clustering problem. Under consideration are the following bio-inspired approaches, used to reveal implicit data structures: small-world networks, ant-based networks, fuzzy logic, neural networks, chaotic map lattices, classical data mining, self-organizing maps. The general view on advantages and delimitations on various bio-inspired methods combinations is proposed in the form of a decision tree. There are so many combinations of bio-inspired methods (Crespo & Weber, 2005; Georgieva & Klawonn, 2008; Jaimes & Torra, 2010; Kaiser & et. al., 2003, 2007; Li & Shen, 2010, Sussillo & Abbott, 2009) with various extent of effectiveness that we tried to propose a systematic approach to reveal best practices. We state that significant advantages in terms of high quality clustering results can be obtained when complexity of both structure and dynamics is commensurable with complexity of problem. This is possible when we tune the harmony of more than two or three techniques. Distributed manner of decision-making processes in nature dictate multiform compensation of possible ineffective functioning of separate system's element by collective dynamics of all other elements.

Detailed analysis of simultaneous clustering techniques application within one method is given on the example of chaotic neural network (Benderskaya & Zhukova 2008, 2009). The synergy of bio-inspired methods combination makes possible the solution of general clustering problem (no a prior information about topology and number of clusters is available). For the first time we managed to demonstrate the flexibility of the developed dynamic data mining technique as it happens to solve not only clustering problem, but classification problem as well. Fragmentary synchronization of thousands nonlinear elements stands to be stable when new players appear in the collective. We found out that chaotic neural network can classify simultaneously not one but many more objects. To demonstrate wide set of CNN applications we introduce the results on texts categorization that aims to improve the quality of search engines in the Internet.

2. Bio-inspired clustering methods

For centuries humans admire animate nature and accessories applied by life creatures to fulfil various functions. At first it was just formal resemblance and mechanistic imitation, then along with sciences maturity the focus shifted on inner construction of living systems.
However due to the complexity of a living system it is reproduced partly. Separate subsystems embody limited set of functions and principals. Just independently showed up artificial neural networks (attempts to mimic neural system), genetic algorithms (data transfer by means of inheritance), artificial immune systems (partial reproduction of immune system), evolutionary modeling (imitation of evolution development principals). The idea of natural self-organization within individuals is the basis for swarm and ant colony technologies (Handl & Meyer, 2007; Blum & Merkle, 2009). It is important to note that nearly all mentioned technologies deal with distributed parallel data processing thanks to numerous simple processing units comprised into self-organized networks that adapt to ever-changing environment (input information).
Of course there exit substantial peculiarities in the types of local cooperation and global behavior mechanisms predetermined by system's goal (as it is well-known systems demonstrate not only interconnectivity of elements but their ability to serve one purpose).
Evolution of society, new computer technologies have in common the idea of small worlds modelling. Communities of various natures (interests clubs, computer clusters, marketing networks, etc.) speak up for strong local linkage of units and weak connectivity outward nearest neighbors (nodes of the net).
Recent research on brain activities gives evidence for its cluster organization (Kaiser, 2007). So we can generalize that small-world models reflect both animate nature and abiocoen. Originally the notion *bio-inspired* comprised problem solving approaches borrowed from living systems but nowadays it is understood more widely. Results in physics in the field of chaos theory and nonlinear dynamics contribute greatly to bio-inspired methodology as soon as nonlinear chaotic models find their application in data mining – first and foremost bio-inspired scientific area. We propose to classify bio-inspired methods on different issues:

a. *structure and connection:* neural networks (macro level) and artificial immune systems (micro level);
b. *collective behaviour:* ant-based networks, swarm methods, multi agent systems, small-world networks;
c. *evolution and selection*: genetic algorithm, evolutionary programming and evolutionary modelling, evolutionary computations;
d. *linguistics*: fuzzy logic.

To step forward with generalization one can note that nearly all mentioned methods realize collective data processing through adaptation to external environment. Exception is fuzzy logic more relative to classical mathematics (interval logic reflects the diversity of natural language descriptions) (Choi & Chung-Hoon Rhee, 2009; Mendel, 2009).

Though bio-inspired methods are applied to solve a wide set of problems we focus on clustering problem as the most complex and resource consuming. The division of input set of objects into subsets (mainly non-overlapping) in most cases is interpreted as optimization task with goal function determined by inter and inner cluster distances. This approach obliges the user to give the a priori information about priorities: what is of most importance - compactness of clusters and their diversity in feature space or inner cluster density and small number of clusters. The formalization process of clustering problems in terms of optimization procedures is one of the edge one in data mining (Handl & Meyer, 2007; Herrmann & Ultsch, 2008, 2009).

Recent modifications of bio-inspired methods are developed as heuristics. The desire to enlarge the abilities of intellectual systems a separate knowledge domain within artificial intelligence field revealed (Lin & Lee, 1998; Georgieva & Klawonn, 2008; Pedrycz & Weber, 2008; Boryczka, 2009). Soft computing (SC) considers various combinations of bio-inspired methods. As a result there appeared such hybrid methods like: neural-fuzzy methods, genetic algorithms with elements of fuzzy logic (FL), hybrid comprised by genetic algorithms (GA) and neural networks (NN); fuzzy logic with genetic algorithm constituent, fuzzy systems with neural network constituent, etc. One of the main ideas of such combinations is to obtain flexible tool that allow to solve complex problems and to compensate drawbacks of one approach by means of cooperation with another.

For example, FL and NN combination provides learning abilities and at the same time formalized knowledge can be represented due to fuzzy logic element (Lin & Lee, 1998). Fuzzy logic is applied as soon as we want to add some flexibility to a data mining technique. One of the main drawbacks of all fuzzy systems are absence of learning capabilities, absence of parallel distributing processing and what is more critical the rely on expert's opinions when membership functions are tuned. In advance to input parameters sensitivity almost all methods suffer from dimension curse and remain to be resource consuming. The efficiency of these methods depends greatly on the parallel processing hardware that simulate processing units: neurons of neural networks, lymphocyte in artificial immune systems, ants and swarms, agents in multi-agent systems, nodes in small-world networks, chromosomes in genetic algorithms, genetic programming, genetic modeling.

We can benefit from synergetic effects if consider not only collective dynamics but also physical and chemical nature of construction elements - nonlinear oscillators with chaotic dynamics. As it is shown in numerous investigations on nonlinear dynamics: the more is the problem complexity the more complex should be the system dynamics. All over the world investigations on molecular level take place to get new materials, to find new medicine, to solve pattern recognition problem, etc. Most of them consume knowledge from adjacent disciplines: biology, chemistry, math, informatics, nonlinear dynamics, and synergetics.

3. Clustering challenge

During the last decade three curses formed an alliance: great volume of information, its increasing variety and velocity of data processing. These 3Vs predetermine strict quality requirements to data mining systems. The costs of wrong decisions increase exponentially as

the environment changes rapidly. Under this condition the development of automatic clustering systems seems to be one of the most pressing problems. At the moment the greater part of existing clustering systems are semiautomatic. And the key reason for this is the multiformity of datasets that cannot be formalized in one unified way.
Clustering problem is the most complex problem among those defined in Data Mining. The set of elements division into non-overlapping groups (clusters) is provided via criterion of similarity that predetermines the result. In terms of neural networks it is solved by means of unsupervised learning or learning without a teacher (Dimitriadou & et. al., 2001), because the system is to learn by itself to extract the solution from input dataset without external aid. Thus the division must be provided automatically.
To illustrate the representative clustering problems a collection of test datasets was generated and arranged in fundamental clustering problems suite (FCPS). FCPS offers a variety of clustering problems any algorithm shall be able to handle when facing real world data. FCPS serves as an elementary benchmark for clustering algorithms.
FCPS consists of data sets with known a priori classifications (Morchen & et. al., 2005; Ultsch, 2005, a) that are to be reproduced by the algorithm. All data sets are intentionally created to be simple and might be visualized in two or three dimensions. Each dataset represents a certain problem that is solved by known clustering algorithms with varying success. This is done in order to reveal benefits and shortcomings of algorithms. Standard clustering methods, e.g. single-linkage, ward und *k*-means, are not able to solve all FCPS problems satisfactorily.

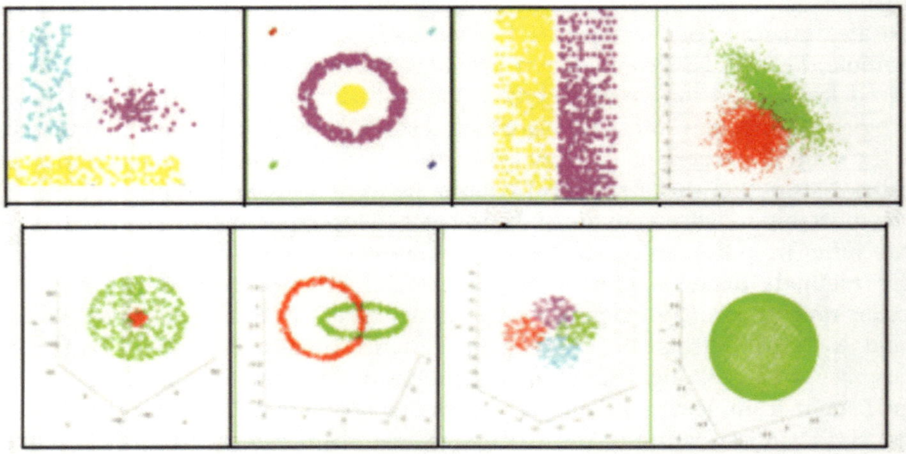

Fig. 1. Fundamental problems clustering suite: 2D and 3D clustering problems vary in density, mutual distance and compactness of clusters (Ultsch, 2005, b).

To solve clustering problem a lot of clustering techniques were developed to reveal most appropriate division of objects in the input dataset in terms of concrete measures of similarity (metrics). There are two types of metrics (Oliveira & Pedrycz, 2007; Han & Kamber, 2005): type 1 - similarity measure between objects within a cluster (euclidean, cityblock, Mahalanobis, Minkowski, cosine, Chebyshev, supremum norm); type 2 - similarity (or dissimilarity) measure between the clusters themselves (single linkage, complete linkage, median clustering, centroid clustering, Ward's method, statistical clustering).

The similarity measure depends greatly on mutual disposition of elements in the input dataset. If we have no a priori information about the type of groups (ellipsoidal, ball-shaped, compact, scattered due to some distribution or just chaotically, and this list is endless) then the probability of erroneous measure choice is very high (Han & Kamber, 2005; Kumar & et. al., 2006; Eidswick, 1973). If our hypothesis about the clusters interrelations or their form or their density does not fulfill then the application of clustering method to this dataset will perform erroneous results.

To overcome the data uncertainty expressed in unformalized variety of possible clusters interrelations usually an expert estimations are used to decide on the choice of clustering technique or interpret clusterization results. Without an expert each time application of a method to concrete dataset (when there is no a priori information available) is a roulette game. This is a serious obstacle on the way to automatic clustering.

To summarize there are three targets to be hit by one clustering technique: it should be fast in terms of calculations, independent to the information about number and topology of clusters, flexible to reveal inner structure of input dataset. So the main question is how to accomplish all this issues in one method.

4. Dynamic data mining

The most perspective direction is based on the attempts to model the work of human brain, which is a highly complex, nonlinear and parallel information-processing system. Complex cortex structure is modelled and formed by artificial neuron lattices, which are joined by great amount of interlinks. This global link of simple neurons provides their collective behaviour. Each neuron carries out the role of a processor. That's why neuron network structure is the most appropriate base for parallel computing - there is no need to prepare data (in neural network input data is already parallelized). For parallel computing to work correctly software should be able to partition its work and data it operates on over hundreds of processors. High speed and with the same time high quality solution of most various complicated problems can be received by means of microsystem's collective behaviour property. The main idea of self-organization is in distributed character of data processing, when one element dynamics means nothing, but at the same time group dynamics define macroscopic unique state of the whole system, that allows this system to reveal capabilities for adaptation, learning, data mining and as one of the results - high computation effectiveness.

Advances in experimental brain science give evidence to the hypothesis (Borisyuk & et. al., 1998; Borisyuk, R.M, & Borisyuk, G.N, 1997) that cognition, memory, attention processes are the results of cooperative chaotic dynamics of brain cortex elements (neurons). Thus the design of artificial dynamic neural networks on the base of neurobiological prototype seems to be the right direction of the search for innovative clustering techniques. Computer science development predetermined promising possibilities of computer modeling. It became possible to study complex nonlinear systems. Great evidence for rich behavior of artificial chaotic systems was accumulated and thus chaos theory came into being (Schweitzer, 1997; Mosekilde & et. al., 2002; Haken, 2004). Dynamics exponential unpredictability of chaotic systems, their extreme instability generates variety of system's possible states that can help us to describe all the multiformity of our planet.

It is assumed to be very advantageous to obtain clustering problem solution using effects produced by chaotic systems interaction. In this paper we try to make next step in the

development of universal clustering technique. Dynamic data mining combines modern data mining techniques with modern time-series analysis techniques.
To mimic nature highly unstable dynamics and distributed data processing were combined. Thus chaotic neural network (CNN) came into being originally in the form of Angelini's model (Angelini, 2003, Angelini & et. al., 2001). We modified the model greatly in order to generate clustering results of a better quality. As it is shown on Fig. 2 CNN is a recurrent neural network with one layer of n neurons. Each neuron corresponds to one point in the input dataset which in general case consists of n objects, each described by p features (p-dimensional image). CNN is a dynamic neural network, where each processing unit changes its state depending on the dynamics of all other neurons

$$y_i(t+1)=\frac{1}{C_i}\sum_{i\neq j}^{n} w_{ij} f(y_i(t)),\ \ t=1...T, \tag{1}$$

$$C_i=\sum_{i\neq j}^{n} w_{ij},\ i,j=\overline{1,n} \tag{2}$$

$$W=\{w_{ij}\}=\exp\left(-d_{ij}^{\ 2}/2a\right),\ \ i,j=\overline{1,n}, \tag{3}$$

$$f(y(t))=1-2y^2(t), \tag{4}$$

where n – number of neurons, w_{ij} - strength of linkage between elements i and j, d_{ij} - Euclidean distance between neurons i and j, a – local scale, depending on k-nearest neighbors, T – time interval. The a value is average number of neighbors, calculated via Delaunay triangulation. The initial state of neural network is described by random values in the range [-1, 1].

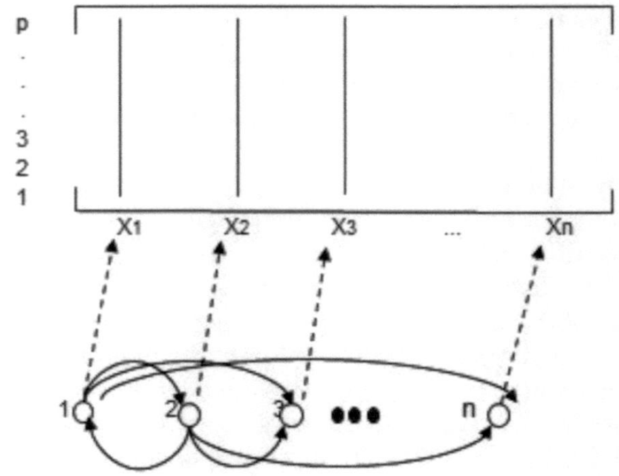

Fig. 2. The relation of input dataset and structure of chaotic neural network.

Key point of CNN functioning is the emergence of cooperative dynamics between neurons outputs via time. After some transition period they start to change states synchronously.

The synchronization extent depends greatly on mean field formed by linkage strengths. Primary results on modeling high dimensional chaotic map lattices were published by K. Kaneko (Kaneko, 1987). These works showed up the fact that globally coupled chaotic map lattices exhibit formation of ensembles synchronously oscillating elements. These ensembles Kaneko called clusters that serve as system's attractors. If there appear to be several clusters then the system is characterized by multistability, when several attractors coexist in the phase space at the same parameters values. He showed that in case of w_{ij}=0 chaotic map lattice dynamics converges to the ordered stage that corresponds to strange attractor (there are several groups of completely synchronized neurons); partly ordered stage (large oscillatory clusters coexist with a lot of small ones); turbulent phase (there are no big clusters only small ones evolve independently from each other).

In Angelini's model uncertainty about topology and number of clusters was replaced by the uncertainty about w_{ij} parameters that depend on a priori unknown value of k-nearest neighbors used in (3). Though the idea to make neural network an inhomogeneous one and set the linkage strengths via (3) is great.

To explore the chaotic neural dynamics (oscillatory clusters) we thoroughly use several visualization techniques: representation of total output dynamics and phase portraits. Exactly because of the deep analysis of the output dynamics we managed to discover new type of synchronization (fragmentary synchronization) and the way to control CNN dynamics.

This paper fully corresponds to the chaotic logic approach that comprises ideas from both humanitarian and natural sciences. Terminology of chaos theory is still a subject of heated discussions. That's why we would like to clear out the language. The key idea of the paper consists in the synthesis of investigations results in such fields as: topology (both structural and spatial), synchronization as a universal concept, control of many-dimensional nonlinear systems, times series analysis, neural networks application as a computing base, data processing and informatics. Due to this great variety of issues we use terminology from different scientific areas slightly interpreting or enriching the vocabulary.

The most crucial word of the paper is chaotic. The word chaos is naturally associated with extremely unpredictable systems dynamics, but not with the stable, and recurrent reproduction of the same results. And in the case of clustering problems we need to generate the only solution every time we use the same method. The chaotic dynamic of CNN is guaranteed by logistic map (4). We want to stress that chaos in CNN dynamics is important only to ensure the sufficient level of instability to make the emergence of self-organizing phenomenon possible. Though instant states of neurons remain to be chaotic mutual synchronization of elements due to the phenomenology of CNN is stable.

The phenomenology of CNN can be examined by the outputs dynamics analysis. The statistics on instant changes of CNN outputs via (1) is gathered after some transition period. To analyse statistics complex time-series analysis should be accomplished. We applied various techniques and realized that none of them is adequate for time series generated by CNN. The reason consists in various types of synchronization that takes placeCNN may produce not only well-known synchronization but also such synchronization when instant output values in one cluster do not coincide neither by amplitude nor by phase and there is even no fixed synchronization lag. In spite of everything joint mutual synchronization exists within each cluster. This synchronization is characterized by individual oscillation cluster melodies, by some unique "music fragments" corresponding to each cluster. From this follows the name we give to this synchronization type - fragmentary synchronization.

Thus dynamic data mining is realized in the form of a shift from static output analysis to dynamic one. The input dataset is given to logistic map network by means of inhomogeneous weights assignment via (3). It means that input dataset is not given to neural network in the classical meaning. On the opposite the structure of chaotic neural network adapts every time to the input image. We want to stress that CNN can equally find clusters in the dataset of any dimension, because the compression via Euclidean metric evaluation is provided. As it is shown on Fig. 2 the number of objects in the input dataset coincides with the number of neurons in CNN. And we can say that each neuron represents its own point in the dataset. On Fig. 3 you can see the dynamics of CNN generated in response to different clustering problems.

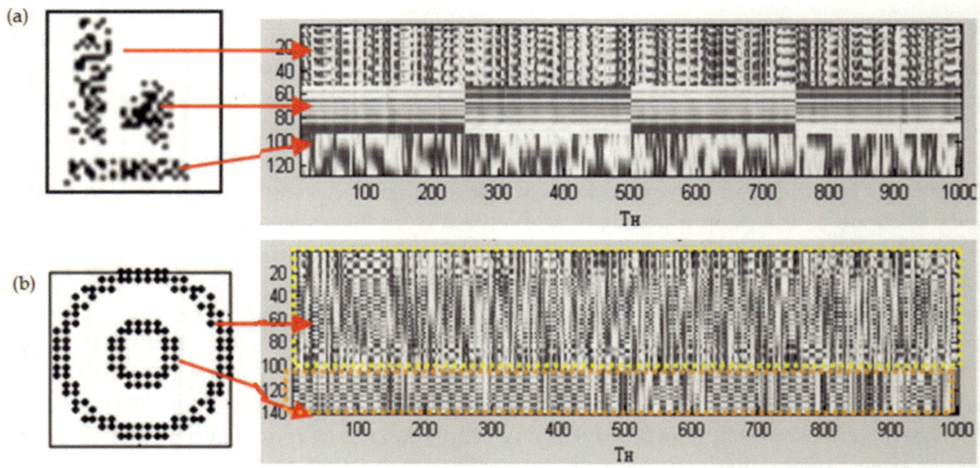

Fig. 3. Result of dynamic data mining consists in oscillatory clusters that in their turn are comprised by fragmentary synchronized outputs of chaotic neural network: (a) – three clusters found by CNN without any a-priori information in response to 2D clustering problem; (b) – two clusters found by CNN without any a-priori information in response to 2D clustering problem.

5. Synergy of bio-inspired methods

Separate class of dynamic neural networks - oscillatory networks - is successfully applied to solve segmentation problems. Thus, to solve highly complicated problems it is appropriate to combine achievements in nonlinear dynamics, self-organization theory and neural networks theory. In our project this integration is represented by investigation of new, complex recurrent neural networks type, that seems to be very perspective in future.

The proposed clustering technique possesses features almost every of bio-inspired methods mentioned above:

a. from *small–world networks* we take irregular, incomplete linkage between elements in (clusters are formed by nearest neighbours);
b. from *ant-based networks* we take parallel performance of elements (the solution is generated both by individual and collective dynamics of elements);
c. from *genetic algorithms* we take iterative improvement of intermediate solution by means of previous experience interchange (extensive search of best fit solution);

d. from *fuzzy logic* we take interval logic in post processing of clustering results (both vertical when we analyse fractal structure of system's output dynamics and horizontal when time-series analysis is conducted);
e. from *neural networks* we take processing element with complex transfer function (logistic map) and stress that in case of new technique its dynamics can be interpreted as learning process;
f. from *classical self-organizing maps* we take k-means metric.

Statistical methods, based on the idea of sample average, bring up to information losses. That's why the information processing must be similar to biological prototype. We solve the problem of CNN processing by accurate time-series analysis.

The clustering of all input datasets from Fig. 1 was successfully fulfilled by CNN thanks to refuse to the avoidance of metrics obtrusion. New method is based on determination of implicit law in data structure by means of self-organization. So CNN can be classified as oscillatory recurrent neural network, comprised by one layer inhomogeneous connected neurons, each with chaotic behaviour. The oscillatory nature of CNN makes it similar to brain dynamics and allows to make hypothesis on wide dynamic data mining abilities.

Further on we show application of proposed clustering technique to solve classification problems and multidimensional text categorization problem.

6. CNN classification and clustering

Classification problem is more simpler than clustering problem because there is information about classes representatives - centres of classes. In self-organizing maps (Kohonen's neural network is one to be easily compared with) learning process stops as soon as the centres of clusters stop changing during the search procedure (Kohonen, 1995, Liu & et. al., 1999). The answer to clustering problem is given by SOM after learning process in the following way: each point in the input dataset is shown to SOM and the nearest centre of cluster attracts the point - thus it is classified. We stress that classical SOM can't generate the answer "I do not know". CNN during learning process does not estimate centres of clusters. Though in this paper we propose to use CNN to solve classification problem as well.

To solve classification problem on the basis of CNN we need to solve previously clustering problem for concrete input dataset and then add new points (new neurons to neural network). For this added neurons we calculate outputs dynamics without recalculation of all other neurons outputs. Further on we analyse joint output dynamics.

We made different experiments on classification of additional points. Fascinating thing we discovered about CNN is that the network can classify at the same time not one or two but a lot more points. These new points, being in the neighborhood of a cluster join this cluster. The criteria of joining one of the clusters deals with the density of new points added to the original dataset. If density of the added points is equal or exceeds the density of the nearest cluster then these new points join the cluster. Otherwise CNN generates a new cluster - that is similar to the answer "I do not know". Thus CNN allows to solve both clustering and classification problems almost simultaneously that expands greatly its application domain.

7. Text categorization application of CNN

In our previous papers we tested CNN on 2D, 3D input datasets from FCSP. Here on we want to check whether CNN can cope with real data - sets of objects, each described by *p*-

dimensional number of features. We made our focus on Internet Search Engines and questionable results they generate as relevant in response to users «keywords sequence» requests. There are a lot of search optimization techniques that we do not take into account, focusing mainly on the quality of clustering results.

The aim of quantitative text analysis is the determination of some textual structure laws and contents laws, expressed in quantitative measure. These laws may concern some style features of an author, belonging to this or that genre, literary or scientific school, etc. Then these laws are used for text systematization by structure or by content.

Nowadays actual problems are such as determination of psychological condition of an author at the moment of text creation, authorship determination, and formal content determination.

To solve these problems it is important to define correlation between words in one document or in group of documents to find out formal structure of texts and as a result quantitative measure of their similarity.

To check the hypothesis whether CNN is applicable to solve text categorization problem we planned an experiment. We chose "neural networks" thematic from "artificial intelligence" domain. To model the situation as close as it is possible to the real information search problem we added texts to the input bunch of documents that belong to adjacent thematic – "fuzzy logic" and "machine learning" (ML). From the input set of documents CNN should find ones that are relevant to "neural networks" thematic. As a result we propose that CNN will divide all documents into clusters and one of them will comprise docs from "neural networks" thematic. In this interpretation of clustering problem the feature space consists of thematic's keywords. Input image for CNN consists of formal document representations – coded texts (the words in texts are replaced by zero if a keyword of the thematic occurs or one if not).

Text analysis methods are based on formal document presentation as some set of features that is previously formed by methods of textual preconditioning or by human being. If there are enough of input patterns (texts) and it is possible to classify each text to only one class in the previously formed set of classes then a solving rule can be used. This rule is received after learning with a teacher (probability classifiers, feed-forward network).

Clustering results reveal implicit law in text structure. Text clustering is characterized by such problems as great correlation between elements (texts), this cause big clusters intersections and absence of a priori information about clusters.

Hence "to measure" the text (its structure and its content as a result) it is proposed to use CNN. The order, created during functioning CNN – is the information that single neurons (or words, or documents) have about each other.

The objects to cluster are described by a set of features (feature vectors) and are represented as points in many-dimensional space. Consequently to verify the clustering results of different methods images with various complexity are applied. This approach allows not only to cluster the images (for example, analyze data taken from satellite image of an area) but produce visual demonstration of any clustering problem, because in this case it is interpreted as pattern recognition problem.

The decision result of the solving rule depends greatly on representation form of input data. In our case input data is the coded text. To form this code new knowledge in computer linguistics is applied: the idea of the text is highly correlated with distribution of clue words in text. To start text categorization we need to solve attendant tasks:

a. create database of keywords for various text categories;
b. choose text representation technique;
c. provide linguistic analysis (exclude prepositions, conjunctions, synonyms, etc.).

One of the reasons of unsatisfactory work of Information Processing Systems underlies in text representation methods drawbacks. There are several approaches to text representation: frequency, binary, compressive. The two first are applied more often. Frequency methods are based on calculations of clue words frequencies - times of appearance in the text. Binary methods fix absence ore presence of clue word in a document (the feature vector that describes a text will consist of nulls and ones: 0 – if the word is present, 1 – if absent. Frequency methods have some drawbacks due to frequency averaging-out of each of the clue words. This causes losses of meaningful information about text structure.

On the one hand it is undesirable when the same term is used several times in one sentence (it is better to apply synonyms). The result of this construction sentence rule is that the total term frequency appearance may be little. On the other hand very frequent usage of a term doesn't guarantee that the document's theme corresponds with the term.

The resent researches in computer linguistics show that the idea of the text is highly correlated with text structure – distributions of single clue words, pairs of clue words, combinations of three words (and so on). Similar in content and level of complexity texts must have similar structures – not only the average frequencies of clue words usage.

In this article a new approach to text representation is proposed. It is based on clue words distributions within texts. To do this a document is divided into M groups of words. N is defined by Sturges rule that tells us how much intervals to choose to construct a bar chart of distribution (for each document its own M is defined). Then usage frequencies of each clue word in each of group are calculated. Than the larger is the document than the larger is the group of word.

The advantage of distributed text frequency representation is in the decrease of information losses. Because with minimum computational spendings on the input of clustering system comes a text representation with little distortion in text specificity. Thus defining correlation in group words usage allows revealing the inner structure of the text and to a certain extent its content-idea.

The results of text clustering showed possibility of practical CNN application. Text collections, represented in D-dimensional feature space of clue words and belonging to three intersected themes were successfully clustered. The text representation method influence on clusterization quality was investigated and the results analysis permits to make a conclusion that proposed frequency distributed method gives better results over classical frequency method. The results of correct clustering are 3-5% more than in classical frequency method. The documents number increase makes better clustering quality.

To solve real clustering D-dimensional problem we can't visualize D-dimensional input objects, but we can preliminary solve by ourselves and compare the results. We created 3 collections of documents that belong to three thematics in different ratio: 30(NN)-30(FL)-30(ML), 50(NN)-20(FL)-20(ML), 20(NN)-40(FL)-40(ML). As a result dynamic data mining technique generated an answer that to the extent of 80% coincide with desired one, 6% of documents were not joined to any cluster as they were considered as noise. To increase the clustering quality we think it is important to expand number of documents in the input dataset.

8. Conclusion

We analyzed the multiformity of existing clustering techniques and concluded that considered CNN model can be related to bio-inspired ones. The ability to solve complex clustering problems in terms of oscillations clustering language in future research can be extended by dynamic inputs (at the moment the *p*-dimensional input dataset is fixed unchangeable during processing time). It was discovered that CNN can also be applied as a classifier. This fact can save a lot of time when working with invariant images (the space rotation of input image has no effect on CNN – the only thing that matters is mutual location of objects). The preliminary results on *p*-dimensional clustering of real data by means of CNN were positive in terms of clustering quality. Successful results were predetermined also by new text representation technique that gave 3-5% better results. But the time, needed to reveal oscillatory clusters prevents from industrial implementation of dynamic data mining technique. The direction of further research deals with the domain of modern time-series data mining – the alternative to algebraic approach, used at the moment.
We highly appreciate partial support of this research by St. Petersburg government, Science and Graduate Education Committee (diploma PSP №090190).

9. References

Aliev, R. A.; Aliev, R. R.; Guirimov, B. & Uyar, K (2008). Dynamic data mining technique for rules extraction in a process of battery charging, *Applied Soft Computing*, No. 8, pp. 1252–1258

Angelini, L. (2003). Antiferromagnetic effects in chaotic map lattices with a conservation law, *Physics Letters* A 307(1), pp.41–49

Angelini, L., Carlo, F., Marangi, C., Pellicoro, M., Nardullia, M. & Stramaglia, S. (2001). Clustering by inhomogeneous chaotic maps in landmine detection, *Phys. Rev. Lett.* N86, pp.89–132

Benderskaya, Elena N. & Zhukova, Sofya V. (2008). Clustering by chaotic neural networks with mean field calculated via Delaunay triangulation, *Proceedings of Third international workshop on Hybrid artificial intelligence systems*, pp. 408-416, ISBN 978-3-540-87655-7, Burgos, Spain, September 24-26, 2008, Lecture Notes in Computer Science, vol. 5271, Springer-Verlag, Berlin-Heidelberg

Benderskaya, Elena N. & Zhukova, Sofya V. (2009). Fragmentary synchronization in chaotic neural network and data mining, *Proceedings of 4th international conference on Hybrid artificial intelligence systems*, pp. 319-326, ISBN 978-3-642-02318-7, Salamanca, Spain, June 10-12, 2009, Lecture Notes in Computer Science, vol. 5572, Springer-Verlag, Berlin-Heidelberg

Blum, Ch. & Merkle, D. (2009). *Swarm Intelligence: Introduction and Applications*, ISBN 978-3642093432, Springer

Borisyuk, R. M., & Borisyuk, G. N. (1997). Information coding on the basis of synchronization of neuronal activity, *Bio Systems*, Vol. 40, No 1., pp. 3-10

Borisyuk, R. M.; Borisyuk, G. N. & Kazanovich, Y.B. (1998). The synchronization principle in modelling of binding and attention, *Membrane & cell biology*, Vol. 11, No. 6, pp. 753-761

Boryczka, U. (2009). Finding groups in data: Cluster analysis with ants, *Applied Soft Computing*, No. 9, pp. 61-70

Budayan, C.; Dikmen, I. & Birgonul M. T. (2009). Comparing the performance of traditional cluster analysis, self-organizing maps and fuzzy C-means method for strategic grouping, *Expert Systems with Applications*, No. 36, pp. 11772–11781

Ceylan, R.; Ozbay, Y. & Karlik, B. (2009). A novel approach for classification of ECG arrhythmias: Type-2 fuzzy clustering neural network, *Expert Systems with Applications*, No. 36, pp. 6721–6726

Chee, B. & Schatz, B. (2007). Document clustering using small world communities, *Proceedings of the 7th ACM/IEEE-CS joint conference on Digital libraries*, International Conference on Digital Libraries, Canada, 2007, pp. 53-62

Crespo, A. & Weber, R. (2005). A methodology for dynamic data mining based on fuzzy clustering, *Fuzzy Sets and Systems*, No. 150, pp. 267–284

Dimitriadou, E., Weingessel, A., Hornik, K. & Voting-Merging (2001). An Ensemble Method for Clustering, *Lecture Notes in Computer Science*, Vol. 2130

Dressler, F. & Akan, O. B. (2010). A survey on bio-inspired networking, *Computer Networks*, No. 54, pp. 881–900

Eidswick, J.A. (1973). On some fundamental problems in cluster set theory, *Proceedings of the American mathematical society*, Vol.39, No.1, pp. 163-168

Georgieva, O. & Klawonn, F. (2008). Dynamic data assigning assessment clustering of streaming data, *Applied Soft Computing*, No. 8, pp. 1305–1313

Choi, Byung-In & Chung-Hoon Rhee, Frank (2009). Intervaltype-2fuzzy membership function generation methodsf or pattern recognition, *Information Sciences*, 179, pp. 2102–2122

Ghosh, A., Halder, A., Kothari, M. & Ghosh, S. (2008). Aggregation pheromone density based data clustering, *Information Sciences*, No. 178, Elsevier, pp. 2816–2831

Haken, H. (2004). Synergetics. Introduction and Advanced Topics, *Physics and Astronomy Online Library*, p. 758, Springer

Han, J. & Kamber, M. (2005). *Data Mining. Concepts and Techniques*, The Morgan Kaufmann Series in Data Management Systems, Morgan Kaufmann

Handl, J. & Meyer, B. (2007). Ant-based and swarm-based clustering, *Swarm Intelligence*, Vol. 1, No. 2. (16 December 2007), pp. 95-113

Herrmann, L. & Ultsch, A. (2008). The Architecture of Ant-Based Clustering to Improve Topographic Mapping, *Proceedings of the 6th international Conference on Ant Colony Optimization and Swarm intelligence*, pp.379-386, ISBN:978-3-540-87526-0, Brussels, Belgium, September 22 - 24, 2008, Lecture Notes In Computer Science, vol. 5217. Springer-Verlag, Berlin, Heidelberg

Herrmann, L. & Ultsch, A. (2009). Clustering with Swarm Algorithms Compared to Emergent SOM, *Proceedings of the 7th international Workshop on Advances in Self-Organizing Maps*, St. Augustine, FL, USA, June 08 - 10, 2009, pp.80-88, ISBN:978-3-642-02396-5, Lecture Notes In Computer Science, vol. 5629, Springer-Verlag, Berlin, Heidelberg

Jaimes, L. & Torra, V. (2010). On the Selection of Parameter m in Fuzzy c-Means: A Computational Approach, *Integrated Uncertainty Management and Applications*, Vol. 68, pp. 443–452

Jang, J-S. R. & Sun, Ch.-T. (1997). *Neuro-Fuzzy and Soft Computing: A Computational Approach to Learning and Machine Intelligence*, ISBN 978-0132610667, Prentice Hall

Kaiser, M. (2003). Mean clustering coefficients - On clustering measures for small-world networks, *Chaos*, Vol. 13, No. 3

Kaiser, M. (2007). Brain architecture: a design for natural computation, *Philosophical Transactions of the Royal Society A*, 2007, Dec 15, 365(1861), pp.3033-3045

Kaiser, M.; Gorner, M. & Hilgetag, C. (2007). Criticality of spreading dynamics in hierarchical cluster networks without inhibition, *New Journal of Physics*, Vol. 8, May 2007, pp. 110

Kaneko K. (1987). Phenomenology of spatio-temporal chaos, *Directions in chaos,*World Scientific Publishing Co., pp. 272-353, Singapore

Kohonen T. (1995). *Self-Organizing Maps*, Springer Verlag, Berlin

Kumar, B. V.; Mahalanobis, A. & Juday, R.D. (2006). *Correlation Pattern Recognition*, Cambridge University Press

Li, Y. & Shen, Y. (2010). An automatic fuzzy c-means algorithm for image segmentation, *Soft Computing,* No. 14, pp.123–128

Liu, Q.; Rui, Y.; Huang, T. & Levinson, S. (1999). Video Sequence Learning and Recognition via Dynamic SOM, Proceedings. International Conference on Image Processing, ICIP-99, vol. 4, pp.93 - 97

Mendel, Jerry M. (2009). On answering the question ''Where do I start in order to solve a new problem involving interval type-2 fuzzy sets?'', *Information Sciences,* 179, pp. 3418–3431

Mörchen, F., Ultsch, A., Nöcker, M. & Stamm, C. (2005). Databionic visualization of music collections according to perceptual distance, *Proceedings 6th International Conference on Music Information Retrieval (ISMIR 2005)*, London, UK, pp. 396-403

Mosekilde, E.; Maistrenko, Yu. & Postnov, D. (2002). *Chaotic synchronization*, World Scientific Series on Nonlinear Science, Series A, Vol. 42

Oliveira, V. J. & Pedrycz, W. (2007). *Advances in Fuzzy Clustering and its Applications*, Wiley

Pedrycz, W. & Weber, R. (2008). Special issue on soft computing for dynamic data mining, *Applied Soft Computing*, No. 8, pp. 1281–1282

Schweitzer, F. (1997). *Self-Organization of Complex Structures: From Individual to Collective Dynamics*, CRC Press

Sussillo, D. & Abbott, L. F. (2009). Generating Coherent Patterns of Activity from Chaotic *Neural Networks, Neuron*, Vol. 63, pp. 544–557

Ultsch, A. (2005, a). Density Estimation and Visualization for Data containing Clusters of unknown Structure, *Proceedings 28th Annual Conference of the German Classification Society (GfKl 2004)*, Dortmund, Germany, Springer, Heidelberg, pp. 232-239

Ultsch, A. (2005, b). Clustering with SOM: U*C, *In Proc. Workshop on Self-Organizing Maps*, Paris, France, pp. 75-82

Xu, R.; Damelin, S.; Nadler, B. & Wunsch, D. (2010). Clustering of high-dimensional gene expression data with feature filtering methods and diffusion maps, Artificial Intelligence in Medicine, No. 48, pp. 91–98

25

Exploiting Inter-Sample Information and Exploring Visualization in Data Mining: from Bioinformatics to Anthropology and Aesthetics Disciplines

Kuan-ming Lin[1] and Jung-Hua Liu[2]
[1]Duke University,
[2]University of Leeds,
[1]USA
[2]UK

1. Introduction

In this data-overabundant world, revealing and representing comprehensible relationships behind complicated datasets have become important challenges in data mining. This chapter presents recent achievements in applying data mining techniques to two application areas—microarray analysis and anthropology study on Wi-Fi networks—and applies visualization techniques to help integrate heterogeneous databases to obtain useful data interpretation.

As the amount of available microarray data has increased exponentially, integration of heterogeneous databases has become necessary. However, direct integration of microarrays is ineffective after normalization because of the diverse types of specific variations in experiments. This chapter reviews two approaches to overcome this issue, and introduces a cube model that combines and outperforms the two approaches by extracting information from yeast genes.

This chapter will continue on a recent anthropology study which applies data mining to visualize urban Wi-Fi networks. In the past, artists could not store and handle with huge data without database, and therefore their works typically failed to communicate with other disciplines. Nonetheless, anthropologists have explored implicit relations and viewed them in multiple ways, and they have created a number of different category principles including binary opposition, functional structure and interpretation. These multiple principles can serve as the basis to visualize human thinking and reasoning in cross-cultural and interdisciplinary study. The anthropology study to be described in this chapter will relate Wi-Fi statics in complicated fieldwork databases with easily-understood cultural phenomena.

Clear visualizations involve data aesthetics as well, which focuses on how to represent data in eye-conscious and categorized forms. This chapter will manifest that aesthetics can help expand existing data mining ideas to visual representations, with the example of combining the cube model introduced for bioinformatics data mining and the representation of regional Wi-Fi networks in spatial-temporal color charts.

2. Exploiting inter-gene information for biological data mining

2.1 Overview

Due to the increasing gap between the enormous content of sequenced genomes and the limited understanding of associating biological functions, computer assistance has been introduced to scientists for analyzing data generated from various biological experiments. In particular, high-throughput gene expression microarrays, which measure the gene expression levels in a number of experimental conditions, efficiently provide extensive amount of information for gene product examinations, and therefore become the most commonly available source of high-throughput biological data.

However, the volume and the diversity of microarray repositories, e.g. Stanford Microarray Database (Gollub et al., 2003) and NCBI Gene Expression Omnibus (Edgar et al., 2002), poses a challenge of integrating microarrays to yield more robust and accurate analysis than that on a single microarray. Direct integration via value normalization is often ineffective because of the diverse types of experiment specific variations such as lab protocols, microarray platforms, sample treatments, etc. A number of sophisticated merging methods have thus been proposed, and in this section we focus on a generalized cube framework (Lin & Kang, 2007; Lin et al., 2009), which can be combined with a variety of metrics and learning algorithms originally applied to single microarray analysis.

2.2 Related work

A representative method which merged multiple cDNA microarrays and calculated the correlations across all arrays was presented in (Eisen et al., 1998). This technique is nonetheless hard to integrate oligonucleotide microarrays because their expression values are typically not comparable. An improvement averaged the Pearson correlations over all datasets (Jansen et al., 2002), but according to (Tornow, 2003), averaging does not reflect any realistic correlation structure of the data.

Bayesian models (Bernard & Hartemink, 2005; Joshi et al., 2004) were also studied for integrating heterogeneous biological data. However, these models have not yet scaled up to large-scale data integration and mining, and applications were limited to analyzing a small subset of regulatory network.

Kernel fusion techniques (Borgwardt et al., 2005; Lanckriet et al., 2004) have been applied to biological data integration. Such techniques, however, assumed a certain underlying representation of the data (e.g., the radius basis function kernel matrix), and relied on kernelized clustering or classification algorithms (e.g., support vector machines), thus restricting the applicability and extensibility to various types of biological data.

2.3 The cube integration model

Suppose we are given a set of k microarray datasets that measure the quantity of gene products from a common set of genes. Thus, each gene of interest will be associated with k features. While conventional analysis simply merges these k feature sets with some normalization, we propose a more comprehensive integration model by considering the inter-gene relations, which is formally defined as follows:

Definition. A model M conforming to the cube framework consists of four elements (g, X, d, f) which generate a set of similarity matrices K and the corresponding cube vectors v:

- The first element $g = (g_1, g_2, \ldots, g_n)$ refers to a set of n genes of interest.

- The second element $X = (X_1, X_2, \ldots, X_k)$ is a collection of k microarray datasets to be integrated, where each microarray experiment X_m is a table of $n \times s_m$ entries storing the expression values of the n genes in g over the s_m samples.
- The third element $d = (d_1, d_2, \ldots, d_k)$ is a set of metric functions. Each metric
  $d_m : X_m \times X_m \rightarrow R$
  maps a pair of genes into a real value. The metrics can be simple functions like indication or difference function, or more sophisticated ones like correlation or kernel functions. With the metrics we associate each X_m with an $n \times n$ similarity matrix K_m by
  $(K_m)_{ij} = d_m(X_{mi}, X_{mjj})$.
  From the k similarity matrices, we thus define a set of k-dimensional similarity vectors v by considering all of the n^2 gene pairs (g_i, g_j):
  $v_{ij} = ((K_1)_{ij}, (K_2)_{ij}, \ldots, (K_k)_{ij})$.
- The fourth element $f : R^k \rightarrow \{keep, discard\}$ works as a filter on all vectors in v. Because microarray data often contain considerable amount of noisy or unavailable entries, the n^2 vectors generated need some filtering to reduce noise. For example, vectors with many low-valued correlation coefficients might be of little interest for gene expression analysis, so they should be eliminated to reduce both noise and computational time. Filtering itself can also select biologically meaningful vectors. As we shall see later, the TSP classifier imposes simple filtering criteria to identify cancer marker genes.

We demonstrate this data model via the cube illustration shown in Fig. 1 and the workflow outline in Fig. 2. As shown in Fig. 1(b), the n^2 similarity vectors can be naturally viewed as n^2 points in a k-dimensional space. Defining a metric in this space will then allow us to analyse the distances among the points and therefore find intrinsic relations among the genes.

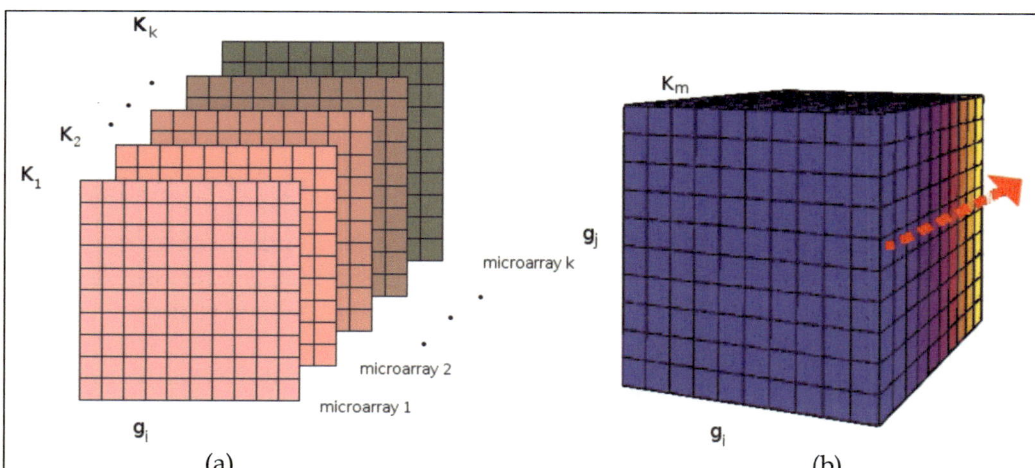

Fig. 1. (a) Each dataset X_m is associated with a gene similarity matrix K_m. Each cell in the similarity matrix is a value defined by a metric. (b) The cube constructed from the gene pairs (g_i, g_j) across the similarity matrices K_m's. The dotted line represents a k-dimensional vector.

The product from the cube framework is a subset of cube vectors labelled with gene pairs, which is demonstrated in Fig. 2. Learning algorithms can then be applied to these vectors. For example, if genes are annotated with their biological functions, these vectors can be the training data for supervised learning algorithms such as k-nearest-neighbor and support

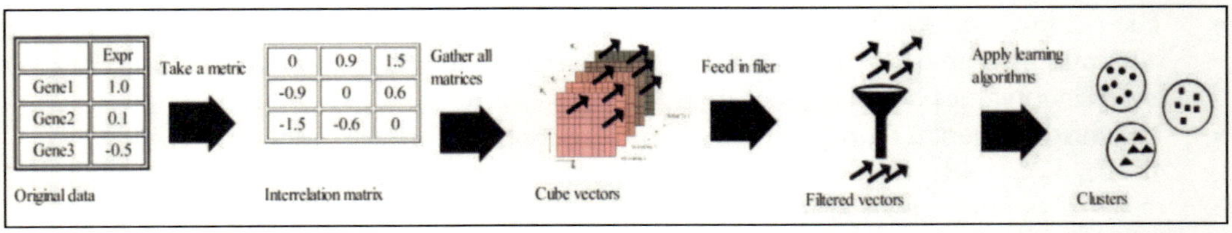

Fig. 2. Outline of the cube integration model. Each data source corresponds to one or more interrelation matrices, and all matrices form a cube. Each vector in the cube represents a gene pair. These vectors are then filtered and finally fed into any suitable learning algorithm.

vector machines. Gene clustering may also be implemented with algorithms such as hierarchical clustering and k-means. Note that kernel machines can be used to learn from the vectors regardless of whether the similarity matrices are in kernel forms, which means the cube framework is more extensible and adjustable than kernel fusion techniques.

2.4 Specialization examples and improvement

We give the outline of two integrative analysis algorithms that actually fits in the cube framework. The first algorithm, Top-Scoring Pairs (TSP) (Xu et al., 2005), translates the expression values into inter-gene comparison indicators, and then computes each gene pair's discriminative effectiveness by the distance of the center of cancer and non-cancer groups. The most discriminative gene pair is used as the marker genes for classifying new samples. Here we show how the TSP algorithm fits in the proposed integration model by identifying the four elements (g, X, d, f) of the model:

- The gene set g comprises $n = 12{,}600$ genes in the TSP paper (Xu et al., 2005).
- The input databases X is a set of profiles grouped into normal and cancer profiles. In the TSP paper three prostate cancer microarray datasets with 223 profiles were used in training, and two additional microarray datasets with 129 profiles were used in testing.
- The metric d for all datasets is the same indicator function
  $(d_m)_{ij} = 1$ iff $(X_m)_i < (X_m)_j$; otherwise $(d_m)_{ij} = 0$.
  With this metric the TSP algorithm constructs a cube with all binary entries.
- The filtering function f, which is the key of the TSP algorithm, is a ranking algorithm according to the average difference between normal profiles and cancer ones:

$$\Delta_{ij} = \left| \frac{1}{k_1} \sum_{m=1}^{k_1} (d_m)_{ij} - \frac{1}{k_2 - k_1} \sum_{m=k_1+1}^{k_2} (d_m)_{ij} \right| .$$

The gene pair achieving the highest rank is then selected as the marker gene pair.

To classify a new profile, TSP compares the expression values of the two genes in the marker gene pair (g_i, g_j). Suppose in the training data the normal profiles have higher average expression value of g_i than that of g_j. During classification the new profile will be classified as normal if and only if in this profile g_i is also more expressed than g_j.

We then show how another algorithm, second-order correlation analysis (Zhou et al., 2005), corresponds to an example in the cube framework. This study found that doublets of the same function may have moderate overall (first-order) correlations but high second-order correlations which were not considered by conventional correlation analyses. Again, we identify the four constructs of the cube model as follows:

- g is a set of 2429 genes from budding yeast *Saccharomyces cerevisiae*. All genes are annotated based on Gene Ontology (Ashburner et al., 2000).
- X consists of 35 cDNA microarrays and four Affymetrix ones. Unlike the TSP algorithm, in each microarray a gene corresponds to a group of profiles.
- The metric d in each microarray is jack-knife correlation, which takes the leave-one-out Pearson's correlation coefficient with the minimum absolute value. The use of jack-knife correlation effectively reduces the number of doublets in the filtering phase.
- The second-order correlation analysis study poses several constraints on selecting doublets to overcome computational difficulties. First, only the gene pairs from the same functional category are included. Furthermore, they consider only the genes where at least eight expressions are available in all microarrays. Finally, a gene pair is defined as a doublet if at least eight and at least a quarter of the correlation values are greater than a cut-off value $\tau=0.6$. The selectivity of the filter f is low, as only 5142 doublets pass the filter.

The doublets thus selected are then clustered using TightCluster (Tseng and Wong, 2005) with the similarity metric in the k-dimensional vector space being correlation again, which gives the name of the second-order correlation analysis. In general, however, the distribution of the points in the vector space might be captured by other metrics like Euclidean distance or normalized inner product. According to the experiments in (Lin & Kang, 2007), the second-order correlation analysis could be improved by applying different metrics or learning algorithms to the filtered vectors. As shown in Table 1, the accuracy of biological function classification was improved by simply changing the metrics or the clustering algorithm.

Metric	Clustering algorithm	Inclusion accurary
correlation coefficient	TightCluster	72% (Zhou et al.)
correlation coefficient	hierarchical clustering with complete linkage	90% (Lin & Kang)
1-norm	hierarchical clustering with complete linkage	93% (Lin & Kang)
1-norm	c-means	89% (Lin & Kang)

Table 1. Functional homogeneous group inclusion rates over the 100 tightest clusters.

2.5 Discussion

Although the two algorithms in the previous subsection seem to differ in both the analysis models and the target applications (i.e., gene functional classification and disease prediction), they both utilize inter-gene information and can be well described under the cube integration model. Therefore, the cube model can server as a general integration framework that provides an easy and efficient way to implement an effective microarray integrative analysis framework.

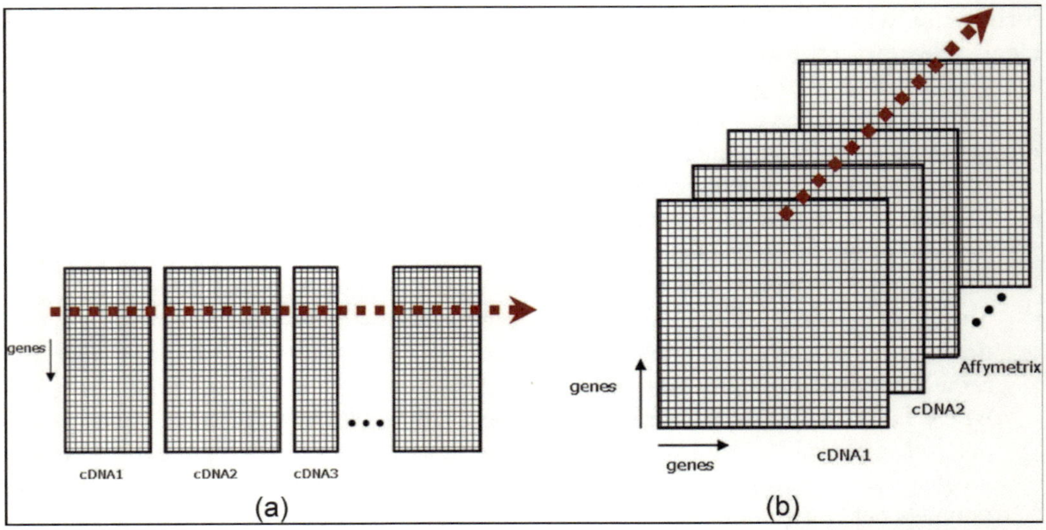

Fig. 3. (a) Illustration of conventional microarray merging technique. The microarrays are concatenated to form a large table. The dotted arrow represents the attributes of a gene. (b) Illustration of the cube framework. The similarity matrices generated from microarrays are piled to form a cube. The dotted arrow represents the attributes of a gene pair.

To summarize the intrinsic differences, a visual comparison between the conventional merging technique and the cube framework is shown in Fig. 4. The cube model is more flexible than the concatenation model and has several immediate advantages. First, the construction of the cube vectors is independent of the analysis, so we can apply any clustering or classification algorithm as long as the pair-wise distances between gene pairs are defined. Also, since now the complexity of each microarray is hidden in a matrix, in the analysis phase there are no normalization or feature selection issues, as long as the number of microarrays is not too large. Moreover, domain knowledge for a specific microarray experiment may be applied by designing the metric function for the dataset to improve the performance of subsequent data analyses. In sum, the integration model not only reduces the effects of experiment specific factors, but also captures vital information of inter-gene relation in biological processes.

3. Exploring urban Wi-Fi landscapes in anthropological fieldwork data mining

3.1 Overview

This section introduces a Wi-Fi (wireless technology for connecting to the Internet) landscape research project which explains how anthropologists study and analyze cyborg (cybernetic organism) identity in large scale Wi-Fi data collected in several cities via contextualized data mining. Conventionally, anthropologists live and study in small scale settlement to observe their participant' activities, and hence they need public and privileged statistics data as complementary data to study urban life. Such methodology however introduces a conflict between participant observations and statistic analysis on data interpretation. While participant observations focus on the data in social and cultural context, statistics concern about the data in related variables. For example, some anthropologists consider crime represents one way to solve social conflicts, but statistics may suggest that crime relates instead to unemployment rate. The disagreement leads to develop new types of contextualized data mining methodology to obtain data and produce statistics from fieldwork.

This fieldwork for the urban Wi-Fi landscpe study explores five cities—Taipei in Taiwan, Chicago and New York in USA, Hong Kong in China, and London in UK—where Wi-Fi is widely adopted to construct the citywide networks. Low cost and easy installation are major factors for cities to promote Wi-Fi as their fundamental digital infrastructure. Beyond technology and infrastructure, Wi-Fi also relates to our habitus (Boudieu 1977) and behaviors, at least in a number of countries. Habitus shape Wi-Fi users as identifiable groups and Wi-Fi access points as the main objects in such groups. Users need Wi-Fi access points to connect to cyberspace and construct their identifiers in the social and hardware networks. Wi-Fi access points build their society, which is similar with the *house society* concept in anthropology, a society whose basic social unit is a *house* (Lévi-Strauss 1982). Here the term *house* can refer not only to physical building, but also to abstract concept.

The relation between Wi-Fi access points and houses is of conceptual metaphor (Lakoff and Johnson: 1980), where they share common properties categorized into *qualities*, *entities* and *functions* (Ahrens 2002, 2010). *Qualities* mean attributes of objects. For example, house and Wi-Fi access points share the *tangible* quality. *Entities* refer to the parts, such as houses' pipe and Wi-Fi access points' antennas. Finally, Wi-Fi access points provide connections and houses provide dwelling places, which explain the *functions* of the two objects.

Above all, the house society theory provides an innovative approach to examine Wi-Fi data in social aspects beyond the amount and distribution of Wi-Fi access points. This is significant in expanding data mining applications to include social contexts as variables in data analysis. In this section, we will introduce the development of Wi-Fi in cities, and argue how conceptual metaphor and *house societies* concept highlight cultural or social context to place Wi-Fi statistics for data mining.

3.2 Literature review

3.2.1 Fieldwork

Fieldwork is the main difference on methodology between anthroplogy and other disciplines. To obain first-handed information, anthropologists stay for a long period in the arena of their study to proceed their research. In particular, to acquire direct and clear data, anthropologists participate local events and activities to observe the society and ask informants questions, called *participant observation*. For anthropologists, *behaving and thinking like a native* is the ideal goal, and *native's point of view* is the basic requirement for explaining and interpreting cultures. Because participant observations are made by directly inquiries, anthropologists applying such apporach can only study small-scale settlement (Evans-Pritchard 1940; Malinowski 1922). Hence, if researchers want to study cities, they need to refer to statistics from government or companies (Low 1996). However, statistics is not easy to integrate into traditional anthropology methodology. To bridge the gaps, in this section conceptual metaphor will be applied.

3.2.2 Wi-Fi development

Wi-Fi, a trademark of Wi-Fi alliance, means wireless technology based on IEEE 802.11 (Wi-Fi Alliance 2010). Wi-Fi has changed the structure and meaning of Web. One decade ago when Wi-Fi were not available, Internet users relied on wired connections at home, offices or cyber cafes to surf online because they are forced to stay at a particular position to connect to the Internet via a network cable. Web surfers were literally points in a web connected via lines. With the new Wi-Fi technology, access points (AP) emit short-distance wireless signals for Internet connection and hence create a temporary cyberspace for Internet connection. As a result, Wi-Fi users are more like residents in houses or apartments and they are connected by spaces rather than lines.

According to geographical surveys (Torrens 2008; Schmidt and Townsend 2003; Jones and Liu 2007), Wi-Fi is now very popular as millions of them are distributed in the world. These studies, however, focused only on the distribution on geographical space and applied statistics to depict Wi-Fi maps. In contrast, in this chapter we will investigate Wi-Fi distribution statistics in social space and cultural context.

3.2.3 House societies theory

Ubiquitous Wi-Fi access points become a new type of houses which locate residents/users in the physical world. For example, the search engine giant, Google, was criticized about its Wi-Fi scanning in Australia, knows so much about individuals, that is driving around and taking photos of every street in Australia, is collecting data that could enable it to physically map that information to a physical street and presumably a physical house. Besides Wi-Fi access points, Wi-Fi-equipped devices also transform human beings to cyborgs (Haraway 1991) dwelling in urban Wi-Fi spaces. To help analyze prevailing urban Wi-Fi access points with visible properties as devices and invisible information as houses, the house societies theory in anthropology is introduced in research.

Anthropologist Claude Lévi-Strauss (1982) employed *house* which contained tangible and intangible properties to study kinship systems in different societies, e.g. American natives, European nobles and medieval Japanese societies. Beyond blood relationships, material objects (e.g., wealth, space) and immaterial properties (e.g., title, fame, power) contribute to construct identities in the same house. As a result, house societies theory posits that a house is an elementary unit where economical and political activities occur, and that these interrelated activities shape house members as a special and identifiable group. This theory together with conceptual metaphors can bridge Wi-Fi access points and houses.

3.2.4 Conceptual metaphor

The connection between houses and Wi-Fi access points can be constructed by metaphor. Metaphor means applying one thing to describe another thing. Conceptual metaphor was proposed by George Lakoff and Mark Johnson (1980). They claimed that conceptual metaphor is based on culture background so we can comprehend the social/cultural relationship behind the link of diverse category of objects. They defined the item to be described as the *Target Domain (TD)* and the item to explains TD as the *Source Domain (SD)*. In this chapter, house is the SD and Wi-Fi AP is the TD.

Houses and Wi-Fi APs are distinctive matters, but conceptual metaphor bridges these two via mapping principles. Mapping principles are the reason which people connect objects of separate domains. The mapping principles concern about shared aspects on both objects. Kathleen Athens (2002) addressed three classifications of aspects—*entities*, *functions*, and *qualities*—to analyse conceptual metaphors and explore mapping principles. *Entities* mean parts such as windows of houses; dwelling is one purpose of houses and it is also the *function* of house; *qualities* are applied to describe attributes like "concrete" or "huge." The three classifications are the variables in statistics and they relate to contextualized objects like houses and Wi-Fi access points. The values of the three variables can give weights in the mapping principles and represent the cultural/social meaning of object-centered study.

3.3 Methodology

In the following table, the three classifications of "Wi-Fi AP is House" metaphor and the examples are listed. The three classifications of conceptual metaphor provide clear criteria to describe the features of Wi-Fi access points.

	House	Wi-Fi AP	Commons
Entities	bricks, cements, windows, doors, addresses, location, ownership, residents, space, house names	box, antenna, signal, location, ownership, users, space, Wi-Fi AP names, membership, appearance	location, community, ownership, users, membership, space, name, appearance
Functions	connection, living, shelter, resting, sharing, storing up, locating person in society, providing resource	connection, transferring information, identifying members, dwelling, accessing Internet	identifying members, resource, connection, dwelling
Qualities	colors, sizes, urban, rural, owned, rented, public, private	colors, sizes, subscribing, private, public, urban, rural	colors, sizes, ownership, public, private, urban, rural

Table 2. Three classifications of the "Wi-Fi AP is House" metaphor.

The above table shows that houses and Wi-Fi APs have commons in specific items and the mapping principles as follows.

- "House and Wi-Fi AP" contains tangible and intangible entities.
- The main function of "House and Wi-Fi AP" concerns about locating people in networks/societies.
- Qualities of "House and Wi-Fi AP" can be private, public, or restricted.
- Wi-Fi AP is the materialized and spatial identity in conceptual metaphor of house.

While mapping principles provide a basis for statistics, fieldwork constitutes the collection of Wi-Fi access points, our basic data sets. This fieldwork was conducted in London, Chicago, New York, Hong Kong and Taipei. Instead of recording all Wi-Fi AP data, the fieldwork focused on how Wi-Fi networks are shaped in different cities. Although there are some organizations providing Wi-Fi distribution maps, there still exists some restrictions such as:

- Data attribute: Pure Wi-Fi machine data cannot give us culture, society, economy and environment information in the cities.
- Legal issue: Commercial companies such as Skyhook collect Wi-Fi positions by their stuff and only allow limited license to query the data from their user interface; full access to their databases is not allowed. Open/Free map groups such as wigle.net collect data by the participants, but the group owner rejects the query request because they consider the use may be unrelated to the purpose of open/free map project.

To collect Wi-Fi hardware information, a Windows batch file run in laptops and an iPod Touch commercial software, *WiFiFoFum*, are employed to automatically record Wi-Fi information while walking around the cities. Besides automatic collections by both devices in different areas of the cities, related culture and environment were also observed and notes were made.

3.4 Result

	New York	Chicago	London	Hong Kong	Taipei	Total
#Records	18428	5196	18743	84437	102047	228851
#Access points	11223	3459	3923	16740	13125	48470
Fieldwork duration	Jan 2009 - Feb 2009	Oct 2008 -Dec 2008	Oct 2007– Mar 2010	Apr 2009 - May 2009	Jul 2006 -Jul 2010	Jul 2006 -Jul 2010
Area	Manhatta n & Queen	Midtown & Northern Area	Zone 1 & 2	Hong Kong, Kowloon, Mong Kok, New Territory	East Area	N/A
Max # recurrence	42	97	178	210	1138	N/A
Average # recurrence	1.64	1.5	4.8	5.0	7.8	N/A

Table 3. Fieldwork statistics of the five target cities.

In this project, we have collected 48,470 Wi-Fi access points in five cities. Table 3 shows the statistics obtained. The total number of access points of this project is far lower than Kipp Jones and Ling Liu's work, where more than 5,600,000 access points were collected in USA by Skyhook (Jones and Liu 2006), and Torrent's work, where 500,000 access points in Salt Lake City in USA were collected (Torrent 2008). The main reason is that the collection approaches differ. Skyhook collected access points by cars with special Wi-Fi detecting facilities, and Torrens searched access points by foot, bicycles and cars with a special signal-detecting device. They aimed to include all access points in every area. Our study instead concerns about the behavior of general users perceiving Wi-Fi access points as (via conceptual metaphor) conceiving houses in their daily life. Thus, to reflect general user experiences in the statistical distribution of Wi-Fi access points, in this project walking, buses, trams, trains and metro trains serve as the main transportions. Furthermore, data were collected by personal laptops and personal mobile devices instead of specific W-Fi detection devices. In contrast to the previous two studies, the statistics context in this study relates to persons in cities rather than to urban infrastructure.

There are several additional findings in the statistics:

- Hong Kong has the highest number of Wi-Fi access points, while Chicago has the fewest ones. As we only stayed at Hong Kong for one month to collect data, we can infer that the density of Wi-Fi access points is the highest in Hong Kong.
- The maximun recurrence is 1,138 in Taipei and the minimun is 42 in Taipei. The result may be caused the familarity of the authors with the city. We can assume if users are familiar with the city more, they have more fixed routes to explore the city.

- The average recurrence presents that Chicago (1.5) and New York (1.64) have the similar average. The average of Hong Kong (5.0) and London (4.8) are also close. This phenomenon indicates that similar historical and cultural background may shape similar Wi-Fi distribution.

Two Wi-Fi access point quantities are reported for each city in Table 3: one is *records* and the other *access points*. The former is the total records without removals of the recurrence of Wi-Fi access points and the latter only counts distinct Wi-Fi APs. Unlike other researchers who filtered out identical access points in the databases to conduct the statistics of Wi-Fi APs in geographical distributions, we retain recurrences to observe two additional properties: frequency and routes. For example, commuters in Taipei shows obvious recurrence location sets, as the same access points always appear in daily routes. In this case, density of Wi-Fi APs only reflects the spatial distributions, but frequency is more meaningful. Because most users have similar places and routes to access Wi-Fi Aps in home, office, cafés, pubs and restaurants, higher frequency can mean more fixed routes.

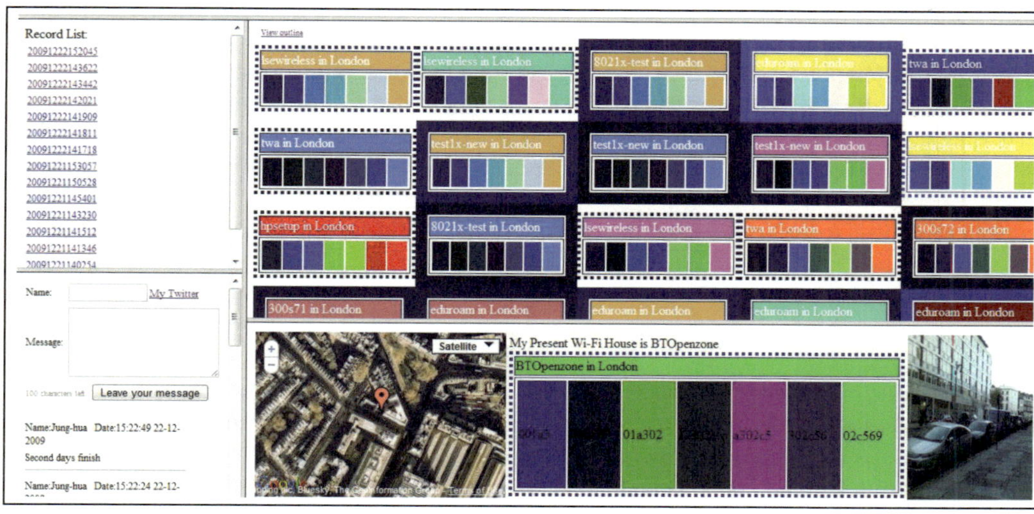

Fig. 4. Sample Wi-Fi records in London containing the location which the data are collected and uploaded, one streetview picture and the color chart of BSSID (Basic Service Set Idendtifier, Wi-Fi APs's unique identifier). The top left part is the record list and the below is the guestbook which link to this project's twitter. Converted color charts of BSSID of a series of Wi-Fi APs are presented in the top right. The bottom of right column is composed of map, one BSSID's color chart and one streetview picture. Color conversion rules are explained in the aesthetic part of the article.

We can see from Table 3 that Wi-Fi access points are popular in all of the five cities. In London, many houses have their own Wi-Fi access points and telecom company BT has installed many commercial Wi-Fi hotspots in most public places. In addition to static access points, Wi-Fi access points also appear on particular trains and coaches, as well as airplanes in London, New York and Chicago. On one hand, most research and advertisements about prevailing Wi-Fi access points emphasize Wi-Fi's easy access, wireless attributes, and commercial business. On the other hand, artists, sociologists, and geographers consider Wi-Fi as a social movement of digital citizenship in our society. They offer an all-encompassing social view to explain and interpret how Wi-Fi technology shapes Internet life in a new, wireless way. Their concerns tend to explore public lifestyles, but Wi-Fi also plays an important role in our private lives. As mentioned, *house* is the keys to understanding the effect of Wi-Fi on the connection between private and public spheres.

3.5 Discussion

Ubiquitous Wi-Fi hotspots not only provide citizens a convenient vehicle to access the Internet but also break the boundary between public and private areas. Wi-Fi users can access the Internet in cafés or train stations in a similar manner to accessing it at home. In addition, Wi-Fi devices are widely adopted in many houses, whether they are supplied by an Internet Service Provider (ISP) or purchased by users. Wi-Fi devices are like tubes that produce heat; however, they are different in that Wi-Fi devices use wireless signals to connect two different worlds – the real world and cyberspace. Internet connections project physical users into cyberspace where they become another identity. In this sense, cyberspace is a metaphor for and a symbol of our real lives and Wi-Fi network devices are important media that create and embody these metaphors and symbols.

In contrast to telephone/modem cables, Wi-Fi devices expand Internet connections from a socket-like tap to a wireless signals. The process is similar to how energy resources create heat that is accessible to every member of the house, no matter where the member is. The main difference is that, while house members can access directly water from taps, heat via gas or electricity, and television reception through television signals, they need extra Wi-Fi equipped devices to access the Internet even though a wireless signal exists in the house.

Through connecting to the Internet via network cables, telephone lines, or modems, computers can be viewed as extensions of these devices, as house members use them in the same way as watching TV programs on television or washing hands by turning on a water tap. Under these circumstances, members use their own body parts to interact directly with the world around them. In contrast, if house members adopt Wi-Fi to access the Internet, their computers are no longer required to be fixed in particular positions. In other words, computers *escape* from modems and telephone cables and are no longer extensions of them. Instead, computers and other mobile devices can be viewed as extensions of the human body, expanding human beings' senses and abilities in order to explore the other world, *cyberspace*.

When we examine wireless maps of broader districts such as street blocks in cities, physical houses may also be defined by Wi-Fi devices as their signal coverage. This correspondence again bridges the maps of real world and cyberspace. Wi-Fi devices create network names that appear on users' computers. Wi-Fi networks are named by either manufacturers or owners, and these names are used to identify ownership of the access points. Using Wi-Fi network names, members can access the Internet via these devices. The members who are granted access know each other because Wi-Fi devices can cover only limited ranges, within a house for example. On the other hand, Wi-Fi networks are a metaphor for houses because Wi-Fi network names, like other kinds of names of houses, can be considered intangible property of houses.

Wi-Fi access points, as Claude Levi-Strauss's *house societies*, shape members into special and identifiable groups. A Wi-Fi network is both a shared property among house members and a resource for members to access the Internet. This resource is limited and restricted to particular target groups, namely family members and house members. It is worth pointing out that house members are different from family members in that house members may be family members, flat mates, tenants and owners, etc. Because Wi-Fi networks are representations of and metaphors for a house, house society theory evokes the consideration that Wi-Fi devices in houses are viewed as more cultural and social than technological, for their influence in daily life shapes and confirms members' relationships.

4. Aesthetic view of inter-sampling for house-like Wi-Fi access points

4.1 Overview

In the previous two sections, we studied two types of data mining targets. The microarray cube framework was applied in gene analysis, and conceptual metaphor between house and Wi-Fi was applied in anthropology investigation. Both studies provide indirect methods to find innovative and interrelated information in huge and complicated data. From aesthetic point of view, such apporach is similar to how Claude Monet applied water and flowers to paint the inexistent light on his work *The water lily pond*, according to French philosophist Alain Badiou (2006). Our two studies utilize simple visible forms, cube representation and metaphoric house respectively, to present sophisticated data structures, gene microarray network and urban Wi-Fi landscape. The new forms contain and reproduce a series of rules, visual elements, orders and patterns.

Beyond algorithms, aesthetics offers data mining a new way to construct its framework to analyse the data. Aesthetics is one kind of cultural form and symbolic system, and in this sense Lin's microarray cube is biologically and Liu's metaphor is anthropologically cultural form and symbolic system. Therefore, in this section we will apply data mining to visualise and materialise these data sets and create Wi-Fi artworks in aesthetical framework. We hope that the synthetic approach will help data mining to expand to cultural/social spheres and to organize and visualize humanity data.

4.2 Literature review

Aesthetics is one of the main topics in art and art history. Different artists have their individual techniques and tastes to construct their artworks. According to Theodor Adorno (1997), a famouse philospher on aesthetic theory, the emprical world is mediated to art with the aesthetics. Aestheitcs is a series of patterns and symbolic forms to represent the world. Contemporary artists' artworks, especially generative art and net art, reflect this concept.

Generative artworks are created by one or a series of algorithms which produce a repetative patterns to present artists' interpretation for what they perceive. An example is Jared Tarbell's *Substrate*, shown in Fig. 5, which creates sets of lines to construct rectacles with algorithm to compose a visually and rythematically aesthetic world.

Net artists also create rule-based artworks with Web browsers. For example, Lisa Jevbratt's famous art project (shown in Fig. 6) converted IP addresses into five interfaces (migration, random, every, excursion, and hierarchical). This project aims to depict web into a visual language with different patterns to mediate IP addresses in physical world to imaginary world.

Above all, aesthetics is not merely a subjective and arbitrary taste for beauty; rather, it is a way to analyze, realize and represent our world in particular patterns to dig out the relations and information behind complicated data. This section will convert Liu's Wi-Fi data with Lin's cube model to create artworks to mine data with aesthetics.

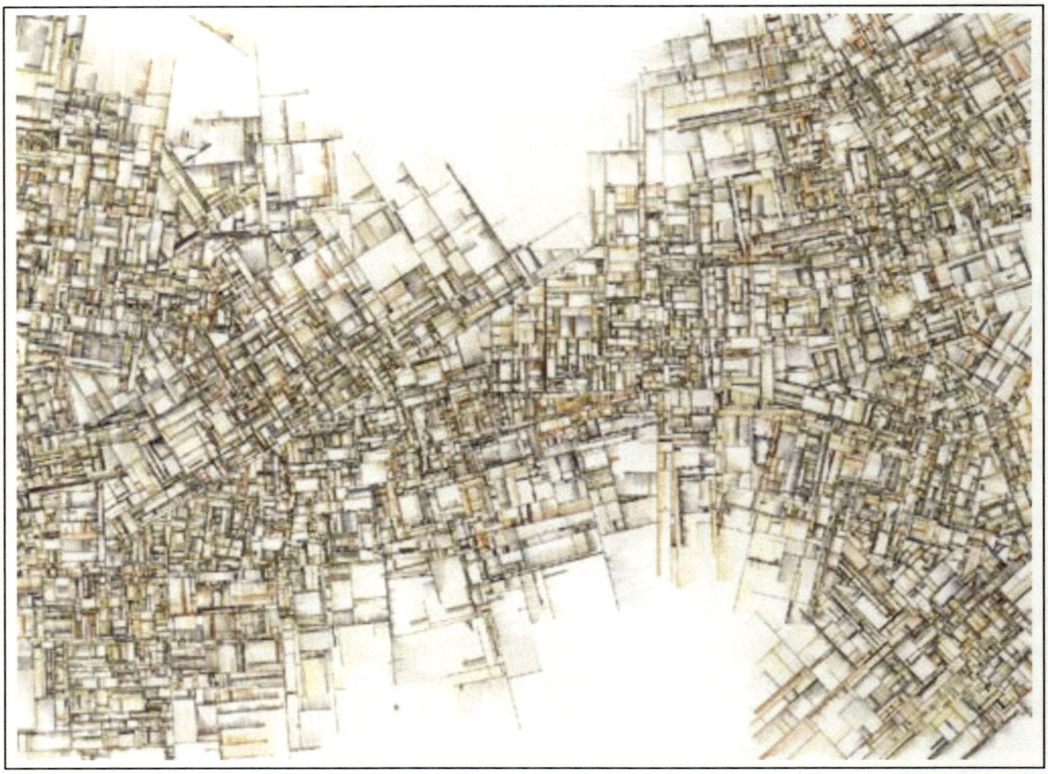

Fig. 5. Jared Tarbell's *Substrate,* a generative artwork.

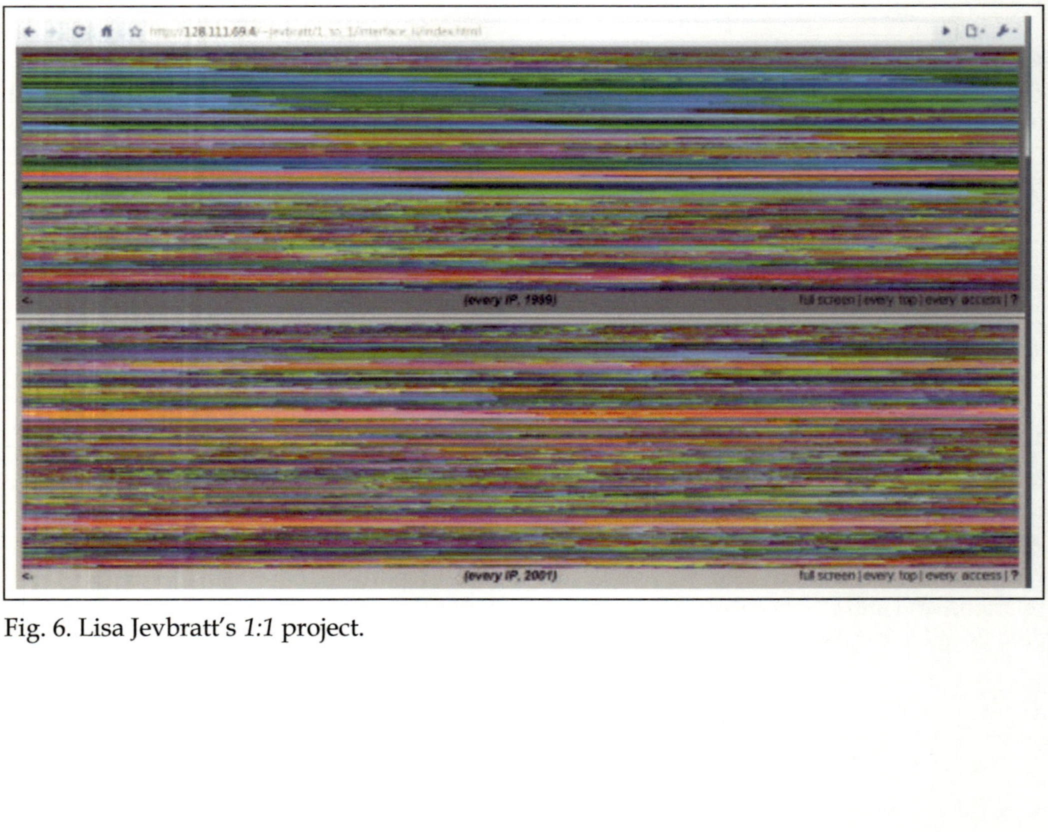

Fig. 6. Lisa Jevbratt's *1:1* project.

4.3 Methodology

To convert urban Wi-Fi landscapes into artworks, an element to bridge the two domains is necessary. We thus introduce BSSID, the unique identifier of Wi-Fi access points like house addresses. A BSSID is a 12-digit hexadecimal code, composed of two parts. The first six digits is the vendor's code and the last six digits is the serial number in the factory.

Inspired by Lin's cube mode, BSSID is mediated to color charts to present the codes (see Fig. 7). For connecting to database and making artworks accessible, the converted color charts are presented in Web pages with PHP (Hypertext Preprocessor, a script language). Web pages show seven colors per BSSID according to HTML's 6-digit hexadecimal coding in BSSID through the following procedure. The first webpage color code is created from the first to the six digits of BSSID, the second color code from the second to the seventh digits, and so forth. The shifting translations reflect the coexistence and interaction between the vendor and the individuality of the Wi-Fi access point. Such transitional charts can be viewed as genes of urban Wi-Fi systems, thus similar with a gene set in Lin's microarray study. Furthermore, artworks composed of charts could provide us a new way to mine data to realize the difference among urban Wi-Fi landscapes.

Incorporated with Liu's house metaphor connection, color charts are then shaped as a *house* image (Fig 5.). The image is composed of the following three parts: (1) the bottom part, which is the color charts computed by the aforementioned method; (2) the top part, where the Wi-Fi access point name and area appear in the color of the final 6-digit color (same as the rightmost color in the chart); and (3) the border that surrounds the top and bottom parts, which is the first 6-digit color (same as the leftmost color in the chart). If the Wi-Fi access point requires authorization for access, the border will be solid; otherwise, it will be dotted.

Most physical houses in cities were built by a few building companies, and hence they usually seem similar to one another. To house members, however, their houses are unique, and our Wi-Fi access point color charts can reflect such personal uniqueness. Therefore, the color transitions in Wi-Fi networks contain both personal and public access.

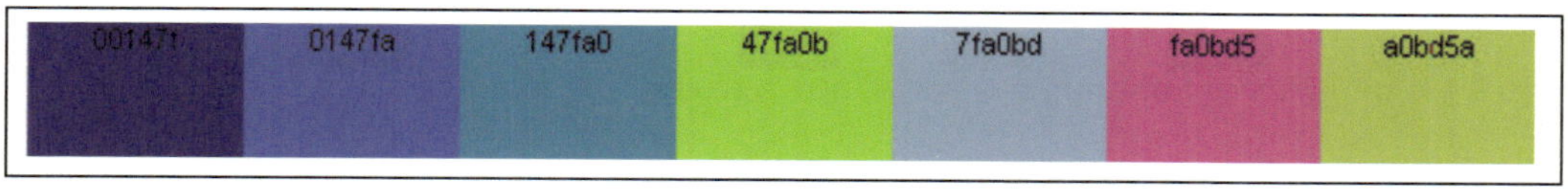

Fig. 7. The seven-color chart of the BSSID *00147fa00bd5a*. The first (leftmost) color encodes the first six digits *00147f* into RGB color code *#00147f*, which corresponds to dark blue.

Fig. 8. House images of two Wi-Fi access points.

4.4 Result

The algorithm of this series of artworks converts BSSID to color and arrange them according to timeline. The order is from top to bottom in the same row from left to right. The arrangement is similar to stripping Lin's cube representation to long patchs, providing a new perspetive to view the data sets. The border represents not only the Wi-Fi access point's degree of openness, but also the color generated from the vendor's code. Since authorization and encryption functions are provided by the manufacturer, borders in metaphor can correspond to the walls of physical houses constructed by building companies.

The charts of London and Chicago are shown in Fig. 9. In both cities there are obvious parts which is full of Wi-Fi access points of solid border, yet Chicago seems more open than London according to the color distribution. Wi-Fi charts in New York and Hong Kong (Fig. 10) show similar patterns, where encrypted and non-encrypted Wi-Fi access points are equally distributed. The difference between the cities is still the degree of openness: New York, like Chicago, is relatively more open than other two cities, and Taipei (Fig. 11.) is the most open city.

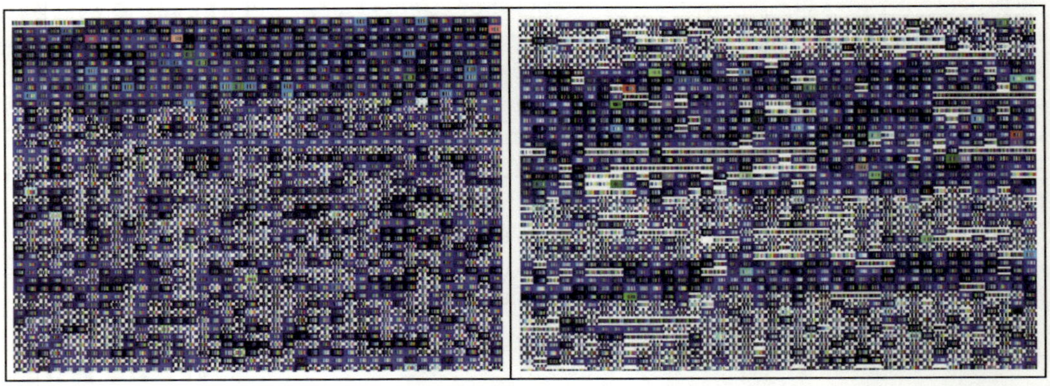

Fig. 9. Color charts of London (left) and Chicago (right).

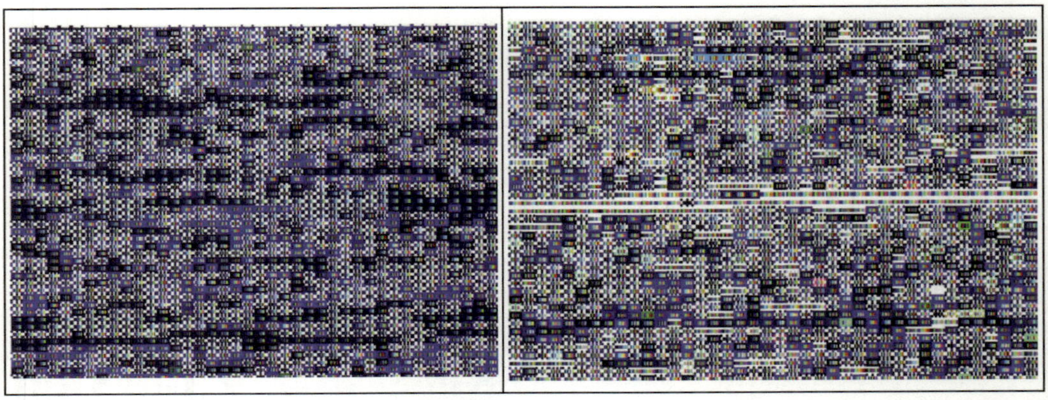

Fig. 10. Color charts of Hong Kong (left) and New York (right).

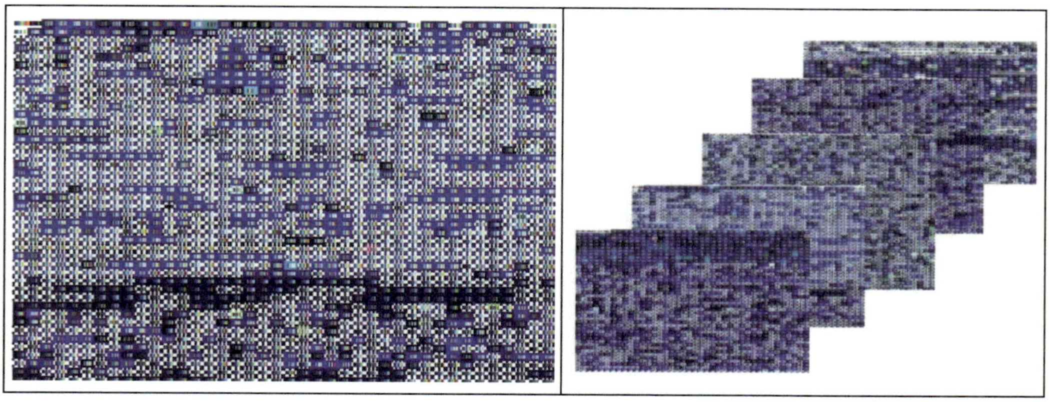

Fig. 11. Color charts of Taipei (left) and microarray inter-samples (right).

4.5 Discussion

Visualization of Wi-Fi networks presents special urban landscapes. Arjun Appadurai (1996) proposed five terms to describe the uneven and disjunctive landscape under globalization, which also applies to urban Wi-Fi landscapes. After modifying the definitions of terms in order to describe Wi-Fi networks in cities, the landscapes described below deepen the meaning of colors and patterns.

- Ethnoscapes: Wi-Fi cyborgs with similar moving routes create specific landscape of diverse cyborg group.
- Technoscapes: They can be distributions of Wi-Fi access points or personal Wi-Fi devices.
- Financescapes: The unequal Wi-Fi distribution reflects financial difference. For example, more Wi-Fi-equipped devices are affordable and needed in wealth area.
- Mediascapes: City-wide Wi-Fi infrastructure provides governments and telecom companies a new and easy way to show advertisement and messages in Wi-Fi login pages.
- Ideoscapes: Freedom, ubiquity, convenience, liberty and surveillance are the ideological landscapes constructed in Wi-Fi slogans and arguments.

By the collaboration of anthropology and linguistics knowledge, artists can communicate with other disciples with conceptualization and contextualization of artworks. The patterns and orders from aesthetics mediated Wi-Fi system to an data-mining artworks. Artworks will not be restricted to aesthetics, which implies that artists can express their idea in more elaborate and appropriate words and forms. The visualizations can also help anthropologists think pictorially to tackle complex and abstract issues with concrete and visible observations and analysis. For example, ordered and colored route charts from the Wi-Fi fieldwork data make abstract artworks conceivable and apprehensible for non-artists.

5. Conclusion

In this chapter, we discussed data mining in three disciplines: bioinformatics, anthropology and aesthetics. Data in these disciplines are usually hard to be directly visualized and hence need data mining to select and transform representative data into comprehensible forms.

Taking microarray analysis as the example in bioinformatics, Lin applied a cube mode to define inter-relations among different samples. Liu visualized the hidden Wi-Fi access points in five cities with house metaphor to analyze the similiarities and differences. Then, aesthetics concepts combined the two studies to visualize inter-sample relationships in different cities, with color charts which constitute Wi-Fi landscapes.

Visualization does not merely reflect data; rather, it offers us visual ways to re-discover important information behind complicate algorithms and huge amount of data. As artist Lev Manovich said, modern browser art "rendering the phenomena that are beyond the scale of human senses into something that is within our reach, something visible and tangible." (Manovich 2002: 8-9) Lin converted invisible gene sets to visible cubes, and therefore inter-relation of gene sets could be discovered and well-formed. Liu viewed Wi-Fi access points as houses to transform invisible Wi-Fi landscapes to visual house societies, which helped us to study Wi-Fi networks in big cities. Aesthetics made anthropology study as artworks through investigations of how patterns and rules in visualization contribute to analyze complicated phenomena. Reversely speaking, artists can also share similar language learned from data visualization with data mining experts and social scientists. Above all, researchers from various disciplines could communicate with each other and strengthen their data-mining skills through broader interpretation on visualization.

6. References

Adorno, T. W. (1997). *Aesthetic theory,* University of Minnesota Press, 081661799-6, Minneapolis

Appadurai, A. (1996). *Modernity at large: cultural dimensions of globalization,* University of Minnesota Press, 081662792-4, Minneapolis

Ahrens, K. (2002). When Love is not Digested: Underlying Reasons for Source to Target Domain Pairing in the Contemporary Theory of Metaphor. *Proceeding of the First Cognitive Linguistics Conference,* pp. 273-302, Taipei, January 2002, Cheng-Chi University, Taipei

Ahrens, K. (2010). Mapping Principles for Conceptual Metaphors, In: *Researching and Applying Metaphor in the Real World,* Cameron Lynne, Alice Deignan, Graham Low, Zazie Todd, (Ed.), 185–208 , John Benjamins,978902722380-7,Amsterdam

Ashburner, M. et al. (2000). Gene ontology: tool for the unification of biology. The Gene Ontology Consortium. *Nature Genetics,* Vol. 25, No. 1, pp. 25-29, 1061-4036

Badiou, A. (2006). Speaking the unspeakable. Original audio recording available at http://www.lacan.com/space/badiou3.mp3

Bernard, A. & Hartemink, A. (2005). Informative structure priors: joint learning of dynamic regulatory networks from multiple types of data, *Pacific Symposium on Biocomputing,* pp. 459-470, 1793-5091, Hawaii, January 2005, World Scientific, Singapore

Borgwardt, K. et al. (2005). Protein function prediction via graph kernels. *Bioinformatics,* Vol. 32, No. 1, pp. 47-56, 1367-4803

Bourdieu, P. (1977). *Outline of a theory of practice,* Cambridge University Press, 052121178-6, Cambridge

Edgar, R. et al. (2002). Gene expression omnibus: NCBI gene expression and hybridization array data repository. *Nucleic Acid Research,* Vol. 30, No. 1, pp. 207-210, 0305-1048

Eisen, M. et al. (1998). Cluster analysis and display of genome-wide expression patterns, *Proceedings of the National Academy of Sciences,* Vol. 95, No. 25, pp. 14863-14868, 1091-6490

Evans-Printchard, E. E. (1940). *The nuer: a description of the modes of livelihood and political institutions of a Nilotic people,* Clarendon Press, 115352163-6, Oxford

Gollub, J. et al. (2003). The Stanford microarray database: data access and quality assessment tools. *Nucleic Acid Research,* Vol. 31, No. 1, pp. 94-96, 0305-1048

Haraway, D. J. (1991). *Simians, cyborgs, and women: the reinvention of nature,* Routledge, 041590386-6, New York

Jevbratt, L. (2002). 1:1, http://128.111.69.4/~jevbratt/1_to_1/interface_ii/index.html

Jansen, R.; Greenbaum, D. & Gerstein, M. (2002). Relating whole-genome expression data with protein-protein interactions. *Genome Research,* Vol. 12, No. 1, pp. 37-46, 1088-9051

Jones, K. & Liu, L. (2006). What where Wi: An analysis of millions of Wi-Fi access points. *Portable Information Devices, 2007. PORTABLE07. IEEE International Conference on,* pp.1-4, 142441039-8, May 2007, Orlando, FL, IEEE, Orlando

Joshi, T. et al. (2004). Genome-scale gene function prediction using multiple sources of high-throughput data in yeast saccharomyces cerevisiae. *OMICS: A Journal of Integrative Biology,* Vol. 8, No. 4, pp. 322-222, 1536-2310

Lakoff, G. & Johnson, M. (1980). Metaphors we live by, *University of Chicago Press,* 022646801-1, Chicago

Lanckriet, G. et al. (2004). Kernel-based data fusion and its application to protein function prediction in yeast, *Pacific Symposium on Biocomputing,* pp. 300-311, 1793-5091, Hawaii, January 2004, World Scientific, Singapore

Lévi-Strauss, C. (1982). *The way of the masks,* University of Washington Press, 029595929-0, Seattle

Lin, K. & Kang, J. (2007). Exploiting inter-gene information for microarray data integration. *Proceedings of the ACM Symposium on Applied Computing,* pp. 123-127, 978-1-60558-166-8, Seoul, Korea, March 2007, ACM, New York

Lin, K. et al. (2009). A cube framework for incorporating inter-gene information into biological data mining source. *International Journal of Data Mining and Bioinformatics,* Vol. 3, Issue 1, pp. 3-22, 1748-5673

Low, S. M. (1996), The Anthropology of Cities: Imagining and Theorizing the City. *Annual Review of Anthropology,* Vol. 25, pp. 383-409, 0084-6570

Malinowski, B. (1922). *Argonauts of the western Pacific; an account of native enterprise and adventure in the archipelagoes of Melanesian New Guinea,* G. Routledge & Sons, 020342126-4, London

Schmidt, T. & Townsend A. (2003). Why Wi-Fi wants to be free. *Communications of the ACM,* Vol. 46, Issue 5, pp. 47–52, 0001-0782

Tarbell, J. (2003). Substrate. Original artwork published online at http://www.complexification.net/gallery/machines/substrate

Tornow, S. (2003). Functional modules by relating protein interaction networks and gene expression. *Nucleic Acid Research,* Vol. 31, No. 21, pp. 6283-6289, 0305-1048

Torrensa, P. M. (2008). Wi-Fi geographies. *Annals of the Association of American Geographers,* Vol. 98, Issue 1, pp. 59–84, 0004-5608

Tseng, G. & Wong, W. (2005). Tight clustering: a resampling-based approach for indentifying stable and tight patterns in data. *Biometrics,* Vol. 61, No. 1, pp. 10-16, 0006-341X

Xu, L. et al. (2005). Robust prostate cancer marker genes emerge from direct integration of inter-study microarray data. *Bioinformatics,* Vol. 21, No. 20, pp. 3905-3911, 1367-4803

Zhou, X. et al. (2005). Functional annotation and network reconstruction through cross-platform integration of microarray data. *Nature Biotechnology,* Vol. 23, No. 2, pp. 238-243, 1087-0156

Wi-Fi Alliance. (2010). Wi-Fi CERTIFIED™ Products. Homepage at http://www.wi-fi.org/certified_products.php

26

Data Mining Industrial Applications

Waldemar Wójcik and Konrad Gromaszek
Lublin University of Technology
Poland

1. Introduction

Novel, advanced sensors, dynamic development of information technologies as well as modern high-performance computers applied in different fields of human activity result in large amount of data.

Consequently, these data, grouped in the data sets are both large and complex. The complexity come from the several mutually excluding factors like acquisition with different sensors at various times, frequencies or resolutions. The increasing size and complexity of data in different practical, often industrial branches stands the challenging problem for nowadays scientific disciplines.

Regarding to above facts, it is notable that these techniques progressively displace many traditional methods (eg. visualization and statistics) that are no longer suitable for the analysis. Like schematic drawings and mathematical equations were formerly necessary to obtain competitive advantage, currently - data mining techniques place similar role. They enable to make scientific discoveries, gain fundamental insights into considered physical process and advance in their better understanding.

Although "data mining" term reflects somehow its idea of mining the data in general, it had a varied origins and history, evolving during time and borrowing and enhancing ideas of different fields. These domains have included statistics, image processing, machine learning, mathematical optimization, information retrieval etc. That's why data mining has multidisciplinary nature (Kamath, C., 2009).

It is worth to point out that in some disciplines like statistics, terms "data mining" or "data dredging" have negative connotation, regarding to the fact they were used to describe extensive searches through data. Statisticians tend to ignore the developments in data mining (Duebel, C., 2003), (Tang, Z., 2005).

The term "data mining" originally referred to a single stage of Knowledge Database Discovery (KDD) process. While KDD is a nontrivial process of identifying valid, useful and understandable patterns in data, data mining means which patterns are extracted and enumerated from data. This idea combines regularities finding (hidden for human) with computer's calculation speed in large amount of data (Jacobson, R. & Misner, S., 2005).

Some practitioners (Simoudis, E., 1996) refer to data mining as the process of extracting valid, previously unknown, comprehensible and actionable information form database and using it to make crucial business decisions. This approach joins data mining with data warehouse and divide the process into four actions carry out on data: selection, transformation, mining and results interpretation.

However circular definition considers it as process of extracting useful information from data. Some data miners preserve distance form terminology debate, focusing on how the ideas from different fields can be combined and enhanced to solve the problems of interest in data analysis.

It is hard to clearly distinguish data from a single component discipline on one hand. But on the other hand these technologies confluent with a new forms of data like natural language processing and comprise data mining.

Considering the golden triangle of research, knowledge and innovation, data mining approach should find also practical application in supervisory and control systems.

The chapter makes the attempt to present data mining techniques usage in various industrial applications.

2. KDD and common data mining themes

Data mining stands one of the stages of Knowledge Database Discovery (KDD) process. Although, there are many data mining techniques, they all have their origins based on science disciplines like statistics (statistical multidimensional analysis) or machine learning. The idea of KDD combines regularities finding (hidden for human, because of time limitations) with computer's calculation speed in large amount of data (Jacobson, R. & Misner, S., 2005).

(Fayyad, U. et al., 1996) defines KDD as the nontrivial process of identifying valid, novel, potentially useful, and ultimately understandable patterns in data.

The additional steps in the KDD process, such as data preparation, data selection, data cleaning, incorporation of prior knowledge, and proper interpretation of the results of mining ensure that useful knowledge is derived from the data.

The necessary stages in overall KDD process applied in manufacturing are delineated in Table. 1. The KDD process is interactive and iterative involving more or less the presented stages (Fayyad, U. et al. 1996; Mitra, S. et al. 2002).

(Choudhary A., et. al., 2009) underlines that data mining is an interdisciplinary field with the general goal of predicting outcomes and uncovering relationships in data.

Bounded with data mining, sophisticated algorithms allow to discover hidden patterns associations, anomalies from large amounts of data stored in a data warehouse or other information repositories.

The authors emphasize, that in the context of industry or manufacturing apart classification, two high level primary goals of data mining are prediction and description.

First of them - descriptive data mining focuses on discovering interesting patterns to describe the data and the second – concentrate on predicting the behaviour of a model and determining future values of key variables based on existing information from available databases.

The above goals can be achieved by using a variety of data mining tools and techniques, although predictive model can be descriptive, so that boundaries between them may not be sharp.

It is crucial to determine the type of knowledge to be mined, because it determines the data mining functions.

In most manufacturing problems, it is necessary to view the summarized data in concise, descriptive terms to provide an overall picture of the manufacturing domain's data or distinguish it from a set of comparative classes. This type of data mining is called **concept description** and includes characterization and discrimination that are basically used to understand the process. Regarding to concept description several functions can be distinguished: quality control, job scheduling, fault diagnosis, maintenance or defect analysis.

No.	Stage name	Description
1.	Understanding the manufacturing domain	Stands the relevant prior knowledge related to manufacturing application and targeted goal.
2.	Collecting the targeted data	This stage includes the collecting raw data, selecting the data sets and focussing on the set of variables affecting the problem partly defined in the first stage.
3.	Data cleaning, pre-processing and transformation	This incorporates the pre-processing of data such as noise removal, and both replacement of missing values and data cleaning. Data are consolidated into forms appropriate for mining.
4.	Data integration	This step includes multiple manufacturing heterogeneous data sources integration.
5	Choosing the functions of data mining	Depending on the problem defined (stage 1) various data mining functions (clustering, classification, prediction, association, regression, summarization etc.) need to be performed to derive the model.
6.	Choosing the appropriate data mining algorithm	The selection of technique is important to perform the desired function for finding patterns in the data.
7.	Data mining	Includes searching for patterns of interest in a particular representational form or a set of such representations.
8.	Interpretation and visualization	Tasks that include the interpretation and visualization of patterns to derive novel knowledge.
9.	Implementation of discovered knowledge	Incorporation of discovered knowledge into the manufacturing domain performance system. The feedback is received and the knowledge can be modified further based on the achieved feedback.
10.	Knowledge storage, reuse and integration into the manufacturing system	This includes the storage of discovered knowledge for future reuse and possible integration in to the manufacturing system.

Table 1. Stages of KDD process in manufacturing (Choudhary A., et. al., 2009)

There is another important domain in industry and manufacturing which is a learning function that maps a data item into one of several predefined categorical classes. Named **classification,** builds to describe a predetermined set of data classes or concepts. This is known as supervised learning regarding performing analyses on the database tuples described by attributes form the training dataset. Next the learned model is represented in the form of classification rules, decision trees, or mathematical formulas.

What is important, obtained model, based on classifier accuracy, is used for classification of the future data or test data. General techniques used for classification are decision tree induction, Bayesian classification, Bayesian belief network and neural networks (NN). Other techniques such as K Nearest Neighbour (KNN), Case Based Reasoning (CBR), GA, RST, Fuzzy Logic (FL) and various hybrid methods are also used for classification purposes (Han, J. & Kamber, M., 2001).

Classification domain is a very useful solution in many areas of manufacturing. It covers semiconductor industry, defects classification to find patterns and derive the rules for yield improvement. One of the example of the classification is online Control Chart Pattern Recognition (CCPR) for SPC. This approach is based on association of unnatural patterns displayed by a control chart with specific causes that adversely impact the manufacturing process.

Nowadays **prediction** in manufacturing processes, maintenance, quality improvement or defects detection become significant element. It is defined as a learning function that maps a data item to a real valued prediction variable. Prediction is usually viewed as the construction and use of a model to assess the class of an unlabelled sample. Rarely as prepared model to assess the value or value range of an attribute that a given sample is likely to have (Choudhary A., et. al., 2009).

3. Industrial data mining applications overview

Since industrial systems become very complex, classical control methods become more sophisticated to lead the process more adequate according to appropriate conditions form economic (cost-effectivenes) to safety.

Both technology development as well as requirements factors are crucial to modern industry. Their main aim is advising process operators or even replace them regarding to human fault elimination and increasing both the level of quality and security.

Such approach is not new. It seems to be the continuation of computational intelligence ideas implementations, stared in early 70'. Development of scientific principles of artificial neural networks, predictive and adaptive control, become a new challenge for scientists and industry practitioners.

It is notable, that pure optimizing of known process lines stands only a part of interests. Using innovative technology allows to gain a competitive advantage on one hand, but it also opens the new possibilities to very complex, nonlinear processes, where it is very hard or impossible to gather precise, direct information from measurement equipment directly, due to high and unforeseen dynamics or extremely hard environment conditions obstacles.

Modern manufacturing facilities are in general highly automated with advanced process monitoring and data archiving systems. Large amount of process parameters and outcome variables over a number of production runs are stored in the data warehouses. Such vast amount of data stands a vital resource to comprehend the complex characteristics of several processes as well as enhance production quality, robustness or any other particular parameters.

Several studies were presented in literature according to implementation of data mining techniques. The use of data mining techniques in industry and manufacturing began in early 1990s regarding to (Lee, M. H., 1993). Generalization the algorithm, predicting the future experiments outcome under various conditions by (Irani, K. et al., 1993) opened a new chapter in of semiconductor manufacturing applications due to diagnosis and process modelling aspects.

Semiconductor industry had enormous influence on data mining appliances, because (Bertino, E. et al., 1999) in 1999 also reported successful applying data mining techniques to wafer manufacturing. Since 2000 more complex and detailed studies were applied regarding to increasing level of technology process. Directly attached computer component manufacturing uses data mining techniques to improve the process as well as to provide management staff exact/appropriate information. This computer component manufacturing was described by (Gibbons, W. et al., 2000).

The quality control automated data mining system was presented in 2001 by (Maki, H., 2001). A novel, perception-based method for automated construction of compact and interpretable models from highly noisy data sets was presented in (Last, M., 2004), where useful and understandable patterns in manufacturing data was extracted from two semiconductor products. Authors also described possible directions for the future use of automated perceptions in data mining and knowledge discovery. (Huang, H. et al., 2005) made an analysis of products quality improvement in ultra-precision manufacturing industry using data mining for developing quality improvement strategies in optical products. Their findings showed that the important factors for percentage of devices were type of processing chain, precision requirement, product classes, and raw material. It is notable, that optimum range of target group in production quality indicators was identified from gains chart.

Review of the several applications of data mining in manufacturing engineering, in determined production processes, operations, fault detection, maintenance, decision support, and product quality improvement contains (Harding, J. et al., 2006). They presented several domains of data mining grouped chronologically from early 1990s to 2005. In (Wang, L. et al., 2006) notices that data mining had created new intelligent tools for automated extracting useful information and knowledge with its profound impact on practices in manufacturing. He discusses the trends of these changes in 2006. Likewise (Rokach, L. et al., 2006) proposed the BOW (Breadh-Oblivious-Wrapper) algorithm for discovering the appropriate decomposition structure, based on idea of decision tree for each projection of subsets.

Studies continuation of data mining in the semiconductor fabrication process in 2007 can be found in (Chien, C. et al., 2007). (Gebus, S. et al., 2009) present knowledge acquisition software implemented for decision support system on electronic assembly line, that supports portability and flexibility.

Regarding to one of the most powerful management innovations in 2007 - cellular manufacturing, the new data mining algorithm for designing the conventional cellular manufacturing systems was developed in (Liu, C., 2007).

Another data mining application concerns the process control in CNC manufacturing presented in (Kumar, S. et al., 2007). The knowledge discovery was used there in designing a STEP-compliant system. Applied self-learning algorithms enabled increasing consistently producing quality of products due to knowledge acquired from previous data and results in eliminating the errors of the manufacturing system.

Two stage cluster approach based framework to generate useful patterns and rules for standard size charts was discussed in (Hsu, C., 2009). This solutions from 2008 had conducted an empirical study in an apparel industry to support manufacturing decision for production management as well as marketing with various customers' needs.

Knowledge-based artificial neural network model for monitoring of the manufacturing process was implemented by (Yu, J. et al., 2008). It was used for fault recognition of products regarding to quality categories. Due to product quality, a genetic algorithm based rule extraction approach was developed by (Yu, J. et al., 2008) to discover the independent relationship between manufacturing parameters.

Return to industry data mining origins in 2009 was described by (Kang, P. et al., 2009) according to a virtual metrology system for semiconductor manufacturing. To reduce the number of variables in developed models two variable selection methods as well as two variable extraction methods (PCA, KPCA) were employed. Another attainment was employing five regression algorithms employed to predict the metrology measurements.
Also automotive industry data mining accents can be found in (Buddhakulsomsiri, J. et al., 2009) where authors present a sequential pattern mining algorithm that allows product and quality engineers to extract hidden knowledge from large automotive warranty database.
The latest publications from 2010 concern a new approach based on particle swarm optimization algorithm for clustering problems description (Durán, O. et al., 2010) or knowledge induction from data to detect and isolate machine breakdowns in carpet manufacturing (Çiflikli, C. & Kahya-Özyirmidokuz, E., 2010) or modern manufacturing facilities for bioproducts to improve robustness of large scale bioprocesses (Charaniya, S., et al., 2010), where authors demonstrate in different stages of the process the power of mining process data in revealing hidden correlations between parameters and outcomes. Separate solution stands (Bartok, J. et al., 2010) where data mining tasks and integration is used for detection and prediction of significant meteorological phenomena due to DMM project (Data Mining Meteo).
Widespread availability of new computational methods and tools both for data analysis and predictive modelling has its successful applications traditionally in business decision making (Seng, J., & Chen, T., 2010), but also in medicine (Bellazzi, R., & Zupan, B., 2008).

4. Crucial meaning of databases

Nowadays knowledge discovery, knowledge management and knowledge engineering stands the important topics to manufacturing researchers and managers intent on exploiting current assets. Database technology is central to all these knowledge-based research and engineering topics. Combining with statistical techniques, databases have been processed to derive the underlying relationships within the data processing, previously associated with statisticians (Harding, J. et al., 2006). Regarding to presented literature overview there are plenty of methods, implemented functions or even frameworks on one hand. On the other hand they are usually dedicated to the appropriate problem solution. The fact is that, the mining techniques require stable and infallible framework. There are several data mining software vendors with leadership of Oracle, Microsoft and IBM.
The complete business intelligence solution is the advantage of Microsoft's SQL Server. Apart from relational database management system (RDBMS)(OLTP database engine), it also offers Integration Services, Analysis Services as well as Reporting Services. The Whole framework hold forth to transfer data between different systems, summary reports creation as well as advanced warehouses implementation.
The common practice shows that several stages of production are handled by different databases In the classic, relational database (OLTP), records are assigned to individual transactions. It contains measured output and control signal values as well as repository states.
Despite of continuous transaction processing from different measuring devices and actuators, the typical relational model is unable to specify the total efficiency or emergency during the particular period of production. Regular finding answer for such a question

requires time consuming summaries in many tables, often using complex join operations. The time absorbing computation need to be repeated, when asked about efficiency in several departments is the main disadvantage.
Such kind of reports are improved by the *MS Analysis Services*, that store pre-processed data in the warehouse and they are more suitable for preparing reports. This kind of database consists of the *fact table* with aggregated values, named *measures* which are divided into time, departments etc. However, the fact table in the typical OLAP (On-Line Analytical Processing) database contains keys (not values) for measures tables, apart from aggregated values.
Data contained in the fact table constitute multidimensional cube. However, there may be more than three dimensions in an OLAP system, so the term hypercube seems to be more suitable. The arrangement of data into cubes avoids a limitation of relational databases which are not well suited for near instantaneous analysis of large amounts of data.
The typical linking the fact table with measures tables uses star schema. Such a structure facilitate queries and reports creation, using Multidimensional Expressions and Data Mining Extensions languages for data analysis.
Analysis Services use previously acquired and pre-processed data by the Integration services, but often they become source for Reporting Services and other applications (Zawadzki, M., 2005), (Żarski, A., 2006).

5. Prediction example

One of the original data mining usage for prediction analysis were marketing research. The technology lets a retailer to predict, for instance, the most preferable goods bought by particular age male at his local supermarket.
This technology can be used for similar purpose, but in completely different area. Many industrial automation systems acquire on-line process data in SCADA (Supervisory Control And Acquisition) systems. They allows for process supervising by the operators. The typical SCADA system workstation block scheme is presented in the Fig.1a, where on-line database and historical data repository was distinguished.
Although human stands the "perfect controller" on one hand, he is failure susceptible, because of his physiology on the other hand. Not optimal (even suboptimal in some cases) controller sets with it's negative process influence are referred to final product quality, and finally increase the total costs.
The solution of that problem could be an advisory system for process operators, that use "faultless operator" behaviour from knowledge base already stored in the system (see Fig. 1b). It's primal aim ought to be optimized control set prediction.
The solution of that problem could be an advisory system for process operators, that use "faultless operator" behavior from knowledge base already stored in the system (see Fig. 2b). It's primal aim ought to be optimized control set prediction.
Crucial functional purposes of considered advisory system:

- storage, processing and integration data from different sources;
- data analysis, ability to implement Business Intelligence (BI) implementation, hierarchical views and several data mining techniques deploy;
- presentation and distribution of achieved results .

Notice, that all above can be solved by the internal services of SQL Server 2005 standard version. Scheme of the proposal advisory system is presented in the Fig. 1b, where apart standard elements analysis SQL Server database are localised.

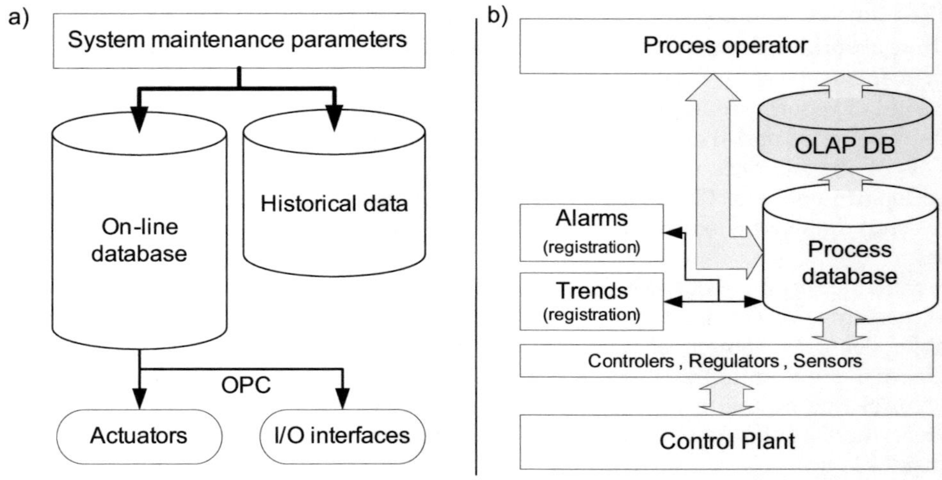

Fig. 2. Process workstation block chart, b)OLAP DB extended SCADA system scheme concept

The information gathered (and later mined) are contained in the warehouse embedded trained data model. Gathering data and making predictions on trained data models is improved by Microsoft's special query language for data mining, called DMX.

5.1 Creating and training a mining model

The prior action in this stage is as set up a connection to Analysis Services 2005 (SSAS) and create a new mining model. The purpose of the model is to predict the velocity set for beet slicer control based on some sugar production process. The DMX statement for model creation is following:

```
String CreateModel = "Create mining model BSVelocity_Prediction" +
"( SampleID long key," +
"BS_DateTime text discrete, BS_No text discrete," +    //which slicer
"BS_Charge real, BS_Efficiency real," +
"BS_VelocityCV real," +                    //measured velocity
"BS_VelocitySP real predict)" +            //setpoint
"Using Microsoft_Decision_Trees";
OleDbCommand CMD = new OleDbCommand(CreateModel, conn);
CMD.ExecuteNonQuery();
```

In the above statement, after the declaration of the data type for each column, there is content type also added. This action inform the algorithm applying to the mining model (in this example, Microsoft Decision Trees) how the data in the columns is to be distributed. The last line of the Create statement uses the predict keyword, telling the algorithm that all other columns will predict the outcome of BS_VelocitySP column for the model.

Training the model consists of two stages: the data mining algorithm input cases testing and looking for correlations in the data. After correlations identification, the model is repopulated with these new patterns. Model processing starts over as new data is introduced into the model. This results in more precise predictions, because the patterns are revised over time. To populate the model with data, the DMX Insert statement is used:

```
String PipeData2Model = "INSERT INTO VelocitySP_Prediction"
+ "(SampleID, BS_DateTime, BS_No, BS_Charge,"
+ " BS_Efficiency, BS_VelocityCV,"
+ " BS_VelocitySP) OpenQuery(btsldbsource, 'Select sampleid, datetime, "
+ " bs_no, charge, efficiency, vel_cv, vel_sp FROM btsl')";
OleDbCommand CMD = new OleDbCommand(PipeData2Model, conn);
CMD.ExecuteNonQuery();
```

Above query seems to be roadmap between a table called Samples in a SQL Server database, defined by the datasource btsldbsource, and the mining model. OpenQuery is a DMX function for performing DMX queries against relational databases from inside an OLE-DB session connection. Nethertheless, for this kind of tasks Integration Services in Business Intelligence Studio are frequently used.

After delivering data to the model, the algorithm may be used to test the cases as well as to identify patterns..

5.2 Control set prediction

Prepared model may be used to predict the best control set of velocity (setpoint), with appropriate efficiency level and current load of the beet slicer. For example, velocity control set is going to be determined with efficiency greater than 62%, efficiency range 55-85%, with a 80% probability or better. DMX Select query statement is used to make predictions on the model:

```
String PredictModel = "Select T.SampleID, VelocitySP_Prediction"
+".BS_VelocitySP From VelocitySP_Prediction NaturalPredictionJoin"
+ " OpenQuery(BTSL, 'select * from NewSamples) As T"
+ " Where T.BS_Efficiency > 62 And T.BS_Charge Between 55 And 85"
+ " And PredictProbability(BS_VelocitySP, '60') >0.8";
OleDbCommand CMD = new OleDbCommand(PredictModel, conn);
OleDbDataReader myReader; myReader = CMD.ExecuteReader();
while (myReader.Read()) { //return data } myReader.Close();
```

Considered query introduces new cases to the mining model from BTSL datasource, containing the table NewSamples. The DMX function NaturalPredictionJoin allows to join the data from the NewSamples table and model without any additional specifications, because both tables have the same columns. Function, PredictProbability is used in conjunction with the Where clause to produce desired results (Smith, J., 2003), (Tang, Z., 2005).

5.3 Industrial usage assessment

To be competitive, the companies ought to adapt to the market changes very quickly, maximizing their profit with simultaneous lowering production costs. The reasonable (cheap) solution is optimization of the most important stages of the production process. The key element allowing to bring the optimization through is processing appropriate information in proper time is the. It gives a stable framework for wise and precise decision making.

Although data mining techniques are mainly addressed to IT branch, banking and stock markets, there are many arguments for industrial usage.

Described solution is intended particularly both to the enterprises that trying to keep up the market and also to these with modern processing lines. The local sugar industry may be a very good example, while it is strongly influenced by the French and German consortiums. To remain competitiveness Polish sugar industry may improve thanks to pro-cessing lines modernization, but it is very expensive and time consuming solution. Alternative idea – efficiency improvement by the production important stages optimization, using data mining seems to be necessary.

6. Conclusion

Data mining is blend of concepts and algorithms from machine learning, statistics, artificial intelligence, and data management. With the emergence of data mining, researchers and practitioners began applying this technology on data from different areas such as banking, finance, retail, marketing, insurance, fraud detection, science, engineering, etc., to discover any hidden relationships or patterns.

Data mining is therefore a rapidly expanding field with growing interests and importance and manufacturing is an application area where it can provide significant competitive advantage (Harding, J. et al., 2006).

The use of data mining techniques in manufacturing began in the 1990s and it has gradually progressed by receiving attention from the production community. These techniques are now used in many different areas in manufacturing engineering to extract knowledge for use in predictive maintenance, fault detection, design, production, quality assurance, scheduling, and decision support systems. Data can be analyzed to identify hidden patterns in the parameters that control manufacturing processes or to determine and improve the quality of products. A major advantage of data mining is that the required data for analysis can be collected during the normal operations of the manufacturing process being studied and it is therefore generally not necessary to introduce dedicated processes for data collection. Since the importance of data mining in manufacturing has clearly increased over the last 20 years, it is now appropriate to critically review its history and application.

Data mining techniques becomes the basic element of modern business. Although the idea is not new, new technologies and implemented standards make a contribution to their growing popularity. Regarding to mining model usage SQL Server 2005 stands breakthrough in this area. Thanks to the DMX language either programmers or database administrators are able to create Data Mining Systems in simple way.

Although economical and business publications are very fruitful of data mining approaches, the described problem is presented rather weak in the international publications. Nethertheless some industrial appliances of data mining technology were considered in (Duebel, C., 2003).

Industrial usage of data mining techniques opens new possibilities in decision making not only for top level management, but also for advisory or control systems. Several prediction, classification or even anomaly detection algorithms implementation may become lucrative tool for industrial process appropriate stages optimization, that combines diagnosis and control functions.

The reviewed literature shows that there is a rapid growth in the application of data mining in industry and manufacturing. However, there is still slow adoption of this technology in some industries for several reasons including both difficulties in determining the type of data mining function to be performed in any particular knowledge area and question of choice the most appropriate data mining technique regarding to many possibilities.

7. References

Bartok J., Habala O., Bednar P., Gazak M. & Hluchy L. (2010). *Data mining and integration for predicting significant meteorogical phenomena.* International Conference on Computational Science, (ICCS 2010), Procedia Computer Science 1, Elsevier, 37-46

Bellazzi R., & Zupan B., (2008). *Predictive data mining in clinical medicine: Current issues and guidelines.* International Journal of Medical Informatics 77, 81-97

Bertino, E., Catania, B. Caglio, E. (1999). (*Applying data mining techniques to wafer manufacturing*), in: Zytkow, J.M., Rauch, J. (Eds.), PKDD'99, LNAI, vol. 1704, Springer-Verlag, Berlin, 41–50

Buddhakulsomsiri, J., Siradeghyan, Y., Zakarian, A., & Li, X. (2006). *Association rule generation algorithm for mining automotive warranty data.* International Journal of Production Research, 44(14), 2749–2770

Charaniya, S., Le, H., Rangwala, H., Mills, K., Johnson, K., Karypis, G. & Hu W. (2010). *Mining manufacturing data for discovery of high productivity process characteristics.* Journal of Biotechnology, 147(3-4), 186-97

Chien, C., Wang, W. & Cheng, J. (2007). *Data mining for yield enhancement in semiconductor manufacturing and an empirical study.* Expert Systems with Applications 33, 192–198

Choudhary, A. K., Harding, J. A., & Tiwari, M. K. (2009). *Data mining in manufacturing: a review based on the kind of knowledge.* Intell Manuf, 20, 501-521

Çiflikli, C. & Kahya-Özyirmidokuz, E. (2010). *Implementing a data mining solution for enhancing carpet manufacturing productivity.* Knowledge-Based Systems (article in press)

Duebel, C. (2003). *Application of Data Mining Techniques to Industrial Processes for Improved Business Performance,* APACT Conference

Durán, O., Rodriguez, N. & Consalter, L.A. (2010). *Collaborative particle swarm optimization with a data mining technique for manufacturing cell design.* Expert Systems with Applications 37, 1563–1567

Fayyad, U. M., Shapiro, G. P., & Smyth P., (1999). *The KDD process for extracting useful knowledge from volume of data.* Communications of the ACM, 39, 27-34

Gebus, S. & Leiviska, K. (2009). *Knowledge acquisition for decision support systems on an electronic assembly line.* Expert Systems with Applications 36 (1) 93–101

Gibbons, W., Ranta, M., Scott, T. et al. (2000). *Information management and process improvement using data mining techniques.* in: Loganantharaj, R., et al. (Eds.), IEA/AIE 2000, LNAI, 1821, Springer-Verlag, Berlin, 93–98

Han, J. & Kamber, M. (2001). *Data mining: concepts and techniques.* Morgan Kaufmann, USA

Harding, J.A., Shahbaz, M., Srinivas, S. & Kusiak, A. (2006). *Data mining in manufacturing: a review.* Journal of Manufacturing Science and Engineering 128, 969–976

Hsu, C. (2009). *Data mining to improve industrial standards and enhance production and marketing: an empirical study in apparel industry.* Expert Systems with Applications 36 (3), 4185–4191

Huang, H. & Wu, D. (2005). *Product quality improvement analysis using data mining: a case study in ultra-precision manufacturing industry.* in: Wang, L. Jin Y. (Eds.), FSKD 2005, LNAI, 3614, Springer-Verlag, Berlin, 577–580

Irani, K.B., Cheng, J., Fayyad, U.M. et al., (1993). *Applying machine learning to semiconductor manufacturing.* IEEE Expert 8 (1), 41–47

Jacobson, R. & Misner, S. (2005). *Microsoft SQL Sewer 2005 Analysis Services. Step by step.* Promise

Kamath, C. (2009). *Scientific Data Mining. A practical perspective.* Society for Industrial and Applied Mathematics, Philadelphia

Kang, P., Lee H-J., Cho, S., Kim, D., Park, J., Park, C-K, & Doh, S. (2009). *A virtual metrology system for semiconductor manufacturing.* Expert Systems with Applications 36, 12554–12561

Kumar, S., Nassehi, A. & Newman, S.T. et al. (2007). *Process Control in CNC manufacturing for discrete components: a STEP-NC compliant framework.* Robotics and Computer Integrated Manufacturing 23, 667–676

Last, M. & Kandel, A. (2004). *Discovering useful and understandable patterns in manufacturing data.* Robotics and Autonomous Systems 49, 37–152

Lee, M. H. (1993). *Knowledge based factory.* Artificial Intelligence Engineering 8, 109–125

Liu, C. (2007). *A data mining algorithm for designing the conventional cellular manufacturing systems.* in: Orgun, M.A. , Thornton, J. (Eds.), AI 2007, LNAI, 4830, Springer-Verlag, Berlin, 715–720

Maki, H. & Teranishi, Y. (2001). *Development of automated data mining system for quality control in manufacturing.* in: Kambayashi, Y., Winiwarter, W., Arikawa, M. (Eds.), DaWak, LNCS 2114, Springer-Verlag, Berlin, 93-100

Mitra, S., Pal., S. K., & Mitra P., (2002). *Data mining in soft computing framework: A survey.* IEEE Transactions on Neural Networks, 13(1), 3-14

Rokach, L. & Maimon, O. (2006). *Data mining for improving the quality of manufacturing: a feature set decomposition approach.* Journal of Intelligent Manufacturing 17 (3), 285–299

Seng J., & Chen T., (2010). *An analytic approach to select data mining for business decision.* Experts Systems with Applications 37, 8042-8057

Simoudis, E. (1996). *Reality check for data mining.* IEEE Expert, 26–33

Smith, J., (2003). *Data mining with C# and ADO.NET,* www.devsource.com

Tang, Z., (2005). *Data Mining with SQL Server 2005,* John Wiley & Sons

Wang, K. (2006). *Data mining in manufacturing: the nature and implications.* in: Wang, Kovacs, G., Wozny, M. et al. (Eds.), International Federation for Information Processing (IFIP) Knowledge Enterprise: Intelligent Strategies in Product Design, Manufacturing, and Management, vol. 207, Springer-Verlag, Boston, 1–10

Yu, J., Xi, L. & Zhou, X. (2008). *Intelligent monitoring and diagnosis of manufacturing processes using an integrated approach of KBANN and GA.* Computers in Industry 59, 489–501

Zawadzki, M., (2005). SQL Server 2005, MIKOM

Żarski, A., (2006). *Data mining using SQL Server 2005,* www.codeguru.pl